ADVERTISING AND PUBLIC RELATIONS LAW

T0313384

Addressing a critical need, *Advertising and Public Relations Law* explores the issues and ideas that affect the regulation of advertising and public relations speech, some of the most dynamic and prevalent areas of professional communications today. This updated third edition explores the categorization of different kinds of speech and their varying levels of First Amendment protection as well as common areas of litigation for communicators such as defamation, invasion of privacy, and copyright and trademark infringement.

Features of this edition include:

- A new chapter on Internet-related laws affecting advertising and public relations speech.
- History and background of major legal theories affecting professional communicators.
- Extended excerpts from major court decisions.
- Overviews of relevant federal and state regulatory schemes, including those promulgated and enforced by the FTC, FCC, FDA and others.
- Appendices providing a legal glossary, a chart of the judicial system, sample model releases and copyright agreement forms.

The volume is developed for upper-level undergraduate and graduate students in media, advertising and public relations law or regulation courses. It also serves as an essential reference for advertising and public relations practitioners.

Carmen Maye is an assistant professor in the School of Journalism and Mass Communications at the University of South Carolina, where she teaches courses in media law and advertising. She holds a J.D. and a Ph.D. from the University of South Carolina and is a member of the South Carolina Bar Association.

Roy L. Moore is a professor emeritus at the University of Kentucky, where he was the associate dean of the College of Communications and Information Studies. He is the former Dean of the College of Mass Communication (now College of Media and Entertainment) at Middle TN State University and a member of the State Bar of Georgia (emeritus) and the Kentucky Bar Association. He holds a Ph.D. in mass communication from the University of Wisconsin and a J.D. from the Georgia State University College of Law.

Erik L. Collins is a professor emeritus in the School of Journalism and Mass Communications at the University of South Carolina, where he was the associate director for graduate studies and research. He holds a Ph.D. from the Newhouse School of Public Communications, Syracuse University, and a J.D. from the Ohio State University School of Law.

Routledge Communication Series

Jennings Bryant/Dolf Zillmann, Series Editors

Selected titles include:

Advertising and Public Relations Law
By Carmen Maye, Roy L. Moore and Erik L. Collins

Mass Communications Research Resources
An Annotated Guide
Edited by Christopher H. Sterling, James K. Bracken, and Susan B. Hill

Perspectives on Radio and Television
Telecommunication in the United States, 4th Edition
F. Leslie Smith, David H. Ostroff, and John W. Wright

Balancing the Secrets of Private Disclosures
Edited by Sandra Petronio

The Business of Sports
Off the Field, in the Office, on the News, 3rd Edition
Mark Conrad

Advertising and Public Relations Law, 3rd Edition
Carmen Maye, Roy L. Moore, and Erik L. Collins

Applied Organizational Communication
Theory and Practice in a Global Environment, 4th Edition
Thomas E. Harris and Mark D. Nelson

Public Relations and Social Theory
Key Figures, Concepts and Developments, 2nd Edition
Edited by Øyvind Ihlen and Magnus Fredriksson

Family Communication, 3rd Edition
Chris Segrin and Jeanne Flora

For a full list of titles please visit: www.routledge.com/Routledge-Communication-Series/book-series/RCS.

ADVERTISING AND PUBLIC RELATIONS LAW

THIRD EDITION

Carmen Maye, Roy L. Moore and Erik L. Collins

NEW YORK AND LONDON

Third edition published 2020
by Routledge
52 Vanderbilt Avenue, New York, NY 10017

and by Routledge
2 Park Square, Milton Park, Abingdon, Oxon, OX14 4RN

Routledge is an imprint of the Taylor & Francis Group, an informa business

First edition published by Lawrence Erlbaum Associates 1998
Second edition published by Routledge 2011
Library of Congress Cataloging-in-Publication Data
Names: Moore, Roy L., author. | Maye, Carmen, author. | Collins, Erik, author.
Title: Advertising and public relations law / Carmen Maye,
    Roy L. Moore, Erik L. Collins.
Description: Third edition. | New York, NY : Routledge, 2019. | Includes
    bibliographical references and index.
Identifiers: LCCN 2019009432 | ISBN 9781138484467 (hardback) |
    ISBN 9781138484481 (pbk.) | ISBN 9781351051743 (ebk)
Subjects: LCSH: Advertising laws—United States. | Public relations
    and law—United States.
Classification: LCC KF1614 .M66 2019 | DDC 343.7308/2–dc23
LC record available at https://lccn.loc.gov/2019009432

ISBN: 978-1-138-48446-7 (hbk)
ISBN: 978-1-138-48448-1 (pbk)
ISBN: 978-1-351-05174-3 (ebk)

Typeset in Interstate
by Apex CoVantage, LLC

Visit the eResources: www.routledge.com/9781138484481

This book is dedicated to Roy's wife of 50 years, Pam; their son Derek and daughter-in-law Michelle; and their precious grandchildren, Elie and Juno.

Also dedicated to Carmen and Erik's cat, Stanley, whose keyboard terpsichorean moves contributed random letters to the manuscript; and dog, Clarence, whose antics provided just the right comic relief to long hours at the keyboard.

CONTENTS

PREFACE

In the early days of the 20th century, the original curriculum of the world's first school of journalism included a required course in communication law. The class dealt with libel and, to a substantial degree, with postal regulations. That made sense at the time: 85 percent of all journalism graduates went to work for community newspapers, and an understanding of law affecting the mail was important.

Today, we operate in a mass media–and social media–environment. Advertising and public relations professionals, and those hoping to enter the professional world, not only need to possess many of the same skills as traditional journalists, but also need to learn a great deal about public opinion and human behavior, management techniques and strategic problem solving. And, as was the case with those pioneering journalists nearly a century ago, today's advertising and public relations professionals must be aware of the laws and jurisprudence affecting their chosen fields.

Some of the legal issues facing journalists equally affect advertising and public relations professionals. However, many other law-related issues and concerns of those in the advertising and public relations professions are different from those of editors and reporters. Designed to serve both the practitioner and the student, this third edition of *Advertising and Public Relations Law* addresses this wide range of legal topics.

Although there are some excellent general media-law texts available, none has been developed to the extent this one has to reflect the distinctive needs of advertising and public relations professionals and aspiring professionals. Some of the specific differences you will notice are (a) two entire chapters devoted to the commercial speech doctrine, including its history and development; (b) separate chapters on public-interest speech, patents and trademarks, and trade secrets and ideas; (c) extensive discussions of how federal agencies beyond the Federal Trade Commission regulate advertising and product promotion; (d) two chapters focusing on privacy rights and concerns; a chapter on traditional journalistic concerns such as privilege and access; and (e) an appendix with model release forms, a diagram of the United States court system and a copy of the United States Constitution. Our concluding chapter, new to this edition, consolidates and discusses laws related to the Internet and online communications that impact the practice of advertising and public relations.

Lawyers sometimes characterize seemingly unimportant, minute differentiations of facts or law as "distinctions without a difference." We believe you will find this volume, in comparison with others on the topic, a distinction *with* a difference. We hope that practitioners and students alike will find our efforts interesting, enjoyable and, most of all, highly informative.

ACKNOWLEDGMENTS

Many individuals contributed to the completion of this text. We want to note the contributions of Ron Farrar, Jay Bender, Eric Robinson and Lisa Sisk (colleagues former and current); and Lauren Von Herbulis, Anna Saunders, Jamie Stancil, Renée Williamson, Rachel Amanda Farris, Jackson Carter and Branden Birmingham (graduate students former and current) who endured hours of discussion, argumentation and copy editing. Christopher S. McDonald, of the Tiencken Law Firm in Charleston, South Carolina, is responsible for sections of the discussion of contract law in Chapter 9 and contributed his expertise in a number of other areas. We especially thank Matthew Telleen for his contributions to the discussion of election law cases in Chapter 3.

We would also like to take this opportunity to acknowledge and thank the contributions to media law made by our current and former contemporaries in schools and departments of journalism and mass communications around the country, including, but not limited to, Jay Wright, Steve Helle, Bob Trager, Bill Chamberlain, Bob Drechsel, Kent Middleton, Ruth Walden, Dwight Teeter, Barton Carter, Kyu Ho Youm, Michael D. Murray, Wat Hopkins, J. Michael Farrell and others too numerous to mention, but nonetheless, deeply deserving of our great respect, who have paved the way for today's younger generation of scholars who make this field vibrant and dynamic.

Equally, if not more deserving of acknowledgment, are the true pioneers of commercial speech law: Jim Goodale, Cam DeVore, Conrad Schumadine, Bruce Johnson, Steve Brody, Diane Zimmerman, Bob Sack and others whose labors have created robust constitutional protection for a category of speech that originally was accorded none at all.

1 The First Amendment

Advertising and public relations students and practitioners picking up a 500-plus page book filled with examples and discussions of laws regulating advertising and public relations speech could be pardoned for being somewhat puzzled. After all, the language of the First Amendment to the federal Constitution clearly mandates that "Congress [and, by logical extension, any lesser unit of government] shall make no law ... abridging freedom of speech or of the press."[1] How can there be laws regulating any speech (let alone advertising or public relations speech) in the face of the Constitution's emphatic statement that there can be "no law"? This puzzle requires us to begin with a brief overview of the First Amendment and how it is interpreted, before we turn our attention to the principal subject matter of this book.

Development of First Amendment Jurisprudence

The dilemma for courts faced with deciding cases that challenge the constitutionality of attempts by government to regulate speech and press is that despite the emphatic "no law" language of the First Amendment (see Appendix A), it is almost impossible to believe that those who helped add the amendment to the federal constitution more than 200 years ago meant to protect all speech without exception, even speech, for example, that is treasonous or criminally threatening or harmful to reputation. Yet judges and justices cannot simply ignore the First Amendment because they personally disapprove of the speech in question. Therefore, they have been obliged to develop a logical, rational and defensible method of interpretation by weighing and balancing the interests of those supporting freedom of expression against those favoring competing interests. To understand how they have accomplished this, we need to take a brief look both at how judges interpret law and how historians interpret history.

Role-play the part of judge for a moment. Not a Supreme Court justice but a judge in a lower level court in which the cases usually involve petty crimes and minor disagreements—the kind of court you often see depicted on afternoon or late-evening cable television programs. The next case on the docket is *City v. Jones*. Testifying for the city is the arresting officer, who reports that the defendant was apprehended at 10 a.m. Saturday and charged with operating a motorized, self-propelled vehicle within a city park. A municipal ordinance (the name often given to laws made at the city or county level) makes such operation illegal for all "persons regardless of status or circumstances." The law specifies that "all persons violating this ordinance shall be sentenced to (a) no more than 30 and no fewer than 10 days in the city jail, and (b) a fine of no more than $100 and no less than $30." Because the defendant, Jones, is pleading guilty, this seems like an open-and-shut case for you to decide.

Figure 1.1 The words of the First Amendment to the Constitution of the United States of America are etched into the facade of Newseum, the museum of the press, in Washington, D.C.

Credit line: Dorti/Shutterstock.com

Before you pass judgment, however, it seems only fair to hear what the defendant has to say. Unfortunately, Mr. Jones apparently is nowhere to be seen. When you ask the arresting officer "Where's Jones?" the policeman gestures for you to lean forward and look over the front of your large, desk-like bench. Upon so doing, you discover that "Mr. Jones" is a curly headed, 7-year-old boy, clutching a gigantic toy truck on which a child can sit and ride by winding up a big key on the toy truck's cab. You're the judge. Now what do you do? It doesn't seem right to issue a fine and throw the little kid in the slammer, but it also doesn't seem right for you to ignore the law that clearly says it applies to all "persons regardless of status or circumstances."

This rather exaggerated hypothetical case is an example that illustrates a very real dilemma that daily confronts those who must interpret and apply the law to a set of facts. We know what the law says—we can read it over and over. The question is, what does the law mean? This is exactly what judges face when asked to interpret the First Amendment.

Let's go back to the courtroom where everyone is awaiting your decision. If you thought about looking at the precedent set by other judges who have looked at this municipal ordinance in the past, you are on the right track. Judges do look to prior decisions and the rationales employed by the judges in earlier cases. But they generally don't stop there. They also may study the literal language of the law or regulation and may take the added step of researching the records of the debate and discussion surrounding its adoption by those who passed it in the first place. Judges often find this legislative history a helpful guide in interpreting and applying the language of the law to the unique set of facts in the cases before them. In addition, they may examine any other historical records that could cast light on the meaning and purpose of a law or regulation.

In our hypothetical case of the little boy arrested for riding on his self-propelled toy truck in the city park, let's suppose the minutes taken at the city council meeting when the ordinance was passed reveal that the purpose of the municipal ordinance was to block off the streets going though city parks. The rationale was to prevent cars, trucks and buses from running over joggers, bike riders and in-line skaters (and children riding toy trucks) using the paved surfaces in city parks on weekends for recreation. Support for this interpretation is reflected in newspaper articles of the time, reporting both the number of mishaps that had occurred and calls for action by concerned citizens to protect city park users.

With this knowledge, you as judge now have a logical and justifiable reason to dismiss the charges against the boy—after all, he was doing what the law was designed to encourage—and perhaps admonish the arresting officer to be a little less zealous in the future in enforcing this particular ordinance.

These same methods of interpretation can be applied to any law, including the First Amendment. For example, a judge asked to decide a case concerning the constitutionality of a law regulating speech could gather evidence to assist in determining what the First Amendment *means* (we know what it *says*) and apply it to the facts of the present case by searching the records of the debates and discussions engaged in by the framers of the First Amendment in 1791.

Strange as it seems, however, such a search would be of little help. The actual discussions were conducted behind closed doors, and it appears the delegates were in enough agreement that the First Amendment should include the words "no law ... abridging speech or of the press" that they did not leave a clear record of what they actually meant by those words.

With little specific evidence for determining the literal meaning of the First Amendment available, judges, lawyers and legal scholars have turned to the next best evidence—the historical context of the writing of the First Amendment. This means that those seeking to interpret the First Amendment rely both on their general knowledge about the events in revolutionary

Figure 1.2 The Supreme Court of the United States has held that "political speech," or speech related to matters of public concern, is entitled to maximum First Amendment protection.

Credit line: Perry Correll/Shutterstock.com

America in the late 1700s and their interpretations of historical evidence found in personal diaries, letters, essays and state constitutional provisions written by the framers of the First Amendment.

The outcome of this historical detective work, combined with judicial precedence and evolving judicial philosophies over a more-than-200-year span, has produced the conclusion, now generally accepted by courts and legal scholars, that the framers of the First Amendment did not intend to protect all speech equally. This conclusion has led courts to differentiate categories or levels of speech that receive differing levels of constitutional protection. This protection can range from speech "fully" protected by the First Amendment to speech with no First Amendment protection at all.

Because the drafters of the Constitution envisioned a country in which the people would govern themselves by a process of achieving consensus through deliberation and debate, virtually all legal scholars and practitioners agree that the most protected speech under the "no law" language of the First Amendment is the speech related to "political speech," what Justice William Brennan once termed "open, robust discussion of public issues."[2] On the other hand, following this analytical approach, speech judged to be obscene or related to criminal activity (e.g., extortion or perjury) is entitled to no First Amendment protection at all. Speech categorized as commercial or over-the-air broadcast falls somewhere in between.

The Tests, Constitutional and Otherwise, for "Fully Protected" Speech

Envision the statue of Lady Justice, blindfolded, holding a set of scales. The scale is perfectly balanced. Normally, if Congress or a federal agency wishes to regulate everyday activities and the government action is subsequently challenged in court as unconstitutional, the government will prevail (i.e., tip the scale in its favor) if it can demonstrate a well-drafted law or regulation designed to accomplish a reasonable government purpose. Sometimes referred to as a "rational basis" test, this historic, court-made rule begins with the assumption that what the government has done is constitutional. It then places the burden on those challenging a government action to demonstrate a lack of rational basis for the law or regulation, usually a difficult burden for the challenger to meet.[3]

Challenging a law or regulation that arguably abridges a fundamental liberty like protected speech, however, automatically differentiates such a case from the norm. The Court has spent more than eight decades developing an appropriate test to preserve constitutional values when a legislature or agency wishes to regulate "those functions essential to effective democracy."[4]

This alternative approach, often referred to as the "compelling government interest test" (sometimes also defined as requiring that a court look with "strict scrutiny" at government attempts to regulate a fundamental liberty) has proven to be a major bulwark in the defense of individual liberties. The test places a heavy burden on the government body wishing to regulate, requiring that it must demonstrate (a) an overriding necessity for its actions, (b) that the law or regulation actually advances the government interest, (c) that it is "narrowly tailored" to accomplish just the limited purpose the government may be permitted and (d) that it is the least restrictive means available to the government for accomplishing its ends.[5]

Although the Court has never set out a definitive list of these "functions essential to effective democracy," clearly the right to freedom of speech and press is among them. Although the test's exact meaning has been altered over the years, a modern-day court, borrowing from 14th

Amendment Equal Protection cases,[6] normally will require the government to meet the equivalent of a "compelling" government interest when seeking an immediate cessation or punishment of protected speech. Even if the government interest in regulating speech is judged to be
compelling, the government will not automatically win a case involving regulation of protected
speech. A court still must weigh and balance the government's interests against the other side's
speech interests. How to do this represents another example of conflicting judicial philosophies
and theories.

Remember the earlier mention of the statue of Lady Justice, holding a set of balanced
scales? One school of judicial thought suggests that in otherwise protected speech cases, a
court first should pile extra weight on the speech side of the scale and then look to the government to pile enough weight on its side to overcome the handicap created in favor of the speech
interests. This method, sometimes referred to as giving speech a "preferred position,"[7] suggests
that a court require the government to meet an extra "heavy burden,"[8] at least when it wants to
regulate fully protected speech (i.e., speech about important political or social issues).

This imbalanced approach to deciding speech cases is by no means the only approach a
court might follow, however. Many jurists and legal scholars argue that the correct approach for
a court to take is to first determine if both the government and speech interests are substantial
and, if so, to adjudicate the actual case before the court by simply balancing the interests of
both parties and arriving at a decision based upon which has the greater weight on its side. For
example, as Justice Harlan noted in his opinion in *Barenblatt v. United States*,[9] "Where First
Amendment rights are asserted to bar government interrogation, resolution of the issue always
involves a balancing by the courts of the competing private and public interests at stake in the
particular circumstances."[10]

Courts have not been uniform in electing to follow either this "ad-hoc-balancing"[11] approach
or the "preferred-position" approach discussed above. This has created some confusion for
those trying to predict the outcomes of cases, as well as those who believe First Amendment
law should develop in a neat and orderly manner. More recent developments, such as the continuing terrorist threats to national security after Sept. 11, 2001, and the use of websites by radical
groups to foment violent protests, pose new challenges for those defending freedom of speech.
Nonetheless, it is still true today that the government at both the federal and state levels faces
a difficult task in defending a law or regulation that either prohibits or punishes speech about
important political or social issues.

The First Amendment: From Its Beginnings Through
the 19th Century

Perhaps somewhat surprisingly, what we understand as the meaning of the First Amendment is
not an 18th-century, but rather a more modern 20th-century concept. Between the ratification
of the First Amendment in the 1790s and the first major court decisions involving challenges to
laws regulating speech in the early 1900s, no significant litigation occurred to define the constitutional limits of the federal government's power to regulate speech. The reasons the 19th century (called by one commentator the "forgotten years" of media law)[12] saw few speech-related
court cases are rooted in history and the new nation's frontier mentality.

Think of America and Americans in the 1800s. Chances are, the stereotypical view is of a
bunch of self-reliant adventurers bent on carving out a livelihood by either taming the wilder-
ness or building empires in business and commerce. Although American history is not that

simple, one should not underestimate the effects of "rugged individualism" and the fear of centralized big government that helped shape our national character. A century and a half ago, Americans readily discussed politics and were far from shy to express their views about highly controversial issues, but rarely were laws passed to limit debate or control ideas. Also, although individuals differed (sometimes violently), those differences were not fueled by ideologies like socialism or communism or other "isms" identified with or supported by foreign governments.

Another reason for the scarcity of First Amendment court decisions was that those who disagreed with their neighbors about political or religious issues and who then encountered hostility or attempts to regulate their speech (believers in the teachings of the Church of Jesus Christ of Latter-day Saints, often referred to as Mormons, come to mind), often just packed up and left—and there was lots of wide-open space for them to settle. Yet another major factor in minimizing First Amendment jurisprudence during this time was an 1833 decision[13] by the Supreme Court of the United States that held the provisions of the "Bill of Rights" in the federal Constitution applied only to actions by the federal government, and thus did not apply to state laws and regulations. Considering all these reasons, the lack of litigation involving the First Amendment during the 19th century becomes more understandable.

By the beginning of the 20th century, however, many of these factors were changing. With the closing of the American frontier in the early 1890s,[14] fewer expanses of desirable land for community sites meant that any large group of people who shared other than mainstream political ideologies or religious practices could no longer easily band together to form isolated communities of their own. The composition of the incoming tide of immigrants also changed, bringing to American shores people from eastern and southern Europe with what some long-time residents regarded as exotic and perhaps threatening customs, traditions and ideologies. By 1914, with war looming in Europe, disagreement over which side, if any, the United States should support in the upcoming conflict sharply divided Americans whose ancestors had settled the country many years before from immigrants of more recent arrival.

This divided public support for an American war effort was a major contributing factor to the passage of the Espionage Act of 1917.[15] This statute made it a federal crime to aid and comfort the enemy, and included provisions that, in certain circumstances, punished speaking out against the war effort as well. When those opposed to the war spoke out anyway, the stage was set for the first series of court cases in which the central issue focused on the determination of just how much protection of speech the First Amendment provides.

The Development of Modern First Amendment Interpretation: The World War I Cases

Schenck v. United States[16] and *Abrams v. United States*[17] were the first two such cases. Both involved groups opposed to wartime activities preceding and during World War I. Schenck and his small band of socialists, antagonistic toward U.S. support for war against Germany and its allies, made their disapproval known by publishing and mailing out a flier that urged young men selected for the draft to refuse to report for induction. Abrams and his anarchist and communist friends were concerned that bullets made to fight Germans might instead be used to kill Russian communists engaged in the civil war in Russia that eventually led to the overthrow of the czar in 1917. To try to prevent this, Abrams helped publish fliers urging workers in American munitions factories to strike.

It is extremely doubtful that either Schenck or Abrams would have been successful in attracting many converts to his cause or in creating any real damage to the American war effort.

Nonetheless, federal authorities arrested both men along with a number of their supporters and convicted them of conspiracy to violate the Espionage Act and other crimes. On appeal of their convictions to the Supreme Court of the United States, both Schenck and Abrams cited the First Amendment as grounds for overturning the lower courts' decisions, arguing that Congress could not constitutionally pass a law that punished mere speech in such a fashion. The Court upheld the convictions in both instances but, in the process, began the development of so-called "speech tests" to be applied in such cases.

Although there was strong historical and precedential evidence supporting the government's claim that the authors of the First Amendment had meant the "no law" language to apply only to government censorship ("previous restraint") and not to punishment of dangerous or disagreeable speech after the fact, the opinion by Justice Oliver Wendell Holmes, Jr. in *Schenck* adopted the alternative position that the speech in question was undoubtedly protected from government interference in "normal" times and "ordinary" circumstances. However, he approved the conviction of Schenck because, as he said,

> [w]hen a nation is at war, many things that might be said in time of peace are such a hindrance to its effort that their utterance will not be endured so long as men fight and that no Court could regard them as protected by any constitutional right.[18]

Because Schenck and his fellow socialists sent anti-war pamphlets to young men about to be drafted into the armed services, Justice Holmes found there was sufficient evidence that they intended their act to hinder the war effort.

For Justice Holmes,

> The question in every case is whether the words used are used in such circumstances and are of such a nature as to create a clear and present danger that they will bring about the substantive evils that Congress has a right to prevent.[19]

This "clear-and-present-danger" test subsequently became the basis for judging the constitutionality of the federal government's attempts to regulate normally protected speech.

Justice Holmes dissented in *Abrams*, however. He conceded that the outcome of Abrams' actions to hinder munitions production might impede the war effort (although even this was highly doubtful), but he argued that the government could not convict Abrams of "espionage" because his purpose was to support his comrades in Russia, not to hinder the war effort against Germany. He thus lacked the specific intent to aid the enemy required by the wording of the Espionage Act.

Justice Holmes used his dissenting opinion as well to present his famous analogy of a free marketplace of ideas that he likened to an early 20th century, economic "laissez-faire" free marketplace of goods and services.[20] According to Justice Holmes, the First Amendment suggests that the antidote to Abrams' "bad" speech is not restricting speech through government regulation or subsequent punishment, but rather to encourage more "good" speech by those with countervailing messages.

In this free "marketplace of ideas" analogy, Justice Holmes reasoned that the "best test of truth" for speech is through the open "competition [with alternative ideas] of the thought to find acceptance in the marketplace." Holmes argued that the true meaning of the First Amendment requires citizens to protect speech from interference by government, even if it is speech they "loath and believe fraught with death," unless the speech poses such a serious and immediate threat that the government must act "to save the country."[21]

A variety of alternative models for thinking about the relationship between freedom of speech and competing social and political values have subsequently been advanced by a host of political theorists, jurists and academic scholars. For example, the free marketplace of ideas concept has been criticized by those who argue economic disparities among speakers means that the marketplace is rigged in favor of major corporations and others who can best afford to flood the marketplace with their ideas on a large scale. Others reject the marketplace model because they believe religious dogma or philosophic principles determine which ideas are true and which are not. Nonetheless, the idea advanced by Justice Holmes a century ago that people should be able to openly discuss and debate virtually any and all ideas and opinions in an open forum without fear of government suppression or punishment remains central to many, if not most, Americans' understanding of the "no law … abridging freedom of speech or of the press" wording of the First Amendment.

Laws Aimed at Curtailing Dissent

When World War I ended in Europe, federal laws regulating speech involving political issues fell into disuse, but a new and potentially equally dangerous threat to the free discussion of public issues was growing. The years between 1920 and 1940 marked a spurt in the growth of labor unions—to a minor degree influenced by socialist and communist ideologies—as workers organized to improve working conditions, hours and benefits. These efforts often were bitterly opposed by the captains of industry and their friends in state legislatures and statehouses, particularly when labor resorted to the ultimate weapon of a strike.

This era of industrial warfare frightened many in power with the specter of organized workers, dominated by "evil" outside forces, bent on destroying the democratic capitalist system by less-than-peaceful means. State lawmakers responded to these fears with the passage of so-called criminal syndicalism or criminal anarchy statutes. Eventually, 21 states adopted such laws aimed at punishing those who spoke out or joined groups advocating in favor of "the duty, necessity or propriety" of overturning lawful governments or "industrial … reform" by "sabotage or violence."[22]

Historically, such state laws would have raised no federal First Amendment issues, but this all changed in 1925 when the Supreme Court of the United States decided *Gitlow v. New York*.[23] Benjamin Gitlow had been convicted of the state crime of criminal anarchy for printing material urging labor unrest. The highest appeals court in New York upheld the conviction, deciding that it did not violate the state constitution's protection of speech. Despite the odds and a century-old history of precedent against the success of such an appeal, Gitlow petitioned the Supreme Court of the United States to hear his case, and the Court surprised many observers by agreeing to do so. Unfortunately for Gitlow, the Court agreed with the New York court and upheld his conviction. Fortunately for free-speech advocates, the Court also found that the Due Process Clause of the 14th Amendment to the federal Constitution gave jurisdiction to federal courts to review state court decisions that arguably infringe upon free-speech rights. This in effect extended First Amendment protections of speech and press to actions by the states as well as by the federal government.

During the decade following *Gitlow*, the Court reviewed a dozen or so speech regulation cases emanating from state courts. These decisions usually upheld the convictions of speakers but also contained dissenting opinions (usually by Justices Holmes and Brandeis) filled with ideas, historical analyses and philosophical points for future arguments in favor of a limited ability for government at any level to regulate speech.

Advocacy Speech

State efforts to regulate protected speech declined in the mid-1930s as the country concentrated on pulling itself out of the Great Depression. Unlike the resistance to the country's participation in World War I, the U.S. entrance into World War II in the early 1940s (with the Soviet Union as an ally) engendered little widespread public speech favoring fascism or advocating organized resistance to fighting Nazi Germany and its allies or the Japanese empire. Not surprisingly, therefore, World War II resulted in virtually no cases concerning the prosecution of speech-related activities parallel to those of *Schenck* or *Abrams* during the previous conflict. This hiatus came to an abrupt end, however, at the end of World War II with the heating up of the so-called Cold War.

Beginning in the mid-to-late 1940s and continuing into the early 1950s, the scare of a Moscow-inspired, communist penetration into all aspects of American life led federal prosecutors and legislative investigating committees to pursue a spate of espionage-related speech cases. Two of the more famous were *Dennis v. United States*[24] and *Yates v. United* States.[25] The Supreme Court of the United States in *Dennis*, perhaps the historic low point of First Amendment protection for political speech, upheld a conviction apparently based solely on membership in the Communist Party. The Court noted that the defendant's participation in a "highly organized conspiracy"[26] ready for violence when "the time had come for action"[27] was enough of a threat to warrant criminal sanctions. The Court appeared to feel that simply by being a communist, Dennis was "advocating" treasonous activity. By 1957 and the *Yates* decision, however, cooler judgment prevailed and the Court returned to the rationale that a showing of actual (rather than presumed) advocacy of illegal activity was necessary before the government could punish mere speech.

This trend toward greater protection of civil rights and fundamental personal liberties (including freedom of speech) begun in the late 1950s, accelerated in the decade of the 1960s. By 1969, the Court had evolved its thinking about the extent of protection for public-interest speech to the degree that in *Brandenburg v. Ohio*,[28] it struck down as unconstitutional an Ohio statute with wording almost identical to that upheld in earlier decisions like *Gitlow*. In overturning the conviction of a Ku Klux Klan leader who spoke out in favor of prejudicially motivated violence, the Court in *Brandenburg* created what's often referred to as the "*Brandenburg* test." This modern-day definition of clear and present danger requires that a state wishing to punish political speech must prove the speech was *intended* to produce "imminent, lawless activity" by those sympathetic to the speaker's cause[21] and that the illegal acts were "likely to occur" (often referred to as "inciting to riot").

Prior Restraints on Speech

In *Schenck v. United States* (discussed above), Justice Holmes began his analysis with the observation that from its inception, almost all observers had agreed that the First Amendment was designed to prohibit "previous restraints." Such censorship measures include court orders, censorship boards, discriminatory taxation policies, licensing schemes, limiting access to the means of production (e.g., newsprint or electric power) and other government actions aimed at preventing speech from entering the marketplace of ideas.

Evidence for this understanding of the First Amendment was provided both by analyzing the steps the British Crown had taken to regulate speech of its colonists (e.g., requiring a government license for printers) and subsequent legislation enacted by Congress shortly after the First Amendment had been adopted that punished seditious libel (i.e., defaming the government or government officials). The Alien and Sedition Acts of 1798 arguably were thought compatible with the "no law" language of the amendment because they did not act as previous, or prior, restraints of speech, but rather punished speakers after they spoke.

Given the nearly unanimous hostility toward any attempts by the government to employ previous restraints as a means of regulating speech, it is not surprising that only a few such cases have reached the Supreme Court. The first of these, *Near v. Minnesota*, involved a newspaper editor who had so outraged authorities in Minneapolis/St. Paul that he was denied the right to continue to publish any newspaper in the state on the basis that for him to do so would constitute a public nuisance. Rightfully seeing this as a prior restraint of speech about important public issues, the Court struck down the state regulation.

Four decades later, the Court reaffirmed its position that prior restraint is the most serious violation of the First Amendment (at least for fully protected speech) when *The New York Times* and *The Washington Post* began to publish the so-called "Pentagon Papers."[29] The classified, top-secret report, subsequently referred to by the Court as "The History of U.S. Decision Making Process on Vietnam Policy," was compiled at the behest of the U.S. Department of Defense during the mid-1960s. Consisting of some 3,000 pages of text and an additional 4,000 pages of supplementary materials, the 47 volumes contained documentary evidence that presidential administrations dating back to the late 1940s had systematically either lied about or covered up the extent of the United States' involvement in the escalating conflict between the North and South Vietnamese.

As this 1971 case unfolded, the federal government asked federal courts in New York and Washington, D.C., for injunctions to stop publication of these highly classified defense documents. Finally, the Supreme Court stepped in, and in a 6–3 decision, noting that "any system of prior restraints of expression comes to the court bearing a heavy presumption against its constitutionality,"[30] determined that the government had not produced the great weight of evidence necessary to meet the "heavy burden" needed to overcome that presumption. The Court then overturned a lower court order prohibiting *The New York Times* from continuing to publish the papers.

Content-Based Regulation of "Lesser Protected" Speech

As discussed previously, much of the development of First Amendment law during the last 10 decades has focused primarily on the attempts to regulate "political speech." Today it is generally agreed that, in most circumstances, a legislature or government agency wishing to regulate this constitutionally protected speech faces a heavy burden of convincing a court that there is a compelling need for the government's actions. Unfortunately for free-speech advocates, courts have proven less vigilant in striking down attempts to regulate speech that does not easily fit under the "political speech" rubric.

As noted earlier, because of confusion about what the framers of the First Amendment actually meant when they wrote "no law," courts historically have differentiated among different kinds of speech by the degree of constitutional protection afforded. This differentiation is critical to understanding the reasons underlying the degree of constitutionally permissible regulation of advertising, public relations and other forms of commercial speech (discussed in more detail in Chapter 2). Suffice it to say that courts have consistently held that "purely" commercial speech does not receive the same level of protection as speech about important public issues.

Figure 1.3 Because the public airwaves that carry broadcast messages are a scarce resource, courts have held that Congress may more freely regulate over-the-air broadcast speech to ensure that broadcasters operate in the public interest.

Credit line: Grasetto/iStockPhoto

Similarly, courts have held that lessened First Amendment protection applies to over-the-air broadcast speech. The logic employed by the courts for so holding is slightly different, however. Initially unregulated, radio broadcasters went to Congress in the 1920s seeking help because broadcasters were impinging on each other's radio frequencies. What they got was the Radio Act of 1927.[31] This soon was supplanted by the more comprehensive Communications Act of 1934[32] that also created the Federal Communications Commission (FCC). The law not only regulated use of frequencies and technical specifications, but also allowed the FCC to police the content of broadcasts to ensure broadcasters operated "in the public interest, convenience and necessity."[33]

Eventually, broadcasters challenged the FCC (and the law itself) as unconstitutionally infringing on their protected speech rights. In the combined *NBC v. United States* and *CBS v. United States*[34] cases in 1943, the Supreme Court upheld the constitutionality of the Act, agreeing that Congress could set content restrictions on broadcasters to police the use of the airwaves, which the government labeled a scarce public resource. The underlying legal premise was that the authors of the First Amendment could not have anticipated over-the-air broadcast speech and, therefore, the government was entitled to more leeway in regulating such speech. The continuing need for such laws and regulations, given today's multitude of media and communication channels, will continue to be one of the major areas of potential free-speech litigation facing lawmakers and communicators in this century.

As mentioned earlier, unlike commercial and broadcast speech, which are protected to some degree from government regulation, courts have held that obscene expression and speech that is criminal in nature (e.g., threatening, extorting or fraudulent) are totally without First

Amendment protection. Although an extensive discussion of this court-sanctioned form of content restriction is beyond the scope of this book, readers should understand that the issue in most cases challenging government restrictions of these kinds of speech is a definitional one (e.g., is the speech obscene or does it contain a real threat?).

The Court has spent decades wrestling with the definitional problems involved in obscenity cases. The wording of the current test is from *Miller v. California*,[35] a case decided by the Court in 1973, involving a conviction under state law of a man accused of mailing sexually explicit advertisements for books and films. Upholding the conviction, the Court said that for a work to be defined as legally obscene, the average person, applying contemporary community standards, must find that the work, taken as a whole, appeals to prurient interest in sex. In addition, the material must describe specifically defined content in a patently offensive manner and the work, taken as a whole, must lack serious literary, artistic, political or scientific value.[36]

Finally, a sort of betwixt and between content-/non-content-based rationale for regulating the dissemination of ideas has been raised by courts in cases involving attempts to regulate expressive conduct rather than pure speech. Some of these controversial decisions have concerned flag burning, nude dancing, spray-painting "hate speech" messages and picketing abortion clinics. Those wishing to engage in such actions argue that their activities are protected by the First Amendment because of the message inherent in their actions. An alternative interpretation, often advanced by the government, argues that conduct is different from speech and, therefore, legally can be more controlled.

This so-called speech/action dichotomy has created conflicting rulings from courts grappling with the issues that such cases raise. Often the outcome has turned on an ad-hoc evaluation of the "importance" of the expression versus the strength of the competing government interest. Thus, the Supreme Court has held that flag burning[37] is expressive conduct that is protected because of its political nature. Nude dancing, on the other hand, is expressive conduct that often is not protected because the message conveyed is of such a minor artistic nature that the government often can ban or control it simply on public policy grounds.[38]

Non-Content-Based Speech Regulations

The First Amendment clearly places barriers to the government's attempts to restrain or punish speech based upon its content. However, other speech-related laws and regulations, although infringing on a speaker's ability to get his or her message across, may not raise the same degree of First Amendment concern for the courts.

One example is regulation based on "time, place or manner." The criteria for such regulations are that they (a) advance a legitimate government interest, (b) be content neutral, (c) be reasonable and (d) not be used to ban or make speech practically impossible. Challenges to time, place or manner regulations often occur when authorities try to regulate such speech-related activities as door-to-door solicitations, parades, demonstrations on public property and so forth. Courts have been faced with a series of cases involving billboards, street signs and news racks resulting from municipalities' attempts to limit the number and placement of signs and vending machines on city streets for safety or aesthetic reasons. A number of these cases involve advertising or other kinds of commercial speech and are discussed later.

New media technology provides yet another problem area for time, place or manner regulations. Government attempts to limit spam e-mail messages and prevent unsolicited telephone marketing efforts raise interesting, and as yet unresolved, First Amendment issues that are just now winding their way through state and federal systems.

Other types of cases raising non-content speech issues involve efforts to gain access to government information, avoid disclosing the sources of information to government agencies or being required by law to publish information. Whether seeking to gain or avoid giving information, those so doing typically claim a right of free speech as the basis for their actions. Government representatives counter that the First Amendment gives lawmakers greater leeway to regulate such speech-related activities because the laws are not content based. Courts dealing with such claims have reacted inconsistently, sometimes recognizing First Amendment claims and sometimes giving them short shrift. Many of these issues also are discussed in subsequent chapters.

Importance of Free Speech

As this introductory chapter concludes, it may occur to the reader that a great number of people have gone to a great deal of trouble to theorize, legislate, argue and fight for the right of the individual to write or speak free of unwarranted government restraint or censure. The logical question that follows is: Why is free speech so important that many believe almost all other interests are subservient to it?

One of the reasons we might ask that question is that we have always lived in a society where free speech is protected. We take it for granted that we have the right to speak or write about almost anything we please without first getting it cleared by the official government censor or fearing the heavy tread of the storm-trooper's boot outside our door. However, the founders of this nation knew what it was like to fear both the censor and the authorities. Therefore, they were adamant in their belief that only in a society where people were free to criticize government and official conduct, as well as to speak out on other important public issues, could a democratic form of government flourish.

This has led scholars like Melvin Nimmer to the conclusion that the chief function of unfettered speech is the "enlightenment function."[39] Nimmer quotes Justice Brandeis, one of the Court's generally acknowledged great champions of freedom of speech and press, to the effect that "freedom to think as you will and to speak as you think are means indispensable to the discovery and spread of political truth."[40]

Professor Alexander Meiklejohn proposed a similar argument. In his viewpoint, freedom of speech is important because it allows intelligent choices by the electorate in a self-governing democracy.[41] Meiklejohn's ideas have been instrumental in formulating the concept that the First Amendment's primary purpose is to protect "political speech" from government regulation. "Its purpose," according to Meiklejohn, "is to give to every voting member of the body politic the fullest possible participation in the understanding of those problems with which the citizens of a self-governing society must deal."[42] But Nimmer argues that focusing solely on political truth is too limiting:

> The search for all forms of "truth," which is to say the search for all aspects of knowledge and the formulation of enlightened opinion on all subjects is dependent upon open channels of communication. Unless one is exposed to all the data on a given subject, it is not possible to make an informed judgment as to which "facts" and which views deserve to be accepted.[43]

Free speech, however, is important to our society beyond its critical role in governance. In a country not controlled by an ideology or dogma, free speech is seen as both a means for continually examining the status quo and as the mechanism for introducing new ideas and concepts into society as a leavening agent of change. The 17th-century philosopher John Milton was one of the first to publicly argue that the best path to truth is through uncensored exchange of ideas.[44] Two centuries later, John Stuart Mill urged the correlative idea that even speech proven to be false is important and needs protection because it forces us to reexamine old ideas rather than just assume them to be true.[45]

Critical to the enlightenment function of free speech is that the system for arriving at the outcome should be equally unrestricted. As Nimmer points out, "Absolute certainty on any issue of fact or opinion is beyond human capability. All determinations of 'truth' are necessarily tentative, subject to modifying or contradictory 'truths' which may later emerge."[46] However, if information that could lead to "contradictory truths" is limited or prohibited, the system becomes stagnant.

Justice Oliver Wendell Holmes, Jr. likened this process to the free marketplace of goods and services in his famous dissenting view in *Abrams*. Writing with a touch of irony, Justice Holmes first noted that

> [p]ersecution for the expression of opinions seems to me perfectly logical. If you have no doubt of your premises or your power and want a certain result with all your heart, you naturally express your wishes in law and sweep away all opposition.[47]

However, Justice Holmes was quick to point out that

> [w]hen men have realized that time has upset many fighting faiths, they may come to believe even more than they believe the very foundations of their own conduct that the ultimate good desired is better reached by free trade in ideas—that the best test of truth is the power of the thought to get itself accepted in the competition of the market and that truth is the only ground upon which their wishes can be carried out. That at any rate is the theory of our Constitution. It is an experiment, as all life is an experiment.[48]

The authors of this text would not be surprised to learn that a large majority of those reading the passage from Justice Holmes' dissent quoted above would strongly affirm his views as their own. Yet when given specific examples of the kinds of ideas and opinions such a free marketplace of ideas would permit, a sizeable number might not be as quick to agree. They may believe either that a consensus idea arrived at in the marketplace simply may be wrong or that a minority viewpoint may be incorrect or obnoxious or dangerous and, therefore, legitimately can and should be suppressed.

Nimmer, among others, responded to the criticism that truth will not always be the result of free marketplace forces by pointing out that such criticism "misses the point."[49] He noted that "Justice Holmes did not state that truth is to be found in the power of the thought to get itself accepted in the competition of the market. He said rather that this constitutes 'the best test' of truth."[50] As Nimmer said,

> What is the alternative? It can only be acceptance of an idea by some individual or group narrower than that of the public at large. Thus, the alternative to competition in the market must be some form of elitism. It seems hardly necessary to enlarge on the dangers of that path.[51]

Justice Holmes himself later responded to critics of a free marketplace who point out that allowing uninhibited free speech might protect a minority view that could prove "bad" or "false."

Rather than government suppression, Holmes' solution was almost always the introduction of more speech. This approach was exemplified by Justice Brandeis in his concurring decision in *Whitney v. California*[52] in which he noted, "The fitting remedy for evil counsels is good ones. ... If there be time to expose through discussion the falsehood and fallacies, to avert the evil by the process of education, the remedy to be applied is more speech, not enforced silence."[53] The reason is obvious for those who believe in free speech. That which the majority believes "bad" or "false" today, if allowed to be tested in the marketplace of ideas, may later prove to be the opposite. As Nimmer concludes, "It is only through the process of testing by hearing more speech from others that a reliable judgment can be made as to the worth of the objectionable speech. This is the very essence of the enlightenment function" of free speech.[54]

Although the enlightenment function may be the primary rationale for free speech recognized by most scholars, it is not the only one. One of the better-known alternative (if complementary) functions was advanced by Vincent Blasi who suggested that the primary value of free speech is to serve as a "checking function"[55] on the affairs of state. Free speech in this concept serves not so much as a means to test the truth of a multiplicity of views and opinions but as a counter balance to the power of government by ensuring that abuses of that power are restrained and exposed when they occur.

Even commentators who dispute the value of free speech as essential to democratic government or an enlightened society generally do not dispute that there are individual as well as societal benefits to free speech. Both as a way to vent frustration, rage or anger and as a means for self-expression, speech is an outlet for personal emotions that otherwise might lead to destructive acts or be repressed at psychological cost to the individual.

Conclusion

Those who do not believe that the best test of truth is in the free marketplace of ideas—who wish to limit or prohibit speech rather than encourage more speech when they encounter ideas and opinions they consider dangerous or odious—often desire to regulate or legislate for what they believe to be the best of motives. Perhaps they see people doing "unacceptable" things and wish to discourage these activities by discouraging speech that promotes the behaviors. Alternatively, they may wish to regulate speech in the name of the afflicted or the weak. Unfortunately, as will be seen is subsequent chapters, these arguments are often raised in support of restricting or restraining advertising, public relations and other commercial speech.

Notes

1. UNITED STATES CONSTITUTION, Amendment I.
2. New York Times v. Sullivan, 376 U.S. 254, 270 (1964).
3. M. B. Nimmer, Nimmer on Freedom of Speech: A Treatise on the First Amendment, §2.05 [B] 2-29 (Matthew Bender, 1988).
4. Whitney v. California, 274 U.S. 357, 377 (1927).
5. *See*, e.g., Shaw v. Hunt, 519 U.S. 804 (1996).
6. U.S. Const. amend. XIV.
7. Nimmer at §2.05 [B] 2-29. *See*, e.g., Marsh v. Alabama, 326 U.S. 501 (1946).
8. *Id*. quoting Bantam Books Inc. v. Sullivan, 372 U.S. 58, 70 (1963).
9. Barenblatt v. U.S., 360 U.S. 109 (1959).
10. *Id*. at 126.

11. Nimmer at §2.02 2-9.
12. D. M. Rabban, *The First Amendment in Its Forgotten Years*, 90 Yale L.J. 514 (1981).
13. Barron v. Mayor of Baltimore, 32 U.S. (7 Pet.) 243 (1833).
14. *See*, e.g., F. J. Turner, The Frontier in American History (Henry Holt Co., New York 1935).
15. C. 30, tit. 1, §3, 40 Stat. 217, 219 (comp. new st. 1917, §1012c).
16. Schenck v. U.S., 249 U.S. 47 (1919).
17. Abrams v. U.S., 250 U.S. 616 (1919).
18. Schenck, 249 U.S. at 52.
19. *Id.*
20. Abrams, 250 U.S. at 630 (Holmes, J., dissenting).
21. *Id.*
22. *See*, e.g., Criminal Anarchy Statute, N.Y. Penal Laws §160,161 (1909), originally enacted 1902.
23. Gitlow v. New York, 268 U.S. 652 (1925).
24. Dennis v. U.S., 341 U.S. 494 (1951).
25. Yates v. U.S., 354 U.S. 298 (1957).
26. Dennis, 341 U.S. at 511.
27. *Id.*
28. Brandenburg v. Ohio, 395 U.S. 444 (1969).
29. *Id.* at 447.
30. New York Times v. U.S., 403 U.S. 713 (1971).
31. 44 Stat. 1162 (1927).
32. 47 U.S.C. §151 (1934).
33. 48 Stat. 1064 (1934) 47 U.S.C.A. §151 et seq.
34. Nat'l. Broadcasting Co. v. U.S., and C.B.S. v. U.S., 319 U.S. 190 (1943).
35. Miller v. California, 413 U.S. 15 (1973).
36. *Id.*
37. Texas v. Johnson, 491 U.S. 997 (1989).
38. Barnes v. Glen Theatre, 501 U.S. 560, 111 S. Ct. 2456 (1991).
39. Nimmer at §1.02 [A], 1-7.
40. *Id.* quoting Whitney v. California, 274 U.S. 357, 375 (1927).
41. Nimmer at §1.02 [H], 1-44.
42. *Id.* at 1-45, quoting A. Meiklejohn, Political Freedom: The Constitutional Powers of the People 75 (Oxford University Press, New York 1965).
43. Nimmer at §1.02 [A], 1-7.
44. J. Milton, Areopagitica (Harlan Davidson, Wheeling, IL 1987).
45. J.S. Mill, On Liberty, 1-8 (Cambridge University Press, New York 1989).
46. Nimmer at §1.02 [A], 1-7.
47. Abrams, 250 U.S. at 630.
48. *Id.*
49. Nimmer at §1.02 [B], 1-12.
50. *Id.* citing Abrams, 250 U.S. at 630.
51. Nimmer at §1.02 [B], 1-12.
52. Whitney, 274 U.S. at 375 (Brandeis, J., concurring).
53. *Id.*
54. Nimmer at §1.02 [G], 1-42.
55. *Id.* at 1.02[I], 1-47, quoting V. Blasi, *The Checking Value in First Amendment Theory*, Am. B. Found. Res. J. (1977) 521.

2 The Development of the Commercial Speech Doctrine

The legal challenges faced by advertising and public relations practitioners are distinctly different than those confronted by journalists and other communicators. A number of prominent scholars have suggested that the framers of the First Amendment intended its freedom of speech and press provisions to apply to debate and discussion of public issues, not advertising or other commercially oriented messages. They argue, therefore, that speech primarily designed to further the economic interests of the speaker can (and perhaps should) be subject to greater government regulation than fully protected "political speech."

Beginning with the first cases interpreting the constitutional protections of speech discussed in the previous chapter, courts have accepted this general premise. Fortunately for advertising and public relations practitioners, courts also have determined that economically inspired speech is not totally devoid of constitutional protection. This chapter looks at the development of the First Amendment body of law focusing on what courts typically refer to as "commercial speech."

Development of Commercial Speech Jurisprudence

Walking down the streets of Colonial Williamsburg in Virginia or Old Sturbridge Village in Massachusetts—or reading one of the newspapers these reconstructed communities of the late 18th and early 19th centuries produce—you might be struck by the virtual absence of advertising compared to the neon signs and commercial-filled mass media of a modern metropolis. This lack of advertising is no historical oversight.

In the days before the advent of regional or national mass distribution of goods, residents of a community bought most items from local craftspeople, with the exception of a few relatively expensive products shipped by sea from England and the continent. A window display, small painted sign or, in larger communities, a classified-sized advertisement in the local weekly or monthly newspaper sufficed to inform a merchant's target market. By the end of the 19th century, however, first the railroads and then the mail-order business had changed all that. Railroads made it possible for local stores to sell mass-produced goods shipped from sites perhaps hundreds of miles away. The mail-order catalog business and rural free delivery, coupled with private carriers like Wells Fargo, meant that a consumer did not need to depend solely on the inventory of a local tradesperson to purchase a desired item.

Mass producers of items such as soap or cereal or clothing depended at first only on local merchants to push their products. Soon, however, smart manufacturers saw the need for their own marketing and advertising campaigns to spur demand for particular brands and to build

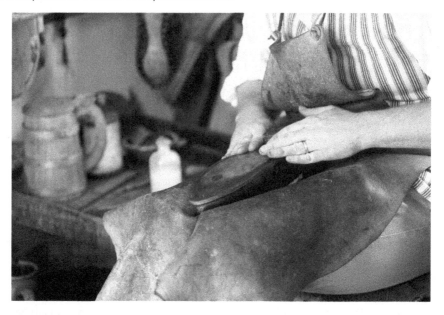

Figure 2.1 Before technology and travel allowed goods to be distributed regionally and nationally, most residents of a community purchased shoes and other personal and household items
from known, local craftspeople who had no need to advertise.

Credit line: BDPhoto/iStockPhoto

brand loyalty. By the turn of the 20th century, techniques of mass marketing and advertising,
particularly the use of display advertising in rapidly expanding mass-circulation newspapers
and magazines, began to catch up with the techniques for the mass production and distribution
of goods.

Until the development of advertising via the mass media, few manufacturers, retailers or
consumers worried about the quality or the truthfulness of commercial speech. Strange as it
seems in modern times, accustomed as we are to consumer watchdog groups and government
regulatory agencies, most people in the 19th century followed the maxim of caveat emptor
("let the buyer beware"). Consumers depended on their proximity to the makers and sellers
of goods to ensure quality control of the items they purchased. If the clientele found the merchant's goods or services disappointing, they were sure to mention it the next time they saw
the merchant in the street or stopped by the shop. Also, much of the commercial speech of
the time communicated simple information such as store hours or featured items. Additionally,
most people saw little advertising or product publicity of any kind as it would be defined today,
and what little they did see generally was dismissed by all but the most gullible as inherently
unbelievable, particularly because of the extravagant claims made for the benefits to be gained
by selecting the touted products or services.

With mass media advertising and publicity becoming key determinants in purchasing behavior, both manufacturers and consumers began to be more concerned with the truthfulness of
the factual claims for products and services. These concerns led to the adoption of so-called
printer's ink statutes at the state level (*Printer's Ink* magazine, a trade publication, had proposed
a model statute in 1911). Conviction of violating these statutes typically subjected those making
false claims in their commercial speech to minor criminal penalties, like a monetary fine.

In response to the growth of business monopolies and cartels, Congress created the Federal Trade Commission (FTC) in 1914. Its mandate was to ensure a level playing field in the competitive arena by preventing, among other things, "deceptive acts and practices."[1] Over time, the Commission interpreted this language to include regulatory overview of commercial speech to ensure truthful, non-deceptive claims. The federal Food and Drug Administration (FDA) and the Securities and Exchange Commission (SEC) were created in the 1930s to regulate specialized products (e.g., medicines, health-care and beauty aids) and the buying and selling of securities, respectively, including the kinds of claims and other information manufacturers could make for these products and services.

These government efforts to control commercial speech paralleled the development of self-regulatory schemes by various trade associations such as the Associated Advertising Clubs of America. These self-regulatory efforts depended largely on the use of moral suasion rather than penalizing offenders (such regulatory efforts will be discussed in more detail in later chapters).

From these early beginnings at the dawn of the 20th century until World War II, federal and state actions to regulate commercial speech continued to grow, albeit in piecemeal fashion. Somewhat surprisingly, however, despite this nearly half century of increasing regulatory developments, it was not until 1942 that such efforts were challenged as inherent violations of the federal Constitution's guarantee of free speech. It took an eccentric individual entrepreneur to see the issue all the way through to the Supreme Court of the United States.

The Commercial Speech "Exception" to the First Amendment: *Valentine v. Chrestensen*

The stage was set for the Court's initial foray into examining the constitutionality of commercial speech regulation with its decision in the 1939 case of *Schneider v. State (Town of Irvington)*.[2] Police arrested Clara Schneider, a Jehovah's Witness, for failing to obtain a permit before proselytizing her religious views door to door. The Court overturned her conviction on First Amendment speech and religion grounds but, in so doing, was careful to note that "[w]e are not to be taken as holding that *commercial* soliciting and canvassing may not be subjected to such regulation."[3] The Court seemed to suggest that rather than control commercial speech by a content-neutral, time-place-and-manner regulation, the community could legitimately discriminate against commercial speech based on the content of the message—the rationale being that commercial speech did not possess the same degree of First Amendment protection as other speech.

This apparent willingness by the Court to distinguish between regulation of commercial speech and other kinds of speech was borne out three year later in *Valentine v. Chrestensen*,[4] the first instance in which the Court decided the First Amendment issues in the case solely on the basis that the content of the speech in question was purely commercial. F. J. Chrestensen, a small-time entrepreneur/showman, hit on the idea of rescuing a decommissioned United States Navy submarine by purchasing it, refurbishing it and charging a small admission fee to tour the ship. After finally gaining permission from New York State officials to tie up at a pier in the East River (New York City officials had refused his initial request to use a city pier), Chrestensen was faced with the problem of how to attract visitors to his exhibit.

In New York City, it was virtually impossible for a small business to use conventional advertising to attract customers. Because of scarcity and economies of scale, generally only large corporations or other organizations could either afford or need to reach the hundreds of thousands of readers, listeners and viewers the city's mass media served. A businessman like Chrestensen might have afforded a small advertisement or two to publicize his submarine tours, but unless he could spend thousands of advertising dollars to get his message across on a much larger scale, his commercial speech was bound to be lost in the clutter of the other commercial messages vying for consumers' attention.

Having no large advertising budget at his disposal, Chrestensen turned instead to another traditional big-city publicity technique—handbills. Determining this to be a cheap (if perhaps less effective) means of reaching potential customers, Chrestensen created and had printed handbills that he distributed to passersby on the city's streets. Unfortunately for Chrestensen, this was in violation of the New York City Sanitary Code which said, in part, "No person shall ... distribute ... any handbill, circular ... or other advertising matter whatsoever in or upon any street or public place."[5] The city ordinance made an exception, however, for "the lawful distribution of anything other than commercial and business advertising matter."[6]

The government interests were straightforward—protecting pedestrians from being accosted and perhaps impeded by street solicitors and preventing litter on city streets caused by the likelihood that those taking the handbills would throw them on the pavement. The countervailing interest of Chrestensen was equally clear—the freedom to advertise his submarine tour using a handbill containing legal, accurate and truthful speech.

After a number of unpleasant encounters with the police, Chrestensen, rather than face the continuing risk of arrest, chose instead to reprint his handbill with the commercial message (minus any mention of a tour fee) on one side and, as the Court later noted, "a protest against the action of the City Dock Department in refusing the respondent wharfage facilities at a city pier"[7] on the other. The police, seeing this as simply an effort by Chrestensen to get around the law by turning his commercial speech into a political protest (which the ordinance specifically allowed), again refused permission to distribute his reprinted handbill, although they conceded that distributing a circular with just the protest message would be legal under the city code.

At this point, Chrestensen turned to the federal courts, seeking a restraining order to stop the police from interfering with the distribution of his handbills. A district court found that the city ordinance indeed went too far and granted a permanent injunction against police enforcement of the disputed regulation.[8] A federal appeals court agreed, upholding the lower court's order in a divided opinion.[9]

The Supreme Court of the United States disagreed. The question, said the Court, is "whether the application of the ordinance to [Mr. Chrestensen's] activity was, in the circumstances, an unconstitutional abridgement of the freedom of the press and of speech."[10] Although noting that previous decisions had "unequivocally held that the streets are proper places for the exercise of the freedom of communicating information and disseminating opinion and that ... states and municipalities ... may not unduly burden or proscribe its employment in these public thoroughfares ... [W]e are equally clear," said the Court "that the Constitution imposes no such restraint on government as respects purely commercial advertising."[11]

The "Commercial Speech Exception" Begins to Narrow

The Court did not return to evaluating the First Amendment status of pure commercial speech until its decision in the 1973 case of *Pittsburgh Press Co. v. Pittsburgh Commission on Human Relations*.[12] The *Pittsburgh Press Co.* case is complex for a variety of reasons, not the least of which is that it requires the reader to think of by-gone times when newspapers like the *Pittsburgh*

Press routinely ran classified advertising for employment under "HELP WANTED—MALE" and "HELP WANTED—FEMALE" columns. Typically, ads under the "MALE" heading included law-yers, physicians and other professionals, whereas ads under the "FEMALE" heading were more likely to be seeking public school teachers, nurses and clerical workers. The arrangement of the advertisements clearly implied that females need not apply for jobs in the well-paid professions or for managerial positions in industry.

The general public gave little thought to such sex-based discrimination until these practices were challenged by civil rights laws passed by Congress in the mid-1960s. These federal stat-utes inspired state and local governments to enact laws and regulations, including the Human Relations Ordinance legislated by the city of Pittsburgh, forbidding sex bias in the workplace. The regulation prohibited hiring based on the job-seeker's sex, and made it unlawful "[f]or any person whether or not an employer, employment agency or labor organization, to aid ... in the doing of any act declared to be an unlawful employment practice by this ordinance ..." including publishing or circulating "any notice or advertisement relating to 'employment' or membership which indicates any discrimination because of ... sex."[13]

In October 1969, the National Organization for Women filed a complaint with the Pittsburgh Commission on Human Relations charging that the *Pittsburgh Press* was in noncompliance with the city ordinance. The Commission agreed and issued a cease-and-desist order instructing the newspaper to discontinue using the sex-based classification scheme. The newspaper's argu-ments that it simply was following the requests of advertisers and that the ordinance violated the newspaper's right to determine the layout and content of its advertising pages were specifi-cally rejected. A local court of common pleas declined the newspaper's appeal of the Commis-sion's action. Subsequently, an intermediate-level Pennsylvania Commonwealth court modified the order slightly, but basically left it intact. The Pennsylvania Supreme Court refused to review the case and the newspaper appealed to the Supreme Court of the United States.

Conceding that protection of speech and press was paramount to a democracy, the Court, nonetheless, held that the city ordinance was not a significant detriment to the newspaper's economic well-being. Based on *Valentine*, the Court also found that the contents of the adver-tisements in question were "classic examples of commercial speech."[14] The newspaper had argued that, unlike *Valentine*, the commercial speech distinction was inapplicable in this case because the issue was the regulation of the editorial judgment of a newspaper rather than the control of commercial content or the actions of an advertiser. The Court rejected this argu-ment, finding that decisions about placement of an advertisement failed to "lift the newspaper's actions from the category of commercial speech."[15]

The Court also rejected the newspaper's final argument that a distinction between commer-cial speech and other kinds of speech was inappropriate and should be abandoned. Saying this argument would be best left until a later day, the Court noted that the discriminatory advertis-ing policy and contents of the advertisements in contention were "not only commercial activity but illegal commercial activity under the Ordinance."[16] The Court concluded that

> [a]ny First Amendment interest which might be served by advertising an ordinary commer-cial proposal and which might arguably outweigh the government interest supporting the regulation is altogether absent when the commercial activity itself is illegal and the restric-tion on advertising is incidental to a valid limitation on economic activity.[17]

At first reading, the decision in *Pittsburgh Press* appeared to be a simple re-affirmation of the Court's commercial speech exception to the First Amendment. However, a more thorough analysis provided hope that the Court's blanket denial of constitutional protection for purely commercial speech was not as absolute as it had seemed. Rather than simply refusing to hear the case or dismissing the newspaper's First Amendment arguments out of hand, the Court was careful to base its decision on the notion that the commercial speech in question was for an illegal purpose and that the government's interests in regulation, therefore, outweighed the newspaper's speech interests. This opened the door ever so slightly to the idea that courts should scrutinize more carefully any government attempts to ban or in other ways regulate *truthful* commercial speech for *legal* products or services.

The unusual circumstances of the next important commercial speech case, *Bigelow v. Virginia*,[18] created the first major breakthrough in the efforts to place commercial speech within the ambit of the First Amendment. The Court's decision in *Bigelow* emanated from a case involving an advertisement for an abortion referral service. Bigelow, a resident of Virginia and the director and managing editor of his self-described "underground weekly newspaper," *The Virginia Weekly*,[19] published a display advertisement that read as follows:

UNWANTED PREGNANCY
LET US HELP YOU
Abortions are now legal in New York.
There are no residency requirements.
FOR IMMEDIATE PLACEMENT IN ACCREDITED
HOSPITALS AND CLINICS AT LOW COST
Contact ... or call any time...
...
AVAILABLE 7 DAYS A WEEK
STRICTLY CONFIDENTIAL.
We will make all arrangements for you
and help you with information and counseling.[20]

All of the information in the advertisement was true, including the legality of regulated abortions in New York State. Unfortunately for Bigelow, the Virginia statute making abortions illegal at that time in his home state also outlawed efforts by "any person by publication, lecture, advertisement, or by the sale or circulation of any publication, or in any other manner, [to] encourage or prompt the procuring of abortion or miscarriage."[21] The statute made such "encouraging and prompting" efforts a misdemeanor.

Bigelow was convicted of violating the statute and fined $500 ($350 of which was forgiven if he promised not to run similar advertisements in the future). The Supreme Court of Virginia upheld his conviction, specifically rejecting his First Amendment-based claim that the statute was unconstitutional. The Virginia court found that the speech in question was a "commercial advertisement" and, therefore, it could "constitutionally [be] prohibited by the state...[when] the advertising relates to the medical-health field."[22]

On appeal, the Supreme Court of the United States vacated Bigelow's conviction and returned the case to Virginia for further consideration without deciding on the merits of his First Amendment claims. It did so because of the Court's intervening decision in *Roe v. Wade*[23] that states have limited ability to regulate abortions. On remand, the Supreme Court of Virginia reaffirmed its earlier opinion, upholding Bigelow's conviction on the basis that *Roe v. Wade* had not "mentioned the subject of abortion advertising."[24] Bigelow again appealed to the Supreme Court of the United States, and the Court reversed his conviction, this time on First Amendment grounds.

The Court began its opinion by stating that reliance on *Valentine* for the proposition that purely commercial speech is unprotected by the First Amendment was misplaced. "The fact that [*Valentine*] had the effect of banning a particular handbill does not mean that [it] is authority for the proposition that all statutes regulating commercial advertising are immune from constitutional challenge."[25]

The Court next distinguished *Pittsburgh Press*, noting that although the classified, help-wanted advertisements in the newspaper were purely commercial speech, even they "would have received some degree of First Amendment protection if the commercial proposal had been legal."[26] In the present case, the Court found that the advertisement in Bigelow's weekly newspaper "did more than simply propose a commercial transaction. It contained factual material of clear 'public interest.' Viewed in its entirety," said the Court,

> [T]he advertisement conveyed information of potential interest and value to a diverse audience—not only to readers possibly in need of the services offered, but also to those with a general curiosity about, or genuine interest in, the subject matter or the law of another State and its development, and to readers seeking reform in Virginia.[27]

It seems reasonable to believe that underlying the Court's decision in *Bigelow* was concern that Virginia's regulation of commercial speech for an abortion referral service was a none-too-subtle attempt to regulate a woman's constitutional right to seek an abortion. Support for this view came from the language of the decision, including a disclaimer by the Court that "[w]e do not decide in this case the precise extent to which the First Amendment permits regulation of advertising that is related to activities the State may legitimately regulate or even prohibit."[28] Later in the opinion, the Court again noted that "[w]e need not decide here the extent to which constitutional protection is afforded commercial advertising under all circumstances and in the face of all kinds of regulation."[29]

However, the Court did determine that

> [t]o the extent that commercial activity is subject to regulation, the relationship of speech to that activity may be one factor among others to be considered in weighing the First Amendment interest against the government interest alleged. Advertising is not thereby stripped of all First Amendment protection.[30]

From now on, said the Court, "a court may not escape the task of assessing the First Amendment interest at stake and weighing it against the public interest allegedly served by the [government] regulation"[31] if the commercial speech is not deceptive or fraudulent and is related to a legal product or service.

Bigelow represented a significant step forward in overcoming the Court's 30-year acquiescence to government regulation of purely commercial speech, but the decision failed to address a number of major issues. Although, after *Bigelow*, courts were required to balance speech interests against government regulatory interests, there was little discussion by the Court about how that balancing was to take place or how much weight should be assigned to either speech or government interests. (Remember that in other earlier cases, the Court placed a "heavy burden" on those who wish to regulate fully protected speech.) Nor was there discussion of the range of activities the Court had in mind when it noted that "the State may legitimately regulate or even prohibit"[32] advertising for some activities.

The Court also did not define the terms "deceptive" and "fraudulent" or the legality of a state limiting non-deceptive, legal advertising in its media for an activity or product illegal in another state (e.g., a New York statute banning advertising of an illegal abortion referral service in Virginia). Finally, the Court did not indicate what the result might have been if Virginia's regulation had been aimed at an advertiser rather than at the newspaper publishing the advertisement or if potential consumers of an advertised service or product had any independent First Amendment rights to receive the information contained in the disputed advertising.

Virginia State Board of Pharmacy: The High-Water Mark for Protection of Commercial Speech

It was this last issue that formed the basis for the Court's next major commercial speech decision, *Virginia State Board of Pharmacy v. Virginia Citizens Consumer Council, Inc.*,[33] still the high-water mark in the development of First Amendment protection for purely commercial speech. The Virginia State Board of Pharmacy is the agency empowered by the state to license and regulate pharmacists and the practice of pharmacy in Virginia. The Pharmacy Board had ruled that advertising the price of prescription drugs was inherently "unprofessional conduct" and that such conduct could subject the pharmacist who violated this rule to sanctions, including license revocation.

These regulations were questioned neither by advertisers nor the media, but rather by a consumer group self-described as representing potential purchasers of prescription medicines. The Consumer Council challenged the Pharmacy Board's anti-advertising rules on the somewhat novel thesis that consumers, who would benefit from information about prescription drug prices, had a First Amendment right to receive such information.

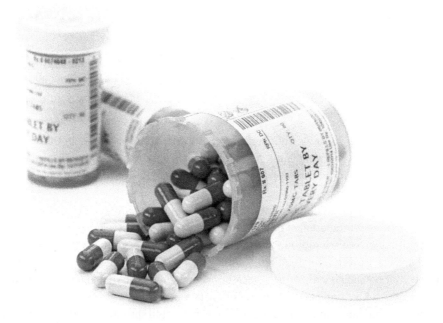

Figure 2.2 Should pharmacists be able to advertise the price of prescription drugs? That was the issue in 1976's *Virginia Board of Pharmacy v. Virginia Citizens Consumer Council* case decided by the Supreme Court of the United States.

Credit line: Ken Weinrich/Shutterstock.com

A special three-judge federal district court weighed the state's stated interests in preventing abuse and deception in the practice of pharmacy against the speech-related arguments advanced by the plaintiff that price information could significantly reduce the costs of prescription medicines. Noting evidence that prices charged for the same drugs could vary as much as 600 percent from pharmacy to pharmacy, the court found that the consumer group's arguments carried greater weight and struck down the anti-advertising regulations on First Amendment grounds. The Pharmacy Board appealed to the Supreme Court of the United States, arguing that Virginia's ban on advertising was a legitimate regulation of purely commercial speech.

The Court characterized the basic issue in the case as

> whether there is a First Amendment exception for "commercial speech." ... Our pharmacist does not wish to editorialize on any subject, cultural philosophical or political. He does not wish to report any particularly newsworthy fact, or to make generalized observations even about commercial matters. The "idea" he wishes to communicate is simply this: "I will sell you the X prescription drug at the Y price." Our question, then is whether this communication is wholly outside the protection of the First Amendment.[34]

To answer this question, the Court stressed four factors favoring disseminating commercial information about the price of prescription drugs. First, said the Court, the economic motivation behind the speech did not serve to disqualify it automatically from First Amendment protection. Second, the Court noted that "consumer's interest in the free flow of commercial information ... may be as keen, if not keener by far, than his interest in the day's most urgent political debate."[35] This was especially true in this case, said the Court, because the poor and elderly represented by the plaintiff tend to spend a disproportionate amount of income on prescription drugs, yet have little ability to comparison shop.

As its third factor, the Court also determined that striking down the ban on this form of commercial speech served to underlie the more general interest society has "in the free flow of commercial information."[36] Commercial information of general public interest (e.g., advertisements discussing the benefits of environmentally friendly products) would likely be protected from such government regulation, the Court said, and it could find little reason for not affording prescription drug advertising similar status.

Finally, acknowledging that the American economic system is based on free enterprise, the Court concluded that the system, "no matter how tasteless and excessive it sometimes may seem, is nonetheless [dependent on] dissemination of information as to who is producing and selling what product, for what reason, and at what price."[37] For the system to work, said the Court, it requires that "decisions, in the aggregate, be intelligent and well informed. To this end, the free flow of commercial information is indispensable."[38]

The Court accepted Virginia's arguments that prescription drug advertising could weaken the professionalism of licensed pharmacists but rejected banning advertising as a legitimate means for the state to accomplish its ends, noting the availability of many other regulations controlling the licensing and practices of the profession. Most such regulations would be permissible, said the Court, but adopting the one that relies "in large measure on the advantages of [keeping the public] in ignorance"[39] is not among them. "It is precisely this kind of choice, between the dangers of suppressing information, and the dangers of its misuse if it is freely available, that the First Amendment makes for us."[40]

In striking down the ban on prescription drug advertising, however, the Court was quick to add that it was not affording fully protected, First Amendment status to purely commercial speech. Legitimate time-place-and manner regulations would still be legal, said the Court, as would regulations restricting false, misleading or deceptive commercial speech. In an extensive footnote, the Court stated that because of the "hardiness" of commercial speech, and because the truth of the statements in such speech "may be more easily verifiable by its disseminator than, let us say, news reporting or political commentary," government could be granted greater leeway under the First Amendment to regulate purely commercial speech.[41]

The court said,

> Since advertising is the *sine qua non* of commercial profits, there is little likelihood of its being chilled by proper regulation and foregone entirely. Attributes such as these, the greater objectivity and hardiness of commercial speech, may make it less necessary to tolerate inaccurate statement for fear of silencing the speaker.[42]

The Court also noted that, at times, it could be appropriate "to require that a commercial message appear in such a form or include such additional information, warnings and disclaimers necessary [so as] to prevent its being deceptive. They may also make inapplicable the prohibition against prior restraints."[43]

The Court concluded that none of these rationales for lawful regulation of purely commercial speech applied in this case. "What is at issue [here] is whether a State may completely suppress the dissemination of concededly truthful information about entirely lawful activity, fearful of that information's effect upon its disseminators and its recipients. [W]e conclude that the answer ... is in the negative."[44]

Despite the Court's reluctance to grant full First Amendment protection to pure commercial speech, the Court's change of focus in *Virginia State Board of Pharmacy* from protecting the rights of the speaker to protecting the needs and the rights of the audience to receive information gave hope to commercial speech advocates that the commercial speech exception to the First Amendment was now limited to speech that touted an illegal product or activity or to commercial claims that could mislead or deceive the potential consumer. Under such a consumer-based approach, the government would be hard pressed to deny readers and viewers the information they needed to make informed choices when deciding how to conduct their personal commercial transactions.

The Supreme Court Begins to Retreat: *Bates et al. v. State Bar of Arizona*

Unfortunately, the euphoria generated by *Virginia State Board of Pharmacy* among free commercial speech advocates was almost immediately tempered by the reasoning of the Court in *Bates et al. v. State Bar of Arizona*[45] just one year later. The case involved John Bates and Van O'Steen, both attorneys practicing law in Phoenix, who formed a partnership to run a legal clinic to provide low-cost legal services for people of moderate income. It became apparent almost immediately that they would need to advertise to build a client base.

As part of this advertising, the partners decided they should include information about the fees charged for standard services such as uncontested divorces and simple personal bankruptcies. Advertising was expressly forbidden, however, by the rules covering the practice of law in Arizona as administered by the state's bar association. When the two attorneys placed an advertisement in the *Arizona Republic*, the state bar president filed a complaint that eventually resulted in both Bates and O'Steen being suspended from the practice of law for one week. Both appealed their suspensions to the Arizona Supreme Court, arguing that the sanctions by the bar violated both antitrust and free-speech laws. The Arizona court upheld the suspensions, and Bates and O'Steen appealed to the Supreme Court of the United States.

The Court dismissed contentions that the state bar rule violated federal antitrust provisions but found merit in the attorneys' First Amendment arguments. Citing *Virginia State Board of Pharmacy* for the proposition that commercial speech was at least somewhat protected by the First Amendment, the Court then turned its attention to the state bar association's arguments that lawyer advertising was an exception to this rule or, in the alternative, that the particular advertising by Bates and O'Steen was inherently false and deceptive.

Ordinarily, said the Court, there is no need for a finding that a specific speaker's rights in fact have been violated before a court should strike down a law or regulation that suppresses speech as an infringement of the First Amendment. This, the Court said, "reflects the conclusion that the possible harm to society from allowing unprotected speech to go unpunished is outweighed by the possibility that protected speech will be muted."[46] In a case involving purely commercial speech, however, the Court noted that this overbreadth doctrine does not apply because there are " 'commonsense differences' between commercial speech and other varieties [of speech]."[47]

One such difference, said the Court, is that because

> advertising is linked to commercial well-being, it seems unlikely that such speech is particularly susceptible to being crushed by overbroad regulations. Moreover, concerns for uncertainty in determining the scope of protection are reduced; the advertiser seeks to disseminate information about a product or service that he provides, and presumably he can determine more readily than others whether his speech is truthful and protected.[48]

The Court characterized the principal issue in *Bates* as "a narrow one"—whether "lawyers ... may constitutionally advertise the prices at which certain routine services will be performed."[49] The bar association had argued that because the costs for legal services could only be determined on a case-by-case basis, advertising fixed prices was inherently false and deceptive. The Court disagreed, holding that the state's total ban on lawyer advertising via the mass media (including advertising the price of standard services) was not permitted under the First Amendment, but also noting that pure commercial speech still could be regulated in ways that fully protected speech cannot. For example, the Court explicitly stated that false, deceptive or misleading commercial speech could be restrained, as could commercial speech about illegal products or transactions. Additionally, the Court noted that time-place-and-manner regulations could apply to commercial speech and that "the special problems of advertising on the electronic broadcast media ... [could] warrant special considerations."[50]

The Court's focus in *Bates*—"whether lawyers [i.e., the commercial speaker] ... may constitutionally advertise"[51]—clearly indicated it was no longer judging the constitutionality of laws regulating commercial speech by evaluating how much such laws infringe on the rights of the audience to receive commercial information. The Court could have characterized the issue in *Bates* as "whether consumers of legal services have a right to information about the prices of standard legal services" but chose not to do so. Although the Court indulged in some discussion of the need for informed decision-making on the part of potential clients, *Bates* signaled the beginning of a continuing retreat from the *Virginia State Board of Pharmacy* audience-centered focus and a return to evaluating attempted regulation of purely commercial speech by balancing the rights of the speaker—and not the receiver—against the interests of the government.

Development of Modern Commercial Speech Regulation: *Central Hudson's* Four-Prong Test

In *Central Hudson Gas & Electric Corp. v. Public Service Commission of New York*,[52] the Supreme Court, perhaps in an attempt to resolve the confusion caused by its nearly four-decades-long, zigzag path of dealing with arguments over First Amendment protection versus commercial speech regulation, set out a four-part test to help potential litigants and lower courts evaluate the probable constitutionality of laws governing commercial speech.

The challenged regulations in *Central Hudson* banned advertising that promoted the use of electricity. Originally, the regulations had been promulgated by the state agency in charge of regulating utilities as a temporary response to an energy crisis in the early 1970s. The Public Service Commission (PSC) extended the advertising ban after the immediate crisis had passed, however, as a general conservation measure. The PSC admitted that prohibiting advertising was not a perfect remedy because it also restricted electric power utilities from publishing advertisements encouraging the most efficient uses of electric power and because the ban did not apply to alternative energy sources like oil or coal. Nonetheless, the Commission continued its ban, in part because it feared that allowing advertising would send "misleading signals"[53] to consumers that conservation of electric power was no longer an important energy conservation goal. Central Hudson Gas & Electric challenged the PSC's ban in state court, but its arguments that the ban violated the corporation's First Amendment rights received little sympathy. Central Hudson then appealed to the Supreme Court of the United States.

Citing *Virginia State Board of Pharmacy*, Justice Powell, writing for the majority, reiterated that the First Amendment protects commercial speech from unwarranted government

Figure 2.3 The challenged advertising regulations in *Central Hudson Gas and Electric Corp. v. Public Service Commission of New York* were a byproduct of an energy crisis in the early 1970s that created fuel shortages across the United States.

Credit line: Everett Historical/Shutterstock.com

regulation, but also noted the Court's decisions recognizing differences in constitutional protection between commercial speech and other kinds of speech. Therefore, he said, protection for commercial speech "turns on the nature both of the expression and of the government interests served by its regulation."[54]

According to Justice Powell, "[i]n commercial speech cases ... a four-part analysis has developed."[55] First, said Justice Powell, the court needs to determine (a) if the speech in question is protected by the First Amendment at all. As examples of non-protected speech, Justice Powell noted there was little constitutional value in commercial speech that promotes illegal activities and products or that contains statements that are false or which tend to mislead or deceive. If the speech in question falls into one of these categories, it fails the first part of the four-part test and the government may regulate as it sees fit.

However, if the commercial speech the government intends to regulate does not fall into any of these categories, it is protected by the First Amendment and, said Justice Powell, "the government's power is more circumscribed."[56] Before regulating constitutionally protected commercial speech, said Justice Powell, the government must first show (b) that such regulation serves a "substantial" [not "compelling"] government purpose and, in addition, (c) that the actual manner in which the government proposes to regulate the speech directly aids the government in achieving its substantial purpose.[57] Finally, said the Court, the regulation must be (d) "narrowly tailored" to ensure that the regulation "is not more extensive than is necessary to further the [substantial government purpose]."[58]

Applying its four-part test to the facts of *Central Hudson*, the Court first found that the Constitution protected the company's commercial speech because there was nothing illegal, false or deceptive about the commercial information the utility company was attempting to convey. Turning to the arguments of the state regulatory commission, the Court agreed that the state's interests in conserving natural resources and encouraging non-wasteful use of electric power were "substantial" government interests. The Court also accepted the Commission's arguments that the method chosen—regulating the utility's commercial speech—helped the state to realize its substantial interest in discouraging excessive consumption of electric power. The Court based its finding on the premise that "there is an immediate connection between advertising and demand for electricity."[59]

The Court found, however, that the actions by the state utility commission could not pass the fourth part of the test because the challenged regulations were overly broad. "The Commission's order," said the Court, "reaches all promotional advertising, regardless of the impact of the touted service on overall energy use."[60] The Court, noting that the utility company had argued that it would have informed consumers how to be more energy conscious if not for the advertising ban, held that "[t]o the extent that the Commission's order suppresses speech that in no way impairs the State's interest in energy conservation, [that] order violates the First and Fourteenth Amendments."[61] Justice Powell pointed out that instead of a complete prohibition, the Court might have accepted alternative methods of regulating the utility company's commercial speech like restricting the format of the advertisements, limiting rather than prohibiting speech or requiring additional content.

Although the four-part *Central Hudson* test gained the approval of a majority of the Court as a cogent summation of the evolution of constitutional protection for purely commercial speech, several justices remained skeptical. Some felt that providing any constitutional protection for commercial speech extended the protective umbrella of the First Amendment to speech the authors of the First Amendment never meant to include. Others feared that such protection for commercial speech could water down protection for speech they considered more important.

The Court Applies the *Central Hudson* Test With Mixed Results

Chief among the critics of *Central Hudson* was Justice Rehnquist. He expressed some of his sharpest criticisms in his dissenting opinion in *Metromedia, Inc. v. San Diego*,[62] the first major commercial speech case to reach the Court after *Central Hudson*. *Metromedia* involved a challenge to the city of San Diego's municipal ordinance banning billboards and other outdoor advertising signs "to eliminate hazards to pedestrians and motorists"[63] and for general aesthetic reasons. A billboard company challenged the ordinance, arguing that the ordinance's exceptions for on-premise advertising of commercial names and/or services and for off-premise signs of a religious, historical or public service nature were not sufficient to protect the commercial billboard company's free-speech interests.

The Court struck down the city ordinance, but the justices strenuously disagreed among themselves about how to apply the *Central Hudson* four-part test (Justice Rehnquist characterized the Court's collective opinions as "a virtual Tower of Babel").[64] Justice White and three other justices agreed that the city's regulatory scheme passed the *Central Hudson* test for legally regulating commercial speech, but they nonetheless disallowed the ordinance on the grounds that permitting on-premise advertising of commercial messages but disallowing noncommercial messages unconstitutionally discriminated against noncommercial speech. Justices Blackmun and Brennan agreed that the ordinance should be struck down but on the grounds that it did not pass any part of the *Central Hudson* test. Chief Justice Burger and Justices Stevens and Rehnquist dissented in separate opinions, but each would have upheld the ordinance, agreeing that both the city's reasons for regulation and the means to accomplish its ends met the requirements of the *Central Hudson* test.

Similar internal divisions within the Court surfaced in a series of subsequent commercial speech cases in which shifting coalitions of justices alternately upheld and struck down government attempts to regulate commercial speech. For example, in *City Council v. Taxpayers for Vincent*,[65] the Court upheld a ban on signs that did not differentiate between commercial and noncommercial speech. Justices Brennan, Marshall and Blackmun dissented on the grounds that the majority had been much too deferential to the city's aesthetics arguments and had not carefully evaluated the competing speech interests. Justice Brennan would have required the city to at least demonstrate that it was engaged in a major, multi-method campaign to eradicate visual pollution and that banning signs was a necessary step in this campaign.

The elasticity of the *Central Hudson* test was best illustrated by the Court's decision in the 1986 case of *Posadas de Puerto Rico Associates v. Tourism Company of Puerto Rico*.[66] The Puerto Rico legislature had passed a statute legalizing casino gambling to encourage economic development of the island, but the statute specified that casinos would not "be permitted to advertise or otherwise offer their facilities to the public of Puerto Rico."[67] A later modification of the statute permitted advertising in "newspapers, magazines, radio, television or other publicity media outside Puerto Rico,"[68] even though such media might find their way into the hands of island residents.

Posadas de Puerto Rico Associates, a corporation operating the Condado Plaza Hotel and Casino, was fined and threatened with suspension of its gambling license by the Tourism Company of Puerto Rico, the agency delegated power by the commonwealth to regulate casinos, for violating the law's advertising provisions. The corporation paid the fine under protest and asked the courts of Puerto Rico to judge the statute's constitutionality. Although the courts agreed that the statute had been interpreted too broadly (apparently even imprinting the name of the casino on matchbook covers had been prohibited), they upheld the statute's prohibition of advertising in the mass media of Puerto Rico.

At the Supreme Court, Justice Rehnquist, writing for a five-person majority, applied the *Central Hudson* test but in a manner that greatly diminished the commercial speech protection provided in that case. The Court said,

> The ... commercial speech at issue here concerns a lawful activity and is not misleading or fraudulent, at least in the abstract. We must therefore proceed to the three remaining steps [of the test]. ... The first of these ... involves an assessment of the strength of the government's interest in restricting the speech.[69]

The Court, without requiring the commonwealth to produce evidence justifying its conclusions, held that Puerto Rico had satisfied the second part of the Central Hudson four-part test, accepting the commonwealth's arguments that "casino gambling ... would produce serious harmful effects on the health, safety and welfare of the Puerto Rican citizens, such as the disruption of moral and cultural patterns, the increase in local crime ... and the infiltration of organized crime."[70] The Court added, "[w]e have no difficulty in concluding that the Puerto Rico Legislature's interest ... [in the] welfare of its citizens constitutes a 'substantial' government interest."[71]

The Court characterized parts three and four of the *Central Hudson* test as requiring "a consideration of the 'fit' between the legislature's ends and means chosen to accomplish those ends."[72] Again without analysis, the Court accepted the commonwealth's "belief" that the "advertising of casino gambling aimed at the residents of Puerto Rico would serve to increase the demand for the product advertised."[73] The fourth part of the *Central Hudson* test proved no more of an obstacle. "We also think it clear beyond peradventure that the challenged statute satisfies the fourth and last step ... namely, whether the restrictions on commercial speech are no more extensive than necessary to serve the government's interest."[74]

Unlike previous cases that involved bans of commercial speech struck down on First Amendment grounds, the commercial speech in *Posadas* was not about a constitutionally protected activity like abortion or birth control. Justice Rehnquist said,

> In our view ... it is precisely because the government could have enacted a wholesale prohibition of the underlying conduct that it is permissible for the government to take the less intrusive step of allowing the conduct but reducing the demand through restrictions on advertising.[75]

The Court added that

> [i]t would be ... a strange constitutional doctrine which would concede to the legislature the authority to totally ban a product or activity but deny to the legislature the authority to forbid the stimulation of demand for the product or activity through advertising on behalf of those who would profit from such increased demand.[76]

Others quickly pointed out that Justice Rehnquist had it exactly backwards. While there is no constitutional protection of casino gambling, the First Amendment is there to protect speech about (and even encouraging) this activity.

If *Virginia State Board of Pharmacy* represents a high-water mark for the protection of commercial speech, *Posadas* may well be the opposite. After *Posadas*, the Court continued to apply and further amplify the four-part *Central Hudson* test in a series of "pure" commercial speech cases. Unfortunately, the Court lurched forward and backward, first finding increased First Amendment protection for commercial speech, then retreating from that position. The sum total of these cases left the so-called commercial speech exception to the First Amendment intact but did little to clarify the exact parameters and permissible extent of government regulation of commercial speech. A pair of cases in 1993, *City of Cincinnati v. Discovery Networks, Inc.*[77] and *Edenfield v. Fane*,[78] however, breathed new life into prongs three and four of the *Central Hudson* test.

Discovery Network, Inc., a provider of "educational, recreational, and social programs to individuals,"[79] published a promotional magazine touting its programs that was distributed via street news racks. Similarly, Harmon Publishing Co., a real estate business, promoted its property listings by using street news rack to distribute free publications describing homes for sale. Both companies had sought and received permission to locate their news racks at approximately 40 sites in the Cincinnati area, but the city council approved an ordinance rescinding this permission in a move the council described as an attempt to beautify the downtown streets as well as to make them safer for pedestrians and drivers. As applied, however, the removal order affected only the news racks of Discovery and Harmon, and not those of actual news publications.

Discovery Network and Harmon challenged the enforcement of the ordinance, claiming First Amendment violations along with due process concerns. City officials, although conceding that application of the ordinance to newspapers and news magazines would raise First Amendment problems, countered that the plaintiffs' speech was commercial in nature and, therefore, the city had greater license to regulate their speech because of the reduced First Amendment protection accorded commercial speech.

A federal trial court disagreed,[80] finding that the city had failed to demonstrate a reasonable fit between its desire for beauty and safety and its actions in banning the approximately 60 news racks owned by the plaintiffs. On appeal, the Sixth Circuit characterized the only issue as "does Cincinnati's ordinance ... prescribe a 'reasonable fit' between the ends asserted and the means chosen to advance them?"[81] The court found that it did not.

The Supreme Court of the United States accepted the city's appeal, observing that the "importance of the court of appeals decision, together with the dramatic growth in the use of newsracks throughout the country, prompted our grant of certiorari."[82] Writing for a six-person majority (Justice Blackman added a concurring opinion as well), Justice Stevens agreed with the Sixth Circuit's interpretation of the third prong of the *Central Hudson* test, holding that "[i]t was the city's burden to establish a 'reasonable fit' between its legitimate interests ... and the means chosen to serve those interests."[83] The Court concluded, "There is ample support in the record ... that the city did not [meet the burden] we require."[84]

In part four of the Court's *Central Hudson* analysis, Justice Stevens briefly dismissed the city's contention that it could ban the specific street racks of the non-news-oriented companies on the theory that commercial speech is less protected by the First Amendment. The Court noted that

> the city contends that the fact that assertedly more valuable publications are allowed to
> use newsracks does not undermine its judgment that its aesthetic and safety interests are

stronger than the interest in allowing commercial speakers to have similar access to the reading public. We cannot agree. In our view, the city's argument attaches more importance to the distinction between commercial and noncommercial speech than our cases warrant and seriously underestimates the value of commercial speech.[85]

The Court concluded that "Cincinnati's categorical ban on the distribution, via newsrack, of 'commercial handbills' cannot be squared with the dictates of the First Amendment."[86]

In *Edenfield*, decided only one month after *Discovery Network*, the Court again went to work on prong three of *Central Hudson*, requiring the government to go beyond speculation and actually offer proof that its regulation serves the government's interests. Scott Fane, a certified public accountant (CPA), found himself at odds with the Florida Board of Accountancy's rule forbidding the state's CPAs from engaging in in-person solicitation for new clients. Prior to relocating to Florida, Fane had owned an accounting practice in New Jersey, a state that allowed such solicitation.

Fane filed suit in the United States District Court for the Northern District of Florida,[87] asking the court for declaratory and injunctive relief to prevent the Board from enforcing its rule. In support of the defendant, a former chairman of the Florida Board testified that the rule was necessary to protect potential clients from unethical practices by CPAs. In his testimony, the former chairman contended that accountants who solicit customers are "obviously in need of business, and may be willing to break the rules."[88]

The court disagreed with the Board's contention that a hungry accountant is necessarily a dishonest one. It issued a summary judgment in favor of Fane and enjoined enforcement of the Florida Board of Accountancy's no-in-person-solicitation rule. The federal Court of Appeals for the Eleventh Circuit upheld the lower court's ruling.[89]

The Supreme Court of the United States affirmed the two lower courts' decisions. Justice Kennedy, delivering the opinion for an eight-justice majority, focused on prong three of *Central Hudson*, stating the Florida Board had not satisfied the burden of proof that its rule "advance[s] the [government] interest" asserted.[90] Addressing this burden, Justice Kennedy noted that

> [t]his burden is not satisfied by mere speculation or conjecture; rather, a government body seeking to sustain a restriction on commercial speech must demonstrate that the harms it recites are real, and that its restriction will in fact alleviate them to a material degree.[91]

Beyond abstract anecdotes and conjecture, the new interpretation offered by the majority in *Edenfield* apparently required *evidence* that the substantial interest articulated by the state was being met by the speech regulation in question.

Distinguishing Speech About Constitutionally Protected Activities/Products: *United States v. Edge Broadcasting Company*

In the midst of the celebration of the apparent resuscitation of the third and fourth parts of the *Central Hudson* test by the Court's holdings in *Discovery Network* and *Edenfield*, the Court handed down its opinion in *United States v. Edge Broadcasting Company*,[92] a case that, at the very least, made any celebration somewhat premature.

Edge Broadcasting was the license holder and operator of WMYK-FM, a radio station broadcasting from Elizabeth City, North Carolina. According to audience research, more than 90 percent of its listeners lived over the border in the nearby Hampton Roads, Virginia, metropolitan area.

The station's legal problems arose when management determined that the North Carolina station could boost advertising revenues if it could air commercials for the Virginia state lottery. Unfortunately, for Edge Broadcasting, WMYK was shut out from cashing in on this lucrative source of revenue because a North Carolina statute made it a misdemeanor to participate in or advertise a lottery.

What complicated matters even more was a federal statute[93] that specifically banned broadcasters like Edge Broadcasting from advertising lotteries in neighboring states if the state in which the station is licensed does not have a lottery. To avoid potentially unpleasant legal consequences, Edge Broadcasting sought a declaratory judgment in federal district court in the eastern district of Virginia that would hold the federal statute to be in violation of the broadcaster's First and Fourteenth Amendment rights.

The district court had little trouble deciding the lottery commercials satisfied the first prong of Central Hudson (i.e., is the speech protected by the First Amendment?) because Virginia had "lawfully created" its lottery program and the information contained in the advertisements the North Carolina station wished to run were neither false nor deceptive. As for the second prong of the test, the court accepted the government's argument that Congress had the right to regulate over-the-air broadcasts in ways it could not constitutionally regulate other media and that such regulation explicitly extended to disseminating information about lotteries. The court also agreed that the government's overall interest in regulating commercial speech about lotteries was legitimately in "furtherance of fundamental interests of federalism, enabling non-lottery states to discourage gambling."[94]

The district court determined, however, that both sections of the federal anti-lottery advertising statute ran afoul of the third prong of the *Central Hudson* test. The requirement that the challenged regulation directly advance an important government interest was not met by the statute's provisions, said the court, because they were "ineffectual means of reducing lottery participation by North Carolina residents."[95] The court added that audience analysis showed that listeners "within the area of the [station's] signal receive most of their radio, newspaper and television communications from Virginia-based media."[96] Conversely, little of the station's listening audience resided in North Carolina and the evidence demonstrated that this audience already was "exposed to significant lottery advertising on television" and print media emanating from Virginia. For these reasons, the court found that "sections 1304 and 1307 [of the federal statute], at most, have only a remote impact on Virginia lottery sales among North Carolina residents."[97]

On appeal, the Fourth Circuit Court of Appeals upheld the trial court in a brief, unpublished opinion.[98] North Carolina then petitioned the Supreme Court of the United States to hear its appeal, which was granted. Despite the state's urging to the contrary, the Court rejected the argument that commercial speech advocating or publicizing gambling was a vice-related activity and thus inherently within the power of government to control in any manner it chose. Instead, the Court elected to treat *Edge Broadcasting* as a normal commercial speech case requiring application of the four-part *Central Hudson* test.

Writing for the majority, Justice White noted that although for much of its long history "purely commercial advertising was not considered to implicate the constitutional protection of the First Amendment,"[99] beginning with *Virginia Board of Pharmacy* such speech was at least somewhat protected. "Our decisions, however," continued the Court, "have recognized the 'common-sense' distinction between speech proposing a commercial transaction … and other varieties of speech."[100] Applying the *Central Hudson* test, the Court agreed with the lower courts that Edge Broadcasting's speech was truthful, for a lawful activity (in Virginia) and non-deceptive. It conversely found that the government had a substantial interest "in supporting the policy of non-lottery States, as well as not interfering with the policy of States that permit lotteries."[101]

The Court disagreed with the lower courts, however, that the government had been unable to meet the third part of the *Central Hudson* test. Characterizing the lower court holdings as failing to "fully appreciate"[102] the government's interests, the Court observed that

> this question cannot be answered by limiting the inquiry to whether the government interest is directly advanced as applied to a single person or entity. Even if there were no advancement as applied in that manner ... there would remain the matter of the regulation's general application to others.[103]

The Court was quick to add that "[t]his is not to say that the validity of the statute's application to Edge is an irrelevant inquiry, but that issue properly should be dealt with under the fourth factor of the *Central Hudson* test."[104]

Having concluded that the lower courts had incorrectly held that the government had not satisfied the third part of the *Central Hudson* test, however, did not end the case. "Left unresolved," said the Court, "... is the validity of applying the statutory restriction to Edge, an issue that we now address under the fourth *Central Hudson* factor" whether the regulation is more extensive than is necessary to serve the government interest.[105] Harkening back to earlier cases, the Court noted that the government was required only to demonstrate "a fit between the restriction and the government interest that is not necessarily perfect, but reasonable."[106] The Court concluded the state had met this burden and overturned the decisions by the lower courts.

Justice Stevens, in dissent, was vehemently opposed to the majority's affirmation of the ban on the acceptance of lottery advertising by Edge Broadcasting. To Justice Stevens, "suppressing truthful advertising regarding a neighboring State's lottery, an activity which is, of course, perfectly legal, is a patently unconstitutional means of effectuating the Government's asserted interest in protecting the policies of non-lottery states."[107] The government, concluded Justice Stevens,

> has selected the most intrusive, and dangerous, form of regulation possible–a ban on truthful information regarding a lawful activity imposed for the purpose of manipulating, through ignorance, the consumer choices of some of its citizens. Unless justified by a truly substantial government interest, this extreme, and extremely paternalistic, measure surely cannot withstand scrutiny under the First Amendment.[108]

Commercial Speech Related to Alcohol Sales and Strength

In 1987, the Coors Brewing Company filed an application with the Bureau of Alcohol, Tobacco and Firearms for permission to print alcohol percentage contents on its beer container labels and in advertisements. Because these practices had been expressly forbidden by Section 205(e) (2) of the 1935 Federal Alcohol Administration Act (FAAA), the Bureau rejected Coors' application. Coors found a more receptive audience in the federal courts. Both the federal district court and the court of appeals agreed that the government had not met part three of the *Central Hudson* test. The government appealed to the Supreme Court.

In *Rubin v. Coors Brewing Co.*,[109] counsel for the federal government first advanced the theory that the law served a substantial government interest (part two of the *Central Hudson* test) in preventing alcohol "strength wars," a practice whereby producers of alcoholic beverages attempted to induce potential consumers to purchase a product on the basis of higher alcohol content. The government argued that the FAAA provisions had the potential effect of deterring "a particular type of beer drinker—one who selects a beverage because of its high potency—from choosing beers solely for their alcohol content."[110] In the government's view, the Act satisfied prong three of *Central Hudson* by "restricting disclosure of information regarding a particular product characteristic ... [thereby] decreas[ing] the extent to which consumers will select the product on the basis of that characteristic."[111]

Understandably, Coors Brewing Company painted a different picture of the FAAA's provisions. First, Coors contended that the labeling restrictions failed part two of *Central Hudson* and did not constitute a substantial government interest because the law had not been created with the *intent* of preventing strength wars. Coors based its primary objections, however, on part three of *Central Hudson*, questioning the validity of the FAAA labeling provisions. If the prohibition of alcohol content labeling truly advanced the government's interest by preventing strength wars, said Coors, why then did the law *require* wine and other distilled spirit manufacturers to provide the very same alcohol content disclosure on labels currently prohibited on beer labels? Coors also argued that there was no longer a substantial interest in enforcing the 1935 Act based on "protecting the health, safety, and welfare of its citizens."[112]

The Court was sympathetic to Coors' prong three arguments, agreeing that "205(e)(2) cannot directly and materially advance [the government's] asserted interest because of the overall irrationality of the Government's regulatory scheme."[113] As evidence of this irrationality, the Court suggested that beer advertisements in the mass media that include statements of alcohol content were of potentially greater danger than product labels themselves, yet the Act did not require an advertising ban by states that elected not to do so. The Court also accepted Coors' argument that the lack of a level playing field between beer, wine and other distilled spirits in advertising and labeling regulations constituted proof that the government's stated interest was not being met by the law. Justice Thomas, writing for the Court, stated that "[i]f combating strength wars were the goal, we would assume that Congress would regulate disclosure of alcohol content for the strongest beverages as well as for the weakest ones."[114]

Beyond the victory for commercial speakers represented by the majority opinion in *Rubin*, perhaps more importantly the case also illustrated the growing sense of disquiet by some members of the Court about *Central Hudson*'s lack of deference to truthful, non-deceptive commercial speech. In his concurring opinion, Justice Stevens noted that suppression of any truthful commercial information "because of the perceived danger of that knowledge is an anathema to the Free Speech Clause."[115] He added, the possibility "that consumers should be misled or uninformed for their own protection ... does not suffice to justify restrictions on protected speech in any context."[116]

Since *Rubin*, the Supreme Court has faced three additional cases involving so-called vice activities (e.g., gambling and consumption of alcohol and tobacco) and, in the process, added bite to prongs three and four of *Central Hudson*.

In the first, *44 Liquormart v. Rhode Island*,[117] the Court addressed constitutional challenges by two liquor retailers to the state's complete ban on non-point-of-sale alcohol price advertising. 44 Liquormart filed suit against the state after being cited and fined $400 for running ads that pictured a number of items with explicit pricing information, as well as pictures of two different brands of liquors accompanied by the word "WOW" (but no prices). Because price information accompanied many of the items in the advertisement, the Rhode Island Liquor Control administrator adjudged the word "WOW" to imply a discount price for the liquor as well.

After paying the fine, 44 Liquormart filed suit in federal district court asking that the state law be overturned on First Amendment grounds. Citing multiple studies that called into question the link between alcohol advertising and alcohol abuse, the trial court concluded that the advertising ban did not satisfy the *Edenfield* requirement that a regulation materially advance the government's asserted interest.[118] A federal appeals court reversed the lower court decision, forcing the liquor retailer to seek relief in the Supreme Court of the United States. In what would prove to be one of the most convoluted commercial speech decisions rendered by the Supreme Court, a shifting coalition of justices determined, among other things, that the Rhode Island alcohol price-advertising ban did indeed run afoul of First Amendment protections for commercial speech.

44 Liquormart is particularly important to those wishing to understand the Court's stance on commercial speech because it illustrates the continuing sharp differences between justices in their commercial speech considerations. Although all nine justices agreed that the Rhode Island law did not pass constitutional muster, their agreement ended with the judgment. The case featured an eight-part opinion written by Justice Stevens (with each part joined by different groups of justices), a three-part opinion penned by Justice Thomas, and a separate concurrence written by Justice O'Connor and joined by Chief Justice Rehnquist and Justices Souter and Breyer.

Specifically addressing the possibility that *Posadas* and *Edge Broadcasting* had created a subdivision of commercial speech for vice-related activities, Justice Stevens wrote that "[t]he respondents misread our precedent. Our decision last term striking down an alcohol-related advertising restriction [in *Rubin*] effectively rejected [a vice exception]."[119] Justice Stevens noted that "[f]urther consideration of [*Posadas*] persuades us that [it] should be rejected."[120] Justice O'Connor's concurrence offered the most traditional *Central Hudson* analysis of the facts in the case, determining that Rhode Island failed to demonstrate a "reasonable fit" between the complete advertising ban and its asserted interest of curbing alcohol consumption.

Justice Thomas used his concurrence in *44 Liquormart* as a platform for advocating a return to the *Virginia State Board of Pharmacy* standard of viewing with strict scrutiny any attempt to silence truthful, non-deceptive commercial messages. Justice Thomas said,

> In cases such as this, in which the government's asserted interest is to keep legal users of a product or service ignorant in order to manipulate their choices in the marketplace, the balancing test adopted in *Central Hudson* … should not be applied.[121]

The principal opinion expressed some of the same unease with censoring truthful, non-deceptive commercial speech. Justice Stevens suggested that the Court should apply *Central Hudson* only in cases in which the regulation in question clearly attempts to protect consumers from false or deceptive commercial information. Conversely, according to Justice Stevens, any regulation not clearly designed to protect consumers from such messages should be treated with a greater presumption of unconstitutionality.

Three years later, in *Greater New Orleans Broadcasting Association v. United States*,[122] the Supreme Court once again granted review to a commercial speech case that challenged the constitutionality of Title 18 U.S.C. §1304 (the same federal statute in question in *Edge Broadcasting*) in banning all broadcast advertising for gaming activities at privately owned casinos. The case was brought by a group of Louisiana broadcasters who had filed suit in federal district court seeking to have §1304 and its companion FCC regulations invalidated on First Amendment grounds.

Unlike *44 Liquormart*, the opinion in *Greater New Orleans* offered very little in the way of ambiguity. The justices unanimously agreed that §1304 and its companion FCC regulations could not be reconciled with First Amendment protections for commercial speech because they failed both parts three and four of the *Central Hudson* test. Justice Stevens, writing for the Court, focused on the irrationality of §1304, noting that the government's "regulatory regime is so pierced by exemptions and inconsistencies that the Government cannot hope to exonerate it."[123] Specifically, the opinion dismissed the government's contention that the advertising ban would lower demand for the service. Indeed, said the Court, casino gambling advertising likely did little more than funnel hardcore gamblers to a particular casino rather than draw new customers into the gambling fold.

Another major "vice" case occurred in *Lorillard Tobacco Company v. Reilly*.[124] In *Lorillard*, the tobacco corporation challenged a set of Massachusetts laws designed to protect children from exposure to tobacco advertising. Among the chief features of the law were prohibitions of billboards and other externally visible advertising within 1,000 feet of school grounds, as well as a prohibition of tobacco point-of-sale advertising less than five feet from the ground. In passing the law, the state had reasoned that small children would be less likely to see advertisements were they above their eye level.

The Court ruled that the outdoor ban violated prong four of *Central Hudson*'s "not more extensive than necessary" clause. The Court found persuasive Lorillard's argument that the close proximity of schools in urban areas of the state would mean that the 1,000-foot rule effectively banned tobacco advertising in as much as 90 percent of the land area in some Massachusetts cities. The Court said this showed strong evidence that the regulations were more extensive than necessary and did "not demonstrate a careful calculation of the speech interests involved."[125]

Considering the five-foot, point-of-sale rule, the Court engaged in a very brief (and almost humorous) dismissal of the regulation based on *Central Hudson* third and fourth prong grounds. Writing for the Court, Justice O'Connor noted that "[t]he 5-foot rule does not seem to advance...[the] goal [of curbing demand for tobacco products among children]. Not all children are less than 5 feet tall, and those who are certainly have the ability to look up and take in their surroundings."[126] The Court, in dismissing the notion that tobacco "is so special, so unlike any other object of regulation, that application of normal First Amendment principles should be suspended," noted that "[n]o such [vice] exemption exists."[127]

The Court's most recent commercial speech decisions involved cases of so-called compelled speech by producers of industry-wide promotional campaigns. For example, in *Johanns v. Livestock Marketing Association*,[128] the plaintiff objected to paying a $1 assessment for each head of cattle required by the federal Beef Promotion and Research Act of 1985. The challenge to the statute focused on objections to the advertising of beef as a generic product (as in the "Beef. It's What's for Dinner" marketing campaign). The plaintiffs argued the promotion on behalf of all producers of beef products harmed their own individual efforts to promote their products as superior in quality compared to the products produced by the rest of the industry, and strongly objected to being required to pay for the campaign.

Because the federal law mandated that all beef producers contribute to the promotional campaign, said the Court, the speech was not normal commercial speech, but rather could be considered as government speech (despite being paid for by private parties). On this basis, said the Court, the government requirements raised no First Amendment issues.

Figure 2.4 Although restrictions on the sale and advertising of alcohol and tobacco products have often stood up to constitutional scrutiny and been upheld by courts, the Supreme Court has stated that normal First Amendment principles apply to speech related to "vices" like cigarettes and beer.

Credit line: Stockcreations/Shutterstock.com

What's So Different About Commercial Speech?

At times, the Supreme Court of the United States has appeared to sympathize with those who wish to regulate commercial speech, while at other times it has sided with those who desire it to be protected from such regulation. As we conclude this chapter, perhaps we need to address a basic question: What is it about this kind of speech that has produced this ambivalence?

Legal commentators Alex Kozinski and Stuart Banner offer some interesting answers. The first is that pure commercial speech is not pure, i.e., it is motivated by monetary desire. Whether it is advertisers, advertising agencies, other corporate speakers or the media that carry the commercial messages, all have a profit-making motive for speaking. A second reason is the content of the speech. Much commercial speech is admittedly hyperbolic in nature, designed to influence and persuade the target market by appealing to psychological variables rather that providing straightforward information about the attributes of a product or service. These two reasons have led many critics of commercial speech to the conclusion that such speech is of little value and, therefore, not deserving of First Amendment protection. Kozinski and Banner note that critics of commercial speech make arguments like "people may think they prefer TV commercials to [the Greek epic poem] *The Iliad*, but if they think harder they'll realize their original preference was wrong."[129]

Additionally, critics of commercial speech may argue that commercial speech is less deserving of First Amendment protection than other forms of speech because of characteristics inherent in the speech itself. Professors Ronald Collins and David Skover,[130] for example, have suggested that the statement that pure commercial speech contains no value is an objective statement of fact. The Supreme Court in *Virginia State Board of Pharmacy* cited "common sense" differences between commercial and noncommercial speech as reasons for different levels of First Amendment protection. The Court noted that commercial speech is "verifiable" and therefore held to a higher standard than other forms of speech. Additionally, the Court found that commercial speech is a "more durable" type of speech because the speech is profit motivated and not as easily chilled by regulations as other forms of speech.[131]

In theory, each of these rationales for commercial speech regulation could be subject to verification. And even if true, it does not necessarily follow that they require a lesser degree of First Amendment protection for commercial speech. Courts, however, have almost universally accepted these rationales without question, as they have the judgment that commercial speech should be a form of lesser-protected speech.

As Kozinski and Banner point out, however, there is no obvious inherent distinction between commercial and noncommercial speech in the wording of the First Amendment. In fact, the term "commercial speech" was not employed by the Court until the *Pittsburgh Press* case in 1973. The two commentators speculate that the reasons courts used the terms "advertising" and "soliciting" prior to this case is significant. "In *Valentine* [the first major case], ... the Court wasn't facing a case about commercial speech; it was facing a case about advertising [a kind of business]."[132] They conclude that "[i]n 1942 ... [*Valentine*] was easy not because the Court thought of commercial speech as a category of speech deserving no protection, but because the Court didn't treat the case as involving speech at all."[133]

Because courts have given their consent to the possibility of greater regulation of pure commercial speech does not mean that either regulators or legislators need to or should make such regulations and laws. Unfortunately for commercial speech advocates, lawmakers often have strong political motivations for doing so. Pure commercial speech may be the means by which consumers learn about the products and services they want and need, but many are ambivalent about the value of this speech, especially as compared to speech about important public issues. Many activists in political, environmental or social organizations go beyond mere ambivalence to argue that commercial speech is, at best, inconsequential or, at worst, evil in the sense that it promotes unwanted behavior or products and services harmful to the individual or the environment.

Not uncommonly, those who are active in promoting such causes believe so strongly in them that, to quote Justice Holmes, they fall into the category of those who see regulation of "expression of opinions ... [as] perfectly logical. If you have no doubt of your premises or your power and want a certain result with all your heart you naturally express your wishes in law and sweep away all opposition."[134] With the bulk of the voting public indifferent, and with only groups of economically self-interested advertisers and media to represent the other side, legislators and regulators have often been persuaded that regulating or banning commercial speech is a cheap, politically expedient and easy way to tackle social ills.

Conclusion

Although the history of constitutional protection for commercial speech often has resembled the health chart of a critically ill patient, the strengthening of prongs three and four of the *Central Hudson* test in the Court's most recent major decisions in this area provides hope that truthful, non-deceptive commercial speech is closer than ever to achieving full First Amendment protection.

Arguably, in any attempt to regulate commercial speech, the speech itself should be the focal point of a court's attention rather than the ways in which the messages are being communicated.

However, the intrusive nature of contemporary media marketing and advertising techniques may hinder efforts to provide more constitutional protection for commercial speech. How much of a hindrance remains to be seen.

Notes

1. Federal Trade Commission Act, 15 U.S.C. §§ 45(1).
2. Schneider v. State, 308 U.S. 147 (1939).
3. *Id.* at 165.
4. Valentine v. Chrestensen, 316 U.S. 52 (1942).
5. §318 of the New York City Sanitary Code.
6. Valentine, 316 at 53 note 1 (emphasis added).
7. *Id.*
8. Chrestensen v. Valentine, 34 F. Supp. 596 (S.D.N.Y. 1940), *aff'd*, 122 F.2d 511 (2d Cir. 1941), *overruled*, 316 U.S. 52 (1942).
9. Chrestensen v. Valentine, 122 F.2d 511 (2d Cir. 1941), *overruled by* 316 U.S. 52 (1942).
10. Valentine, 316 U.S. at 54.
11. *Id.*
12. *See*, e.g., Pittsburgh Press Co. v. Pittsburgh Commission on Human Relations et al., 413 U.S. 376 (1973).
13. Pittsburgh Press, 413 U.S. 376.
14. Bigelow v. Virginia, 421 U.S. 809 (1975).
15. Pittsburgh Press, 413 U.S. at 385.
16. *Id.* at 387.
17. *Id.* at 389.
18. Bigelow, 421 U.S. 809.
19. *Id.* at 811 note 1.
20. *Id.* at 812.
21. *Id.* (quoting Va. Code Ann. §18.1-63 (1960)).
22. *Id.*
23. Roe v. Wade, 410 U.S. 113 (1973).
24. Bigelow, 421 U.S. at 815.
25. *Id.* at 818.
26. *Id.* at 821.
27. *Id.* at 822.
28. *Id.* at 825.
29. *Id.*
30. *Id.* at 826.
31. *Id.*
32. *Id.* at 825.
33. Va. State Bd. of Pharmacy v. Va. Citizens Consumer Council, 425 U.S. 748 (1976).
34. *Id.* at 749.
35. *Id.* at 761.
36. *Id.* at 763.
37. *Id.*
38. *Id.* at 765.
39. *Id.* at 769
40. *Id.* at 770.
41. *Id.* at 772 note 1.
42. *Id.*
43. *Id.* at 772 note 24.

44. *Id*. at 773.
45. Bates v. State Bar of Arizona, 433 U.S. 350 (1977).
46. *Id*. at 380.
47. *Id*. at 381.
48. *Id*.
49. *Id*. at 366–367.
50. *Id*. at 384.
51. *Id*. at 367.
52. Central Hudson Gas & Elec. v. Public Serv. Comm'n, 447 U.S. 557 (1980).
53. *Id*. at 560.
54. *Id*. at 563.
55. *Id*. at 566.
56. *Id*. at 564.
57. *Id*. at 599.
58. *Id*. at 569.
59. *Id*.
60. *Id*. at 570.
61. *Id*.
62. Metromedia, Inc. v. City of San Diego, 453 U.S. 490 (1981).
63. *Id*. at 493.
64. *Id*. at 543.
65. Members of City Council v. Taxpayers for Vincent, 466 U.S. 789 (1984).
66. Posadas de Puerto Rico Assocs. v. Tourism Co., 478 U.S. 328 (1986).
67. *Id*. at 332.
68. *Id*.
69. *Id*. at 340.
70. *Id*. at 341.
71. *Id*.
72. *Id*.
73. *Id*. at 342.
74. *Id*. at 343.
75. *Id*.
76. *Id*.
77. City of Cincinnati v. Discovery Network, Inc., 507 U.S. 410 (1993).
78. Edenfield v. Fane, 507 U.S. 761 (1993).
79. City of Cincinnati, 507 U.S. 410.
80. Discovery Network, Inc. v. City of Cincinnati, 1990 S.D. Ohio 90-00437.
81. Discovery Network, Inc. v. City of Cincinnati, 946 F.2d 464, 468 (6th Cir. Ohio, 1991).
82. Discovery Network, 507 U.S. at 415.
83. *Id*. at 416.
84. *Id*.
85. *Id*. at 419.
86. *Id*. at 431.
87. Fane v. Edenfield, 1990 U.S. Dist. LEXIS 18829 (N.D. Fla. Sept. 13, 1990).
88. Edenfield, 507 U.S. at 765.
89. Fane v. Edenfield, 945 F.2d 1514 (11th Cir. 1991).
90. Edenfield, 507 U.S. at 767.
91. *Id*. at 770–771.
92. United States v. Edge Broadcasting Co., 509 U.S. 418 (1993).
93. 18 U.S.C. §§1304 & 1307.

94. *Id.*

95. *Id.* at 639.

96. *Id.*

97. *Id.* at 641.

98. Edge Broadcasting Co. v. United States, 5 F.3d 59 (4th Cir. 1992).

99. Edge, 509 U.S. at 426.

100. *Id.* citing Ohralik v. Ohio State Bar Ass'n, 436 U.S. 447, 455–456 (1978).

101. *Id.* at 426.

102. *Id.* at 428.

103. *Id.* at 427.

104. *Id.*

105. *Id.* at 429.

106. *Id.*

107. Discovery Network, 507 U.S. at 419.

108. *Id.* at 439.

109. Rubin v. Coors Brewing Co., 514 U.S. 476 (1995).

110. *Id.* at 484.

111. *Id.*

112. *Id.* at 485.

113. *Id.* at 488.

114. *Id.*

115. *Id.* at 497 (Stevens, J., concurring).

116. *Id.*

117. 44 Liquormart, Inc. & People's Super Liquor Stores, Inc. v. Rhode Is. & Rhode Is. Liquor Stores Ass'n, 517 U.S. 484 (1996).

118. 44 Liquormart v. Racine, 829 F. Supp. 543 (D.R.I., 1993).

119. 44 Liquormart, 517 U.S. at 513.

120. *Id.* at 488.

121. *Id.* at 518.

122. Greater New Orleans Broad. Ass'n, Inc. v. United States, 527 U.S. 173 (1999).

123. *Id.* at 190.

124. Lorillard Tobacco Co. v. Reilly, 533 U.S. 525 (2001).

125. *Id.* at 562.

126. *Id.* at 566.

127. *Id.* at 586.

128. Johanns v. Livestock Marketing Ass'n, 544 U.S. 550 (2005).

129. A. Kozinski and S. Banner, *The Anti-History and Pre-History of Commercial Speech*, 71 Tex L. Rev. 747, at 757 (1992-1993).

130. R. Collins and D. Skover, *Commerce and Communication*, 71 Tex L. Rev. 697 (1993).

131. Virginia State Bd. of Pharmacy v. Virginia Citizens Consumer Council, Inc., 425 U.S. 748, 771 note 24 (1976).

132. Kozinski and Banner, *The Anti-History and Pre-History of Commercial Speech*, 747, at 757.

133. *Id.* at 758.

134. Abrams v. U.S., 250 U.S. 616 at 630 (1919), (Justice Holmes, dissenting).

3 Defining Commercial Speech and Related Issues

Chapter 1 traced the somewhat erratic course the Supreme Court of the United States has followed to create and implement "tests" that speakers, government regulators and lower courts should employ to gauge the degree of constitutional protection afforded different kinds of speech. As discussed in Chapter 2, although noncommercial speech about public issues is protected from regulation in all but truly unusual situations, commercial speech often has been treated as a First Amendment second-class citizen. Specifically, the Court's *Central Hudson* test allows regulation when the government interest asserted as the basis for regulation is substantial, there are no other means the government reasonably could employ that are less restrictive of speech and the government has been careful not to regulate any more speech than necessary.

Paid-For Public-Interest Speech by Not-For-Profit Organizations

In *Valentine v. Chrestensen*,[1] the Court's initial foray into establishing the constitutional limits on the regulation of commercial speech, the Court made no attempt to define the terms it used in determining New York City's legal right to ban handbills that advertised tours of Chrestensen's submarine. Chrestensen's disputed handbills did not contain any mention of an admission fee, but city authorities and the Court treated them as "commercial and business advertising matter"[2] forbidden by a municipal ordinance. The Court said that although in most cases the city could not prohibit citizens from using city streets to disseminate opinion, "[w]e are equally clear that the Constitution imposes no such restraint on government as respects purely commercial advertising."[3]

The Court noted that Chrestensen could not avoid regulation simply by adding a discussion of public issues if his speech still remained basically commercial in purpose. In so doing, the Court's opinion foreshadowed issues that continue to haunt commercial-speech cases: an unambiguous definition of what constitutes commercial speech, the constitutional status of speech that takes the form of commercial speech but is not related to commercial activity, and the differences, if any, in the protection of that speech depending on the nature of the speaker.

Nearly two decades passed after *Valentine* before the Court again made a major clarification about the definition of commercial speech. It did so in its discussion of a variety of issues in *New York Times v. Sullivan*.[4] In *Sullivan*, the Court carved out an important exception for what today are often called "advertorials," as well as for other forms of paid-for speech used by not-for-profit organizations to discuss matters of public interest.

The backdrop of the case originated in the desegregation efforts led by Dr. Martin Luther King, Jr. in Southern states in the late 1950s and early 1960s. On March 29, 1960, *The New York*

Times carried a full-page advertisement entitled "Heed Their Rising Voices." Included in what the advertising copy called "the wave of terror" directed against the civil rights activities of Dr. King and other activists were charges that Dr. King and his followers had been arrested on trumped-up charges.

The plaintiff in the subsequent defamation suit, L. B. Sullivan, served as a Montgomery city commissioner whose duties included supervising the police department. Claiming that the statements in the advertisement about police misconduct libeled him, Sullivan brought suit against a number of African-American clergymen who had purchased the advertisement and against the *New York Times* for publishing it. An Alabama jury eventually awarded Sullivan $500,000 (more than $4 million in today's economy)—a verdict that eventually was appealed all the way to the Supreme Court of the United States.

All parties (and the Court) recognized the fact that the allegedly libelous statements were published in an advertisement was an important factor in the case. Based on the wording of the Court's opinion in *Valentine*, Sullivan's attorney argued that the Supreme Court lacked jurisdiction even to hear the newspaper's appeal on the premise that *Valentine* had determined that commercial speech had no special constitutional protection and that the harmful speech in this case was admittedly in the form of a full-page advertisement.

The Court disagreed and elected to hear the newspaper's appeal. In eventually deciding in favor of the newspaper, the Court noted that those relying on *Valentine* for the proposition that "the constitutional guarantees of freedom of speech and of the press are inapplicable here ... because the allegedly libelous statements were published as part of a paid, 'commercial' advertisement"[5] were guilty of misinterpreting the Court's earlier intent.

According to the Court, the crucial distinguishing factor in its earlier holding in *Valentine* was the conclusion that the speech consisted primarily of purely commercial advertising. By contrast, "[t]he publication [in *Sullivan*] ... was not a 'commercial' advertisement in the sense in which the word was used in [*Valentine*]," said the Court. "It communicated information, expressed opinion, recited grievances, protested claimed abuses, and sought financial support on behalf of a movement whose existence and objectives are matters of the highest public interest and concern."[6]

Saying that failure to provide First Amendment protection would discourage others from buying or running what the opinion called "editorial advertisements,"[7] the *Sullivan* Court noted that this result "might shut off an important outlet for the promulgation of information and ideas by persons who do not themselves have access to publishing facilities—who wish to exercise their freedom of speech even though they are not members of the press."[8] The Court concluded that "we hold that if the allegedly libelous statements would otherwise be constitutionally protected from the present judgment, they do not forfeit that protection because they were published in the form of a paid advertisement."[9]

This procedural decision allowed the Court to decide the *Sullivan* case on its merits. In the process, however, the opinion strongly called into question the widely held belief that the determination of whether speech should be defined as commercial was based on whether the speech occurs in paid-for space or time. In effect, the Court's decision meant that after *Sullivan*, courts must assess whether the speech the government wishes to regulate is commercial in nature by evaluating the *content* of the speech.

Such a content-based definition arguably requires an unambiguous line of demarcation differentiating commercial speech from noncommercial speech. Surprisingly, despite the passage of more than five decades since the *Sullivan* decision, the Court has yet to provide this

Figure 3.1 Might an organization's statements by a representative at a news conference be regarded as commercial speech subject to greater limitation and punishment? For organizational speakers, a broad definition of commercial speech means more speech is at risk for sanction by the government.

Credit line: Wellphoto/Shutterstock.com

"bright-line" definition. The problems presented by this failure to agree on one standard definition of commercial speech are discussed in detail later in this chapter.

Paid-For Public-Interest Speech by For-Profit Organizations

Roughly a decade and a half after *New York Times v. Sullivan*, the Court returned to the subject of paid-for speech used to addresses public issues in *First National Bank of Boston v. Bellotti*.[10] Unlike *Sullivan*, this time it was in the context of a case involving the government's efforts to regulate public-interest speech by a profit-making corporation.

At issue was an attempt by the state of Massachusetts to enforce its statute prohibiting banks, telephone companies, public utilities and most business corporations (and their officers) from spending money "for the purpose of … influencing or affecting the vote on any question submitted to the voters, other than one materially affecting any of the property, business or assets of the corporation."[11] Another provision of the statute specified that no questions "submitted to the voters solely concerning the taxation of the income, property or transactions of individuals shall be deemed materially to affect the property, business or assets of the corporation."[12]

First National Bank and other corporations questioned the validity of the statute when planning to purchase advertising space and time to express their opposition to a proposed state constitutional amendment authorizing the state to institute a graduated personal income tax. They were informed by the state's attorney general, Francis X. Bellotti, that he would enforce the state's statutory prohibitions against such advertisements if the corporations persisted in their efforts to state their views via media advertising.

The penalties provided in the statute were severe (a fine of up to $50,000 for a corporation and/or a fine of up to $10,000 or imprisonment of up to one year, or both, for an officer or director of the corporation). Rather than violating the statute and then appealing the imposition of such penalties, First National Bank and its corporate allies sought a declaratory judgment—a sort of advisory opinion—to test the statute's constitutionality in advance.

The state's highest court held the statute to be a valid limitation on the speech interests of the plaintiffs, finding that the First Amendment rights of a corporation could constitutionally be "limited to issues that materially affect its business, property or assets."[13] The state court characterized the issue as whether a corporation's First Amendment rights were the equal of individuals and found as a matter of law that they were not. The court noted that the statute did not prohibit speeches on the topic by corporate executives or statements to the press, internal newsletters, bulletins to stockholders or other typical corporate public relations activities, so long as they did not involve contributions or "expenditure of corporate funds."[14]

On appeal, the Supreme Court of the United States made short work of the state's arguments. Refusing to frame the issue as the nature and extent of corporate First Amendment rights, the Court instead said,

> The proper question ... is not whether corporations 'have' First Amendment rights and, if so, whether they are co-extensive with those of natural persons. Instead, the question must be whether [the statute] abridges expression that the First Amendment was meant to protect. We hold that it does.[15]

The Court rejected arguments that allowing for-profit corporations to spend corporate assets to campaign against such referenda or to speak out on public issues would overwhelm the marketplace of ideas by drowning out other voices. There was no evidence of such a threat, said the Court, and there were other less drastic measures a state might take in order to alert its citizens about potential abuses of the marketplace of ideas such as requiring advertisements placed by corporations to carry information identifying the source of the speech. In short, said the Court, when a for-profit corporation wishes to use advertising or other forms of paid-for speech to discuss matters of general public interest not connected with its commercial activities, such speech should receive the same degree of constitutional protection as speech from other sources.

Four years after *Bellotti*, the Court, in *Consolidated Edison Co. of New York, Inc. v. Public Service Commission of New York*,[16] reversed a lower court decision that had upheld a Commission policy banning the utility company's discussion of public issues in brochures and flyers included with monthly customer billings. Citing *Bellotti*, Justice Powell reiterated "the inherent worth of the speech in terms of its capacity for informing the public does not depend on the identity of its source."[17] Despite what Justice Blackmun (in dissent) called a "free ride"[18] for the utility company's propaganda at ratepayer expense, the majority held that such a total ban "strikes at the heart of the freedom to speak."[19]

The vast majority of decisions in cases with fact patterns resembling *Bellotti* have been decided in favor of the paid-for speech interests. For example, in *C & C Plywood v. Hanson*,[20] a federal appeals court, citing *Bellotti*, struck down a Montana statute that banned corporate financial contributions in support of ballot issues. In *Let's Help Florida v. McCrary*, a federal appeals court similarly held unconstitutional a Florida law limiting corporate contributions "[t]o any political committee in support of, or in opposition to, an issue to be voted on in a state-wide election." [21]

Paid-for Speech by For-Profit Speakers in Support of Candidates for Public Office

The rules change considerably when financial contributions—including paying for political advertising and other forms of communication—are made to assist candidates for public office. For example, the 1971 Federal Elections Campaign Act[22] (FECA) regulates the amount individuals and organizations may contribute directly to candidates for federal office and creates rigorous disclosure and reporting requirements for those making such contributions. Many states have passed similar statutes to regulate campaigns at the state level.[23]

The constitutionality of the federal act (as amended in 1974) was challenged in *Buckley v. Valeo*.[24] The Supreme Court ruled that restricting direct contributions to candidates was constitutional, but it struck down the provisions of the Act limiting the amounts that could be spent on behalf of a candidate by groups or organizations working independently of the candidate.

The general euphoria that free-speech champions derived from the holdings in *Buckley* and a series of subsequent decisions was dealt a nearly fatal blow, however, by the opinion of the Court in the 1990 case of *Austin v. Michigan Chamber of Commerce*.[25] In *Austin*, the Court upheld government restrictions on a corporation's political speech involving independent expenditures for or against candidates for public office, ruling that regulations governing such efforts satisfied the definition of a compelling government interest needed to outweigh the speaker's First Amendment rights.

Section 54(1) of the Michigan Campaign Act expressly prohibited corporations from expenditures that could lead "to the nomination or election of a candidate."[26] The Act defined such contributions as "a payment, donation, loan, pledge, or promise of payment of money or anything of ascertainable monetary value"[27] although it allowed corporations to spend money for such purposes if the money was maintained in a separate fund.

The Michigan Chamber of Commerce, a corporation established to encourage economic development and improve the state's business climate, normally does not engage in direct political support of candidates. However, faced with a special election to fill a vacancy in the state legislature, Chamber officials desired to buy advertising space in a local newspaper to support a pro-business candidate. Fearing that the campaign act would prohibit such activity, the Chamber sought a declaratory judgment in federal district court that the statute should be unenforceable on First Amendment grounds.

Although a federal district court upheld the act as a legitimate limitation on corporate activity[28] (the state statute was modeled in part on a similar federal statute), on appeal, the Sixth U.S. Circuit Court of Appeals ruled that the Michigan Campaign Act could not, for First Amendment reasons, apply to the Chamber because it was not a traditional corporation and was formed expressly to spread economic and political messages.[29] The federal appeals court found no compelling interest that would justify infringing the speech interests of the Chamber.

On appeal by the state, the Supreme Court disagreed. Although it was appropriate for the court of appeals to apply the compelling government interest test to this case, said the Court's majority, the lower court had erred in not recognizing that the state had met this requirement. The Court held that Michigan obviously was concerned with "the corrosive and distorting effects of immense aggregations of wealth that [are] accumulated with the help of the corporate form and that have little or no correlation to the public's support for the corporation's political ideas."[30]

The Court conceded both that the desire to support candidates for public office via advertising is speech that "constitute[s] 'political expression at the core of our electoral process and of the First Amendment freedoms,'" and that "[t]he mere fact that the Chamber is a corporation does not remove its speech from the ambit of the First Amendment."[31] However, said the Court, "the unique state-conferred corporate structure that facilitates the amassing of large treasuries warrants the limit in independent expenditures."[32] The Court also concluded "the Chamber does not possess the features that would compel the State to exempt it from restriction on independent political expenditures."[33]

In dissent, Justice Kennedy noted that in this situation involving the regulation of advertising constituting "a paradigm of political speech,"[34] the Court clearly "adopts a rule that allows Michigan to stifle the voices of some of the most respected groups in public life on subjects central to the integrity of our democratic system."[35] Justice Kennedy continued,

> Those who thought that the First Amendment exists to protect all points of view in candidate elections will be disillusioned by the Court's opinion today; for that protection is given only to a preferred class of nonprofit corporate speakers: small, single-issue nonprofit corporations that pass the Court's own vague test for determining who are the favored participants in the electoral process.[36]

The holding in *Austin* cast a pall over those who believed that the Court in prior opinions had recognized an almost absolute First Amendment protection for corporate speech about public issues and campaigns. That dark cloud only deepened with the passage in 2002 of the

Figure 3.2 A 2006 movie critical of presidential candidate Hillary Clinton, who was seeking the Democrat party nomination, led to *Citizens United v. Federal Elections Commission*, a major Supreme Court opinion on campaign-contribution limits.

Credit line: Jose Gil/Shutterstock.com

Bipartisan Campaign Reform Act (BCRA). Also known as the McCain-Feingold Act,[37] the BCRA significantly regulated the raising and spending of so-called soft money by national political parties. In addition, the BCRA restricted the use of corporate and union funds for broadcast messages within 60 days of a general election. The bill, signed into law by President George W. Bush, withstood a later court challenge in *McConnell v. Federal Elections Commission*.[38]

Citizens United v. FEC

In 2006, Citizens United, a nonprofit corporation with a multi-million-dollar annual budget supplied mostly from donations by individuals but also partly funded by for-profit corporations, produced a film entitled *Hillary: The Movie*. The 90-minute documentary about Hillary Clinton was clearly unsympathetic to the senator, who was seeking to become the 2008 Democratic Party nominee for president.

In addition to showings in theaters, Citizens United sought to distribute the movie through a video-on-demand provider. In so doing, however, the organization became concerned that it might run afoul of §203 of the BCRA (which modified §441b of the 1971 FECA). The "law prohibit[ed] 'electioneering communication,' defined as 'any broadcast, cable, or satellite communication' that 'refers to a clearly identified candidate for Federal office' and is made within 30 days of a primary or 60 days of a general election."[39]

Seeking clarification of its status, Citizens United went to federal court seeking a declaratory judgment that §203 should not be applicable to *Hillary: The Movie*.[40] The district court denied Citizens United's request, and subsequently granted the FEC's motion for summary judgment.[41] The case was first argued on its merits at the Supreme Court, which deferred judgment until all parties could file supplemental briefs addressing whether "either or both *Austin* and the part of *McConnell*" should be overruled.[42]

Writing for a five-justice majority, Justice Kennedy began his opinion by noting that

> Section 441b's prohibition on corporate independent expenditures is … a ban on speech. As a "restriction on the amount of money a person or group can spend on political communication during a campaign," that statute "necessarily reduces the quantity of expression by restricting the number of issues discussed, the depth of their exploration, and the size of the audience reached."[43]

Thus, said Justice Kennedy, "[i]ts purpose and effect are to silence entities whose voices the Government deems to be suspect."[44]

According to Justice Kennedy, such a law raises significant constitutional issues. "The First Amendment protects speech and speaker, and the ideas that flow from each. We find no basis for the proposition that, in the context of political speech, the Government may impose restrictions on certain disfavored speakers."[45]

In addition, said Justice Kennedy, "[t]he Court has recognized that First Amendment protection extends to corporations (citations omitted). This protection has been extended by explicit holdings to the context of political speech."[46] Citing *Bellotti*, Justice Kennedy noted that "[t]he Court has … rejected the argument that political speech of corporations or other associations should be treated differently under the First Amendment."[47]

Justice Kennedy next turned to the issue of efforts to restrict independent campaign expenditures generally. "The *Buckley* Court explained that the potential for quid pro quo corruption distinguished direct contributions to candidates from independent expenditures," said Justice

Kennedy, and "invalidated ... restrictions on independent expenditures."[48] Although *"Bellotti,"* he continued, "did not address the constitutionality of [Massachusetts'] ban on corporate independent expenditures to support candidates, ... that restriction would have been unconstitutional under *Bellotti's* central principle: that the First Amendment does not allow political speech restrictions based on a speaker's corporate identity."[49]

Turning to the Court's decision in *Austin*, which, according to Justice Kennedy, "uph[eld] a direct restriction on the independent expenditure of funds for political speech for the first time in [this Court's] history,"[50] he noted that "the *Austin* Court identified a new governmental interest in limiting political speech: an anti-distortion interest" defined as "preventing 'the corrosive and distorting effects of immense aggregations of wealth that are accumulated with the help of the corporate form and that have little or no correlation to the public's support for the corporation's political ideas.'"[51]

The Court is thus "confronted," continued Justice Kennedy, "with conflicting lines of precedent: a pre-*Austin* line that forbids restrictions on political speech based on the speaker's corporate identity and a post-*Austin* line that permits them."[52] Observing that "the Government does little to defend" *Austin's* anti-distortion rationale, Justice Kennedy also gave it little credence.[53] "The rule that political speech cannot be limited based on a speaker's wealth," he said, "is a necessary consequence of the premise that the First Amendment generally prohibits the suppression of political speech based on the speaker's identity."[54] In addition, "[i]t is irrelevant for purposes of the First Amendment that corporate funds may 'have little or no correlation to the public's support for the corporation's political ideas.'"[55]

Saying that "[f]or the most part [the government] relinquishe[s] the antidistortion rationale"[56] as the basis for its justification of independent expenditures, Justice Kennedy noted that "the Government falls back on the argument that corporate political speech can be banned

Figure 3.3 Justice Anthony Kennedy, who retired in 2018 from the Supreme Court of the United States, authored several notable free-speech opinions, including *Citizens United v. Federal Elections Commission*.

Credit line: Rob Crandall/Shutterstock.com

in order to prevent corruption or its appearance. In *Buckley*, the Court found this interest 'sufficiently important' to allow limits on contributions but did not extend that reasoning to expenditure limits."[57] Similarly, that interest "is not sufficient to displace the speech here in question. For the reasons explained above, we now conclude that independent expenditures, including those made by corporations, do not give rise to corruption or the appearance of corruption."[58] As for the government's argument about unfairness to dissident corporate shareholders, Justice Kennedy, citing *Bellotti*, suggested that "[t]here is ... little evidence of abuse that cannot be corrected by shareholders 'through the procedures of corporate democracy.' "[59]

If "Congress finds that a problem exists," Justice Kennedy observed, "we must give that finding due deference."[60] However, he continued,

> the remedies enacted by law ... must comply with the First Amendment; and, it is our law and our tradition that more speech, not less, is the governing rule. An outright ban on corporate political speech during the critical pre-election period is not a permissible remedy.[61]

Post-*Citizens United*

The Court's *Citizens United* opinion was immediately controversial.[62] The decision provoked severe criticism by President Barack Obama,[63] political commentators and editorialists. Legislative proposals to restrict independent campaign expenditures were introduced in Congress, but all failed to pass.[64] The uproar continues, and the impact of the decision on political campaigns continues to be discussed routinely in newspapers[65] and blogs,[66] as well as in legal scholarship.[67] It also has been debated in legislatures[68] and courthouses[69] around the country, and it is possible the issue will find itself before the Supreme Court once again.[70]

The two most significant decisions since *Citizens United* are *SpeechNow.org v. FEC*[71] ("*SpeechNow*") and *Arizona Free Enterprise Club's Freedom Club PAC v. Bennett*[72] ("*Arizona Free Enterprise Club*"). The *SpeechNow* decision is particularly significant in that it is directly responsible for the so-called Super-PACs that received much of the criticism from campaign-finance-reform advocates during the 2012 and 2016 presidential primary seasons.[73]

Although individuals were allowed to make unlimited individual expenditures prior to the *Citizens United* ruling, groups categorized by the FECA as "political committees" were subject to specific provisions that limited the amount of money any one person could contribute.[74] The limit for contributions from an individual to a political committee was $1,000 per committee, with a possible total of $69,900 for contributions to all political committees.[75] *SpeechNow* involved a challenge to these provisions as being unconstitutional in that they limited an individual's ability to make independent expenditures on political issues.[76]

An individual's right to make independent expenditures on political speech had been established in *Buckley*[77] and was not at issue in *Citizens United*. Therefore, not surprisingly, the trial court opinion in *SpeechNow*, which was initiated before *Citizens United*, was not dependent on that decision for its opinion.[78] However, the subsequent ruling by the Court of Appeals for the District of Columbia came after the *Citizens United* decision, and that court relied heavily (in fact almost exclusively) on *Citizens United*.[79]

The appellate court ruled that contribution limits must be closely drawn to serve a sufficiently important interest and that the Supreme Court has "recognized only one interest sufficiently important to outweigh the First Amendment interests implicated by contributions for political speech: preventing corruption or the appearance of corruption."[80] In *Citizens United*,

Justice Kennedy's majority opinion stated specifically that "independent expenditures ... do not give rise to corruption or the appearance of corruption."[81] According to the court in *SpeechNow*, "this simplifies the task of weighing the First Amendment interests implicated by contributions to *SpeechNow* against the government's interest in limiting such contributions."[82]

In overturning the trial court's decision, the appellate court essentially said that something always outweighs nothing. If "independent expenditures do not give rise to corruption," any level of burden would be inappropriate when justified on the basis of possible corruption. And if the corruption interest is the only compelling interest the government has for burdening political speech, as was the case in *SpeechNow*, all such burdens of political speech are, by definition, unconstitutional.[83]

A second post-*Citizens United* decision that has affected the balance between campaign finance reform and free speech also relied heavily on *Citizens United*. In *Arizona Free Enterprise Club*,[84] the Supreme Court considered the constitutionality of Arizona's matching funds provisions for political candidates. At issue were provisions of Arizona's Clean Elections Act (ACEA)[85] that allowed political candidates who received a minimum number of $5 donations from Arizona voters to opt to receive public funding for their campaigns.[86] By choosing public funding, candidates agreed to limit the amount of their own, private campaign funding in return for a set amount of public money.[87]

How much money any one candidate would receive from the state depended on a number of factors, including provisions of the Act that called for "equalizing" or matching funds.[88] This provision mandated that if another candidate chose to opt out of public financing and use private funds, that amount would dictate how much money the publicly funded candidate would receive.[89] If the privately funded candidate exceeded the public-funding allotment, §16-952(B) of ACEA provided additional money to the publicly funded candidate in an attempt to equalize funding.[90] If a privately funded candidate faced a number of publicly funded candidates, each would receive equalizing funds.[91]

In addition to matching money spent by the privately funded candidate, ACEA would match funds spent on behalf of that candidate by independent groups.[92] Once the public funding limit was surpassed, any additional money spent either by or on behalf of the privately funded candidate would result in additional money being given to any publicly funded candidate in the same race.[93]

Citizens United and *SpeechNow* focused on whether the burdening of speech by the challenged regulation was justified by a compelling interest. Both the Supreme Court and the District of Columbia Circuit Court said it was not. *Arizona Free Enterprise Club*, on the other hand, focused more on whether the underlying regulation actually burdened speech at all. The Court of Appeals for the Ninth Circuit held that ACEA posed only a minimal burden to speech because privately financed candidates could still spend unlimited funds on political speech and upheld the Arizona law as constitutional.[94] The Supreme Court disagreed, and, in a 5-4 decision, held that the relevant provisions of the ACEA violated the First Amendment.[95]

According to Chief Justice Roberts' majority opinion, "The matching funds provision 'imposes an unprecedented penalty on any candidate who robustly exercises [his] First Amendment right[s].'"[96] The provision "forces the privately funded candidate to 'shoulder a special and potentially significant burden' when choosing to exercise his First Amendment right to spend funds on behalf of his candidacy."[97]

Once establishing that the provision imposed a burden, the Court was left to consider whether there was a compelling governmental interest sufficient to justify the infringement of

First Amendment rights. The parties in *Arizona Free Enterprise Club*, however, failed to agree about which government interest was at issue in the case.[98] The plaintiffs believed the ACEA was aimed at "leveling the playing field" in terms of candidate resources.[99] Possibly because of the precedent against considering an equalizing interest as a compelling one, the defendants countered that the government interest being served by the ACEA actually was the elimination of corruption or the appearance of corruption.

The Court first rejected the idea that leveling the playing field is a compelling government interest.[100] In fact, in *Davis*, the Court held that "discriminatory contribution limits meant to 'level electoral opportunities for candidates of different personal wealth' did not serve 'a legitimate government interest' let alone a compelling one."[101] Leveling the playing field, added the Court, had also been dismissed as a compelling interest in *Buckley* and *Citizens United*. "The Court is troubled by the fact that efforts to level the playing field means allowing the government to have an impact in the choice over who governs, and this is 'a dangerous enterprise that cannot justify burdening protected speech.' "[102]

Prior to *Citizens United*, the defendants' arguments about the elimination of corruption might have had a chance. Although the Court discussed in some detail whether the ACEA is actually aimed at eliminating corruption,[103] in the end, because the Court held that the provisions limit or burden independent expenditures (as opposed to contributions), the same language from *Citizens United* that was controlling in *SpeechNow* was controlling here.[104] In other words, if independent expenditures cannot give rise to corruption or the appearance of corruption, then any provision aimed at limiting or burdening these expenditures will fail under this justification.[105]

The legislation at issue in *Citizens United* barred corporations from spending general treasury funds on independent campaign expenditures, but as *SpeechNow* and *Arizona Free Enterprise Club* indicate, the reach of the *Citizens United* opinion has spilled over into other areas. The language from the majority opinion has played a large role in shaping (indeed, striking down) two pieces of campaign-finance legislation that were not specific to corporations.

For example, the *SpeechNow* decision allows corporations to give money without limitation to organizations for the purpose of political speech but extends that same right to individual citizens as well. And, while the Arizona provision triggered matching funds when corporations (in a post-*Citizens United* world) spent money on speech in support of a privately funded candidate, the provision actually paid no attention to whether the speakers were corporate or individual.

Clearly, *Bellotti* and *Citizens United* have dramatically altered the landscape of efforts to limit the role corporate big money plays in referendums and elections. What it has not done is still the voices of those who, nonetheless, argue that ways must be found to restrict what they see as its pernicious influence. Nonetheless, it still seems safe to say that in most instances paid-for speech by for-profit corporations will be free from regulation if that speech discusses matters of general public interest or independently supports or opposes candidates for public office and there is not a countervailing government interest of great importance.

Admittedly, corporate and other organizational paid-for speech on matters of public interest usually is of little concern to most advertising professionals who make their fortunes promoting the goods and services a corporation sells for profit. For public relations professionals, however, the continuing viability of full First Amendment protection for such speech is particularly important as it provides protection for an important weapon in the arsenal of public relations techniques for communicating organizational messages to important publics.

Commercial and Quasi-Commercial Speech

It seems clear that courts will accord a lesser degree of First Amendment protection for speech by a corporate speaker if the speech is determined to be in direct pursuit of its commercial interests. Unfortunately, in a series of rulings, the Supreme Court has made this determination much more complex than one might assume. In addition, it is by no means clear how the courts or regulatory agencies will (or should) react to speech by for-profit companies that does not directly urge the purchase of goods or services, but, nonetheless, arguably is commercial in nature.

Resolving these issues is particularly important to advertising and public relations professionals because those who advocate limitations on the speech of for-profit corporations are likely to continue to press for greater regulation of such quasi-commercial corporate speech on public policy grounds. If successful in convincing a court that a corporation's speech should be classified as commercial speech, such a ruling opens the door to imposing a variety of legally acceptable means for speech regulation impermissible if the speech were fully protected under the First Amendment.

As discussed in Chapter 1, prior restraint of speech—including commercial speech—in the form of bans or limitations is the least preferred remedy that courts and regulators may employ. However, there are other remedies that have found favor with the Supreme Court and with lower courts when regulating commercial speech. For example, in *Central Hudson*, Justice Powell, citing *Banzhaf v. FCC*,[106] noted that requiring the advertising to include "information about the relative efficiency and expense of [the utility company's] offered service, both under current conditions and for the foreseeable future"[107] would be acceptable and preferable to the banning-of-speech remedy sought by the state's public service commission. Critics of commercial speech have suggested such other measures as (a) limiting appeals especially targeting racial or ethnic groups (tobacco and liquor advertising); (b) requiring commercial speakers to include additional information representing other points of view (e.g., drug warning labels); and (c) banning cartoon characters, illustrations or pictures of users of the product or service in the graphic design of commercial speech (so-called tombstone ads).

Alternatively, regulation of corporate commercial speech might take the form of requirements, like those of the Federal Trade Commission (FTC) that the commercial speaker bears the burden of demonstrating that its speech, if challenged, is neither false nor illegal nor deceptive. Additionally, such regulatory bodies have legally required speakers to back up factual claims with scientific data or results of rigorously conducted public opinion polls.

Assuming that speech designated as commercial continues to be accorded only second-class constitutional protection by the Court, it would seem essential that the Court draw a "bright line" that unambiguously provides a clear division between speech defined as commercial and speech classified as noncommercial (or, perhaps more to the point, speech that is fully protected and speech that is not). Despite numerous opportunities, the Court has failed to provide this demarcation. What is worse, the Court has continued to waiver in its handling of definitional issues related to commercial speech, depending on the nature and the facts of the case it is deciding.

Almost all would agree that advertisements and marketing promotional material for goods and services fall directly within the definition of commercial speech. Less clear is whether marketing-related public relations efforts by a profit-making corporation (e.g., a press conference announcing a new product) fall within this definition. Advertising and public relations speech not directly focused on a for-profit organization's goods or services (e.g., a company's advertisement in the local newspaper publicly thanking its employees for community service efforts) finds itself in an even more ambiguous position vis-à-vis its relation to commercial speech. Advertising and public relations speech advancing a social issue or discussing important public problems (e.g., company-sponsored public service advertisements warning about environmental issues related to climate change) may not fit the definition of commercial speech at all.

For example, what is the First Amendment status of a cigarette company's advertisement questioning the validity of anti-smoking research claims; a news release by an automobile manufacturer touting the virtues of its new models; a magazine or brochure containing some information of general interest, but obviously intended to promote the publisher's instructional programs; or a brewing company that prominently affixes its logo design on the side of a NASCAR racer? All of these examples are taken from real-life cases (some of which are discussed later in this chapter), producing results that are confusing and often appear to be in direct conflict with each other over the issue of whether they fall within the definition of commercial speech.

The definition of commercial speech most preferred by partisans of as little restriction of speech as possible is the narrow definition mentioned in the Court's first modern-day "purely commercial speech" case—*Pittsburgh Press*.[108] Reacting to the split in rationales and outcomes in the *Valentine* and *Sullivan* decisions, the Court attempted to position the sex-based, help-wanted ads at issue in *Pittsburgh Press* as more like those prohibited in *Valentine*. Characterizing the ads as "classic examples of commercial speech,"[109] the Court noted that the "critical feature" of the speech in question was that it "did no more than propose a commercial transaction."[110]

The Court subsequently employed this language in *Virginia State Board of Pharmacy*.[111] According to Justice Blackmun, writing for the majority, this definition means that it would be improper to characterize all speech that is published in paid-for space or time as commercial speech, citing the civil-rights-related advertisement in *Sullivan*. Similarly, said the Court, speech should not be classified automatically as commercial just because it appears in a medium that has a profit-making motive, citing cases involving bookstores and movies. Also, the Court noted that speech soliciting financial contributions is not necessarily commercial, even if paid for, again citing *Sullivan*. Finally, neither speech about subjects generally related to commerce (e.g., arguments for or against free trade) nor paid-for speech that simply communicates facts (e.g., portions of the abortion clinic advertisements in *Bigelow*) automatically makes the speech commercial.

Justices hostile to regulating commercial speech (e.g., Stevens and Blackmun) consistently used the narrow "commercial transaction" definition in subsequent opinions. For example, employing this definition, the Court in *Board of Trustees of the State University of New York v. Fox*[112] noted that although speech involved in soliciting sales of Tupperware in college dormitories was commercial speech, it would be overly broad to encompass all "paid" speech within the definition of commercial speech. Expanding the definition beyond speech that "does no more than propose a commercial transaction," said the Court, would impermissibly define commercial speech occurring when, for example, payment is made for services like tutoring students, providing counseling sessions or offering advice on medical or legal matters.[113] Similarly, in *City of Cincinnati v. Discovery Network, Inc.*,[114] Justice Stevens rejected the city's contention that it could regulate the placement and number of news racks on city streets because it would be too difficult to determine the differences between regular newspapers that are sold for profit and contain commercial messages versus the primarily commercial publications the city sought to control. Although not the deciding factor in the case, it is clear that at least some members of the majority in *Discovery Network, Inc.* rejected the city's reliance on language that first sur-faced in *Bates*[115]—and was used again by the Court in the cases of *Friedman v. Rogers*[116] and *Central Hudson*[117]—that the correct method for determining if the speech in question is commercial speech is to evaluate the "economic motivation" for the speech.

This alternative definition—"economic motivation" rather than "speech proposing a com-mercial transaction"—has found favor, however, with a number of other justices. In *Central Hud-son*, for example, Justice Powell expressly rejected the contentions of Justice Stevens that the Court's use of "economic interests" as the basis for defining commercial speech would sweep more speech than was constitutionally permissible under the commercial speech umbrella. Judging the utility company's speech to not be commercial speech, said Justice Powell, "would grant broad constitutional protection to any advertising that links a product to a current public debate. But many, if not most, products may be tied to public concerns."[118]

Subsequently in *Dun & Bradstreet, Inc. v. Greenmoss Builders, Inc.*,[119] a credit reporting agency being sued for defamation argued it should receive First Amendment protection for its alleged defamatory statements. (Other constitutional issues involved in defamation commer-cial-speech cases are discussed in Chapter 4.) The Court held that such reliance was improper, in part because the credit report that falsely accused the plaintiff of bankruptcy was like com-mercial speech in that it was "solely motivated by the desire for profit, which, we have noted is a force less likely to be deterred than others."[120] The dissent, in vain, vigorously challenged this formulation, arguing that economic motivation was too broad a term and that the "do no more than propose a commercial transaction"[121] language of *Pittsburgh Press* should be employed when defining commercial speech.

Perhaps the most notable use of the "economic motivation language" as the definition of commercial speech appears in the majority opinion in *Bolger v. Youngs Drug Products Corp.*,[122] a case in which the classification of the speech in question was one of the key issues confront-ing the Court. *Bolger* involved an alleged violation of a federal postal regulation prohibiting the mailing of "[a]ny unsolicited advertisement of matter ... designed, adapted, or intended for preventing conception."[123] Postal officials' interpretation of the statute excluded from this ban any "unsolicited advertisements in which the mailer has no commercial interest."[124]

Youngs Drug Products Corp. manufactured a variety of contraceptive devises typically mar-keted through wholesalers who in turn would sell the products to pharmacists for eventual sales to the public. To stimulate demand, Youngs employed a number of marketing tactics including sending unsolicited, direct mail publications to the general public. Among these were a multi-page flyer promoting the company's entire inventory of products, circulars devoted only to mar-keting prophylactics, and what the company characterized as "informational pamphlets" about the virtues of using prophylactics, especially those manufactured by Youngs.

When complaints from customers concerned about receiving Youngs' direct-marketing mate-rials reached postal authorities, the postal service warned Youngs that continuing to mail such materials would violate the anti-mailing statute. Because violating the statute could include both criminal and civil penalties, the company sought relief in the federal courts in the form of a declaratory judgment, arguing that threats to apply the statute's provisions would interfere with Youngs' First Amendment rights. The lower courts held that all three direct mail publications were examples of commercial speech but held also that the government's arguments for banning the mailing of the publications were insufficient to withstand a First Amendment challenge based on the *Central Hudson* four-part test.[125]

The Supreme Court agreed that the government had not been able to satisfy the *Central Hudson* four-part test and also agreed, over Justice Stevens' objections, that all three types of marketing materials mailed by Youngs were examples of commercial speech. Noting that the Court had long recognized a "'common-sense' distinction"[126] between commercial and noncommercial speech and that the Court had also determined that commercial speech is only entitled to limited First Amendment protection, Justice Marshall characterized the Court's first task in *Bolger* as "determin[ing] the proper classification of the mailings at issue here. Appellee contends that his proposed mailings constitute 'fully protected' speech ... [while] Appellants argue ... that the proposed mailings are all commercial speech."[127] The job of the Court, said Marshall, is to make sure "that speech deserving of greater constitutional protection is not inadvertently suppressed."[128]

The Court found that although most of the mailings in question "fall within the core notion of commercial speech—'speech which does no more than propose a commercial transaction,'"[129] the company's publications containing general information about the merits of prophylactics posed "a closer question."[130] In attempting to answer this question, the Court began by observing that just because the publication was admittedly a direct mail advertisement did not automatically classify it as commercial speech (citing *Sullivan*). Neither did the fact that the publications referred to the products manufactured by Youngs. In addition, the Court noted that economic motivation, by itself, would normally not be a sufficient determinant of the status of the publication (citing *Bigelow*).

But, the Court continued, "[t]he combination of all these characteristics ... provides strong support for the ... conclusion that the informational pamphlets are properly characterized as commercial speech. The mailings constitute commercial speech notwithstanding ... that they contain discussions of important issues."[131] The Court added, "We have made clear that advertising which 'links a product to a current public debate' is not thereby entitled to the constitutional protection afforded noncommercial speech. A company has ... protections available to its direct comments on public issues," said Justice Marshall, "so there is no reason for providing similar constitutional protection when such statements are made in the context of commercial [speech]."[132]

In a footnote, Justice Marshall pointed out, however, that his three-part analysis was not meant to be a generalized test like the Court's four-prong *Central Hudson* test. The Court, said Marshall,

> (does not) mean to suggest that each of the characteristics present in this case must necessarily be present in order for speech to be commercial. For example, we express no opinion as to whether reference to any particular product or service is a necessary element of commercial speech.[133]

Not surprisingly, lower courts and government agencies trying to interpret and apply the Court's varying definitions of commercial speech have produced a decidedly mixed bag of decisions and policy statements. A number of courts have rejected government attempts to regulate speech based on judgments that the speech in question did not fall within the narrow "commercial transaction" definition of commercial speech. For example, in *New York City v.*

American School Publications,[134] a New York court[135] rejected claims that the defendant's magazine was commercial speech despite arguments by the plaintiff that much of the content of, and the motivation for publishing, the magazine was intended to market the defendant's school course offerings. The court based its decision on the rationale that it was the content of the speech rather than the intent of the speaker that should rule in a definitional argument. Citing *Pittsburgh Press* and *Sullivan*, the court noted that the defendant's speech should be fully protected if it "communicates information, expresses opinion, recites grievances, protests claimed abuses or solicits financial support on behalf of a movement whose existence and objective are matters of public concern."[136]

Other courts have upheld government regulations based on a more expansive definition of commercial speech. In a decision that would appear to be the direct opposite of the opinion in *American School*, in *In re Domestic Air Transportation Antitrust Litigation*, a federal appeals court in the Eleventh Circuit (Alabama, Florida and Georgia)[137] upheld an order issued in an antitrust dispute that required an airline's in-flight magazine to carry notice of the antitrust suit against the airline. The court reasoned that the publication was designed to further the company's economic interests, even though most of the publication carried articles of general interest and there was little content that actually promoted the company. In *National Commission on Egg Nutrition v. FTC*,[138] a federal appeals court held that an advertisement claiming "there is no scientific evidence that eating eggs increases the risk of ... heart disease"[139] fit within the definition of commercial speech and thus was subject to government regulations involving potentially false or misleading advertising claims. According to the court, despite the language of the Supreme Court in *Pittsburgh Press* and *Virginia State Board of Pharmacy*, the definition of commercial speech

> was not intended to be narrowly limited to the mere proposal of a commercial transaction, but extend[s] to false claims as to the harmlessness of the advertiser's product asserted for the purpose of persuading members of the reading public to buy the product.[140]

An example that highlights the continuing disagreement over the proper definition of commercial speech involved the R.J. Reynolds Tobacco Company, a major cigarette manufacturer. The company ran a series of advertisements reporting on the results of a federally funded study of health risk factors called "MRFIT." According to the tobacco company, the results of the study, which tracked long-term health records of a large sample of regular citizens, demonstrated there was no evidence of the high positive correlation between smoking and various diseases claimed by anti-smoking forces. The advertisement concluded with the statement, "We at R.J. Reynolds do not claim this study proves that smoking doesn't cause heart disease ... [only] ... that the controversy over smoking and health remains an open one."[141]

Although the advertising copy contained no mention of a specific brand or any hint of a sales pitch, the Federal Trade Commission claimed jurisdiction over the advertisements on the basis that their real purpose was to induce people to continue smoking cigarettes and, therefore, constituted commercial speech that the FTC said was false or misleading. An administrative law judge threw out the complaint, holding that the advertisements were not commercial speech but rather editorial statements published as advertisements.[142] In rejecting the FTC's position, the judge found that deciding in favor of the government would make it virtually impossible for

> any business firm ... [to] ever be able to publish an opinion in a newspaper or magazine ad on a controversial public issue which concerns one of its products without losing the full

protection of the First Amendment and subjecting the firm and the ad to the Commission's jurisdiction.[143]

The FTC then overruled its own administrative law judge (FTC procedures will be discussed more fully in a later chapter) on the basis that the judge had mishandled the classification of the advertisements as noncommercial speech.[144] Acknowledging that the FTC would lack jurisdiction to regulate the advertising if the speech were not commercial, the FTC concluded that the Supreme Court had not set forth a definitive test of that term. Therefore, said the FTC, it would be necessary in each individual case to evaluate the factors to be considered as found in the decisions by the Court and lower courts in relation to the facts of the case.

According to the FTC, among the factors to be considered were whether (a) the speech was published in paid-for time or space, (b) there was an economic motivation behind the speech, (c) the speech was designed to market or promote a product or service and (d) the copy mentioned a particular product or service. Applying this formulation of the attributes of commercial speech to the advertisements by R.J. Reynolds, the agency concluded that the administrative law judge's decision was too hasty in that it failed to take these factors sufficiently into account. "A message that addresses health concerns that may be faced by purchasers or potential purchasers of the speaker's product," said the FTC, "may constitute commercial speech."[145] At this point, R.J. Reynolds decided to throw in the towel and signed a consent decree that did not admit any violation but contained an agreement not to misrepresent the data from the "MRFIT" study in future advertising.

The California Supreme Court Expands the Definition of Commercial Speech in *Kasky v. Nike*

For free-speech advocates, the California Supreme Court offered a most ominous omen for greater regulation of commercial speech in the 2002 case of *Kasky v. Nike*.[146] The case originated in reaction to a late 1990s, classic corporate-reputation campaign undertaken by Nike to answer critics of its overseas labor practices. Already the subject of numerous accusations by international labor-rights advocacy groups that Nike was engaged in so-called sweatshop labor practices, the company decided to respond aggressively to its critics after a negative critique of Nike's practices aired on the CBS newsmagazine *48 Hours*.

As one of its first reputation reclamation efforts, Nike commissioned an audit of its corporate labor policies by Atlanta-based corporate consulting firm GoodWorks International, LLC. The choice of GoodWorks seemed a strategically wise move. The chairman of GoodWorks, Andrew Young, has been hailed throughout his life as a champion of human rights, including his work as the United States' ambassador to the United Nations. Young is perhaps best known, however, for being a close adviser and confidant of Dr. Martin Luther King, Jr. during the 1960s civil rights struggles.

On Nike's behalf, Young made a 10-day trip to China, Indonesia and Vietnam, visiting 12 factories, including four that had been widely reported as being among the chief abusers of workers' rights. Upon his return, Young summarized his conclusions in a press release prepared by Nike with the statement, "It is my sincere belief that NIKE is doing a good job in the application of its Code of Conduct. But NIKE can and should do better."[147] Young wrote that he found no evidence of illegal or unsafe working conditions at any of the factories he visited.

The press release marked Nike's opening salvo in a comprehensive public relations effort built around the GoodWorks report. Several days after the initial release, Nike purchased advertising space in various newspapers featuring headlines such as "Nike Passes Inspection—No

Sweat." Andrew Young publicly defended Nike, writing letters to editors refuting attacks on Nike and questioning the motives of the corporation's critics. To quell the rising sense of unease about buying Nike products for college athletic teams, Nike CEO Phil Knight penned letters to college athletic directors touting the GoodWorks study findings. Response to the campaign predictably was mixed. Although some hailed Nike's audit as a step in the right direction, critics of the corporation denounced Nike's campaign as simply the latest effort by the company to pull the wool over the eyes of the public.

Any positive uptick for Nike's image was short-lived. During the three months following the corporation's initial efforts, new allegations regarding both Nike and the GoodWorks report surfaced. Anita Chan, professor at the Australian National University's Contemporary China Center, wrote a letter to the editor of the *Journal of Commerce* stating that the GoodWorks report had erroneously listed her as an information resource. Additionally, Chan wrote that "Mr. Young's report is oblivious to the whole issue of worker safety" because it ignored the labor abuses that were taking place in Asian factories. Chan concluded, "[s]ending a sincere novice on a quick jaunt of Asia has the earmarks of a PR exercise. It appears that Mr. Young was taken for a ride."[148]

Additionally, still looming over Nike's head was the criticism that the corporation did not pay a living wage to its workers, a charge unanswered in the GoodWorks report and Nike's press statements. The company then issued a new release touting an additional Nike-commissioned study recently completed by a group of MBA students at Dartmouth University. The study determined that, contrary to the findings of the original *48 Hours* report, Nike workers in Vietnam and Indonesia were paid significantly higher than their countries' living wages. The critics answered the Dartmouth study less than three weeks later and, ironically, used Nike's own information against the corporation. The Transnational Resource and Action Center, a San Francisco-based corporate-responsibility advocacy group, released a leaked, year-old memo from an accounting firm study of one of Nike's Vietnam factories. The audit detailed a host of Nike's labor and safety violations ranging from allowing employees to work without protective clothing to requiring overtime for no extra pay. Nike acknowledged the accuracy of the report but noted that the year-old problems outlined in the audit had already been addressed.

Watching this public debate with interest was Californian Marc Kasky, a self-described environmentalist and community activist. Addressing Nike's corporate practices, Kasky later told a reporter from the *San Francisco Chronicle*, "I saw something that I thought was wrong, and I wanted to do something about it."[149] Kasky consulted attorney Alan Caplan (who had been an attorney of record in the lawsuit that eventually caused R.J. Reynolds Tobacco Company to shelve its Joe Camel advertising logo), inquiring about the feasibility of suing Nike for its recent public relations misstatements. Caplan suggested that Kasky invoke provisions of the state's Business and Professions Codes[150] that would allow him to file suit against Nike for false advertising and unfair trade practices as a "private attorney general" representing the people of the state.

Kasky filed suit in California Superior Court alleging four causes of action. Among other claims, the suit alleged that Nike had engaged in "unfair business practices within the meaning [of the law]" and that the company had violated the state's false advertising laws.[151] As remedies for Nike's alleged misdeeds, Kasky demanded that Nike engage in a court-supervised campaign to correct its misstatements and cease making false and misleading statements regarding its overseas labor practices. Kasky also demanded that Nike "disgorge all monies that it acquired by the alleged unlawful and unfair practices" in California.[152]

In reply, Nike challenged the constitutionality of the application of the Business and Professions Codes, relying on the First Amendment and portions of the California constitution.

Specifically, Nike argued that its speech was noncommercial in nature and, therefore, not subject to California's false advertising and unfair competition laws. A superior court judge agreed and dismissed Kasky's case without leave to amend.[153] Kasky appealed this decision, but the California appeals court also dismissed Kasky's claim.[154]

Nike had won the first two rounds in the California court system, but its most serious challenge lay ahead. Kasky petitioned for review in the California Supreme Court, which reversed the appeals court decision.[155] Seizing on the federal Supreme Court's ambiguous definitions of commercial speech and the presumed false and deceptive elements of Nike's statements (even though not part of marketing or promotional efforts but rather in a public relations campaign), the *Kasky* majority determined that the facts in this case demanded a new and more comprehensive definition for commercial speech. The court said:

> We conclude that when a court must decide whether particular speech may be subjected to laws aimed at preventing false advertising or other forms of commercial deception, categorizing a particular statement as commercial or noncommercial speech requires consideration of three elements: *the speaker, the intended audience*, and *the content of the message*.[156]

The court then applied its new definition of commercial speech to Nike's public relations management campaign. Addressing the "speaker" element of the test, the court noted that "the first element—a commercial speaker—is satisfied because the speakers—Nike and its officers and directors—are engaged in commerce. Specifically, they manufacture, import, distribute, and sell consumer goods in the form of athletic shoes and apparel."[157] Next, addressing the "intended audience" portion of the test, the court said that "an intended commercial audience is also satisfied because Nike's letters to university presidents and directors of athletic departments were addressed directly to actual and potential purchasers of Nike's products."[158] The court also accepted the argument that "Nike's press releases and letters to newspaper editors, although addressed to the public generally, were also intended to reach and influence actual and potential purchasers of Nike's products."[159]

Finally, addressing the "content of the message" in Nike's campaign, the court, in a breathtakingly expansive interpretation of commercial speech, said that factual statements

> describing [Nike's] own labor policies, the practices and working conditions in factories where its products are made, [t]he wages paid to the factories' employees … the way they are treated, and whether the environmental conditions under which they work violate local health and safety laws[160]

all fall within the court's definitional conceptions of "commercial character" and "product references," thus satisfying the third part of the court's definition.

Summing up its analysis, the four-justice majority determined that Nike's public relations campaign did indeed amount to commercial speech and, therefore, was subject to a *Central Hudson* analysis. The case was sent back to the court of appeals to determine if Nike's statements were false. If so, the state's Business and Professions Codes would allow Kasky to claim damages on behalf of California's citizens.

Rather than accept the California Supreme Court's decision, Nike appealed to the Supreme Court of the United States. After hearing oral arguments, the Court dismissed the case on procedural grounds and returned the case to the courts of California. Three months before a new trial date was set, Kasky and Nike issued a joint press release announcing a settlement in the case. According to the terms, Nike would commit $500,000 to maintain its overseas factories'

Figure 3.4 Nike, which markets athletic shoes, equipment and clothing, was compelled to answer critics of its manufacturing practices in both courts of law and public opinion. Nike asked the Supreme Court of the United States to declare its communications in its own defense to be First Amendment protected expression, rather than commercial speech.

Credit line: August_0802/Shutterstock.com

worker-education programs and donate $1 million to the Fair Labor Association, an offshoot of the Clinton administration-created Apparel Industry Partnership.

Because of *Kasky*, and because of the broad reach of California's Business and Professions Codes, any for-profit corporation doing business in that state (even if not physically located there) may now assume that virtually all of its messages will fall within the state court's sweeping new definition of commercial speech. Potentially even more troubling to for-profit corporate communicators is that the *Kasky* commercial speech definition provides a roadmap for other states that may wish to create their own commercial speech definitions.

Perhaps the best illustration of *Kasky*'s potential impact on future corporate communications practices is demonstrated by the advice published in the *Los Angeles Lawyer*, the local bar association's principal publication, to all attorneys representing corporate clients that do business in California. The article warned "when advising a business client on how to publicly address certain issues that the client considers noncommercial, practitioners should alert the client that the safest choice is silence."[161]

Defamation and Commercial Speech: Definitional Constitutional Issues

Perhaps no better illustration of the problems caused by the failure of the Court to provide a precise definition of commercial speech exists than in the differences in outcomes that could occur in a lawsuit involving a for-profit corporation alleging harm to reputation. Much depends upon whether the libelous statements are classified as commercial or noncommercial speech.

A lawsuit for defamation of character typically arises in response to a false statement of fact about the plaintiff, published or disseminated in other ways to a third party by the defendant, causing harm to reputation. Such cases are examples of state-based, civil tort laws designed to permit recovery of monetary damages for harm to persons or personal property (a more thorough analysis of commercial communication torts is found in later chapters).

Until *New York Times v. Sullivan* in 1964, federal constitutional issues played almost no role in the resolution of such suits. However, in *Sullivan*, the Supreme Court was faced with a complex case, involving political speech, civil rights and editorial advertising that the Court felt demanded a constitutional rule providing First Amendment protection for false and defamatory speech directed against public officials acting in their official capacity. This rule was later extended to public figures in the combined cases of *Curtis Publishing Co. v. Butts* and *A.P. v. Walker*,[162] and, to a lesser degree, to private plaintiffs suing media defendants in *Gertz v. Welch*.[163] Although the levels of constitutional protection differ, the underlying rationale for First Amendment protection of false and defamatory speech is the same: a commitment to encouraging "wide open discussion of public issues"[164] that could be chilled by overly stringent defamation laws.

Prior to *Sullivan*, state laws generally favored the plaintiff's cause in a defamation suit, holding the defendant to a strict standard for imposing liability. The holdings in *Sullivan* and *Butts* turned the tables almost 180 degrees, making it impossible for the plaintiff to win (if the plaintiff is a public person) unless the plaintiff can show actual malice—defined as whether the defendant either knew the defamatory statements were false or that the defendant entertained serious doubts about the truth of the statements before publishing them. *Gertz* extended this logic to private plaintiffs suing media defendants in matters of public interest, although only requiring that private plaintiffs in such situations prove that the defendant acted at least negligently.

Most corporations are extremely concerned about maintaining and protecting their good name within their business or professional communities. Therefore, they not only have reputations to defend, but often are quick to do so. Corporations and other legally recognized organizations also can be guilty of issuing defamatory statements about individuals (e.g., a statement about reasons for employee termination) or other organizations (e.g., statements impugning the motives or activities of a competitor). For these reasons, it is not unusual to find defamation suits involving corporations and other organizations as either plaintiffs or defendants. In such situations, two competing First Amendment issues may intersect.

The potential conflict is straightforward. Normally, if the plaintiff in a defamation suit is a public person, the burden of proof is difficult and the defendant can count on constitutional protection for the speech in question unless the defendant knew the harmful speech was false or published with reckless disregard for the truth. If the plaintiff in such a suit is private, and the opposing party is a media defendant, the plaintiff's case is less difficult to meet, but the defendant knows that the plaintiff must prove that the defamatory statements were made at least negligently.

But what if the defamatory speech is also defined as commercial speech? In *Central Hudson*, the Supreme Court determined that false or deceptive commercial speech merits no protection under the First Amendment and that even truthful, non-deceptive commercial speech is deserving of less protection than other kinds of speech. Should the plaintiffs and defendants in a defamation-by-commercial-speech case benefit from the constitutional protections erected by the Court to the same degree as other defendants or are these First Amendment requirements lost because the defamatory speech is commercial and, therefore, less protected?

The Court has obliquely recognized this conundrum but never directly addressed it. In *Bates v. State Bar of Arizona*, the Court cited *Virginia State Board of Pharmacy* for the proposition that commercial speech should be differentiated from other speech in the context of advertising by attorneys and other professionals. "Since advertising is linked to commercial well-being, it seems unlikely that such speech is particularly susceptible to being crushed by overbroad regulation....[P]resumably [the advertiser] can determine more readily than others whether his speech is truthful and protected."[165] Similar sentiments surfaced in a footnote in *Central Hudson*.

In *Dun & Bradstreet, Inc. v. Greenmoss Builders*,[166] the Court was faced with the appeal of a Vermont case involving a false credit report harming the business reputation of a corporation. While the Court was badly fragmented in its ruling, one of the rationales advanced by some members of the Court for denying First Amendment protection to the defendant's speech was that the speech in question did not address matters of general interest or concern. This was true, said the Court, in part because the credit reports were economically motivated and, therefore, less like constitutionally protected commercial speech.

In *U.S. Healthcare Inc. v. Blue Cross of Greater Philadelphia*,[167] a federal Court of Appeals for the Third Circuit directly addressed the defamation-in-the-context-of-commercial-speech issue. The case arose out of the entry of U.S. Healthcare into the health insurance market that had been dominated by the insurance programs provided by Blue Cross. The cornerstone of the new type of insurance plan was the concept of health maintenance organizations (HMO) that provided savings in the costs of medical insurance, but required the participants in such plans to forego the freedom to choose their own health-care providers. The HMO programs became so popular that Blue Cross decided to mount a marketing campaign to convince both potential consumers and former customers that the more traditional insurance plans offered by Blue Cross were preferable.

As part of this campaign, Blue Cross sponsored advertisements in newspapers and broadcast stations and sent direct mail circulars touting the benefits of its insurance plans, "in particular, Personal Choice [a Blue Cross preferred provider system] ... at the expense of HMO products."[168] The Blue Cross-sponsored advertisements, which did not mention U.S. Healthcare, consisted of informational comparative advertising claims (e.g., "I don't like those HMO health plans. You get one doctor. No choice of hospitals.")[169] and claims designed to appeal to the emotions (e.g., an obviously saddened woman lamenting that "[t]he hospital my HMO sent me to just wasn't enough. It's my fault.").[170] In a counter move, U.S. Healthcare rolled out its own "responsive advertising campaign" to "counteract the Blue Cross/Blue Shield message."[171] Like the Blue Cross advertisements, the campaign consisted of informational and emotional messages, although, unlike its competition, a number of U.S. Healthcare's advertisements directly challenged Blue Cross and its Personal Choice plan by name.

Not content simply to duel in the media, U.S. Healthcare also filed a lawsuit charging, among other things, that the Blue Cross-sponsored advertisements defamed U.S. Healthcare's products and its standing in the community. Blue Cross responded with counter suits alleging similar claims. Trying to sort out the various claims and counter-claims, the jury in the federal district court trial[172] eventually rejected all of the claims by Blue Cross but was unable to reach agreement on the claims by U.S. Healthcare. Before a new trial could begin, Blue Cross asked the court to rule that the First Amendment required a dismissal of U.S. Healthcare's libel claims. According to Blue Cross, because the Supreme Court of the United States had established that public persons defamed in a matter of public concern must show that the defendant knew the defamatory statements were false or was reckless about the truth of the statements, and because U.S. Healthcare could not meet this constitutionally imposed burden, the trial court should enter a judgment in favor of Blue Cross without the need for another trial. The district court agreed the constitutional standards did apply and granted the defendant's motion to terminate the libel claims.

On appeal, the court of appeals divided the advertisements into four categories, two of which, said the court, could give rise to a cause of action for defamation. The appeals court disagreed with the lower court, however, on the issue of whether constitutional protections should apply, holding that the commercial speech in question was not entitled to the "heightened protection under the First Amendment"[173] merited by fully protected speech. In reviewing the line of Supreme Court decisions involving defamation beginning with *Sullivan*, the appeals court found that principal factors underlying the balancing of speech versus reputational interests were (a) the status of the plaintiff and (b) the classification of the speech. Focusing on the latter of these two criteria, the court noted that the Supreme Court had established that commercial speech, although accorded some constitutional protection, nonetheless received "protection somewhat less extensive than that afforded 'noncommercial speech.'"[174] Therefore, noted the court, if the speech in question were truly commercial in nature, the First Amendment protections extended to other kinds of false and defamatory speech need not apply.

Allowing states greater latitude in regulating defamatory commercial speech, said the court, would not inhibit such speech because the speaker, driven by economic considerations, would not be "deterred by proper regulation."[175] The court found that intolerance of false and defamatory statements of fact was justifiably higher in a situation in which commercial speakers were "uniquely qualified to evaluate the truthfulness of their speech"[176] because of their familiarity with both the goods and services they provide. On a more theoretical note, the court added that "requir[ing] a parity of constitutional protection for commercial and noncommercial speech alike could invite dilution, simply be a leveling process, of the force of the amendment's guarantee with respect to the latter kind of speech."[177]

The question that remained was whether any of the defamatory speech by either of the two health-care insurers should be defined as commercial speech. Taking its definition from *Bolger*, the court answered this question affirmatively, finding that the speech was in commercial form, was economically motivated and referred to specific products or services. In addition, because of the large financial interests involved on both sides, the court observed that "it would have to be a cold day before these corporations would be chilled from speaking about the comparative merits of their products."[178] Also, the court noted that a significant number of the advertisements had little or no true informational content, but rather were emotional appeals designed to discourage participation in the competitor's programs.

Finally, the court rejected the arguments advanced by Blue Cross that its advertisements were part of an ongoing public controversy about health-care systems therefore deserving of heightened First Amendment protection. Quoting *Central Hudson*, the court noted that there was "[little] reason for providing constitutional protection when such statements are made only in the context of commercial transactions."[179] The Supreme Court refused to accept the case on appeal, making *U.S. Healthcare* the only important major decision on the issue of the constitutional protections accorded defamatory commercial speech to date.

Two lower court decisions have wrestled with this issue with conflicting results. In *Castleman v. Internet Money Ltd.*, the Texas Court of Appeals refused to dismiss the plaintiff's case of defamation on the basis that "commercial speech historically has not been afforded the expansive protections under the First Amendment as has other forms of speech."[180] On a more positive note for free-speech advocates, an Arizona court of appeals in *Sign Here Petitions, LLC v. Chavez* held that a corporation's defamatory speech merited full First Amendment protection, at least in situations when "speech has a mixture of commercial and non-commercial elements."[181] The court based its rationale on the premise that "the presence of [commercial speech] does not diminish the constitutional protection of the whole [message]."[182]

The federal circuit court's rationale in *U.S. Healthcare* has been criticized, and the issue may still be decided differently by the Supreme Court. Nonetheless, the decision stands as a warning sign for advertising and public relations practitioners that their speech may not be afforded heightened First Amendment protection if their organization is sued for defamation, particularly when that speech involves criticism of the commercial products or practices of the competition.

There are no major cases raising similar constitutional issues involving commercial speech and other communication-related torts (e.g., invasion of privacy or intentional infliction of emotional distress). There is little reason on the face of it to assume that courts would accord heightened First Amendment protection for commercial speech in cases raising such claims.

The Importance of the Definitional Issues

From an advertising or public relations point of view, if the Court continues to hold that commercial speech is entitled to only limited First Amendment protection, the narrow definition of commercial speech as "speech that does no more than propose a commercial transaction" is, by far, preferable. Unfortunately, the continuing viability of this definition as the one employed by future courts, legislatures and regulatory agencies is suspect.

The reasons for pessimism are simple: the Court's "commercial transaction" language has proven both unclear and inadequate. Perhaps this is because the Court, beginning in *Pittsburgh Press*, meant to use the term only as a "classic example" or as "the core meaning" of commercial speech rather than as the final comprehensive definition. It is unfortunately true (at least from the point of view of clarity and consistency in the law) that even those on the Court who defend this definition have not uniformly employed the "commercial transaction" definition in subsequent commercial speech cases.

The greatest reason for concern, however, is that the "commercial transaction" language just does not work. For example, it is reasonable to believe that (a) marketing press releases announcing and touting the virtues of a company's new product; (b) direct mail pieces that are "instructional" in nature, but clearly require the purchase of a product for the instruction to be effective; (c) billboards depicting only a red bulldog with no other words or images (advertising Red Dog Beer); (d) broadcast advertisements featuring various physical feats of daring followed by the slogan "JUST DO IT" (a Nike commercial); or (e) letterhead stationery of physicians or attorneys claiming special skills will all be treated by courts and government regulatory agencies alike as commercial speech, despite the absence of any language proposing an actual commercial transaction. These examples are only a few of the myriad ways that profit-making organizations communicate in furtherance of their economic well-being.

Although of academic interest, all this might be of little practical significance if no one were motivated to seek regulation of broadly defined commercial speech. Unfortunately for free-speech advocates, this is far from the case. Social engineers, government regulators, special interest representatives and a whole host of others who believe that members of the public need protecting from their own freely made choices are often dismayed to find that despite information campaigns and logical arguments to the contrary, some people simply persist in doing what others feel is bad for them. Whether it's smoking cigarettes, not wearing seat belts or eating trans-fat foods, there seem to be the recalcitrant few who will not fall in line with the prevailing winds from Vichy.

Other critics of commercial speech argue that for-profit corporations, particularly if large, are inherently dangerous unless kept in check, and that restrictions on corporate speech are one of the few means of reining them in. Still others represent or claim to represent those characterized as inherently unable to make informed choices about corporate activities (e.g., children or the mentally or physically impaired).

Some social activists are content to limit their efforts to moral suasion. Others, recognizing it would be difficult or perhaps impossible to regulate or ban the underlying corporate activity or product (e.g., Prohibition), have adopted the tactic of lobbying for governmentally imposed limits on speech about activities or products by an "offending" corporation. Such efforts often seem to be a siren-like call for legislators and regulators who, by passing legislation or creating regulations, claim credit for attacking important social problems without spending any tax dollars or adding to government bureaucracy.

However, expansive efforts to regulate corporate speech likely will not succeed unless that speech falls under the definition of "commercial speech"–as noted earlier, a lesser-protected speech category. Therefore, those who wish to regulate for-profit corporations will be doing their level best to say that most or all for-profit corporate speech activity should be classified as commercial speech. This clearly includes advertising, but also such marketing "speech activities" as billboards, ballpark signage, race-car sponsorship and a host of other promotional efforts, as well as broadly defined, marketing-oriented public relations speech. It seems inevitable that such efforts to sweep corporate speech into a regulatory framework also will focus on more traditional public relations speech (e.g., speeches by company executives, news releases about general corporate activities or community relations campaigns).

The question then becomes: How successful will these efforts be?

Conclusion

It seems a reasonable prediction that courts and regulators seeking a definitive definition of commercial speech will be inclined to adopt a term akin to the more inclusive "economic motivation" language of *Central Hudson* rather than the alternative, more restrictive "does no more than propose a commercial transaction" language of *Pittsburgh Press*. This prediction is based on the assumption that those seeking to define and regulate commercial speech will choose the definition that those actually engaged in speaking commercially have long recognized and, increasingly, are making a cornerstone of their marketing efforts.

If this prediction becomes a reality, joining all or significant parts of a corporation's public relations functions with advertising and marketing communications efforts, and then locating them all within the framework of an integrated marketing communications department–an increasingly seen corporate communications structure–becomes problematic from a legal perspective. In so doing, for-profit corporations may well be seen as making the tacit (if not overt) admission that the corporation's public relations speech is speech made directly for economic motives.

It would appear that the safest strategy is to plan for a future in which any communication activities by a profit-making company (except news media or other mass communication companies) reasonably related to the company's products or services will likely be defined as commercial speech. If this proves true, for the time being, advertising and public relations professionals should let the California Supreme Court's *Nike* decision be their guide and make sure that all such speech be accurate, truthful and non-deceptive.

Notes

1. Valentine v. Chrestensen, 316 U.S. 52 (1942).
2. *Id.* at 53.
3. *Id.* at 54.
4. New York Times Co. v. Sullivan, 376 U.S. 254 (1964).
5. *Id.* at 265.
6. *Id.* at 266.
7. *Id.*
8. *Id.*
9. *Id.*
10. First National Bank of Boston v. Bellotti, 435 U.S. 765 (1978).
11. *Id.* at 767.
12. *Id.* at 768.
13. *Id.* at 767.
14. *Id.* at 793.
15. *Id.* at 776.
16. Consolidated Edison Co. v. Public Service Comm'n, 447 U.S. 530 (1980).
17. *Id.* at 533.
18. *Id.*
19. *Id.*
20. C & C Plywood Corp. v. Hanson, 420 F.Supp. 1254 (1976).
21. Let's Help Florida v. McCrary, 621 F.2d 195 (5th Cir. 1980).
22. 2 U.S.C. §441 (a) 1988
23. To date, some 27 states have done so.
24. Buckley v. Valeo, 424 U.S. 1 (1976).
25. Austin v. Michigan St. Chamber of Commerce, 494 U.S. 652 (1990).
26. *Id.* at 655.
27. *Id.*
28. Michigan State Chamber of Commerce v. Austin, 643 F. Supp. 397 (D. Mich., 1986).
29. Michigan State Chamber of Commerce v. Austin, 856 F.2d 783 (6th Cir. 1988).
30. Austin, 494 U.S. at 660.
31. *Id.* at 657; citing Buckley v. Valeo, 424 U.S. 39, 96 (1976); quoting Williams v. Rhodes, 393 U.S. 23 (1968).
32. *Id.* at 665-666.
33. *Id.* at 698.
34. *Id.*
35. *Id.* at 696.
36. *Id.* at 700.
37. Bipartisan Campaign Finance Act of 1997, S. 25, 105 Cong. (1997) (enacted).
38. McConnell v. Federal Election Commission, 540 U.S. 93 (1993).
39. 2 U.S.C.S §434(f)(3)(A).
40. Citizens United v. FEC, 530 F. Supp. 2d 274 (D.C. Cir. 2008).

41. *Id.*
42. Citizens United v. FEC, 557 U.S. 932 (2009).
43. Citizens United v. FEC, 558 U.S. 310, 339 (2010) (quoting Buckley v. Valeo, 424 U.S. 1, 19 (1976) (per curiam).
44. *Id.*
45. *Id.* at 342.
46. *Id.*
47. *Id.* at 343 (citing First Nat. Bank of Boston v. Bellotti, 435 U.S. 765, at 776 (1978)).
48. *Id.* at 345. (Buckley did not consider §610's separate ban on corporate and union independent expenditures. Had §610 been challenged in the wake of Buckley, however, it could not have been squared with the reasoning and analysis of that case).
49. *Id.* at 347.
50. *Id.*
51. *Id.* at 348.
52. *Id.*
53. *Id.* at 349.
54. *Id.* at 350.
55. *Id.* (quoting Austin v. Michigan Chamber of Commerce, 494 U.S. 652, 657 (1990)).
56. *Id.* at 356.
57. *Id.*
58. *Id.* at 358.
59. *Id.* at 477 (quoting First Nat. Bank of Boston v. Bellotti, 435 U.S. 765, at 794(1978)).
60. *Id.*
61. *Id.*
62. See *Money Grubbers: The Supreme Court Kills Campaign Finance Reform*, SLATE, Jan. 21, 2010, www.slate.com/id/2242209/pagenum/all; Jeffrey Toobin, *Bad Judgment*, New Yorker, Jan. 22, 2010, www.newyorker.com/online/blogs/newsdesk/2010/01/campaign-finance.html; Editorial, *The Court's Blow to Democracy*, N.Y. Times, Jan. 22, 2010, www.nytimes.com/2010/01/22/opinion/22fri1.html
63. Jackie Calmes & Carl Hulse, *Obama Assails Republicans on Campaign Finance*, N.Y. Times, July 27, 2010, at A10.
64. *See* Michael A. Menoli, *Disclose Act Fails to Advance in Senate*, Los Angeles Times, Sept. 24, 2010, http://articles.latimes.com/2010/sep/24/nation/la-na-disclose-act-20100924; Paul Blumenthal, *Congressional Democrats Seek Corporate Disclosure Post-Citizens United*, Huffington Post, July 13, 2011, www.huffingtonpost.com/2011/07/13/congressional-democrats-corporate-disclosure_n_897404.html
65. See George Will, *Super Pacs Can't Crown a King*, Wash. Post, Feb. 29, 2011 www.washingtonpost.com/opinions/super-pacs-cant-crown-a-king/2012/02/28/gIQAAxOAjR_story.html; Gail Collins, *Who Wants to Be a Millionaire?*, N.Y. Times, Jan. 13, 2011 at A21.
66. See Richard L. Hasen, *The Numbers Don't Lie*, Slate, Mar. 9, 2012, www.slate.com/articles/news_and_politics/politics/2012/03/the_supreme_court_s_citizens_united_decision_has_led_to_an_explosion_of_campaign_spending_.html; Dan Abrams, *The Media's Shameful, Inexcusable Distortion of the Supreme Court's Citizens United Decision*, Mediate, Feb. 8, 2012, www.mediaite.com/online/the-medias-shameful-inexcusable-distortion-of-the-supreme-courts-citizens-united-decision/
67. See Richard L. Hasen, *Citizens United and the Illusion of Coherence*, 109 Mich. L. Rev. 581 (2011), Richard A. Epstein, *Citizens United v. FEC: The Constitutional Right That Big Corporations Should Have But Do Not Want*, 34 Harv. J.L. & Pub. Pol'y 639 (2011).
68. Citizens United v. FEC Constitutional Remedies: List of Local, State and Federal Resolution Efforts, People for the American Way, www.pfaw.org/issues/government-the-people/citizens-united-v-fec-constitutional-remedies-list-of-local-state-and-f (last retrieved Nov. 20, 2018).
69. Editorial, *Montana Takes on Citizens United*, N.Y. Times, Jan. 23, 2012, at A26.

70. Ed Kilgore, *Court Gets Second Chance on Citizens United*, Washington Monthly, Feb. 22, 2012, www.washingtonmonthly.com/political-animal-a/2012_02/court_gets_second_chance_on_ci035574.php

71. SpeechNow.org v. FEC, 599 F.3d 686 (D.C.Cir.2010).

72. Arizona Free Enterprise Club's Freedom Club PAC v. Bennett, 131 S.Ct. 2806 (2011).

73. Sam Stein, *2012 Campaign Super Pac Mega-Donors Feel Burn of Political Spotlight*, Huffington Post, Mar. 14, 2012, www.huffingtonpost.com/2012/03/14/super-pac-2012-campaign-donors_n_1344932.html

74. SpeechNow.org v. FEC, 599 F.3d 686 at 691 (D.C.Cir.2010).

75. *Id*.

76. *Id*.

77. Buckley, 424 U.S. 1 (1976).

78. *See* SpeechNow.org v. Federal Election Com'n, 567 F.Supp.2d 70 (D.D.C., 2008).

79. SpeechNow.org v. FEC, 599 F.3d 686 (D.C.Cir.2010).

80. *Id*. at 692.

81. *Id*. at 694 (quoting Citizens United v. FEC, 555 U.S. at 314).

82. *Id*. at 695.

83. *Id*.

84. Arizona Free Enterprise, 131 S.Ct. 2806 (2011).

85. Ariz.Rev.Stat. Ann. §16–940 et seq. (West 2006 and Supp.2010).

86. Arizona Free Enterprise Club's Freedom Club PAC v. Bennett, 131 S.Ct. at 2813–14.

87. *Id*.

88. *Id*.

89. *Id*.

90. *Id*.

91. *Id*. at 2816.

92. *Id*.

93. *Id*.

94. McComish v. Bennett, 611 F.3d 510, (9th Cir.(Ariz.)2010).

95. Arizona Free Enterprise Club's Freedom Club PAC v. Bennett, 131 S.Ct. 2806 (2011).

96. *Id*. at 2818 (quoting Davis v. FEC, 554 U.S. 724, 739 (2008)).

97. *Id*.

98. *Id*. at 2824–25.

99. *Id*.

100. *Id*.

101. *Id*. at 2825 (quoting Davis v. FEC, 554 U.S. at 741).

102. Arizona Free Enterprise Club's Freedom Club PAC v. Bennett, 131 S.Ct. at 2826.

103. *Id*.

104. *Id*.

105. *Id*.

106. Banzhaf v. FCC, 405 F.2d 1082 (1968).

107. Central Hudson, 447 U.S. at 571 citing Banzhaf, 405 F.2d 1082.

108. Pittsburgh Press Co. v. Human Rel. Comm'n, 413 U.S. 376 (1973).

109. *Id*. at 385.

110. *Id*.

111. Va. State Bd. of Pharmacy v. Va. Citizens Consumer Council, 425 U.S. 748 (1976).

112. Board of Trustees of the State Univ. of N.Y. v. Fox, 492 U.S. 469 (1989).

113. *Id*. at 487.

114. City of Cincinnati v. Discovery Network, Inc., 507 U.S. 410 (1993).

115. Bates v. State Bar of Ariz., 433 U.S. 350 (1977).

116. Friedman v. Rogers, 440 U.S. 1 (1979).

117. Central Hudson, 447 U.S. 557.

118. *Id.* at note 5.

119. Dun & Bradstreet, Inc. v. Greenmoss Builders, 472 U.S. 749 (1985).

120. *Id.* at 762.

121. *Id.* at 790, quoting Pittsburgh Press, 413 U.S. at 385.

122. Bolger v. Youngs Drug Products Corp., 463 U.S. 60 (1983).

123. *Id.* at 61.

124. *Id.* at 62.

125. Central Hudson, 447 U.S. at 561.

126. *Id.* at 563 note 5.

127. Bolger, 463 U.S. at 68.

128. *Id.* at 61.

129. *Id.* at 62.

130. Youngs Drug Prods. Corp. v. Bolger, 526 F. Supp. 823 (D.D.C., 1981).

131. Bolger, 463 U.S. at 65.

132. *Id.* at 66.

133. *Id.* at note 14.

134. New York City v. American School Publications, 505 N.Y.S.2d 599 (July 31, 1986).

135. New York City v. American School Publications, 119 A.D.2d 13 (N.Y. App. Div. 1986).

136. American School Publications, 505 N.Y.S.2d at 603.

137. In re Domestic Air Transportation Antitrust Litigation, 141 F.R.D. 534 (N.D. Ga. 1992).

138. National Comm'n on Egg Nutrition v. F.T.C., 570 F.2d 157 (7th Cir. 1978).

139. *Id.* at 159.

140. *Id.* at 163.

141. In re R.J. Reynolds Tobacco Co., [1983–1987] Trade Reg. Rep. (CCH) ¶ 22, 385 at 23, 467 (Aug. 6, 1986) *rev'd* Trade Reg. Rep. (CCH) ¶ 22, 522 at 22, 180 (Apr. 11, 1988), *stay denied*, Trade Reg. Rep. (CCH) ¶22, 549 at 22, 231 (June 3, 1988).

142. *Id.*

143. *Id.*

144. *Id.*

145. *Id.*

146. Kasky v. Nike, Inc., 119 Cal. Rptr. 2d 296 (Cal. 2002).

147. Press Release, Vada O. Manager, *NIKE Responds to Ambassador Young's Report on the NIKE Code of Conduct* (June 24, 1997) (on file with PR Newswire).

148. Letter from Anita Chan, Professor, Contemporary China Centre, Australian National University, to Editor, *Journal of Commerce* 8A, Jul. 25, 1997 (on file with *Journal of Commerce*).

149. Steve Rubenstein, *S.F. Man Changes from Customer to Adversary*, San Francisco Chronicle, May 3, 2002, at A6.

150. Cal. Bus. & Prof. Code §§17200–17204; Cal. Bus. & Prof. Code §17500; Cal. Bus. & Prof. Code §17535.

151. Kasky v. Nike, Inc., 93 Cal. Rptr. 2d 854, 857 (Cal. Ct. App. 1st Cir. 2000), *rev'd and rem'd*, 119 Cal. 4th 296 (2002).

152. Kasky v. Nike, Inc., 119 Cal. Rptr. 2d at 302.

153. Kasky v. Nike, Inc., 93 Cal. Rptr. 2d 854.

154. *Id.*

155. Kasky v. Nike, Inc., 119 Cal. Rptr. 2d 296.

156. *Id.* at 311.

157. *Id.* at 313.

158. *Id.* at 313–314.

159. *Id.* at 314.

160. *Id.*
161. Jonathan A. Loeb and Jeffrey A. Sklar, *Practice Tips: The California Supreme Court's New Test for Commercial Speech*, 25 L.A. Lawyer 13, 13 (2002).
162. Curtis Pub. Co. v. Butts, 388 U.S. 130 (1967).
163. Gertz v. Welch, 418 U.S. 323 (1974).
164. Sullivan, 376 U.S. at 270.
165. Bates, 433 U.S. at 381.
166. Dun & Bradstreet, 472 U.S. 749.
167. U.S. Healthcare, Inc. v. Blue Cross of Greater Philadelphia, 898 F.2d 914 (3d Cir. 1990).
168. *Id.* at 918.
169. *Id.*
170. *Id.*
171. *Id.* at 919.
172. U.S. Healthcare, Inc. v. Blue Cross of Greater Philadelphia, 1988 U.S. Dist. LEXIS 1832 (E.D. Pa., 1988).
173. U.S. Healthcare, 898 F.2d at 920.
174. *Id.* at 932.
175. *Id.*
176. *Id.* at 934.
177. *Id.*
178. *Id.* at 935.
179. *Id.*
180. Castleman v. Internet Money Ltd., 545 S.W.3d 682 (Tex. App. Amarillo, Apr. 19, 2017).
181. Sign Here Petitions, LLC v. Chavez, 243 Ariz. 99, 105 (Ariz. App., Aug. 29, 2017).
182. *Id.*

4 Defamation, Product Disparagement and Related Torts

The First Amendment declares, "Congress shall make no law ... abridging the freedom of speech, or of the press."[1] That "no law" language sounds absolute. However, as discussed in the previous three chapters, it is not, at least according to a century's worth of decisions by the Supreme Court. A business executive may have the right to criticize the local government, but inspiring others to engage in its violent overthrow could lead to criminal punishment. Advertising agencies and business entities have broad liberty to disseminate messages extolling products and services but not to make deceptive, false or unfair claims that may mislead the public.

The subjects of this chapter are *defamation*, *product disparagement* and related torts—areas in which the First Amendment plays only a limited role. Although this chapter cannot provide a definitive treatment of these complex topics, it does explore many of the major legal dilemmas advertising and public relations specialists may encounter in their professional roles. We will also examine how the courts, including the Supreme Court, have balanced the constitutional right of freedom of expression with the right to protect the reputation of an individual, corporation or product.

Background

Whether it's within their families, religious sects, social orders or local communities, individuals have been resolute in protecting their reputations and personal standing. Dating back to the dawn of civilization, the remedy for those who believed their reputations had been unfairly harmed was to step outside to engage in a fistfight or, if members of the aristocracy, in a duel (often referred to as an "affair of honor").

Over time, recognizing that these violent remedies were inefficient in maintaining social order the courts of law in England developed the common law of *defamation* that substituted lawsuits and courtrooms as a more expeditious and humane approach for resolving such conflicts. Not surprisingly, when the British colonized the New World, they brought with them their common law, including defamation law. When the colonists broke away to form a new country, British common law evolved into American common law. Today, American and British laws of defamation resemble first cousins rather than siblings—with many similarities but some noticeable differences.

American common law is state-made law; there is no federal common law. Therefore, technically, there are 50 different sets of defamation laws in the United States. But because of the way the common law evolved, beginning with the original 13 states and then adoption by each new addition to the union, the laws of defamation from Alaska to Wyoming look remarkably alike.

That's why the discussion below is generally applicable to all jurisdictions, with a few variations around the edges such as the legal effect of a retraction or length of time to bring a suit (statute of limitations).

Terminology

Traditionally, printed defamation was referred to as *libel* and spoken defamation as *slander*. In today's more technologically complex communications world, a more apt way to think of libel is as communication that is "fixed" rather than transitory. Although postings and messages on social media such as Facebook, Twitter, Instagram, Snapchat and Tumblr may be quickly deleted by the sender and, therefore, might be considered transitory, courts have generally interpreted such content to be governed by libel law, not slander law, unless individual state laws say otherwise. Even ad-libs—spontaneous comments broadcast live (which are relatively rare in today's environment of timed delays)—would more likely be classified as libel, not slander.

Because of its more enduring nature, legislatures and courts have tended to classify libel as more serious than slander. Virtually all defamation involving the mass and social media, including advertising and public relations, will most likely be treated as libel. For this reason, the terms defamation and libel are used interchangeably throughout the rest of this chapter to refer to the tort of defamation.

Figure 4.1 Although postings and messages on social media such as Facebook, Twitter, Instagram, Snapchat and Tumblr may be quickly deleted by the sender and, therefore, might be considered transitory, courts have generally interpreted such content to be governed by libel law, not slander law, unless individual state laws say otherwise.

Credit line: Gil C/Shutterstock.com

Criminal libel, in which the police and the prosecuting attorney get involved, is exceedingly rare. The overwhelming majority of libel and slander cases are handled as civil wrongs to be litigated in lawsuits between individuals or other entities (e.g., corporations, associations, partnerships and so forth). This involves a branch of *tort* law—defined for our purposes as claims of harm to persons or personal property (e.g., automobile mishaps, determinations of negligence in medical malpractice cases and so forth). Those who lose a civil libel suit in court are not "found guilty" of libel, but are simply held *liable* for the injury caused by the defamatory communications.

Almost any news release, website posting or advertisement holds the potential for a libel suit. Although libel actions can and often do arise out of major advertising campaigns or major stories originating in news releases, libel suits can just as likely be prompted by what may initially appear to be innocuous or minor messages that are, for that reason, sometimes carelessly handled. Libel suits are expensive, time-consuming and fatiguing for both sides. The individual, organization or other entity instigating the action (the plaintiff) typically seeks money damages to pay for repairing a sullied reputation. However, judges and juries often are hard pressed to place precise monetary values on an individual's, organization's or product's reputation, as well as the depreciation caused by a libelous statement. As a result, libel suits often lead to frustration for everyone involved.

Although it might be tempting to turn to the courts to repair the besmirching of the good name of an organization or its products, public relations professionals have the responsibility to inform their organization or their client about the potential far-reaching consequences of filing defamation suits. For example, each court appearance or motion could lead to additional, potentially adverse media coverage because fair and accurate accounts of trials, legislative sessions and government actions and documents may contain further unfavorable and even damaging statements about the plaintiff.

Some individuals and businesses suing for libel may be less interested in obtaining financial damages than in moral vindication. At the urging of some judges (and even Supreme Court justices), the courts, working with other members of the legal profession, have developed mechanisms outside the judicial system for resolving or attempting to resolve some of the civil disagreements that severely clog both federal and state courts. This has led to a variety of processes under the umbrella of what is called *alternative dispute resolution*, including the creation of advertising review boards and other mediation and arbitration services.

For now, however, and probably for the near future, defamation questions are likely to be ultimately resolved in courts and, when plaintiffs win, the results usually mean the awarding of money damages. This may seem a crude and inappropriate means to restore so intangible a thing as reputation, but it appears to have worked over time. If nothing else, payment of cold, hard cash translates the harm into a language everybody can understand.

Who Can Sue and Be Sued?

Any living individual person or entity recognized by the law as a person (e.g., corporation, partnership or similar entity) can bring a cause of action for defamation. The dead are ineligible, as are their estates or relatives (e.g., an individual cannot sue for libelous statements about a deceased relation). In most instances, units of government cannot sue for defamation, but note that individual government office holders as individuals are permitted to do so.

For defamation (and product disparagement and trade libel), each repetition of offending statements may be regarded as a separate publication for which damages may be recovered.

Every person or organization with a hand in the publication of the statements could, in theory, be a defendant. Specifically, defendants can be categorized as primary publishers, republishers or secondary publishers:

Primary publishers. Advertising and public relations professionals, as well as reporters and editors, who actually prepare the harmful messages, clearly will be named as defendants in a defamation suit, although in actual practice, the agency or organization for which they created the message will likely be the primary defendants in such a suit. In an agency situation, the client most likely also will be equally liable. The owner of a newspaper or television station carrying a defamatory statement will be considered a primary publisher and thus held accountable for the message to the same extent as the original publishers. Everything that appears in print or on the air—including letters to the editor, advertising messages, news releases and other communications—becomes the responsibility of the publisher. As discussed later in this chapter, this publication rule is also true for original material posted on a website or transmitted in a twitter account.

Republishers. Anyone who repeats or passes along a defamatory statement will be held accountable in the same was as a primary publisher, even if, in repeating the libel, the speaker makes it clear that the defamatory message is not believed. For example, suppose a news release issued by a public relations agency quotes an outside expert as claiming that a competitor of your client has construction standards that are too low, resulting in the competitor building unsafe structures. Attributing the statement to the outside expert does not protect the agency or client. Because of the Communications Decency Act (see Chapter 13), this rule does not apply to third-party postings in social media.

Secondary publishers. Those who help circulate the defamatory materials (e.g., the person who delivers the newspaper or a technician who disseminates the defamatory video or the owner of the bookstore) may also be held accountable, but only if they had knowledge, or should have had knowledge, of the defamatory content.

The Elements of Libel

Before a plaintiff can win a libel suit, that person or entity must prove that (a) defamatory statements (words, pictures, illustrations, etc. are classified in the law as "statements") have been made (*defamation*); (b) the statements were of and concerning the plaintiff (*identification*); (c) the statements have been disseminated to at least one third party by the defendant (*publication*); (d) injury to the plaintiff was caused by the actions of the defendant (*causation*); and (e) the defamatory statements were published with the required degree of fault established by law (*fault*).[2]

Defamation

The plaintiff must demonstrate that the words or images, in fact, did have defamatory meaning. Some statements may be libelous *per se* (i.e., in and of themselves) and require no further explanation for a judge or jury as to why they damaged the plaintiff's reputation. This is the first category of libel. Examples include *swindler, fraudster, blackmailer, forger, tax-evader, crook* and *AIDS carrier.* The second category of libel is libel *per quod.* Such statements may initially appear to be non-defamatory, but the manner or context in which the words or images are understood by those familiar with the person who is the subject of the statement may be defamatory.

The actual words or images themselves need not be false and clearly defamatory to be actionable. In what is often called "libel by implication," courts have consistently held that if reasonable people exposed to the message draw a defamatory meaning from how the statements in the message relate to each other or from how an illustration suggests a meaning perhaps not intended by the communicator defendant, the message will be considered libelous even if, technically, each fact in the message is true. Thus, a Boston newspaper was found liable in a defamation case when it published an article on teenage sexual practices alongside a picture of a number of readily identifiable teenagers, even though a careful reading of the cutline underneath the photo would have informed a reader that the picture was unrelated to the article.

Advertising and public relations professionals should develop the habit of routinely and meticulously reviewing their communications, regardless of the medium, before they are published for statements that may be seen as defamatory. One method is to list every person and organization mentioned or depicted in the communication and note exactly what is being said about each. Another is to take a moment and stand back from ensuring the details of a message are accurate in order to see how an observer might interpret the overall message. Finding and eliminating potentially libelous material prior to public dissemination is not only the best method for avoiding a possible lawsuit, but the mark of true professional communicators who understand their business.

Publication

The offending statements must reach an audience, if only a small one. For example, Person X may defame Person Y in a confidential memo, but Person Y will not have a legitimate basis for claiming defamation unless Person X has shown the offending statements to at least one additional third party.

Technically, publication occurs the moment a third person has seen the communication. In *Dun & Bradstreet v. Greenmoss Builders, Inc.*,[3] the Supreme Court affirmed a substantial judgment against a credit reporting company for publicizing false and defamatory information, although only five copies of the plaintiff's credit report had been sent to the company's subscribers. The Alton, Ill., *Telegraph* was hit with a $9.2 million libel judgment (enough to force the paper into bankruptcy) stemming from an internal memorandum that was never published.[4] The internal memo, written by two of the paper's reporters, accused a local contractor of having ties with a savings and loan institution that the reporters apparently believed was connected to organized crime.

Unfortunately for an advertising or public relations professional as defendant, a plaintiff typically has little difficulty demonstrating that publication has occurred because the defendant agency or organization has disseminated the defamatory information to thousands, if not millions, of individuals in network or local advertising, through widely distributed news releases, or in campaigns on YouTube, Facebook, VImeo, Twitter, Pinterest, Snapchat or other social media.

Identification

To be actionable, a defamatory statement must be "of or concerning" the specific person or entity. This is commonly known as *identification*. If the audience, or even a small segment of it, reasonably believes the defamatory statements refer to the plaintiff, that person or entity has likely been identified for purposes of libel. A plaintiff identified in a news release or social media message by name, age, title, place of business and hometown probably will have little or no difficulty convincing a court that the plaintiff is the subject of the defamatory comments.

However, identification by name may not be necessary. Veiled references may be sufficient for consumers to know, or believe they know, to whom the story refers. When libelous statements concern a group as a whole, courts consistently have determined that the larger the group, the tougher it is to establish that the defamatory information is "of or concerning" an individual plaintiff. According to Dean William Prosser, considered to be the preeminent authority on the law of torts, a group needs to have about 25 or fewer members before individual plaintiffs will be able to prove defamatory statements identify them. When the defamatory statements are about large groups (e.g., all dentists or members of a professional football team), establishing identification of specific individuals in such cases ranges from difficult to impossible.

Causation

As with any tort, the plaintiff in a defamation suit must allege and prove that the actions of the defendant were the logical and proximate cause of the claimed injury. Often this is easily accomplished because the plaintiff is simply charging that the defendant published libelous statements seen by acquaintances who now think less of the plaintiff or clients who have withdrawn their business or customers who are now former customers.

However, demonstrating causation is not always so straightforward. Suppose a new restaurant, The Pickled Beet, has recently opened and is doing well in its first few months of operation. The food critic for the local entertainment blog site reviews the new eatery and offers a less than positive critique. A sample comment: "The steer my steak came from must have died of old age." Following the review, the restaurant begins a slow decline in revenue. The owners file suit for libel, claiming the review harmed the restaurant's reputation and caused the decline in business.

The reviewer would likely argue that even if one assumes the statements in the published review about the quality of food at The Pickled Beet are false (which the critic would claim they are not, of course) the plaintiff cannot demonstrate the loss of revenue has been caused solely or primarily by the actions of its food critic. The restaurant's economic downturn might be attributable to the usual decline in patrons experienced by new restaurants once the "initial tryers" have dined there once or by worsening economic conditions in the area or perhaps a seasonal slump (or some combination of all of these factors). Clearly, the owners of The Pickled Beet will have their work cut out for them in proving that the review was the primary or even a contributing cause of the loss in business.

Damages

Traditionally, a plaintiff seeking compensation for harm to reputation has been entitled to seek four different kinds of monetary awards: *nominal* damages, *special* damages, either *presumed* or *actual* damages (in some jurisdictions these two and special damages are sometimes lumped together into "general" or "compensatory" damages) and *punitive* damages.

The general rule in American law is that a plaintiff has to be awarded something of value to win a lawsuit—the common law generally does not recognize moral victories. Therefore, plaintiffs not interested in seeking a large award but interested in vindication of their reputations, might simply seek a small or *nominal* damage award. Traditionally, "$1.00" (and sometimes attorney fees) was the typical amount of such an award. It is also possible that although a plaintiff is actually seeking millions for the supposed harm to reputation, a judge or jury could determine that although the plaintiff technically has proven defamation, no real harm was done and, therefore, the plaintiff deserves no more than nominal damages.

Special damages are often described as "out-of-pocket dollar losses." To secure special damages, a plaintiff must produce evidence sufficient to prove that the libelous statements cost the plaintiff demonstrable monetary loss. In the example of the disputed restaurant review above, the restaurant, if successful in the case, most likely would be limited to special damages for the provable loss of revenue attributable to the negative review.

The third category of damages, *presumed* or *actual* damages, developed over time in response to the situation in which a plaintiff could prove the first four elements of defamation but was unable to place a specific economic value on damages to reputation (e.g., how much is losing your best friend worth?). In reaction to this anomalous situation, the law eventually created a category of damages (called presumed damages) requiring no proof of actual monetary loss on the part of the plaintiff. This means that a judge or jury may presume that harm occurred and grant a monetary award presumed to compensate the plaintiff for that harm.

In *Gertz v. Robert Welch, Inc.*,[5] the Supreme Court limited this category of damages to actual damages in cases brought by private plaintiffs against media defendants when reporting on matters of public interest. Although actual damages differ from presumed damages by requiring at least some evidence that the harm to reputation has occurred, once established, judges or juries may award any amount of money thought necessary to compensate plaintiffs. The possibility of such mega-verdicts should be an impetus for advertising and public relations professionals to take all possible precautions to avoid a libel suit.

Punitive damages are not awarded to compensate the plaintiff, but rather to punish the defendant and to serve as a deterrent against future such actions. Generally, courts award punitive damages only when the defendant's actions are so outrageous that they offend the conscience of judges or juries. In a defamation suit, punitive damages might be awarded if the statements of the defendant were not only false and defamatory, but the defendant knew they were false when published, and the statements were purposefully meant to harm the plaintiff. Like presumed damages, punitive damage awards can reach mega-amounts and are as dangerous, if not more so, for defendants.

The Supreme Court has established criteria for determining whether a punitive damages award is excessive—i.e., whether the defendant had fair notice of the conduct for which it could be punished and the severity of the penalties. In *BMW of North America v. Gore* (1977),[6] the Court said the three guideposts a court must look at are (1) "the degree of reprehensibility of the defendant's conduct," (2) "the ratio between the plaintiff's compensatory damages and the amount of punitive damages," and (3) the difference between the punitive damages and "the criminal or civil sanctions that could be imposed for comparable misconduct."[7] The case involved the discovery by a physician that his newly purchased BMW sports car had been repainted after suffering acid rain damage but still sold as new. A jury awarded him $4,000 in compensatory damages and $4 million in punitive damages, which the judge in the case approved. On appeal, the Alabama Supreme Court cut the punitive damages in half. The Supreme Court remanded the case back to the state supreme court, which then reduced the punitive damages to $50,000.

Falsity

Today, in a defamation lawsuit, it must be established that the complained-about statements made by the defendant are both harmful to reputation and false before the plaintiff has any chance of winning. This was not always the case. An oddity of British common law, brought to the colonies from England beginning in the late 1600s, was that truth or falsity made no difference in determining whether someone could successfully sue for defamation. However, in the celebrated 1735 trial of John Peter Zenger,[8] a newspaper publisher in colonial New York, an American jury determined that if the defamatory statements were true, the defendant would not be held liable for the harm to reputation. Note, however, that this verdict placed the responsibility for proving truth on the defendant, rather than requiring the plaintiff to first show the statements were false.

For some plaintiffs and defendants, this allocation of the burden of truth and falsity is still the rule. But in 1964, in the landmark case of *The New York Times v. Sullivan*,[9] the Supreme Court altered this allocation of burden for public officials so they, not the defendants, have to prove the defamatory statements are false. In *Curtis Publishing Company v. Butts*, decided two years later, the Court recognized a category of defamation plaintiffs called "public figures" and eventually placed the burden of proving falsity on them as well. Subsequently, beginning with *Gertz v. Welch* (1974),[10] the Court effectively also changed the burden for private plaintiffs, at least when the defendants could be characterized as "press or broadcast media."[11]

It is legally unsettled whether those engaged in advertising and public relations communications should be treated as media defendants when sued by a private plaintiff. Advertising and public relations professionals, thus, may face the possibility of a defamation suit by a private plaintiff in which they will have to bear the burden of proving the truth of their statements.

Defendant Fault

In addition to defamation, publication, identification, causation, damages and (often) falsity, the plaintiff bringing a libel suit must show that the defendant has acted with the degree of *fault* required by the law in permitting the offending material to be disseminated. The fault standard depends on whether the person or corporation bringing the suit is, in the eyes of the court, "private" or "public."

American libel law is far more protective of private citizens or organizations than public officials or public figures. Historically, the fault standard in a defamation suit was the equivalent of "no fault" or "strict liability." This unusual fault standard required plaintiffs to prove only defamation, publication, identification, causation and damages. The defendant was strictly liable for the harm to reputation, no matter how carefully the defendant had acted. This meant that even if the defamation was accidental (e.g., a made-up name for a character that actually turned out to be similar to the name of a real person), the defendant, unless having some other defense, lost the case.

The strict liability fault standard for all defendants changed dramatically with the Supreme Court's opinion in *New York Times v. Sullivan*. The controversy arose over a full-page advertisement that appeared in *The New York Times* on March 29, 1960, that attempted to raise money to support civil rights crusades in the South. The ad called attention to the leadership of a dynamic, young minister, Dr. Martin Luther King, Jr., who was leading the resistance against racial segregation policies in Montgomery, Alabama. The ad copy contained strong statements, many of which were later proven to be untrue, about the treatment accorded African-American leaders and their sympathizers. For example, the ad claimed:

> In Montgomery, Alabama, after students sang "My Country, 'Tis of Thee," on the state capitol steps, their leaders were expelled from school, and truckloads of police armed with

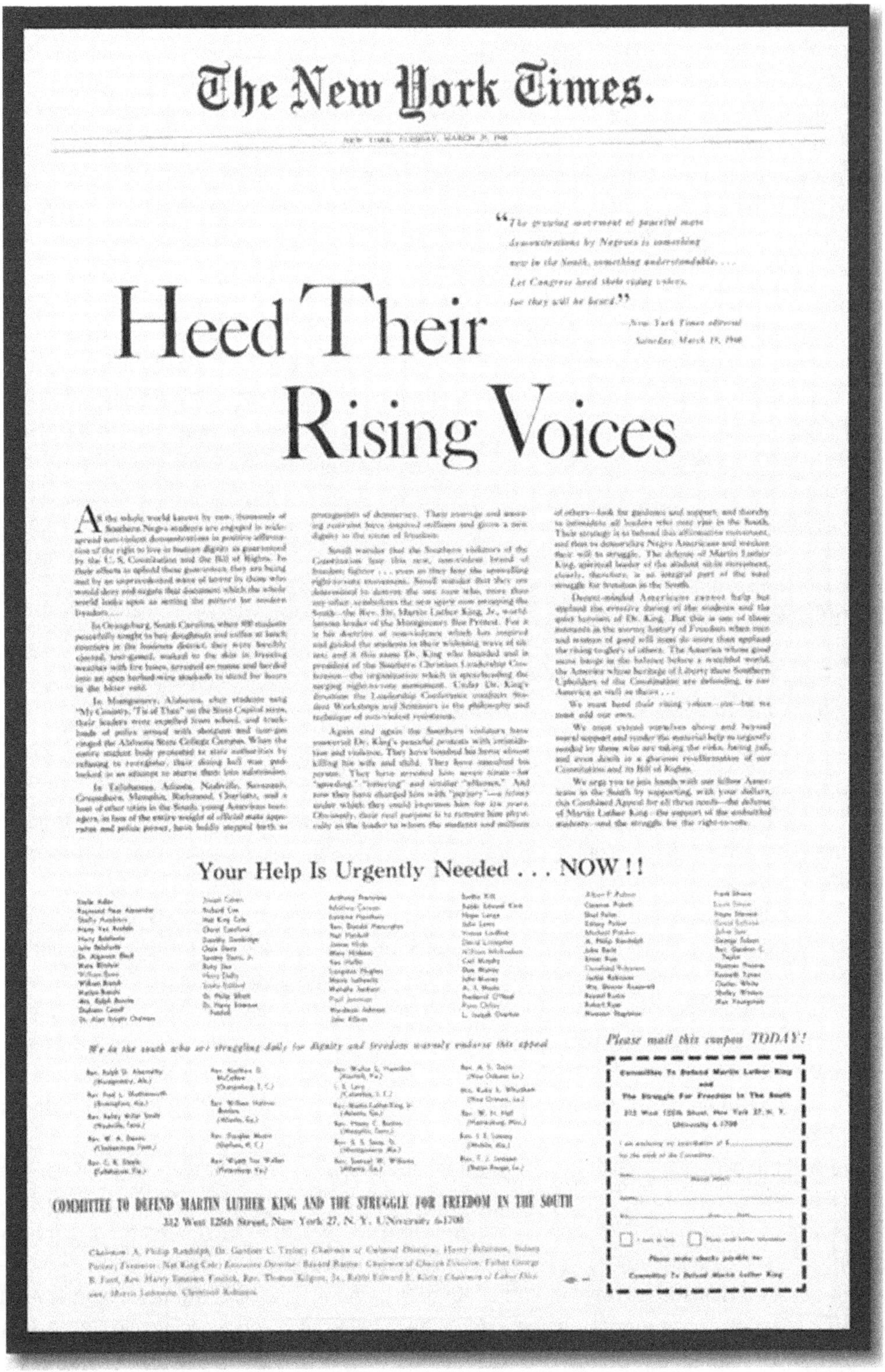

The New York Times.

"The growing movement of peaceful mass demonstrations by Negroes is something new in the South, something understandable. . . . Let Congress heed their rising voices, for they will be heard."

—New York Times editorial
Saturday, March 19, 1960

Heed Their Rising Voices

Your Help Is Urgently Needed . . . NOW !!

Please mail this coupon TODAY!

COMMITTEE TO DEFEND MARTIN LUTHER KING AND THE STRUGGLE FOR FREEDOM IN THE SOUTH
312 West 125th Street, New York 27, N. Y. UNiversity 6-1700

Figure 4.2 The full-page *New York Times* advertisement that was the subject of the landmark Supreme Court decision in *New York Times v. Sullivan* (1964).

Credit line: Committee to Defend Martin Luther King and the Struggle for Freedom in the South—This image is available in the holdings of the National Archives and Records Administration, cataloged under the National Archives Identifier (NAID) 2641477. This work is in the public domain in the United States; it was published in the United States between 1923 and 1977 without a copyright.

shotguns and tear gas ringed the Alabama State College campus. When the entire student body protested to state authorities by refusing to register, their dining hall was padlocked in an attempt to starve them into submission. ... Again and again Southern violators have answered Dr. King's peaceful protests with intimidation and violence. They have bombed his home, almost killing his wife and child. They have assaulted his person. They have arrested him seven times—for "speeding," "loitering," and similar "offenses." And now they have charged him with "perjury," a felony under which they could imprison him for ten years.[12]

These statements were embellished accounts of what actually transpired in Montgomery. There were no padlocks, no tear gas, and Dr. King did not suffer the number of arrests suggested. When Montgomery city officials sued *The Times* saying they had been defamed, the newspaper, to its embarrassment, could not plead truth as a defense because it had not verified the assertions in the ad.

The first of what eventually led to 11 lawsuits against the *Times* was filed by L.B. Sullivan, one of three elected city commissioners of Montgomery and the man responsible for overseeing the police department. At trial, the judge instructed the jury that the statements in the ad reflected adversely on the police department and its leaders and were libelous per se.[13] The jurors awarded Sullivan $500,000 in presumed and punitive damages. After this judgment was upheld by the Alabama Supreme Court,[14] the *Times* carried its appeal to the Supreme Court.

In a unanimous ruling, the Court reversed the judgment against *The Times* and, in the process, established a new fault standard—*actual malice*—that public officials, criticized in their official capacity, would need to meet in order to win a defamation suit.[15] Acknowledging that the newspaper may have been negligent in not checking for errors in the ad copy, the Court rejected the argument that the newspaper had published the errors knowingly and, therefore, *The Times* had not published with actual malice.

It is important to note that the term actual malice in the law of defamation does not refer to hatred or spite directed toward the plaintiff. Actual malice is defined as knowledge of falsity or reckless disregard for the truth. The defendants need only show that they neither knew that what they were disseminating was false, nor seriously doubted what they were disseminating was true to defeat a claim of actual malice. Actual malice is usually difficult but not impossible to prove. As a result, most public officials and figures do not bring libel suits and those who do generally lose.

Later decisions by the Court expanded the *Sullivan* doctrine to include public figures as well as public officials. In the eyes of the Court, public figures could be individuals who have achieved celebrity status, either because of their involvement in public issues or because they have become famous through their exploits as entertainers, sports figures or newsmakers. Melania Trump, Jimmy Fallon, Britney Spears, LeBron James and Bill Gates come to mind. Alternatively, individuals might become public figures in certain limited areas of interest if they are defamed as a result of their attempts to influence the outcome of a public controversy (e.g., legalization of marijuana or prayer in schools). Because they voluntarily stepped into the spotlight, they might be considered limited public figures for purposes of any libel action arising out of that particular controversy.

During the highly contentious and partisan Senate confirmation process for Supreme Court Justice Brett Kavanaugh in 2018, outrageous accusations and claims were leveled for weeks online and throughout the mass and social media against both then-Judge Kavanaugh and his primary accuser of sexual and physical assault, Dr. Christine Blasey Ford. Judge Kavanaugh was already a public official, but Dr. Ford (reluctantly) became a public figure when she made her accusations public and testified before the Senate Judiciary Committee. There were literally thousands of ads attacking both individuals broadcast on television and radio and in social media. Although neither Kavanaugh nor Ford sued for defamation, if they had done so, they would have had to prove that such statements were not only false and defamatory but also disseminated with actual malice.

Efforts to determine what advertising and public relations professionals believed before publishing controversial web postings, advertisements or news releases have prompted libel lawyers to probe the communicators' "state of mind," as reflected in private conversations, internal memoranda, e-mail communications and social media messages. In *Herbert v. Lando* (1978),[16] the Supreme Court held that when a media defendant is alleged to have circulated defamatory falsehoods and is sued for harm to the plaintiff's reputation, there is no First Amendment privilege barring the plaintiff from "inquiring into the editorial processes of those responsible for the publication where the inquiry will produce evidence material to the proof of a critical element of the plaintiff's cause of action."[17] Advertising and public relations professionals would be well advised to have a memorandum or e-mail record of responding affirmatively to superiors questioning the accuracy and validity of sources of information, and to refrain from any asides or personal commentary that might suggest that they have doubts or disbeliefs about what they are about to publish.

As with individuals, corporations, partnerships and other similar organizations may be classified for purposes of a libel suit as either public or private plaintiffs. In making this important determination, courts traditionally take into account the following factors:

- *The size of an organization.*
- *The character and volume of an organization's marketing communications.* Not every organization that advertises or in other ways communicates with its publics is necessarily a public figure, but organizations that attempt to influence events through advertising or other similar means are likely to yield their private-figure status. Evidence that an organization has advertised heavily or has conducted extensive reputation management campaigns may convince a court that it has ready access to the channels of communication, and, like public officials and public figures, it can readily respond to negative statements about its activities.
- *The history of an organization's involvements in controversies.* If an organization has previously been involved in a public dispute, such participation may contribute to a decision to classify the organization as a public figure.
- *Whether an entity exists in a heavily regulated industry and is publicly owned.* Examples include media, insurance and privately owned utility companies. For purposes of libel, such organizations would likely be treated as public figures.

To further complicate matters, a decade after *Sullivan*, the Court in *Gertz v. Robert Welch, Inc.* changed the fault standard for private persons as well, at least when suing media defendants in a matter of general public interest.[18] The new standard, although varying from state to state, is at least negligence. For example, a media defendant could not be held liable for an accidental mistake but could be held liable for a negligent error like sloppy editing. There is considerable doubt, however, that courts will treat advertising and public relations practitioners or their organizations as media defendants. Prudent advertising and public relations professionals, therefore, should assume they may be held to a fault standard that means they are strictly liable for any mistake, no matter how carefully they acted, and recognize the dangers inherent in not taking every precaution to avoid such lawsuits.

Affirmative Defenses

Once a libel plaintiff has made a *prima facie* case (i.e., established defamation, publication, identification, etc.), the other side is entitled to mount a defense. Called affirmative defenses, these traditional, common-law defenses have evolved over time to include *truth*, *absolute or conditional privilege*, and *fair comment* and *opinion*.

Truth is now generally regarded as a complete defense, but truth is often difficult to prove. In reality, it often boils down to one person's word against another's. Thus, one may know that something is true but face enormous difficulty proving it before a judge and jury. Information sources who speak fearlessly while a news story or news release is being developed have been known to lose their nerve or their memories while under oath in a deposition or on the witness stand.

Absolute privilege is the freedom to discuss certain aspects of the public's business with impunity. For example, absolute privilege is conferred on members of Congress during debates and hearings. Likewise, society has determined that prosecuting attorneys, judges, mayors, city council and school board members or zoning commissioners, for example, should be able to comment fully and freely while performing official duties. If such individuals had to worry about speaking the absolute truth in everything they said, they might well become too inhibited to do the public's business.

Those who report information stemming from someone who has absolute privilege enjoy a *conditional (or qualified) privilege*. Conditional privilege extends to reports of governmental documents as well. Journalists and other citizens can quote from privileged documents without fear of successful libel suits, so long as the published or broadcast accounts are complete, fair and accurate. Other common-law forms of conditional privilege may apply, especially when commercial speech is concerned. For example, a competitor is privileged to make boastful, embellished claims about its own products or services compared to those offered by the competition, so long as the comparison does not contain false assertions of fact (e.g., "Our products are far superior to the other leading brands").[19] This puffery, or exaggerated praise of one's own goods or services, is not considered defamatory, even if it is sharply critical of the competition, so long as the boasting is couched in general, nonspecific terms. Note, however, that if a claim states a product is superior, perhaps because the competition has employed substandard materials in its product, the statement has become specific (capable of being proved or disproved). The statement would no longer be covered by a qualified privilege because it would no longer be treated as puffery.[20]

A defendant may also have an *interest privilege*. This conditional privilege allows a reply to communications by others to serve one's own interests—in other words, to defend against the defamation of another, even if the reply itself may be defamatory. However, this does not mean that the response can be a knowing falsity or reflect a reckless disregard for the truth. Deliberate, specific untruths constitute an abuse of privilege, and such statements will forfeit their protection.

Fair comment and criticism protects expression of opinions about things offered to the public for acceptance or rejection. A politician's voting pattern, a company's environmental record, an architect's creativity or a restaurant's cuisine are all examples of acceptable targets of public discussion, even though such adverse criticisms might hurt the business or the professional reputation of the organization or individual.

In *Gertz*, the Supreme Court created a possible additional affirmative defense for *opinion* statements. According to the Court,

> We begin with the common ground. Under the First Amendment there is no such thing as a false idea. However pernicious an opinion may seem, we depend for its correction not on the conscience of judges and juries, but on the competition of other ideas.[21]

Opinion statements are not susceptible to a truth or falsity test.

The danger in mixing factual statements with opinions is exemplified in the Supreme Court's decision in *Milkovich v. Lorain Journal Company* (1990).[22] The case involved a sports column that claimed a high school wrestling coach "had beat the system with the big lie" and that "anyone who attended the meet ... knows in his heart that [Milkovich, the plaintiff] lied at the hearing after giving his solemn oath to tell the truth."[23] The Court, in reversing a trial court's summary judgment in favor of the defendant newspaper, said that despite the opinion-like language, a "reasonable fact finder could conclude that the statements in the ... column imply an assertion [of fact] that Milkovich perjured himself in a judicial proceeding."[24]

Other Defenses

In addition to truth, conditional privilege, fair comment and opinion, so-called secondary defenses, often called defenses in mitigation or incomplete defenses, may provide at least some protection for defendants in defamation cases. Secondary defenses do not allow the defendant to avoid a judgment, but they can lessen the blow of an adverse libel decision by reducing the amount of money a court might award.

One of these secondary defenses is *retraction*—a voluntary action that demonstrates a good faith effort on the part of the communicator to set the record straight and to atone for a defamatory statement. Note, however, that for a court to find it persuasive, the retraction should be timely, prominent and complete. For example, if, in an angry political ad, your client mistakenly accuses a prominent businessman of tax evasion, your retraction should not say, "We are *sorry* that we said he is a tax dodger," but rather, "He is *not* guilty of tax evasion." Another secondary defense is to offer the offended persons the *right of reply*—to provide space to those who have been wronged, or think they have been, to tell their side of the story. Neither a retraction nor a right of reply can be imposed. The courts recognize the rights of publishers to control the contents of their publications.[25]

Product Disparagement

Although it is much like defamation, the tort of *product disparagement* involves injurious false-hoods that disparage the quality of a product or service but do not defame the company that provides and produces them.

Terminology

The common law criteria for establishing product disparagement are: (a) the disparaging statement has been made; (b) the statement has been published to a third party by the defendant; (c) the statement is about a specific product or service; (d) the statement is the direct cause of the actual harm suffered by the plaintiff; (e) the plaintiff is entitled to be compensated by money damages because the statement results in financial damage or is likely to do so; (f) the statement is false; and (g) the defendant acted with actual malice—meaning that the defendant knew the statement is untrue or entertained serious doubt whether the statement is true or false.

A good example is the "pink slime" case in which the Walt Disney Company was sued by Beef Products Inc. (BPI), a family-owned company based in Dakota Dunes, South Dakota. The case centered on a series of broadcast and online reports by ABC News, owned by Disney. According to opening statements by BPI's lead attorney during the trial, ABC News used the term "pink slime" at least 350 times in stories on different media platforms to describe BPI's beef product known as "Lean Finely Textured Beef (LFTB)." (The term "pink slime" was coined by a government biologist in a private e-mail to his colleagues to describe the product, which results from spinning off fat from beef trimmings with highly sophisticated equipment.)

At the time of the reports, LFTB, which had FDA approval, was contained in about 70 percent of the ground beef in the country, including that sold in several leading major grocery chains and in fast-food restaurant chains such as McDonald's. After the reports, according to trial testimony, BPI suffered an 80 percent drop in sales and was forced to close three of its four plants and lay off 700 of its 1,300 employees. ABC claimed its reports were accurate, fair and complete.

BPI sued under a South Dakota statute that allows for triple damages if a defendant knowingly lies about the safety of a food product. The company's suit sought $1.9 billion in damages,

Figure 4.3 In the so-called "pink slime" case, the Walt Disney Company was sued by Beef Products Inc., a family-owned company based in South Dakota, for product disparagement. The case centered on a series of broadcast and online reports by the Disney-owned ABC News, whose New York headquarters is pictured here.

Credit line: NYCStock/Shutterstock.com

which, if tripled, would translate to $5.7 billion. The case was finally settled in 2017 after a con-fidential out-of-court agreement was reached that cost Disney at least $177 million,[26] based on Disney's litigation costs listed in the company's 2017 second quarter regulatory filing.

Product Disparagement Versus Defamation

Although defamation and product disparagement represent concerns over somewhat different interests, at times, they may overlap. If a statement reflects merely on the quality of what the plaintiff is selling, it is product disparagement alone. If, however, the statement also alleges that the plaintiff is not honest, lacks integrity or is defrauding the public by selling something known to be defective or a health hazard, the statement may also be defamatory. Actions may be brought in the same lawsuit to cover both torts, so long as the damages are not duplicated. For example, in *Steaks Unlimited, Inc. v. Deaner*,[27] a charge of false advertising concerning the value of meat sold by the plaintiff was made by a local TV newscast. The court found both product disparagement and corporate defamation.

Many product disparagement claims, if they involve charges of false advertising, are brought under the federal Lanham Act, which permits recovery for "any person who is or who believes he or she is likely to be damaged by a misrepresentation of the nature, characteristics, qualities, or geographic origin of his or her or another person's goods, services, or commercial activi-ties."[28] Provisions of the Lanham Act include:

Civil action:

(1) Any person who, on or in connection with any goods or services, or any container for goods, uses in commerce any word, term, name, symbol, or device, or any combination thereof, or any false designation of origin, false or misleading description of fact, or false or misleading representation of fact, which–

   (A) is likely to cause confusion, or to cause mistake, or to deceive as to the affiliation, con-nection, or association of such person with another person, or as to the origin, spon-sorship, or approval of his or her goods, services, or commercial activities by another person, or

   (B) in commercial advertising or promotion, misrepresents the nature, characteristics, qualities, or geographic origin of his or her or another person's goods, services, or commercial activities, shall be liable in a civil action by any person who believes that he or she is or is likely to be damaged by such act.[29]

Trade Libel

The term *trade libel* is an ancient one, coined to describe defamation about the quality of com-mercial goods and services. Casting aspersions on the quality of goods and services was likened to personal defamation. In recent years, the expansion of the concept of product disparagement has left trade libel a rather narrow area. However, trade libel is different from product dispar-agement in several respects.

In trade libel: (a) special damages–pecuniary losses resulting from the offending state-ments–must be proved, and (b) under certain conditions, it is possible to obtain an injunction to stop the trade libel (e.g., cessation of a continuing advertising campaign), whereas in product disparagement, such speech cannot be enjoined. In some states, trade libel laws are referred to as "slander of goods" or "slander of title."

Conclusion

The Supreme Court has not decided any major cases for some time in the areas of defamation, product disparagement or trade libel, leaving the law to evolve at the state and lower federal court levels. Although the lower courts are generally applying the settled principles of defamation to newer media, including social media, they continue to grapple with a number of difficult procedural issues related to unique aspects of Internet-based and electronic communication.

Advertising and public relations professionals should be aware that the chances are not remote that they and their clients and organizations might have difficulty in bringing defamation-related suits in their home states against out-of-state defendants and, conversely, in a Catch-22-like situation, they may be held liable in out-of-state jurisdictions for statements made on a website that are accessed in locations far away.

Challenges presented by defamatory statements made online and the associated jurisdictional issues raised by the Internet and World Wide Web will likely require continued reexamination by courts of how to ensure a means of redress for reputational harm without throttling online communications as we have come to know them.

Notes

1. U.S. Const. amend. I.
2. Restatement (Second) of Torts 558 (Am. Law Inst. 1977).
3. Dun & Bradstreet v. Greenmoss Builders, Inc., 472 U.S. 749 (1985).
4. Paper Loses $9.2 Million Libel Suit, N.Y. Times, July 20, 1980, §1, Part 2, at 29.
5. Gertz v. Robert Welch, Inc., 418 U.S. 323, 349 (1974).
6. BMW of North America v. Gore, 517 U.S. 559 (1977).
7. *Id.*
8. James Alexander, Ed. S. N. Katz, A Brief Narrative of the Case and Trial of John Peter Zenger, Printer of the New York Weekly Journal, John Harvard Library (Belknap Press of Harvard University Press, Cambridge, MA, 1972).
9. New York Times v. Sullivan, 376 U.S. 254 (1964).
10. Gertz v. Robert Welch, Inc., 418 U.S. 323, 349 (1974).
11. *Id.*
12. New York Times Co., 376 U.S. 254.
13. *Id.* at 262.
14. New York Times Co. v. Sullivan, 273 Ala. 646, 679 (1962).
15. New York Times Co., 376 U.S. 254, 280.
16. Herbert v. Lando, 441 U.S. 153 (1979).
17. *Id.*
18. Gertz418 U.S. 323, 349.
19. Restatement (Second) of Torts §649 (Am. Law Inst. 1977).
20. *Id.* §650A.
21. Gertz v. Welch, 418 U.S. 323, 339–340 (1974).
22. Milkovich v. Lorain Journal Company, 497 U.S. 1 (1990).
23. *Id.*
24. *Id.*

25. *See* Miami Herald v. Tornillo, 418 U.S. 241 (1974).
26. See for example, Timothy Mclaughlin, *ABC TV Settles with Beef Product Maker in 'Pink Slime' Defamation case*, Reuters, June 28, 2017, www.reuters.com/article/us-abc-pinkslime-idUSKBN1APOFY; Jeff John Roberts, *Disney Paid $177 Million to Settle ABC 'Pink Slime' Case*, Fortune Mag., Aug. 10, 2017, http://fortune.com/2017/08/10/disney-pink-slime/
27. Steaks Unlimited, Inc. v. Deaner, 468 F. Supp. 779 (D.C. Pa. 1979).
28. 15 U.S.C.A. §1125.
29. 15 U.S.C.A. §1125(a) False designations of origin, false descriptions and dilution forbidden.

5 Invasion of Privacy
False Light, Private Facts, Intrusion and Other Related Torts

In the 21st century, notions about personal privacy seem almost quaint. In addition to the information that many people voluntarily share on social media or exchange in commercial transactions, specialized data collection agencies store and often sell salary, employment, credit, home-mortgage, health-care and other personal information even more sensitive. With access to more data than ever, the mass media also are capable of disseminating a great deal of information about each of us, including physical likenesses, even if we might urgently wish the media not to do so. In response, courts are seeing an exponential growth in suits demanding that those who have invaded the personal privacy rights of others, thereby causing mental anguish, be made to pay money damages.

Privacy Law Origins

Although today's invasions of our personal privacy occur in many outlets, other than the news media, it was unrestrained, sensational press coverage in the late 1800s that prompted legal scholars to advocate the first privacy laws. The lurid era of yellow journalism in the late 19th century found reporters prying feverishly into the personal affairs of the rich and famous.

An aristocratic Boston lawyer and businessman, Samuel Warren, was particularly offended by what he regarded as steamy, voracious press attention paid to the forthcoming wedding of his daughter. Because no remedies were available under existing law to deal with such journalistic excesses, Warren decided that a novel approach was needed. In collaboration with his former law partner, Louis Brandeis, Warren pounded out an angry, sweeping article for the *Harvard Law Review*[1] that proposed the legal system recognize a new principle, which they described as an individual's right to privacy:

> [T]he press is overstepping in every direction the obvious bounds of propriety and decency. Gossip is no longer the resource of the idle and of the vicious, but has become a trade, which is pursued with industry as well as effrontery. ... To occupy the indolent, column upon column is filled with idle gossip, which can only be procured by intrusion upon the domestic circle. The intensity and complexity of life, attending upon advancing civilization, have rendered necessary some retreat from the world...[because] modern enterprise and invention have, through invasions upon his privacy, subjected him to mental pain and distress, far greater than could be inflicted by mere bodily injury.[2]

Courts and state legislatures did not react immediately to provide citizens (in the Warren and Brandeis phrase) "some retreat from the world," but clearly the privacy thesis struck a responsive chord within the legal profession. Subsequently, several privacy invasions were alleged in lawsuits, although a court would not allow the first recovery for damages until some 15 years later. Over the next several decades, privacy law continued to evolve—sometimes slowly, often inconsistently—in response to technological and social change.

Because of this inconsistency, eventually, noted legal scholar William Prosser suggested that an analysis of the facts and issues in the majority of reported cases indicated most invasion of privacy complaints could be categorized as belonging to one of four different types: (a) unreasonably placing an individual in a false light before the public; (b) unjustifiably publishing embarrassing private facts; (c) unreasonably intruding into one's physical solitude; and (d) misappropriating one's name, identity or likeness.[3] Prosser's suggested taxonomy proved to be just the ticket for making order out of chaos, and most legal scholars, state courts and legislatures subsequently adopted his four-part invasion of privacy classification scheme.

A general discussion of the basic elements of an invasion of privacy suit often proves difficult because a plaintiff's case might involve one or more of the four different types (e.g., proving a defendant committed an unreasonable act in an intrusion case versus demonstrating that a statement is not true in a false light case). Nonetheless, some issues are common across most types.

First, courts usually make no distinction between oral speech and written or otherwise recorded communication. Additionally, the right to privacy is considered an individual personal right and, therefore, generally cannot be the subject of a lawsuit by family members or by the plaintiff's estate if the plaintiff is no longer living. For similar reasons, most jurisdictions have held that only individuals—and not corporations or other similar entities—may bring a cause of action for invasion of privacy because such organizations have no "feelings and sensibilities" of human beings (misappropriation, in some instances, being the exception to this rule).

This chapter discusses *false light*, *public disclosure of private, embarrassing facts* and *intrusion*. These three subcategories of the tort of invasion of privacy (generally defined as the wish to be left alone) are part of civil tort law defined in Chapter 4 as involving claims of harm to persons or personal property. The chapter concludes with a brief discussion of *infliction of emotional distress*. Misappropriation, the fourth subcategory of invasion of privacy and the one of most concern to advertising and public relations professionals, is the subject of Chapter 6.

False Light

The *Restatement of Torts* defines *false light privacy* as:

> One who gives publicity to a matter concerning another that places the other before the public in a false light is subject to liability to the other for invasion of his privacy, if
>
> (a) the false light in which the other was placed would be highly offensive to a reasonable person, and
> (b) the actor [perpetrator] had knowledge of or acted in reckless disregard as to the falsity of the publicized matter and the false light in which the other would be placed.[4]

In some respects, false light privacy is much like defamation, a point we return to later. But there are important differences—enough of them to make false light, in the eyes of most courts, a separate matter entirely. What might be considered among the first successful false light courtroom victories occurred in England in 1816. The winner was Lord Byron, one of the most colorful of all the English romantic poets. Angry because someone had falsely attributed a mediocre poem to him—one he swore he had not written—Byron persuaded a British court to issue an order halting further publication and circulation of the poem.[5]

In the United States, false light evolved slowly from the beginnings of privacy law in the early 1900s, but the tort sprang forth after a more than five-decade gestation period in the mid-1960s to become identified by most commentators as a separate subcategory of invasion of privacy. Today, a majority of states have adopted some form of false light and courts in a number of the remaining states have hinted that they might adopt the tort if presented with the appropriate case.

However, false light invasion of privacy continues to be severely criticized by many in the mass media and the legal community as being so substantially like the tort of defamation that it should cease to be recognized as a separate cause of action. This line of thinking has recently led a number of states, including Florida,[6] Massachusetts,[7] Texas[8] and North Carolina,[9] to explicitly decline to recognize false light as cognizable by their courts. It is still too early to determine whether this is a trend that will continue.

The Elements of False Light

Similar to a suit for defamation, the plaintiff must first prove that (a) a false statement has been made that offends ordinary decency (but, unlike libel, not necessarily harmful to reputation); (b) the offending material has been shown to at least one other person by the defendant; (c) the plaintiff has been identified in the statements; (d) the actions of the defendant are the true cause of the actual harm suffered by the plaintiff (in this case, mental anguish rather than injury to reputation); (e) the plaintiff is entitled to be compensated by money damages for that harm; and (f) the defamatory statements appeared because the defendant has done all this with the required degree of fault established by law. Let's take a closer look at each of these points in turn.

False Statements That Offend Ordinary Decency

The false light statement must be found offensive to a reasonable person. With few clear-cut guidelines to follow, judges and juries are given broad latitude to define what is "highly offensive," and the results are not always consistent or predictable.

When she was 10 years old, Eleanor Sue Leverton of Birmingham, Alabama, was struck by a car, knocked down and nearly run over. As a woman bystander lifted the injured child from the pavement, a newspaper photographer, who happened to be nearby, shot a picture of the scene. His powerful, dramatic photograph was published the following morning in a Birmingham newspaper.

Nearly two years later, the *Saturday Evening Post* magazine used that same picture—it had been purchased from a photo syndicate house—to illustrate an article on pedestrian carelessness. The story was entitled "They Ask to Be Killed," and underneath the photograph was this subheading: "Safety education in schools has reduced child accidents measurably, but unpredictable darting through traffic still takes a sobering toll." Beside the title was a box that read: "Do you invite massacre by your own carelessness? Here's how thousands have committed suicide by scorning laws that were passed to keep them alive."

Miss Leverton and her parents resented the implication that her misfortune was brought on by her own carelessness. Indeed, the Birmingham police concluded at the time that the accident happened not because of her own carelessness, but because the motorist had run through a red light. The Levertons sued for an unwarranted invasion of their daughter's privacy and were awarded $5,000 (the equivalent of approximately $56,000 in today's economy). An appeals court agreed that the judgment was appropriate: "The sum total of all this is that this particular plaintiff, the legitimate subject for publicity for one particular accident, now becomes a pictorial, frightful example of pedestrian carelessness. This, we think, exceeds the bounds of privilege."[10] In other words, Miss Leverton had been placed in a false and offensive light.

A wrong or misleading context alone, however, may not win a false light privacy suit if the conduct depicted is not found to be offensive. For example, consider the case of Clarence W. Arrington, whose photograph was used on the cover of *The New York Times* magazine in connection with a lengthy article entitled "The Black Middle Class: Making It."[11] The photograph, published without his consent, showed him walking down a Manhattan street wearing an expensive business suit, carrying a briefcase and, in general, looking prosperous.

Indeed, Arrington was doing well. He had earned an M.B.A. from Columbia University, and, at the time his photo was taken, was a financial analyst with General Motors. Still, he resented being associated with the *Times* magazine article, a harsh indictment of materialistic and status-conscious African Americans who, the article contended, were becoming less and less concerned about the plight of their less fortunate African-American brothers and sisters.

Arrington sued the *Times*, claiming that he did not fit the theme of the article or the materialistic views of the persons who had been interviewed. He was placed in a false light, he argued, and, as a result, he was exposed to contempt and ridicule from his friends and suffered mental anguish. The trial court agreed, but the appeals court did not, holding that the *Times* article neither depicted him personally as being insensitive nor portrayed him in an offensive manner.[12]

Publication

Like defamation, the offending words must reach an audience. Also like defamation, a false light plaintiff often has a relatively easy time demonstrating that publication has occurred because the defendant advertising agency or public relations department has disseminated the false information to thousands, if not millions, of readers or viewers in network television advertising, press release material published in hundreds of news outlets or in campaigns on YouTube, Facebook or other social networking sites.

Unlike defamation, most courts have held that the audience must be substantial in size. Technically, however, publication occurs the moment a third person has been exposed to the communication. There is no formula for determining when an audience will be deemed large enough to be substantial; rather courts tend to evaluate the overall context of the statements and the plaintiff's relationship to the audience. For example, statements on signs posted on a public street have been deemed to be published, even though the geographic area of distribution was small,[13] and statements disseminated to a few people may be regarded as "published" if members of the small audience had a special or particular connection to the plaintiff.[14]

On the other hand, statements made at work in the context of employment evaluations usually fail to meet the publication requirement.[15] Also, information disseminated about a potential plaintiff on a "need-to-know" basis is generally not considered to be published. For example, suspicions about a house vandal shared with the police and homeowner's association were held as not satisfying the publication requirement.[16] But the dissemination of statements to an audience of several hundred in a "private" event may constitute publication.[17]

Identification

The plaintiff in false light invasion of privacy cases faces virtually the same requirements as a libel plaintiff to prove an audience, or even a tiny portion of it, believes that the statements refer to him or her. Unfortunately for the professional communicator, identification also is often made easy for the plaintiff because of the emphasis on clarity that is inherent in the training of professional communicators. Identification of group members for false light purposes is also identical. Like libel, each member of a small group, traditionally about 25 members or fewer, may sue and be able to collect, even if he or she is not personally identified in the false and shocking or outrageous communication.

This a good place to again note who can be a plaintiff in a false light suit because this is one area in which false light differs significantly from defamation. The reason that individual members of a small group can sue is that each member of the group is recognized in the law as having legal standing. In defamation, so does any entity that is recognized as an individual in the eyes of the law, such as a company, partnership or other legal entity. Although they may have a reputation to defend for libel purposes, these fictitious "individuals" generally cannot bring a cause of action for false light because they cannot demonstrate suffering mental anguish caused by the published false statement central to a plaintiff's case in proving false light invasion of privacy.

Causation

As in any tort, the plaintiff in a false light invasion of privacy suit must allege and prove that the actions of the defendant were the logical and proximate cause of the alleged injury. Often this is easily accomplished because the plaintiff is simply claiming that he or she has suffered legitimate mental anguish when the defendant published false and outrageous statements seen by acquaintances or clients or customers.

Problems involving proving causation might arise when a plaintiff can be shown to be mentally unstable in general or is responding negatively to a false statement that, in the opinion of a judge or jury, should not have caused mental anguish severe enough to warrant compensation. Also, if the false but not defamatory statement has been already widely circulated by others, the plaintiff may experience difficulty in convincing a jury that the defendant's repetition of the statement legitimately could be seen as causing any significant additional harm to the plaintiff's mental well-being.

Compensation

Although the devil is in the nuances differentiating the laws of false light from state to state, a plaintiff seeking compensation for harm to his or her mental well-being caused by an outrageous, false statement generally will be entitled to seek four different kinds of monetary awards: *nominal* damages, *special* damages, *actual* damages (in some jurisdictions, the second and third awards are sometimes combined and called "general" or "compensatory" damages) and *punitive* (or "exemplary") damages. Although these are discussed more thoroughly in Chapter 4, let's briefly look at each of these in turn.

The general rule in American law is that a plaintiff has to be awarded something of value to win a suit in law as opposed to a suit in equity—the common law generally does not recognize moral victories. Therefore, a plaintiff not interested in seeking a large award, but interested in proving to the world that the embarrassing or outrageous statements are false, might simply seek a small or *nominal* damage award. This is relatively rare, however, in false light cases. More typically, a plaintiff, actually seeking thousands (if not millions) of dollars for the supposed mental anguish is found by a judge or jury to have suffered no real harm and, therefore, not deserving of more than a nominal award of damages, even though, technically, the plaintiff has proven all the elements of his or her false light case.

Special damages are often thought of as out-of-pocket dollar loss. To obtain special damages, a plaintiff must produce evidence sufficient to prove that the false and outrageous statements cost the plaintiff demonstrable monetary loss. Expenses for psychiatric care, counseling services or prescribed medications, as well as evidence of wages lost or other financial reverses because the plaintiff was too upset to function normally, are examples of special damages often claimed by plaintiffs in false light cases.

The third category of damages, *actual* damage, needs no proof of actual monetary loss on the part of the plaintiff, but often requires the plaintiff to demonstrate that the alleged mental anguish caused by the false and outrageous statements did, in fact, exist. In jurisdictions that ask for some evidence of mental anguish, plaintiffs seeking actual damages, in addition to their own testimony about how upset they feel, typically introduce testimony from friends and medical and/or counseling professionals to meet this requirement.

Punitive damages are awarded not to compensate the plaintiff, but to punish the defendant. Because they are meant to punish instead of compensate, punitive damages, generally, are awarded only when the defendant's actions are so outrageous that they offend the conscience of judges or juries. In a false light invasion of privacy suit, punitive damages might be awarded if the statements of the defendant were not only false, but the defendant both knew they were false when published and were purposefully meant to harm the plaintiff.

If a judge or jury accepts that the harm has occurred, and the defendant has no additional defenses, money will be awarded to the plaintiff to compensate him or her based on the judge's or jury's estimation of the harm—an invitation for large damage awards for the plaintiff that many courts seem unable to resist. The possibility of such large verdicts should be all the impetus needed for advertising and public relations professionals to take all possible precautions to avoid becoming embroiled in a false light suit.

Defendant Fault

To be successful in a false light invasion of privacy lawsuit, the plaintiff must show that the offending publication occurred because the defendant who published the material did so with the *fault* standard established by law. Although fault in tort law often is defined as an error in judgment or conduct (i.e., negligence, or any departure from normal care because of inattention, carelessness or incompetence), in false light invasion of privacy, the Supreme Court has decreed that the fault required is "actual malice" (i.e., the publication of a deliberate lie, or publishing with a reckless disregard as to whether the statement is true).

Actual malice, the fault standard required for public officials and public figures in defamation cases (discussed in Chapter 4), is a very difficult hurdle for a plaintiff to overcome. Because all plaintiffs in false light invasion of privacy suits must show actual malice, regardless if they are public or private, one might conclude that false light cases would be few and far between. For reasons discussed later in this chapter, however, proving actual malice in false light cases is often much easier because of the outrageous actions of defendants in publishing the complained of material.

Time, Inc. v. Hill

The two criteria essential for winning a false light invasion of privacy suit are (a) that the false light in which the other person is placed would be highly offensive to a reasonable person and (b) that the person who publicized the false and offensive information knew it was false at the time or acted in reckless disregard of whether the material was true. The latter criterion—the actual malice fault requirement—was first applied by the Supreme Court to false light invasion of privacy in 1967, in *Time, Inc. v. Hill*.[18] In this case, the first major invasion of privacy case ever ruled on by the Supreme Court, members of a quiet, private family became the subject of intense and poorly handled media coverage because of the crush of events quite out of their control.

The case began with a jailbreak. In 1952, three convicts escaped from a maximum-security facility and rather than head for the hills, slipped into the peaceful suburb of Whitemarsh, Pa., just outside Philadelphia. The three convicts, apparently selecting a private home at random, invaded the residence and held the owners, James Hill and his wife, and their five children hostage for 19 hours.[19] The family members were not harmed or molested; in fact, they reported that they had been treated with courtesy despite the tenseness of the situation. Police, acting on a tip, found out about the hostages and surrounded the Hill home. When the convicts attempted to escape, two of the three were shot and killed in a gun battle with the police.

Early in the following year, a writer named Joseph Hayes published a novel about a family held hostage by three escaped convicts. Entitled *The Desperate Hours*,[20] the novel was inspired by the Hill family drama, although the author drew on other similar hostage situations as well. The book differed from actual events in several aspects. For one thing, the convict characters in the novel, far from being courteous, were portrayed as mean and abusive, especially toward the daughter of the family. The upcoming publication of the book that was expected to become a bestseller, plus the trauma of the original experience and the subsequent intensive media and public attention surrounding the 19-hour standoff, prompted the Hill family to move to Connecticut where none of their new acquaintances knew of the hostage-related events.

The publication of the novel, however, was only the beginning. A short time later, Hayes decided to turn the book into a play. Drawing favorable attention from theatrical producers, the play was cast and then taken on the road to various cities on the East Coast to test different versions of the play in preparation for possible production in New York City. After positive reviews in regional newspapers, the now definitely Broadway-bound play was scheduled to have its last out-of-town performances in Philadelphia.

At this juncture, editors at the country's leading news and photo magazine, *Life*, decided to do a piece about the play. To give the story a unique angle, *Life*'s editors elected to dredge up the Hill family's ordeal and relate it to the fictional treatment depicted in *The Desperate Hours*.

"The play," the *Life* article exclaimed, "is a heart-stopping account of how a family rose to heroism in a crisis."[21] A series of photographs, taken both inside and outside the former Hill residence, depicted posed actors illustrating scenes from the play. One photo showed "the son" being roughed up by one of the convicts. Another photo, captioned "daring daughter," showed an actor depicting the daughter in the play biting the hand of a convict, forcing him to drop a pistol on the floor, while another photo was of the supposed father hurling the pistol out of a window. None of these things had happened to the Hill family.

The Hills had finally had enough, especially when it was announced that the play would become the basis of a major motion picture. A text and photo-illustrated article, clearly linking the Hills to the dramatized events, published in the one magazine that, at the time, was on every coffee table in every home and office in America, meant there was no place the Hills could live without seemingly forever being defined by the one trauma-causing event they had hoped to put behind them.

In their suit for invasion of privacy, the Hills' complaint was that the *Life* article placed them in a false light by implying that the fictionalized, sensationalized events shown in the photographs reflected their own experiences as hostages. The trial court jury[22] agreed that the magazine had been careless in linking the Hills to the play (at least in the photo captions) and found in their favor, as did the appeals court.[23] Eventually, the case made its way to the Supreme Court of the United States, with *Life* arguing that a constitutional issue—freedom of the press to discuss matters that are newsworthy—was involved.

The Court decided the case in the wake of its recent ruling in *New York Times v. Sullivan*,[24] which changed the fault standard in some defamation cases to actual malice (discussed in Chapter 4). The decision in *Hill* was a sweeping victory for freedom of the press. Although the connection between reporting on public events like the struggle for civil rights in Southern states that was at the heart of the *Sullivan* decision and an article about an upcoming play supposedly based on the Hill family's private ordeal struck some observers as tenuous, the Court made it, nonetheless. Ruling in favor of *Life* magazine, the Court sent the case back for another trial, holding that the Hill family (and apparently all plaintiffs in future false light cases) could win only if actual malice could be proven.[25] *Life* magazine was careless, sloppy and negligent, perhaps, but its behavior clearly did not rise to the level of actual malice. At this point, the Hill family threw in the towel.

Affirmative Defenses

Once a false light invasion of privacy plaintiff has made a *prima facie* case (proved a false and outrageous statement, publication, identification and so forth), the other side is entitled to mount a defense. These affirmative defenses include *conditional privilege, opinion* and *consent*.

Those who report information stemming from someone who has absolute privilege enjoy a *conditional* (or *qualified*) *privilege* (this concept is discussed more fully in Chapter 4). Conditional privilege extends to reports of government documents as well. Journalists and other citizens may quote from privileged documents without fear of false light suits so long as the published or broadcast accounts are full, fair and accurate.

In *Gertz v. Robert Welch, Inc.* the Supreme Court apparently created an additional affirmative defense for *opinion* statements. The Court commented,

> We begin with the common ground. Under the First Amendment there is no such thing as a false idea. However pernicious an opinion may seem, we depend for its correction not on the conscience of judges and juries, but on the competition of other ideas.[26]

Opinion statements are truly opinion—not susceptible to a truth or falsity test—and, therefore, cannot be the basis of a false light case.

Consent is a third affirmative defense to a charge of false light. Although, technically, a defense to libel as well, few consent to have their good names tarnished. It might be the case, however, that individuals who expect to or find material published about them that makes them look better than they actually are, would initially agree to the publication. Remember that the Hill family was depicted falsely as behaving heroically in the face of danger. A signed, or in other ways documented, consent is almost always a foolproof affirmative defense to invasion of privacy suits unless the defendant has somehow gone beyond the scope of that consent.

Other Defenses

In addition to *conditional privilege*, *opinion* and *consent*, there are secondary defenses, often called defenses in mitigation or incomplete defenses. One of these is *retraction*. As discussed in Chapter 4, a voluntary retraction can show good faith on the part of the communicator–an attempt to set the record straight and atone for a false statement. For the court to find it persuasive, the retraction should be timely, prominent and complete. Another secondary defense is to offer the offended people the *right of reply*–to provide space to those who have been wronged, or think they have been, to tell their side of the story.

Neither a retraction nor a right of reply can be imposed. The courts recognize the rights of communicators to control the contents of their communications. Corrections, retractions and rights of reply are all provided voluntarily, when they are provided at all. Secondary defenses do not allow the defendant to avoid a judgment, but they may reduce the amount of money a court might award.

Subcategories of False Light

The subcategory of invasion of privacy called false light can itself be subdivided into three categories, typically labeled as *embellishment*, *distortion* and *fictionalization*.[27] *Time, Inc. v. Hill* is an example of an embellishment case where the defendant has truthfully reported major facts about the plaintiff, but then has "embellished" the particulars by adding extra material to make it a better story. Let's look at each of these sub-subcategories in turn.

Embellishment

In *Hill*, the Supreme Court held that all plaintiffs in a false light case must show the defendants acted with actual malice. As mentioned above, a plaintiff often finds it easier to prove this fault standard than in a defamation suit. *Cantrell v. Forest City Publishing, Co.* is an example of a false light, *embellishment* case that demonstrates this principle.[28]

In 1967, the Silver Bridge across the Ohio River collapsed, killing 44 people, including Melvin Cantrell. The Cleveland *Plain Dealer* sent reporter Joseph Eszterhas and a photographer to the scene. Eszterhas, who subsequently went on to become a Hollywood film writer (including scripts for *Basic Instinct* and *Showgirls*), wrote several powerful, human-interest articles about the disaster. One of these pieces focused on the funeral of Mr. Cantrell and the impact of the tragedy on his family.

Five months later, Eszterhas was sent back to the Cantrell neighborhood to write a follow-up article. Eszterhas and a photographer visited the Cantrell home and talked with the Cantrell children, but Margaret Cantrell, the widow, was not present. The article that Eszterhas developed from his revisit, later published in the Sunday magazine section of the *Plain Dealer*, emphasized the family's poverty-stricken condition. At one point, the text read:

> Margaret Cantrell will talk neither about what happened nor about how they are doing. She wears the same mask of non-expression she wore at the funeral. She is a proud woman. Her world has changed. She says that after it happened, the people in town offered to help them out with money and they refused to take it.[29]

Beyond the misleading impression that the reporter had personally interviewed Cantrell, there were a number of other flaws in the piece. In particular, statements about the family's poverty were exaggerated. Cantrell sued for false light invasion of privacy, alleging that the *Plain Dealer* article caused her family members to become objects of pity and that she and her son suffered mental distress, shame and humiliation.

The trial court awarded her $60,000 in damages, but the appeals court reversed.[30] The Supreme Court, however, agreed to review the case. In only the second invasion of privacy case to reach the Court, the Court ruled in favor of Cantrell. "These were calculated false-hoods," the Court's opinion said of the *Plain Dealer* article, "and the jury was plainly justified in finding that Eszterhas had portrayed the Cantrells in a false light through knowing or reck-less untruth."[31]

Another example of an embellishment, false light invasion of privacy decision was the case of baseball star Warren Spahn, who sued a company that published a fictitious biography about him. Entitled *The Warren Spahn Story*, the book was a highly flattering portrait of the famous left-handed pitcher who won more than 300 games and was a National League fan favorite for many years. The "biography" embellished Spahn's life in many ways, adding luster to his World War II record, for example, and including, as the trial court put it, "a host, a preponderant percentage, of factual errors, distortions and fanciful passages."[32] Spahn's stature as a public figure might allow for some latitude, the court conceded, but in this case "the findings of fact go far beyond the establishment of minor errors in an otherwise accurate biography."[33]

The lesson to be learned for advertising and public relations professionals is to not yield to the temptation to jazz up an ad, story or any other type of communication by adding a few extra, colorful comments or facts. The temptation is there because "we're not saying anything bad about somebody, so why would they object?" As these cases tell us, the plaintiffs may object not for what you said, but that you said anything at all—especially if you embellished the truth.

Distortion

Distortion false light privacy cases arise when the defendant, typically through visual or graphic means, allegedly "distorts" the personality of the plaintiff. Often this distortion is caused when the defendant uses a photo or illustration, originally intended for one purpose, to satisfy another. Both the *Leverton* case, involving the misuse of the photo of the child hit by the car to illustrate a subsequent story about careless pedestrians, and the *Arrington* case, where the photo of a young, prosperous male was used in an article about middle-class blacks turning their backs on their less fortunate brethren, are classic false light, distortion cases.

Unfortunately, such cases are numerous in legal annals. For example, the *Saturday Evening Post* magazine provided what a court found to be a false and offensive context for a photograph it used to illustrate an article about taxicab drivers in Washington, D.C. Entitled "Never Give a

Passenger an Even Break," the piece dwelled on what it said was the rude and conniving behavior of cabbies in the nation's capital, characterizing them as "ill-mannered, brazen, and contemptuous of their patrons." Accompanying the *Post* article was a photograph of a cab driver, Muriel Peay, who evidently was neither impolite, nor brazen. Peay sued and won on the claim that the article and photo had placed her in a false light.[34]

Another example is the case of Sue S. Crump, a coal miner in West Virginia, who agreed to be photographed to illustrate a newspaper article about women coal miners. Two years later, the same photograph was dug out of the files to illustrate a different article, this one about problems facing female coal miners. Entitled "Women Enter 'Man's' World," the article recounted various hazing incidents inflicted on female miners by their male counterparts. The article used as examples a Virginia woman miner who was physically attacked twice while underground, and a Wyoming woman miner who "was dangled off a 200-foot water tower accompanied by the suggestion that she quit her job. She did."

None of these kinds of incidents had happened to Crump. When friends and associates began questioning her about them, she said the unfavorable attention prompted by the publication of her photograph in this different context caused her a great deal of embarrassment and humiliation.[35]

In *Jumez v. ABC Records*, a New York court awarded musician Jean-Pierre Jumez almost $150,000 in damages in a distortion false light case for the packaging of a recording of solo classical music for the guitar. Unfortunately for the recording company, the cover photo pictured a bearded half-clad (no trousers) male model strumming the instrument. Given the circumstances of the situation, Jumez was concerned that consumers naturally would assume that the man in the photo was the musician performing in the recording. He was not amused.

The lesson for communicators is clear. Advertising and public relations professionals should make certain that any photograph used to illustrate a story, brochure or website is used appropriately. For example, a public relations employee preparing an article for the company website about worker carelessness should not simply grab a file photo of employees working on the assembly line. This same admonition applies to an advertising agency art director who may be tempted to illustrate a public service TV spot about kids and handguns by using old file footage from a school playground video.

Fictionalization

Fictitious, according to *Black's Law Dictionary*, is defined as, "having the character of a fiction; pretended; . . . imaginary, not real."[36] *Fictionalization* false light, invasion of privacy involves enhancing a news article, book, play or film by inventing additional dialogue, thoughts, ideas or actions to characters portrayed as fictitious, but who, in fact, closely—perhaps too closely—resemble real people.

A classic example involved the case of *Bindrim v. Mitchell*.[37] In the course of writing her newest novel, Gwen Davis Mitchell, an author, asked to take part in something called nude encounter therapy. Dr. Paul Bindrim, a psychologist and leading exponent of this technique, agreed to her request but stipulated that she should not write about the actual session she attended or identify Dr. Bindrim or his treatment center in any way.

The novelist promised to abide by these restrictions and, although including a fictional nude therapy group session in her novel, took pains to disguise the actual facts upon which it was based. Among other things, the writer coarsened the language of the group leader, described him in a manner that did not resemble Dr. Bindrim and changed both his academic credentials and the location of the session by placing it in a different state.

Dr. Bindrim, nonetheless, sued for false light, fictionalization invasion of privacy, claiming that, despite the changes, because of his celebrated status as the guru of nude encounter therapy, everyone reading the book would automatically think the alleged fictional character and situation were really about him and his practice. The court agreed that the measures adopted to disguise Bindrim were not only inadequate, but actually made him look worse than he actually was.

Those advertising and public relations professionals feeling especially creative need to remember that taking their frustrations out against former significant others, estranged family members, high school principals or landlords who cheated them out of their security deposits by thinly disguising them as antagonists in a piece of fiction should fight the feeling. It would be foolish to exact an ounce of revenge at the price of paying a pound's worth of damages to an aggrieved plaintiff.

The Future of False Light Lawsuits

Whether the tort of false light invasion of privacy will survive as an independent cause of action is certainly a matter of some doubt. The tendency for states either to question their adoption of false light or to outright refuse to recognize this invasion of privacy subcategory, coupled with decisions for defendants in recent false light cases, does not bode well for those who advocate for false light as separate from defamation or infliction of emotional distress.

Nonetheless, it still may be too early to plan the memorial service for a fallen tort. The majority of states still recognize some form of false light and the proliferation of social websites, filled with rumor and outright falsehoods, may yet provide the impetus for a renaissance of actions brought by the aggrieved subjects of such communications. This is especially true for the *distortion* subcategory of false light, given the advent of computer software programs like Photoshop and smart phone apps capable of digitally adding, subtracting or modifying visual material in ways that easily could lead to claims that defendants knowingly cast plaintiffs in a false light. In one well-known example, a candidate for governor of Massachusetts was made to look angrier and more threatening during a debate in a political advertisement paid for by his opponent.

Prudent advertising and public relations professionals, therefore, should continue to be vigilant that their messages live up to the traditional professional standards of truth and accuracy. Specifically, they would be wise to avoid the temptation to slim down the fashion model, alter the complexion of a cover subject, or remove or add in a missing individual in a group photo, all real-life examples of the ease of digitally creating a false impression that could lead to false light suits. Plaintiffs in a false light case may not be complaining that anything good or bad was said about them, but rather that anything was said at all. They want to be left alone.

Public Disclosure of Private, Embarrassing Facts

When Samuel D. Warren and Louis D. Brandeis wrote their famous *Harvard Law Review* article calling for the recognition of an individual's right to privacy, it was public disclosure of private, embarrassing facts they had in mind. "Gossip [even if true]," they wrote, "... has become a trade, which is pursued with industry as well as effrontery."[38]

According to the *Restatement of Torts*:

> One who gives publicity to a matter concerning the private life of another is subject to the other for invasion of his privacy, if the matter publicized is of a kind that
>
> (a) would be highly offensive to a reasonable person, and
> (b) is not of legitimate concern to the public.[39]

Disclosure of private information is one of the few media-related situations in which truth is not an absolute defense. The key phrases, again, are *highly offensive* and *legitimate public concern*. If the disclosed information were false, clearly the plaintiff would bring a defamation suit or a false light case. In both of these torts, finding that the allegedly false statements were actually true would defeat the plaintiff's case. In contrast, the disclosed information in a private facts case, while true, is of such a highly private and embarrassing nature that making public such personal facts might persuade a judge or jury that those who disclosed this information have acted so outrageously that they should be made to pay the plaintiff money damages.

Legal problems arising from the public disclosure of private facts are far more likely to involve news reporters and editors (i.e., journalists) than advertising and public relations professionals. However, it should be noted that several of the first lawsuits brought in this area were indeed prompted by public notices published as advertisements—one published in a newspaper, another posted prominently on a busy street, a third shouted from the highway—that certain debtors, identified by name, did not pay their debts, allegations that were as embarrassing in 1918, when such suits were first filed, as they might be today.

The tort of public disclosure of private, embarrassing facts really emerged in the mid-1960s to become identified by most commentators as a subcategory of invasion of privacy and recognized by courts as a separate cause of action. Today, most states have adopted some form of public disclosure of embarrassing facts. However, New York,[40] Virginia,[41] Indiana[42] and North Carolina[43] either have severely limited private facts cases or have declined to recognize the tort at all.

Public relations professionals, especially, would do well to familiarize themselves with this aspect of privacy law. Public relations writers prepare publicity releases and other types of organizational communications on any number of topics and issues, and some of these messages could easily concern the public disclosure of private facts (e.g., explaining the complexities of a sensitive personnel decision or backgrounding the issues in a heated proxy fight for control of a corporation). These and numerous other possible scenarios hold the potential for invasion of privacy suits.

Under current interpretations, unless the private facts disclosed are outrageously offensive and outside the broad realm of legitimate public interest, they may be publicized. Nonetheless, even if the law would eventually protect disclosure, the public relations professional and/or his or her organization or client might win in a court of law only to lose in the court of public opinion because the disclosure is considered beyond the bounds of ordinary decency.

The Elements of Private, Embarrassing Facts

Like false light invasion of privacy, public disclosure of private, embarrassing facts resembles defamation. For a private facts case, the plaintiff must first show that (a) a statement has been made that discloses truthful, private, embarrassing facts and the disclosure of which offends ordinary decency; (b) the material must be shown to at least one other person by the defendant;

(c) the plaintiff has been identified in the statements; (d) the actions of the defendant are the true cause of the actual harm suffered by the plaintiff (in this case, mental anguish); (e) the plaintiff is entitled to be compensated by money damages for that harm; and (f) the statements appeared because the defendant has done all this with the required degree of fault established by law. Let's take a closer look at each of these points in turn.

Statement of Private, Embarrassing Facts

The statement of embarrassing private facts must contain the kinds of information that reasonable people recognize as being so personal that public disclosure would be considered highly offensive. Thus disclosing information already in public records or giving publicity to matters that occur in public or in places where a potential plaintiff would not have a legitimate expectation of privacy (e.g., a place of business or an event open to the public) likely would not give rise to a successful private facts cause of action.

"Offensiveness" in such cases often involves disclosing matters related to sexual practices or preferences, financial or educational records, and health or medical information. For example, on September 11, 1975, a deeply disturbed young woman named Sara Jane Moore approached President Gerald R. Ford as he was about to make a speech at Union Square in San Francisco. As President Ford was shaking hands with onlookers and well-wishers in the crowd, Ms. Moore edged her way toward the front of the spectators, brandishing a revolver. President Ford's secret service bodyguards failed to spot her, but Oliver W. Sipple, standing nearby, did. As she raised the pistol to fire, Sipple grabbed her arm causing the bullet to miss its mark, almost certainly saving the President serious injury. Sipple was hailed as a hero and, inevitably, subjected to massive local and national publicity.

Figure 5.1 In 1975, a citizen named Oliver Sipple thwarted an assassination attempt of President Gerald R. Ford, seen here in a campaign stop the next year. After his act of heroism drew media and public attention, Sipple filed an invasion of privacy lawsuit over the publication of private facts about his life.

Credit line: Thomas J. O'Halloran/Library of Congress, Prints and Photographs Division, Washington, D.C.

Within hours, popular local columnist Herb Caen published an item in his *San Francisco Chronicle* column suggesting that Sipple was homosexual.[44] An article the next day in the *Los Angeles Times* theorized that President Ford's failure to promptly thank Sipple for his heroism was a direct result of Sipple's sexual orientation, and questions were raised in the gay community whether the White House was shunning Sipple because of his associations.[45]

From these articles, Sipple, who was, in fact, homosexual, said his parents, brothers and sisters learned for the first time of his sexual orientation. As a result, he said, he felt abandoned by his family and exposed to contempt and ridicule, causing him mental anguish, embarrassment and humiliation. Sipple sued the *Chronicle* for invasion of privacy because, he said, they published private, embarrassing information about his life. Sipple's membership in the local gay community was known in San Francisco. His concern was that the news of his sexual orientation was not known in the Midwest, where his parents and siblings lived.[46]

The court sided with the defendant news organization in the Sipple case because, the court said, the very public nature of the event would create legitimate news value in reporting the details about the person who possibly saved the life of the President. Other courts, however, have held that displays of confidential autopsy photographs, [47]publishing a photograph of a nursing mother,[48] disclosing private information about medical health details,[49] publishing the name of a victim of child sexual abuse[50] and publicizing the name of an individual accused of failure to pay debts[51] do constitute publication of information that would be classified as highly embarrassing.

Clearly, determining what is "highly offensive to a reasonable person" can be a vague and uncertain business, but it is in this arena that most public disclosure of private, embarrassing facts actions are brought. Courts generally will disallow cases based on hypersensitive hurt feelings by insisting on an "ordinary decency" standard, but with few clear-cut guidelines to draw upon, judges and juries are given broad latitude to define what they consider private information that should be protected from disclosure, and the results are not always consistent or predictable.

Publication

As with defamation, a private facts plaintiff often has a relatively easy time demonstrating that publication has occurred because the defendant advertising agency or public relations department has disseminated the private, embarrassing information to thousands, if not millions, of readers or viewers in network television advertising, press release material or in campaigns on YouTube, Facebook or other social networking sites. However, publication must be attributable to actions by the defendant. Thus cases involving potential plaintiffs active in social causes like AIDS prevention or anti-abortion campaigns in which the plaintiff has disclosed personal information or in which they have provided interviews to media outlets about aspects of their private lives likely would fail because plaintiffs would have little basis for complaining about subsequent publication of what once might have been considered private facts.

While technically publication occurs the moment a third person has seen the communication, like false light, to be actionable, the offending words typically must reach a broad audience rather than just a few. Many jurisdictions refer to publication as giving "publicity" to the private, embarrassing information. Note, however, that a sizable minority of states has found the publication requirement satisfied in situations in which, for example, the offending information was made public to the plaintiff's co-workers or in other situations "when a relationship exists between the plaintiff and the [special] public to whom the information was disclosed."[52]

Identification

The plaintiff in a private, embarrassing facts privacy case must meet virtually the same require-ments as a defamation or false light plaintiff to prove that an audience believes that the state-ments refer to him or her. Identification is often not difficult for the plaintiff because the defendant, as a professional communicator, has clearly identified the subjects in the communications.

Identification of group members for private, embarrassing facts purposes is identical to defa-mation and false light cases. A member of a small group, traditionally about 25 members or fewer, may sue and be able to collect, even if he or she is not identified individually in a shocking and outrageous communication. Like false light, the tort of disclosure of private facts is limited to individuals because organizations cannot demonstrate they have suffered mental anguish about the published information.

Causation

The plaintiff in a disclosure of private, embarrassing facts suit must allege and prove that the actions of the defendant were the logical and proximate cause of the claimed injury. Often this is easily accomplished because the plaintiff is simply charging that he or she has understand-ably suffered mental anguish when the defendant outrageously disclosed private, embarrassing statements seen by acquaintances, clients or customers.

Problems involving proving causation might arise when a plaintiff is complaining about the disclosure of private, embarrassing facts that, in the minds of a judge or jury, should not have caused mental anguish severe enough to warrant compensation. Also, if the private facts are already widely known by others, the plaintiff may experience difficulty in convincing a judge or jury that the defendant's disclosure of the statement legitimately could be seen as the sole cause of the alleged harm to the plaintiff's mental well-being.

Compensation

A plaintiff seeking compensation for harm to his or her mental well-being resulting from dis-closure of private, embarrassing facts generally will be entitled to seek three different kinds of monetary awards: *nominal* damages, *general/compensatory* damages (like libel, in some juris-dictions these awards are sometimes split into "special" and "actual" damages) and *punitive* (or "exemplary") damages. Although these are discussed more thoroughly in Chapter 4 and in the false light section above, let's briefly revisit each of these in turn.

A plaintiff seeking a small or *nominal* damage award is relatively rare in public disclosure of private, embarrassing facts cases. More typically, a plaintiff actually seeking a large sum to com-pensate for the supposed mental anguish is found by a judge or jury to have suffered no major harm and, therefore, not deserving of more than a nominal award of damages.

To obtain *general/compensatory* damages, plaintiffs may show actual out-of-pocket dollar loss, by producing evidence of expenses for psychiatric care, counseling services or prescribed medications, as well as wages lost or other financial reverses attributable to the plaintiff being too upset to function normally. In addition, plaintiffs can attempt to demonstrate through their own testimony that the alleged mental anguish caused by the outrageous disclosure does, in fact, exist, even if there is no evidence of actual financial loss. In jurisdictions that ask for some evidence of this supposed mental anguish, plaintiffs typically introduce testimony from friends and medical and/or counseling professionals about their observations of such psychic harm as "humiliation,"[53] "depression,"[54] "memory lapses"[55] or "insomnia."[56].

If a judge or jury accepts that the harm has occurred and the defendant has no additional defenses, money will be awarded to the plaintiff as compensation based on the judge or jury's estimation of the harm—an invitation for large damage awards for the plaintiff. The possibility of such large verdicts should be the impetus needed for advertising and public relations professionals to take all possible precautions to avoid becoming embroiled in a private, embarrassing facts suit.

Punitive damages, generally, are awarded when the defendant's actions are so outrageous that they offend the conscience of judges or juries. In a private, embarrassing facts invasion of privacy suit, punitive damages might be awarded if the information was disclosed with a purposeful intent to harm the plaintiff or, as one court said, "a callous and conscious disregard" of the plaintiff's right to privacy, possibly adding mega-amounts to the defendant's tab.

Defendant Fault

As with defamation and false light, private, embarrassing facts cases require the plaintiff to show the offending disclosure resulted because the person who published the material met the *fault* standard established by law. It is by no means clear, however, what that standard is.

The majority of states recognizing this tort have adopted negligence as the requisite fault standard. Alternatively, a number of states have adopted a standard that requires a showing of reckless disregard for the offensive disclosure of information. Others have opted for an intentional standard, meaning that carelessness would not be sufficient. Unlike defamation, even in those jurisdictions that have adopted stricter standards, generally there appears to be no differentiation between public and private plaintiffs in disclosure of private, embarrassing facts cases.

Affirmative Defenses

Once a private, embarrassing facts privacy plaintiff has made a *prima facie* case (i.e., a statement containing sensitive private information, publication, identification and so forth), the other side is entitled to mount a defense. Affirmative defenses include *conditional privilege, consent* and, unlike defamation and false light privacy, *newsworthiness*.

Those who report information stemming from someone who has absolute privilege enjoy a *conditional* (or *qualified*) *privilege* (a concept discussed more fully in Chapter 4). Conditional privilege extends to reports of government documents as well. Courts have consistently held that information in public records cannot be considered private. Journalists and other citizens can quote from privileged documents without fear of private, embarrassing facts suits so long as the published or broadcast accounts are full, fair and accurate.

The Supreme Court has created a constitutionally based privilege as well. The landmark case in this regard—the first time the Court acted on a private, embarrassing facts case—came in 1975, with *Cox Broadcasting v. Cohn*.[57] This invasion of privacy case arose when, during court proceedings involving a rape and murder case, a reporter from WSB-TV, the Cox-owned television station in Atlanta, asked the court clerk for copies of the charges to check the accuracy of the details. The victim's name was listed in the documents, and the journalist disclosed the young woman's name in his televised report that evening. The story was rebroadcast the following day.

Normally, only the victim in a disclosure of private information action can instigate a suit, but at that time, a Georgia law permitted close relatives of a rape victim to file the suit on her behalf. Additionally, Martin Cohn, the victim's father, brought suit against Cox Broadcasting, claiming that the disclosure of his daughter's name and other information invaded his privacy as well. After Georgia trial and appeals courts found in the plaintiff's favor, Cox Broadcasting appealed to the Supreme Court.

At issue was this: Could the news media be punished for publishing facts already in records made public by a court? In an 8-1 decision, the Court said no. As Justice White, writing for the majority, noted,

> We are reluctant to embark on a course that would make public records generally available to the media but forbid their publication if offensive to the sensibilities of the supposed reasonable man. Such a rule would make it very difficult for the media to inform citizens about the public business and yet stay within the law. The rule would invite timidity and self-censorship and very likely lead to the suppression of many items that would otherwise be published and that should be made available to the public.[58]

Some court records, such as juvenile proceedings, might not be open to the public. The Court's opinion in *Cox* avoided addressing any questions on the constitutionality of sealed court records. The thrust of the *Cox* holding was this: If made available to the public, the mass media (or anyone else) cannot be held liable for money damages for publishing truthful information based on court records.

Essentially the same reasoning prevailed in another Court ruling—*The Florida Star v. B.J.F.*[59] This 1989 case also involved publication of a rape victim's name. A cub reporter for a Jacksonville weekly newspaper, leafing through the incident report prepared by officers in the sheriff's department based on their activities that day, ran across an item in which a woman had complained that she had been raped and robbed. The Jacksonville sheriff's department routinely made incident reports available to the press, but, normally, did not include the names of sexual assault victims. In this case there was a lapse—the full name of the rape victim was included and subsequently reported in the newspaper's story.

Obviously, the sheriff's department had carelessly included the rape victim's name in the report. Even so, there were signs in the pressroom where the report was made available that victims of sex crimes were not to be identified. There also was a Florida statute forbidding disclosure of a rape victim's name. Beyond that, *The Florida Star*'s own editorial policy forbade the publication of a rape victim's identity.

The victim, subsequently referred to in court records as B.J.F., sued for private, embarrassing facts invasion of privacy, claiming that the publication caused her mental anguish, forced her to change her telephone number to avoid harassing phone messages and prompted her to seek psychiatric counseling. At trial, the judge found the newspaper to have been negligent, leaving it to the jury to determine the amount of damages. The jury awarded B.J.F. $100,000.[60]

On appeal, the Florida Supreme Court affirmed the judgment.[61] However, the U.S. Supreme Court reversed, ruling that the newspaper should not be punished for publishing truthful information from an official source, even though the information was not part of a court proceeding and the information was obtained by mistake.

Consent is a second affirmative defense to a private embarrassing facts charge. Anyone who watches reality television programs or uses Facebook or views YouTube knows that it is not unusual for individuals who seek attention or simply don't care about revealing private information about themselves to post material that others might think would normally be the kinds of matters generally not discussed.

Consent can be either actual (e.g., expressed in a signed waiver) or implied. Implied consent often is found when plaintiffs have either engaged in conduct that points to acquiescence (listing a former employer as a credit reference) or participated in activities of a public nature (e.g., being a guest on a television talk show). As long as the defendant has a signed document or in other ways demonstrates consent, perhaps by showing that the plaintiff posted website information, consent is almost always a foolproof affirmative way to defuse a potential private, embarrassing facts case unless the defendant has somehow gone beyond the scope of that consent.

However, advertising and public relations practitioners would be well advised to ensure that a giving of consent to publication of potentially sensitive or potentially embarrassing information is full and "knowing" consent by explaining in detail how the information will appear. Employees, for example, may not realize how revelations about personal matters may be taken by co-workers or clients until they encounter subsequent jokes or rude comments at their expense. Also, employees or those dependent on the organization in other ways may feel pressured by a representative, seen as from "corporate headquarters," to consent to publication of material to which normally they might otherwise object. Legally, evidence of consent may stand up in a court of law but at the cost of hurt feelings on the part of people of concern to the organization.

Because the information published by the defendant in a private, embarrassing facts case is true, not surprisingly, defendants often argue that publication was in the public interest because it was of legitimate *newsworthiness*, a third affirmative defense. The central purpose of the First Amendment, according to the distinguished scholar Alexander Meiklejohn,

> is to give to every voting member of the body politic the fullest possible participation in the understanding of those problems with which the citizens of a self-governing society must deal. ..... Nor ... is freedom of the press confined to comment upon public affairs and those persons who have voluntarily sought the public spotlight. ... The scope of the privilege thus extends to almost all reporting of recent events, even though it involves the publication of a purely private individual's name or likeness.[62]

The desire to keep information private is bound to collide with the right to disseminate information to the public. Over the years, much to the dismay of many who may not wish to see their affairs splashed on the front page or aired on the nightly news, courts have been quite liberal in defining public interest, not just as something people necessarily *should* read about, but as something they do read about, or almost anything in which people are interested.

Individuals who seek the public limelight are thought to deserve less protection when someone discloses private information about them than those individuals who prefer to live out their lives quietly. Private persons often find themselves drawn into an event that happens in a public place (an accident, as the victim of a crime or simply happening by chance to be present) that creates a newsworthy moment. The *Restatement of Torts* points out that even involuntary subjects may not always have their privacy protected:

> These persons [involuntary public figures] are regarded as properly subject to the public interest, and publishers are permitted to satisfy the curiosity of the public as to its heroes, leaders, villains and victims, and those who are closely associated with them. As in the case of the voluntary public figure, the authorized publicity is not limited to the event that itself arouses the public interest, and to some extent includes publicity given to facts about the individual that would otherwise be purely private.[63]

A South Carolina case, however, suggests that the public interest in a news story might take a back seat to protecting the privacy of an individual, under certain circumstances. In a lengthy story dealing with teenage pregnancies, the *Greenville News* interviewed a male high school student who had been identified—by the unwed mother—as the father of her baby.

The young man said he had been led to believe he was talking to a data gatherer for a research study of teen pregnancies, not to a newspaper reporter, and that he had no idea his statements, including his identification by name and his admission that he fathered the child, would appear in the newspaper. When the newspaper printed the article, the young man sued. The newspaper argued that the information was newsworthy and of legitimate public concern. The South Carolina Supreme Court, however, determined that this was a matter for a jury to decide. The jury found the name of the father was not of great public concern and decided on a substantial judgment against the newspaper.[64]

Subcategories of Private Facts

The subcategory of invasion of privacy called public disclosure of private, embarrassing facts can itself be subdivided into three categories, typically labeled as *extent of intimacy versus newsworthiness*, *passage of time* and *consent exceeded*.[65]

Extent of Intimacy Versus Newsworthiness

The case of Oliver Sipple, outed by the media in examining the life of the man who likely saved the life of the President of the United States, is an example of an intimacy versus newsworthiness case. The defendant truthfully reported major facts about the plaintiff, including the particulars of his sexual orientation, that Sipple would have preferred be kept from public knowledge.

In making the determination on a case-by-case basis about who should win in the straightforward contest between the plaintiff's wish to keep certain intimate details of his or her life secret versus the news media's determination that the public has a right to know, courts have taken into account such factors as the way the communication was presented, the nature of the information being publicized, the degree of intimacy such disclosure represents and the value of the disclosure—as measured in newsworthiness—to the general public. What often emerges, as Dean Prosser theorized some years ago, "is something in the nature of a 'mores test,' by which there will be liability only for publicity given to those things which the customs and ordinary views of the community will not tolerate."[66]

One of the saddest cases in this area, and one of the most often referred to in legal circles, is that of William James Sidis. Young Mr. Sidis was known far and wide for his mathematical prowess at an early age. By the time he was 11, he had already become an authority on the subject of four-dimensional bodies, and he lectured to distinguished mathematicians on that and other matters. At 16, and amid much public fanfare, he was graduated from Harvard College. However, Sidis' youthful genius did not prepare him for later life, and he never seemed comfortable as an adult. He lived as unobtrusively as possible and eventually became something of a recluse.

Twenty years later, the *New Yorker* magazine decided to develop a profile on Sidis, another in its series entitled "Where Are They Now?" The *New Yorker* writer found Sidis living in a hall bedroom in "Boston's shabby south end" and reported in great detail that, among other things: (a) Sidis' room was severely unkempt; (b) he had developed a curious and hollow laugh; (c) he had suffered a nervous breakdown; (d) he regarded his former fame with contempt; (e) he was presently employed as an insignificant clerk, a position in which he would never use his astonishing mathematical gifts; (f) he maintained a bizarre collection of streetcar tokens; and (g) his consuming interest was now focused on the folklore of the Okamakammesset Native American tribe.[67]

As the court in Sidis' subsequent suit for disclosing private embarrassing facts would later point out:

> It is not contended that any of the matter printed [in the *New Yorker* profile] is untrue. Nor is the manner of the author unfriendly; Sidis today is described as having "a certain child-like charm." But the article is merciless in its dissection of intimate details of its subject's personal life, and this in company with elaborate accounts of Sidis's passion for privacy and the pitiable lengths to which he has gone in order to avoid public scrutiny. The work possesses great reader interest, for it is both amusing and instructive; but it may be fairly described as a ruthless exposure of a once public character, who has since sought and has now been deprived of the seclusion of private life.[68]

After weighing all factors, the trial court found that the unfortunate Sidis, many years later, was still newsworthy and, somewhat reluctantly, found in favor of the *New Yorker*.

The court said,

> We express no comment on whether or not the news worthiness of the matter printed will always constitute a complete defense. Revelations may be so intimate and so unwarranted in view of the victim's position as to outrage the community's notions of decency. But when focused upon public characters, truthful comments upon dress, speech, habits, and the ordinary aspects of personality will usually not transgress this line. Regrettably or not, the misfortunes and frailties of neighbors and "public figures" are subjects of considerable interest and discussion to the rest of the population. And when such are the mores of the community, it would be unwise for a court to bar their expression in the newspapers, books, and magazines of the day.[69]

Apparently, the massive publicity about Sidis' childhood would continue to haunt him so long as audiences remembered him as a one-time celebrity.

Compare the outcome in *Sidis* with the result in *Barber v. Time*,[70] a case involving Dorothy Barber who suffered from a rare metabolic disease; although she ate constantly, she continued to lose weight. Eventually she was hospitalized for treatment. The case was something of a medical curiosity, and several news media, including *Time* magazine, decided to do a piece about it. Bursting into her Kansas City hospital room, a news service photographer got a picture of Barber, which, when it later appeared in *Time*, portrayed the unfortunate young woman in terms not unlike those that might be used to describe a freak: "Insatiable Eater Barber" read the caption accompanying the photograph. In the piece, she was referred to as "Starving Glutton" and "she eats for ten."

The publication of the article prompted Barber to sue. The court agreed that, although the story might well be newsworthy, the specific identification of her by name and the way she and her medical problem were characterized were so odious as to represent an invasion of her privacy,[71] and decided the case in favor of the plaintiff.

More notable cases pitting claims of harm from disclosure of private facts versus arguments about the newsworthiness of the published information have centered on videos of sexual activities by prominent public figures. For example, the actress Pamela Anderson and rock musician Bret Michaels successfully brought suit in federal court in California to stop a company from distributing the couple's stolen, private sex tape via the Internet. The court ruled that while the existence of the tape might be newsworthy, this finding did not extend to actually displaying the tape.

More recently, the professional wrestler Hulk Hogan (real name Terry Bollea) sought money damages from Gawker Media for writing about and displaying parts of a secretly recorded video showing Hogan and the wife of a friend in a sexual relationship. The friend subsequently gave the video to Gawker that argued the newsworthiness of the tape should outweigh any privacy interests of Hogan. A jury eventually disagreed and awarded Hogan more than $100 million for disclosure of the embarrassing information. The amount of the award resulted in the defendant filing for bankruptcy that spelled the end of Gawker Media.

Although courts accord great deference to arguments by journalists that the newsworthiness of the disclosed sensitive information should outweigh individual privacy interests, such an argument may fall on deaf ears if made by advertising or public relations professionals. Prudent professionals would be wise to obtain documented consent for the disclosure of sensitive information rather than rely on arguments about the value of the disclosure.

Passage of Time

Is there a point in which one's past can be safely buried? Does the law's concept of rehabilitation—as, for example, with convicts who, on being released from prison, are said to "have paid their debt to society "—apply to one's private life, formerly made public, or, as in the case of William Sidis, discussed above, must they remain public forever? Again, the law is not clear.

For example, consider the case of Marvin Briscoe, who once hijacked a truck. He was arrested, convicted and served time in prison. Thereafter, as his lawyer subsequently noted, Briscoe "abandoned his life of shame and became entirely rehabilitated and thereafter lived an exemplary, virtuous, and honorable life … he has assumed a place in respectable society and made many friends who were not aware of the incident in his earlier life."[72]

A magazine writer aware of Briscoe's past, used the unfortunate man's criminal example to illustrate an article entitled "The Big Business of Hijacking," later published by *Reader's Digest* magazine. At one point, the article read: "Typical of many beginners, Marvin Briscoe and [another man] stole a 'valuable looking' truck in Danville, Ky., and then fought a gun battle with the local police, only to learn they had hijacked four bowling-pin spotters."[73]

Although the account was truthful, there was nothing in it to suggest that the incident had happened more than a decade previously. Briscoe, who had since moved to California, found himself "scorned and abandoned" by his friends; his 11-year-old daughter learned of her father's conviction from the publication. He sued. The trial court decided Mr. Briscoe had no cause of action and effectively dismissed the case.[74]

On appeal, the California Supreme Court reversed this decision and sent the case back for trial. Briscoe's claim that he had been rehabilitated, the appeals court said, should be examined seriously by a jury. Ideally, said the court,

> his neighbors should recognize his present worth and forget his past life of shame. But men are not so divine as to forgive the past trespasses of others, and plaintiff therefore endeavored to reveal as little as possible of his past life. Yet, as if in some bizarre canyon of echoes, petitioner's past life pursues him through the pages of *Reader's Digest*, now published in 13 languages and distributed in 100 nations, with a circulation in California alone of almost 2,000,000 copies.[75]

In public disclosure of private, embarrassing facts, as in much else involving the First Amendment, courts generally presume that the balance is weighted in favor of free expression. The decision of the California appeals court in *Briscoe* warns, however, that public disclosures of delicate private facts can still carry grave consequences for the privacy interests of individuals. As the court noted,

> A publisher does have every reason to know, *before* publication, that identification of a man as a former criminal will be highly offensive to the individual involved. It does not require close reading of *Les Misérables*[76] or *The Scarlet Letter*[77] to know that men are haunted by the fear of disclosure of their past and destroyed by the exposure itself.[78]

Prudent advertising and public relations professionals should recognize that dredging up an occurrence that took place decades earlier, especially if it was not a criminal matter or otherwise reported in the public record, can have dangerous consequences. This is a good place to remind the reader that, for example, a now prominent and successful businessperson might be highly embarrassed by the revelation of his or her past childhood spent in impoverished circumstances, even though disclosure of the information was intended by the communicator to convey a positive statement about the level of achievement of the subject of the publication.

Consent Exceeded

The case of *Virgil v. Time Inc.*[79] was triggered by an article about famed body surfer Mike Virgil, portrayed in *Sports Illustrated* magazine as one of the most fearless members of a daredevil band of surfers at The Wedge, dangerous waters near Newport Beach, California. Virgil apparently was as uninhibited on dry land as in the water.

During interviews with Curry Kirkpatrick of *Sports Illustrated*, Virgil spoke freely about his private life. He recounted that he had devoured insects and spiders, extinguished a lighted cigarette inside his mouth and won a bet by burning a hole through a dollar bill with a lighted cigarette while the dollar bill rested on the back of his hand. Also, that he had never learned to read, had thrown himself down a flight of stairs at a ski resort "to impress these chicks" and periodically contrived to injure himself by "div[ing] off billboards or drop[ping] loads on myself so that I could collect unemployment compensation so that I could surf at The Wedge."[80]

When a fact-checker from the magazine telephoned to verify these assertions, Virgil developed second thoughts about the article. Conceding that he could not stop the publication of information about him the magazine had learned from others, Virgil specifically asked *Sports Illustrated* not to print anything connected with his private life that he himself had told the writer. The magazine published the piece with the personal details included, and Virgil sued for invasion of privacy.

Although he eventually lost his case because of a tortured reading of the California invasion privacy statute by a federal court (the judges in California may have been in the sun too long), the lesson to be learned is plain. If an individual reveals personal, private information generally considered highly embarrassing if given publicity, but prior to publication retracts permission to use the information that was obtained solely from that individual, prudent advertising and public relations professionals should respect that withdrawal of consent and not disclose the information.

The Future of Disclosure of Private, Embarrassing Facts Litigation

In recent private facts cases where the defendants have prevailed, the decisions often are based on a finding that the speech in question does not constitute private facts, either because the information is already known (e.g., *Smith v. NBC Universal, et al.*)[81] or because it comes from the public record (e.g., *Mendelson v. The Morning Call, Inc.*).[82]

Unlike false light, however, lawsuits over the disclosure of private, embarrassing facts as invasions of privacy are poised to explode in frequency as technology makes it easier to obtain, process and disseminate information many still consider to be nobody else's business.

Nontraditional media, in particular, have traveled into unexplored territory in private facts cases, encountering consumer and data privacy issues (like those discussed in Chapter 13) along the way. What is the safest course of action? If the information would be considered private and is neither known, nor available in public records (it should be remembered that not all government information is, by definition, public information), prudent advertising and public relations professionals should steer a wide course away from disclosure.

Intrusion

According to the *Restatement (Second) of Torts*, intrusion is defined as:

> One who intentionally intrudes, physically or otherwise, upon the solitude or seclusion of another or his private affairs or concerns, is subject to liability to the other for invasion of privacy, if the intrusion would be highly offensive to a reasonable person.[83]

Often referred to as the "news-gathering tort," intrusion invasion of privacy is of lesser concern to advertising and public relations professionals because they typically do not engage in the types of actions (e.g., use of hidden video recorders or taping telephone conversations) that are often the subject of intrusion suits.

Figure 5.2 The tort of intrusion is a type of invasion of privacy that involves the highly offensive intrusion into the solitude or seclusion of another. In the era of drones and nanotechnology, intrusion lawsuits are increasingly common outside the context of newsgathering, where it has most often been an issue.

Credit line: Dmitry Kalinovsky/Shutterstock.com

The history of the development of intrusion invasion of privacy parallels the subcategories of false light and public disclosure, maturing in the latter part of the 20th century. Today, with the advent of sophisticated electronic recording devices and computer savvy experts, intrusion is becoming one of the more common invasion of privacy lawsuits. The vast majority of states currently recognize some form of intrusion as a separate tort.

The Elements of Intrusion

The elements of an intrusion claim differ markedly from the other subcategories of invasion of privacy. In a lawsuit for intrusion invasion of privacy, the plaintiff must first show that: (a) an intrusive act has been committed by the defendant that is highly offensive to a reasonable person; (b) the actions of the defendant are the true cause of the actual harm suffered by the plaintiff (in this case, mental anguish); (c) the plaintiff is entitled to be compensated by money damages for that harm; and (d) the intrusive action has been done by the defendant with the required degree of fault established by law.

Intrusive Act

Because the tort of intrusion invasion of privacy focuses on the acts of the defendant, there is no requirement that the plaintiff prove publication of damaging information or deal with issues of truth or falsity. The essence of whether an intrusive act rises to the level of an infliction of mental anguish sufficient to warrant an award of damages turns on the judgment of what is, as one court noted, "outrageous to a person of ordinary sensibilities." Thus, the complained of act cannot be judged solely on the basis of a plaintiff who is highly and unusually sensitive to the presence of others.

It also is necessary that plaintiffs be in a situation in which they have legitimate expectations to be free of unreasonable intrusive acts. Taking a picture of the plaintiff on a public street, while perhaps unwanted, is not actionable. Taking a picture of the plaintiff in his or her hospital room without permission would likely be a different matter. For this reason, advertising and public relations professionals are less likely to fall prey to intrusion lawsuits than journalists because potential plaintiffs would have a difficult task showing that actions by the defendants in a business setting took place in a private location. Cases on this point have concluded that there is no expectation of privacy from intrusion when an employer monitored employee calls on a company phone, installed surveillance cameras in an office area, or tape-recorded a conversation with an employee in a disciplinary proceeding.

However, those who work in places that deal with sensitive information (e.g., educational institutions) or in which employees, clients or customers might have legitimate reasons to be highly offended by unwelcomed information gathering actions (e.g., health-care organizations) need to be especially mindful of personal privacy concerns. Courts also have allowed intrusion claims by employees when management broke into a locker secured by an employee's lock or in other ways led employees to believe that they had a reasonable expectation of personal privacy in a workplace situation.

Finally, it should be noted that liability for the tort of intrusion invasion of privacy usually requires a showing that the defendant actually committed an intrusive act (or at least ordered or authorized the intrusion). Simply acquiring sensitive information from a source who may have intruded into the solitude of another to acquire it normally will not subject the recipient to an intrusion lawsuit (but might lead to liability for some other media tort, depending on the nature of the disclosed information).

Causation

Plaintiffs in an intrusion suit must allege and prove that the actions of the defendant were the logical and proximate cause of the claimed injury. Often this is easily accomplished because the injured parties are simply charging that they have understandably suffered mental anguish when the defendant outrageously invaded their private space.

Problems involving proving causation might arise when a plaintiff is complaining about an intrusive act when, in reality, it is the dissemination of the information obtained that proved upsetting. Alternatively, if in the minds of a judge or jury, the complained of act should not have caused mental anguish severe enough to warrant compensation, the plaintiff may experience difficulty in convincing the court that the defendant's acts legitimately could be seen as the sole cause of the alleged harm to the plaintiff's mental well-being.

Compensation

A plaintiff seeking compensation for harm to his or her mental well-being resulting from an outrageous intrusive act generally will be entitled to seek three different kinds of monetary awards: *nominal* damages, *general/compensatory* damages (like libel, these awards are sometimes split into "special" and "actual" damages) and *punitive* (or "exemplary") damages. These are discussed more thoroughly in the false light section above.

Defendant Fault

As with defamation, false light and private, embarrassing facts cases, an intrusion lawsuit requires the plaintiff to show the offending disclosure resulted because the person who committed the outrageous act did so with the *fault* standard established by law. The majority of states recognizing this cause of action have adopted an intentional fault standard, meaning that carelessness would not be sufficient. Generally, there appears to be no differentiation between public and private plaintiffs in intrusion privacy cases.

Affirmative Defenses

Consent is an affirmative defense to an intrusion charge. Consent can be either actual (e.g., expressed in a signed waiver) or implied. Implied consent often is found when plaintiffs have stepped out into a public space or placed themselves in a location in which they have no reasonable expectation of privacy. Consent is almost always a foolproof affirmative way to defuse an intrusion case unless the defendant has somehow gone beyond the scope of that consent.

Subcategories of Intrusion

The tort of intrusion invasion of privacy traditionally has been subdivided into three categories: *surreptitious surveillance* (e.g., hidden recording devices or taping telephone conversations), *trespass* (e.g., entering onto property of another for information gathering purposes) and *consent exceeded* (i.e., situations in which the defendant has gone beyond the limits of the actual or implied consent of the plaintiff).[84] Let's look briefly at each of these in turn.

Surreptitious Surveillance

Surreptitious surveillance is normally associated with the use of hidden recording devices, either visual or auditory. In analyzing potential liability for surreptitious surveillance intrusion, courts generally look at three factors: (a) the plaintiff's level of legitimate expectation to be free of unconsented-to, intrusive acts; (b) the openness of the defendant; and (c) the "hidden-ness" of the recording device.

Courts have held that the highest level of legitimate expectation to be free of unconsented-to, intrusive acts is in one's place of residence. At the other extreme, courts generally have held that people have almost no legitimate expectation to be free of such acts in public places. The contentious issues involving this factor often focus on the places in between (one's office, automobile, health club locker room and so forth).

For example, in the classic case of *Dietemann v. Time, Inc.*,[85] reporters posing as a patient and the patient's friend surreptitiously recorded the activities of an unlicensed medical practitioner in Dietemann's home in an effort to obtain evidence about his alleged unauthorized practice of medicine. The defendants were found liable for intrusion invasion of privacy based on these actions.

In contrast, in *Crow v. Crawford & Co.*,[86] an employer surreptitiously videotaped the activities of a worker and members of his family in a public park. The court held that this was not an intrusive act, even though the taping took place in a "wooded and secluded" area, because of the lack of legitimate expectation to be free of such an intrusive act in a public place.

Advertising and public relations professionals should think not twice, but three times before engaging in surreptitiously audio recording, photographing or video recording individuals in places where those individuals have a reasonable expectation to be free from intrusive acts. Although the news media are often victorious in defending intrusive acts in the process of news gathering, advertising and public relations professionals, in most circumstances, would have a much more difficult time justifying such actions. Prudent advertising and public relations professionals should have a really good reason to engage in such activities even when the potential plaintiff is in a public place.

Recording telephone conversations poses additional risks because of federal and state regulations. Although some states allow telephone recording to take place if one party has knowledge of the taping, other states require both parties to be aware. The better course of action for advertising and public relations professionals would be to always obtain consent from all parties before recording a conversation. Taping telephone conversations not involving one of the parties can lead to serious legal troubles (law enforcement officials need a wiretap order—similar to a warrant—to do so) as will surreptitiously recording discussions between individuals when the recorder is not present (often in violation of so-called eavesdropping laws).

Trespass

Trespass intrusion invasion of privacy typically involves the unauthorized entry onto the private property of another. For example, in *Quinn Emanuel Urquhart Oliver & Hedges, LLP v. LaTorraca & Goettsch*,[87] a court held in favor of the plaintiff in a trespass invasion of privacy claim involving a comedian whose shtick was gaining admittance to events without buying a ticket. After being arrested on a complaint by the Academy Awards, the plaintiff successfully sued the Academy for trespass because private investigators, hired by the Academy, eavesdropped on the plaintiff's conversations while in an area of the plaintiff's apartment complex clearly marked as a "no trespassing" zone.

Members of the media have no less, but no more rights to go onto private property as any other citizen. Therefore, in situations where reporters are demanding entrance to an organization or a client's premises, it is perfectly legitimate for organizations to deny the news media access to places such as emergency rooms, corporate operating facilities or private events, even if newsworthy activities have occurred. Similarly, even if the media have entered private property in the same manner as other citizens, they may be denied continued access if they exceed the consented to presence by engaging in news-gathering activities unwanted by the owners of the property.

It also may be possible to "trespass" to information. For example, in *Bilney v. Evening Star*,[88] a newspaper published confidential information about the academic records of the University of Maryland's basketball team. Although the intrusion claim was eventually dismissed because the reporters, themselves, did not ask for, or actually observe, confidential records, clearly those who, without authorization, had access to and provided these records to the reporters would likely have been liable for an intrusion invasion of privacy claim. Advertising and public relations professionals who are not authorized to access sensitive health, personnel or personal information should neither surreptitiously obtain records of such information, nor employ or suggest to those who are authorized that they provide them with such records.

Consent Exceeded

This sub-subcategory of invasion of privacy usually involves individuals who go beyond the plaintiff's actual or implied consent to tolerate acts that might otherwise be regarded as intrusive. The classic case is *LeMistral, Inc. v. Columbia Broadcasting System*[89] where television reporters, with cameras running, entered a prominent restaurant for a story related to health code violations. The court held that although the restaurant was open to the public as a place of public accommodation, the defendant had vitiated the restaurant's implied invitation to the public because the defendant had not intended to purchase the products and services offered there.

More recent cases often have dealt with paparazzi photographers stalking movie stars and other entertainers or reporters attempting to obtain photographs or video of events in quasi-public view. In 2006, California put into effect an expansion of its privacy law, popularly called the "Anti-Paparazzi Act."[90] The law provides for liability for trespass for the purposes of obtaining visual images or audio recordings and provides for significant money damages from those who violate its provisions. Perhaps of more interest to advertising and public relations professionals, it holds equally liable those who direct, solicit or induce others to engage in either physical or constructive invasion of privacy.

Advertising and public relations professionals should take heed. Although potential plaintiffs initially may have consented to have their privacy intruded upon, this does not provide *carte blanche* for actions that reasonable people would consider to be overstepping the boundaries of that consent.

The Future of Intrusion as Invasion of Privacy

As communication technology grows more sophisticated, so too does the use of that technology in committing what many may see as intrusive acts. Although it may be tempting for advertising and public relations professionals to secretly video- or audio-record recalcitrant employees, conferences with unruly clients or participants in special events, it is advisable to fight the temptation.

The same is true for soliciting a confederate to obtain information posted on an otherwise restricted-access Facebook page, snooping into an employee's private Twitter account or accessing others' personal e-mails. Related cases have arisen involving the actions of organizations to access personal hard drives or software attached to computers given to employees for use at home. All of these activities might, under some circumstances, be considered outrageously intrusive unless the "snooper" has obtained knowing, demonstrable consent and not gone beyond that consent in their actions.

Infliction of Emotional Distress

The final subject of this chapter is a brief mention of the tort of *infliction of emotional distress*. The issue here refers to the ability of communications to damage one's psyche. In some respects, infliction of emotional distress is much like invasion of privacy. In others, it resembles defamation. In actual practice, lawsuits have been brought alleging all three—defamation of character, invasion of privacy and infliction of emotional distress—leaving it to the courts to sort out which torts, if any, might apply in a given situation.

According to the *Restatement (Second) of Torts*, "One who by extreme or outrageous conduct intentionally or recklessly causes severe emotional distress to another is subject to liability (a) for such emotional distress, and (b) if bodily harm to the other results from it, for such bodily harm."[91]

Until the mid-20th century, the law generally shied away from protecting an individual's interest in emotional and mental tranquility. As late as the mid-1930s, the *Restatement of Torts* declared that

> [t]he interest in mental and emotional tranquility and, therefore, in freedom from mental and emotional disturbance is not, as a thing in itself, regarded as of sufficient importance to require others to refrain from conduct intended or recognizably likely to cause such disturbance.[92]

Beginning in the 1940s, however, courts began to recognize that sometimes mental distress can be so extreme as to bring on physical or mental illness, and a person intentionally subjecting another to such intense mental suffering could be found liable for the harm that results. Today, most states have adopted some form of this tort. Some states have incorporated infliction of emotional distress into their defamation or privacy laws, whereas others regard infliction of emotional distress as a separate wrong, particularly in situations where a public disclosure of private, embarrassing facts case is not appropriate because the facts, although of such a nature to cause mental distress, are not private.

The Elements of Infliction of Emotional Distress

Before awarding a judgment in an infliction of emotional distress suit, a court must be satisfied that: (a) a statement has been made that offends ordinary decency; (b) the offending material has been shown to at least one other person by the defendant; (c) the plaintiff has been identified in the statement; (d) the actions of the defendant are the true cause of the actual harm suffered by the plaintiff (in this case, emotional distress); (e) the plaintiff is entitled to be compensated by money damages for that harm; and (f) the distressing statements appeared because the defendant has published all this with the required degree of fault established by law. Most jurisdictions recognize only intentional actions as the fault standard, but a growing number are also allowing a claim of negligent behavior in appropriate circumstances.

Because the elements of emotional distress resemble the elements of defamation if the statements are false, and disclosure of private, embarrassing facts invasion of privacy if the statements are true, it would be redundant to discuss them in detail. Rather, a number of examples should be sufficient to illustrate these elements.

Examples of Emotional Distress

Cases alleging infliction of emotional distress have been brought in situations involving excommunication from a church, religious harassment and religious shunning,[93] hounding for collection of an overdue bill,[94] a false report that the plaintiff was suffering from a fatal illness[95] and even an unexpected eviction notice.[96] In more recent years, a number of cases have arisen directly out of mass media-related situations, becoming another tort affecting mass communications professionals.

A major case in this area was decided by the Supreme Court in *Hustler Magazine v. Falwell*.[97] The key players were the Rev. Jerry Falwell—a nationally known minister, commentator on public affairs and leader of The Moral Majority, a conservative action group—and Larry Flynt, publisher of an irreverent and often-raunchy magazine. The inside front cover of *Hustler's* November 1983 issue contained what the magazine referred to as a "parody" of a Campari liquor advertisement featuring the name and picture of Mr. Falwell. Entitled "Jerry Falwell Talks About His First Time," the format resembled actual Campari ads in which celebrities recounted their "first times" of sampling the liquor. *Hustler* being *Hustler*, one may imagine what the rest of the ad contained. In tiny print at the bottom of the offending page was a disclaimer that read, "ad parody—not to be taken seriously."[98]

Falwell, however, did take it seriously, filing lawsuits for libel, invasion of privacy and intentional infliction of emotional distress. A Virginia judge summarily threw out the invasion of privacy claim and the trial jury found against Mr. Falwell on the libel allegation. But the jury did award Falwell a total of $200,000 on the intentional infliction of emotional distress claim.[99] The federal court of appeals affirmed the judgment.[100] The Supreme Court, however, reversed, holding that to punish a media defendant for its parody of a public figure such as Mr. Falwell could effectively silence political cartoonists, satirists and others who attempt to poke fun at public personalities, and curtail the free flow of ideas and opinions on matters of public interest and concern.[101]

Because of this, public officials and public figures—as defined in *Sullivan* (see Chapter 4)—cannot win an intentional infliction of emotional distress lawsuit alleging false statements without showing actual malice. Early indications are that courts may hold private plaintiffs to a lesser standard in such cases in years to come, but this remains an open question.

Infliction of emotional distress cases that are complaining about true but distressing facts are equally difficult to win, especially if they involve a mass media defendant. For example, in *Hood v. Naeter Brothers Publishing Co.*,[102] a newspaper in Cape Girardeau, Missouri, published the name and address, accurately taken from police reports, of the plaintiff, an eyewitness to a liquor store robbery in which one person was killed. At the time, the suspects were still at large. Hood sued the newspaper, stating that as a result of the publication he had lived in constant fear, had to change his residence repeatedly and had to submit to the care of a psychiatrist.

The information published by the newspaper was not injurious to reputation, it did not cast him in a false light, and the court determined that the information disclosed about Hood were not private, embarrassing facts. Hood sued for infliction of emotional distress, claiming that the newspaper knew, or should have known, that his exposure as an eyewitness while the killers were still at large constituted outrageous behavior. Both the trial court and the court of appeals ruled in favor of the newspaper.[103]

The most recent prominent case, also decided in favor of the defendant, was *Snyder v. Phelps*. Members of the Westboro Baptist Church make it a practice to picket the funerals of U.S. soldiers to highlight their belief that God is offended by the acceptance of homosexuality, especially in the military. Mathew Snyder, the father of one of these dead soldiers, sued Pastor Fred Phelps and other church congregants for intentional infliction of emotional distress, intrusion and civil conspiracy. Although awarded millions of dollars in damages by the trial court, Snyder's victory ultimately was overturned by the Supreme Court on the basis that the First Amendment protected this speech about public matters and because the church members had conducted their picketing activities in a lawful manner, well away from the actual site of the funeral.

Cases of more relevance to advertising and public relations professionals include a former employee suing city agency personnel for statements made about the reason for his termination, a teacher complaining about her public treatment by school authorities during an investigation of violation of testing standards and harassing behavior by a mortgage company threatening home foreclosure. Either linking individuals to products or services they may abhor or providing information of a derogatory, if truthful, nature about individuals to the media may give rise to emotional distress cases as well as false light or private facts suits.

The Future of Infliction of Emotional Distress as a Cause of Action

Although infliction of emotional distress cases are difficult to win against media defendants, advertising and public relations professionals should recognize that their communications may not always be treated by courts as meeting the definition of media. The Supreme Court and lower courts have consistently differentiated between media and non-media defendants and, just as consistently, provided less protection for non-media defendants. Moreover, if "bad behavior" online continues unchecked, courts may be receptive to expanding the application of emotional distress lawsuits to a broader range of communications and defendants, even those clearly definable as members of the media. This potentiality should provide continued motivation for public relations and advertising professionals to double-check the rationales behind communications that may exceed conventions of ordinary decency.

Conclusion

Because of the intemperate nature of many communications found online, outraged and aggrieved individuals who are the subjects of such communications are increasingly turning to the courts to seek a remedy for the dissemination of information they argue has caused emotional distress. Public relations professionals, in particular, should be extremely vigilant to protect themselves and their organizations or clients from releasing the kinds of information or taking the kinds of actions related to their employees, competitors or critics that could provoke these types of lawsuits.

Commercial speakers should also beware of the increasing frequency of "outrage" or copycat suits arising from claims of harm based on actions taken by plaintiffs encouraged by the media to engage in risky behaviors. For example, in *Strange v. Entercom Sacramento LLC*,[104] a radio station was assessed a more than $16 million damages award when a contestant in a station-sponsored contest later died after ingesting a lethal quantity of water.

Whether depicting drivers performing tricks in an automobile ad or sponsoring or conducting wacky promotional schemes, prudent advertising and public relations professionals should take steps to ensure that children or gullible adults are strongly discouraged from attempting to duplicate what they have seen, and that they are not exposed to potential harm caused by participation in an event.

Notes

1.   Samuel Warren & Louis Brandeis, *The Right to Privacy*, 4 Harv. L. Rev. 193 (1890).
2.   *Id.* at 196.
3.   William L. Prosser, *Privacy*, 48 Cal. L. Rev. 383 (1960).
4.   American Law Institute, Restatement of the Law of Torts (2d ed.), §649 (American Law Institute Publishers, St. Paul, MN, 1975).
5.   *Id.* at 398.
6.   Jews for Jesus, Inc. v. Rapp, 997 So. 2d 1098 (Fla. 2008).
7.   Ayash v. Dana-Farber Cancer Institute, 443 Mass. 367 (2005).
8.   Cain v. Hearst Corp., 878 S.W.2d 577 (Tex., 1994).
9.   Renwick v. News & Observer Pub. Co., 310 N.C. 312 (1984).
10. Leverton et al. v. Curtis Publishing Co., 192 F.2d 974 (1951).
11. William Brashler, *The Black Middle Class: Making It*, N.Y. Times Magazine, Dec. 3, 1978, 147–148.
12. Arrington v. New York Times, 5 Media L. Rep. 2581 (1980).
13. Wilson v. Yerke, 2011 U.S. Dist. LEXIS 8739 (M.D. Pa. Jan. 31, 2011).
14. Sims v. Humane Soc'y of St. Joseph County Ind. Inc., 758 F. Supp. 2d 737 (N.D. Ind. 2010).
15. Smith v. PNC Bank, 2011 U.S. Dist. KEXIS 74279 (W.D. Pa. June 2, 2011); Stewart v. XRimz, LLC, 2011 U.S. Dist LEXIS 27988, 16–17 (M.D. Pa. Mar. 18, 2011).
16. Curry v. Whitaker, 943 N.E.2d 354 (Ind. Ct. App. 2011).
17. Smith v. McGraw, 2011 WL 1599579 (D. Md. Apr. 27, 2011).
18. Time, Inc., v. Hill, 385 U.S. 374 (1974).
19. *Id.*
20. *Id.*
21. *Id.*
22. Hill v. Hayes, 18 A.D.2d 485 (N.Y.A.D. 1963).
23. Hill v. Hayes, 15 N.Y.2d 986 (N.Y. 1965).
24. New York Times v. Sullivan, 376 U.S. 254 (1964).
25. Time, Inc., v. Hill, 385 U.S. 374 (1974).
26. Gertz v. Robert Welch, Inc., 418 U.S. 323, 339–340 (1974).
27. Practising Law Institute, Communications Law, Vol. 1, 526 (Practising Law Institute, New York 2005).
28. Cantrell v. Forest City Publishing Co., 419 U.S. 245 (1974).
29. *Id.*
30. Cantrell v. Forest City Publishing Co., 484 F.2d 150.

31. Cantrell, 419 U.S. at 253.
32. Spahn v. Julian Messner, 221 N.E.2d 543, 545 (1966).
33. *Id.*
34. Peay v. Curtis Publishing Co., 28 F. Supp. 305 (1948).
35. Crump v. Beckley Newspapers Inc., 320 S.E.2d 70 (1984).
36. Black's Law Dictionary (West Group, St. Paul, MN, 6th ed. 1990).
37. Bindrim v. Mitchell, 92 Cal. App. 3d 61(Cal. App. 1979).
38. 4 Harv. L. Rev. at 196 (1890).
39. Restatement (Second) of Torts, §652D.
40. Wojtowicz v. Delacorte Press, 43 N.Y.2d 858 (1978).
41. WJLA-TV v. Levin, 264 Va. 140 (2002).
42. Doe v. Methodist Hosp., 690 N.E.2d 681 (1997).
43. Hall v. Post, 323 N.C. 259 (1988).
44. Sipple v. Chronicle Publishing Co., 154 Cal. App. 3d 1040 (1984).
45. *Id.*
46. *Id.*
47. Reid v. Pierce County, 136 Wash. 2d 195 (1998).
48. Restatement (Second) of Torts §652D, illus. 10 (1977).
49. Horn v. Patton, 291 Ala. 701 (1973).
50. M.G. v. Time Warner, Inc., 89 Cal. App. 4th 623 (2001).
51. Trammell v. Citizens News Co., 285 Ky. 539 (1941).
52. McSurely v. McClellan, 753 F.2d 88, 112 (D.C. Cir. 1985).
53. *Id.* at 109 (D.C. Cir. 1985).
54. Diaz v. Oakland Tribune, Inc., 139 Cal. App. 3d 118 (1983).
55. *Id.*
56. *Id.*
57. Cox Broadcasting Co. v. Cohn, 420 U.S. 469 (1975).
58. *Id.* at 496.
59. The Florida Star v. B.J.F., 491 U.S. 524 (1989).
60. *Id.* at 529.
61. Florida Star v. B.J.F., 499 So. 2d 883 (Fla. App. 1 Dist., 1986).
62. Quoted in George C. Christie & James E. Meeks, Cases and Materials on the Law of Torts (Gale Cengage, Florence, KY, 2nd ed. 1990) at 1116.
63. Restatement (Second) of Torts §652D.
64. Hawkins v. Multimedia, 344 S.E.2d 145 (1986).
65. 1 Practising Law Institute, Communications Law, 524 (Practising Law Institute, New York 2005).
66. William L. Prosser, *Privacy*, 48 Cal. L. Rev. 383, 397 (1960).
67. Sidis v. F-R Publishing Corp., 113 F.2d 806 (1940).
68. *Id.* at 807-808.
69. *Id.* at 809.
70. Barber v. Time, Inc., 159 S.W.2d (1942).
71. *Id.*
72. Briscoe v. Reader's Digest Association, 483 P.2d 34 (1971). Overruled 2004.
73. *Id.*
74. *Id.*
75. *Id.* at 41-42.
76. Victor Hugo, Les Miserables (Hurst & Blackett, London 1862).
77. Nathaniel Hawthorne, The Scarlet Letter (Ticknor & Fields, Boston, MA. 1850).
78. Briscoe v. Reader's Digest Association, 483 P.2d at 44 note 18 (1971).

79. Virgil v. Time, Inc., 527 F.2d 1122 (1975).

80. *Id.* at 1124 note 1.

81. Smith v. NBC Universal, et al. 524 F. Supp. 2d 315 (S.D.N.Y. 2007).

82. Mendelson v. The Morning Call, Inc., 2007 Pa. Dist. & Cnty. Dec. LEXIS 256 (C.P. Leh. Sept. 4, 2007).

83. RESTATEMENT (SECOND) OF TORTS §652B (1977).

84. See for example, 3 COMMUNICATIONS LAW IN A DIGITAL AGE, 286 (Practising Law Institute, New York 2008).

85. Dietemann v. Time, Inc., 449 F.2d 245 (9th Cir. 1971).

86. Crow v. Crawford & Co., 259 S.W.3d 104 (2008).

87. Quinn Emanuel Urquhart Oliver & Hedges, LLP v. LaTorraca & Goettsch, 2006 Cal. App. Unpub. LEXIS 1706, 34 Med. L. Rptr. 1453 (2006).

88. Bilney v. Evening Star, 43 Md. App. 560, 406 A.2d 652 (1979).

89. LeMistral, Inc. v. Columbia Broadcasting System, 61 A.D.2d 491 (1978).

90. CAL. CIV. CODE §1708.8 (2006).

91. RESTATEMENT (SECOND) OF TORTS §46 (1965).

92. RESTATEMENT (FIRST) OF TORTS §46, cmt. c (1934).

93. Bear v. Reformed Mennonite Church, 462 Pa. 330, 342 A.2d 105 (1975).

94. Ford Motor Credit Co. v. Sheehan, 373 So. 2d 956 (1979).

95. Chuy v. Philadelphia Eagles Football Club, 595 F.2d 1265 (3rd cir. 1979).

96. Meiter v. Cavenaugh, 40 Colo. App. 454 (1978).

97. Hustler Magazine v. Falwell, 485 U.S. 46 (1988).

98. *Id.* at 48.

99. *Id.* at 49.

100. Falwell v. Flynt, 797 F.2d 1270 (1986).

101. Hustler Magazine, 485 U.S. at 51.

102. Hood v. Naeter Brothers Publishing Co., 562 S.W.2d 770 (1970).

103. *Id.* at 771.

104. Strange v. Entercom Sacramento LLC, Case no. 07AS00377 (Cal. Super. Ct. Sacramento County, 2009).

6 Invasion of Privacy
Misappropriation and Right of Publicity

This chapter focuses on the tort of *misappropriation* invasion of privacy and its offshoot, the right of publicity. Both involve the non-consented use of a person's name or likeness, often for commercial purposes. The cause of action differs somewhat depending upon whether the plaintiff is a private individual who is mentally anguished about the non-permitted use (misappropriation) or a celebrity who wishes to be compensated when his or her name or likeness was used without permission (right of publicity).

Misappropriation Background

When Warren and Brandeis were advancing their radical ideas for the *Harvard Law Review*[1] more than 100 years ago (see Chapter 5), they probably were not thinking in terms of misappropriation as a factor in their proposed right. Yet misappropriation cases were among the first to be presented as invasions of privacy. Over the years, such exploitation has become a major aspect of the ever-evolving laws of privacy and publicity.

The first attempts to recover monetary damages in misappropriation cases were not successful, although one plaintiff, an actress, was able to stop publication of a picture of her in a costume she thought to be scandalous.[2] Among the most famous of the early misappropriation cases was that of Abigail Roberson of Albany, New York, whose picture, published without her consent, appeared in 1902 on thousands of posters advertising Franklin Mills Flour. The attractive young woman, mortified at seeing pictures of her splashed across the city and with the accompanying copy describing her as "the flour of the family," brought suit for what she regarded as an invasion of privacy. The New York Court of Appeals, in *Roberson v. Rochester Folding Box Co.*,[3] rejected the arguments that had been advanced by Warren and Brandeis and issued a majority opinion insisting that:

> an examination of the authorities leads us to the conclusion that the so-called "right of privacy" has not yet found an abiding place in our jurisprudence, and, as we view it, the doctrine cannot now be incorporated without doing violence to settled principles of law by which the profession and the public have long been guided.[4]

This ruling, allowing Miss Roberson no relief for what had clearly been commercial exploitation of her physical appearance, touched off a firestorm in the next session of the New York State legislature and, in 1903, led to the passage of a statute making it both a criminal offense (a misdemeanor) and a civil wrong to make use of the name or likeness of an individual for "advertising purposes or for the purposes of trade" without first obtaining written consent.[5] The new law permitted the person whose privacy had been invaded to seek monetary damages as well as an injunction to halt further publication of the offensive material. This statute, which later became part of the New York Civil Rights Law, was the first ever to deal with the right of privacy, and it remains on the books to this day.

The first common-law acceptance of the right of privacy came two years after *Roberson* by the Georgia Supreme Court in 1904. An insurance company's advertising featured the name and picture of an Atlanta artist, Paolo Pavesich. The ad copy also presented a testimonial, falsely attributed to him, as to the value of having a sound insurance portfolio. Pavesich sued for $25,000 and won. The Georgia Supreme Court expressly rejected the New York decision regarding Abigail Roberson and endorsed the earlier views of Warren and Brandeis:

> The form and features of the plaintiff [Pavesich] are his own. The defendant insurance company and its agents had no more authority to display them in public for purposes of advertising ... than they would have had to compel the plaintiff to place himself upon exhibition for this purpose.[6]

Once the misappropriation right of privacy was accepted in *Pavesich*, most other jurisdictions—but by no means all—began to follow suit. For example, a Washington court came down hard on an advertiser who used a customer's name as an endorsement without permission:

> Nothing so exclusively belongs to a man or is so personal and valuable to him as his name. .... Others have no right to use it without his express consent, and he has the right to go into any court at any time to enjoin or prohibit any unauthorized use of it.[7]

Today, the vast majority of states have adopted some form of misappropriation and the right of publicity.

Terminology

The *Restatement (Second) of Torts*, much referred to in this book, defines misappropriation and the right of publicity as:

> One who appropriates to his own use or benefit the name or likeness of another is subject to liability to the other for invasion of privacy.[8]

The key to understanding the tort of invasion of privacy by misappropriation is that it requires exploitation by another for purposes of trade or other benefit. The injury is personal.

Elements of Misappropriation and the Right of Publicity

Although the specifics are defined somewhat differently from state to state, generally the individual hoping to present a solid misappropriation case must demonstrate that: (a) statements that appropriate the plaintiff's identity—or an identity licensed to or in other ways belonging to some other individual or organization bringing the lawsuit—have been made; (b) the offending material has been shown to other persons by the defendant; (c) the plaintiff has been identified in the statements; (d) the actions of the defendant are the true cause of the actual harm suffered by the plaintiff; (e) the plaintiff is entitled to be compensated by money damages for that harm; and (f) the statements appeared because the defendant has done all this with the required degree of fault established by law. Let's take a closer look at each of these points in turn.

Misappropriation Statement

The statement at the center of the misappropriation complaint must contain information about the plaintiff used in such a way that reasonable people would find offensive if it happened to them. Misappropriation in such cases often involves the use of a person's name, likeness or persona in a manner that offends, or in other ways upsets, the plaintiff.

Consider two hypothetical examples. First, Joe Piscoonyak works at Old Sandlapper Brewing Company and indeed consumes a substantial quantity of Old Sandlapper beer. Without his knowledge or consent, your photographer takes a photograph of Joe headed for the checkout stand in a local supermarket, his shopping cart filled with cartons of Old Sandlapper. The photograph is subsequently published as part of an advertisement and in a company promotional brochure. Although the photograph truthfully depicts his enthusiastic choice of brews, and despite the fact that he is an employee of the company, you have nevertheless invaded Joe's privacy by appropriating his likeness.

Second, Sally Sunshine's engagement picture, a splendid photographic portrait, is displayed without her knowledge and consent in the window of the photographer's studio as an example of the superior quality of work done by that studio. The work is indeed of admirable quality, yet Miss Sunshine's privacy similarly has been invaded.

These two hypothetical situations, and the thousands of actual cases that could be employed as real-life examples, should alert the reader to the care that should be exercised before using

Figure 6.1 New York's Times Square is known for a variety of commercial signs and billboards. Many of these displays feature celebrities and other models who have given their consent for their likenesses to be associated with the sale or promotion of goods and services.

Credit line: Luciano Mortula/Shutterstock.com

any public or private individual's name or likeness without permission, even if the use is by a not-for-profit organization. The reader should remember that the basis of a claim for invasion of privacy by misappropriation may not be because of concern about *what* was said or published, but rather that anything was said or published about the complainant *at all*. "Leave me alone" is the essence of this tort.

Publication

While technically publication occurs the moment a third person has seen the communication, the offending message must typically reach a broad audience, rather than just a few, to be actionable. Many jurisdictions refer to publication as giving "publicity" to the misappropriated information.

As with defamation, a misappropriation invasion of privacy plaintiff often has a relatively easy time demonstrating that publication has occurred. This is because the defendant advertising agency or public relations department has disseminated the information to thousands, if not millions, of readers or viewers in network television advertising; press release material published in hundreds of news outlets; or in campaigns on YouTube, Facebook or other social networking sites.

Identification

The plaintiff in a misappropriation privacy case must meet virtually the same requirements as a defamation plaintiff to prove that an audience of concern to the plaintiff (e.g., fellow employees) believes that the statements are about him or her. Identification is often not difficult for the plaintiff because the defendant, as a professional communicator, has clearly identified the subjects in the communications.

The tort of misappropriation is limited to individuals if the claim involves a private person because organizations cannot demonstrate they have suffered mental anguish about the published information. However, if a celebrity has in some way conveyed the rights to the use of his or her name, likeness or persona to an organization, that organization can bring a misappropriation right of publicity claim for the loss of financial income attributable to the unauthorized use by the defendant.

Causation

The plaintiffs in a misappropriation privacy suit must allege and prove that the actions of the defendant were the logical and proximate cause of the claimed injury. Often this is easily accomplished because the plaintiffs, if private citizens, are simply charging that they have understandably suffered mental anguish when the defendant outrageously misappropriated their names or likenesses and the results have been seen by acquaintances or clients or customers. Celebrity plaintiffs, similarly, may have an easy time if the misappropriation claim simply involves a complaint that their names have been linked to activities the celebrities find distasteful.

Problems proving causation might arise when private plaintiffs are complaining about the misuse of their identity in situations where, in the minds of a judge or jury, they have not suffered mental anguish severe enough to warrant compensation. Celebrities may experience difficulty in proving causation if their claims involve complaints of economic harm because they may find it difficult to provide evidence that the value of their endorsement appeal has declined or that they have been cheated out of potential income because of the actions of the defendant.

Compensation

A private plaintiff seeking compensation for harm to his or her mental well-being resulting from misappropriation of his or her identity generally will be entitled to seek four different kinds of monetary awards. These are *nominal* damages, *special* damages, *actual* damages (in some jurisdictions, the second and third awards are sometimes combined and called "general," or "compensatory" damages) and *punitive* (or "exemplary") damages.

For a plaintiff to seek a small or *nominal* damage award is relatively rare in misappropriation cases. More typically, a private plaintiff, actually seeking a large sum to compensate for the supposed harm, is found by a judge or jury to have suffered no real harm and, therefore, not deserving of more than a nominal award of damages. The same is true for celebrities.

To obtain *special* damages, often thought of as "out-of-pocket dollar loss," plaintiffs must produce evidence sufficient to prove that the misappropriation of identity cost the plaintiff a demonstrable monetary loss. Expenses for psychiatric care, counseling services or prescribed medications, as well as evidence of wages lost or other financial reverses because the plaintiff was too upset to function normally, are examples of special damages often claimed by private plaintiffs. Celebrity plaintiffs, normally, are seeking reimbursement either for expenses linked to their mental anguish that are similar to a private plaintiff or for losses to their financial balance sheet (e.g., "I charge $10,000 for a product endorsement").

The third category of damages, *actual* damage, requires no proof of actual monetary loss. However, all plaintiffs must demonstrate that the alleged mental anguish caused by the misappropriation does, in fact, exist. In jurisdictions that ask for some evidence of mental anguish, plaintiffs seeking actual damages typically, in addition to their own testimony, introduce testimony from friends and medical and/or counseling professionals about psychic damages. It should be noted that these damages are only available to a celebrity who is claiming mental anguish in addition to financial loss.

If a judge or jury accepts that the harm has occurred and the defendant has no additional defenses, money will be awarded to the plaintiff as compensation based on the judge or jury's estimation of the harm—an invitation for large damage awards for the plaintiff. The possibility of such large verdicts should be all the impetus needed for advertising and public relations professionals to take all possible precautions to avoid becoming embroiled in a misappropriation suit.

Punitive damages, generally, are awarded when the defendant's actions are so outrageous that they offend the conscience of judges or juries. In a private misappropriation invasion of privacy suit, punitive damages might be awarded if the misappropriation was done in a way that was considered outrageous and shocking (e.g., purposely linking the plaintiff to a controversial product). Punitive damages in celebrity misappropriation cases might be awarded either because the celebrity is linked to an outrageous activity, or the usage has severely damaged the plaintiff's ability to capitalize on his or her own celebrity status. Like actual damages, punitive damage awards can reach mega-amounts in misappropriation suits and are as dangerous, if not more so, to defendants.

Defendant Fault

Fault in tort law often is defined as an error in judgment or conduct, such as negligence or any departure from normal care because of inattention, carelessness or incompetence. However, in misappropriation invasion of privacy, the majority of states and state courts have decreed that the fault required is intentional or purposeful action, while others go further to mandate a fault standard that resembles common law malice (i.e., the taking of the name or likeness was an intentional act designed to harm the plaintiff).

Affirmative Defenses

Once a misappropriation privacy plaintiff has made a *prima facie* case–a statement appropriating the name or likeness of another without consent, publication, identification and so forth–the other side must mount a defense. Affirmative defenses include *personal consent, property releases, incidental use, transformative use, satire, parody* and *newsworthiness.* New York's ground-breaking Right of Privacy law says, in part:

> Any person whose name, portrait or picture is used within this state for advertising purposes or for the purposes of trade without … written consent … may maintain an equitable action in the supreme court of this state against the person, firm or corporation so using his name, portrait or picture, to prevent and restrain the use thereof, and may also sue and recover damages for any injuries by reason of such use.[9]

Experienced public relations practitioners and advertising professionals know the value of obtaining signed *personal consent* on release forms from their subjects and to ensure that those they hire to obtain or create information (e.g., a freelance videographer) obtain them as well. A photograph used purely for news reporting purposes does not require consent (this issue is discussed further later in this chapter). However, if the news organization reprints or sells the photo for later use in advertising or promotional materials, the newsworthiness defense might not apply, and some additional protection–in the form of a signed consent–may be necessary.

A photographer attempting to freelance a picture or a freelance writer seeking to publish an article will find that a signed release to accompany the material will make it more marketable. Two example model releases are shown in Appendix C. Most professional photographers and writers routinely carry around pads of such blank release or consent forms to use as needed. Other, simpler versions of a release form may also be used; there is no single, uniform standardized release.

The consent form allows the person who is being used for commercial purposes to decide how much right of privacy to give up and on what terms. Even so, problems with consent can arise. The following are ways to avert some of them:

A. The consent should be written. A number of states do not recognize oral agreements or handshakes where misappropriation lawsuits are concerned.
B. It should be understandable to persons of average intelligence.
C. The person giving the consent must be a competent adult. Minors–people under 18 years of age–cannot sign consent forms that are legally binding; a parent or guardian must sign the consent form on their behalf.

This latter point was sorely tested in prolonged litigation in New York by the actress Brooke Shields and her mother during the 1980s. At the age of 10, Miss Shields posed semi-nude for a picture story that appeared in a Playboy Press book, *Sugar and Spice*. Her mother had signed the appropriate consent forms. Five years later, however, Shields, by then a promising young actress, had attained a measure of notoriety and the owner of the consent forms marketed the photos to other magazines, at least one of which published them with the caption "Brooke Shields Naked." Mrs. Shields sued on her daughter's behalf and, in a complex series of trials, ultimately lost. The consent forms she had signed took away her and her daughter's rights to recovery.[10]

In some cases, the consent may become invalid. In a 1961 Louisiana case, a health club owner obtained written consent to use photographs of a customer, Cole McAndrews, to illustrate the before-and-after effects of a rigorous exercise program. However, the health club owner waited for 10 years before deciding to use the photos. During that time, the physical condition of McAndrews had changed a bit; he presumably resembled the "before" rather than the "after" photos. Thus, the health club ads featuring his photos subjected him to a certain amount of embarrassment, and he sued. The trial judge was sympathetic, noting that, under the circumstances, the permission forms McAndrews had signed should have been renewed.[11]

If there is no consideration—something of value given in return for the consent—the consent can be withdrawn before the photographs are published. The consideration may be payment of as little as $1, or it may be something else of value. Without "valuable consideration," a consent form, as with other types of contracts (see Chapter 9), may be difficult to enforce.

Finally, if the photos are altered or the context in which they are used is materially changed from what the model thought it would be, the consent may not be binding. Retouching the photo, changing the background scene or using the photo to advertise one product when the model believed it to be for another can effectively undermine a consent agreement. In an era when digital imaging makes it possible to alter photographs easily, this point becomes especially important.

The American Magazine Photographers Association offers its members this useful nuts-and-bolts advice:

1. Get a release whenever possible.
2. If you do not have a release, and if a person could be recognized by anyone, retouch the face and/or figure to eliminate all possibility of recognition when people might appear in: (a) paid ads; (b) promotional matter; or (c) any published use that could be deemed embarrassing or in incorrect context (no matter how remote).[12]

Similar to obtaining a release from individuals before using their name or likeness, it is also a good idea to obtain a *property release* from the owners of buildings and other real estate that might be used in photographs for advertising or other trade purposes. These owners do not have a "right of privacy" as such to be invaded by such photos, but courts have determined that there are property rights that cannot be unjustly exploited for commercial purposes. Property releases, signed by the owners or agents for the owners, may be needed for photographs of such places.

If the building is merely incidental or part of the background—a photograph of a street scene or other public gathering place—a property release probably is not necessary. Although most buildings in public places can be safely photographed and used in advertisements, there have been instances of successful claims that the photographs in an advertisement of an identifiable building in a public location constituted a legal infringement of the owner's property rights. Property rights can be and have been extended to owners of animals when the animals have been photographed for purposes of trade without the owner's consent. Again, specific consent forms signed by the owners should be obtained.[13]

As a general rule, use of names and likenesses in news contexts are protected, whereas use of names and likenesses in press releases, promotional materials and advertising messages may not be. Sometimes the distinctions are blurred. Professional football legend Joe Namath brought suit in 1976 against *Sports Illustrated* claiming that the use of his photograph, which had been on the magazine's cover, was actually intended as advertising and promotional materials to attract new readers. The New York Jets quarterback's claim was rejected when the court held that this was *"incidental use"* of his photograph to illustrate the "quality and content" of the publication and that this was a "necessary and logical extension" of the otherwise newsworthy photograph.[14]

If the photograph had been used in a manner to suggest that Namath was personally endorsing the magazine, however, the photograph would likely have been found to be misappropriation. The same reasoning applies to public relations messages, particularly in the preparation of employee publications.

Another factor to be considered in determining incidental use is whether the use of an individual's photo is sufficiently related to the commercial use as to constitute misappropriation. For example, a crowd shot to illustrate an advertisement may indeed have identifiable faces in it. If these faces are merely that—faces—and otherwise immaterial to the selling message, it is unlikely that a misappropriation action could be won by any of the individuals depicted in the photo. Again, it is the identity of the individual, not merely the incidental use of it, which must be appropriated. So long as these people are not shown as specifically endorsing the product in the ad, and so long as their presence is incidental to—and not directly supportive of—the selling message, an action for invasion of privacy would likely not succeed.

Recently, courts have begun dismissing misappropriation claims on the basis that the allegedly infringing use created a *"transformative"* work. In *Comedy III Productions Inc. v. Gary Saderup Inc.*,[15] the California Supreme Court, while upholding the plaintiff's claim that use of images of The Three Stooges on T-shirts was actionable, noted that courts should balance the plaintiff's publicity interests against an "affirmative defense that the [disputed] work is protected by the First Amendment [if] it contains significant [artistic] transformative elements" that makes it a new creative effort.[16]

This was true for golfer Tiger Woods, who sued an artist for selling prints of a painting depicting past winners of a major golf tournament with Woods' likeness as the predominant image. A federal appeals court held that not only was the work of art a transformative creation protected under the First Amendment, but that the painting and prints artistically depicted historic events and the inclusion of Woods' image was an incidental use.[17] Note, however, that the use of the painting as an illustration in an advertisement for golf clubs might have produced a very different result.

Artistic "transformation" may be in the eyes of the beholder. Former hockey player Anthony "Tony Twist" Twistelli sued the creators of a comic book series after they gave his nickname to a character portrayed as a mafia don. The trial court in Missouri employed a "predominant use" test to find that the combination of the specific marketing of the comic books to hockey fans and admitting that the comic book character was named after Twistelli (both he and the character were considered tough-guy "enforcers") were enough to demonstrate that the plaintiff's publicity rights had been violated. A jury award of $15 million was upheld on appeal, suggesting that perhaps comic books were not thought to merit an artistic transformative defense.[18]

The bottom line is that truly artistic or trivial uses of names or likenesses most likely will not constitute misappropriation or right of publicity invasion of privacy. Still, if there is any doubt about using a photograph showing a number of identifiable likenesses for commercial purposes, it may be a good idea to find another way to illustrate the concept. Either that or obtain consent to use the names and/or likenesses in this commercial context. Consent provides protection, but only if the consent is properly obtained and not exceeded.

Entertainers who make their living by performing impressions of celebrities in nightclubs or in media appearances generally are immune from right-of-publicity suits by the celebrities they imitate. This exception also protects late-night television comics, parachuting Elvis Presley look-alikes and satirists of contemporary social and political figures. It should be clear, however, that this defense of *satire* or *parody* would not hold up if these imitators use their talents to promote the commercial interests of others. Thus, it would be perfectly acceptable, from a legal perspective, for an impressionist to imitate the distinctive speaking voice of the actor James Earl Jones as part of the impressionist's act, but not to perform such a vocal impersonation as part of a commercial to sell a particular brand of soft drink.

In addition, particularly in the case of impressionists who attempt to physically resemble a celebrity, the performer should take care not to create a performance that, in effect, duplicates all or a sizable portion of the original celebrity's act or to make use of symbols or images associated with the real celebrity in promoting the impressionist's performances.

Individuals cannot prevent publication of their names when they take part or become involved in the news or a public event. In matters "concerning *newsworthy* events or matters of public interest,"[19] the news media's right to inform the public will take precedence over an individual's right to privacy. A Kentucky resident, an innocent bystander at the scene of a brutal knife assault, sued when a local newspaper published a photograph of the incident. The Kentucky Supreme Court held that the man's privacy had not been unjustly violated:

> The right of privacy is the right to live one's life in seclusion, without being subjected to unwarranted and undesired publicity. In short, it is the right to be left alone. ... There are times, however, when one, whether willing or not, becomes an actor in an occurrence of public or general interest. When this takes place, he emerges from his seclusion, and it is not an invasion of his right or privacy to publish his photograph with an account of such occurrence.[20]

Thus, a name or photo of a person involved in a newsworthy situation may be used without that person's permission. This holds true despite the fact that most newspapers, magazines and broadcast stations are commercial enterprises attempting to make a profit. The primary consideration in newsworthiness is the attempt to inform the public about matters of general interest. The profit motive—that of selling newspapers or increasing audience share for advertising purposes—is regarded as secondary. The *Restatement (Second) of Torts* puts it this way:

> The value of the plaintiff's name is not appropriated by mere mention of it, or by reference to it in connection with legitimate mention of his public activities. ... The fact that the defendant is engaged in the business of publication, for example of a newspaper, out of which he makes a profit, is not enough to make the incidental publication a commercial use of the name or likeness.[21]

Much depends, however, on how the material is used. A photograph might be newsworthy in one context, but appropriation in another. For example, a Page 1 photograph of a victim of a hit-and-run driver would obviously be considered newsworthy. However, that same photo used in an advertisement to promote the newspaper's photographic talents as a reason to subscribe to the paper might well invade the victim's privacy.

Consider two other examples. First, a Sunday supplement news feature on spring styles, accompanied by photos of fashion models, would likely be newsworthy. The same photos in trade advertisements would not be protected. Second, a spectacular photograph taken in New York City's Times Square of a sailor kissing a nurse in celebration of the end of World War II could safely appear in *Life* magazine as being newsworthy. The same photo, reproduced and sold as a poster, would not.[22]

From the beginnings of privacy law, courts have recognized the conflict between an individual's desire for privacy and the public's concern about being informed. In the landmark *Pavesich* case, the Georgia Supreme Court held that it believed the right of privacy to be a natural right, recognized by "the law of nature."[23] But it also warned that enforcing an individual's right of privacy could "inevitably tend to curtail the liberty of speech and of the press," which, the court said, is also a natural right. "It will therefore be seen," the court predicted, "that the right of privacy must in some particulars yield to the right of speech and of the press."[24] This has proved to be the case.

Traditionally, the news media's most useful defense against invasion of privacy lawsuits has been the concept of "newsworthiness." But reports in the news media are very different, insofar as privacy laws are concerned, from advertising and public relations messages. Newsworthiness as a defense may be of little benefit whatsoever to an advertising agency or corporate public relations department threatened with a misappropriation invasion of privacy lawsuit.

The Right of Publicity

Although misappropriation is designed to protect everyone, the *right of publicity* has evolved primarily to protect celebrities' hard-won fame—as reflected in their names, likenesses and voices—from unauthorized exploitation. The right of publicity has developed as an offshoot of a combination of misappropriation, the laws of unfair competition and protecting property rights as well. In some states, the rights of privacy and publicity are merged to protect private citizens and celebrities alike under one common-law tort of "appropriation of name or likeness."[25] In other states, statutes expressly protect a right of publicity as something distinct from misappropriation, although a common-law right of action may still be available to an aggrieved plaintiff. According to Professor Jennifer Rothman, more than 30 states have laws that address the right of publicity apart from misappropriation, and in at least 25 of those states, the right of publicity extends beyond the death of the one whose image is being exploited.[26]

The landmark ruling in right of publicity law is *Haelan Laboratories v. Topps Chewing Gum.*[27] This 1953 case involved major league baseball players who had consented to "an exclusive license" with a bubblegum company to publish their photographs on baseball cards. When a second company wanted to use some of the same players' photos, a lawsuit ensued. At issue was whether the players' rights to privacy could be assigned to a third party, the company with the license. The court of appeals held that the rights, under these circumstances, had economic value and could be protected as such. Judge Jerome Frank, in writing the opinion, described this unique characteristic as the "right of publicity."[28]

In numerous cases since that time, the right of publicity has become more clearly defined. Although much like misappropriation, it is different in a number of respects. In misappropriation, the nature of the damages is personal; it results in mental anguish, embarrassment, indignity or emotional distress. Celebrities have feelings too, of course, but in rights of publicity cases, the damage is largely economic. Not unlike copyright or patent law, the right of publicity allows these individuals to reap the rewards of their endeavors. The right of publicity often has less to do with emotional distress and more to do with protecting one's commercial interests as a celebrity.

The mass media and society have conferred celebrity status on vast numbers of people: film and TV stars, musicians, ballplayers, authors, fashion designers and a great many others. To these individuals, celebrity status has profound economic implications; unauthorized use of the names or images of the famous is, in effect, a form of thievery. Although police and prosecutors are unlikely to get involved in such cases, private attorneys can and do file lawsuits to protect their celebrity clients' interests.

This fast-moving area of the law, pursued with vigor by celebrities and their agents, has important consequences for advertisers, public relations specialists and promoters. The law is clear. Trading on the celebrity status of public people for commercial purposes without their express permission could prove to be a costly mistake that should never be made.

The right of privacy is essentially an individual matter, whereas the right of publicity is recognized in some jurisdictions as having a commercial life even after the death of the celebrity, unlike the right of privacy, which is limited to living people.[29] Examples of such deceased celebrities who have achieved commercial life after death include John Wayne, Fred Astaire, Elvis Presley, Kurt Cobain and Michael Jackson. In the case of *Martin Luther King, Jr., Center for Social Change v. American Heritage Products*,[30] the Georgia Supreme Court noted that a right of publicity survived the death of Dr. King even though he had never exploited his fame for commercial purposes during his lifetime.

Celebrity Identification Through Use of Name, Likeness or "Persona"

Increasingly, courts are willing to entertain claims based on the unauthorized use of a celebrity's likeness even where the person's image has not been used or might previously have been thought to be unrecognizable—in other words, a perception that the likeness is that of a Michael Jackson, a Muhammad Ali or a Vanna White. This reference by "persona," or that which brings to mind an individual even if no name or actual likeness is present, can encompass the protection of a nickname if the person associated with it can prove that someone else was using it for commercial gain, as the former University of Wisconsin and professional football star "Crazy Legs" Hirsch proved in a lawsuit against the maker of "Crazy Legs" pantyhose.[31]

Muhammad Ali, the heavyweight-boxing champion, won an injunction to halt further publication in *Playgirl* magazine of a frontally nude black male sitting in a corner of a boxing ring. This was a drawing, not a photograph, but the face resembled that of Ali and the accompanying text referred to the figure as *The Greatest*—a term Ali had often used to describe himself in promoting boxing matches. In this context, the court held the nickname and likeness were indeed identified with Ali in the public mind and thus could be protected from unauthorized use.[32]

In some ways, such unauthorized use may be regarded as *deception*—akin to a violation of the Lanham Act that prohibits unfair competition (the Lanham Act,[33] as well as infringement on copyrighted material, is discussed at length in other chapters). In one such case, a court found that the likeness of a model used in promoting a video rental store looked enough like the actor and director Woody Allen to cause confusion in the minds of customers. The ad implied that Woody Allen was, in some fashion, involved with the video rental operation or endorsing it.

Indeed, as New York's Chief Justice Motley wrote, the imitation in the advertising photograph was highly specific, portraying:

> a customer in a National Video Store, an individual in his forties, with a high forehead, tousled hair, and heavy black glasses ... his face, bearing an expression at once quizzical and somewhat smug, is leaning on his hand. ... The features and pose are characteristic of the plaintiff. The staging of the photograph also evokes associations with plaintiff. Sitting on the counter are videotape cassettes of *Annie Hall* and *Bananas*, two of plaintiff's best-known films, as well as *Casablanca* and *The Maltese Falcon*. The latter two are Humphrey Bogart films of the 1940's associated with plaintiff primarily because of his play and film, "Play It Again, Sam," in which the spirit of Bogart appears to the character played by Allen and offers him romantic advice. In addition, the title "Play It Again, Sam" is a famous, although inaccurate, quotation from *Casablanca*.
>
> The individual in the advertisement is holding up a National Video V.I.P. Card, which apparently entitles the bearer to favorable terms on movie rentals. The woman behind the counter is smiling at the customer and appears to be gasping in exaggerated excitement at the presence of a celebrity.[34]

Allen's objections, the court decided, were well founded. The comedian/film star/writer/director seemed to be personally offended. In Judge Motley's words, Allen, "to paraphrase Groucho Marx, wouldn't belong to any video club that would have him as a member."[35]

In *Onassis v. Christian Dior-New York, Inc.*,[36] a court found that an advertising photograph of a fictional wedding scene, where some of the guests were real celebrities, featured a model who too closely resembled Jacqueline Kennedy Onassis. She was able to get the advertisement stopped. Particularly hurtful to the defendant's case was the fact that the fashion photographer had specifically asked the modeling agency for a Jackie Kennedy look-alike. When photographed with the real-life celebrities, the model gave the advertisement a persuasive illusion of authenticity. Justice Edward J. Greenfield wrote:

> Defendants knew there was little or no likelihood that Mrs. Onassis would ever consent to be depicted in this kind of advertising campaign for Dior. She has asserted in her affidavit, and it is well known, that she has never permitted her name or picture to be used in connection with the promotion of commercial products. [37]

The woman who had posed for the picture, a secretary named Barbara Reynolds, argued that she could not be prevented from using her own face. But the court held otherwise. "Where [the] use [of one's own face] is done in such a way as to be deceptive or promote confusion," the court said, "that use can be enjoined."[38]

To win a right of publicity case, a celebrity must convince a court that the defendant has benefited financially from the association with the celebrity. The association need not always be explicit. In *Cher v. Forum International, Ltd.*,[39] the singer won a substantial judgment on the basis of an interview article that was promoted as her personal endorsement of the magazine. The article, developed by a freelancer, was originally planned for *Us* magazine. Cher, who had stipulated before granting the interview that she wanted to approve any additional uses of the material, was unhappy with the way the interview had gone and requested the editors of *Us* not to use it. When the editors agreed, the freelancer then sold copies of the tape-recorded interview to *Forum* and to a supermarket tabloid, *The Star*.

Forum quickly used the tape to prepare a cover story about Cher and promoted the article with advertising that said, "There are certain things that Cher won't tell *People* and would never tell *Us*."[40] The copy also urged audiences to "join Cher and *Forum's* hundreds of thousands of other adventurous readers today."[41] When Cher sued, the court agreed with her that the advertising copy could reasonably be interpreted as being Cher's personal endorsement of the magazine and thus a violation of her right of publicity.

Advertisers and other commercial speakers may violate a celebrity's right of publicity in ways other than unauthorized use of a name or likeness. A number of court decisions have held commercial speakers liable for damages in connection with the unauthorized use of a particular expression associated with the celebrity, a vocal sound-alike, a character created by the celebrity or even, in *Motschenbacher v. R.J. Reynolds Tobacco Co.*,[42] for unauthorized altering of the unusual decorations used by the owner of a racing car. The opinion noted:

> plaintiff [Lothar Motschenbacher] has consistently "individualized" his [racing] cars to set them apart from those of other drivers and to make them more readily identifiable as his own. Since 1966, each of his cars has displayed a distinctive narrow white pinstripe appearing on no other car. This decoration has adorned the leading edges of the cars' bodies, which have uniformly been solid red. In addition, the white background for his racing number "11" has always been oval, in contrast to the circular background of all other cars.[43]

When these were altered slightly, and the cigarette brand name "Winston" was added to the markings of the car, the court found the driver's right of publicity had been violated.

In *Carson v. Here's Johnny Portable Toilets*,[44] the talk show host and comedian Johnny Carson objected to the phrase, "Here's Johnny!" as the name for a line of portable restrooms. Carson, who was not asking for monetary damages but instead to have the company adopt another name for its product, argued that he had been introduced for many years to the national television audience of the NBC "Tonight Show" with that phrase and that the public associated it with him. Additionally, Carson owned stock in a line of clothing that used "Here's Johnny!" in its advertising.

The manufacturer of the "Here's Johnny!" portable restrooms countered with the argument that "john" and "johnny" had been used by the public for years to describe restroom facilities but admitted that he did indeed have Carson in mind when he named his business. In advertising the product, he referred to his company as "The World's Foremost Commodian." The majority of a divided court sided with Carson, holding that he had been unfairly capitalized upon—that the phrase had indeed become a part of his identity—and thus he should be permitted to control its use.

Another court determined that unique characters developed by actors can be protected—in this case the characters of Groucho, Chico and Harpo, creations of the Marx Brothers.[45] But the mere portrayal of a role does not give the actor publicity rights to it, as the heirs of Bela Lugosi learned when they attempted to control the character of Count Dracula that Lugosi played in a famous early 1930s movie. Tartly, the court noted that Lugosi did not have exclusive rights to Dracula any more than the actor Charlton Heston might have to Moses, a part he played in *The Ten Commandments*.[46] But note, however, that by the same token, depicting either Dracula or Moses as actually resembling either the actors Lugosi or Heston could result in a different outcome.

Bert Lahr, the comedian and film actor, and Bette Midler, the singer, among others, have been able to recover damages (in Ms. Midler's case, $400,000) for unauthorized imitations of their voices. Lahr, who played the part of the Cowardly Lion in the well-known film version of *The Wizard of Oz*, sued over an imitation of his voice in an advertisement. The court agreed with the actor, noting that the advertisement "had greater value because its audience believed it was listening to [Lahr]."[47]

In Midler's case, the advertising agency Young & Rubicam invited her to sing one of her hit recordings ("Do You Want to Dance?") in commercials for the Ford Motor Company. When she declined, the agency hired one of her former backup singers to imitate her voice, which she did, highly successfully. Midler sued, and the federal court found in her favor, commenting that "the human voice is one of the most palpable ways identity is manifested," and the unauthorized imitation was a violation of her right of publicity.[48] In a later case, a federal jury in Los Angeles found that a sound-alike commercial violated the publicity rights of Tom Waits and awarded the singer nearly $2.5 million in damages.[49]

There are those who would argue that in these and other decisions, the right of publicity, still in its relative youth, has already been stretched to the point that it could muzzle certain aspects of freedom of expression where advertising and promotion are concerned. Legal scholar Christopher Pesce warns, "Allowing celebrities to recover in cases where advertisers loosely imitate limited aspects of their 'personae' protects interests unworthy of the status of property, chills creative endeavor, and creates an unpredictable standard of recovery."[50]

Richard Kurnit, whose Manhattan law firm represents a number of publishers and advertising agencies, put it this way:

> The idea that entertainment properties are akin to explosives—if you hit someone you are strictly liable—is particularly frightening when you consider that publicity claims result in uncontrollable damage awards for emotional distress and punitive damages at the whim of a jury.[51]

A First Amendment Threat?

Beyond the hazards posed by the right of publicity to creative people in the advertising and public relations fields, some First Amendment concerns have emerged as well. As noted above, a traditional defense in privacy cases—and, by extension, cases involving the right of publicity—has been newsworthiness. But a bizarre case, *Zacchini v. Scripps-Howard Broadcasting*,[52] blurred the distinction between commercial and noncommercial use and, in effect, changed the nature of misappropriation law.

Hugo Zacchini, billed as "the human cannonball," earned his living as an entertainer by allowing himself to be blasted from a huge cannon into a safety net some 200 feet away. His act, in its entirety, took only a few seconds. One evening, as Zacchini was about to perform in the Cleveland area, a TV news crew showed up and, over his protests, filmed the act (all 15 seconds of it) and showed the segment on the late-evening news. Zacchini sued, claiming this showing violated his right of publicity and cost him thousands of dollars in lost revenue. Once his entire act had been shown on television, he argued, few people would be willing to pay money to watch him perform in person.

The TV station, for its part, argued that Zacchini's act had legitimate news value and that newscasts were securely protected by the First Amendment. Also, the station contended, the Zacchini segment represented only a tiny fraction of the newscast, and the station did not realize any revenue, directly or indirectly, from reporting this particular news story. The Supreme

Court of the United States ultimately agreed, but in a tortured 5-4 decision, sided with Zacchini anyway. In Justice White's opinion:

> The broadcast of petitioner's [Zacchini's] entire performance, unlike the unauthorized use of another's name for purposes of trade or the incidental use of a name or picture by the press, goes to the heart of petitioner's ability to earn a living as an entertainer. Thus in this case, Ohio has recognized what may be the strongest case for a "right of publicity"—involving not the appropriation of an entertainer's reputation to enhance the attractiveness of a commercial product, but the appropriation of the very activity by which the entertainer acquired the reputation in the first place.[53]

The *Zacchini* decision, the first ruling ever by the Supreme Court of the United States in this sector of the law, could lead to further confusion in determining what is commercial exploitation and what is simply news. Some months after *Zacchini*, the ABC television network began to prepare a docudrama on the life of the celebrated actress Elizabeth Taylor. Taylor objected on the grounds that her life story was her own and that she might one day write her autobiography. A movie about her life now, she contended, might take away income that should be hers. Rather than risk a court suit, ABC decided to shelve the project.[54]

Because of the zany facts of the *Zacchini* case—few celebrities will find their total act being filmed for a newscast—it is unlikely that the case will have much in the way of direct influence on the rapidly emerging law of publicity. To the extent that it represents a judicial propensity to protect a celebrity's right of publicity, however, *Zacchini* might well be regarded as an important case.

The Most Likely Tort?

The dynamic growth of advertising, public relations and the mass media industry in recent years has given the concepts of misappropriation and right of publicity new status in the law of invasion of privacy. For example, mass media coverage, advertising, marketing campaigns, public relations messages and social media posts have helped create thousands of celebrities, although many of them, obviously, may enjoy only a few fleeting moments of fame. (Think early-round contestants on talent competition-shows, someone doing something regrettable on a social media site that receives millions of views, or the here-today, gone-tomorrow notoriety of reality television participants whose dinner choices no longer command attention.) No matter how brief, during their time in the spotlight, they understandably wish for some authority to protect their "professional personalities" from unauthorized exploitation.

To an ever-increasing degree, the courts seem inclined to grant that protection to them as well as to those plaintiffs who can legitimately demonstrate mental anguish as a result of defendants taking their name or likeness. The number of cases of misappropriation, and especially the right of publicity, is on the increase, and the forecast is for more of the same. Simply put, the plaintiffs seem to be winning the cases they should win while losing those that involve more novel applications of privacy law.

For example, courts have found for the plaintiffs in cases involving the unconsented-to use of plaintiffs name or likeness (a) on a sex-oriented website that attributed a fictitious personal profile to the complainant;[55] (b) for continued use of a chef's name to promote a catering business after the chef had left the organization's employment;[56] (c) when an employer argued it maintained the rights to the names of former hosts of a radio program;[57] and (d) in a suit by a former NFL star who no longer wished to have his name attached to a trophy awarded by a sports group to the best college linebacker in the country.[58]

On the other hand, courts have found for the defendants in cases where:

A.   The plaintiff was not considered to be a public figure (despite the plaintiff's rather exalted personal opinion to the contrary).[59]

B.   A rock band complained that the defendant's inclusion of a song attributed to them in a video game violated their rights of publicity.[60]

C.   The Mars candy company displayed a giant M&M dressed (or rather undressed) like the plaintiff who has achieved some local celebrity status for his "Naked Cowboy" character (we don't make these up).[61]

In a much-watched case, *C.B.C. Distribution and Marketing, Inc. v. Major League Baseball Advanced Media, L.P.*,[62] Major League Baseball lost its attempt to limit the use of player names and stats by a fantasy baseball league through a misappropriation claim because, the courts said, the information was readily available in the news media and prohibiting its use by the defendant, even for financial gain, would be in violation of the defendant's First Amendment rights. More recent cases pushing the new media envelope include the football Hall of Famer Jim Brown[63] who sued the NFL claiming a computer-game avatar referred to him because it "played" the same position as Brown in his playing days, and numerous individuals suing for misappropriation because they appeared in the "Borat"[64] movies.

Conclusion

We have devoted an entire chapter to misappropriation and the right of publicity because this is the privacy tort most likely to trip up unwary advertising and public relations professionals. Clearly, the safest course of action for wise and prudent practitioners is to be sure that consent, either voluntarily given or purchased, has been obtained before using anyone's name, likeness or persona for any advertising or public relations purposes.

Notes

1.   Samuel Warren & Louis Brandeis, *The Right to Privacy*, 4 Harv. L. Rev. 193 (1890). As later scholarship has noted, Warren's daughter was only 7 years old at the time. In *Demystifying a Landmark Citation*, 13 Suffolk U.L. Rev. 875, Professor Jerome Barron suggests that Warren was in fact angry at press criticism of his father-in-law, Thomas Bayard, Sr., who had been a U.S. Senator and a member of President Grover Cleveland's cabinet.

2.   Jennifer E. Rothman, The Right of Publicity: Privacy Reimagined for a Public World (Harvard University Press, Cambridge, MA 2018).

3.   Roberson v. Rochester Folding Box Co., 171 N.Y. 538, 556 (1902).

4.   *Id.*

5.   N.Y. CLS Civ. R. §§50–51.

6.   Pavesich v. New England Life Ins. Co., 50 S.E. 68, 79 (1905).

7.   State v. Hinkle, 131 Wash. 86, 93 (1924).

8.   American Law Institute, Restatement of the Law of Torts (2nd ed.), Sec. 652d (American Law Institute Publishers, St. Paul, MN 1975).

9.   Quoted in an excellent discussion of privacy in George C. Christie & James E. Meeks, Cases and Materials on the Law of Torts (Gale Cengage, Farmington Hills, MI 1990) at 1088ff.

10. Shields v. Gross, 563 F. Supp. 1253 (D.N.Y. 1983).

11. McAndrews v. Roy, 131 So. 2d 256 (La. Ct. App., 1961).

12. Michael Heron, Stock Photography Handbook (American Society of Media Photographers, 2nd ed. 1990), at 123-139.

13. *Id.* at 127.

14. Namath v. Sports Illustrated, 48 A.D.2d 487 (N.Y. App. Div. 1975).

15. Comedy III Productions, Inc. v. Gary Saderup, Inc., 25 Cal. 4th 387 (2001).

16. *Id.* at 407.

17. ETW Corp. v. Jireh Publ'g, Inc., 332 F.3d 915 (6th Cir. 2003).

18. Doe v. McFarlane, 207 S.W.3d 52 (Mo. App. E.D. 2006).

19. Allen v. National Video, Inc., 610 F. Supp. 612 (S.D.N.Y. 1985).

20. Jones v. Herald Post Co., 18 S.W.2d 972, 973 (Ky. 1929).

21. Restatement (Second) of Torts, §652D.

22. Mendonsa v. Time Inc., 678 F. Supp. 967 (D.R.I. 1988).

23. Pavesich v. New England Life Ins. Co., 50 S.E. at 69.

24. *Id.* at 74.

25. Christopher Pesce, *The Likeness Monster: Should the Right of Publicity Protect Against Imitation?*, 65 N.Y.U. L. Rev. 782, 782 (1990).

26. Rothman, The Right of Publicity, 87.

27. Haelan Laboratories v. Topps Chewing Gum, 202 F.2d 866 (2d Cir. 1953); *cert. denied,* 346 U.S. 816 (1953).

28. *Id.* at 868.

29. There is some dispute on this point. William L. Prosser, Handbook of the Law of Torts (West Publishing Company, Eagan, MN, 4th ed. 1971), found slim evidence to suggest the possibility of descendability (a 1945 Arizona case, Reed v. Real Detective Pub. Co., 63 Ariz. 294), but as he noted, "there is no common law right of action for a publication concerning one who is already dead."

30. Martin Luther King, Jr., Center for Social Change, Inc. v. American Heritage Products, Inc., 250 Ga. 135 (1982).

31. Hirsch v. S. C. Johnson & Son, 90 Wis. 2d 379 (1979).

32. Ali v. Playgirl, 447 F. Supp. 723 (S.D.N.Y. 1978).

33. Lanham Act (15 U.S.C. §1051-1127).

34. Allen v. National Video, Inc., 610 F. Supp. 612 (S.D.N.Y. 1985).

35. *Id.* at 617.

36. Onassis v. Christian Dior-New York, Inc., 122 Misc. 2d 603 (NY Misc., 1984).

37. *Id.* at 605.

38. *Id.* at 612.

39. Cher v. Forum International, 692 F.2d 634 (9th Cir. 1982).

40. *Id.* at 638.

41. *Id.* at 639.

42. The Motschenbacher v. R.J. Reynolds Tobacco Co., 498 F.2d 821 (9th Cir. 1974).

43. *Id.* at 822.

44. Carson v. Here's Johnny Portable Toilets, 698 F.2d 831 (6th Cir. 1983).

45. Groucho Marx Prods., Inc. v. Day & Night Co., 523 F. Supp. 485, 491 (S.D.N.Y. 1981).

46. Lugosi v. Universal Pictures, 25 Cal. 3rd 813 (1979), as reported by Plevan & Siroky, Advertising Compliance Handbook, at 557.

47. Lahr v. Adell Chemical Co., 300 F.2d 256 (1st Cir. 1962).

48. Midler v. Ford Motor Co., 849 F.2d 460 (9th Cir. 1988).

49. Paul Feldman, *Tom Waits Wins $2 ½ Million in Voice-Theft Suit*, L.A. Times, May 9, 1990, Metro; Part-B, Metro Desk.

50. Pesce, *Likeness Monster, supra* note 25, at 818.

51. Richard Kurnit, *Right of Publicity*, Ent. & Sport Law. 4, 3 (Winter/Spring 1986), at 15.
52. Zacchini v. Scripps-Howard Broadcasting Co., 433 U.S. 562 (1977).
53. *Id.* at 576.
54. Tamar Lewin, *Whose Life Is It, Anyway? It's Hard to Tell*, N.Y. Times, Nov. 21, 1982; Ralph L. Holsinger, Media Law (McGraw-Hill, New York c.1991) at 231.
55. Doe v. Friendfinder Network, Inc., 540 F. Supp. 2d 288 (D.N.H. 2008).
56. Lewis v. Marriot Int'l, 527 F. Supp. 2d 422 (E.D. Pa., Dec. 20, 2007).
57. Amigo Broad. v. Spanish Broad. Sys., Inc., 521 F.3d 472 (5th Cir. 2008).
58. Butkus v. Downtown Athletic Club of Orlando, Inc., 2008 W.L. 2485524 (C.D. Cal., March 31, 2008).
59. Ji v. Bose Corp., 526 F. Supp. 2d 349 (D. Mass. 2008).
60. The Romantics v. Activision Publishing Inc., 532 F. Supp. 2d 884 (E.D. Mich. 2008).
61. Burck v. Mars, Inc. et al., 2008 W.L. 2557427 (S.D.N.Y. 2008).
62. C.B.C. Distribution & Marketing, Inc. v. Major League Baseball Advanced Media, L.P., 505 F.3d 818 (8th Cir. 2007).
63. Katie Thomas, *Retired NFL Player Jim Brown Loses Lawsuit Against Video Game Publisher*, N.Y. Times, Sept. 29, 2009.
64. Jay Reeves, *Borat Wins Court Case Against Etiquette Teacher*, Huffington Post, Jan. 19, 2008.

7 Copyright

Copyright, trademarks and patents are typically grouped into an area of the law known as *intellectual property*. Because copyright is an area of the law that has a substantial impact on advertising and public relations, this chapter deals exclusively with copyright law. The next chapter focuses on trademarks and includes a brief discussion of patents.

Historical Background

American copyright law can be traced back to England and, specifically, the Statute of Anne[1] passed by Parliament in 1710 to recognize and protect the rights of authors. From the 1400s on, English printers and publishers were concerned about preventing competitors from pirating their works. These efforts culminated with the Act of Parliament that recognized the right of authors to ownership of their original works. Of interest, however, for subsequent American copyright law, the Act recognized such rights for only a limited amount of time (generally 14 years, with the possibility of renewal for an additional 14 years).

Because British law, including the law of copyright, formed the basis of American colonial law, it is not surprising that when the framers of the United States Constitution drafted that document, they included authority for federal copyright law in Article I, Section 8. This section gives Congress authority "To Promote the Progress of Science and Useful Arts, by securing for limited Times to Authors and Inventors the exclusive Right to their respective Writings and Discoveries."[2] This provision effectively grants a limited monopoly to "Authors" that enables them to profit from their "Writings" as an inducement for them to contribute to the "Useful Arts." Today, copyright protection by extension applies not only to authors, but to artists, photographers and others who produce original creative works ("original works of authorship"). Exclusive federal jurisdiction over copyrights (and patents) is justified under both the Supremacy Clause (Article VI) and the Commerce Clause (Article I, Section 8) of the Constitution.

Congress enacted the first federal copyright statute in 1790, one year after the Constitution was ratified and a year before the Bill of Rights took effect. The 19th century brought many revisions to the federal copyright scheme embodied in numerous revisions of the statute. What developed was a two-tiered system, with the federal statute protecting mainly published works and state common law governing unpublished works.

That system continued into the 20th century with the revised 1909 law, which itself was revised on numerous occasions over the next six decades to accommodate new technologies and philosophies about what should be protected. In 1909, for example, radio had reached only an experimental stage. The Internet, social media, computers, photocopiers, CDs, DVDs,

Figure 7.1 Copyright symbol
Credit line: notbad/Shutterstock.com

satellites and even television were yet to be created. Under the 1909 law and its many revisions, copyright infringement was certainly possible, and creators definitely needed protection, but it was much more difficult than it is today to make unauthorized use of a person's creative work.

That all changed when, pushed by technological innovations, the Copyright Act of 1976 took effect on January 1, 1978, and the pieces of what was once a colossal mess were assembled into some long-needed order. The 1976 Act, which is the basis for copyright protection today, brought significant changes; even the premises of the old and new statutes were at odds. Unlike previous copyright laws, including the 1909 law, the new law was clearly designed to be an author-oriented statute offering broad and extensive protection to the creators of original works of authorship. Implementation of the copyright law and the copyright registration process is the responsibility of the United States Copyright Office, a part of the Library of Congress in Washington, D.C.

Creation of Copyright

Have you ever wondered, "How can I copyright my great idea?" The "shocking" answer is: "Sorry. You can't copyright an idea; you can only copyright your expression of that idea."

A work can be copyrighted only if it exists outside the mind of the creator; under the current copyright statute, that occurs "when it is fixed in a copy or phonorecord for the first time."[3] Once a work is fixed in a tangible medium, the protection begins. When a work is developed over time, the portion that is fixed at a particular time is considered the work at that time. For instance, the copyrighted portion of this book at the time these words are being composed on the computer is everything written thus far to the end of this sentence. If a work is prepared in different versions, each version is a separate work for purposes of copyright. The third edition of this book is considered a separate work from the second edition and so on.

Probably the most important difference between the old and new copyright statutes is the point at which copyright protection begins. Under the 1909 federal statute, federal copyright protection generally could not be invoked until a work had been published along with notice of copyright. There were a few exceptions to this rule, but unpublished works were basically protected only under state law, or what was known as *common law copyright*. Common law copyright certainly had some advantages, including perpetual protection for unpublished works, but with each state having its own common law, there was little uniformity.

The 1976 Copyright Law solved this problem: copyright exists automatically "in original works of authorship fixed in any tangible medium of expression, now known or later developed, from which they can be perceived, reproduced, or otherwise communicated, either directly or with the aid of a machine or device."[4] No registration is necessary. No publication is required.

Not even a copyright notice has to be placed on the work for it to be copyrighted. The copyright exists automatically upon creation.

This is one of the most misunderstood aspects of copyright by advertising and public relations professionals who wish to make use of the creative works of others—a work is copyrighted the very second it is created in a tangible medium. Nothing could be simpler. No hocus-pocus, smoke and mirrors or other magic. Not even a government form to complete.

"Fixing" an Idea

When does an idea become a work actually fixed in a medium? According to Section 101:

> A work is "fixed" in a tangible medium of expression when its embodiment in a copy or phonorecord, by or under authority of the author, is sufficiently permanent or stable to permit it to be perceived, reproduced, or otherwise communicated for a period of more than transitory duration. A work consisting of sounds, images, or both, that are being transmitted, is "fixed" for purposes of this title if a fixation of the work is being made simultaneously with its transmission.[5]

Suppose an enterprising skywriter composes a love poem in the sky to her fiancé during halftime of the Super Bowl. A few miles away, another romantic scribbles in the ocean sand his cartoon sketch of his spouse. Can both original works of authorship be copyrighted? Each faces a major obstacle—it is not "fixed" in a tangible medium of expression. Almost as soon as the love poem is created in the sky, it literally evaporates into thin air. Its transitory nature prevents it from being "fixed" for purposes of copyright. The same holds true for the cartoon in the sand when it is washed away by the tide.

How does one "fix" these creative efforts? An easy way is to put them on a piece of paper or perhaps photograph them on a smartphone before they fade. But won't paper or even digital photos eventually deteriorate or disappear? Fixation does not require permanency; only that the medium be sufficiently permanent or stable to allow it to be perceived, copied or otherwise communicated for more than a transitory duration.

Similar Ideas

What if two individuals have a similar idea and both express it in tangible terms? Can the one who first fixes the idea in a creative work prevent the other from profiting from his or her later efforts if the expression is the same, but the creative efforts appear to be independent of each other?

In *Hoehling v. Universal City Studios, Inc.*,[6] a federal appellate court ruled that Universal had not infringed on the copyright of A. A. Hoehling's book, *Who Destroyed the Hindenburg?*, in a movie about the explosion of the German dirigible at Lakehurst, New Jersey, in 1937. The film was based on a book by Michael Mooney published in 1972, 10 years after Hoehling's work. Both books theorized that Eric Spehl, a disgruntled crew member who was among the 36 people killed in the disaster, had planted a bomb in one of the gas cells. Although the 1975 movie, which was a fictionalized account of the event, used a pseudonym for Spehl, its thesis about the cause of the tragedy was similar to that in Hoehling's book. (Investigators concluded that the airship blew up after static electricity ignited the hydrogen fuel, but speculation has always abounded about whether this was the actual cause.)

Figure 7.2 The German passenger airship Hindenburg seconds after catching fire, May 6, 1937. In *Hoehling v. Universal City Studios, Inc.*, a federal appellate court ruled that Universal had not infringed on the copyright of A. A. Hoehling's book, *Who Destroyed the Hindenburg?*, in a movie about the explosion of the German dirigible at Lakehurst, New Jersey, in 1937. The film was based on a book by Michael Mooney published in 1972, 10 years after Hoehling's work.

Credit line: Everett Historical/Shutterstock.com

A federal district court judge issued a summary judgment in favor of the defendant, Universal City Studios, and a federal circuit court of appeals upheld the decision. According to the appeals court:

> The protection afforded the copyright holder has never extended to history, be it documentary fact or explanatory hypothesis. The rationale for this doctrine is that the cause of knowledge is best served when history is the common property of all, and each generation remains free to draw upon the discoveries and insights of the past.[7]

Hoehling claimed there were other similarities, including random duplication of phrases and the chronology of the story, but the court saw no problem with such overlap. The U.S. Supreme Court denied certiorari in the case.[8]

Protected Works

Under Section 102, copyright protection extends to "original works of authorship fixed in any tangible medium of expression, now known or later developed, from which they can be perceived, reproduced, or otherwise communicated, either directly or with the aid of a machine or device."[9] This section enumerates eight categories under works of authorship: (1) literary works;

(2) musical works, including any accompanying words; (3) dramatic works, including any accompanying music; (4) pantomimes and choreographic works; (5) pictorial, graphic and sculptural works; (6) motion pictures and other audiovisual works; (7) sound recordings; and (8) architectural works.[10]

Section 102(b) notes that copyright protection does not extend to "any idea, procedure, process, system, method of operation, concept, principle, or discovery, regardless of the form in which it is described, explained, illustrated, or embodied in such work."[11] Some of these items may enjoy protection as trademarks, trade secrets or patents, but they cannot be copyrighted even though works in which they appear can be copyrighted.

In the case of compilations or derivative works, Section 103 specifies that only the material contributed by the author of a compilation or derivative work is granted new copyright protection; any preexisting material used in the derivative work or compilation does not gain additional protection, but maintains the same protection it had originally. In other words, you cannot expand the protection a work originally was granted by using it in another work such as a derivative work or compilation.

Section 101, which contains definitions of terms in the statute, defines a *compilation* as: "A work formed by the collection and assembling of preexisting materials or of data that are selected, coordinated, or arranged in such a way that the resulting work as a whole constitutes an original work of authorship."[12] Compilations also include *collective works*, defined as: "A work, such as a periodical issue, anthology, or encyclopedia, in which a number of contributions, constituting separate and independent works in themselves, are assembled into a collective whole."[13]

A *derivative work* is defined as:

> A work based upon one or more preexisting works, such as a translation, musical arrangement, dramatization, fictionalization, motion picture version, sound recording, art reproduction, abridgment, condensation, or any other form in which a work may be recast, transformed, or adapted. A work consisting of editorial revisions, annotations, elaborations, or other modifications, which, as a whole, represent an original work of authorship, is a "derivative work."[14]

Unprotected Works

People unfamiliar with copyright law wrongly assume that any creative work can be protected by copyright. Although the 1976 statute is broad, certain types of works do not fall within its protection. The most obvious example is a work that has not been fixed in a tangible medium. But, as discussed above, the Act also excludes "any idea, procedure, process, system, method of operation, concept, principle, or discovery."[15] Note, however, that although such works have no protection in and of themselves, *expressions* of them can be copyrighted. For example, a university professor who writes a textbook based on his ideas about advertising and public relations law cannot protect his ideas per se, but the expression of those ideas—a book—is copyrighted the moment it is created and put in a tangible medium.

Titles (e.g., "The Voice" and "The Big Bang Theory"), names (e.g., Harry Potter and Nemo), short phrases (e.g., "Rub some dirt on it" and "If no pulse, start CPR"), slogans (e.g., "A Diamond is Forever" and "They're GR-R-R-reat"), familiar symbols and designs (e.g., the Nike "swoosh") and mere listings of ingredients and contents cannot be copyrighted, although these may enjoy other forms of legal protection, such as trademark protection. Four more categories of works that lack copyright protection include works by the U.S. Government, works of common information, works in the public domain and works consisting of basic facts.

Government Works

The Copyright Act of 1976 generally prohibits the federal government from copyrighting works it creates. The major exception to this rule is that the government can acquire copyright for works it did not create. For example, U.S. postage stamp designs are copyrighted, as witnessed by the copyright notice in the margins of sheets and booklets, despite the fact that the U.S. Postal Service is a semiautonomous federal agency.

Works of Common Information

Like works of the U.S. Government, works consisting wholly of common information having no original authorship such as standard calendars, weight and measure charts, rulers, etc. cannot be copyrighted. Note, however, that works that contain such information can be copyrighted even though the information cannot be. As an illustration, a calendar with pictures of herbs for each month could be copyrighted, but the copyright would extend only to the photographs and any other original work on the calendar, not the standard calendar itself.

Works in the Public Domain

Under the 1909 law, copyright protection lasted for a maximum of two terms of 28 years each for a total of 56 years. Works copyrighted before changes made by the 1976 law took effect had the period of protection extended, but any work that was copyrighted prior to 1903 and any work whose copyright was not timely renewed no longer have protection. Thus, some works copyrighted as late as 1949 have gone into the public domain because no copyright renewal application was filed. Works that had already gone in the public domain by January 1, 1978, when the 1976 copyright law took effect, continued in the public domain. As discussed later in this chapter under "Copyright Duration," the 1976 Copyright Act was amended in 1998 by the Sonny Bono Copyright Term Extension Act (CTEA) to extend protection for most author-identified works to the lifetime of the author plus 70 years and for what are known as "work made for hire" works and anonymous or pseudonymous works to 120 years from creation or 95 years from publication, whichever is shorter.

Once a work becomes public domain property, no royalties have to be paid and no permission needs to be sought from any owner before use.

Facts

Facts alone are not eligible for copyright protection. The *expression* of facts, however, does enjoy protection. Thus, although news cannot be copyrighted, newscasts can be.

In *Miller v. Universal City Studios*,[16] a federal court of appeals overturned a district court decision that Universal had infringed the copyright of Gene Miller, a Pulitzer Prize-winning reporter for the *Miami Herald*, in a book entitled *83 Hours 'Til Dawn*. The nonfiction work focused on a young woman named Barbara Mackle who was rescued after being kidnapped and buried underground for five days in a box in which she could have survived for no more than a week. Markle's kidnapper, 23-year-old Gary Steven Krist, was convicted and sentenced to life in prison in 1969,

Figure 7.3 Works consisting wholly of common information having no original authorship, such as standard calendars, cannot be copyrighted. Works that contain such information can be copyrighted even though the information cannot be. A calendar with pictures of herbs for each month could be copyrighted, but the copyright extends only to the photographs and any other original work on the calendar, not the standard calendar itself.

but he was released on parole in 1979. His female accomplice was convicted and sentenced to seven years in prison and then paroled after serving four years. She was deported to her native Honduras. In 2006 Krist and his stepson were arrested and pleaded guilty to drug smuggling. Krist was sentenced to more than five years in jail.[17] After his release, Krist eventually attended medical school and became a licensed physician in Indiana in 2001.[18]

The trial court in *Miller* was impressed by the approximately 2,500 hours that the author said he had spent researching and writing the book:

> To this court it doesn't square with reason or common sense to believe that Gene Miller would have undertaken the research required ... if the author thought that upon completion of the book a movie producer or television network could simply come along and take the profits of the books and his research from him.[19]

Although there were several similarities between Miller's book and the script for Universal's docudrama, *The Longest Night*, including some of the same factual errors, the appellate court ordered a new trial on the ground that "the case was presented and argued to the jury on a false premise: that the labor of research by an author [unearthing the facts in the case] is protected by copyright."[20]

In 1991, the Supreme Court of the United States attempted to clarify the concept of "originality," which is closely linked to the facts-versus-compilation-of-facts distinction. In *Feist Publications, Inc. v. Rural Telephone Service Co.*,[21] the Court unanimously held that the white pages of a telephone directory could not be copyrighted. The case involved a telephone book publisher that used the names and telephone numbers from a competing telephone company's directory to compile its own areawide telephone directories. The Court noted that, although the telephone company could claim copyright ownership in its directory as a whole, it could not prevent a competitor from using the elements of its compilation of names, towns and phone numbers to create the competitor's own directory. Facts are not copyrightable, the justices said, but the compilations of facts can generally be copyrighted.

The decision stressed that hard work or "sweat of the brow" is not enough; there must be originality of creative expression, which the Court characterized as the *sine qua non* of copyright. However, it should be noted that the *amount* of originality is not the test. "To be sure, the requisite level of creativity is extremely low; [but] even a slight amount will suffice,"[22] Justice O'Connor wrote for the Court.

Copyright Ownership and Transfer

There is a world of difference between the treatment of copyright ownership under the 1909 statute and coexisting common law versus the treatment under the current Copyright Act of 1976 and the Sonny Bono Copyright Term Extension Act of 1998 (discussed later in this chapter). Under the old law, when an author, artist or other creator sold his or her copyright, the presumption was that all rights had been transferred unless rights were specifically reserved by the creator, usually in writing. For instance, an artist who sold his or her original painting to someone effectively transferred copyright ownership as well because the common law recognized that the sale of certain types of creative works invoked transfer of the copyright to the purchaser.

The presumption now works in the opposite direction. None of the exclusive rights (discussed later in this chapter), nor any subdivision of those rights, are legally transferred in the sale of a

Figure 7.4 In 1991, the Supreme Court of the United States attempted to clarify the concept of "originality" in copyright law. In *Feist Publications, Inc. v. Rural Telephone Service Co.*, the Court unanimously held that the white pages of a telephone directory could not be copyrighted. The Court noted that, although the telephone company could claim copyright ownership in its directory as a whole, it could not prevent a competitor from using the elements of its compilation of names, towns and phone numbers to create the competitor's own directory. Justice Sandra Day O'Connor, shown here visiting Jamestown Settlement, Virginia, in 2007, wrote the opinion.

Credit line: Joseph Sohn/Shutterstock.com

copyrighted work unless the transfer is in writing and signed by the original copyright owner or the owner's legal representative.

Under the current statute, the copyright is immediately vested in the original creator/author. If more than one creator (i.e., there is joint authorship), the copyright belongs to all of them. The creator or creators can, of course, transfer their rights, but the transfer of any exclusive rights must be in writing.

Oral agreements are sufficient for the transfer of nonexclusive rights. For example, a free-lance artist could have a valid oral agreement with an advertising agency to create a series of drawings to be used in commercials for a life insurance company. At the same time, he or she could have an agreement with a magazine to do similar illustrations for a feature story. However, if the artist chose to transfer (a) an exclusive right, such as the sole right to reproduce the drawings; (b) a subdivided right, such as the right to reproduce the drawings in commercials; or (c) the right to produce a derivative work, such as a training video based on the drawings, such a transfer would need to be in writing to be binding. (See Appendix D for Sample Copyright Agreements.)

Is copyright ownership restricted to works created by humans? In late 2014 the U.S. Copyright Office included in its *Compendium of U.S. Copyright Office Practices*, Third Edition, a clarification that

> only works created by a human can be copyrighted under United States law, which excludes photographs and artwork created by animals or by machines without human intervention. ... Because copyright law is limited to "original intellectual conceptions of the author," the office will refuse to register a claim if it determines that a human being did not create the work. The Office will not register works produced by nature, animals, or plants.[23]

The clarification was in response to a series of selfies taken by a monkey that eventually led to a widely publicized three-year legal battle over whether animals (through an agent) could claim copyright protection and thus file infringement suits under U.S. Copyright law for works they created. The works at issue were created in 2012 by a 6-year-old, black-haired crested Indonesian macaque named Naruto who snapped a series of photos with an unattended camera owned and set up by wildlife photographer David John Slater. When Slater asserted copyright ownership of the photos after he published them in a book and they were subsequently published online without his permission, People for the Ethical Treatment of Animals (PETA) sued Slater in U.S. District Court in 2015, claiming Naruto was the proper copyright owner. PETA filed suit as a "next friend" of the macaque. Ultimately, a three-judge panel of the Ninth Circuit U.S. Court of Appeals unanimously upheld a lower court decision, ruling that the Copyright Act of 1976 did not specifically authorize a right of nonhuman animals to sue for copyright infringement. The panel also granted the defendant's request for attorney fees.[24]

Ownership of Compilations and Derivative Works

Ownership in compilations and derivative works becomes more complicated. Remember that the key differences between a compilation and a derivative work are that (a) a compilation consists of pulling together separate works or pieces of works already created, whereas a derivative work can trace its origins to one previous work, and (b) the key creative element in a compilation is the way in which the preexisting works are compiled to create the whole (i.e., the new work), whereas the creative dimensions of a derivative work are basically independent of the previous work.

An anthology of poems by Robert Frost, which consists of poems previously published on their own, is an illustration of a compilation that is also a collective work. With certain exceptions, the owner—who is usually the creator—of an original work of authorship has exclusive rights that only he or she can exercise or authorize others to exercise. Thus the poet would normally own the copyright in his works, absent his assigning the rights to another party (his publisher, for example). If Frost did make such an assignment with five of his poems contained in the compilation, there would be three copyright holders in the work—the poet for most of the poems, the publisher for the five poems earlier obtained from Frost and the compiler of the final book, *Collected Works of Robert Frost*, for the ways the poems are arranged in the book, the typeface used in the printing of the work, any original commentary, etc.

Prudent advertising and public relations professionals should recognize that in any one collective work like a movie or music recording, there may be a number of copyright owners. In the film, the director, the writer of the screenplay, the film editor and the creator of the original musical score may all have independent copyrights in the various elements that make up the finished product. Likewise in the music recording, the composer, lyricist and music arranger may all have separate ownership interests that need to be satisfied before the recording may be used.

The novel *Gone with the Wind* and its subsequent history provide an example of ownership of a derivative work. Margaret Mitchell's heirs, who inherited the rights to her novel after she was killed by an auto in 1949, nixed any sequels to the enormously popular book and movie for more than four decades. A series of sequels, including books and movies, probably would have brought in millions of dollars in royalties, but *Gone with the Wind* devotees, dying to learn the fate of Rhett and Scarlett, had to wait until 1991 when agents representing the estate finally chose Alexandra Ripley to write *Scarlett: Tomorrow Is Another Day*. The 768-page sequel was published simultaneously in 40 countries, with excerpts appearing a month earlier in *Life* magazine. The television movie followed in 1994—all six hours plus commercials.

Joint Authorship

Section 101 of the Copyright Act defines a *joint work* as "a work prepared by two or more authors with the intention that their contributions be merged into inseparable or independent parts of a unitary whole."[25] Unless there is a written agreement stating otherwise, joint authors are considered co-owners of the copyright in a work. According to Section 201(a), joint authorship, where present and intended, is advantageous to the hiring party because a joint author has an undivided interest in the work and can, therefore, make use of the work without seeking permission from the other joint owner or owners unless all the owners expressly agree in writing how the copyright ownership in the work is to be divided. Section 201(a) has been interpreted, however, to mean that one who hires a freelancer may not claim joint authorship based solely on their input into the direction of and their supervision of the production of a copyrighted work.

Works Made for Hire

An exception to the rule of author-as-copyright-owner is a "work made for hire," which exists in two situations:

A. A work prepared by an employee within the scope of his or her employment, or

B. A work specially ordered or commissioned for use as a contribution to a collective work, as part of a motion picture or other audiovisual work, as a translation, as a supplementary work, as a compilation, as an instructional text, as a test, as answer material for a test, or as an atlas, if the parties expressly agree in a written instrument signed by them that the work shall be considered a work made for hire.[26]

In the case of a work made for hire, the employer is considered the author for purposes of copyright and automatically acquires all rights, exclusive and nonexclusive, unless the parties have signed an agreement to the contrary. Thus, the employer effectively attains the status of creator of the work.

For instance, a full-time copywriter for an advertising agency would have no rights to the copy created for the agency. In contrast, a photo sold by a freelance photographer to a public relations firm for use in a press release normally would not be a work made for hire unless the photographer, who is contractually an independent contractor, had signed a contract specifically stating that the photo shall be considered a work made for hire.

Suppose a public relations writer writes a novel about a fictional head of a public relations firm who solves major crime mysteries on the side. The book is written at home on the public relations professional's own time, but much of the inspiration comes from his or her observations at work. Is the novel a work made for hire? Clearly not; although the public relations professional may have gotten some ideas from interactions with her colleagues, the writing was completed outside the scope of employment. Serving as a source of inspiration alone is not enough for an employer of an individual to claim copyright. An employer–employee relationship must have existed in the context in which the work is created.

Copyright terms that resemble those of a work made for hire also may be designated by contract. Suppose, for example, that Acme Corporation's in-house marketing communications team hires an advertising agency to prepare a new product promotional campaign. The default position under the Copyright law is that the agency owns the copyright in any creative works produced for Acme. Acme and its agency are free, however, to enter into an agreement that would treat any agency-produced works as "works made for hire," meaning that Acme would then, by the terms of the agreement, possess the copyrights in its campaign materials. Communications professionals hiring outside agencies should take care to recognize and distinguish works-made-for-hire-scenarios and commemorate their intentions in writing if they deviate from the law's standard provisions. Similarly, agencies and freelancers should be mindful of the chain of copyright creation and ownership to protect their own interests and minimize the potential for agency-client conflicts over creative property.

Working With Freelancers

Freelancers create much of the copyrighted material existing today and work-made-for-hire principles play a major role in the copyright status of much of this creative output. Unfortunately, although the 1976 law defines dozens of terms, from an *anonymous work* to a *work made for hire*, it does not define *employer, employee* or *scope of his or her employment*. In 1989, however, the Supreme Court settled some perplexing questions regarding works made for hire by enunciating a clear principle for determining whether an individual is an "employee." In *Community for Creative Non-Violence v. Reid*, the Court unanimously held:

> To determine whether a work is for hire under the Act [Copyright Act of 1976], a court must first ascertain, using principles of general common law of agency, whether the work was prepared by an employer or an independent contractor. After making this determination, the court can apply the appropriate subsection of §101.[27]

The Court then indicated factors under the general common law of agency to be applied in determining whether the hired party is an employee or an independent contractor, including:

> the hiring party's right to control the manner and means by which the product is accomplished. Among the other factors relevant to this inquiry are the skill required; the source of the instrumentalities and tools; the location of the work; the duration of the relationship between the parties; whether the hiring party has the right to assign additional projects to the hired party; the extent of the hired party's discretion over when and how long to work; the method of payment; the hired party's role in hiring and paying assistants; whether the work is part of the regular business of the hiring party; whether the hiring party is in business; the provision of employee benefits; and the tax treatment of the hired party. ... No one of these factors is determinative.[28]

Community for Creative Non-Violence v. Reid established the presumption that a work is not a work made for hire unless there is a written agreement to treat it as such. As the justices noted, the legislative history of the 1976 Act provides strong evidence that Congress meant to establish two mutually exclusive ways for a work to acquire work-made-for-hire status. The Court also pointed out that "only enumerated categories of commissioned works may be accorded work for hire status ... [and that the] ... hiring party's right to control the product simply is not determinative."[29]

The Court specifically rejected an "actual control test" that the Community for Creative Non-Violence argued should be determinative. Under such a test, the hiring party could claim the copyright if it closely monitored the production of the work, but the Court said this approach "would impede Congress' paramount goal in revising the 1976 Act of enhancing predictability and certainty of copyright ownership."[30] The Court went on to note that "[b]ecause that test hinges on whether the hiring party has closely monitored the production process, the parties would not know until late in the process, if not until the work is completed, whether a work will ultimately fall within §101(1)."[31] Congress intended in the 1976 law that it must be clear who owns the copyright at the time a work is created, said the Court. As one intellectual property attorney notes,

> Because the categories are generally narrow ones, most types of works fall outside them. As a result, many intended 'work for hire' agreements are ineffective in creating a valid work made for hire, and the copyright remains the property of the creator.[32]

A 2001 case looked at the rights of individual copyright owners whose individual works were included in a collective work, namely specific editions of *The New York Times*, *Newsday* and *Sports Illustrated*. The issue, in *New York Times Company v. Tasini*,[33] concerned whether freelancers' copyrights in their individual articles were infringed when the articles were subsequently reproduced in electronic form without authorization. The freelancers had been compensated for the use of their works in print but argued they were entitled to additional royalties for subsequent electronic uses such as inclusion in searchable CD-ROMs or databases. The Supreme Court found for the freelancers. Writing for the Court, Justice Ginsburg said:

> If there is a demand for a freelance article standing alone or in a new collection, the Copyright Act allows the freelancer to benefit from that demand. ... It would scarcely "preserve the author's copyright in a contribution" as contemplated by Congress ... if a newspaper or magazine publisher were permitted to reproduce or distribute copies of the author's contribution in isolation or within new collective works.[34]

Figure 7.5 A 2001 case, *New York Times Company v. Tasini*, concerned individual works included in a collective work, namely specific editions of *The New York Times*, *Newsday* and *Sports Illustrated*. The issue was whether freelancers' copyrights in their individual articles were infringed when the articles were subsequently reproduced in electronic form without authorization. The Supreme Court found for the freelancers.

Credit line: Helena G.H./Shutterstock.com

The practical effect of *Tasini* was to encourage organizations to seek all-encompassing releases from freelancers at the time of engagement. Freelancers, on the other hand, gained potential leverage to be used in negotiating fees and terms of use for their copyrighted contributions.

The Copyright Owner's Exclusive Rights

Copyright laws give the copyright owner a series of exclusive rights the owner may sell, lease, give away or otherwise transfer as desired. Under Section 106, the copyright owner has the exclusive right to:

- Reproduce the copyrighted work in copies or phonorecords.
- Prepare derivative works based upon the copyrighted work.
- Distribute copies or phonorecords of the copyrighted work to the public by sale or other transfer of ownership, or by rental, lease or lending.
- Perform the work publicly if it is a literary, musical, dramatic or choreographic work; a pantomime; or a motion picture or other audiovisual work.
- Display the work publicly if it is a literary, musical, dramatic or choreographic work; a pantomime; or a pictorial, graphic or sculptural work. This right also applies to the individual images of a motion picture or other audiovisual work.
- Perform the work publicly by means of a digital audio transmission if the work is a sound recording.[35]

Termination of Transfer

Under certain limited conditions, a copyright owner who has transferred any of these exclusive rights to another may elect to terminate the transfer. Under Section 203, a copyright owner can terminate a grant of any exclusive or nonexclusive right after 35 years by notifying the individual or organization to whom the right was transferred.[36] This is an often-overlooked provision that can certainly work to the advantage of a copyright owner, especially when a work is slow in gaining popularity. This special termination-of-transfers provision applies neither to works made for hire, nor to grants to prepare specific derivative works.[37]

An illustration of how this provision could work is a legal dispute that *The Hollywood Reporter* characterized as "a case that had the potential to rock the music industry to its core."[38] Invoking Section 203, Sir Paul McCartney sued Sony/ATV in 2017 in U.S. District Court in Manhattan.[39] He requested a declaration that he could reclaim more than 260 copyrights he and John Lennon owned, including "I Want to Hold Your Hand," "Yesterday," "Hey Jude" and "Love Me Do."[40] Michael Jackson outbid McCartney in 1985 for the rights to the Beatles songs and later set up a joint venture with Sony/ATV Music Publishing. Jackson's estate sold its part of the venture to Sony for $750 million in 2016. McCartney had sent termination notices for the songs, beginning with "Love Me Do," for which notice had to be given by October 5, 2018. He decided to seek the declaration after Sony/ATV successfully fought the pop group Duran Duran's attempts to exercise such termination rights for its songs in a British court.[41]

McCartney and Sony/ATV settled out-of-court in a confidential agreement several months after McCartney filed his lawsuit. As one writer noted, "Now that the McCartney and Sony/ATV have resolved the issue themselves, copyright watchers won't have the satisfaction of knowing how a stateside court would rule in the case."[42]

Owning the Object Versus Owning the Copyright

In contemplating copyright ownership rights, it is necessary to distinguish between the actual work and the *copyright* in the original work. Ownership of a work, as opposed to ownership of the copyrights to a work, does not convey any copyrights. For example, if Jan Smurf purchases a 4K Ultra HD video of Walt Disney's *Cinderella* at her local retailer or online, she can play the video to her heart's content in her own home, and even invite her friends for an evening of viewing on her 4K Ultra HD big-screen television. However, she does not have the right to make a copy of the video or even to play it at a neighborhood fundraiser.

In other words, purchasing the video merely gave her the right to use it in the form in which it was intended to be used—nothing more. She could, of course, loan the disc to a neighbor or even sell her copy to a stranger, just as she could with a book or other physical object. Her rights are strictly tangible; she has no intangible property rights.

Under the "first sale" doctrine incorporated in the U.S. Copyright Act,[43] when a book, video, painting, sound recording or similar creative work is lawfully purchased, whether from the copyright owner or other authorized individual or entity, the copyright owner cannot control its resale nor is the copyright owner entitled to a portion of any profits. For example, if a painter sells an original painting she created, she cannot prevent the resale of that work nor the public display of it by the new owner. She also may not collect a cut of the resale price. Similarly, if you purchase a bestseller or other book in a bookstore or other outlet, the publisher of that book is not entitled to any resale royalty rights. In 2014 a California statute[44] that attempted to create such a right for visual artists was struck down in the U.S. Court of Appeals as a violation of the U.S. Copyright Act.[45] Outside the United States, however, royalty rights associated with the resale of creative works may give artists the rights to claim a percentage of any re-sales of their works.[46]

Moral Rights

One of the more controversial issues in the debate over whether the United States should join the Berne Convention (discussed later in this chapter) was Article 6*bis* that requires Convention members to protect the moral rights or *droit moral* of authors.[47] Although the United States does not recognize such rights to the same degree as its other Convention signees, the Visual Artists Rights Act (VARA),[48] adopted by the United States Congress in 1990, amended the Copyright Act to provide limited moral rights for the visual works of art created on or after June 1, 1991. These moral rights fall into two categories under VARA: attribution rights and integrity rights, both of which have been more broadly recognized in many other countries for some time.

Attribution rights involve the right to be credited as the author of a work and to prevent others from attributing a work to you that is essentially not your work. For example, both a publisher who, without consent, omitted the name of the primary author from a book and a magazine editor who falsely claimed an article was written by a well-known author to sell more copies or lend credibility to the magazine would be violating attribution rights.

Integrity rights basically involve "the right to object to distortion, other alteration of a work, or derogatory action prejudicial to the author's honor or reputation in relation to the work."[49] An example of the latter was a 1976 federal court of appeals decision to grant a preliminary injunction against the ABC Television Network on the ground that the copyright of the British comedy troupe known as Monty Python of "Monty Python's Flying Circus" fame was violated when the network extensively edited the troupe's programs, primarily to make room for commercials.[50] Although the comedy team had granted the British Broadcasting Corporation the right to license the programs overseas, that right did not include allowing licensees to significantly distort the programs.

Public Performance Rights and Performance Licenses: Music

Of the copyright owner's exclusive rights listed above, the right "to perform the copyrighted work publicly" is among the most misunderstood, particularly with regard to the public performance of music. Many businesses use music in communicating with customers to establish a mood or tone. Music frequently is featured in advertising, on websites, at special events, at sales meetings, in stores and during phone contact with customers. Because these and other uses of music may implicate the public performance rights and result in possible copyright infringement, advertising and public relations practitioners should become familiar with public performance rights and understand when to seek permission prior to using copyrighted material.

Where recorded music is concerned, copyright law applies to the copying of both the musical work—the composer's music and/or any lyrics—as well as the sound recording itself. The musical work also is protected by the public performance right, which means anyone who wishes to publicly perform the work must obtain permission from the composer and/or lyricist. That's right, the band at a local watering spot "covering" a song they have learned is potentially infringing a copyrighted work.

Radio stations, bars and other businesses that rely on music would be quite busy if required to contact individual composers to secure licenses prior to playing (causing the public performance of) music in their respective establishments—a ridiculously time-consuming and prohibitively expensive proposition. Fortunately for businesses and other entities wishing to publicly use copyrighted music, there is a mechanism—the performance license—that enables a potential user to avoid having to negotiate with individual copyright owners.

Performance licenses, typically acquired through performance rights societies, allow licensees to publicly perform music for which the society has acquired a nonexclusive right. The two primary licensing societies in the United States are the American Society of Composers, Authors and Publishers (ASCAP) and Broadcast Music, Inc. (BMI).[51] Both organizations serve similar functions. ASCAP, founded in 1914, has a membership of more than 680,000 songwriters, composers and music publishers, and nonexclusive rights to more than 11.5 million songs and scores.[52] BMI, a nonprofit corporation formed in 1939, has about 400,000 writer and publisher affiliates, and holds nonexclusive rights to the public performance of more than 6.5 million musical compositions.[53] Both societies grant blanket licenses to broadcast stations and other entities (including Internet-only stations) so they can use any of the music licensed to the societies without having to obtain the permission of individual copyright owners.

Performance licensing is an efficient mechanism for collecting royalties because individual copyright owners are not faced with the onerous task of monitoring broadcast stations and performing venues around the country to catch copyright violators. Instead, the licensing society can handle this. The income from the fees garnered by each society is distributed, after a deduction for administrative expenses, to the copyright owners with whom the society has an agreement. Typically, the composer of a licensed song gets the same share of royalties as the publisher.

Performance licenses are often confused with two other types of licenses that apply to the use of music in movies or television shows: "synchronization" licenses and "master use" licenses. The use of music in film or video requires a synchronization license. A "sync" right allows the licensee to copy a musical recording onto the soundtrack of a film or other video production in synchronization with action so a single work is produced. Specialized agencies, such as the Harry Fox Agency,[54] typically administer synchronization licenses on behalf of composers or those to whom copyrights have been transferred. If the music featured in the film or video (or commercial) is a *particular* sound recording of a musical work (not one produced especially for the film or video), a master use license is required. This gives the licensee the right to reproduce the "master" sound recording. Record companies that own sound recording copyrights usually administer master use licenses.

Broadcasters and film and television producers are not the only ones affected by licensing. Generally, an office, store or other business (whether for-profit or nonprofit) does not have the right to rebroadcast radio signals because the radio station's blanket license covers only its original broadcast, not any other "public performance." The key here is the retransmitting or amplification of a radio or television broadcast, as opposed to merely turning on the radio as background music in a business or workplace. The latter is allowed as a "homestyle exemption" under Section 110.[55] The homestyle exemption allows for televisions and radios carrying copyrighted programming to be played in commercial settings as long as (a) the receiving device is like that typically used in private homes; (b) there is no charge for seeing or hearing the broadcast; and (c) the transmission is not "retransmitted" to the public in any way.[56] Thus, the office worker who listens to a favorite radio station at the office each day is not engaging in copyright infringement, but a metropolitan newspaper that, without consent, retransmits the music being played by a local top-rated radio station to the newspaper's individual offices in its corporate headquarters could be in violation.

As an alternative, dozens of music services, such as Mood Media[57] and InStore Audio Network,[58] offer audio services to stores and other public facilities. Most are delivered via satellite. They cannot be broadcast without consent, which involves paying subscription fees with the proceeds shared with owners of the copyrighted music, including composers and publishers.

It is no secret that licensing societies routinely monitor radio and television stations and visit entertainment events, restaurants, bars, retail stores and other public facilities to spot potential copyright infringers. Copyright violators are usually warned and threatened with a lawsuit if they do not halt infringement or obtain a performance or other appropriate license.

Although the Copyright Act of 1976 has been amended numerous times since its enactment to respond to new technologies as well as other obvious gaps in the law, several copyright issues remained unaddressed for music and audio recordings. In October 2018, President Donald Trump signed into law the Orrin G. Hatch–Bob Goodlatte Music Modernization Act (MMA) that, as its title indicates, aims to modernize copyright issues related to music and audio recordings, including new technologies such as digital streaming. It was an extensive revision of Section 115 of the Copyright Act of 1976. According to an announcement from the U.S. Copyright Office, "The [Music Modernization Act] promises to serve as one of the most significant pieces of copyright legislation in decades."[59]

In an unusual show at the time of bipartisan lawmaking, both houses of Congress unanimously approved the statute, which combined three bills that had been brought before the federal legislative body. Much of the Act's popularity likely may be attributed to the fact that it offers something for everyone involved in the creation, production, distribution and licensing of music and music and audio recordings, including even some protection for those first published before 1923.

The MMA contains three major provisions. Title I ("Music Licensing Modernization"), as one industry publication summed it up, "streamlines the music-licensing process to make it easier for rights holders to get paid when their music is streamed online."[60] Title II ("Classics Protection and Access") brings pre-1972 sound recordings partially into the federal copyright system by extending remedies for copyright infringement to owners of sound recordings fixed before February 15, 1972. Title III ("Allocation for Music Producers"), according to *The Verge*, "improves royalty payouts for producers and engineers … when their recordings are used on satellite and online radio."[61] The publication noted, "This is the first time producers have ever been mentioned in copyright law."[62] As of this writing, the Copyright Office was soliciting public input and feedback for rules associated with the implementation of the MMA. Advertisers, in particular, and their agents who handle music usage should consult the Copyright Office website (www.copyright.gov) for updates regarding MMA rulemaking.

Compulsory Licensing

One of the most controversial and complicated aspects of the Copyright Act of 1976 is the set of compulsory licensing provisions (contained in several sections of the Act). These provisions cover (1) secondary transmissions of broadcast programming by cable,[63] (2) nonsubscription digital audio,[64] (3) subscription digital audio,[65] (4) nondramatic musical works,[66] and (5) non-commercial broadcasting.[67] Compulsory licensing provides a mechanism by which an entity such as a cable or satellite system, broadcaster or Internet audio service provider, for example, can make specific use of a copyrighted work without contacting the copyright owner for permission. This is done by notifying the Licensing Division of the U.S. Copyright Office and paying royalties to be distributed to the copyright owner according to a fee schedule set by three copyright royalty judges reporting to the Copyright Office.

Copyright Duration

Although a particular creative work may qualify for copyright protection, the Constitution places limits on the duration of such protection. Article I, Section 8 says: "To promote the Progress of Science and useful Arts, by securing for limited Times to Authors ... the exclusive Right to their respective Writings."[68] What is meant by "for limited Times" has frequently been the subject of debate. Over the decades, Congress has extended the duration of copyright protection from time to time, granting authors increased protection and delaying the passage of works into the public domain.

With some exceptions, the 1976 law did not change copyright duration for works deemed protected prior to the new law taking effect. Under the old law, copyright lasted for 28 years and could be renewed for an additional 28 years for a possible total of 56 years. For these works, the 1976 law works the same way, but the length of the second (renewal) term was increased to 67 years. Thus, for works copyrighted before the 1976 law went into effect, the specific duration of protection depends on several factors, including whether the work was in its first term under the old law when the new law went into effect or whether the copyright had already been renewed when the new law went into effect.

The Copyright Act of 1976 is much more generous than the 1909 statute when it comes to duration, and even the 1976 Act has been amended to further increase the term of protection (the 1998 Sonny Bono Copyright Term Extension Act [CTEA] extended the original Act's copyright protection by 20 years).[69] Today, in general, works created under the 1976 Act on or after January 1, 1978, are protected for the lifetime of the author, plus 70 years. That means that a 21-year-old songwriter who lives to be 91 will have the benefit of exclusive rights to his or her song for 70 years and the songwriter's heirs (assuming copyright has not been sold or otherwise transferred) will benefit an additional 70 years for a total of 140 years before the song goes into the public domain. The protection of a joint work (the songwriter contributed the music and a buddy wrote the lyrics) is measured by the lifetime plus 70 of the longest living contributor.

Works made for hire and anonymous or pseudonymous works are protected for 120 years from creation or 95 years from publication. Anonymous works are defined as works "of which no natural person is identified as author"; pseudonymous works are those on which "the author is identified under a fictitious name."[70]

As expected, the CTEA was challenged in court as unconstitutional, including on First Amendment grounds. Both the U.S. District Court and the U.S. Court of Appeals upheld the constitutionality of the CTEA. On further appeal, the U.S. Supreme Court held in *Eldred v. Ashcroft* (2003)[71] in a 7-2 majority opinion written by Justice Ruth Bader Ginsburg, that Congress had not exceeded its authority under the U.S. Constitution in enacting the CTEA and that the statute did not violate the First Amendment.

Copyright Notice

One of the most persistent myths about copyright, perhaps because the 1909 statutory require-ments were so rigid, is that a copyright notice cannot be placed on a work unless the work has been officially registered. As noted earlier, this is not the case. The new law not only permits posting of the copyright notice on all works—registered and unregistered—but actually encour-ages this practice.

Under the 1909 law, published works that did not bear a copyright notice were lost forever in the twilight zone of the public domain. Copyright notice is still mandatory for works published before March 1, 1989, although failure to include the notice or giving an incorrect notice does not automatically negate the copyright, as it did under the 1909 law. Instead, the copyright owner is permitted to take certain steps, as provided in Sections 405 and 406 of the statute, to preserve the copyright. These steps include registering the work before it is published, before the omission took place or within five years after the error occurs and making a reasonable effort to post a correct notice on all subsequent copies.[72]

Although not mandatory for works first published on or after March 1, 1989, a copyright notice is highly recommended. It gives the world notice that the work is protected and provides useful infor-mation, including the copyright owner and year of publication, to anyone who may wish to seek permission to use the work. Providing the notice also prevents an individual or organization from claiming innocent infringement (discussed later in this chapter) as a defense to unauthorized use.

Proper Copyright Notice

For purposes of notice, the copyright law divides creative works into two categories: visually perceptible copies ("copies from which the work can be visually perceived, either directly or with the aid of a machine or device")[73] and phonorecords or sound recordings.[74] The distinction is important because the notices are different for the two.

The key three elements of notice are:

- The copyright symbol © or (p) for phonorecords, the word "Copyright" or the abbreviation "Copr."
- The year of first publication of the work (or of creation if the work is unpublished).
- The name of the copyright owner, an abbreviation by which the name can be recognized or a generally known alternative designation.

A notice should be affixed to copies or phonorecords of a work in a way that gives reasonable notice of the claim of copyright. Using a copyright notice is optional for unpublished works, foreign works and works published on or after March 1, 1989.[75]

Examples of a proper notice are:

- © 2019 Carmen Maye.
- Copyright 2019 Roy L. Moore.
- Copr. 2019 Erik L. Collins.

The first example is the one most recommended because it is the only form acceptable under the Universal Copyright Convention (UCC), of which the United States is a member. The UCC was founded in 1952 in Geneva, Switzerland, to bring international uniformity to copyright. If a work is unpublished, there is no mandatory form for notice because notice is not required, but a recommended form is: Unpublished work © 2019 Roy L. Moore.

Placement of Notice

The Copyright Office has issued regulations that are quite specific, although flexible about where a copyright notice should be placed.[76] The statute says simply that for visually perceptible copies, "The notice shall be affixed to copies in such manner and location as to give reasonable notice of the claim of copyright."[77]

Congress delegated authority to prescribe regulations regarding notice to the Copyright Office in the same provision.[78] Before the United States officially joined the Berne Convention on March 1, 1989, copyright notice was generally required for all published works. Leaving off the notice or even making a mistake in using copyright notice meant the work likely lost copyright protection in the U.S. However, as noted earlier, copyright notice is not required for works published on or after March 1, 1989. As the U.S. Copyright Office points out in *Copyright Notice* (Circular 3), there are specific legal benefits of copyright notice.[79]

Copyright Registration

Under the 1976 statute, a work is automatically copyrighted at the time it becomes tangibly fixed. The registration of a copyright, as opposed to its creation, is another matter. Although registration is no longer required for copyright protection,[80] there are major advantages to registration and the process is relatively simple. The advantages include:

- Public record of the copyright.
- Standing in court to file suit for infringement.
- If made within five years of publication, *prima facie* evidence in court of the copyright's validity.
- If made within three months after publication or prior to infringement, the availability of statutory damages and attorney's fees.

Registration may be made at any time during the duration of the copyright by either mailing in a paper application form or by submitting an electronic application online, which is the preferred registration process. Registration must be made prior to filing suit for copyright infringement. As noted above, there are benefits to filing prior to or soon after infringement occurs, particularly in the assessment of damages. For works registered in timely fashion, the copyright owner may be entitled to statutory damages and attorney's fees. Failure to timely register requires the copyright owner to prove actual damages if litigation ensues.

Depending on the type of work being registered and the method of application, the applicant must deposit either electronic or hard copies of the work. Copies of published books, for example, must be sent in hard-copy form; unpublished manuscripts and certain other works, on the other hand, may be submitted electronically so long as they meet certain digital formatting and size requirements.

The electronic system features a single form, Form CO, for copyright registration. For paper filing, specific forms are required (Form TX, VA, PA, etc.) for registration, depending on the type of work being registered. Forms and more information are available at www.copyright.gov, the

Figure 7.6 All copyrighted works published in the United States must comply with the mandatory deposit provision of the U.S. Copyright statute. Two complete copies of the "best edition" of the published work must be sent to the Copyright Office in the Library of Congress, pictured here in Washington, D.C., no later than three months after publication.

Credit line: RobertDodgei/iStockphoto

official Copyright Office website. The site also features eCO tutorials that explain the registration process.

All copyrighted works published in the United States, whether registered or not, must comply with the mandatory deposit provision of the U.S. Copyright statute. Under this requirement, which has a few exceptions, two complete copies of the "best edition" of the published work must be sent to the Copyright Office no later than three months after publication. "Best edition" is defined as "the edition, published in the United States at any time before the date of the deposit, that the Library of Congress determines to be most suitable for its purposes."[81] The purpose of this provision was to ensure the Library of Congress has "copies of every copyrightable work published in the United States for its collection or for exchange with or transfer to any other library."[82] The mandatory deposit provision does not require registration of the work, but copyright registration automatically fulfills the requirement. Failure to comply with the mandatory deposit requirement can result in penalties. The statute assumes that the deposit will be voluntarily made, but if that does not occur and a demand is made by the Copyright Office to the copyright owner, the owner has three months to comply or possibly face the following penalties:

- A fine of not more than $250 for each work.
- The total retail price of the work demanded or, in the absence of a retail price, the reasonable cost of acquiring the work.
- For willful or repeated failure to comply with the demand, a fine of $2,500.[83]

Copyright Infringement

An *infringer* is defined as "[a]nyone who violates any of the exclusive rights of the copyright owner ... or who imports copies or phonorecords into the United States in violation of section 602" ("Infringing importation of copies or phonorecords").[84] The Copyright Act of 1976 has considerable teeth for punishing infringers. Chapter 5 of the Act provides a wide variety of remedies, including civil and criminal penalties and injunctions. The 1989 revision, implementing the Berne Convention treaty, increased the penalties even more. The statute sends a clear message that copyright infringement does not pay. The list of individuals and organizations who have been sued (many successfully) for copyright infringement is legion.

Contributory Infringement

Despite its best efforts, Congress left some gaps in the 1976 copyright law, many of which have been closed with various amendments enacted since the legislation originally passed. The most prominent gap, at least from the consumer perspective, was revealed in *Sony Corp. of America v. Universal City Studios, Inc.*[85]

The case developed when Universal Studios, Walt Disney Productions and other television production companies sued the Sony Corporation, the largest manufacturer of videocassette recorders (VCRs)[86] sold in the United States at that time, for contributory copyright infringement. The Supreme Court looked to patent law for help in defining contributory infringement:

> We recognize that there are substantial differences between the patent and copyright laws. But in both areas the contributory infringement doctrine is grounded on the recognition that adequate protection of a monopoly may require the courts to look beyond actual duplication of a device or publication to the products or activities that make such duplication possible.[87]

Thus, those who enable copyright infringement to occur may be liable for contributory infringement if their contribution advances infringement more so than legitimate, non-objectionable ends. In *Sony*, the production companies claimed the Japanese firm marketed to the public the technology to infringe on copyrighted works they owned. This infringement occurred, according to the plaintiffs, when consumers used Sony's Betamax VCRs[88] to record copyrighted programs broadcast on local stations, specifically "time-shifting" (the Court characterized this practice as the principal use of a VCR by the average owner).

A U.S. District Court judge for the Central District of California ruled that recording of broadcasts carried on the public airwaves was a fair use of copyrighted works, and thus Sony could not be held liable as a contributory infringer even if such home recording were infringement. In a narrow decision that dealt only with Sony's liability for manufacturing and marketing the recorders, the Supreme Court agreed with the district court that the company was not guilty of contributory infringement. In a 5-4 opinion written by Justice Stevens, the Court concluded that home time-shifting was fair use:

> First, Sony demonstrated a significant likelihood that substantial numbers of copyright holders who license their works for broadcast on free television would not object to having their broadcasts timeshifted by private viewers. And second, respondents failed to demonstrate that time-shifting would cause any likelihood of nonminimal harm to the potential market for, or the value of, their copyrighted works. The Betamax is, therefore, capable of

substantial noninfringing uses. Sony's sale of such equipment to the general public does not constitute contributory infringement of respondents' rights.[89]

The Court went on to note that there is no indication in the Copyright Act that Congress intended to make it unlawful for consumers to record programs for later viewing in the home or to prohibit the sale of recorders.

> It may well be that Congress will take a fresh look at this new technology, just as it so often has examined other innovations in the past. But it is not our job to apply laws that have not yet been written.[90]

After the decision, several bills were proposed in Congress to respond to the Court's holding, such as taxing recorders and blank tapes, but most legislators apparently felt the political fallout from such legislation would be too great.

The *Sony* decision, which barely attracted a majority of justices, left many unanswered questions. Is videotaping at home an infringement? Although the Court said that home time-shifting was fair use, the fair use doctrine does not mention such use as permissible. Since *Sony*, new technology has raised similar questions, particularly with respect to home audio recording. For example, XM (now Sirius XM), the satellite radio service, for a time allowed current subscribers to keep copies of songs on special receivers.[91]

Liability for Infringement Online

Most traditional copyright jurisprudence involves direct copyright infringement, which occurs when one party copies, distributes, displays or otherwise abridges one of the "exclusive" rights afforded copyright owners.[92] In some cases, however, a party may be liable for contributory infringement if they take certain steps that enable a third party to engage in copyright infringement. A general exception exists, however, for online service providers (e.g., YouTube, Pinterest, etc.) that provide a forum for others to post content—even infringing content—online. The Digital Millennium Copyright Act (DMCA)[93] passed in 1998 increases penalties for copyright infringement on the Internet. It also gives interactive service providers (ISPs) limited immunity from the legal harm caused by third-party posters. Like Section 230 of the Communications Decency Act (introduced in Chapter 4 and summarized in Chapter 13), which gives online service providers limited immunity from the legal harm caused by third-party posters, the DMCA "limits ISPs from copyright infringement liability for simply transmitting information over the Internet."[94] Additional provisions of the DMCA, including steps ISPs should take after learning of copyright-infringing materials on their sites, are discussed in Chapter 13.

Proving Infringement

Under Section 501(a) of the current copyright statute, anyone who violates any of the exclusive rights of the copyright owner is an infringer, absent a legitimate defense. The statute provides a wide range of remedies from injunctions to criminal penalties. To prove infringement, a plaintiff must demonstrate that he or she owns the copyright to the infringed work and the defendant(s) copied the work. The latter involves proving the defendant(s) had access to the work and that the two works are substantially similar.

Proving ownership is usually not difficult because the owner simply has to produce sufficient evidence that he or she created the work or that the rights to the work were transferred to him or her. Registration is one way to establish this because it constitutes *prima facie* evidence of the validity of the copyright if registration is made prior to or within five years after publication.

Demonstrating access, the second major requirement for proving infringement, is usually a relatively simple matter, especially when a work has been widely distributed. But occasionally a defendant is able to prove lack of access. An example occurred in 1988, when rocker Mick Jagger successfully fought a copyright infringement suit against him for his hit song, "Just Another Night."[95] Reggae musician Patrick Alley claimed the chorus from Jagger's song had been lifted from a song Alley had recorded earlier. Alley claimed that Jagger had access to his song through a drummer who had played on both records, and that Jagger probably heard Alley's song when it was played on several smaller New York radio stations. Jagger denied he had heard the song, and a U.S. District Court jury in New York ruled in his favor after hearing testimony from the defendant that included him singing some of his lyrics.[96]

Figure 7.7 In 1988, rocker Mick Jagger, shown here in 2016, successfully fought a copyright infringement suit against him for his hit song "Just Another Night" by demonstrating that he lacked access to the original work. Reggae musician Patrick Alley claimed the chorus from Jagger's song had been lifted from a song Alley had recorded earlier.

Credit line: JStone/Shutterstock.com

Substantial similarity is typically the key in proving an infringement case. Although it was rendered prior to enactment of the current copyright statute, a 1977 ruling by the Ninth Circuit has become a leading case on the criteria for evaluating substantial similarity. In *Sid and Marty Krofft Television Productions, Inc. v. McDonald's Corp.*,[97] the creators of the show "H.R. Pufnstuf" successfully claimed that some McDonald's television commercials infringed on their copyright because the McDonaldland setting in the hamburger chain's ads and the characters portrayed in them were substantially similar to those in "H.R. Pufnstuf."

The court of appeals applied a two-prong test in reaching its conclusion. First, is there substantial similarity between the underlying general ideas of the two works? If the answer is "no," there is no infringement. If "yes," the second question is: Is there substantial similarity in the manner of expression of the two works? If "yes," there is infringement. If no, the lawsuit fails. Both of these are questions of fact for a jury to determine (or for the judge in a bench trial).

A classic case of substantial similarity involved the classic movie *Jaws*. In 1982, a federal district court in California found that the movie *Great White* was substantially similar to *Jaws* and, therefore, an infringement.[98] The similarities were quite striking, as the court noted, including similar characters (an English sea captain and a shark hunter who together track down a vicious shark), a similar plot and even opening and closing sequences that were virtually identical. The judge in the case felt that it was obvious that "the creators of *Great White* wished to be as closely connected with the plaintiff's motion picture *Jaws* as possible."[99] The producers of the infringing movie were ordered to pay damages, and an injunction was issued to further ban distribution of the film.

The similarities were also striking in a 1989 Seventh Circuit U.S. Court of Appeals decision involving greeting cards.[100] For two years, Ruolo designed distinctive greeting cards for Russ Berrie & Company under a contract granting the latter the exclusive right to produce and sell the cards in its "Feeling Sensitive" line. When the contract expired and Ruolo notified the company that it would not be renewed, Russ Berrie marketed a similar line of cards known as "Touching You." The appeals court upheld a jury decision awarding $4.3 million for Ruolo on the basis that the cards were substantially similar, including being designed for similar occasions and identical in size and layout.

This same "look and feel test" is often applied in determining infringement in computer software cases, although a seminal article on the issue concluded that, "while broad protection may be given by some courts to the structure, sequence and organization of a program, copyright law provides no general protection for the overall 'look and feel' of a computer software."[101]

Remedies for Infringement: Injunctions, Impoundment and Disposition

Under Section 502 of the Copyright Act, federal courts can grant both temporary and permanent injunctions to prevent further infringement once infringement has been proven. The permanent injunction against *Great White*, mentioned earlier, is an example of how this form of equitable relief can be effective. With the injunction, the movie could no longer be distributed, shown or sold anywhere in the United States.

Although injunctions are clearly a form of prior restraint, the courts have indicated they are constitutionally permissible to prevent further infringement of intellectual property rights. A mere threatened infringement is usually not sufficient to warrant an injunction, but once infringement is proven, an injunction becomes a potent weapon available for the copyright owner. As with all injunctions, violations can subject a defendant to citation for contempt and fines as determined by the court.

Section 503 provides two other effective remedies—impoundment and disposition. Impoundment involves the government seizing potentially infringing materials or forcing a defendant to turn them over to the custody of the court until the case is decided. In its final decision, the court can also "order the destruction or other reasonable disposition of all copies or phonorecords" determined to violate copyright.[102] The federal courts rarely resort to these remedies, but they clearly have the authority to use them.

Remedies for Infringement: Damages and Profits

The most common remedy for infringement is an award of damages. A copyright owner who files suit against an alleged infringer can opt at any time before the court issues its decision to claim either actual damages (along with any additional profits) or statutory damages, but he or she cannot recover both.

Under Section 504, an infringer can be liable for actual damages caused by the infringement, plus any profits attributable to the infringement. All the copyright owner needs to show at trial to establish the amount of profit is the infringer's gross revenue.[103] There is no limit on the amount of actual damages the copyright owner can recover, so long as there is sufficient evidence to demonstrate the extent of the harm suffered. As with all civil suits in federal courts, judges have a responsibility to ensure that awards are not excessive in light of the evidence presented at trial. However, the judge and jury have considerable discretion in determining what is reasonable.

The 1988 revision of the Copyright Act[104] and subsequent amendments substantially increased the amount of statutory damages available. If the copyright owner of an infringed work chooses statutory damages instead of actual damages and profits, he or she can obtain an award from $750 (minimum) to $30,000 (maximum) for each infringement of the work, depending on what the court considers an appropriate amount. If the copyright owner can prove that the infringement was willful, he or she can recover, at the court's discretion, up to $150,000 for each infringement.[105] However, if the infringer can convince the court that he or she was not aware and had no reason to believe that he or she was infringing (i.e., innocent infringement), the court can reduce the statutory damages to as low as $200.[106]

There is a "fair use" provision tucked away in Section 504, under which "an employer or agent of a nonprofit educational institution, library or archives acting within the scope of his or her employment" cannot be held liable for statutory damages for infringement in reproducing a work if the person "believed and had reasonable grounds for believing that the use was a fair use."[107] A similar exception is made for public broadcasting employees who infringe by performing or reproducing a published, nondramatic literary work.

Other Remedies for Infringement

Under Section 505, a court can award court costs (i.e., the expenses involved in pursuing the litigation) and reasonable attorney's fees to whichever side wins.[108] These remedies are at the discretion of the judge. Under certain circumstances, anyone who willfully infringes for commercial or private financial gain additionally can be fined up to $250,000 and/or imprisoned for a maximum of five years. Such willful actions include reproduction or distribution, during any

180-day period, of one or more copies or phonorecords of at least one work valued at more than $1,000 retail, and distribution of "a work being prepared for commercial distribution … if such person knew or should have known that the work was intended for commercial distribution."[109]

The FBI is the primary police authority for enforcing the criminal provisions of the copyright statutes. The statutes also include a provision making it a federal crime to traffic in counterfeit labels for phonorecords and copies of motion pictures and other audiovisual works.[110]

International Protection Against Copyright Infringement

There is no universal or worldwide copyright. However, copyright owners are able to take criminal and civil action against infringers in other countries because of various international agreements the United States has signed and conventions and treaties it has joined. Because there is no universal international copyright, the treatment afforded works copyrighted in the United States differs considerably from country to country.

The most sweeping changes in international copyright have been wrought by the ongoing Berne Union for the Protection of Literary and Artistic Property (Berne Convention), which met first in Paris in 1896 and was most recently amended in 1979.[111] The United States, however, did not join the convention until March 1, 1989, after 78 other nations were already members. The major impact of joining was that the United States must now treat the works copyrighted in other Berne Convention countries the same as it treats works of its own citizens, and member countries must offer at least the same protection for U.S. works as they do for those of their own citizens.[112]

On January 1, 1996, the International Agreement on Trade-Related Aspects on Intellectual Property Rights (TRIPS), which was part of the General Agreement on Tariffs and Trade (GATT), took effect. The agreement, which affects all members of the World Trade Organization (WTO) including the United States, allows copyright protection to be automatically restored under certain conditions to works from other countries that had gone into the public domain in the United States. For example, this restoration of copyright applies to works from countries that had no copyright agreements with the United States at the time the work was published, or works that did not have the requisite copyright notice before the Berne Implementation Act removed that formality.[113]

Despite these international guidelines, international enforcement is difficult and piracy of copyrighted goods remains a huge problem for copyright owners. China is an example of a country that seems of two minds where protecting foreign copyrights is concerned. China is a signatory to the Berne Convention and has pledged to cooperate with the WTO's calls for it to honor its copyright protection obligations. However, the International Intellectual Property Alliance maintains that global piracy causes significant economic losses to U.S. publishers, software manufacturers and motion picture producers.[114] President Donald Trump, in particular, singled out China in criticizing intellectual property violations and also hinted that the United States may withdraw from the WTO.

Defenses to Infringement

There are four key defenses to copyright infringement, although the first one is technically not a defense, but a mitigation of damages: (a) *innocent infringement*, (b) *statute of limitations*, (c) *license* and (d) *fair use* (including parody).

Innocent infringement occurs when a person uses a copyrighted work without consent on the good faith assumption that the work is not copyrighted because it has been publicly distributed without a copyright notice. The innocent infringer must prove that he or she was misled by the omission of such notice. He or she can still be liable, at the court's discretion, for profits made from the infringement, although not liable for actual or statutory damages.

There are two major limitations to this "defense." First, an individual cannot claim innocent infringement in the case of works published after March 1, 1989–the effective date of the Berne Convention Implementation Act of 1988. The Berne Convention does not require a copyright notice on any works–published or unpublished–and thus effectively prohibits a claim of innocent infringement. Second, innocent infringement can only be claimed for published works, not for unpublished works, because a copyright notice was not required for unpublished works even before March 1, 1989.

As for the statute of limitations, according to Section 507, "[N]o criminal proceeding shall be maintained … unless it is commenced within 5 years after the cause of action arose,"[115] and "No civil action shall be maintained … unless it is commenced within three years after the claim accrued."[116] If such actions are not initiated within that time, the *statute of limitations* imposes a complete bar, no matter how serious or extensive the infringement.

For example, an unscrupulous writer who uses another writer's chapter without consent in his or her book published in January 2020 could be sued anytime until January 2023 for the initial publication. However, if the unscrupulous writer continues to publish a book with the pirated chapter, the writer can still be held liable in February 2026 for a book the writer permitted to be sold in March 2015, although the initial infringement occurred more than three years previously. Each publication, sale and so forth constitutes a separate and new infringement. Because the statute of limitations is relatively long, it is rarely used as a defense to either criminal or civil infringement.

The typical way in which a copyright is transferred is through a written contract granting a *license*. Therefore, a valid license is a strong defense to a charge of copyright infringement. The Copyright Office does not publish a model contract, but there are dozens of copyright and intellectual property handbooks–some geared to attorneys and others aimed at laypersons–that provide sample agreements.

Section 205 of the 1976 Copyright Act allows, but does not require, parties to record transfer agreements in the Copyright Office.[117] With such a recording, the individual to whom a right or rights have been transferred gains some important legal advantages, including serving as constructive notice[118] of the terms of agreement to other parties to ward off or to answer a charge of copyright infringement.[119] Recording the transfer also provides a public record of the terms of the agreement and establishes priorities in the event of conflicting transfers.[120]

Recording of transfers must comply with the provisions in Section 205 and rules of the Copyright Office. A fee must also be paid for each document. All transfer documents are first checked by the Copyright Office for completeness and then cataloged for the public record.[121] Anyone can gain access to copies of the documents through the Copyright Office's public records website (https://cocatalog.loc.gov/cgi-bin/Pwebrecon.cgi?DB=local&PAGE=First) or by using the equipment in the Copyright Card Catalog in the Library of Congress in Washington, D.C.[122]

Fair use is the most familiar defense to copyright infringement, but for public relations and advertising professionals, it's often a tough defense to successfully use in most alleged infringement cases. However, because fair use is a significant component of copyright law and often one of the most misunderstood, it is worthy of some discussion here, despite its limited applicability to public relations and advertising efforts.

Congress included dozens of definitions in the Copyright Act of 1976, but *fair use* is deliberately not among them because the legislators had difficulty defining the concept. Congress chose instead to incorporate four criteria into Section 107 that had evolved from court cases attempting to determine fair use. In determining whether the use made of a work in a specific case is a "fair use," the factors to be considered include:

1.   The purpose and character of the use, including whether such use is of a commercial nature or is for nonprofit educational purposes.
2.   The nature of the copyrighted work.
3.   The amount and substantiality of the portion used in relation to the copyrighted work as a whole.
4.   The effect of the use upon the potential market for or value of the copyrighted work.[123]

Section 107 mentions specific examples of purposes that can involve fair use, including "criticism, comment, news reporting, teaching (including multiple copies for classroom use), scholarship, or research."[124]

Congress chose to establish broad guidelines and trust the courts to determine, on a case-by-case basis, what is and is not fair use, and that is exactly what the courts have done. Hundreds of court decisions have dealt with fair use, under both the 1909 and 1976 statutes. Each of the four "fair-use factors" listed above is important, but none is, by itself, determinative. Instead, the courts evaluate each situation in light of all four and attempt to strike a balance among them.

For example, in the 1985 opinion in *Harper & Row v. Nation Enterprises*,[125] the Supreme Court held that *The Nation* magazine had infringed the copyright jointly owned by Harper & Row and Reader's Digest Association to the unpublished memoirs of former President Gerald Ford. In early 1977, shortly after he stepped down as president, Ford signed a contract with Harper & Row and Reader's Digest to publish his then-unwritten autobiography. Ford granted the two publishers the right to publish the manuscript in book form and as a serial ("first serial rights"). In 1979, they sold the exclusive right to excerpt 7,500 words from Ford's account of his pardon of former President Richard M. Nixon to *Time* magazine prior to publication. Subsequently, an unidentified source furnished the editor of *The Nation*, a monthly political commentary magazine, with a copy of the unpublished manuscript.

Before *Time* could publish its excerpt, *The Nation* carried a 2,250-word feature that included verbatim quotes from the original manuscript. According to the Court, these quotes comprised about 13 percent of the *Nation's* article and its editor neither made independent commentary nor did any independent research before publication because, as he admitted at trial, he wanted to scoop *Time*. *Time* decided not to publish its excerpt and refused to pay Harper & Row and Reader's Digest Association the remaining $12,500 of the $25,000 it had agreed to pay for pre-publication rights. Harper & Row and Reader's Digest Association then filed suit for copyright infringement against *The Nation*.

Nation Enterprises argued fair use as a defense, which the Supreme Court ultimately rejected. The Court analyzed the case in light of each of the four factors, but paid particular attention to the fourth factor:

> In evaluating character and purpose [factor one] we cannot ignore *The Nation's* stated purpose of scooping the forthcoming hardcover and *Time* abstracts. *The Nation's* use had not

merely the incidental effect but the intended purpose of supplanting the copyright holder's commercially valuable right of first publication. [126]

On the third factor (amount and substantiality), the Court noted that, although "the words actually quoted were an insubstantial portion" of the book, *The Nation*, as the district court said, "took what was essentially the heart of the book."[127] The Court cited *The Nation* editor's own testimony at trial as evidence that he selected the passages he ultimately published "precisely because they qualitatively embodied Ford's distinctive expression."[128]

On the last factor (effect of the use on the potential market), the Court was particularly critical of *The Nation*'s action and its impact. Noting that this factor "is undoubtedly the single most important element of fair use," the majority pointed to the trial court's finding of an actual effect on the market, not simply a potential effect: "*Time's* cancellation of its projected serialization and its refusal to pay the $12,500 were the direct result of the infringement. ... Rarely will a case of copyright infringement present such clear-cut evidence of actual damage."[129]

Another test case of fair use is of particular relevance to organizations that systematically photocopy and share subscription materials among employees. In 1992, in *American Geophysical Union v. Texaco*,[130] a federal district court judge ruled it was not fair use under Section 107 when a Texaco scientist made single copies of articles from the *Journal of Catalysis*.

According to the testimony at trial, Texaco scientists routinely had the company library make single copies of articles from journals to which the company subscribed. The advantages of this procedure include permitting the workers to keep easily referenced files in their desks or on their office shelves, eliminating the risks of errors when data were transcribed from articles and then taken back to a lab for research and making it possible for them to take articles home to read.

The trial court judge held this was not fair use, and thus an infringement, because Texaco's use was for commercial gain, substantial portions of the works were copied and Texaco's use deprived the copyright holder of potential royalties.

The Second Circuit U.S. Court of Appeals, in an interlocutory appeal[131] from the district court, upheld the trial court's decision, but with somewhat different reasoning.[132] The appellate court held that three of the four fair use factors, including the purpose and character of use (first factor) and the effect on potential market and value (fourth factor), favored the publisher. The majority opinion disagreed with a dissenting opinion filed by Circuit Judge Jacobs, who contended that the majority's ruling would require that an intellectual property lawyer be posted at each photocopy machine. As the majority saw it, all Texaco had to do in the specific circumstances of the case was to simply take advantage of existing licensing schemes or work out one on its own.

The court noted,

> We do not deal with the question of copying by an individual, for personal use in research or otherwise, recognizing that under fair use doctrine or the *de minimis* doctrine, such a practice by an individual might well not constitute an infringement.[133]

The problem in this case was that Texaco had a policy of encouraging the photocopying—at least of single copies—by its scientists as a group, which meant there was the potential for hundreds of copies of articles being made, thereby presumably depriving the publishers of potential royalties.

Section 107 of the 1976 statute specifically mentions criticism, comment and news reporting as purposes that can be considered fair use. However, as the courts have made clear, these uses do not always enjoy protection in an infringement suit. For example, in May 1991, a federal district court judge in Atlanta awarded WSB-TV $108,000 plus attorneys' fees and court costs against TV News Clips for videotaping portions of the station's local newscasts and selling them to the public. The court also issued a permanent injunction barring the company from making any further copies of newscasts or offering them for sale.[134] In a similar ruling, a federal appellate court held in 2018 that TVEyes, a service that records myriad content from television broadcasters and places the captured video in searchable databases, was not able to claim fair use of plaintiff Fox News's programming. The service allowed third-party users to watch specified segments up to 10 minutes long. According to the Second Circuit Court of Appeals, the "redistribution" of Fox's copyrighted content "makes available virtually all of Fox's copyrighted audiovisual content—including all of the Fox content that TVEyes's clients wish to see and hear" and "deprives Fox of revenue that properly belongs to the copyright holder."[135]

Parodies

In 1994 the Supreme Court handed down its first major parody copyright decision in *Luther R. Campbell a.k.a. Luke Skyywalker v. Acuff-Rose Music, Inc.*[136] involving the original song "Oh, Pretty Woman," written by Roy Orbison and William Dees in 1964. Twenty-five years later, Luther R. Campbell wrote a song, "Pretty Woman," which was intended to satirize the original work.

Campbell asked Acuff-Rose Music, Inc., the copyright owner of the original song, for a license to use the song in a rap version by 2 Live Crew, but Acuff-Rose refused. 2 Live Crew recorded its version anyway on the album "As Clean as They Wanna Be," which sold almost 250,000 copies in less than a year. In response, Acuff-Rose filed a copyright infringement suit in U.S. District Court. The trial court granted a summary judgment for the defendants on the ground that the 2 Live Crew song was a parody of the original, and thus fair use under the Copyright Act of 1976. On appeal, the Sixth Circuit U.S. Court of Appeals reversed the trial court in a 2–1 decision, holding that the 2 Live Crew song's "blatantly commercial purpose ... prevents this parody from being fair use."[137]

The Supreme Court invoked the four factors and came to a different conclusion. The Court noted that, on the first factor, parodies by definition must draw to some extent on the original work they are criticizing:

> For the purposes of Copyright law, the nub of the definitions, and the heart of any parodist's claim to quote from existing material, is the use of some elements of a prior author's composition to create a new one that, at least in part, comments on the author's works.[138]

The Supreme Court spent little time with the second factor, noting that this criterion had never been much help "in separating the fair use sheep from the infringing goats in a parody case." The Court differed substantially with the court of appeals on the third factor. However, the opinion noted that, although parodists cannot "skim the cream and get away scot free," the lower court "was insufficiently appreciative of parody's need for the recognizable sight or sound when it ruled 2 Live Crew's use unreasonable as a matter of law."

The Supreme Court could not make a final determination from the record on the fourth factor. It did, however, criticize the appellate court for applying the presumption that commercial use was unfair use on this factor. Parodies and the originals usually serve different markets, according to the justices.

> We do not, of course, suggest that a parody may not harm the market at all, but when a lethal parody, like a scathing theater review, kills demand for the original, it does not produce a harm cognizable under the Copyright Act,[139]

the Court said. The key is whether the parody is acting as a substitute or as criticism. In reversing the judgment and remanding it back to the trial court, the Supreme Court held:

> It was error for the Court of Appeals to conclude that the commercial nature of 2 Live Crew's parody of "Oh Pretty Woman" rendered it presumptively unfair. No such evidentiary presumption is available to address either the first factor, the character and purpose of the use, or the fourth, market harm, in determining whether a transformative use, such as parody, is a fair one. The court also erred in holding that 2 Live Crew had necessarily copied excessively from the Orbison original, considering the parodic purpose of the use.[140]

In 2016, Dr. Seuss Enterprises sent a cease-and-desist order alleging copyright infringement to the author of an Off-Broadway play that was written in rhyme to parody the style of Dr. Seuss' book, *How the Grinch Stole Christmas!* According to the U.S. Copyright Office's summary of the resulting court case, "Who's Holiday" incorporated Seuss' "characters, plot elements, and distinctive rhyming style into a 'bawdy, off-color Christmas comedy that imagines Cindy Lou Who, a *Grinch* character, in middle-age.'"[141] As one reporter described the plot of the 75-minute, one-woman play, it "finds the Seuss character ... recently paroled and living in a trailer." And "middle-aged Cindy-Lou Who has traded roast beast for bong rips of 'Who-hash'".[142]

The author, Matthew Lombardo, halted production of the play and filed suit against Dr. Seuss Enterprises, seeking a declaratory judgment that the play constituted fair use. Dr. Seuss Enterprises countersued for copyright and trademark infringement. At the suggestion of the U.S. District Court judge in the case, the plaintiffs filed a motion for judgment on the pleadings so the case could be resolved by conducting a side-by-side comparison of the two works.[143]

Applying the four-factor test used in *Campbell v. Acuff-Rose Music* (1994), discussed above, the trial court found in *Lombardo v. Dr. Seuss Enterprises* (2017)[144] that, on the first factor (purpose and character of use), *Who's Holiday* was a transformative parody. On the second factor (nature of the copyrighted work), the court pointed out that this factor is usually of little importance in the case of a parody because such works, as with *Grinch*, are sufficiently creative to be parodied. With regard to the third factor (amount and substantiality of the use), the judge said the play's "use of *Grinch* is not excessive in relation to the parodic purpose of the copying."[145] Finally, on the fourth factor (effect on the potential market of the copyrighted work), the district court noted:

> Here, there is virtually no possibility that consumers will go see the Play in lieu of reading *Grinch* or watching an unauthorized derivative work, such as the 2000 film *Dr. Seuss' How the Grinch Stole Christmas. Grinch* is a children's book intended for an all-ages audience, whereas the Play is a bawdy, off-color parody of *Grinch* that is so clearly intended for adult audiences. ... The Play is not an unauthorized sequel of Grinch, and given the clear differences in tone and content, it is unreasonable to assume that audiences might confuse the Play for a theatrical version of *Grinch*, or that the Play would usurp the market for *Grinch*.[146]

The Second Circuit U.S. Court of Appeals in *Lombardo and Who's Holiday v. Dr. Seuss Enterprises* (2018)[147] upheld the trial court decision, ruling the court had correctly analyzed each of the four factors. On the first factor, the appellate court agreed that it weighed in Lombardo's favor because it "is a parody, imitating the style of the Grinch for comedic effect and to mock the

Figure 7.8 Shown here are several best-selling books by Dr. Seuss, widely known for his children's books. In 2016, Dr. Seuss Enterprises sent a cease-and-desist order alleging copyright infringement to the author of an Off-Broadway play that was written in rhyme to parody the style of Dr. Seuss' book, *How the Grinch Stole Christmas!*

Credit line: Julie Clopper/Shutterstock.com

naïve, happy world of the Whos."[148] The court of appeals also agreed with the trial court that the second factor is rarely useful. On the third factor, the appellate court noted,

> Here, the Play's use of material from the Grinch weighs in favor of finding fair use. While the Play does use the Grinch's character, setting, plot, and style, it is in the service of the parody. The Play does not copy verbatim or quote from the original book, and while it does recount the plot, it does so to invoke the original.[149]

Finally, the court of appeals supported the trial court's conclusion on the fourth factor, noting "there is little likelihood of harm to either market here."[150] The appellate court also agreed there was no trademark infringement.

Conclusion

In the digital era, articles, photographs, graphics and many other types of information are just a few clicks or screen touches away; copying, downloading or sharing digital files is incredibly easy. Rather than thinking of the Internet as an information superhighway, one could be tempted to view it as an information super "buffet." Judging from the number of copyright infringement and lawsuits regarding online piracy, this view of the Internet as an all-you-can-eat smorgasbord of information appears to be quite common.

This is unfortunate. The problem is that the Internet provides many easy opportunities for copyright (and trademark) infringement. This means intellectual property owners who are "ripped off" online effectively lose the preferred position afforded to them by the law. Detecting infringement and identifying the culprits can be time-consuming and costly. Nonetheless, intellectual property owners with the resources to do so are ramping up efforts to identify and pursue infringement lawsuits.[151] Congress has stepped up to the plate as well with specific legislation to define the scope of potential liability for copyright and trademark infringement arising from use of the Internet.

Because success in advertising and public relations necessarily involves assimilating existing information as well as creating new information, those who work in the fields should pay particular attention to copyright laws when using the Internet. Advertising and public relations professionals also should note that even small amounts of copied material transmitted by e-mail, texting or tweeting can lead to copyright infringement suits. Wise and prudent practitioners, therefore, should be vigilant in their own practices and be alert to head off potential problems caused by others in their organizations or their clients' organizations who may not be aware of the dangers posed by improper attention being paid to avoiding the violation of the copyrights of others.

Notes

1. Statute of Anne (1710), *Primary Sources on Copyright* (1450–1900), eds. L. Bently & M. Kretschmer, www.copyrighthistory.org (last retrieved Nov. 11, 2018).
2. U.S. Const art. I, §8.
3. 17 U.S.C. §101 (2019).
4. 17 U.S.C. §102 (a) (2019).
5. *Id.*
6. Hoehling v. Universal City Studios, Inc., 618 F.2d 927, 6 Med. L. Rptr. 1053 (2d Cir. 1980).
7. *Id.*
8. Hoehling v. Universal City Studios, Inc., *cert. denied,* 449 U.S. 841 (1980).
9. 17 U.S.C. §102 (2019).
10. *Id.*
11. *Id.*
12. 17 U.S.C. §101 (2019).
13. *Id.*
14. *Id.*
15. 17 U.S.C. §102 (2019).
16. Miller v. Universal Studios, Inc., 650 F.2d 1365, 7 Med. L. Rptr. 1735 (5th Cir. 1981).
17. *See* https://justcriminals.info/2017/01/27/barbara-jane-mackle-1968/ (last retrieved Oct. 20, 2018).
18. *See* https://abcnews.go.com/US/story?id=91055&page=1 (last retrieved Oct. 20, 2018).
19. Miller v. Universal Studios, Inc., 460 F. Supp. 984 (S.D. Fla. 1978).
20. *Id.*
21. Feist Publications, Inc. v. Rural Telephone Service Co., 499 U.S. 340, 111 S. Ct. 1282 (1991).
22. *Id.*
23. *See* www.copyright.gov/comp3/docs/compendium-12-22-14.pdf (last retrieved Nov. 11, 2018).
24. Naruto v. Slater, 888 F.3d 418 (9th Cir., 2018).
25. 17 U.S.C. §101 (2019).
26. 17 U.S.C. §101. Also see U.S. Copyright Office, *Works Made For Hire* (Circular 30) (2019), at 2.
27. Community for Creative Non-Violence v. Reid, 490 U.S. 730 (1989).
28. *Id.*
29. *Id.*
30. *Id.*
31. *Id.*
32. Will Montague, *Copyright Law: The Basics*, 82 KY Bar Assoc. Bench & Bar Magazine 16 (Mar./Apr. 2018).
33. New York Times Co., Inc. v. Tasini, 533 U.S. 483 (2001).
34. *Id.*
35. 17 U.S.C. §106 (2019). See also U.S. Copyright Office, Copyright Basics (Circular 1) (2019) at 2, www.copyright.gov/circs/circ01.pdf (last retrieved Nov. 11, 2018).
36. *See* www.copyright.gov.
37. 17 U.S.C. §203(b)(1) (2019).

38. *See* www.hollywoodreporter.com/thr-esq/paul-mccartney-reaches-settlement-sony-atv-beatles-rights-dispute-1018100. (last retrieved November 11, 2018).

39. McCartney v. Sony/ATV Music Publishing LLC et al., U.S.D.C. (S.D. N.Y.) (2017), No. 17-00363.

40. *See* www.reuters.com/article/us-people-paulmccartney/paul-mccartney-settles-with-sony-atv-over-beatles-music-rights-idUSKBN19L2ET (last retrieved Nov. 7, 2018).

41. *Id.*

42. *See* www.hollywoodreporter.com/thr-esq/paul-mccartney-reaches-settlement-sony-atv-beatles-rights-dispute-1018100 (last retrieved Nov. 7, 2018).

43. *See* 17 U.S.C. §109.

44. California Resale Royalty Act (Civil Code §986).

45. Sam Francis Foundation, Inc. v. Christie's, 769 F.3d 1195 (9th Cir. 2014).

46. Brian L. Frye, *Art in the Shadow of Copyright Law*, 82 KY Bar Assoc. Bench & bar magazine 7 (Mar./Apr. 2018).

47. U.S. Copyright Office, Copyright Law of the United States and Related Laws Contained in Title 17 of the United States Code, Appendix M: The Berne Implementation Act of 1988, www.copyright.gov/title17/ (last retrieved Nov. 11, 2018).

48. *See* 17 U.S.C. §106A (2019).

49. *Id.*

50. Gilliam v. American Broadcasting Cos., Inc. 538 F.2d 14 (2d Cir. 1976).

51. Another licensing agency is SESAC, Inc. (www.sesac.com/#/), originally known as the Society of European State Authors and Composers), but ASCAP and BMI dominate the field. Two other licensing entities are Pro Music Rights (https://a2im.org/groups/global-affiliates-music-group/) and Global Music Rights (https://globalmusicrights.com/)

52. See www.ascap.com/.

53. *Id.*

54. *See* www.harryfox.com/.

55. The Fairness in Music Licensing Act (FIMLA), part of the Sonny Bono Copyright Term Extension Act referenced in note 60, is codified at Pub. L. No. 105-298, 112 Stat. 2827, 17 U.S.C. §512 (2019).

56. 17 U.S.C. 110 (5)(A) (2019).

57. *See* https://us.moodmedia.com/.

58. *See* http://instoreaudionetwork.com/.

59. U.S. Copyright Office, *Orrin G. Hatch-Bob Goodlatte Music Modernization Act*, (2018), www.copyright.gov/music-modernization/ (last retrieved Nov. 11, 2018).

60. Dani Deahl, *The Music Modernization Act Has Been Signed Into Law*, The Verge, Oct. 11, 2018, www.theverge.com/2018/10/11/17963804/music-modernization-act-mma-copyright-law-bill-labels-congress (last retrieved Nov. 11, 2018).

61. *Id.*

62. *Id.*

63. 17 U.S.C. 111 (2019).

64. 17 U.S.C. 114(d)(1) (2019).

65. 17 U.S.C. 114(d)(2) (2019).

66. 17 U.S.C. 115 (2019).

67. 17 U.S.C. 118 (2019).

68. U.S. Const. art. 1, §8.

69. Copyright Term Extension Act (CTEA), Pub. L. 105-298, §102(b) and (d) (1998), 17 U.S.C. §304 (2019).

70. 17 U.S.C. §101 (2019).

71. Eldred v. Ashcroft, 537 U.S. 186 (2003).

72. 17 U.S.C. §§405 and 406 (2019).

73. 17 U.S.C. §401(a) (2019).

74. *Id.*

75. U.S. Copyright Office, *Copyright Basics* (Circular 1) (2019) at 6, *supra*, note 36.

76. *See* 37 C.F.R. §201.2 (Copyright notice) for the complete regulations, summarized in U.S. Copyright Office, *Copyright Notice* (Circular 3) (2019), www.copyright.gov/circs/circ03.pdf (last retrieved Nov. 11, 2018).

77. 17 U.S.C. §401(c) (2019).

78. *Id.*

79. U.S. Copyright Office, *Copyright Notice, supra*, note 75.

80. Public Law 103-307, enacted on June 26, 1992, made even renewal registration optional by automatically extending the duration of copyright obtained between January 1, 1964, and December 21, 1977, to an additional 47-year period. No registration renewal needs to be filed for this extension. There are some advantages to renewal registration, however. See U.S. Copyright Office, Renewal of Copyright (Circular 6A) (2019), www.copyright.gov/circs/circ06a.pdf.

81. *See* U.S. Copyright Office at 8, supra, note 75. Also see U.S. Copyright Office, *Best Edition of Published Copyrighted Works for the Collections of the Library of Congress* (Circular 7D) (2019), www.copyright.gov/circs/circ07b.pdf (last retrieved Nov. 11, 2018).

82. *See* U.S. Copyright Office, *Mandatory Deposit of Copies or Phonorecords for the Library of Congress* (Circular 7B) (2019), www.copyright.gov/circs/circ07d.pdf (last retrieved Nov. 11, 2018).

83. *See* U.S. Copyright Office at 7, *supra* note 89.

84. 17 U.S.C. §501(a) (2019).

85. Sony Corp. of America v. Universal City Studios, Inc., 465 U.S. 1112, 104 S. Ct. 1619, 80 L. Ed. 2d 1480 (1984).

86. At the time of the Court's decision, these devices were called videotape recorders or VTRs, but the terminology changed to videocassette recorders (VCRs).

87. *Sony Corp. of America*, 464 U.S. 417, 442.

88. Betamax VCRs used the Beta format, which ultimately lost out to the VHS format, but at the time of the suit, Beta was the dominant format. Even Sony abandoned Beta for VHS in VCRs for home use. These devices are no longer marketed to consumers. They have been superseded by video streaming that uses devices such as Roku, Amazon, Apple TV, Fire TV (Amazon) and Google Chromecast as well as cable and satellite recorders and digital recorders such as TiVo.

89. *Sony Corp. of America* 464 U.S. 417.

90. *Id.*

91. *See* Atlantic Recording Corp. v. XM Satellite Radio, Inc., 2007 WL 136186 (S.D.N.Y. July 17, 2006) (No. 06 Civ. 3733).

92. 17 U.S.C. §§101 *et seq.*

93. Pub. L. 105-3-4, Oct. 28, 1998, 112 Stat 2860.

94. *Id.*

95. *See Jagger Gets Satisfaction in Lawsuit Over Song*, Lexington (KY.), Herald-Leader (Associated Press), Apr. 27, 1988, at A22, col. 3.

96. *Id.*

97. Sid and Marty Krofft Television Productions, Inc. v. McDonald's Corp., 562 F.2d 1157 (9th Cir. 1977).

98. Universal City Studios, Inc. v. Film Ventures International, Inc. 543 F. Supp. 1134 (C.D. Calif. 1982).

99. *Id.*

100. Ruolo v. Russ Berrie & Co., 886 F.2d 931 (7th Cir. 1989).

101. Ronald Abramson, *"Look and Feel" of Computer Software*, Case and Comment, Jan.-Feb. 1990 at 3.

102. 17 U.S.C. §503(b) (2019).

103. 17 U.S.C. §504(b) (2019).

104. Pub. L. No. 100-568, 102 Stat. 2853, 2860.

105. The amounts prior to the October 31, 1988, enactment of the new law were $250 and $10,000, respectively.

106. 17 U.S.C. §504(c)(2) (2019).

107. *Id.*

108. 17 U.S.C. §505 (2019).

109. *See* 17 U.S.C. §506 (2019) and 18 U.S.C. §2319(b)(1)(A) (2019).

110. 18 U.S.C. §2318 (2019).

111. *See* www.wipo.int/treaties/en/text.jsp?file_id=283698 (last retrieved Nov.11, 2018).

112. *See* U.S. Copyright Office, International Copyright Relations of the United States (Circular 38A) (2019) at www.copyright.gov/circs/circ38a.pdf for a complete list of countries having copyright agreements with the United States.

113. *See* U.S. Copyright Office, *Copyright Restoration Under the URAA* (Circular 38B) (2019) at www.copyright.gov/circs/circ38b.pdf.

114. *See* International Intellectual Property Alliance website at https://iipa.org/ (last retrieved on Nov. 11, 2018).

115. 17 U.S.C. §507(a) (2019).

116. *Id.*

117. 17 U.S.C. §205 (2019).

118. *Constructive notice* is a legal term implying or imputing that the public has been notified in the eyes of the law by being provided a means for learning such information. In other words, by recording the agreement in the Copyright Office, the transferor and transferee have met any public notice requirements because anyone who examined the copies of the documents in the Copyright Office would know the terms of the agreement. This contrasts with *actual notice*, in which the parties have formally provided other parties with actual copies of the documents.

119. *See* 17 U.S.C. §205(c)(1)-(2) (2019).

120. *See* 17 U.S.C. §205(d) and (e) (2019).

121. See U.S. Copyright Office, *Recordation of Transfers and Other Documents* (Circular 12) (2019), www.copyright.gov/circs/circ12.pdf (last retrieved Nov. 11, 2018).

122. *Id.*

123. 17 U.S.C. §107 (2019).

124. *Id.*

125. Harper & Row Publishers, Inc. and The Reader's Digest Association, Inc. v. Nation Enterprises, 471 U.S. 539, 105 S. Ct. 2218, 88 L. Ed. 2d 588, 11 Med. L. Rptr. 1969 (1985).

126. *Id.*

127. *Id.*

128. *Id.*

129. *Id.*

130. American Geophysical Union v. Texaco, 85 Cov. 3446, 802 F. Supp. 1 (S.D.N.Y. 1992).

131. Under the Federal Interlocutory Appeals Act, 28 U.S.C. §1292 (b), a U.S. Court of Appeals can review any interlocutory order (an interim order pending final disposition of the controversy) in a civil case if the district court judge states in the decision that there is a controlling question of law on which there is apparent disagreement in the courts. The judge in this case had issued such an order so the appellate court could make the final determination.

132. American Geophysical Union v. Texaco, 37 F.3d 881, 32 U.S.P.Q.2d 1545 (2d Cir. 1992).

133. American Geophysical Union v. Texaco, 60 F.3d 913 (2d Cir. 1995).

134. *Court Clips Wings of Atlanta Video Clipping Service*, BROADCASTING, June 10, 1991 at 63, 65.

135. Fox News Network, LLC v. TV Eyes, Inc., 883 F.3d 169, 174 (2d Cir. 2018).

136. Luther R. Campbell a.k.a. Luke Skyywalker v. Acuff-Rose Music, Inc., 510 U.S. 569 (1994).

137. Luther R. Campbell a.k.a. Luke Skyywalker v. Acuff-Rose Music, Inc., 929 F.2d 700 (6th Cir. 1991).

138. Campbell v. Acuff-Rose 510 U.S. 569.

139. *Id.*

140. *Id.*

141. See www.copyright.gov/fair-use/summaries/matthewlombardo-drseuss.pdf (last retrieved Nov. 11, 2018).

142. Josh Russell, *Off Broadway 'Grinch' Parody Defeats Copyright Claims*, Courthouse News Service, Sept. 18, 2017, at www.courthousenews.com/off-broadway-grinch-parody-defeats-copyright-claims/ (last retrieved Nov. 11, 2018).

143. See www.copyright.gov/fair-use/summaries/matthewlombardo-drseuss.pdf, *supra*, note 142.

144. Lombardo v. Dr. Seuss Enterprises, 279 F.Supp.3d 497 (S.D. N.Y.2017).

145. *Id.*

146. *Id.*

147. Lombardo and Who's Holiday v. Dr. Seuss Enterprises, No. 17-2952-cv (2d Cir. 2018).

148. *Id.*

149. *Id.*

150. *Id.*

151. The Recording Industry Association of America (RIAA) and the Motion Picture Association of America, for example, have initiated hundreds of copyright infringement lawsuits.

8 Patents and Trademarks

Public relations and advertising professionals routinely encounter copyright issues. In many organizations, patents (which relate to inventions) and trademarks (which identify goods) can play an important day-to-day role as well. That's why an understanding of these types of intellectual property is essential.

As with copyrights (discussed in Chapter 7), the constitutional origins of patents can be traced to Article I, Section 8, of the U.S. Constitution, which gives Congress the authority "[t]o promote the Progress of Science and useful Arts, by securing for limited Times to Authors and Inventors the exclusive Right to their respective Writings and Discoveries."[1] Just as copyright law provides a limited monopoly—and therefore, an economic incentive—to those who produce original works of authorship, patent law provides a similar monopoly that allows inventors to profit from their innovations. Because of their clear origin in Article I, Section 8, patents and copyrights are regulated almost exclusively by federal statutes.

By contrast, trademarks involve both state and federal statutes, as well as common law. Federal trademark law arises out of the Constitution's "commerce" and "supremacy" clauses. The commerce clause, also in Article I, Section 8 of the U.S. Constitution, provides that Congress shall have the power "[t]o regulate Commerce with foreign Nations, and among the several States, and with the Indian Tribes."[2] This authority for Congress to regulate interstate ("among the several States") commerce has been interpreted broadly; one offshoot is federal trademark law, codified primarily in Title 15 of the United States Code (known as the "Lanham Act" or the "Trademark Act of 1946").[3]

The supremacy clause, in Article VI of the U.S. Constitution, gives federal law the right of preemption over state law. It provides, in part:

> This Constitution, and the Laws of the United States which shall be made in Pursuance thereof and all Treaties made, or which shall be made, under the Authority of the United States, shall be the supreme law of the Land; and the Judges in every State shall be bound thereby, any Thing in the Constitution or Laws of any State to the Contrary notwithstanding.[4]

As a result, trademarks may be registered and have protection under either state or federal statutes, the latter occurring if the mark is used in interstate commerce. Because of federal preemption, however, state trademark laws are not permitted to conflict with federal trademark laws.

Patents

The U.S. Patent and Trademark Office (USPTO), which, as the name indicates, handles both patents and trademarks, is an agency in the Department of Commerce headed by the commissioner of patents and trademarks, an assistant secretary of commerce. Patents, trademarks and copyright are all forms of exclusive (i.e., monopolistic) control that owners, who can be individuals or companies, can exercise to ensure that others generally cannot market, use or sell the work, invention or mark without the owner's consent.

There are three basic types of patents: utility, plant and design. Patents on mechanical devices, electrical and electronic circuits, chemicals and similar items are known as *utility patents*.[5] *Plant patents* apply to the invention or asexual reproduction of a distinct new variety of a natural plant,[6] and *design patents* are issued for new, original and ornamental designs of manufactured items.[7] In 1994, the U.S. Court of Appeals for the Federal Circuit, which hears all appeals from all decisions in patent infringement suits,[8] ruled that computer software could be patented, although mathematical formulas and algorithms cannot be. In *In re Alappat*, the court reasoned that software "creates a new machine, because a general purpose computer in effect becomes a special purpose computer once it is programmed."[9]

Creation and Duration

Under the current law, patents generally are protected for a 20-year term, measured from the filing date. In some cases, the 20-year period can be extended for a maximum of five years when marketing time was lost because of regulatory delay.[10] The 20-year period was chosen because it has been the standard of the rest of the industrialized world for some time. The law also creates a means by which a provisional application can be filed while the inventor prepares the regular application, which must be filed within one year. During that year, the invention is protected from infringement even if it has not already been built and used, which is a requirement

Figure 8.1 If sufficiently novel, inventions such as this lathe machine may be eligible for patent protection thanks to the Intellectual Property Clause of the Constitution of the United States, found in Article I, Section 8.

Credit line: Pixel B/Shutterstock.com

for protection under traditional patent law. This gives the inventor one year to market the invention without fear of it being stolen.

Securing a patent is typically only the first step in the process. Before the invention can be marketed, approval from other federal and state agencies may be needed. For example, a new food or drug product would probably require a green light from the U.S. Food and Drug Administration. Protecting a name under which the invention is to be sold would require compliance with provisions of trademark laws and probably trademark registration at some point. Unlike trademark and copyright laws, patent law is incredibly complex and the process of obtaining a patent is expensive, time-consuming and complicated. Attorneys who handle patent applications must be specially admitted to the Patent Bar. The filing fee for registering a patent is $360–$960 (if the company has at least 500 employees), and the costs of a search, which may be necessary to establish the novelty of the invention, can add up to thousands of dollars more. The cost for filing a provisional patent application is $280, plus additional fees when non-provisional patent status is sought.

Patent Infringement

Because the stakes can be quite high, patent holders for popular inventions rigorously defend their rights even against small-time entrepreneurs and companies. Infringement of a patent can result in extensive damages, as illustrated in the infringement suit filed by Polaroid against Eastman Kodak over instant photography.[11] When the dust settled in 1986, Eastman Kodak was ordered to pay Polaroid more than $1 billion in damages and was prohibited from further sales of instant photo cameras, film and related products. The suit was based on patents granted to Polaroid in the 1970s.

Patents are generally granted on a first-come, first-served basis, and the race to the finish line can be intense when competitors battle. When two or more claimants apply separately for a patent on essentially similar inventions, the USPTO will hold an interference proceeding, complete with motions and testimony, to ascertain the rightful inventor.

Trademarks

Under the Lanham Act, a trademark is defined as "any word, name, symbol, or device, or any combination thereof adopted and used by a manufacturer or merchant to identify his or her goods or services."[12] Thus, a trademark can be a name, slogan, design or distinct sound so long as it identifies and distinguishes the trademarked goods or services from those of others. The key characteristics are identification and distinction. Classic examples are the Nike Corporation's use of the name Nike, the "swoosh" symbol that appears on Nike products and the slogan "JUST DO IT."

Colors were recognized as potential trademarks in the 1995 Supreme Court decision *Qualitex Company v. Jacobson Products, Inc.*[13] A unanimous Court held that the Lanham Trademark Act of 1946 allows trademark registration of a color. The opinion, written by Justice Breyer, said that the special shade of green-gold used to identify dry cleaning press pads made by Qualitex had acquired the requisite "secondary meaning" under the Lanham Act. A color acquires secondary meaning when consumers strongly associate it with a particular product. Jacobson Products, a competitor to Qualitex, had challenged the trademark registration, unsuccessfully arguing that such registration would create uncertainty about what shades of color a competitor could use and that it was unworkable because of the limited supply of colors. Sounds, such as the roar of the MGM lion, have enjoyed trademark protection for some time, although registration for sounds is harder to come by. As with colors, sounds can attain trademark status only if they have acquired secondary meaning. In 1978, the Trademark Trial and Appeal Board recognized the combination of the musical notes "G, E, and C" used by the National Broadcasting Company as a valid trademark.[14] Harley-Davidson, Inc., which already owns the rights to the word *hog* for motorcycles, applied for a trademark on its engine sound in 1994, but several competitors, including Suzuki, Honda and Kawasaki, opposed the registration. After six years of litigation, Harley-Davidson abandoned its sound trademark application.

Service Marks

Service marks are essentially the same as trademarks, except that they identify the source of services rather than goods. Bank of America, for example, the name for the institution that provides banking and financial services, is a service mark, as is the red and blue stylized mark that appears on the company's checks, ATMs and brick-and-mortar banking centers. Other famous service marks include Hertz, Allstate, Netflix, Citicorp and True Value. The distinction between trademarks and service marks is semantic; the law operates identically for both. To avoid repetition, the term *trademark* is used hereinafter to refer to both trademarks and service marks.

Purpose

Trademarks are extremely important in advertising and public relations. Through the effective marketing and communication of its trademark, an owner can build invaluable market goodwill. Think about the value of trademarks such as Apple, Coca-Cola, McDonald's, Verizon, Xerox, Sony and Walt Disney; it is no wonder that trademark battles can be intense and drawn out, with large sums of money at stake.

The basic purpose of a trademark is to enable consumers to identify the origin of a product or service. Identifying the origin does not necessarily mean knowing the specific manufacturer, distributor or franchise—it simply indicates an association with a particular source. The idea is that the consumer should be able to have confidence that all goods with a specific trademark are associated with the owner of the mark.

For example, when a viewer sees a television commercial for Hershey's Kisses, it is reasonable for a person to assume that all Kisses come from Hershey's. That does not mean, however, that the consumer can assume that all candy bearing the Hershey's trademark is necessarily actually made by the same company, but simply that Hershey's has given its consent for, and presumably imposed its standards on, the distribution of the products under its name. In other words, trademarks provide some indication of quality assurance.

The Coca-Cola Company, for example, has licensed its own line of clothing. Disney Enterprises, Inc. licenses or produces thousands of products, including toys, movies, clothes, games, paint and, of course, its own entertainment complexes throughout the world. Neither Disney nor Coca-Cola actually manufactures all the goods bearing their names; instead, they have contracts with other firms granting permission for the use of their marks.

Trademarks, like patents and copyrights, can be sold and transferred by a written agreement or contract just as with other types of property. When corporations merge and large companies acquire smaller ones, the trademarks are often among the most valuable assets. Consumers rely heavily on brand names or trademarks in their decisions, which is why a company will pay hundreds of millions of dollars to acquire an already well-established trademark for a brand of candy bar, for example, rather than market a similar candy bar under a new trademark. The existing brand is likely a sure winner; a new name could be a huge risk.

Creation and Ownership

The USPTO handles both trademarks and patents, but trademark registration is much different and less expensive than for patents. In fact, copyright and trademark registration involve quite similar processes, although they are administered by different federal agencies. The similarities, however, between trademarks and copyright end there. Unlike copyright and patents, trademarks do not derive their origin from the U.S. Constitution. The authority of Congress to regulate trademarks and service marks, however, does come from the Constitution—more specifically, the commerce clause referenced earlier in this chapter. Unlike copyrights and patents, which have limited duration, trademarks can last indefinitely as long as the owner continues to use and register the trademark and takes appropriate steps to ensure that infringers are prosecuted and that the mark does not go into the public domain.

Trademarks are statutory creations of state and federal government. Before a trademark can be registered under federal law (i.e., the Lanham Act, passed in 1946 and named after its Congressional sponsor), the owner must either use the mark on goods that are shipped or sold in interstate or international commerce or have a bona fide intention to use the mark in such commerce.[15] Trademarks that are not used or intended to be used in interstate and/or international commerce can be registered and protected only under state law. Because trademark laws vary considerably from state to state, state laws will not be discussed here. Prudent advertising and public relations professionals, however, should be aware of state trademark laws that might affect their or their clients' business.

Trademark Infringement

Trademark infringement occurs generally in one of two ways. Either unscrupulous manufacturers produce "knockoff" items that improperly (and illegally) display legitimate trademarks owned by others or a product displays a mark that is confusingly similar to another, similar product. If a street vendor offers to sell what appears to be designer merchandise on the cheap, one can assume the goods are trademark-infringing knockoffs. This is clear trademark infringement with definite negative economic consequences for the owner of the trademark.

A second type of trademark infringement—based on a likelihood of consumer confusion—is less straightforward but may be equally detrimental to the trademark owner. Consumers are likely to be confused when similar marks appear on similar categories of goods. For example, a company that sells winter coats with the "Bobwhite" trademark probably would be concerned about someone else selling "Bobwhite" boots—consumers may reasonably think the boots are made by the coat people. This might give rise to a legitimate trademark infringement lawsuit because of the likelihood of confusion. Bobwhite coats would likely have no legitimate complaint, however, about someone who sells "Bobwhite" birdseed. No reasonable consumer would confuse birdseed with coats, and such a lawsuit would likely be unsuccessful.

Even when a likelihood of confusion is slim, companies with valuable marks often are aggressive in discouraging *any* use of similar trademarks. In 1996, for example, some coffee companies who sell their products on the Internet got a warning from Sun Microsystems, which owns the trademark "Java" for its computer programming language. Sun was concerned that its trademark was being infringed by the use of the term *java* in some of the coffee companies' Internet addresses. According to press reports, there was a bit of irony in that several of the companies had used Sun's Java language to create their own websites.[16]

Even when there is no threat of litigation, companies sometimes change or cease using trademarks—even non-infringing ones—because of consumer perceptions, changing marketing strategies, or at the behest or urging of governmental entities. Often, the decision to change or abandon a trademark is made because of public relations or related concerns. For example, the famous L'eggs package for women's hosiery is now history because the Sara Lee Corporation phased out the containers in 1992 in favor of cardboard packaging that is less taxing on the environment. The Procter & Gamble (P&G) Company redesigned its decades-old moon and stars trademark, eliminating curls in the trade character's beard that looked like the number "6." The company had filed lawsuits and repeatedly issued statements attempting to dispel rumors that P&G supported Satan because of the sixes that appeared in the symbol's beard. (The number 666 is mentioned in the *Book of Revelation* in connection with the devil.) The company introduced two newer symbols—a cursive Procter & Gamble and the abbreviated P&G—but has continued using the older trademark in its revised form.

Sometimes, trademarks are removed from the market for reasons related to brand identity and strategy development. For example, the Washington, D.C.-based team that competes in the National Basketball Association (NBA) was previously known as the Washington Bullets but now competes as the Washington Wizards, a name team management believed better reflected contemporary values. In other cases, trademark owners have maintained registration for established marks but reduced their visibility in the market, only to reintroduce the marks later as nostalgic throwbacks with renewed market value. Nike's "JUST DO IT" tagline is an example of a trademark whose registration has been constant but whose visibility in the marketplace has ebbed and flowed. Trademark owners who engage in this strategy must be sure to maintain some use of their registered marks to prevent others from claiming abandonment and seeking to make use of a mark themselves.

In other cases, entities with registered trademarks have yielded to governmental pressure over the use of certain marks even when their legal risk for failing to do so is unclear. In 1991, the Kellogg Company changed the name of its Heartwise cereal to Fiberwise under pressure from the FDA, which has a policy of discouraging the use of *heart* in a brand name.

Trademark Dilution

Even where there is no likelihood of confusion, trademark owners who believe their trademarks have been lessened in value, or had their meanings diluted, may be able to bring a dilution lawsuit. Trademark dilution occurs when the unauthorized use of a mark causes the distinctive quality of the mark to be lessened, or diluted, as Coca-Cola, Inc. alleged when posters urging readers to "Enjoy Cocaine"—instead of "Enjoy Coca-Cola"—appeared on the market, displayed in a style that mimicked Coke's own trademarked materials. Recognizing the vulnerability of famous marks like Coca-Cola's to have their goodwill diminished in this manner, Congress passed the Federal Trademark Dilution Act[17] (FTDA) of 1995. The law gave owners of famous trademarks an avenue for bringing a dilution action if they believe a mark's distinctive quality has been negatively affected. Early cases in which courts were required to interpret the dilution statute resulted in mixed signals regarding whether potential, or actual, dilution was required. In 2003, the Supreme Court of the United States decided *Moseley v. V Secret Catalogue, Inc.*[18] and held that proof of actual dilution was required. In that case, lingerie seller Victoria's Secret unsuccessfully complained that "Victor's Little Secret" (for a store selling adult-oriented merchandize, including lingerie) diluted the Victoria's Secret trademark. In its opinion, the Supreme Court said the fact that consumers may see the Victor's Little Secret mark and think of the more famous Victoria's Secret was not enough for dilution; proof of actual harm was required.[19]

Congress clarified its intent with the Trademark Dilution Revision Act of 2006,[20] effectively overturning *Moseley*. The revised Act provides that the likelihood of dilution, not actual dilution, is sufficient. It also attempts to define "blurring"[21] and "tarnishment"[22] and specifies that dilution claims must be based on one of these two grounds.

In 1999, Congress directed its attention to cyberspace, providing an option for owners of famous trademarks to address dilution in the form of Internet domain names registered by third parties who have "a bad faith intent to profit from that mark." The Anticybersquatting Consumer Protection Act[23] (ACPA) concerns "cybersquatting" practices from disputes such as *Panavision International v. Toeppen*, in which the makers of Panasonic products sued an individual who registered Internet domain names featuring famous trademarks and then attempted to sell them for profit. The defendant registered www.panavision.com,[24] preventing the internationally known electronics maker from registering this most obvious of domain names. The Ninth Circuit Court of Appeals affirmed the lower court's finding that the defendant had diluted the Panasonic mark by making it more difficult for potential customers to find the legitimate Panasonic website.[25] The ACPA and other issues related to trademarks in cyberspace are discussed more fully in Chapter 13.

Registration

Contrary to popular understanding, it is not necessary for a trademark to be registered to be protected. Without registration, marks are protected where they are in use by common-law principles of ownership, but registration certainly is a good idea. The registration process and term of protection—10 years—under federal law for trademarks and service marks are the same. At one time, trademarks owners who wished to register a mark were required to begin using the mark in commerce prior to receiving any legal protection under the federal trademark statute. With the Trademark Law Revision Act of 1988, Congress added an "intent to use" option that allows trademark owners to apply to register their marks if they have a bona fide intention of using the marks in commerce within six months of submitting the application. The complete registration process commences after the user submits evidence to the Patent and Trademark Office verifying that the mark is actually in use in commerce. As long as the applicant maintains and can demonstrate a bona fide intention to use the mark in commerce, an "intent to use" application may be extended—generally not longer than six additional months—by submitting a written request prior to the end of the original extension.

As with copyright, there are some important advantages to registration, including:

A.	Providing *prima facie* evidence of first use of the mark in interstate commerce and the validity of the registration.
B.	Permitting the owner to sue in federal court (U.S. District Court) for infringement.
C.	Allowing lost profits, court costs, attorneys' fees, criminal penalties and treble damages, in some cases, to be sought.

D. Serving as constructive notice of an ownership claim, preventing someone from claiming that the trademark was used because of a good faith belief that no one else had claim to it. In other words, once the mark is registered, any potential user has an obligation to check the registry to ascertain that no one else owns the mark.

E. Establishing a basis for foreign registration.

Registration is a fairly simple process. The owner files an application (online filing is preferred and available at www.uspto.gov), supplies a drawing of the mark, pays a filing fee for each class of goods or services for which the owner is applying and provides three specimens showing the actual use of the mark on goods or services if the mark already has been used in commerce. Online, electronic filing fees for an initial application range from $225 to $400. Paper filings submitted by mail are permitted but discouraged, and fees are much higher—around $600. In some cases, additional fees are required. The fees for renewals, necessary every 10 years, begin at $425 for each class of goods for which the mark is registered.

Once the USPTO has received the application materials, a trademark examining attorney must decide if the mark can actually be registered. Not all registration attempts are successful. For example, Anheuser-Busch Inc.'s effort to register the mark "LA" for a low-alcohol beer failed. The name "LA" was deemed merely descriptive and thus lacking the requisite secondary meaning or distinctiveness. According to the court,

> Initials do not usually differ significantly in their trademark role from the description words that they represent ... [and thus] ... there is a heavy burden on a trademark claimant seeking to show an independent meaning of initials apart from the descriptive words which are their source.[26]

A registration refusal can be appealed to the Trademark Trial and Appeal Board, an administrative tribunal in the USPTO. Further refusal can be appealed to the federal courts. The Supreme Court of the United States has jurisdiction to hear further appeals but rarely does so.

If approval is granted, the mark is published in the *Trademark Official Gazette*, a weekly bulletin from the USPTO. Anyone opposing the registration has 30 days after the publication to file a protest with the Trademark Trial and Appeal Board, which acts like a trial court. If there is no opposition, in about three months after publication, the registration then becomes official if the application was based on actual use in commerce. If the application is based on an intention to use the mark in commerce, the trademark owner has six months to either use the mark in commerce or request a six-month extension. As of January 1, 2010, there is a rebuttable presumption that if a trademark is not used for three years, it has been abandoned. Under a rebuttable presumption, the owner would have the burden of demonstrating that the trademark was in use in any subsequent infringement suit.

Once federal registration is issued by the USPTO, the owner must provide notice of registration by using (a) the ® symbol; (b) the phrase, Registered in U.S. Patent and Trademark Office; or (c) the abbreviation, Reg. U.S. Pat. & Tm. Off. These registration symbols cannot be used before registration. Prior to registration, an owner is free to use ™ or SM as symbols of a trademark and service mark, respectively, although he or she is not required to do so. Recall that registration is not required for trademark protection, although there are many advantages to registration.

The Lanham Act provides several grounds on which trademark registration may be denied. For much of its existence, the Lanham Act contained a "disparagement provision" that allowed the USPTO to deny registration of marks that "consist of or comprised matter which may disparage persons, institutions, beliefs, or national symbols, or bring them into contempt or disrepute."[27] Based on this provision, the USPTO denied an application for trademark registration for a band consisting of Asian-born musicians who called themselves "The Slants."[28] The band challenged the ruling and in keeping with the discussion on First Amendment principles from Chapter 1, the Supreme Court ruled in 2017 that the government may not refuse to register a trademark based on its content.[29] Writing for the Court, Justice Alito said the provision "offends the bedrock First Amendment principle: Speech may not be banned on the ground that it expresses ideas that offend."[30]

The opinion means that otherwise eligible trademarks like the Washington Redskins will not forfeit protection if government officials find them to be controversial or objectionable. Although "edgy" or potentially controversial trademarks may serve some entities well, most organizations seek to cultivate trademarks that are not likely to result in negative associations. Courts also have considered a similar challenge to the Lanham Act's "scandalousness provision" that bars registration of marks consisting of immoral or scandalous matter. The United States Court of Appeals for the Federal Circuit, for example, has held that the scandalousness provision used to bar registration of the mark "FUCT" is unconstitutional.[31] Even though the mark was correctly deemed to be scandalous or immoral based on its vulgarity, the denial of registration on that basis was impermissibly content based. In light of these recent court outcomes, the valid grounds for denying a registration application include that the mark:

A. Falsely suggests a connection with people, organizations, beliefs or national symbols.
B. Consists of or simulates the flag, coat of arms or other insignia of the United States, a state, a city or any foreign country.
C. Is the name, portrait or signature of a living person unless he or she has given permission.
D. Is the name, portrait or signature of a deceased U.S. president while his surviving spouse is alive unless the spouse has given consent.
E. Is so similar to a mark previously registered that it would be likely to confuse or deceive a reasonable person.
F. Is simply descriptive or deceptively misdescriptive of the goods or services.[32]

With respect to the last ground, "descriptiveness," an exception exists: if an applicant can demonstrate that a mark already being used in commerce has become distinctive enough that the public now identifies the goods or services with the mark, it can be registered even if it is merely descriptive. For example, *World's Finest* is a registered trademark of World's Finest Chocolate, Inc.

Trademark registration is not restricted to commercial enterprises. Individuals, as well as nonprofit organizations, trade associations and other groups, can register trademarks. For example, the Society of Professional Journalists (SPJ) registered its name and logo—along with the name, Sigma Delta Chi—as trademarks in 1991. Trade names such as International Business Machines Corporation and Pepsi-Cola Bottling Company ordinarily may not be registered as trademarks under the federal statute, but names associated with the product or service (i.e., International Business Machines, IBM, Pepsi-Cola and Pepsi) may be registered, and the corporation name can be filed and registered with the appropriate official (usually the Secretary of State) in each state.

Prudent advertising and public relations professionals should be familiar with the registration process because it can play a major role in determining the outcome of an infringement suit

Figure 8.2 Trade names such as Pepsi-Cola Bottling Company ordinarily may not be registered as trademarks under the federal trademark statute, but names associated with the product or service (i.e., Pepsi-Cola and Pepsi) may be registered, and the corporation name can be filed and registered with the appropriate official (usually the Secretary of State) in each state.

Credit line: Apollo51x/Shutterstock.com

or a suit over ownership of the mark. A good start is the USPTO website, which features *Basic Facts About Trademarks*.[33] The International Trademark Association, a private organization in New York City, also distributes informative materials, as does the American Bar Association's Section on Intellectual Property Law.[34]

Transferring or Assigning a Trademark

As noted earlier in this chapter, trademarks routinely change hands or ownership. Often, the transfer of ownership of a trademark—called an assignment—is the result of a corporate merger or acquisition. Sometimes, a trademark owner will simply sell or even give a registered trademark to another entity. In yet other cases, trademark owners may maintain ownership of their marks but change their own names. When assignments of registered marks or name changes occur that affect the record of ownership, the USPTO requires that corresponding registration records be updated. This may be done by completing an online form or submitting a paper filing to the Assignment Recordation Branch of the USPTO. Trademark owners also are urged to modify their registration records to correct any clerical or typographical errors in the listed owner name.

Protecting a Trademark

The owners of popular trademarks such as Xerox, IBM, Kleenex and Kodak sometimes purchase ads in professional publications informing journalists and others that their names are registered trademarks and should be identified as such. Many famous former trademarks, such as cornflakes, linoleum, mimeograph, escalator and raisin bran, went into the public domain and thus lost their protection as trademarks because they were abandoned or the owners did not aggressively fight infringers. Some companies send out press releases and buy ads in trade publications requesting that their trademarks be used as a proper adjective in connection with their products and services, and not as a verb. For example, one may use the search engine, Google, but should not "google" the search, especially when using a competing search engine.

Advertisers find it particularly irksome when news stories and other communications mention trademarks without identifying them as such. *The Associated Press Stylebook and Briefing on Media Law* notes, in its "trademark" entry, "In general, use a generic equivalent unless the trademark name is essential to the story."[35] The *Stylebook* also says that trademarks should be capitalized when they appear.

Some companies have a reputation for diligence in notifying newspapers, magazines and radio and television stations when they believe their trademarks have been used inappropriately. They do this because it is one way to demonstrate a strong effort to protect the marks in case an infringement occurs and they must counter the claim from a defendant that the mark has become generic and no longer worthy of protection. Although a company would have no real basis for claiming infringement simply because a news or feature story made generic use of a trademark, the savvy advertiser and public relations professional should remind reporters, editors and other journalists from time to time that good journalistic practice dictates appropriate acknowledgment of trademarks. When registered slogans, names or symbols are used in an advertisement, press release or other publication, the registered trademark symbol—®—or the common-law designation—™—should be used, as appropriate, to alert the world to the trademark's status.

Remedies for Infringement

Thousands of battles have been fought about trademarks over the years for products ranging from apples to zippers. Trademark owners who discover trademark infringement have several options, ranging from friendly negotiation to intense litigation. Often, enforcement of trademark rights begins with a friendly (but firm) letter from the trademark owner's attorney pointing out the infringement and requesting that it cease immediately. If such a letter is ineffective, or if compensation is sought, the owner may ultimately turn to litigation in federal court. The traditional remedy for trademark infringement is injunctive relief. In other words, a court can require that an infringer take certain actions or cease taking certain actions. The Lanham Act gives courts power to grant injunctions in a variety of ways. Injunctive relief may include requiring the infringer to run corrective advertising and recall and destroy all goods bearing the infringing trademark.[36] In 2004, for example, Adidas America, Inc., the athletic apparel maker famous for its three stripes, filed suit against Ralph Lauren Corp., complaining about a Polo jacket featuring sleeves with two stripes. Adidas requested that the court order the defendant to recall all the two-striped apparel and any related advertising materials so that it could be impounded and destroyed.

Sometimes a court will award monetary relief to a trademark owner. Monetary relief is not guaranteed in trademark litigation, but it can be significant when awarded. The sum may include the defendant's profits, the cost for corrective advertising, attorney's fees, costs and triple the plaintiff's damages. In cases involving counterfeit goods, the Lanham Act allows for statutory damages of not less than $1,000 or more than $200,000 per counterfeit mark per type of goods or services.[37] If the use of the counterfeit mark was willful, the statute allows the court to award up to $2 million per counterfeit per type of goods or services.[38]

Trademarks and Parody

The Trademark Law Revision Act of 1988 permits a trademark owner to recover damages and get an injunction for product or service misrepresentation. It applies, however, only to commercial misrepresentation and not to political communication, editorial content or parodies.

An example of the latter is the case of *L.L. Bean, Inc. v. Drake Publishers, Inc.*[39] When Drake published a sex-oriented catalog parodying L.L. Bean's famous clothing catalog, L.L. Bean filed suit seeking an injunction against the parody, claiming that Drake's *Back-To-School-Sex-Catalog* violated Maine's anti-dilution statute. Such statutes are aimed at protecting trademarks and similar names from suffering disparagement, and thus having their commercial value chipped away through unauthorized use. The First Circuit U.S. Court of Appeals ruled that, because the sex catalog was noncommercial use, the anti-dilution statute could not be used to prohibit its publication because of First Amendment concerns.[40]

Note, however, that had the sex catalog been an attempt to actually market products rather than simply an artistic endeavor, and had it been published after the new Act took effect on November 16, 1989, the Court probably would have ruled in favor of L.L. Bean. Recall that Larry Flynt's notorious Campari parody about Jerry Falwell (discussed in Chapter 5) had First Amendment protection according to the Supreme Court of the United States. The manufacturer of Campari took no legal action against Flynt, but probably would have been unsuccessful because the ad was editorial commentary, not commercial material.

Conclusion

Trademarks have considerable protection under both state and federal law, but trademark holders must take aggressive steps to ensure that their marks do not become diluted and risk going into the public domain. Prudent advertising and public relations professionals representing commercial and noncommercial enterprises should constantly monitor the use of their trademarks for possible infringement, while making sure that they treat the trademarks of others with appropriate respect.

Notes

1. U.S. Const. art. I, §8.
2. *Id.*
3. 15 U.S.C. §1051 *et seq.*
4. U.S. Const. art. VI.
5. *See* 35 U.S.C. §101.
6. *See* 35 U.S.C. §161.
7. *See* 35 U.S.C. §171.
8. All patent infringement suits must be brought in U.S. District Court. Other federal courts and state courts have no jurisdiction. Appeals from a U.S. District Court are then heard exclusively by the U.S. Court of Appeals for the Federal Circuit. Upon a *writ of certiorari*, a discretionary writ, the U.S. Supreme Court can, if it so chooses, hear any appeals from the Federal Circuit.
9. In re Alappat, 33 F.3d 1526, 13 U.S.P.Q.2d 1545 (Fed. Cir. 1994).

10. Pub. L. No. 98-417 (1984) and Pub. L. No. 100-670 (1988) had granted such an extension for drugs, but the 1989 Act broadened the extension to include patents for other inventions and discoveries.

11. Polaroid v. Eastman Kodak, 789 F.2d 1556, 229 U.S.P.Q. 561 (Fed. Cir. 1986); *cert. denied,* 479 U.S. 850.

12. 15 U.S.C. §1051.

13. Qualitex Company v. Jacobson Products, Inc., 514 U.S. 159, 115 S. Ct. 1300, 131 L.Ed.2d 248 (1995).

14. In re General Electric Co., 199 U.S.P.Q. 560 (T.T.A.B. 1978).

15. www.uspto.gov/trademarks/basics/index.jsp (last retrieved Dec. 8, 2009).

16. *See Java Can Get You in Hot Water,* Lexington (KY), Herald-Leader, June 15, 1996, at A11, col. 1.

17. Federal Trademark Dilution Act of 1995, Pub. L. No. 104-98, H.R. 1295 104th Cong. (1996) (amending the Trademark Act of 1946 to revise the protection of famous marks).

18. Moseley v. V Secret Catalogue, Inc. 537 U.S. 418 (2003).

19. *Id.*

20. Trademark Dilution Revision Act of 2006, Pub. L. No. 109-312, H.R. 683, 109th Cong. (amending the Trademark Act of 1946 with respect to dilution by blurring or tarnishment).

21. Dilution by blurring is "association arising from the similarity between a mark or trade name and a famous mark that impairs the distinctiveness of the famous mark." *Id.*

22. Dilution by tarnishment is "association arising from the similarity between a mark or trade name and a famous mark that harms the reputation of the famous mark." *Id.*

23. 15 U.S.C. §1125(d)(1)(A).

24. The corresponding website showed a photograph of Pana, Illinois.

25. 141 F.3d 1316 (9th Cir. 1998).

26. G. Heileman Brewing Co., Inc. v. Anheuser-Busch, Inc., Nos. 88-1223, 88-1309, 88-1310 (Apr. 26, 1989); *see LA Law,* 75 A.B.A. J. 92, Aug. 1989.

27. 15 U.S.C. §1052(a).

28. Matal v. Tam, 137 S. Ct. 1744 (2017).

29. *Id.*

30. *Id.* at 1751.

31. *In re Brunetti,* No. 15-1109 (Fed. Cir. 2017).

32. *See* 15 U.S.C. §1052.

33. www.uspto.gov/trademarks/basics/index.jsp (last retrieved Dec. 8, 2009).

34. *See* American Bar Association, What Is a Trademark?, 1995.

35. D. Christian et al. eds., *Associated Press 2008 Stylebook and Briefing on Media Law* (The Associated Press, New York 2011).

36. 15 U.S.C. §116(a).

37. 15 U.S.C. §117(c).

38. *Id.*

39. L.L. Bean, Inc. v. Drake Publishers, Inc., 811 F.2d 26, 13 Med. L. Rptr. 2009 (1st Cir. 1987).

40. *Id.*

9 Contracts and Other Ways to Protect "Ideas" and Intangible Property

As discussed in the preceding chapters, intellectual property laws generally do not protect ideas that have not been expressed and fixed in some kind of tangible form. A best-selling novel, as expressed on paper or in a Word-processing program, is covered by copyright law but is unprotected in the ideas stage. A concept for building a better mousetrap is unprotected until recorded in the form of specific blueprints. The lack of legal protection generally available for ideas prompted one court to describe ideas, once shared, as being "free as the air."[1] This, however, is a bit of an overstatement; although legal protection for ideas is skimpy, avenues of redress may exist for those whose ideas or other intangible property have been improperly taken, or misappropriated.

Creative people typically enter the uncertain legal territory that is the law of ideas in one of three ways. The first is when proprietary information—such as a trade secret—that is unique and vital to an organization is misappropriated (think "stolen") and shared with a third party. The second is when unique concepts—such as a big idea for an advertising campaign—are shared with prospective clients or investors and are then used or pursued without the creator's permission or involvement. The third is when original, creative materials, such as newspaper articles or website content, are re-purposed—but not necessarily "copied" in a way that violates copyrights—by another entity for its own commercial ends.

While intellectual property law is likely of little assistance in these circumstances, legal schemes that address the misappropriation of trade secrets, ideas and other intangible property may come to the rescue of those who operate in the realm of creativity. This chapter addresses each of these types of misappropriation, beginning with a necessary introduction to contracts, whose principles impact the law of ideas in multiple ways. Readers should note, however, that the types of misappropriation discussed here differ from the "invasion of privacy" kind of misappropriation presented in Chapter 6, which dealt with the unconsented use of another's name or likeness, often for commercial purposes.

Contracts as a Means for the Protection of Ideas

Almost all the means of protecting ideas discussed in this chapter involve, at some point, an evaluation of whether or not the parties have been bound by some kind of contractual obligation. Short of specific statutory protection (e.g., the Copyright Act of 1976) found in legislative schemes, contracts provide the most certainty when it comes to protecting creative output. Contracts literally may be used to define the boundaries of almost any relationship among bargaining parties, from employment and procurement of services, to the present context of protecting personal intellectual output from exploitation by others. Consequently, a number of disputes over ideas are ultimately decided using contract principles to determine the rights and responsibilities of the parties. To understand how contract law impacts the protection of ideas and creative expression, it is beneficial to first understand the basic components of contracts.

When someone mentions the word "law" in casual conversation, those within earshot might immediately think of the law created within a legislative chamber or courtroom. In fact, however, those thousands of volumes of codes, regulations and court opinions make up a mere fraction of the complex organism that is American law. Much of the legal system consists of little bits of "private" law, more commonly known as contracts.

It is useful to think of a contract as a kind of private statute that defines the behaviors, risks and obligations of the parties who have entered into it. The contract could be immensely complex, such as an agreement governing the exchange of billions of dollars for the construction of a new metropolitan airport. More commonly, though, it may be as simple as a customer in a local grocery store signing a credit card slip to purchase a six-pack of Miller Lite. Each of the millions of credit sale transactions that occur every day is a contract, or an enactment of private law, that defines the performances of the parties to the transaction: the credit card company (who has agreed to pay the retailer), the cardholder (who signs the slip and agrees to pay the credit card company at a certain time each month and at a certain interest rate) and the retailer (who performs the store's obligation by surrendering the six-pack to the purchaser).

Express Contracts and the "Bargained-For Exchange"

Classical contract law is based on the concept that two sophisticated parties capable of exercising free will may enter into a private agreement that, if valid, will take its place alongside statutes and regulations as enforceable law. If one party to the contract fails to perform as promised (called a "breach"), the other party may then call upon public institutions such as courts to help the deprived party enforce a remedy against the breaching party. Courts may enforce a variety of remedies, ranging from awarding money damages to requiring the breaching party to live up to the letter of the contract, called "specific performance."

In simple terms, a valid contract requires a bargained-for exchange: one party makes an offer in the form of a promise to perform an act, and the other party has a right to accept the offer, either through a return promise or by performing an act. Each party's return promise or performance is referred to as "consideration" for the other person's promise or performance. To be enforceable as a contract, all promises must be supported by consideration. Without consideration, the parties merely have an informal agreement, which is not legally enforceable.

To illustrate the concepts of offer, acceptance and consideration, contemplate the scenario in which an enterprising, artistic teen hopes to make a little extra money by creating logos for local businesses. She approaches her neighbor, a pet-store owner, and promises to design a new logo by the end of the week for a payment of $75. The neighbor happily accepts the teen's offer. In this situation, the girl made an offer to perform a service that was accepted by the neighbor's return promise to make a payment of $75 when the job was completed satisfactorily. Each promise served as consideration for the other. On its face, this situation creates a valid, enforceable contract. If the girl designed the logo to the exact terms of the agreement but was not paid, the teen could be reasonably assured that a court would enforce a judgment for breach of contract against the nonpaying neighbor.

Changing the scenario slightly, however, might create different results. If the girl had gone to the neighbor and offered to design a logo for free but then did not follow through with her promise, the neighbor could not expect to win a judgment against the teen for breach of contract because a court would likely say "no consideration = no contract."

Consideration may not be based on the performance of some past act.[2] This becomes an important concept for the discussion of protection of ideas. For example, in our scenario, if the teen were feeling spontaneously creative, sat down and designed a new logo for the neighbor's pet store "just to be nice," the neighbor's subsequent promise to reward the teen with $75 would not create an enforceable contract at law if the promise slipped the neighbor's mind. The teen's past act of creating the logo would not serve as consideration for the neighbor's promise to pay her.

Note, however, the potential in this particular hypothetical example for copyright law to kick in: once the teen fixes the logo design in a tangible medium—in a sketch on paper or in digital form on the computer—the logo becomes her copyright-protected property. Although the pet-store owner would not be required, under contract principles, to pay the teen for creating the unsolicited logo, his later decision to use it without obtaining her permission would be copyright infringement. And, of course, trademark law could come into play here, as well: once the pet-store owner uses the logo in commerce, it will serve as his business's trademark according to the principles discussed in Chapter 8.

With these basic contract examples in hand, it becomes somewhat easier to understand the challenges independent creative communications consultants face in protecting their ideas from misappropriation.

Implied Contracts

The discussion of contracts has thus far been about contracts whose terms are stated—often in writing—with specificity. Not all potentially binding agreements are clearly spelled out, however, and the creative process does not necessarily lend itself to ordered thinking in which the sharing of ideas is neatly preceded by the calling of a contract attorney. In fact, the creative process often is spur-of-the-moment and spontaneous. Before "blurting out" a potentially great idea, however, creatives should be aware that, in doing so, they may risk losing control.

In dealing with prospective clients, idea generators should make it known that they are proposing a business transaction and are not simply sharing their valuable ideas out of the goodness of their hearts. That is because in some situations, contractual obligations may be assumed from the statements and behavior of the parties, the circumstances of the interaction or even industry custom. These types of contracts are called "implied contracts" or "contracts implied in fact." Implied contracts operate like express contracts and may be created when two conditions are met. The first condition is that the idea creator makes clear an idea will be shared with the understanding that the recipient has an obligation to pay for the idea if it is used. The second condition is that the recipient of the idea clearly knows about and accepts the obligation to pay before the idea is disclosed. Implied contracts may ultimately be binding on the parties, but unlike express contracts whose terms may ultimately be disputed in court, implied contracts likely require the intervention of a court to declare that they even exist. And the terms of implied contracts tend to be even more difficult to discern.

More rarely, courts find the existence of another type of legal obligation: an "implied-in-law-contract," or "quasi contract." Note that again, the terminology may be confusing. The type of "implied-in-fact" contract discussed above is essentially an after-the-fact contract based on circumstantial evidence of the parties' actual intentions. Quasi contracts, by contrast, are not really contracts at all—they are "fictitious" contracts that impose an obligation on one party to pay another party, even when there is no express or implied contract in place and the parties did not necessarily intend for one to exist. These "quasi-contractual" obligations are based on principles of fairness and equity. In fact, courts sometimes use terminology such as "restitution" and "unjust enrichment" to describe what occurs when one party has conferred a benefit upon another party but has not been justly compensated.

In the realm of ideas, quasi contracts are difficult to establish, which makes the application of promissory restitution principles to the protection of raw ideas highly speculative. Instead, when "idea people" are compensated for their ideas under contract principles, it almost always is because they have convinced a court that an implied-in-fact contract existed, as evidenced by some kind of "meeting of the minds" of the parties.

The primary hurdle for plaintiffs in quasi-contract actions concerns the requirement that there be something "of value" at issue for which equity requires compensation. Where the dispute is about ideas, most courts specify that "value" be measured in terms of novelty and originality. One federal court case, *Phillips v. Avis, Inc.*,[3] illustrates these principles at work. In that case, entrepreneurs Frances and Peter Phillips approached several rental car companies pitching an idea to offer customers tape-recorded street directions. After considerable negotiation between Avis and the Phillips failed to result in a contractual agreement between the parties—although the parties progressed in their negotiations to the point of discussing the amount of compensation should Avis decide to use the Phillips' Drive Time USA service—news leaked that Avis planned to offer a direction service using the NorthstarTM system via cellular telephones and vehicle-tracking technology.

The Phillips sued Avis, claiming misappropriation of a trade secret, unfair competition, misappropriation of an idea and breach of an implied contract. The United States District Court for the Northern District of Illinois rendered summary judgment for Avis on the first three claims. The court rejected a quasi-contract theory, stating that a lack of novelty and originality made the ideas presented to Avis worthless. Thus, said the court, Avis was not unjustly enriched by anything of value retained from its negotiations with the Phillips.[4]

However, the district court did allow the possibility that the Phillips might be able to recover based on the existence of a contract implied in fact, whereby "the conduct of the parties...[allows a court] to infer the terms of a contract."[5] In this case, wrote the court, it was relatively obvious that the Phillips would not have disclosed their idea to Avis had the corporation not offered assurances of compensation should the idea be used. "The Phillips did not present Drive Time USA to Avis as a gift; this was a business proposition. Indeed, by inviting the Phillips to their offices and allowing them to present their idea, Avis consented to the contract [implied in fact]."[6]

An additional hypothetical scenario illustrates the challenges of introducing contracts—even express ones—into the creative and idea-sharing process. (If the following hypothetical scenario rings a bell, it is for good reason. It is loosely based on actual litigation from the early 2000s involving Taco Bell.) Suppose a creative team approaches a fast-food restaurant chain with an idea for a new trade character to represent one of the chain's brands that serves Mexican-style food. The restaurant's in-house brand managers agree to meet with the creative team. At the appointed hour, the creative team pitches an idea for a new trade character: "A little dog, with attitude." The creative team orally describes a feisty, Spanish-speaking, sombrero-wearing

Chihuahua dog and then outlines some of the situations in which the character could be placed. Further ideas are suggested regarding specific ad concepts and human characters who would be ideal antagonists for the hypothetical main trade character.

The restaurant-chain representative tells the creative team that the idea is "great" and that the company will "be in touch" regarding the possibility of collaborating on a campaign featuring the trade character. No one from the company, however, ever does get back in touch. Some months later, while flipping through the channels one evening, a member of the creative team sees what appears to be an almost identical trade character in a commercial whose scenario seems very familiar—a trade character representing the restaurant chain that goes on to become wildly popular in a successful advertising campaign.

Any redress of this grievance for the creative team? Even with the existence of an express contract, this is not necessarily clear. If the creative team had hired an attorney to draft a non-disclosure/confidentiality contract to protect the ideas prior to their being pitched (the wise course of action), the question of whether a pre-disclosure agreement would be binding on the parties presents a difficult question. In the pre-disclosure scenario, the creative team makes an offer to share an idea with the restaurant chain in exchange for the promise that the chain will not appropriate the idea for its own use without properly compensating the creative team. The terms of the agreement are direct, complete and unambiguous—seemingly setting the foundation for an enforceable contract that the writer may use as a basis for legal action when the trade character-based commercial wins awards without the creative team having received credit or compensation.

Unfortunately, problems with consideration might invalidate the creative team's hypothetical pre-disclosure contract. Recalling discussion of the underlying theory for copyright protection in Chapter 7, copyrighted material derives value as property because the creative expression in question has moved beyond the idea stage of development and has been tangibly fixed in some way. To state this concept in the negative, ideas that have not been tangibly fixed and have not developed beyond the "mere idea" stage are outside the protection of federal copyright laws.

In the hypothetical, our creative team's idea for a trade character has not been tangibly fixed (there were no character sketches or prototypes) and thus could not have been copyrighted because, according to federal copyright law, ideas have no value. Because consideration must possess some actual value, the agreement proposed by the creative team and accepted by the restaurant chain arguably may not have been supported by adequate consideration, making the contract unenforceable at law.

But this may depend on the particular court that hears the contract claim. Some courts might hold that "novel" ideas possess intrinsic value and thus can serve as valid consideration in a confidentiality/nondisclosure contract. Others may find that separate, specific consideration is required. The unsettled nature of these issues often means communicators simply must place blind faith in the party sitting across the table unless the creative material is so tangibly fixed as to be copyrightable. In such a scenario, the most optimistic result for the creative team likely would be a finding by a jury that the parties entered into an implied contract that the restaurant chain ultimately breached.

Indeed, this was the outcome in the actual Taco Bell litigation. The real lawsuit, however, featured facts that more clearly established an implied contract than did those contained in the hypothetical here. For example, the actual Taco Bell lawsuit revealed that a Taco Bell licensing manager had approached the creative team at a trade show about licensing its "Psycho Chihuahua" character for use by Taco Bell and had requested a specific proposal including financial terms. In the real example, the creative team had actually developed the character and given it physical form through sketches and cartoons, which it had affixed to goods presented to Taco Bell. When Taco Bell moved ahead with a similar trade character in ads created by its new agency, the same licensing manager expressed concern about the similarity and predicted it would invite a lawsuit. It did, and a jury found that Taco Bell had entered into an implied contract and breached the terms of that contract by failing to compensate the creative team. The creative team was awarded $52 million in damages, including $40 million from the jury and $12 million in interest added by the federal judge.

Returning to the hypothetical "little dog" scenario, note that not even an implied-contract theory would save the creative team if the nondisclosure contract was presented and accepted *after* the disclosure of the trade-character idea. When this happens, courts tend to give short shrift to the creative team's argument that an enforceable contract exists. From almost any angle, breach of contract judgments in the idea-sharing context can be difficult to secure. These types of disputes often boil down to "we said/they said"-style fights, in which the creative team claims the idea and the organization disputes that claim—at great hassle and expense for both parties.

Non-Compete and Confidentiality Agreements

Organizations that trade in ideas or that possess proprietary information frequently turn to contracts to try and keep such information from falling into the hands of competitors or entering the public domain. Disputes over this type of content often arise when former employees are hired by competing organizations and take their "insider" knowledge with them to their new jobs, to the benefit of the new employer. Other disputes occur when third parties—prospective clients, for example—are given access to secret information and misappropriate it at the expense of the organization that created and shared it.

Two kinds of contracts—non-compete agreements and confidentiality/nondisclosure agreements—may be of use in these situations. As with any contract, a mere agreement between the parties is not sufficient—it must be accompanied by valuable consideration. For newly hired employees, the job offer itself may serve as consideration; for existing employees asked to sign such contracts, some courts may regard the promise of continued employment as consideration; others may look for additional consideration, such as a promotion or bonus pay. Where former employees are concerned, the existence of a reasonable, properly executed non-compete contract may discourage unauthorized sharing or provide a means of recourse if the agreement is breached.

Non-compete contracts generally specify the conditions under which a former employee may work for another employer in the same industry. People who work in sales, for example, often are asked to sign non-competes that require them to avoid working for a competitor for a specified period of time, or to refrain from taking with them customer lists developed using their former employer's resources. For employees who may have access to an organization's trade secrets, non-compete contracts tend to include language prohibiting their disclosure.

Where non-employees, such as prospective clients or other third parties, are concerned, confidentiality/nondisclosure contracts offer similar protection. Of course, if an idea has taken shape into expressible form, the most obvious avenue of protection is to tangibly fix the expression so that it becomes subject to the protections of federal copyright law. When the idea is still just an idea, however, and thus not yet copyrightable, a formal confidentiality or nondisclosure agreement may be the best approach for the creator. Such a contract might provide a way to prohibit someone from appropriating the creative communicator's idea or even disclosing the idea in any context unless the communicator was compensated for its use.

Misappropriation of Trade Secrets

A trade secret is information with commercial value derived from the fact that competitors do not have access to it. Trade secrets can take many forms, including formulae, plans, processes, devices and compounds. Classic examples of trade secrets include Colonel Sanders' secret recipe for KFC fried chicken and the original formula for the soft drink Coca-Cola.

Until 2016, companies seeking legal redress for the theft of trade secrets were, for the most part, limited to filing civil actions in state court. That changed with the enactment of the federal Defend Trade Secrets Act[7] (DTSA) of 2016, which allows entities to file civil lawsuits in federal court for the misappropriation of trade secrets "related to a product or service ... in interstate or foreign commerce."[8] The DTSA does not preempt state laws, however, which means plaintiffs may choose to file in state court or file in both state and federal court if circumstances merit doing so.

For the most part, the purpose and language of the DTSA mirrors the language of most state statutes. Most state trade secrets laws, in turn, consist of language adopted from the Uniform Trade Secrets Act[9] (UTSA). The UTSA is a "model" law drafted by an independent commission that seeks to promote uniformity among state statutory laws; 48 states[10] have adopted or introduced trade secrets legislation based on the UTSA. As an example of the wording of a typical state law, the Illinois Trade Secrets Act defines a trade secret as "information, including but not

Figure 9.1 Trade secrets can take many forms, including formulae, plans, processes, devices and compounds. Classic examples of trade secrets include Colonel Sanders' secret recipe for KFC fried chicken and the original formula for the soft drink Coca-Cola.

Credit line: Luciano Mortula/Shutterstock.com

limited to, technical or non-technical data, a formula, pattern, compilation, program, device, method, technique, drawing, process, financial data."[11] Under both the federal law and state statutes based on the UTSA, the distinguishing characteristics of a protectable trade secret are: (a) the trade secret has commercial value by virtue of the fact that it gives the owner a business advantage over competitors who are not familiar with it; and (b) those in possession of the trade secret have made reasonable efforts to protect it from detection.

One of the most challenging aspects of trade secrets law is determining when proprietary information is an actionable trade secret. In addition to the two distinguishing characteristics noted above, courts—both federal and state—tend to require that trade secrets be novel in some way. The novelty requirement has to do with the fact that non-novel concepts are generally known to the public and, by definition, are not properly regarded as secrets. The novelty requirement is not as stringent as that required to obtain a patent, but non-novel materials are not likely to be classified as trade secrets. As the Supreme Court has described it, "That which does not possess novelty is usually known; secrecy, in the context of trade secrets, thus implies at least minimal novelty."[12]

Some courts have required that a trade secret be "continuously used in one's business"—as is the formula for Coca-Cola—while others have held that marketing campaign ideas and ideas for new products may be trade secrets even though they have not yet been implemented.[13] On balance, state-level trade secrets laws embracing the UTSA lean toward protecting even ideas that are not in continuous use.

Under federal and state laws, the key to trade secret protection is secrecy, particularly from competitors or potential competitors. For example, North Carolina defines misappropriation of a trade secret as the "acquisition, disclosure, or use of a trade secret of another without express or implied authority or consent"[14] unless disclosed by someone who had authority to release the secret. The language in the federal statute is similar: appropriation means

> acquisition of a trade secret of another by another person who knows or has reason to know that the trade secret was acquired by improper means; or … disclosure or use of a trade secret of another without express or implied consent.[15]

Unauthorized disclosure of trade secrets often occurs when an "insider" (e.g., an employee or prospective client) reveals the information to a competitor. To protect against such eventualities, organizations may require insiders to sign formal agreements imposing a duty of nondisclosure. Properly drawn, such contractual agreements generally are upheld by courts as a legitimate restriction on commercial speech. Additionally, an organization may require a contractual agreement between itself and those employees with access to trade secrets promising not to accept future employment with competing companies or agencies for a reasonable period of time following departure from the original organization. The enforcement by the courts of such agreements ("covenants not to compete") often depends on the reasonableness of the provisions of the employment contract as they relate to a particular employee challenging their application.

Even without any written agreement not to disclose, courts may uphold sanctions for unauthorized disclosure of trade secrets in cases involving employees or business partners, who have a duty to keep the secrets. Such an implied "duty of non-disclosure" might arise in situations in which the courts find that those with access to the trade secret (e.g., partners in a firm) acted in such manner as to indicate that it was the expectation that the information not be disclosed.

For example, at the height of the 1980s beverage-marketing wars, Pepsico successfully obtained a court injunction to prevent one of its former officers from assuming a position with Quaker Oats for six months after leaving his position and forever prevent him from disclosing trade secrets regarding the company's annual operating plan.[16] The annual plan included marketing strategies for Pepsico to position its AllSport drink to compete with Quaker's Gatorade. More recently, Waymo, a developer of self-driving cars, sued Uber Technologies in 2017 over 14,000 computer files copied and allegedly transferred to Uber by a former Waymo employee.[17] Waymo filed a variety of legal actions alleging patent infringement and the theft of trade secrets in federal and state court. Prior to the end of the federal trial, the parties reached a settlement in which Uber agreed to give Waymo a portion of its $72 billion equity—a payout worth approximately $245 million.[18]

Sometimes the disclosure of a trade secret comes not from an employee or business partner but from an "outsider." Obviously, stealing or engaging in criminally fraudulent activity to acquire trade secrets may well bring civil and criminal penalties. However, the methods employed to gain a competitive advantage by means of learning a rival's trade secrets need not rise to this level to be actionable. For example, in *E.I. du Pont de Nemours & Co., Inc. v. Rolfe Christopher et al.*,[19] the defendants, who ran an aerial photography business, were found liable for illegally acquiring the plaintiff's trade secrets involving the building of a new chemical plant when they flew an airplane over the partially completed facility to photograph its construction in an attempt to discover du Pont's new manufacturing techniques.

Not all disclosures of trade secrets are legally actionable. These types of disclosures include those that occur (a) without the recipient's awareness of the secret nature of the information (e.g., an innocent third party given or sold an idea by an unauthorized source); (b) as a result of deconstructing or "reverse engineering" a product to determine its structure or ingredients; and (c) through legitimate use of freedom of information requests to a government office to obtain public documents (discussed in Chapter 12).

Court-sanctioned remedies for the appropriation of trade secrets may include injunctions, especially when (a) it is likely that a trade secret will be further disclosed if such a court order is not issued; (b) such disclosure likely would result in irreparable harm to the non-disclosing party; and (c) the information is still secret at the time the request for the injunction is made. More typically, those claiming disclosure of trade secrets may recover actual and/or punitive money damages to compensate for the harm done by the revelation of the information.

The Supreme Court of the United States has decided few cases directly involving trade secrets, probably because the lower federal courts generally are not involved in such cases unless they involve parties from two or more states ("diversity jurisdiction") or concern federal employees or federal law. Since 1974, the Court has decided only a handful of cases focusing on trade secrets. In a 1974 case, *Kewanee v. Bicron*,[20] the Court held that Ohio's trade secret law may coexist with federal patent law. The Court noted, among other points, that the federal patent office policy of encouraging invention is not harmed by the existence of other incentives for invention like state trade secrets statutes.

In 1986, in *Dow Chemical v. United States*[21] (a case based on the same facts as *E.I. du Pont de Nemours v. Rolfe Christopher* discussed above), the Court held that the U.S. Environmental Protection Agency (EPA) was acting within its authority when it employed a commercial aerial photographer to take photographs from public airspace of a chemical plant after the company denied the EPA access for an onsite inspection. The Court said such observations were legitimate even though the company's competitors might be barred from such action under state trade secrets laws. The opinion noted that government agencies generally do not try to appropriate trade secrets from private enterprises and that state unfair competition laws do not define the Fourth Amendment's provision regarding unreasonable searches.

In *Ruckelshaus v. Monsanto Co.*,[22] the Court held that, under certain conditions, disclosure of a trade secret by a government agency could constitute a "taking" under the Fifth Amendment, particularly when such disclosure interferes with what the Court called "reasonable investment-backed expectations."[23] Without deciding whether there actually was a Fifth Amendment violation in the case, the Court said that trade secrets that enjoy protection under state law could constitute "property" for purposes of the Fifth Amendment, despite their intangible nature. The Court pointed out that the federal EPA had promised confidentiality in exchange for disclosure of the information to the Agency that the company had designated as trade secrets at the time of submission.

Misappropriation of Ideas

Advertising and public relations professionals are creative people. Creative people often look at a problem or situation and are struck with insights about how to resolve issues, improve on a company's performance or add to a corporation's intellectual property stock-in-trade. Many advertising or public relations professionals have dealt with prospective clients who seemed enthusiastic about implementing proposed ideas tailored for them but instead pursued similar concepts on their own or with the aid of competing agencies.

Figure 9.2 In dealing with prospective clients, idea generators should make it known that they are proposing a business transaction and are not simply sharing their valuable ideas out of the goodness of their hearts. That is because in some situations, contractual obligations may be assumed from the statements and behavior of the parties, the circumstances of the interaction or even industry custom.

Credit line: Antonio Diaz/Shutterstock.com

The nature of advertising and public relations practice often requires the sharing of insights with others before they have taken a form that qualifies for clear legal protection under either copyright or trademark law. In such situations, lawsuits claiming the misappropriation of ideas—some courts call them "submission-of-idea" cases or "idea-theft" cases—may provide what little protection the law allows against those who "borrow"—some might say steal—and use others' creative output or ideas.

Before proceeding, it will be useful to note several characteristics that generally define these types of legal actions. First, like a work-for-hire under copyright law, the tort of misappropriation of ideas is not applicable to ideas suggested by regular, full-time employees of an organization who are paid to be creative as part of their normal, job-related requirements. Second, generic concepts do not typically merit protection. An idea for "a television program about single women living in a big city and how they cope with modern life" might be a commercially viable idea, but most courts likely would find nothing so original or unique in such a concept that it could give rise to a successful misappropriation lawsuit if, after the idea was pitched to a television executive, the network later aired a program with a similar theme. Even if the creative concept constitutes a genuinely breakthrough thought, evidence that another party independently also conceived of a similar notion might defeat such a lawsuit.

Third, courts usually decide misappropriation-of-ideas cases as either "property" cases or "contract" cases. With a property-based claim, the plaintiff alleges the theft of some kind of valuable creative property. With a contract-based claim, the plaintiff alleges the breach of an express or implied contract, as discussed above. Most jurisdictions have different requirements for winning property-based claims, as opposed to contract-based ones. New York courts, for example, require proof of novelty for both types of claims. But to win a property-based misappropriation claim, the plaintiff must offer proof that the idea was novel *in general* and not just as to the defendant. To win a contract-based claim, the plaintiff has to merely offer proof that the idea was novel *as to the defendant* at the time it was disclosed. Some jurisdictions, on the other hand, generally do not allow misappropriation-of-ideas lawsuits unless the misappropriation resulted from a breach of contract. California courts, for example, have a long history of dismissing idea-theft lawsuits because of the near-impossibility of establishing that raw ideas are "property." Most courts, however, including those that apply California law, allow plaintiffs to pursue *contract-based claims* even when the idea at issue is not novel or original. According to a California appellate court, "An idea which can be the subject matter of a contract need not be novel or concrete. It may be valuable to the person to whom it is disclosed simply because the disclosure takes place at the right time."[24]

A case out of New York, *Nadel v. Play-By-Play Toys & Novelties, Inc.*,[25] illustrates the distinction between misappropriation-of-ideas cases claiming "stolen property" versus those claiming a breach of contract. In *Nadel*, a New York-based federal court of appeals (applying New York state law) described the plaintiff as a "toy idea man. Toy companies regularly do business with independent inventors such as Nadel in order to develop and market new toy concepts as quickly as possible."[26] Nadel took the "eccentric mechanism" used in other toys

> then on the market and placed the mechanism inside of a plush toy monkey skin to develop the prototype for a new table-top monkey toy. This plush toy figure sat upright, emitted sound, and spun when placed on a flat surface.[27]

Nadel met with representatives of Play-By-Play who "expressed interest in adapting the concept to a non-moving, plush Tasmanian Devil toy that Play-By-Play was already producing under license from Warner Bros."[28] When Play-By-Play subsequently introduced its "Tornado Taz" product at the New York Toy Fair, Nadel sued for misappropriation (of his idea), claiming that, like his model, the defendants' toy "is a plush toy that emits sounds (including 'screaming,' 'laughing,' 'snarling,' and 'grunting'), sits upright, and spins by means of an internal eccentric vibration mechanism."[29]

In denying Nadel's allegations, Play-By-Play argued that "even if it did use Nadel's idea to develop 'Tornado Taz,' Nadel is not entitled to compensation because Nadel's concept was unoriginal and non-novel to the toy industry." A district court granted Play-By-Play's motion for summary judgment on the grounds that the plaintiff's "claims must ... fail for lack of novelty or originality because 'numerous toys containing the characteristics of [Nadel's] monkey were in existence prior to [the plaintiff's creation in] October 1996.'"[30] The court of appeals noted that if Nadel's claim had been based on contract law, the plaintiff only needed to show that the toy mechanism idea was unknown to Play-By-Play. A misappropriation claim, on the other hand,

> require[s] that the idea at issue be original and novel in absolute terms. This is so because unoriginal, known ideas have no value as property and the law does not protect against the use of that which is free and available to all.[31]

It is advisable for plaintiffs to file both breach of contract and property-type claims, as courts are permitted only to rule on what has been complained of; they may not transform a misappropriation-of-ideas (as property) case into a contract case unless the plaintiff has argued that a contract existed. That said, courts generally have held that plaintiffs may not win under both property and contract-based theories. In other words, if the litigation at its core concerns a breach of an express or implied contract, courts are likely to dismiss simultaneously filed tort claims that basically duplicate the breach-of-contract claims. The real-life lawsuit discussed above involving Taco Bell, for example, began with multiple tort claims, including for misappropriation and trademark dilution. By the end of the litigation, only a claim for breach of implied contract was left standing.

Finally, courts in states with statutes that address the theft of ideas are likely to dismiss common-law misappropriation claims. These courts tend to regard common-law claims related to idea-theft as being preempted by state statutes and, therefore, barred. For example, an Illinois court held that the Illinois Trade Secrets Act, which had been enacted to protect ideas, prohibited the filing of a misappropriation-of-ideas lawsuit that had formerly been allowed as a matter of common law.[32]

The bottom line is these kinds of tort claims are difficult to win if you are the plaintiff, and expensive and hassle-filled if you are the defendant. Because it not unusual for different individuals to think of similar creative concepts or for creative people to firmly believe that someone else has appropriated their good ideas (even in the face of evidence to the contrary), courts place a heavy burden on those seeking legal redress for the misappropriation of ideas.

Misappropriation of Intangible Property

A final category of tort claim relevant to those in the ideas business is the misappropriation of intangible property. An oft-cited example of such "stolen" intangible property is that of a radio station with no news reporters that requires its announcers to simply "rip and read" slightly edited news stories taken directly from the local daily newspaper. The newspaper clearly expects many customers to buy individual copies of the paper but does not appreciate these individual consumers (especially the radio station) then entering into competition with the newspaper by repackaging the creative efforts of the newspaper's reporting staff.[33] In these types of cases, the principal question for disputants is whether one party (a) appropriated another party's creative material that (b) was originally intended only for specific distribution, and then (c) redistributed it to an alternative public in order to make a profit.

The reader should note the difference between possible copyright infringement and a misappropriation of intangible property claim in the above scenario. If the radio station personnel simply read the newspaper's reports verbatim over the air, the newspaper might have a violation-of-copyright case. However, if the station makes changes in the wording of the newspaper's material and then uses it without permission, the newspaper's only remedy might be a lawsuit claiming misappropriation of intangible property. Similarly, if an advertising agency presents a client with a finished design for an ad that the client then distributes without permission, a potential copyright claim would exist. But an agency's mere description to the client of a concept for a finished ad would not trigger copyright protection. Nor would the client's use of an ad whose concept was similar but whose execution was not; in those cases, the agency's most viable option may be a misappropriation claim.

A 1978 case provides an additional example where a copyright infringement lawsuit was unavailable to the plaintiffs, who turned to a theory of misappropriation. In *Columbia Broadcasting System, Inc. v. Melody Recordings, Inc.*,[34] CBS complained that Melody Recordings engaged in the systematic process of re-recording records produced by the plaintiff and selling them under their own label. For technical reasons, the plaintiffs were unable to pursue copyright claims, but the court agreed that New Jersey law applied and that it barred such copying and usage. "What is involved in this case," said the court, "is the direct taking of the artistic and highly creative work of [CBS]. ... Defendants have thus appropriated the unique product of CBS by rerecording its original records."[35] Characterizing the case as a clear misappropriation case, the court noted that:

> [t]he actionable unfairness of this practice inheres in a combination of factors—the substantial investment of time, labor, money and creative resources in the product by the plaintiff, the utilization of the actual product by the defendant, the misappropriation or use of the appropriated product by defendant in competition with plaintiff, and commercial damage to plaintiff.[36]

In addition to looking at the creative efforts of the plaintiff and the actions of the defendant in making use of the material to make a profit (usually with little effort to modify or change the original), courts recognizing this misappropriation tort also examine both the financial harm already suffered by the plaintiff and the probability that the plaintiff will be discouraged from continuing to produce the creative product if relief is not granted.

Remedies for misappropriation of intangible property interests usually involve money damages reflecting the amount lost by the plaintiff or gained by the defendant, although court orders (injunctive relief) ordering the defendant to stop the offending practices may be available in some instances.

Conclusion

To remove as much speculation from the equation as possible, a creative communicator should understand that the most sure-fire method of protecting ideas is to reduce them to a tangible enough form that they merit the protection of federal copyright or trademark laws. When this is impossible, the other methods discussed in this chapter may be all that are available.

In a relatively easy-to-enter, digital media world, courts have seen an increase in cases alleging the stealing of trade secrets as insiders with access to private information make it available in Web-based communications. Whether for personal gain or as a means of striking out against a current or former employer, disclosures by anonymous online posters of company secrets increasingly pose potential problems for those wishing to maintain secrecy about product formulas, new business plans or potential advertising or public relations campaigns.

In addition, the practice of sending unsolicited e-mail or social media messages to organizations proposing ideas and product suggestions has produced an uptick of cases involving disgruntled individuals convinced that a company has relied on their suggestions if the organization actually begins to produce products or take other steps that resemble the business schemes suggested in the unasked-for messages. Prudent advertising and public relations professionals are wise to increase efforts to guard against disclosure of trade secrets by creating or strengthening existing policies and procedures designed to inhibit such disclosures by employees and other insiders within their organizations and to discourage discussions between company employees and those who have contributed unsolicited ideas that could be considered trade secrets.

For similar reasons, when many users seem to have the unwarranted belief that information found on the Internet is free of copyright or trademark protection, it may not be surprising to find an increase in incidents of misappropriation of intangible property. While perhaps it is understandable that individuals may think little about the dangers of rewriting or repackaging information obtained from online sources, prudent advertising and public relations professionals should be vigilant in protecting their own intellectual efforts and in not misusing the protected works of others.

To avoid the charge of misappropriation of ideas, agencies and other entities dealing in intellectual material should continue to erect and maintain rigid barriers between their creative departments and the individuals within the organization to whom unsolicited creative ideas are directed. In addition, organizations should require an individual submitting unsolicited ideas that might constitute a protected business scheme to immediately sign an agreement specifying that any payments or other compensation that might be forthcoming are at the discretion of the purchasing organization.

Notes

1. Int'l. News Service v. Associated Press, 248 U.S. 215, 250 (1919).
2. The concept of consideration evolved significantly in the early 20th century, embracing the concept that past acts could not serve as consideration for a future contractual arrangement. Justice Benjamin Cardozo addressed this rule in the oft-cited contract case of Dougherty v. Salt, 227 N.Y. 200, 125 N.E. 94 (1919). In the case, a woman issued a promissory note due upon her death to her nephew for several thousand dollars (an exceptional sum during the time period) because the boy had always treated her well. When the nephew sought to enforce the promissory note upon her death as a valid enforceable contract, Justice Cardozo wrote that the note was little more than an executory (to be performed in the future) gift and *not* an enforceable contract, because the boy's past acts had no present value as consideration.
3. Phillips v. Avis, Inc., 1996 U.S. Dist. LEXIS 7342 (N.D. IL, May 28, 1996).
4. *Id.* at 13–14.

5. *Id.* at 14.
6. *Id.*
7. Defend Trade Secrets Act of 2016, Pub. L. 114-153, 130 Stat. 376, enacted May 11, 2016, codified at 18 U.S.C. 1836, et seq.
8. *Id.*
9. Unif. Trade Secrets Act (Nat'l Conf. of Commissioners on Uniform State Laws, Proposed Official Draft with 1985 Amendments), www.uniformlaws.org/shared/docs/trade%20secrets/utsa_final_85.pdf
10. As of this writing, New York and North Carolina had yet to adopt the provisions of the Uniform Trade Secrets Act; the Act, however, was introduced in New York in 2018 for potential adoption.
11. 765 ILCS 1065/2 (2005).
12. Kewanee Oil Co. v. Bicron Corp., 416 U.S. 470, 476 (1974).
13. The requirement that a trade secret be "continuously used in one's business" is reflected in the Restatement of Torts (First). The Uniform Trade Secrets Act includes the broader definition, extending protection to "a plaintiff who has not yet had an opportunity or acquired the means to put a trade secret to use."
14. *See* N.C. Gen. Stat. §66-152 (1) (2005).
15. Pub. L. 114-153, 130 Stat. 376, enacted May 11, 2016, codified at 18 U.S.C. 1836, et seq.
16. Pepsico, Inc. v. Redmond and the Quaker Oats Co., 54 F.3d 1262, 35 U.S.P.Q.2d (BNA) 1010 (7th Cir. 1995).
17. Waymo LLC v. Uber Techs., Inc., No. 3:17-cv-00939-WMA (N.D. Cal. Jan. 18, 2018).
18. *See* Aarian Marshall, *Uber and Waymo Abruptly Settle for $245 Million*, Wired, Feb. 9, 2019, 12:17 pm, www.wired.com/story/uber-waymo-lawsuit-settlement/
19. E.I. du Pont de Nemours & Co., Inc. v. Rolfe Christopher, 431 F.2d 1012 (5th Cir. 1970).
20. Kewanee v. Bicron, 416 U.S. 470 (1974).
21. Dow Chemical v. United States, 476 U.S. 227 (1986).
22. Ruckelshaus v. Monsanto Co., 467 U.S. 986 (1984).
23. *Id.* at 1005.
24. Donahue v. Ziv Television Programs, Inc., 245 Cal. App. 2d 593 (Cal. App. Oct. 14, 1966).
25. Nadel v. Play-By-Play Toys & Novelties, Inc., 208 F.3d 368 (2d Cir. 2000).
26. *Id.* at 371.
27. *Id.* at 372.
28. *Id.*
29. *Id.* at 373.
30. *Id.*
31. *Id.* at 380.
32. Learning Curve Toys, LP v. PlayWood Toys, Inc., 1999 U.S. Dist. LEXIS 11262, N.D. Ill., July 19, 1999.
33. *See* International News Serv. v. The Associated Press, 248 U.S. 315, 39 S. Ct. 68, 63 L. Ed. 211 (1918).
34. Columbia Broadcasting System, Inc. v. Melody Recordings, Inc., 341 A.2d 348 (N.J. Super. 1975).
35. *Id.* at 353-354.
36. *Id.* at 354.

10 The Federal Trade Commission and Other Federal Agencies Concerned With Advertising and Public Relations Speech

Numerous federal and state agencies have the authority to regulate specific categories of commercial speech, but the Federal Trade Commission (FTC) remains the agency most involved on a day-to-day basis in regulating the totality of commercial speech. This agency, established at the beginning of the last century, originally was given power to regulate unfair trade practices between and among business competitors. Eventually, Congress expanded the FTC's role to investigate and remedy a variety of marketplace abuses—including false or deceptive commercial speech.

History and Jurisdiction of the FTC in Relation to Commercial Speech

The FTC traces its roots to the growth of monopolistic practices in industries like petroleum production, meat packing and cigarette and steel manufacturing beginning in the early 1880s. Even in those times—the heyday of laissez-faire, ungoverned, free-market economic policy—many in the business community urged the federal government to combat these anticompetitive practices that, it was feared, could result in a few powerful interests gaining control over the free marketplace of goods and services.

In response, Congress passed the Sherman Antitrust Act of 1890[1] to curb these abuses by the trusts and cartels. Although an important first step, the law proved ineffective in combating the major ills associated with economic monopolies. Continuing abuses led to demands that the federal government enact further legislation and set up a mechanism for ensuring that its provisions be enforced. To answer these demands, Congress passed the Federal Trade Commission Act in 1914.[2]

The Act specified that "[u]nfair methods of competition in commerce are hereby declared unlawful."[3] It focused on maintaining a competitive marketplace for business and industry but contained little of direct concern to consumers. The Act further created the FTC, consisting of five commissioners and support staff, to oversee the enforcement of the Act by promulgating rules and regulations ultimately enforceable by civil lawsuits in federal courts.

A major modification of the Act, with direct significance to those engaged in commercial speech, occurred when Congress passed the Wheeler–Lea Amendment in 1938.[4] The addition of the words *unfair or deceptive acts or practices in commerce* in the amended law gave the FTC authority for the first time to protect consumers by taking action against those who attempt to deceive the public about the nature or quality of their products, malign their competitors and/or engage in unfair competitive practices. Such practices specifically included false or deceptive advertising or other commercial messages.

Figure 10.1 The Federal Communications Commission regulates interstate and international communications by radio, television, wire, satellite and cable in the United States, the District of Columbia and U.S. territories.

Credit line: naral chal/Shutterstock.com

The FTC Today

The basic structure of the FTC remains the same as originally established by the 1914 Act. The President, with the advice and consent of the Senate, appoints five commission members. No more than three members may be from the same political party. Each commissioner is appointed to a seven-year term and may be reappointed to additional terms. To ensure both continuity and a minimum of partisanship, FTC members serve staggered terms to avoid a complete turnover in personnel at any one time. The President appoints one member to chair the FTC.

Originally staffed by a small number of employees transferred from other government agencies, today the FTC features an expanded staff that encompasses numerous offices and bureaus including public information, general counsel, administrative law judges and compliance and litigation divisions. Of particular significance to commercial speech interests is the Bureau of Consumer Protection that contains within it the Division of Advertising Practices. This division investigates and enforces FTC regulations in cases of alleged deceptive or unfair advertising and marketing practices. The FTC also maintains seven regional offices across the country to spot and deal with problems at the regional level.

The FTC provides guidance to commercial speakers through a variety of communications and publications such as industry guides, informal responses to inquiries and detailed advisory opinions issued when a commercial speaker wishes to determine in advance if proposed commercial messages meet FTC standards. Consulting FTC advisory materials, most of which are available on the agency's website, is advisable for commercial speakers who have questions or doubts about the legality of their proposed commercial messages and desire guidance about how to proceed.

Deceptive advertising cases arise when the FTC receives requests from consumers, competitors or Congress to investigate an alleged violation of law or FTC regulation. Commissioners or their staff also may note possible violations on their own initiative. The FTC receives millions of complaints each year, which means not every alleged deceptive advertising is pursued or punished; the majority of FTC resources are devoted to national or regional advertising associated with higher priced items that consumers cannot readily evaluate on their own, or whose use or consumption has the potential to cause physical injury or significant economic harm. Sometimes, the FTC focuses on individual advertisers; at other times, the Commission examines the overall advertising practices as to specific industries. In 2014, for example, the commission announced "Operation Steer Clear" to address dubious advertising practices in the automobile sales industry. That initiative involved multiple actions against multiple car dealers across the country and was intended, in part, to send a cautionary message to other industry advertisers who may have been tempted to disseminate similar advertising.

FTC staff members, usually from the Bureau of Consumer Protection, determine whether further procedures seem merited. If the investigators' conclusion is affirmative, the FTC typically sends an informal request for more information to the party under investigation. Should this request be ignored, or if the staff believes the information provided is non-responsive or inadequate to meet the request, the investigators usually seek authority from the FTC for a more formal investigation in which advertiser participation is compulsory.

Congress has granted the FTC sweeping subpoena power to obtain data and other relevant information from parties under investigation. The courts have held that the FTC may use its power to demand information before launching lawsuits or other more formal judicial proceedings even if there is only mere suspicion that a party may be in violation of a law or regulation. After the staff completes its investigation, a formal report is prepared suggesting what next steps need to be taken, if any. Should the conclusion be that a legitimate complaint exists, the FTC may then authorize formal enforcement proceedings. As a first, formal, investigative step, the FTC generally issues to the advertiser a document called a "civil investigative demand" (CID) that functions like a subpoena. CIDs may direct a recipient to appear before a Commission investigator at a designated time and place to testify and/or produce documents or other materials responsive to the request.

If the Commission believes it necessary to adjudicate a matter with an advertiser, it next issues a written complaint "sufficient to inform each respondent with reasonable definiteness of the type of acts or practices alleged to be in violation of the law." Advertisers have 14 days to answer the allegations in the complaint. Typically, parties resolve such complaints with a consent agreement, in which the offending party, often without admitting any violation of the law, agrees to stop the actions challenged by the FTC. The wording of such a consent order often is open to negotiation with the FTC so as to minimize damaging publicity. If no agreement is reached, however, the FTC possesses broad authority to seek other remedies to enforce its orders. Enforcement actions available to the FTC are discussed in more detail later in this chapter.

The FTC's Regulation of False or Deceptive Commercial Speech

Until the 1970s, few gave much thought to the constitutionality of the FTC's regulations covering commercial speech, especially after the Supreme Court's decision in *Valentine v. Chrestensen*[5] (see Chapter 2) that purely commercial speech merited no First Amendment protection. However, with the development of limited constitutional protection for such speech beginning with *Pittsburgh Press Co. v. Pittsburgh Commission on Human Relations*,[6] critics of the FTC began to question both its jurisdiction and its rulings on First Amendment grounds.

These issues were resolved in the FTC's favor by the Court's opinion in *Virginia State Board of Pharmacy v. Virginia Citizens Consumer Council*.[7] Justice Blackmun, while according commercial speech shelter under the umbrella of the First Amendment, also noted that "we ... do not hold that it can never be regulated in any way."[8] Categories of commercial speech specifically mentioned as candidates for regulation included *untruthful speech*, which the Court defined as "false or misleading."[9] The Court added that "obviously, much commercial speech is not provably false, or even wholly false, but only deceptive or misleading. We foresee no obstacle to a State's dealing effectively with this problem."[10]

Although *Virginia State Board of Pharmacy* did not end challenges to the FTC's rulings on First Amendment grounds in lower courts, the Supreme Court has declined to hear such cases. The Court has repeatedly reiterated its support for the constitutionality of the FTC's power to regulate commercial speech in a number of decisions, including *Young v. American Mini Theatres, Inc.*,[11] in which the Court observed that the FTC's "power ... to restrain misleading, as well as false, statements in labels and advertisements has long been recognized."[12]

At the heart of the FTC's activities involving commercial speech are attempts to eliminate speech considered "deceptive or misleading." Section 5 of the Federal Trade Commission Act (the FTC's basic enabling legislation) provides that the FTC shall be empowered to prevent "unfair or deceptive acts or practices in or affecting commerce."[13] Included in such "acts or practices" are what Section 12 of the Act calls "[disseminating] or ... causing to be disseminated ... any false advertisement"[14] involving the wide range of products and services covered in the Act. By *false advertisement*, the Act means:

> an advertisement ... which is misleading in a material respect; and in determining whether an advertisement is misleading, there shall be taken into account (among other things) not only representations made or suggested by statement, word, design, device, sound, or any combination thereof, but also the extent to which the advertisement fails to reveal facts material in the light of such representations or material with respect to consequences which may result from the use of the commodity to which the advertisement relates under the conditions prescribed in said advertisement, or under such conditions as are customary or usual.[15]

Although the language of the statute refers to *advertising*, the FTC's jurisdiction presumably extends to all forms of communication, including websites and social media, brochures, direct mail publications, press releases and so forth, if used for publicity or marketing purposes. This broad definition of advertising has been used by courts in other areas of the law as well. For example, in *Levitt Corporation v. Levitt*,[16] a federal Court of Appeals for the Second Circuit[17] upheld a lower court's injunctive order prohibiting the defendant from issuing press releases and other materials in a trademark infringement claim. Similarly, in *Smith-Victor Corporation v. Sylvania Electric Products, Inc.*,[18] a federal district court[19] found the defendant guilty of a product disparagement violation in which the offending speech was disseminated by both advertisements and press releases.

False and Deceptive Defined

It is important to note that, under the statute's definition, the determination of whether commercial speech is *false* is based on the perception or possible perception of the commercial message by the receiver of the message. The FTC's definition of *false* is quite broad. It includes statements or other commercial speech content (including pictures, graphic depictions or sound) that, although not technically false, reasonably might mislead the receiver of the message. If the reader or listener could reasonably interpret the message to receive a false impression or in other ways be deceived by the message, the message will be considered false. Thus, it will not necessarily avail a speaker to argue that actually no false statement appears in the advertisement or other communication. Commercial speakers also should note that the "reasonableness" requirement applies to the belief that a commercial speech claim makes a promise of performance and not to whether anybody should have believed the claim.

This broad definition includes sins of omission as well. Therefore, it is equally unavailing for the commercial speaker to avoid liability for false and deceptive speech by including only statements that are true (and that the receiver interprets correctly) if there is any significant information left out of the original message. This is particularly so if including the omitted information could change the receiver's evaluation of the claim by casting it in a negative or different light. For example, in *Chrysler Corp. v. FTC*,[20] the FTC found that advertisements claiming superior gas mileage for Chrysler products equipped with six-cylinder engines were deceptive because the ads failed to note that the same models with eight-cylinder engines were less fuel-efficient than similar models made by other manufacturers.

The FTC established its current definition of a *deceptive* act or practice in a policy statement in 1983.[21] Subsequently ratified by the FTC in *In re Cliffdale Assocs., Inc.*,[22] the statement defines such practices as messages that contain: (a) a representation, practice or omission likely to mislead consumers; (b) content that consumers are interpreting reasonably under the circumstances; and (c) a material representation that could influence a consumer's decision with respect to the purchase of a product.[23]

The FTC defines a *material claim* as a statement or omission of a statement that is "likely to affect a consumer's choice of or conduct regarding a product or service."[24] Such statements or omissions "pertain to the central characteristics of the products or services being marketed, such as their performance, quality, cost or purpose."[25] The FTC is concerned with the likelihood that the average consumer might rely on a claim and suffer possible detriment. Therefore, the FTC may take action even without proof that a consumer actually has so relied and suffered actual harm. Representations involving material claims can be either express or implied. Express verbal claims—such as "Contains No Alcohol" or "Swiss-Made Clock"—that prove false almost certainly will be judged by the FTC to be deceptive. Similarly, the FTC will find visual messages deceptive if they expressly promise more than the product or service can deliver.

Merely listing every complaint filed by the FTC against a business for deceptive advertising during the last 10 years would probably take as much space as a chapter in this book. As the Rosdens note in their multi-volume work *The Law of Advertising*, statements challenged by the FTC as factually untrue have ranged from:

> [M]erchandise ... called "antique" without justification, and "bonded" when it was not bonded ... [to] goods [that] were "fireproof" when they were only fire-resistant ... goods [that] were "handmade" when they were not ... [to claims] that meat products were "kosher" when they were not; that goods were made of "leather" when they were not ... that merchandise was "shock-proof," "skid proof," "waterproof" when it was not and was merely shock-resistant, skid-resistant, or water-resistant. Other goods were called "natural" in circumstances that did not permit the use of that appellation; or they were called "rayon"

when they consisted of a different textile. Other merchandise has been called "safe" when it was demonstrably unsafe [footnotes omitted].[26]

In a contest between a commercial speaker and the FTC, the government nearly always wins, although occasionally a business may achieve a partial victory. Traditionally, the courts defer to the FTC because the agency has the necessary expertise to make such decisions.

A series of examples from the mid-to-late 1990s illustrates the FTC's approach. In late 1996, the FTC announced that Van Den Bergh Foods Co., one of the largest marketers of margarines in the United States, had signed a consent order agreeing to halt its national advertising campaign for Promise margarine that used the slogan "Get Heart Smart" and included heart-shaped pats of Promise on food items. Under a consent order, the FTC agrees to take no further action against a business if the company agrees to immediately halt the activity. The FTC alleged the ads implied that using Promise helped cut the risk of heart disease and contained false claims regarding low fat. According to the FTC, Van Den Bergh had not adequately substantiated its claims.[27]

In *In re Häagen-Dazs Company*,[28] the FTC issued its final order in a settlement with the company in which the ice cream producer agreed to immediately halt advertising claims that its frozen yogurt was "low fat" and "98% fat free" and that its frozen yogurt bars had only 100 calories and one gram of fat. The ads included a disclaimer in small type noting that the claims were for frozen yogurt and sorbet combinations. The FTC claimed only two of the nine frozen yogurt flavors actually had three grams of fat or less per serving and thus were low fat as defined by the Food and Drug Administration. Some of the flavors made by Häagen-Dazs had as many as 12 grams of fat, and three had as many as 230 calories.[29]

In yet another example, the FTC filed a complaint against Third Option Laboratories, Inc. for claiming that its drink called "Jogging in a Jug" acted "like a natural solvent for the body, cleaning crystal deposits that are the base of clogged arteries and arthritis."[30] In a $480,000 settlement, the company agreed to stop making false or unsubstantiated claims for any food, drug or dietary supplement and to notify its distributors and consumers who ordered the drink directly from the company about the settlement.[31]

Implied deceptive commercial speech claims usually involve a combination of true statements or visual representations that could cause deception because of the implications the recipient takes away from the overall message. One advertising technique determined by the FTC to be potentially deceptive involves descriptions of characteristics or properties of a product that are truthful, but that have little to do with the product's actual intended use.

For example, assume that to demonstrate the superiority of brand "X" paper towels, an advertising campaign features a single sheet of the product that has been dunked in water. The advertisement then shows the towel supporting the weight of an apple while two sheets of the competition's brand disintegrate under a similar weight. The FTC might find such a demonstration deceptive if the advertising claims focus on the greater absorbency of brand "X" compared to its competitor's products because there is no actual evidence that brand "X" is superior to its competition when it came to absorbing liquids—the logical (and misleading) interpretation the FTC might feel the average consumer would take away from the advertisement's strength test.

Although the FTC provides no specific guidelines for what evidence is necessary to prove how those receiving the information interpret such "representations," it has held (in *In re International Harvester Co.*)[32] that some omissions of fact are acceptable as long as the omitted facts concern "a subject upon which the seller has simply said nothing, in circumstances that do not give any particular meaning to his silence."[33] What the FTC called "pure omissions" are not actionable because they are not omissions that "presumptively or generally reflect a deliberate act on the part of the seller,"[34] and therefore the FTC finds no reason to seek sanctions against the speaker. Any other approach to analyzing the effects of omitted information, said the FTC, would expand the definition of a deceptive act "virtually beyond limits,"[35] given the almost infinite range of possible consumer misinterpretations based on missing information.

The FTC has determined that the speaker may not argue that a consumer should have been smart enough *not* to have relied on the claims made in the commercial message. According to the FTC, the test hinges upon whether a consumer's interpretation of the message, broadly speaking, is reasonable. Reasonableness, says the FTC, is determined by an analysis of the totality of the message. However, the FTC has held that reasonableness does not extend to interpretations of a message that are silly or bizarre, or to claims that would be inherently unbelievable to the average viewer or listener. If consumers reasonably can interpret the message in two ways (one deceptive and one not), the FTC generally will categorize the speech as deceptive.

Commercial claims directed to more vulnerable members of the audience (e.g., children, older adults and those suffering from illness) may be judged deceptive based on the likelihood that the members of that segment of the audience might be deceived. Thus, (a) claims that a toy oven "Means You Can Bake Bread Just Like Your Mom and Dad"; (b) advertisements not disclosing that more parts are needed to equal what the child sees in an advertisement; or (c) failure to mention that calling 900-numbers creates phone charges could run afoul of the FTC's prohibitions on deceptive claims (although no reasonable, normally functioning adult would likely be deceived by such claims).

In almost all cases, straightforward express claims will be considered "material" and contain the potential for deception on their face. In less straightforward situations, the FTC may rely on consumer research to determine such things as the nature and extent of the deception, the importance of the claim to the decision to purchase or use the product or the reasonableness of interpretation. Research techniques favored by the FTC include public opinion polls, focus groups and content analyses.

Deception by Visual Simulation

Perhaps the most notable instance of visual deception prompted the case of *FTC v. Colgate-Palmolive*.[36] Colgate-Palmolive, makers of Rapid ShaveTM, produced a commercial that gave the appearance the shaving cream was so good at softening beards for easy shaves, it could literally soften sandpaper. To demonstrate this softening power, the company simulated the process because, the company said, real sandpaper did not show up well on television. The FTC filed a complaint against Colgate-Palmolive alleging that the ads were false and deceptive because the type of sandpaper used in the commercials required about 80 minutes of soaking to soften, a fact not disclosed in the advertising, Additionally, the commercials did not use sandpaper, but instead used a mock-up of Plexiglas and sand. A hearing examiner dismissed the complaint on the ground that neither misrepresentation was a material misrepresentation that would mislead consumers.[37] The FTC overruled the hearing examiner, holding that the company had misrepresented the moisturizing abilities of the shaving cream because it could not shave sandpaper within the time implied by the commercials. The FTC also held that the Plexiglas ploy was a separate deceptive act and issued an order forbidding the future use of undisclosed simulations in TV commercials.

The Supreme Court agreed with the FTC and rejected Colgate-Palmolive's argument that such simulations were really no different from the practice of substituting a scoop of mashed potatoes for what appears to be ice cream in a commercial, which the FTC had permitted. According to the Court:

> [W]e do not understand this difficulty [making a distinction between the two practices]. In the ice cream case, the mashed potato prop is not being used for additional proof of the product claim, while the purpose of the Rapid Shave commercial is to give the viewer objective proof of the claim made. If in the ice cream hypothetical the focus of the commercial becomes the undisclosed potato prop and the viewer is invited, explicitly or by implication, to see for himself the truth of the claims about the ice cream's rich texture and full color, and perhaps compare it to a "rival product," then the commercial has become similar to the one now before us. Clearly, however, a commercial which depicts happy actors delightedly eating ice cream that is in fact mashed potatoes or drinking a product appearing to be coffee but which is in fact some other substance is not covered by the present order.[38]

In re Campbell Soup Co.,[39] the FTC held that the addition of glass marbles to a saucepan of Campbell soup created deception by visual simulation. The vat of soup, shown bubbling merrily on a stove (marbles and all), formed the visual centerpiece of a television commercial. The advertisement, said the Commission, misrepresented "the quantity or abundance of solid ingredients in a can of Campbell's soup [and] therefore the aforesaid advertisements are false, misleading, and deceptive."[40] Campbell Soup Company argued that the added marbles did nothing more than make the soup appear as it would if observed by a consumer when cooking the soup at home. Nonetheless, the company agreed to cease running the disputed commercial.

Unfair Commercial Speech

The FTC's working definitions of *unfair* and *deceptive* commercial speech have varied over time and with the political and economic philosophies of FTC members. In the early 1980s, Congress took away the FTC's authority to deal with unfair, as opposed to deceptive, advertising or other commercial speech. From then until 1994, the FTC was funded from year to year, in part because of the controversy over the regulation of unfair commercial speech. The Agency was finally reauthorized after an agreement between the House and the Senate that the FTC could not regulate an "unfair" act or practice unless it "causes or is likely to cause substantial injury to consumers that is not reasonably avoidable by consumers themselves and not outweighed by countervailing benefits to consumers or to competition,"[41] or promotes activities contrary to public policy or exploits vulnerable populations. This is a tough standard to meet, and there continue to be fewer complaints filed by the FTC for unfair commercial speech (especially commercial speech that is truthful) than for deceptive commercial speech.

But examples do exist. As one illustration, a study in 1993 by the U.S. Centers for Disease Control and Prevention (CDC) in Atlanta found that the three most heavily advertised brands of cigarettes—Marlboro, Camels and Newport—controlled 86 percent of the market share for smokers ages 12 to 18, compared with only 33 percent of the U.S. market share overall (Marlboro had 60 percent while Camels and Newport each had 13 percent).[42] According to the CDC survey, 3 million adolescents were smoking 1 billion packs of cigarettes each year.[43]

In response, FTC staff recommended the ban of ads for Camel cigarettes that included the character "Old Joe" or "Joe Camel." Studies allegedly showed that even young children associated the character with Camels.[44] Within three years after Joe appeared, said the complaint, the illegal sale of Camels to children under 18 reportedly rose from $6 million to a whopping $476 million a year.[45]

The FTC then launched a much-heralded investigation of the "Joe Camel" advertising campaign. R.J. Reynolds Tobacco Company had spent $42.9 million in major market advertising for Camels the previous year.[46] In June of the same year, the FTC formally announced it was ending the investigation, saying there was no evidence to support claims that children were lured to smoke by the campaign, thus accepting the arguments of the tobacco industry. However, after a series of setbacks in court cases brought against the tobacco industry by anti-smoking groups and the publication of the results of more studies, the FTC announced that it planned to reverse its earlier decision and issue a complaint against R.J. Reynolds for unfair advertising for its Joe Camel ads. The company subsequently abandoned its irreverent, dromedary spokesman.

Other issues noted by the Rosdens that have triggered the FTC's unfairness jurisdiction include: (a) falsely suggesting a product is being offered at a reduced price; (b) not revealing additional charges beyond the advertised price; (c) advertising goods as "free" when there actually are hidden costs or requirements; and (d) "adverting prices as wholesale or factory prices when they are not."[47] The FTC also may treat changes in the ingredients, elements or terms of products or services as creating unfairness concerns unless commercial speakers first modify their marketing messages to alert potential consumers about these changes.[48]

The difficulty in defining an unfair commercial speech act or practice that will withstand a First Amendment challenge has severely limited the applicability of this concept in commercial speech situations. The concept of "unfairness" is also controversial because it implies that commercial speech that is neither false nor deceptive can nonetheless be subject to sanction by the FTC.

The FTC's Disclosure Requirements

Early in its commercial speech jurisprudence, the Supreme Court observed that advertising "does not provide a complete foundation on which to" make certain purchasing decisions. In holding that states may not prohibit truthful advertising by attorneys, the Court reasoned that, rather than denying consumers access to correct but incomplete information, the preferred remedy is "more disclosure, not less." The Court went on to note that, for some commercial messages, some type of "warning or disclaimer or the like, might be required."[49]

In keeping with this approach, the FTC has embraced disclosure requirements as one means of reducing the potential for advertising deception in the commercial marketplace. The Commission's *Policy Statement on Deception* indicates that "some cases involve omission of material information, the disclosure of which is necessary to prevent the claim, practice or sale from being misleading."[50] In general, the Commission requires that qualifying disclosures be "clear and conspicuous." In the context of print advertising, clear and conspicuous essentially means "legible and understandable."

For television commercials, the FTC requires that affirmative disclosures be presented simultaneously in both the audio and video portions of the advertisement. Letters used to convey the disclaimer must be of sufficient size to be easily seen and read on all television sets and should be on a contrasting, solid background. The audio portion of the disclosure should be devoid of other sounds, including music. The Commission also expects disclosures to be made in conjunction with the offers to which they apply, or immediately adjacent to the major sales theme of the commercial if not linked to a specific product representation. Finally, disclosures should be crafted with the target audience of the advertising in mind "to assure that such persons can understand the full meaning of the disclosure."[51]

The Commission also has issued specific guidance for online advertising disclosures that take into consideration the use of smartphones with small screens and the popularity of social media marketing. These ".com" disclosure requirements, along with other potentially deceptive features of advertising, such as the formatting and presentation of "native advertising," are discussed in more detail in Chapter 13.

The *Policy Statement*, addressing deception generally, cites specific Commission cases in which the FTC determined that "written disclosures or fine print may be insufficient to correct a misleading representations (sic)" or that "pro forma statements or disclaimers may not cure otherwise deceptive messages or practices."[52] In addition, subsequent communications aimed at consumers, such as oral statements, label disclosures or point-of-sale materials "will not necessarily correct an initial deceptive representation or omission."[53] The Commission has recognized "that in many circumstances, reasonable consumers do not read the entirety of an ad or are directed away from the importance of the qualifying phrase by the acts or statements of the seller."[54] It tends to regard disclosures that comply with written policy as being generally adequate and notes that "less elaborate disclosures may also suffice."[55]

The bottom line regarding disclosures is that an advertiser may be unaware of the inadequacy of a disclosure until after an advertising campaign begins. Advertisers would do well to keep in mind that the FTC will evaluate the entire advertising, rather than a single aspect of the message to determine how reasonable consumers are likely to respond. Advertisers should take care that "the entire mosaic," including individual disclosures, contributes to an accurate representation of product claims and related offers.

The FTC's Requirements for Prior Substantiation

By far, the most common complaints about false or deceptive commercial speech focus on the failure of the touted products or services to live up to the claims made for them. To discourage such practices, the FTC requires commercial speakers to be ready to provide evidence that all of the material claims made in their commercial speech have been substantiated in advance. In a high-profile adjudication that spanned nearly six years, *In the Matter of POM Wonderful LLC*, the FTC issued a cease and desist order to marketers of a beverage whose advertising promised "that the products could treat, prevent, or reduce the risk of heart disease, prostate cancer, and erectile dysfunction, and were clinically proven to have such benefits." The FTC found that research referenced in the marketing materials claims was inadequate or failed to support the specific claims. The Commission's order, which was affirmed by the Court of Appeals for the District of Columbia, requires POM's "future disease treatment and prevention claims to be supported by at least one randomized, well-controlled human clinical trial, and other health benefit claims to be supported by competent and reliable scientific evidence."[56]

The prior substantiation policy was originated in the FTC's 1972 decision in *In re Pfizer Inc*.[57] In advertising for a sunburn remedy called "Un-Burn," Pfizer claimed that its product "anesthetizes nerves in sensitive sunburned skin" and that it "relieves pain fast."[58] A complaint to the FTC resulted in an action for issuance of a cease-and-desist order on the basis that Pfizer had failed to back up its claims with "well-controlled scientific studies or tests prior to the making of such statements."[59] Although the FTC eventually dropped its investigation of Pfizer, it informally adopted a prior substantiation rule on the basis that a "consumer ... cannot make the necessary tests or investigations to determine whether the ... claims made for a product are true."[60]

The FTC, noting the unequal status between those making product claims and those potentially using those products, added that "it is more rational, and imposes far less cost on society, to require a manufacturer to confirm his affirmative product claims rather than impose...[that] burden upon each individual consumer to test, investigate, or experiment for himself."[61]

The FTC upheld and refined its prior substantiation rules in a series of subsequent cases. By 1976, just three years after *Pfizer*, the FTC, in *In re National Commission on Egg Nutrition*,[62] could describe its rules requiring "substantiation" of product claims as established policy. The FTC explained that "[t]he justification for such a requirement is ... [that] consumers are likely to assume that when a product claim is advanced which is in theory subject to objective verification, the party making [the claim] possesses a reasonable basis for so doing."[63] The FTC concluded that consumers have a right to expect that "advertising claims couched in objective terms are not merely statements of unsubstantiated opinion."[64]

The 1984 Policy Statement on Advertising Substantiation[65] codified these decisions. The policy expressly stated that those seeing or hearing claims of a factual nature about a product can reasonably expect that such claims are based on objective evidence. If advertisers refer to specific tests or experiments, consumers should legitimately expect that claims based on these tests have been substantiated to the degree claimed in the message.

When the FTC says prior substantiation, it means *prior* substantiation. To inhibit commercial speakers from gambling on the mere possibility that their claims may later be substantiated, the FTC holds that the burden of proof rests with those making commercial speech claims to demonstrate that the claims have been substantiated prior to publication.[66] This means that the FTC may act to regulate commercial speech when there is a complaint about an objective material claim made for a product or service even if it eventually turns out that the speech contains no demonstrably false statement of fact.

For example, a claim that a product increases the speed of operation by 30 percent compared to a competing product's performance might lead to FTC action if the claimant cannot show evidence to substantiate those claims prior to publicizing the product. This despite the fact that subsequent research conducted after the claims were challenged might prove the statements to have been true.[67]

Not all claims require the same degree of prior substantiation. The FTC requires the highest levels of proof for statements that readers or viewers reasonably interpret as based on specific evidence for objective claims. Such claims may include wording like "four clinical trials" or "the results of two surveys reveal." For example, in *Pfizer*, the FTC noted that the company's testing "consisting of injections of [the drug] benzocaine could not indicate the probable anesthetic effect of a topical [on the skin] application of this substance."[68] The FTC concluded that Pfizer's commercials were unacceptable because they implied clinical trials supporting the claims made for pain relief although the company, in fact, "did not conduct adequate and well-controlled scientific studies or tests prior to marketing Un-Burn to substantiate the efficacy claims made for Un-Burn."[69] Similarly, the use of such terms as "scientific proof" and "lab-tested evidence," although not establishing the amount or specific level of proof, normally must be substantiated by the kinds of evidence those terms would imply to the reasonable consumer.

Commercial speech that sets specific performance standards—"Lasts Twice as Long as Any Other Leading Brand" or "Gets 30 mpg at Highway Speeds"—requires prior substantiation that demonstrates the accuracy of these claims. The case of *Firestone Tire & Rubber Co. v. FTC*[70] illustrates this heightened prior substantiation requirement for specific claims. Firestone asserted that its "wide oval" tires stopped "25% quicker" than other tires. Finding these claims raised a safety issue, the FTC ordered the company to stop advertising such claims unless and until they could be substantiated.

Often, however, the offending commercial speech does not expressly or by implication refer to specific levels or standards of substantiation. In these instances, the FTC sets the prior substantiation requirements for an objectively testable claim at a "reasonableness" level, based on the legitimate expectations of the consumer. Although the FTC has not established a "bright-line test" to determine reasonableness of prior substantiation in such cases, analysis of the evidence used by the speaker in arriving at the claims and the potential harm to consumers relying on these claims normally will be factors contributing to the FTC's evaluation. For example, claims for health-related products likely will call for more exacting "reasonable" prior substantiation than claims for another kind of product because of the physical risks posed for the unwary consumer.

Reasonable prior substantiation might also involve analyzing the practices of comparable companies or evidence of industry-wide standards. For example, objective claims for a medical product might be compared to a testing-within-the industry standard (e.g., three scientifically controlled tests) if the FTC determines the existence of generally accepted standards established by the medical community for such products. However, if a product is widely used, and consumers themselves could easily verify objective claims, the FTC normally will not require submission of evidence of industry-wide tests to demonstrate the reasonableness of a claim. The FTC also will give great weight to the findings of other agencies (e.g., the Bureau of Alcohol, Tobacco, Firearms and Explosives or the Food and Drug Administration) in accepting the reasonableness of commercial speakers' objective claims.

Balancing the costs of regulation against the benefits such regulation might bring to the consumer may also be considered by the FTC in evaluating the reasonableness of an objective claim. Setting reasonableness standards at too high a level might discourage the introduction of beneficial new products and services into the marketplace. Recognizing that, because of the inductive logic of scientific testing, critics could almost always argue "we need one more study," the FTC normally tempers its requirements for prior substantiation by employing an *ad-hoc*, cost-benefit analysis. Factors in the balancing process might include an evaluation of the likelihood that additional testing could change the evidence supporting the claim, the cost and time needed to conduct such additional tests and the degree of risk to the consumer if the objective claims turned out to be false.

The FTC and Substantiation Standards for Commercial Claims About Health and Beauty and "Green" Products

Based on a pattern of recurring complaints by consumers and consumer groups, the FTC generally looks with special scrutiny at complaints about commercial claims for health-care products because of the potential for immediate, serious physical harm such products could cause. The last few decades also have brought increased scrutiny to so-called green issues involving claims about the environmental impact of goods in the commercial marketplace.

On the diet and weight-loss claim front, the FTC is especially critical of such claims as:

- Consumers who use the advertised product can lose two pounds or more per week (over four or more weeks) without reducing caloric intake or increasing their physical activity.
- Consumers who use the advertised product can lose substantial weight while still enjoying unlimited amounts of high calorie foods.
- The advertised product will cause permanent weight loss even when the user stops using the product.
- The advertised product will cause substantial weight loss through the blockage of absorption of fat or calories.[71]

After years of extensive hearings and litigation, the FTC established a requirement that commercial claims for medicines or personal-care products based directly or indirectly on clinical or scientific evidence must be substantiated by a minimum of two independent clinical trials. The FTC created this standard because it felt that consumers would likely be deceived by claims allegedly based on "clinical studies," believing such procedures had been conducted "scientifically." Also, the FTC reasoned the average consumer would be unable to independently evaluate such claims.

For example, in *In re Thompson Medical Co.*,[72] the company marketing Aspercreme™ claimed that using its topical skin product reduced aches and pains attributed to arthritis as well as, if not better than, ingesting regular aspirin. Unfortunately for Thompson, these claims were not based on evidence the FTC considered scientifically valid. The FTC ordered the manufacturer to stop making any claims about the pain-relieving qualities of Aspercreme unless it conducted "at least two adequate and well-controlled, double-blinded clinical studies"[73] that met what the FTC felt were the standards of accepted scientific research.

In instances involving nonspecific claims for health-care products, the FTC generally has been content with only one clinical trial. These are rare, however, and usually involve claims about either attributes of a product not considered potentially harmful or involving physical properties that can be measured by instrumentation.

To meet FTC substantiation requirements, clinical tests and trials normally must be conducted by qualified independent investigators following an acceptable plan of research. At a minimum, this research plan should be specified in advance of the actual clinical trials and should establish sample sizes, statistical tests and levels of significance that experts in the field recognize as appropriate.

As might be expected, numerous differences in interpretation have arisen between the FTC and commercial speakers over the definitions and implementation of requirements for approved clinical test procedures. Generally, the FTC requires that investigators in different clinical trials be different researchers and operate independently of each other. In *Thompson*, the FTC affirmed that "[t]he personnel who administer the test should also be experienced, as well as properly trained and instructed in using the measures involved in the clinical trial."[74] The FTC has also held that when comparing two products, clinical test procedures should normally include the use of a placebo or its equivalent as a control.

Because it is possible for two products to prove virtually identical in everyday use but to differ when measured by statistical tests, the FTC usually requires claims of superiority for one of the products to be based on both empirical and practical, real-world differences. The FTC also may permit claims that rely on chemical or laboratory test results in lieu of clinical trials if the testing procedures prove acceptable within the scientific community. If the commercial speech about a product also involves claims about freedom from unpleasant side effects ("And It Doesn't Upset Your Stomach"), the FTC normally requires such claims to be substantiated in the same manner as primary claims.

As for "green" claims, in its *Guides for the Use of Environmental Marketing Claims*,[75] the FTC provides guidelines for "environmental claims ... about ... the attributes of a product or package in connection with the sale ... or marketing of such product or package" to individuals and commercial enterprises.[76] The FTC is especially concerned with the use of such terms as *recyclable*, *biodegradable* and *environmentally friendly* and has created guidelines that detail the degree of prior substantiation for such claims.

"Puffing": A Special Prior Substantiation Problem

Although objective claims create the problem of evaluating the reasonable prior substantiation of such claims, other kinds of statements about a product or service—"It's the Best," "There's No Other One for You" or "No Competing Brand Comes Close"—have forced the FTC to create a workable definition of just what constitutes a nonobjective (or "puffing") statement. *Puffing* has been defined as commercial speech "that is not deceptive [because] no one would rely on its exaggerated claims."[77]

Typically, the FTC and courts are more likely to find a claim to be puffing if the statements in the commercial speech refer to a product or service taken as a whole rather than to any specific attributes of the product or service. The statement "It's a Great Truck" would be more likely treated as simple puffery than would the statement "It Gets Great Gas Mileage." Adding the statement "It Gets 5 Miles More Per Gallon at Highway Speeds" would almost certainly turn the statement into an objective claim requiring prior substantiation.

Thus, for example, in *In re Dannon Milk Products, Inc.*,[78] the FTC held that a description of yogurt as one of nature's perfect foods constituted more than puffery because it stated an objective fact about a product's nutritional attributes.

Employing similar reasoning, the FTC and courts usually treat a company's general comparative advertising claims of superiority for its product or service as puffery but tend to require prior substantiation for specific comparative statements about individual characteristics of its products or services because they are objective claims.

The FTC also looks at a claim to determine whether it can be factually verified. Some statements ("You'll Just Feel More Assured Wearing Acme Shoes") are opinion statements and almost always treated as puffery. However, if the statement appears to be based on factual information ("If You Could See the Results of the Studies I've Seen, You'd Agree That Acme Shoes Are Better"), the statement might be treated as expressing fact. The reader should note that simply placing an "I believe ..." or "In my opinion ..." in front of a fact statement will not turn that statement into an opinion statement and therefore free of a prior substantiation requirement.

Perhaps the most troubling element of its puffing-versus-fact standard from the commercial speaker's point of view is the FTC's definition of an *average consumer* standard. The FTC's (and the courts') evaluation of the intelligence the "average consumer" displays often differs sharply from the estimations held by commercial speakers.

In *In re Matter of Better Living, Inc.*,[79] the court agreed with the FTC that the statement that the company guaranteed "the world's lowest price"[80] was a claim of objective fact (and not puffery) requiring substantiation, despite arguments to the contrary that no reasonable consumer could be misled or deceived by such statements. Similarly, in *Gillette Co. v. Wilkinson Sword, Inc.*,[81] the court found that "smoothest, most comfortable shave possible" was "a performance claim for one of the most important characteristics of the product being sold,"[82] although it is open to question whether the "average consumer" would be that easily fooled by such a claim.

The frequent use of the term *new*—as in "New and Improved"—in commercial claims has led the FTC to issue a special policy statement concerning the use of that term. Describing a product or service on the market for more than six months as *new* will be considered questionable unless the product or service provider is conducting a test-marketing campaign. The FTC has indicated that, in such a situation, it will enforce its six-month policy only after the product or service is introduced into the marketplace in final form.

The FTC and Games of Chance

Although the terms are often used interchangeably by commercial speakers, the FTC makes sharp distinctions between and among *lotteries, contests, games of chance, drawings* and *sweepstakes*. Lotteries, unless permitted by statute and conducted by a government agency, are banned by law in most states. Generally, a contest is treated as an illegal lottery if contestants must pay money or take any other kind of action that could be considered to be payment of "consideration," including, in some states, the purchase of a product or service. In addition, a contest risks being judged a lottery if the contestant can win by chance alone, rather than by demonstrating any special skill, and the winners are awarded prizes of economic value.

The FTC is concerned that commercial speech about legal contests, drawings, sweepstakes and other such promotional techniques creates a risk of deception for potential consumers. In an attempt to minimize this risk, the FTC publishes specific guidelines for disclosure of information that apply to games of chance when used by commercial speakers promoting the sale of either food items or gasoline.[83] Those representing these industries would be wise to be in contact with the FTC before creating such contests. The FTC also has used its general supervisory powers to challenge the use of contests and other similar techniques when employed by commercial speakers to promote products or services in other industries.

Although a comprehensive discussion of the wide range of rules covering such techniques is beyond the scope of this chapter, it would be prudent for a commercial speaker contemplating use of a promotional contest to, at a minimum, include clearly written and displayed information in all promotional material about (a) the true chances of winning any prize of value; (b) a description of all prizes (including their value); and (c) the number of prizes to be awarded. Also, the rules and conditions (including any deadlines) for entering the contest or sweepstakes should be publicized, as should information about who is eligible to be a contestant.

FTC Regulation of Testimonials and Endorsements

The FTC has long been concerned about the use of endorsements and testimonials by celebrities or other non-company spokespersons to promote products and services. In 1987, the commission released a policy guide for its regulation of such practices, which it revised in 2009 to better address issues specific to social media and other online endorsements. The updated *FTC Guides Concerning Use of Endorsements and Testimonials in Advertising*[84] primarily impacts the use of disclaimers to accompany true endorsement claims that do not reflect the average experience and the types of endorsements companies can receive from new media sources like blogs and message boards. The Guides do not create law, but they do explain the way the FTC will interpret the law. The Guides state that an endorsement is "any advertising message (including verbal statements, demonstrations, or depictions of the name, signature, likeness, or other identifying personal characteristics of an individual or the name or seal of an organization) that consumers are likely to believe reflects the opinions, beliefs, findings or experience of a party other than the sponsoring advertiser."[85]

According to the FTC, the Guides "reflect the basic truth-in-advertising principle that endorsements must be honest and not misleading."[86] The FTC has emphasized the need for online endorsements to make clear when there is a connection between the endorser and marketer the consumers would not expect, especially when knowledge of the connection may affect how consumers evaluate the endorsement. Social media "influencers," for example, who tout the benefits of certain products must disclose to readers or viewers if they have been paid or given something of value in exchange for mentioning the product. FTC standards regard such endorsements to constitute misleading advertising unless the connection has been clearly disclosed. Both advertisers and their endorsers "may be subject to liability for false or unsubstantiated statements made through endorsements, or for failing to disclose material connections between themselves and their endorsers."[87] The FTC's position is that endorsement statements, whether offered on blogs or social media or in more traditional media vehicles must meet the same substantiation requirements as other material claims.

In *In re Cliffdale Associates, Inc.*,[88] the advertiser of the Ball-Matic Gas Saver Valve claimed that the product was "the most significant automotive breakthrough in the last 10 years"[89] and produced several advertisements with testimonials by alleged users of the product claiming that the valve gave them substantial improvement in miles per gallon of gasoline. The FTC challenged the accuracy of these and other claims for the product. In response, Cliffdale Associates tried to argue that because the consumers providing the testimonials legitimately believed that they had obtained improved gas mileage, no other proof was necessary to justify the claims. The FTC would have none of it. "[C]onsumer tests and testimonials," said the FTC, "are not a recognized way of testing fuel economy."[90] It went on to note that "irrespective of the veracity of the individual consumer testimonials, use of the testimonials to make underlying claims that were false and deceptive was, itself, deceptive."[91]

In its Guides, the FTC describes typical examples of endorsements to help commercial speakers understand and follow its directives. For example, if a consumer posts an item on her personal blog about how much her dog seems to like a new brand of dog food she purchased on her own, the FTC would not consider this to be an endorsement and no disclosure would be necessary. If, however, the consumer joins a network marketing program in which she receives new products, including the dog food, and writes reviews about them, the positive review would be considered an endorsement under FTC Guides. Other examples are less straightforward. For example, if a celebrity has been a long-term spokesperson for a company or product, the use of the celebrity in commercial speech normally would not constitute an endorsement because consumers likely recognize the celebrity is speaking on behalf of the company and not a specific product or service. However, if a company employs a popular sports figure or entertainer with no long-term association with a company as part of the company's marketing campaign for a product, the FTC may consider that to be an endorsement, even if the celebrity never actually makes any overt testimonial statements. Similarly, the FTC may consider statements by critics or reviewers favorable to a product or service that are subsequently used by a company in commercial messages to be endorsements because of the possible confusion in the mind of the consumer about which are the critics' views and which are the company's.

Companies that use celebrities to endorse their products or services must be able to demonstrate that the endorsements are both genuine and accurate in all important details. For example, in *In re Cooga Mooga, Inc.*,[92] the FTC held that statements by singer Pat Boone and members of his family endorsing "Acne-Statin," an anti-acne skin product, were false and deceptive. The commercials claimed, among other things, that Boone's daughters had used the product and that it produced satisfactory results. In finding that most of the health claims for the product were false or exaggerated, the FTC also noted that not all of Boone's daughters had used the medication and that the implication that all had done so constituted an additional untrue claim.

The use of a celebrity endorser must be limited to the time that the celebrity actually uses the product or service. Statements to the effect that a celebrity "drives the Terraplane Z6" would constitute false and deceptive claims if the celebrity either never or no longer drives this automobile. The reader should also remember that those employing the celebrity endorser may be liable for engaging in illegal practices in a Lanham Act cause of action (discussed in Chapter 10).

Regardless of whether the providers of a testimonial are celebrities or individuals portrayed as typical consumers, the claims they make must reflect what the average consumer would experience in normal usage of the product or service. This means that although the endorser may truthfully testify that he or she experienced a phenomenal response or improvement after using a product or service, such claims may be considered deceptive if scientific or statistical evidence reveals such experiences to be significantly different from what the typical user of the product or service might find.

One method of possibly avoiding the need to substantiate an endorsement claim is the use of a disclaimer statement. The FTC's guidelines indicate that adequate disclosure—stating the more typical performance record of the product or service and phrasing and displaying it in such a manner as to be readily understood by the listener or viewer—may be sufficient to satisfy the FTC's requirements for non-deceptive commercial speech. However, simply stating that the endorsement claim "may not be typical" or other similarly worded general disclosures normally are not sufficient. The reader also should note that the more extravagant the claim, the less likely the FTC will accept a simple disclosure or disclaimer to avoid a charge of deceptive commercial speech.

In addition to celebrities and individuals portrayed as average citizens, commercial speakers often employ professionals described as experts to recommend the speaker's product or service. Not surprisingly, the FTC guidelines on testimonials and endorsements make special provision for such endorsers because of the tendency for consumers to believe such experts and their greater capacity to deceive consumers. A commercial speaker employing an expert should be able to demonstrate the expert actually has evaluated the product or service and has done so in a manner "as extensive as someone with the same degree of expertise would normally need to conduct in order to support the conclusions presented in the endorsement."[93] When the endorsement contains claims that the product or service is the equal of, or better than, a competitor, the expert endorser similarly must also have evaluated the competitor's product or service.

A claim made by an expert must be based on the standards employed by the industry involved or by other experts in the field. Similarly, the credentials of the expert providing the endorsement must demonstrate that the expert is qualified to provide such testimonial endorsement.

For example, it would be inappropriate to use a medical doctor in an advertisement endorsing a product if that product is outside the medical specialty of the physician. In *In re Cooper*,[94] the former astronaut Gordon Cooper, a stakeholder in a company that manufactured and sold the "G-R Gas Saver Valve," appeared in the company's advertising wearing what appeared to be his space suit, touting the virtues of the product. Cooper was billed as an expert engineer who had performed tests of the valve in his "independent engineering laboratory."[95] The FTC, although not questioning Cooper's credentials as an astronaut with NASA, ordered the company to cease and desist using Cooper as an endorser of the valve in the company's commercial efforts because he was unqualified to serve as an expert in evaluating and recommending automobile products, despite his scientific and engineering expertise.

FTC guidelines do not prohibit an expert in one field from endorsing a product in another if the endorsement is merely a personal rather than a professional endorsement and the endorsement meets the other requirements for testimonials discussed earlier. When a group or organization supplies the testimonial statement, the FTC requires that the statement reflect the overall consensus of its members. Such groups or organizations must have performed the appropriate tests or in other ways evaluated the product or service in question if the commercial message states or suggests that they have done so. For example, in *Niresk Industries, Inc. v. FTC*,[96] the FTC ordered the company to stop advertising that its products were endorsed by *Good Housekeeping* magazine's "Seal of Approval," when, in fact, that organization had not endorsed them.

Commercial speakers should beware of employing statements published by consumer groups that claim to objectively test products or services even if the quotes are true and accurate. Such consumer organizations jealously guard their reputations as independent evaluators and may resort to legal action to prevent the appearance of an endorsement.

The FTC and Retail Sales

Unlike commercial speech by manufacturers or service providers, commercial speech by retailers usually involves claims about the conditions of the sales situation, including special sales, low prices or unusual merchandising practices. The FTC, recognizing that such commercial speech can be equally as deceptive to the average consumer as claims for products or services, publishes an extensive set of rules governing retail sales. Although a comprehensive review of these rules is beyond the scope of this chapter, a brief overview of the FTC's efforts in this area may serve to alert retail commercial speakers to the need to familiarize themselves with regulations affecting their activities.

One of the FTC's greatest concerns is potentially deceptive claims involving the pricing of goods and services. The FTC publishes its *Guides Against Deceptive Pricing*[97] to provide retail commercial speakers with guidance in this area. Some of the regulations covered in these and other guidelines involve specific rules describing when speakers legitimately may claim that an item is reduced in price from its "usual" or "regular" price. To meet FTC requirements, such sales claims must be based on a comparison with the normal price charged for the item or, if no specific dollar amount or percentage of savings is mentioned, the sale price must be low enough to constitute what the average consumer reasonably would consider a legitimate savings.

If a commercial speaker claims that its prices are lower than its competition's prices or are at manufacturer or wholesale prices, the FTC normally requires such claims to be based on legitimate comparisons with its nearby competitors' normal pricing policies or the usual manufacturers' or wholesalers' prices.

Other FTC guidelines for retailers cover practices such as using the terms *"Introductory Sale"* or *"Buy One, Get One Free"* or *"Free Gift,"* as well as prohibitions on so-called bait-and-switch advertising. This latter term is defined by the FTC as "an alluring but insincere offer to sell a product or service…[for the purpose of switching] consumers from [the advertised item] to … something else, usually at a higher price or on a basis more advantageous to the advertiser."[98] Retail commercial speech practices involving mail-order sales and sales of such items as household furniture, electronics, jewelry and luggage are addressed by specific industry standards. Readers of this text who engage in commercial speech involving these and related practices should refer to guidelines from the FTC if they have concerns about their retail commercial claims.

In an area closely related to retail sales, the FTC oversees implementation and enforcement of the Fair Packaging and Labeling Act (FPLA), which requires that certain products carry labels identifying the contents, source, item quantity and other information to help consumers compare products. FTC regulations exempt certain product categories, including, among other items, meat, poultry and tobacco products and items under the jurisdiction of the Food and Drug Administration (FDA). The FLPA, which was enacted in 1966, was designed to enable consumers to obtain accurate package quantity information to facilitate value comparisons and prevent unfair packaging and labeling of food, devices, cosmetics or any other article or product that "is customarily produced or distributed for sale through retail sales agencies."[99] The FTC also monitors and regulates aspects of commercial speech involving offers of credit extended by retailers to consumers under provisions of the federal Truth-in-Lending Act.[100] The Act, which covers all those who advertise or offer consumer credit, regardless of whether they are actual creditors, calls for non-deceptive commercial speech about the conditions to be met, the actual credit rate the consumer can expect to receive, how any finance charge is computed and other pertinent information. The Act also covers offers of lease agreements and requires similar disclosures of terms, conditions and so forth. The reader engaged in commercial speech involving offers of consumer credit is urged to be in contact with the FTC for guidance to avoid running afoul of its regulations in this area.

The FTC and Consumer Privacy

As online shopping and financial transactions have become a way of life for many consumers, the protection of consumer privacy has taken center stage. Chapter 13 describes data privacy laws enacted recently to address a variety of online data collection, storage and usage. Consumer privacy, however, is a concern wherever consumer data are collected and stored, whether online or not. Over the last two decades, a number of large companies have reported breaches that may have placed consumers' personal information into the hands of identity thieves. An early example involved the data collection company ChoicePoint, which revealed that identity thieves had swiped personal information for almost 150,000 consumers, at least 750 of whom reported being the victims of identity theft.[101] Banks, universities and other organizations also have reported the loss or theft of personal information about consumers, including Social Security numbers and other important sensitive information.

In response, the FTC has used its power under Section 5 of the FTC Act (to condemn "unfair or deceptive acts or practices") to regulate a broad range of business behaviors including consumer privacy violations. One of the most notable involved BJ's Wholesale Club, which, according to the FTC, engaged in an unfair trade practice by failing to secure customers' sensitive information embedded in the magnetic strip on the back of credit cards.[102] The club settled with the FTC and agreed to establish and maintain a "comprehensive information security program that includes administrative, technical and physical safeguards."[103]

After the BJ's Wholesale case, the FTC published in 2007 a so-called Red Flags Rule,[104] requiring certain creditors to develop and implement written Identity Theft Prevention Programs to detect signs of possible consumer identity theft. Covered creditors also must implement measures to increase the accuracy of consumer credit reports and describe appropriate responses that would prevent and mitigate the crime and detail a plan to update the program.[105] The programs "must be managed by the Board of Directors or senior employees of the financial institution or creditor, include appropriate staff training, and provide for oversight of any service providers,"[106] words of importance to public relations professionals working in such organizations.

Such "red flags" might include "unusual account activity, fraud alerts on a consumer report, or attempted use of suspicious account application documents." [107] In 2012, Congress lessened the scope of the Red Flags Rule by narrowing the definition of "creditor"; it did not, however, lessen the potential impact of the rule for covered creditors who fail to comply.

FTC Enforcement: Cease-and-Desist, Consent and Corrective Orders

Without the ability to enforce its rules and regulations, the FTC's function would be limited to advisory status. The Federal Trade Commission Act provides the FTC with the power to "issue and cause to be served on such person, partnership, or corporation [in violation of the law] an order requiring such person, partnership, or corporation to cease and desist from using such method of competition or such act or practice."[108] These "cease-and-desist" orders may be imposed by the FTC itself without resorting to the courts for enforcement.

Although the normal standard for imposition of such a "cease-and-desist order" is a finding that a violation will cause immediate and irreparable harm, at least one court has held that deference by the judiciary to rulings by the FTC means that the FTC need only meet a general-public-interest standard. A court-ordered temporary injunction could become permanent if the court finds that the public would best be served by following this course of action.[109]

When a cease-and-desist order has been ignored or disobeyed, the FTC likely will seek a civil law remedy from the courts by invoking Section 45(m) of the Federal Trade Commission Act.[110] This section permits a court to impose stiff financial penalties for each day the defendant is in violation of the order. For example, in *United States v. Readers Digest Association*,[111] the court assessed a 10-cent penalty for each simulated sweepstakes check the publication had disseminated. Unfortunately for *Readers Digest*, the total number of checks reached more than 17 million, resulting in a fine of $1,750,000.

Almost without exception, a cease-and-desist order comes only after a series of negotiations during the investigation phase of the FTC's preliminary inquiry. Only if the FTC and the commercial speaker cannot agree on an informal alternative course of action to resolve their disagreements will the FTC initiate a more formal complaint procedure.

The overwhelming bulk of cases are settled, usually as a result of a negotiated, signed consent order. By agreeing to discontinue the challenged practice, the commercial speaker can avoid the potentially negative publicity of litigation and need not admit wrongdoing.

Given the normally short shelf life of most commercial speech, consent orders often satisfy all parties. However, commercial speakers may object to signing a consent order if they feel it is unjustified or would seriously interfere either with an ongoing or a planned commercial campaign. In that eventuality, typically the next step after issuance of a formal complaint is a hearing before an administrative law judge (ALJ), who adjudicates legal proceedings involving federal agencies. The ALJ is empowered to obtain evidence through subpoena and, in many respects, the hearing is like a trial. At its termination, the judge must render a decision within 90 days. The ALJ may decide that a cease-and-desist order be entered, determine that some other remedy is called for or decide in favor of the party charged with violating the regulation and dismiss the complaint.

If the judge decides that a cease-and-desist order should be issued and the FTC is in accord with that judgment, the party against whom the order is issued must file a compliance report within 60 days, spelling out a compliance plan. If the FTC disagrees with the ALJ, it may elect to overrule the decision and impose its own sanctions. Rather than comply with the FTC, the party against whom an order is entered may then elect to appeal the FTC's actions in the federal appeals court system.

In its simplest form, the purpose of a cease-and-desist order is to remedy the problem by ordering the offending commercial speaker to stop. However, the FTC is not limited to such a remedy if, in its opinion, additional steps are needed to correct the existing problem or to prevent similar problems from recurring. In such instances, the FTC may issue a broad order that covers commercial speech for other products or services produced by the offending company as well as for claims already found to be false or deceptive.

These so-called fencing-in orders, extending to commercial speech about other products or services the offending organization provides, are the FTC's method of attempting to ensure that the company does not make deceptive claims in future commercial speech. Fencing-in cease-and-desist orders may apply to some or all of the products or services a company provides, or they may be applied to some or all of the claims made for a particular product or service. Normally the FTC only expands its cease-and-desist order to fence in a commercial speaker in circumstances in which there is evidence that the offending speaker has both a history of deceptive commercial speech claims and when there is a future "likelihood of … committing the sort of unfair practice"[112] complained of in the present case.

In more extreme cases, the FTC may ban future commercial speech about a product or service unless affirmative disclosures accompany the speech. Perhaps the best-known example of such an affirmative disclosure order is the agreement reached by the FTC with cigarette manufacturers to include the Surgeon General's warning label in all commercial speech about their products.[113]

When the FTC finds a pattern of long and persistent publication of false and deceptive speech, it may also take the additional step of requiring a commercial speaker to publish corrective information. Although the line between affirmative disclosure and corrective information is not well drawn, the triggering mechanism for FTC action appears to be (a) the longevity of the party's advertising or other commercial speech campaign; (b) the nature and extent of the claims the FTC finds to be false and deceptive; and (c) the hypothesized continuing effects the prior speech might have on the decisions by consumers in the future.

In one of the more notable corrective commercial speech cases, *Warner-Lambert Co. v. FTC*,[114] a federal appeals court upheld the FTC's directive to require corrective information in future advertisements for Listerine. The claim that Listerine somehow could prevent colds and related symptoms had been a part of the product's advertising and marketing campaigns for decades. The FTC's remedy was to require Warner-Lambert to insert information clearly refuting such claims in each future advertisement until the company had spent as much money correcting its advertising as it had spent on all its advertising during the preceding 20 years—approximately $10 million. The court of appeals agreed with the FTC that such a drastic remedy was justified on the basis that the "deceptive advertisement[s] ... played a substantial role in creating or reinforcing in the public's mind a false and material belief which lives on after the false advertising ceases."[115]

FTC Enforcement: Civil Lawsuits

In addition to using its own systems and processes enforced with the aid of ALJs and the federal courts, the FTC can turn directly to federal courts to remedy false or deceptive commercial speech claims within its authority. Advertisers may be susceptible to civil lawsuits brought by the FTC even if they have not received specific cease-and-desist orders or other directives indicating a potential problem with their advertising claims. The FTC is likely to use this option for new, questionable practices likely to be adopted across emerging industries, and in industries where it already has issued a number of such orders, constructively putting competitors and others within that industry on notice that their similar commercial claims may be violations. Available remedies include injunctions, fines and disgorgement of any associated ill-gotten gains, which generally are sought to be refunded to consumers. In 2017, for example, the Commission sought a permanent injunction and monetary judgment against Vizio, the electronics manufacturer, for what it regarded as deceptive and unfair acts or practices over the company's smart televisions. According to the FTC's complaint filed in federal district court in New Jersey, Visio was unfairly collecting and sharing consumers' television viewing data and deceiving consumers about the function of its "Smart Interactivity" feature. Ultimately, the court approved Vizio's agreement to pay the FTC $1,500,000 and implement specific reforms to protect consumer privacy. The FTC has traditionally reserved disgorgement efforts, in which it seeks significant financial redress in order to compensate consumers, for situations involving fraud or where consumers have suffered some kind of tangible harm. But tangible injury is not a prerequisite for seeking financial penalties; as in the Vizio case, the Commission may ask a court to approve significant monetary sanctions even where tangible consumer harm does not exist.

If the situation warrants, the FTC may initiate criminal proceedings with a referral to the Department of Justice seeking to hold a commercial speaker guilty of a criminal misdemeanor. This, however, generally is limited to cases involving commercial claims for medicines or health-related products when an average consumer, believing in the claims for the product, could be seriously harmed and the offending party has ignored earlier warnings or orders by the FTC.

Not surprisingly, the use and reach of the FTC's remedial powers comprises a substantial percentage of the disputes between the FTC and commercial speakers. Much of this litigation has come from challenges to the scope of cease-and-desist orders. Although the FTC is generally victorious, sometimes the courts have found the Commission guilty of overreaching.

For example, in *Chrysler Corp. v. FTC*,[116] the FTC ordered the automobile manufacturer to not only cease potentially deceptive claims for the fuel efficiency of its products but to avoid misrepresenting the results of any tests or other research in its future advertising. A federal court of appeals in the District of Columbia approved the general order but found that the FTC had overreached to the extent of the order limiting discussion of tests and research results.[117] The court noted that such a prohibition was "potentially limitless,"[118] that Chrysler's infractions "were unintentional and non-continuing" and that the offending speech had appeared in only "two out of a campaign of fourteen advertisements."[119]

Similarly, in *ITT Continental Baking Co. v. FTC*,[120] a federal appeals court struck down the FTC's limitations on the company's comparative advertising claims as overbroad, in large measure because the company's statements about the nutritional value of its products were found to be accurate in 11 of the 12 cases discussed. In *American Medical Association v. FTC*,[121] a federal Court of Appeals in the Second Circuit modified the FTC's cease-and-desist order directed against the AMA by limiting it to a simple requirement that the association add the words "respondent reasonably believes" to its medical advertising.[122]

At times, courts may disagree with the scope of the FTC's orders when the offending commercial speaker has already discontinued the disputed practices prior to the FTC's investigation and issuance of the cease-and-desist mandate. However, if the cessation occurs after an investigation is initiated, courts generally are reluctant to overturn or modify FTC rulings.

The FTC and Commercial Speakers: Who Is Liable for What?

The FTC's regulations and enforcement procedures apply both to independent commercial speakers, such as advertising or public relations agencies, and to the original manufacturers or providers of the products or services for which allegedly false and deceptive claims are made. The FTC typically excuses independent agencies from liability for violations of the law if the agencies can demonstrate good faith efforts to ensure that the claims made for their clients' goods and services are truthful. The criteria for these good faith efforts usually can be satisfied if an agency has reasonably relied on information supplied by the client and if the agency has no cause to believe that such information is untrue or deceptive.

However, advertising or public relations agencies can be held vicariously liable as defendants in product liability suits, especially when a product harms a consumer, and directly liable for false, misleading or deceptive commercial speech created for clients. In *Standard Oil v. Federal Trade Commission*,[123] the FTC issued its cease-and-desist order against both the oil company and its advertising agency, Batten, Barton, Durstine & Osborn, Inc. (BBD&O) for broadcasting the company's "F-310" commercials. A federal court of appeals upheld the FTC's decision. As the court noted:

> BBD&O contends the Commission acted improperly in holding it liable under section 5. The standard of care to be exercised by an advertising agency in determining what express and implied representations are contained in an ad and in assessing the truth or falsity of those representations increases in direct relation to the advertising agency's participation in the commercial project. [citations omitted] The degree of its participation is measured by a number of factors including the agency's role in writing and editing the text of the ad, its work in creating and designing the graphic or audio-visual material, its research and analysis of public opinions and attitudes, and its selection of the appropriate audience for the advertising message. Precisely these factors were weighed in reaching the conclusion that BBD&O knew or should have known of the deceptive nature of the F-310 advertising.[124]

The two factors considered by the FTC and the courts in determining whether an agency will be held liable are whether the agency "knew or should have known of the deceptive nature" of the commercial speech and the degree to which the agency participated in the creation and display of the message. The second factor is probably weighed more in the determination. An agency with actual knowledge of an attempt by a client to deceive the public (or which it could have known about if it had acted in a reasonable matter by exercising appropriate diligence) will have a difficult time convincing the FTC and the courts that the agency should not be held jointly liable with the advertiser. Active participation by the agency in the creative process is strong evidence that the agency had actual or constructive knowledge of the deception.

Agencies are liable if the claims made in the commercial speech questioned by the FTC are the product of the creative efforts of the agency, regardless of whether such claims are express or implied. Agencies also have an affirmative duty to modify commercial claims if the agencies acquire new information about the products or services from their clients or other sources. This duty extends to being in compliance with FTC regulations or orders directed against their competitors. The FTC generally presupposes that an agency is responsible for the claims made for a product or service and therefore carefully scrutinizes arguments made by an agency that it had no reason to question whether the information supplied by the agency's clients was false or deceptive.

If an agency is held liable, it can be subjected to the same remedies as its client. Of particular concern have been attempts by the FTC, some successful and some not, to extend its "fencing-in" requirements to all of the commercial speech an agency creates for all of the products and services of any and all clients the agency represents. Agencies may also be liable for fines up to $10,000 per day for each violation of an FTC cease-and-desist order.

The FCC and Other Federal Agencies Concerned With Advertising

Although the Federal Trade Commission is the agency that exercises the most pervasive, day-to-day regulation of commercial speech, numerous government agencies, commissions and boards deal with commercial speech as a result of jurisdiction over specific modes of transmission or certain types of goods or services. Three prominent examples are the Federal Communications Commission (FCC), the Food and Drug Administration (FDA) and the Securities and Exchange Commission (SEC).

The Federal Communications Commission

The Federal Communications Commission (FCC) regulates the transmission of messages carried by radio, television, wire, satellite and cable in the United States and its territories. Like the FTC, the FCC is an independent government agency created and overseen by Congress. It is the country's "primary authority for communications law, regulation and technological innovation."[125] Congress established the FCC with passage of the Communications Act of 1934. The Act replaced the Federal Radio Commission, which had been established in 1912, and broadened the Commission's scope to include all forms of electronic communication in the United States. The FCC regulates television and radio station licensing and aspects of the technology that enables broadcast or wire transmissions. In some cases, the FCC regulates the content of those messages, as well. In fact, the FCC is able to regulate certain broadcast messages in ways that would be unconstitutional for messages carried via print media. The FCC's ability to regulate message content springs from a 1969 Supreme Court ruling in which the Court reinforced the FCC's authority to not only license users of the broadcast spectrum, but to control content in some circumstances.[126] The lesser First Amendment protection accorded print and broadcast media has to do with the fact that the broadcast airwaves are regarded as a form of public property with finite capabilities: only so many signals may be transmitted on the broadcast spectrum at once, which makes it a scarce resource. According to the Supreme Court's "scarcity rationale," as it has come to be known, broadcasters and others who make use of the electromagnetic spectrum to transmit messages over the public airwaves have an obligation to be good public stewards and may be subjected to more stringent regulation to make sure they act in the public interest. In addition to the scarcity rationale, the Court also has referred to the potential intrusiveness of broadcast messages as a rationale for its more stringent regulation; unlike subscription cable or satellite programming, which viewers or listeners invite into their homes, broadcast messages are freely available and accessible to adults and children alike.

Although the FCC does not directly regulate commercial expression, it sometimes partners with the FTC and other agencies in ways that impact advertisers and other commercial speakers. For example, since 2003, the FCC and the FTC have teamed to manage practices associated with telephone marketing calls, better known as telemarketing. According to the FCC, unwanted calls generate more than 200,000 consumer complaints each year, or about 60 percent of all complaints received by the Commission. Congress first addressed telemarketing with the Telephone Consumer Protection Act (TCPA) of 1991, which regulates telemarketing calls. In particular, the TCPA restricts the use of automatic telephone dialing systems and artificial or prerecorded voice messages. In 2003, the FCC supported the FTC in establishing a national Do-Not-Call registry, administered by the FTC as part of its Telemarketing Sales Rule, that allows consumers to opt out of receiving telemarketing calls by placing their telephone numbers in a national database. The Do-Not-Call rules require telemarketers to routinely check the database and purge from their call lists telephone numbers that appear there. Exceptions exist for callers conducting independent research, emergency calls, legitimate fundraising for charitable organizations and political-campaign calls. Companies that have an "established business relationship" with consumers also are allowed to telephone those consumers within 18 months of a purchase or other consumer contact unless the customers ask not to be called. Both the FTC and FCC field consumer complaints about violations of the Telemarketing Sales Rule.

More recently, the FCC has focused on the practice of "robocalling," and/or "spoofing" by telemarketers, practices that, according to the FCC, generate the most complaints from consumers and are the Commission's top consumer priority. The FCC defines robocalls as "calls made with an autodialer or that contain a message made with a prerecorded or artificial voice."[127] Because many robocalls are legal, the FTC has said it seeks to strike a balance between identifying and blocking illegal robocalls in real time, without unduly blocking lawful calls. In general, FCC rules require telemarketers to obtain express consent from consumers before robocalling either their home or wireless phone numbers. The consent requirements for robocalls apply even to telemarketers that have an "established business relationship" with customers through purchases or other contacts within the preceding 18 months.

Spoofing refers to the practice of deliberately and maliciously falsifying the information transmitted to a phone's caller ID display to disguise the identity of the caller. "Neighbor spoofing" is the practice of displaying a phone number similar to the one being called, to increase the likelihood the consumer will answer. Spoofing is not always illegal, but under the federal Truth in Caller ID Act, spoofing with the intent to defraud, cause harm or wrongly obtain anything of value can draw penalties of up to $10,000 for each violation. In 2018, for example—in its first major enforcement action aimed at spoofing—the FCC proposed a fine in excess of $37 million against an Arizona company "for apparently making millions of illegally-spoofed telemarketing calls that appeared to originate from consumers and other numbers not assigned to the company."[128] During a 14-month span, the company allegedly made more than 2.3 million maliciously spoofed telemarketing calls to sell home-improvement and remodeling services. According to

FCC rules, a telemarketer must transmit or display its telephone number, or the number on whose behalf the call is being made, along with the name of the company, if possible. The display must include a telephone number consumers can call during regular business hours to request that they not receive such calls in the future.

The FCC also plays a role in regulating certain types of advertising messaging and placement, including advertising aimed at children, advertising for contests and non-state-sponsored lotteries, and for political advertising and campaign appearances by candidates and their representatives. For example, during the broadcast of television programming directed at children 12 and under, advertising on FCC-licensed stations may not exceed 10.5 minutes an hour on weekends and 12 minutes an hour on weekdays. Federal law also largely prohibits the broadcast of advertisements for a lottery or information concerning a lottery, which is defined as any game, contest, or promotion that contains the elements of prize, chance and consideration. Only the following lottery-related broadcast advertising is permitted:

- State-run lotteries where the advertising is broadcast by a station licensed to a location within that state.
- Advertisements for gaming legally conducted by an Indian tribe.
- Advertisements for both in-state and out-of-state lawful casino gambling.
- State-authorized lotteries if they are conducted by a not-for-profit or governmental organization or as a promotional activity by a commercial organization when the lottery is not the organization's primary business.
- Certain fishing contests.[129]

Special rules also apply to elections. During specified periods before a primary or general election, broadcast stations licensed by the FCC must sell political advertising time to legally qualified federal, state or local candidates at the rate charged for the station's most-favored commercial advertiser. FCC regulations also require that broadcast stations provide "reasonable access" to their airwaves for candidates for federal elective office. This includes the ability to buy commercials during the station's normal broadcast schedule. In addition, the "equal opportunities" provision of the Communications Act requires that stations that provide access to a candidate for office must give other candidates for the same office an opportunity to avail themselves of similar airtime if they so desire. The only exception for these political access requirements is the broadcast of *bona fide* news coverage. A candidate who is the subject of on-the-spot news coverage, including interviews, debates, political conventions and incidental activities, will not trigger the equal opportunity requirement.

The Food and Drug Administration

The FDA is part of the larger U.S. Department of Health and Human Services. Headquartered in the Washington, D.C., area, the FDA employs more than 17,000 people in Washington and in regional offices across the country. Its missions include: (a) approving new drugs, medical devices and certain food additives for safety and, in some cases, effectiveness; (b) setting standards for foods and the labeling of foods and then ensuring via testing that such foods meet these standards; (c) inspecting sites where drugs, cosmetics, medical devices and foods are produced to ensure these products meet the FDA's public safety standards; and (d) issuing public warnings or taking legal action when unsafe products threaten the public welfare. The FDA's

Figure 10.2 Bottled water packaging and labeling falls under the authority of the Food and Drug Administration, which also is responsible for dietary supplements, food additives, infant formulas and other food products, as well as prescription and nonprescription drugs.

Credit line: Wavebreakmedia/Shutterstock.com

professional staff consists mainly of biologists, chemists, nutritionists, pharmacologists, attorneys and other compliance personnel and consumer-affairs officers.

Although its name might imply a wider jurisdiction, for the most part the FDA's direct interest in commercial speech is limited to regulating information about the contents and safety of drugs available only by prescription when advertised or promoted through the mass media or direct marketing to consumers. The federal Food, Drug and Cosmetic Act (FD&C Act),[130] which provides the framework for FDA operations, defines a *prescription drug* as a drug "not safe for [human] use except under the supervision of a licensed practitioner"[131] because of potential harm to the consumer either as the result of its use or from employing the methods necessary for its use. Any new drug may be defined as a "prescription drug" following the FDA's policy of labeling all such products as initially needing "the professional supervision of a practitioner licensed by law to administer such drug[s]"[132] unless the Agency is satisfied that the new drug can be safely introduced and sold over the counter without this requirement.

The FDA's jurisdiction over prescription-drug-related commercial speech emanates, in part, from its original grant of power to regulate "labels and any written, printed or graphic matter (1) upon any article [drug] or any of its containers or wrappers, or (2) accompanying such article."[133] Although the statute does not specifically define what is meant by "printed or graphic matter ... accompanying such [an] article," the FDA and the courts have treated this language as authorizing broad authority over commercial messages that are part of a promotional campaign, including retail sales promotion materials and direct mail pieces.

The FDA's authority to regulate commercial speech was made more explicit by a series of amendments to the FD&C Act, beginning in the 1960s, that specifically gave the FDA jurisdiction over commercial speech involving prescription drugs, reserving the power to regulate nonprescription drug commercial speech to the FTC.

Usually the FDA will treat commercial speech as falling within its regulatory authority if the prescription drug information is disseminated through broadcast or print commercials or through public relations activities aimed at the mass media. FDA jurisdiction over non-media promotional techniques is neither expressly defined nor directly suggested by the statute. However, in *Nature Food Centres, Inc. v. U.S.*,[134] a series of lectures touting the alleged virtues of a dietary supplement was permitted to be entered as evidence on the question of whether the supplement was mislabeled.

In *U.S. v. Articles of Drug, etc.*,[135] and *U.S. v. Guardian Chemical Corp.*,[136] courts held that printed brochures and pamphlets need not directly accompany a drug to be considered part of the drug's "label" and therefore are subject to FDA regulation. Similarly, in *U.S. v. Diapulse Mfg. Corp. of America*,[137] the court ruled that the sending of reprints of medical journal articles constituted "labels" accompanying a medical device. However, despite these rulings, marketing campaigns carried out by direct personal contact with physicians or public relations tactics such as news conferences announcing the creation or availability of new drugs may not be within the FDA's regulatory reach.

Although the FDA retains jurisdiction over the content of the labeling of over-the-counter drugs, cosmetics and foodstuffs, Sections 5 and 12 of the Federal Trade Commission Act give the FTC regulatory power over commercial mass media advertising and other forms of non-label commercial speech involving these products.

Although normally the FTC will follow its own guidelines for regulation of over-the-counter drugs, cosmetics and foodstuffs, including requirements for prior substantiation and appropriate clinical trials, the two agencies usually work closely together in determining what will be considered false or deceptive commercial speech. For example, the FDA publishes guidelines that specify appropriate requirements for the labels of products falling under its jurisdiction. These include uses and levels of effectiveness for many over-the-counter medications and health claims related to food. The FTC will normally take these specifications into account in determining its regulations of commercial speech in the media involving such products.

FDA Content-Based Regulation of Prescription Drug Commercial Speech

The specific regulations promulgated and enforced with respect to the content of commercial speech within the FDA's jurisdiction are primarily designed to ensure consumer safety. Such content-based regulation would appear to be constitutional under *Virginia State Board of Pharmacy* (discussed earlier) if the commercial speech in question falls within the speech the Supreme Court of the United States defines as "false or misleading." As the Court noted, "Obviously, much commercial speech is not provably false, or even wholly false, but only deceptive or misleading. We foresee no obstacle to a State's dealing effectively with this problem."[138]

FDA regulations normally require that a detailed list of the ingredients appear in a prominent and readable manner within a prescription drug advertisement or other commercial speech. Additionally, the message must indicate the percentage of each ingredient and the list of ingredients must follow the same order as found on the prescription drug's label.

Beginning in the early 1960s, the FDA also mandated that commercial advertising must contain the prescription drug's generic name each time the brand name of the product is mentioned. As might be imagined, the requirement that the generic name accompany the brand name proved to be a pain for copywriters and designers attempting to use advertisements, brochures and other communication vehicles. The regulation eventually was challenged in federal court by the pharmaceutical industry in *Abbott Laboratories v. Celebrezze*.[139] The case was eventually settled when the FDA agreed to modify its requirements. The generic name now needs to appear in conjunction with the brand name when the brand name is "featured" in the advertisement but not when subsequently appearing in body copy on the same page of the advertisement. However, the generic name must be included with the brand name in statements specifying benefits of the drug or detailing side effects.

FDA regulations also require that generic drug names be visually or aurally prominent and must be located close to the brand name in the text of the advertisement. Typically, this may be accomplished by placing the generic name in brackets after the brand name or by adding such wording as "... a brand of (generic name)." The regulations also specify that the generic name must be set in type that is at least half the size of the brand name.

FDA Requirements for a "True Summary" of Side Effects and Effectiveness

The FD&C Act mandates that each commercial message promoting a prescription drug include a "summary" of specified information about its safety and effectiveness.[140] FDA regulations specify that the information within this summary must reflect the wording accepted by the FDA for the drug's package labeling, including a description of all the specific side effects and "contraindications" that could result from taking the drug as well as any warnings or cautions for its use.[141]

The regulations prescribe that the requirements for a truthful summary apply to the entire advertisement. "[U]ntrue or misleading information in [one part] of the advertisement" cannot be corrected by inclusion of correct information in another.[142] However, even if part of the advertisement "would make the advertisement false or misleading by reason of the [*omission*] of appropriate qualification," the overall advertisement still will be in compliance if a "prominent reference [is included] of a more complete discussion of such qualification or information."[143]

The requirements for information about effectiveness and side effects are limited to information about the purposes for which the drug is intended and as promoted in the commercial message. The FDA does not require an advertisement for a prescription drug that promotes a specific use for the drug to contain statements of side effects or effectiveness for all the other possible purposes for which a drug might be adopted or recommended by the medical or pharmaceutical communities. However, the FDA has ruled that it is impermissible to group a number of side effects or contraindications together under one general warning unless the language of the warning conforms with the FDA's previously approved language. Also, specific information about possible side effects must be included for each "contraindication" or claim.

Commercial speakers need beware inadvertently suggesting uses for drugs not given prior approval by the FDA for fear the commercial claims may cause the drug to be reclassified as a "new drug." Uses for a drug "generally recognized as safe and effective among experts qualified by scientific training and experience to evaluate the safety and effectiveness"[144] will not be seen as creating a "new drug" so long as well-conducted clinical evaluations or documentation in medical literature provide evidence the drug meets FDA requirements.

FDA regulations detailing the kinds of information or omissions of information the Agency might find to be false or misleading are extensive. Clearly, commercial speech about prescription drugs will be judged false and deceptive if it (a) fails to indicate possible side effects; (b) exaggerates the effectiveness of a drug compared to its drawbacks; (c) neglects to specify the negative effects of long-term usage; (d) contains "a representation ... that a drug is better, more effective, [or] useful in a broader range of conditions or patients" than can be justified by at least two appropriate clinical trials;[145] or (e) claims that a drug is safer than a competitor's product without appropriate scientific evidence.

Additionally, a number of FDA regulations specifying the kinds of commercial speech claims the agency might find false or deceptive concern the inappropriate use of statistical tests, sample sizes and levels of statistical significance. Examples include statements such as "pooling data from various insignificant or dissimilar studies"[146] in such a way as to incorrectly suggest statistical significance, erroneously using a statistical finding of "'no significant difference' ... to deny or conceal ... real clinical difference,"[147] or employing "reports or statements represented to be statistical analyses ... that are inconsistent with or violate the established principles of statistical theory."[148]

A third general category of potentially misleading statements involves misrepresentations about the subjects taking part in clinical trials. For example, it is false and deceptive to include "normal individuals without disclosing that [they] are normal"[149] unless the drug is marketed to such individuals. Similarly, commercial messages that fail to disclose the potential side effects of a drug when administered to a "selected class" of subjects for whom the drug is actually intended would likely draw the FDA's fire. So too would claims for a drug's effectiveness when the test data are "derived with dosages different from those recommended in approved or permitted labeling,"[150] or when they "represent or suggest that drug dosages properly recommended for use in the treatment of certain classes of patients ... are safe and effective for the treatment of other classes of patients [e.g., children] ... when such is not the case."[151]

A fourth category of deceptive statements involves inclusion or reference to literature that either is false or could be construed in a misleading way. For example, commercial speakers should be careful not to publish testimonials about a drug's effectiveness that exceed the product's actual tested effectiveness or that have been made questionable by scientific studies published more recently than those cited in the testimonials. Additionally, commercial statements may run afoul of FDA regulation if they tout a drug's effectiveness that could be attributed to either a combination of drugs or to the psychological "placebo effect" of taking any medication.[152]

The FDA also might find problems with the manner in which commercial information is presented. For example, false or misleading statements may arise from a failure "to present information relating to side effects ... with [appropriate] prominence and readability ... taking into account ... [such] factors as typography, layout, contrast headlines ... [and] white space."[153] Similar concerns also could arise in broadcast advertisements.

The FDA has recognized a number of limited exceptions to its "brief summary" requirements for prescription drugs. Commercial speech that simply "reminds" providers or consumers of a drug by mentioning its name and/or the costs of such a drug need not provide information on side effects, contraindications or ingredients. Similarly, advertisements for sale of drugs in bulk to be repackaged or relabeled and advertisements intended for drugs used as ingredients of medications pharmacists create for their clientele are exempt as long as the advertisements do not contain claims for a drug's safety or effectiveness.[154]

A more general exception to the "brief summary requirements" for commercial speech about prescription drugs was created by the FDA to encourage dissemination of information about new drugs or new uses for existing drugs through scientific colloquia and professional conferences. Even when a new drug has not officially passed FDA standards, the agency will usually permit information about the existence and properties of the drug to be communicated in these forums, so long as such meetings are conducted under the auspices of disinterested parties, such as scientific societies or universities, and the information presented is factually correct and balanced. However, although there has been little litigation on this issue to date, the FDA may not be as willing to forego its information requirements for new drugs if the information is communicated by means of manufacturer-sponsored conventions, press conferences, news releases or other public relations techniques.

Enforcement of FDA Prescription Drug Advertising Regulations

Although the FDA's enabling legislation provides for a number of legal remedies by which the agency may enforce its regulations of prescription drug-related commercial speech, for the most part these remedies remain weapons for threatening legal action rather than for actual use. The mere threat of legal action has proven to be a virtual guarantee the offending party will voluntarily take the steps necessary to bring the criticized commercial speech within FDA guidelines.

The FD&C Act provides the FDA with the power to seek injunctive relief, seize offending products and seek criminal penalties for advertising of prescription drugs the FDA believes have been "misbranded."[155] Short of these drastic remedies, the offending party must notify physicians or others to whom the commercial speech has been addressed when the information or omission of information the FDA feels is a problem is corrected, and it then must become part of the drug manufacturer's commercial message.

The Securities and Exchange Commission

The Securities and Exchange Commission (SEC), which oversees the regulation of stock markets as well as the companies and investors that trade securities in these markets, is of vital concern to large segments of both the advertising and public relations communities.

The SEC's history of regulating the buying and selling of securities dates back to the late 1880s, when a recurring cycle of financial good times and periods of economic chaos created a pattern of boom-or-bust that eventually brought calls for reform of the nation's economic system. Initial efforts at regulation at both the federal and state levels proved ineffective, however. Finally, the financial crises that led to the Great Depression in the early 1930s provided the impetus for real reform. These efforts began with passage of the Securities Act of 1933[156] and the Securities Exchange Act of 1934.[157] The latter Act established the SEC and charged it with the responsibility of ensuring that timely, complete and truthful information be made available to the public about publicly traded securities.

Until the 1960s, the SEC largely went about its business of enforcing existing regulations involving disclosure of information. However, revisions of the Securities Exchange Act in 1964,[158] coupled with a greater willingness by the SEC's staff to initiate investigations of investment companies, set the SEC on a collision course with many existing business practices throughout the 1960s and 1970s. This eventually led to a number of further reforms in financial marketplace

Figure 10.3 Companies whose stock is publicly traded must take care to adhere to Securities and Exchange Commission guidelines for statements regarding company finances and performance.

Credit line: lev radin/Shutterstock.com

activities. Although the 1980s brought a lessening in the SEC's aggressiveness, the events sur-rounding the collapse of the Enron Corporation and revelations of other corporate improprieties at the beginning of this century inspired Congress to pass tough new financial accountability laws and reinvigorated the SEC as a major player in maintaining the stability of the securities market today.[159]

The Commission itself is composed of five commissioners, appointed for five-year terms by the President with the concurrence of the Senate. One of these appointees is selected by the President to chair the SEC. To reduce partisanship, no more than three commissioners may be members of the same political party. Headquartered in Washington, D.C., the SEC maintains eight regional offices across the country. The SEC's professional staff includes securities analysts, accountants, attorneys and various regulatory and enforcement personnel. The SEC's activities are segmented into divisions. The most important for commercial speakers is the Division of Cor-poration Finance. This division, among other duties, oversees corporate registration statements, annual and quarterly reports and other corporate financial communication activities.

SEC Regulation of First-Time or Additional New Offerings of Securities

According to the SEC, the primary purposes of the 1933 Securities Act were to "provide inves-tors with material financial and other information" and "to prohibit misrepresentation, deceit, and other fraudulent acts and practices in the sale of securities generally."[160] The Supreme Court, in *Ernst and Ernst v. Hochfelder*,[161] characterized the purpose of the statute as provid-ing "full disclosure of material information concerning public offerings ... to protect investors against fraud and, through the imposition of specified civil liabilities, to promote ethical stand-ards of honesty and fair dealing."[162]

The Act's definition of a *security* includes:

> [A]ny note, stock, treasury stock, bond, ... certificate of interest or participation in any profit-sharing agreement, ... investment contract, ... certificate of deposit for a security, fractional undivided interest in oil, gas, or other mineral rights, or, in general, any interest in an instrument commonly known as a "security"... or guarantee of, or warrant or right to subscribe to or purchase any of the foregoing.[163]

With the exceptions of private securities offerings, offerings sold completely within one state (and therefore subject to state rather than federal regulation) and those within a certain dollar amount, Section 5 of the Act specifies that before a security can be offered for sale, a "registration statement" must be formally filed with the SEC. Prior to the filing of this statement of registration, the law mandates that no press releases, news conferences, mass media advertising or sales promotions issued with the intent or effect of encouraging the sale of the company's securities are permitted. For this reason, commercial speakers must be extremely wary of disseminating any information that the SEC might interpret as promoting the sale of new securities, including disseminating information about the price of new securities or claims for the safety or benefits of investing.

After the required registration statement is filed with the SEC, the Securities Act requires a waiting period, during which the party offering the securities for sale may communicate limited information about the issuance of the securities. Typically, this is done by means of a formal preliminary "prospectus." No actual purchase offers can be accepted until the waiting period expires. The preliminary prospectus must conform to the format and contain the copious detailed information specifically called for by the Act to meet SEC approval. The Securities Act provides an exception to its no-advertising policy during the formal waiting period for "tombstone advertisements," so called because their appearance is strictly curtailed by the SEC's rules. Such advertisements are generally restricted to a straightforward presentation of information about the price of a security, who is offering it for sale and how it may be purchased.[164]

Disregard of the no-promotional-activities strictures in the Securities Act by commercial speakers can lead to unfortunate results. In *S.E.C. v. Arvida Corporation*,[165] a press release, issued by the brokerage firm Loeb, Rhoades & Co., touted the virtues of the stock offered by a new company, the Arvida Corporation. The release described the company's financial stability and the extensiveness of its land holdings. Unfortunately for Arvida, the news release was issued and distributed to the nation's leading financial publications before the formal processes mandated by the Act had been completed, causing the SEC to determine that the requirements for a formal registration statement had been breached.

In a companion action, *In re Carl M. Loeb, Rhoades & Co.*,[166] the SEC challenged the issuance of a press release as a violation of Section 5 of the Securities Act on the basis that it had "set in motion the processes of distribution ... by arousing and stimulating investor and dealer interest in Arvida securities."[167] Loeb, Rhoades argued that the news release was exactly that—news—and therefore could not be grounds for a Section 5 violation. The SEC disagreed, holding that "astute public relations activities" had created the "news," and that this was "precisely the evil which the Securities Act seeks to prevent."[168]

The court concluded that, "[a]lthough it appears that defendants acted in good faith ... and although [they] continue to deny [liability] ... nevertheless the Court finds that defendants violated Section 5(c) of the Securities Act"[169] and ordered the parties not to offer common shares of Arvida unless a registration statement was filed with the SEC and all other agency require-ments were met.

SEC Regulation of the National Securities Marketplace

Congress passed the Securities Exchange Act of 1934 to regulate the ongoing trading of securi-ties after the first-time offering for sale in stock exchanges and by brokers. Like the Securities Act, the Securities Exchange Act's basic purpose is to ensure that investors are assured of full disclosure of all timely and pertinent information necessary to make a reasoned and informed decision about selling or purchasing a security. A second purpose is to prevent "any manipula-tive or deceptive device or contrivance"[170] that could lead to fraud in the securities market, including false or deceptive advertising or other commercial speech. In 2018, for example, the SEC filed a civil complaint against Elon Musk, the Chief Executive Officer of the automaker Tesla, Inc., alleging that Musk's statements disseminated on the social media platform Twitter violated the Securities Exchange Act. Musk dispatched several statements via Twitter regarding his plans for the company and its financing that were, according to the SEC, false and mislead-ing, and that Musk knew to be so at the time he made them. According the complaint, "Musk's false and misleading public statements and omissions caused significant confusion and disrup-tion in the market for Tesla's stock and resulting harm to investors."[171] Musk reached a settle-ment with the SEC that required him and Tesla to pay a combined $40 million in penalties and in which Musk agreed to step down as Chairman. In addition, Tesla agreed to appoint additional independent directors to its board and implement additional controls and procedures to over-see Musk's communications.[172]

In addition to monitoring the more spontaneous public statement issued by those in con-trol of publicly traded companies, the SEC enforces the Securities Exchange Act's disclosure provisions by requiring that companies whose stock is offered for sale to the public provide regular, periodic reports that accurately detail the state of the company, its future plans and other similar financial information. Every publicly traded company, except for small or intrastate corporations, must keep a registration statement on file with the SEC that provides informa-tion similar to the statement required under the Securities Act. In addition, they are required to file an annual comprehensive report (Form 10-K), regular updates and various other reports as needed to meet the SEC's regulations for timely disclosure of new information about a com-pany's financial status. This information includes changes in senior management or board of directors, initiation of bankruptcy proceedings or any other "material" event.

Congress broadened normal reporting requirements with its passage of the Williams Act in 1968.[173] The Act mandated that a company proposing to take control of another company by acquiring a majority of outstanding shares from current stockholders (a so-called "tender offer") must disclose (a) detailed information to the SEC, the target company and current share-holders about the take-over company; (b) the reasons behind the tender offer; and (c) what the purchaser plans to do with the acquired company. If such disclosure is not complete, or if the SEC finds the information provided either false or misleading, the SEC can initiate legal action to ensure compliance.

Because tender offers often are made via the mass media or other publicity techniques, public relations and advertising professionals should be aware of SEC rulings about what con-stitutes the actual commencement of an official tender order. Otherwise, making statements in advertisements or other forms of publicity that the SEC might consider as sufficient to create such an offer could trigger requirements that the tender offeror submit the requisite copious financial information on appropriate forms and within specified time limits or risk legal sanction by the SEC.

Under Section 14(d) of the Act, for example, publicity about the possible or impending purchase of another company has been held to create a tender offer if it is published in newspaper advertisements or disseminated to security holders or investors by other means. If such publicity is interpreted as creating a tender offer, Section 14(e) mandates that the communication must include everything from the identity of the bidder to a statement that stockholder lists are being used to reach securities holders. Also, the communication must include the expiration date of the offer, the degree to which the offer will result in control of the target company by the bidder and how securities holders may obtain information from the bidder.

SEC Regulation of False or Deceptive Commercial Speech

The SEC's enabling legislation and regulations demand that commercial speech involving securities must be truthful, non-deceptive and comprehensive. The SEC's interpretation of Section 14(a) that broadly defines deceptive information involving tender offers was upheld in *Gillette Company v. RB Partners*.[174] In that case, a chart in a newspaper advertisement was judged to misrepresent the conditions of the offer even though all of the information presented was true. The problem, said the SEC, was that the design of the chart made it appear that foreign parties predominated in the group seeking to make the offer when such was not the case.

Like the FTC, the SEC looks with especial disfavor on statements that could mislead potential consumers or investors in the ultimate decision to purchase. In the selling and buying of securities, such deceptive statements might include speculative or untruthful information about (a) changes in senior management of a corporation; (b) potential mergers or takeovers; (c) revenues or profits; (d) significant new markets; or (e) plans for new securities offerings. Omission of information in corporate public statements that could deceive investors in any of the ways noted above raises equally problematic issues for corporate communicators.

Allegedly deceptive statements can be disseminated in press releases, speeches before public bodies, media interviews or company publications. If a misstatement occurs, the company (and its public relations counsel) must publicly correct the error or risk liability. Such affirmative action is also required if statements initially true have been made false by changes in the company or in the marketplace. There is no affirmative duty, however, to correct the misstatements of outside third parties (e.g., market analysts or financial reporters) if the company had no hand in preparing or distributing the allegedly deceptive information.

The extent of the SEC's reach in regulating commercial speech involving tender offers and proxy solicitations is exemplified by the case of *Long Island Lighting Company (LILCO) v. Barbash*.[175] In *LILCO*, a coalition of politicians and activists initiated a proxy fight to change the utility's board of directors and forestall the construction of a nuclear power plant. As part of this campaign, those opposed to the current operation of the utility purchased a newspaper advertisement urging stockholders to vote for replacing management and in favor of turning the utility into a municipally run company.

The utility, challenging the advertisement as false and misleading, sought an injunction to prohibit "solicitation" of the company's shareholders "until the claimed false and misleading statements had been corrected" and information to that effect had been filed with the SEC.[176] The company argued that the purpose of the advertisement was to "influence the exercise of proxies by LILCO shareholders" and that the statements were "false and misleading in numerous respects relating to alleged advantages for ratepayers."[177]

A federal district court judge dismissed the complaint, holding that the SEC's rules about the permissible use and content of commercial speech involving proxy solicitations did not apply because the advertisement in question was not specifically directed toward shareholders.[178] The judge also noted significant First Amendment concerns because "[a]llowing injunctive relief on the ground that the advertisement constitutes an improper proxy solicitation would pervert the legitimate protective function of the regulation into an unconstitutional licensing of political speech."[179]

A federal court of appeals, however, overruled the trial court, holding that the SEC's rule could apply even when there was no direct appeal to shareholders.[180] The rules apply, said the appeals court, "not only to direct requests to furnish, revoke or withhold proxies, but also to communications which may indirectly accomplish such a result or constitute a step in a chain of communications designed ultimately to accomplish such a result."[181] According to the court, "[d]etermination in every case is whether the challenged communication, seen in the totality of circumstances, is 'reasonably calculated' to influence the shareholders' votes."[182]

Noting that SEC rules require that "solicitations in the form of 'speeches, press releases, and television scripts' be filed with the SEC,"[183] the court agreed with the SEC's brief in favor of LILCO's position that "it would 'permit easy evasion of the proxy rules' to exempt all general and indirect communications to shareholders,"[184] including the advertisement in question, even if the information it contained also concerned matters of general public interest.

Securities and Exchange Commission v. Texas Gulf Sulphur Co.[185] illustrates the problems that public relations and advertising professionals face in determining (a) the kinds of information a company can and should make public if that information could impact the trading of its securities; (b) when that information should be released; and (c) the ramifications of either carelessness or deliberate deception in the information-dissemination process.

The case began in the early 1960s when Texas Gulf Sulphur's geophysical surveys revealed the possibility of significant deposits of copper, zinc and other valuable ores in land owned by the company in eastern Canada. Testing at the site confirmed the high probability that a valuable strike had been located. This information was kept strictly confidential so that Texas Gulf Sulphur could acquire additional lands adjoining its holdings. Further chemical testing convinced the company's scientists and senior management that, if anything, the initial estimates of the worth of the discovery significantly underestimated its value.

Approximately six months later, with most of its land acquisition complete, the company again began to drill into the ore to obtain additional samples. During this time, a number of Texas Gulf Sulphur's management officials (and people alleged to have received tips from these officials about the value of the discovery) purchased significant amounts of the company's stock. In addition, the company issued stock options to its highest paid employees, several of whom knew about the findings revealed by the analysis of the samples from the Canadian site.

With exploratory drilling underway, rumors of a potentially valuable discovery by Texas Gulf Sulphur began to circulate in the financial community. Concerned that the company's strategic and tactical plans for announcing the findings could be compromised, the company, with the help of a public relations consultant, drafted a press statement that was released to major daily newspapers. The statement announced that, although a strike had been made and early results appeared favorable, the rumors of a major discovery exaggerated "the scale of operations and mention plans and statistics ... that are without factual basis." According to the release, "[t]he work done to date [on the Canadian site] has not been sufficient to reach definite conclusions and any statement as to size and grade of ore would be premature and possibly misleading."[186]

In the SEC's opinion, the statements made or implied in Texas Gulf Sulphur's press release about the potential value of the ore, as well as the omission of information known to the company but not included in the release, involved "material" facts. This satisfied the legal requirement, specified by the Securities Exchange Act, that before a company's commercial speech can be challenged under Rule 10(b)(5)[187] as fraudulent it must contain information that allegedly could have influenced investors or shareholders to purchase, dispose of or fail to trade in a company's stock (or how to vote in a proxy dispute).

Although the extent of actual detriment to potential investors and shareholders who might have either not purchased additional shares or prematurely disposed of their stock in the company based on the information contained in the press release was questioned by both the federal district court and the federal appeals court that subsequently heard the case on an appeal by the company, both courts concluded that the SEC and aggrieved investors and shareholders had sufficient evidence to pursue suits that eventually cost the company hundreds of thousands of dollars and much negative publicity.

Texas Gulf Sulphur illustrates a number of important issues for those engaged in communication activities involving securities transactions or proxy issues. The courts noted that there was nothing wrong with withholding information about the potential value of the discovery until additional land purchases were completed. However, Texas Gulf Sulphur had an affirmative duty to disclose the information promptly once the acquisitions were completed and drilling had resumed or it would risk violating the SEC's rules requiring timely disclosure of material information.

Although the courts found that the company had partly satisfied the requirement for timely disclosure, they also found that the SEC's rules mandating that the dissemination of material information be made so as to give the information wide distribution had been violated. In defending themselves against accusations of fraud, several of Texas Gulf Sulphur's corporate officials involved in the case argued that the information about the strike was already public, based on limited publication by Canadian media. The court gave short shrift to this argument, finding that, "rumors and casual disclosure through Canadian media, especially in view of the [earlier] 'gloomy' ... release denying the rumors ... hardly sufficed to inform traders on American [stock] exchanges."[188]

Although ultimately not a factor in the outcome, the efforts of the company's outside public relations counsel in drafting the fraudulent press release also could have subjected the public relations agency to legal liability if a court determined that the agency either knew or should have known that false or misleading material statements of fact were being disseminated. Additionally, although the courts held that Texas Gulf Sulphur had no duty to correct speculation or misstatements made by the financial press to which the company made no contribution, such a duty could arise if misinformation began to circulate based on the company's own statements unless the company's clearly articulated message was simply misquoted or misunderstood by the media.

Finally, although the SEC and the courts focused on the content of the communication and not its form, it seems likely that Texas Gulf Sulphur would have been found equally liable for disseminating misleading information if the information had been conveyed by an internal newsletter, in-person briefing, news conference, quarterly or annual report, company website or other public relations tactic, so long as there was evidence that the information was "material" and that investors or shareholders learned of it and relied on it to their detriment.

Insider Trading

Yet another issue of importance to advertising and public relations professionals illustrated in the *Texas Gulf Sulphur* case is the possibility of violating a fiduciary relationship through "insider trading" or "tipping."[189] The primary duty of those who oversee the management of a corporation is to represent the best interests of the company's shareholders. Thus, using nonpublic information about a company's financial status to trade in a company's securities or engage in stock option plans without first publicly disclosing such information might constitute a breach of fiduciary responsibility that could subject the company and individual officials—including those who manage the company's communication efforts—to legal liabilities.

Similarly, "tipping off" confidants or financial consultants about nonpublic material information that could influence trading in a company's securities may constitute a violation of fiduciary trust. As the appeals court in *Texas Gulf Sulphur* noted, the SEC's regulations are

> also applicable to one possessing the information who may not be strictly termed an 'insider' within the meaning of [the Act]. Thus, anyone in possession of material inside information must either disclose it to the investing public or, if disabled from disclosing to protect a corporate confidence … must abstain from trading in or recommending the securities concerned.[190]

Clearly, such requirements apply to public relations or advertising counsel. Violations of the anti-tipping rules could subject both those who pass along the information and those who profit from it to legal sanctions. For example, the court in *Texas Gulf Sulphur* concluded that "all transactions in TGS stock or [stock option] calls by individuals apprised of the drilling results … were made in violation of [SEC] Rule 10(b)(5)."[191]

Perhaps the best-known incident involving communication professionals and insider trading involved Anthony Franco, who, at the time of the incident, was president of the Public Relations Society of America (PRSA). According to the SEC, Franco was guilty of a violation of fiduciary trust for allegedly purchasing stock in a company to which he was a consultant, based on insider information that the company would soon be acquired by another corporation. Although formally admitting no wrongdoing, Franco eventually resigned the PRSA presidency and pledged not to act on insider information in the future.

The Franco incident raises yet another concern for those engaged in commercial speech. Even when not officially acting as an agent or consultant to a company, and therefore technically with no fiduciary responsibility to its shareholders, advertising and public relations professionals may learn of material information about a company's financial status. The SEC and the courts have held in a number of instances that there is a duty for these "market" insiders, as well as for those actually inside the company, to divulge such information or forego trading in the securities to avoid the risk of being found in violation of Rule 10(b)(5).

In *Carpenter v. U.S.*,[192] the Supreme Court refused to overturn a finding that fraud had been committed by a financial columnist for the *Wall Street Journal* who was convicted of using information learned "on the street" for his own gain and for tipping off investors in advance about companies he would tout or condemn in his column. Although the columnist was judged not to possess any fiduciary relationship to the companies mentioned in his column or to the market, he nonetheless was held liable under SEC rules prohibiting fraud.

Enforcement of SEC Regulations

Congress has given the SEC power to seek civil and criminal remedies for violations of the securities laws and regulations. In addition, the courts have interpreted the securities laws as providing private citizens with the right to go to court to seek money damages from companies and individuals who have, through omission or misrepresentation of material information, induced the investors to buy or sell securities to their disadvantage.

The *Texas Gulf Sulphur* case provides illustrations of how these sanctions may be imposed. After finding that the press release downplaying the magnitude of the ore deposit discovery could mislead stockholders and investors (and that actions by the company's senior officials and their friends acting on their tips constituted illegal insider trading), the federal appeals court turned its attention to establishing liability and assessing damages. The court found that, contrary to the lower court's opinion, Texas Gulf Sulphur could be subjected to an injunction sought by the SEC to desist from future insider trading. The court remanded the case to the district court for further action on this issue.

Similarly, the appeals court sent back for further proceedings the assessment of liability for the company officials who had violated Rule 10(b)(5) either by insider trading or by exercising stock options during the period before full public disclosure was made. The court also opened the door to later civil suits by stockholders and traders who could demonstrate that they had been materially misled by the fraudulent activities of both the company and its managers.

In a series of subsequent cases, the lower courts decreed that the individuals within the company who had purchased stock based on insider information would be forced to disgorge their profits from such purchases and enjoined from future insider trading practices. Although it was judged that the company could be the subject of the injunction sought by the SEC if there were evidence of continuing or probable future wrongdoing, more troubling for the company was the filing of more than 100 civil lawsuits by disgruntled investors against the company and its management. Depending on how the value of the shares traded based on the misrepresentation by the company was determined, at one point the damages claims against the company ranged from roughly $80 million to as much as $390 million—a figure more than the total worth of the company.

The lessons to be learned for advertising and public relations professionals are clear. Prudent professionals should be extremely careful in counseling senior management about the needs for a company's broad and timely disclosure of securities information as well as to create a system of checks and balances within the department or agency by instituting a "disclosure compliance program."[193] Such programs could help forestall the risk of inadvertently publishing information or running afoul of other provisions of the securities laws that could lead to violations of SEC regulations and possibly subject the company or client to crippling lawsuits.

Additionally, advertising and public relations professionals should be wary of trading in securities based on material information they acquire by virtue of their status as company or marketplace insiders as well as passing along tips about such information to friends or brokers. It would be wise to pursue such efforts only after seeking sound investment advice from financial consultants knowledgeable about the most up-to-date rulings by the SEC regarding the obligations and legal liabilities of those who engage in such trading practices.

Conclusion

As this chapter indicates, federal administrative agencies have not been reluctant to exercise their congressionally granted authority. Often, the myriad federal regulations that emanate from federal agencies has a direct impact on commercial expression created and disseminated by advertising and public relations professionals. Although the FTC is the primary concern for commercial speakers, other administrative agencies may impact specific communications, such as those concerned with the offering or sale of securities. Commercial speakers would be wise to continually keep in mind the harm an investigation by a federal regulatory agency could have not only on the life of a particular commercial campaign, but on the long-term reputations of both the product or service and the organizations responsible for creating the problematic commercial message.

Notes

1. 15 U.S.C. §§1-7 (1890).
2. *Id.* at §§41-58, as amended.
3. *Id.*
4. *Id.* at §53.
5. Valentine v. Chrestensen, 316 U.S. 52 (1942).
6. Pittsburgh Press Co. v. Human Rel. Comm'n, 413 U.S. 376 (1973).
7. Va. State Bd. of Pharmacy v. Va. Citizens Consumer Council, 425 U.S. 748 (1976).
8. *Id.* at 770.
9. *Id.* at 771.
10. *Id.*
11. Young v. American Mini Theatres, Inc., 427 U.S. 50 (1976).
12. *Id.* at 69 note 31.
13. 15 U.S.C. §45 (a)(6).
14. *Id.* §52 (b).
15. *Id.* §55 (a)(1).
16. Levitt Corp. v. Levitt, 201 U.S.P.Q. (BNA) 164 (E.D.N.Y. 1978), *aff'd* 593 F.2d 463 (2d Cir. 1979).
17. Levitt Corp. v. Levitt, 593 F.2d 463 (2d Cir. 1979).
18. Smith-Victor Corp. v. Sylvania Electric Products, Inc., 242 F. Supp. 302 (N.D. Ill. 1965).
19. *Id.*
20. Chrysler Corp. v. Federal Trade Com., 182 U.S. App. D.C. 359 (D.C. Cir. 1977).
21. 45 Antitrust and Trade Reg. Rep. (BNA) no. 1137, at 684 (Oct. 14, 1983).
22. In re Cliffdale Assoc., 103 F.T.C. 110 (1984).
23. K. A. PLEVAN & M. L. SIROKY, ADVERTISING COMPLIANCE HANDBOOK 109 (Practising Law Institute, New York, NY, 2nd ed. 1991) (citing *In re International Harvester Co.*, 104 F.T.C. 949, 1056 (1984)).
24. In re Southwest Sunsites, Inc., 105 F.T.C. 7, 149 (1985); *aff'd* 785 F.2d 1431 (9th Cir. 1986); *cert. denied,* 479 U.S. 828 (1986).
25. *Id.*
26. 2-18 George E. Rosden & Peter E. Rosden, *Part V: Basic Principles of Federal Trade Commission Control of Advertising,* in THE LAW OF ADVERTISING §18.03 (Matthew Bender).
27. Federal Trade Commission File No. 912 3336 (11/7/96). See Federal Trade Commission Press Advisory No. C-3582 (6/7/95).
28. *See Get the Scoop: Haagen-Dazs Not Low Fat,* Lexington (KY) HERALD-LEADER (The Washington Post), Nov. 22, 1994, at A-5, col. 3.
29. *Id.*

30. *See Followup: Bogus Health Drink, Latecomer Air-Conditioner*, 60 Consumer Rep. 447 (1995).

31. In re Third Option Laboratories, 120 F.T.C. 973 (1995).

32. In re International Harvester Co., 104 F.T.C. 949 (1984).

33. *Id*. at 1059.

34. *Id*.

35. *Id*.

36. F.T.C. v. Colgate-Palmolive Co., 380 U.S. 374 (1965).

37. *Id*.

38. *Id*.

39. In re Campbell Soup, 1970 F.T.C. LEXIS 116 (May 25, 1970).

40. *Id*. at 4.

41. H.R. 2243.

42. *See Hooked on Tobacco: The Teen Epidemic*, 60 Consumer Rep. 142 (1995).

43. *Cigarette Ads Found to Affect Teen-Agers Most*, Lexington (KY) Herald-Leader (Associated Press) Aug. 18, 1994, at A3, col. 4.

44. *See Hooked on Tobacco, supra* note 42.

45. *Can First Amendment Save Camel's 'Old Joe'?*, Lexington (KY) Herald-Leader.

46. *See Hooked on Tobacco, supra* note 42. at 144.

47. 2-18 Rosden, *Unfair Methods of Competition*, in The Law of Advertising §18.06 (Matthew Bender) (citations omitted).

48. *Id*.

49. Bates, 375-385.

50. Fed. Trade Comm'n, FTC Policy Statement on Deception, appended to Cliffdale Associates, Inc., 103 F.T.C. 110, 174 (1984), www.ftc.gov/system/files/documents/public_statements/410531/831014deceptionstmt.pdf

51. Fed. Trade Comm'n, Commission Enforcement Policy Statement in Regard to Clear and Conspicuous Disclosures in Television Advertising, CCH Trade Regulation Reporter, 75609.09 (Oct. 21, 1970).

52. *Id., supra* note 51.

53. *Id*.

54. *Id*.

55. *Id*.

56. Final Order at 2, In the Matter of Pom Wonderful LLC v. Resnick, No. 9344 2013, www.ftc.gov/sites/default/files/documents/cases/2013/01/130116pomorder.pdf

57. In re Pfizer, Inc., 81 F.T.C. 23 (1972).

58. *Id*. at 24.

59. *Id*. at 24-25.

60. *Id*. at 62.

61. *Id*.

62. In re Natl. Comm'n on Egg Nutrition, 88 F.T.C. 84 (1976); modified, Nat'l. Comm'n on Egg Nutrition v. F.T.C., 570 F.2d 157 (7th Cir. 1977); *cert. denied*, 439 U.S. 821 (1978).

63. *Id*. at 191 (citations omitted).

64. *Id*. n.14.

65. 47 Antitrust and Trade Reg. Rep. (BNA), n.1176 at 234 (Aug. 2, 1984).

66. Plevan at 114. *See, e.g.*, Firestone Tire and Rubber Co. v. F.T.C., 481 F.2d 246 (6th Cir. 1973).

67. *See, e.g.*, Leon A. Tashof v. F.T.C., 14 F.2d 707 (D.C. Cir. 1970).

68. In re Pfizer, Inc., 81 F.T.C. 23, 66 (1972).

69. *Id*.

70. Firestone Tire & Rubber Co. v. F.T.C., 481 F.2d 246 (6th Cir. 1973).

71. F.T.C. Guidelines §b–ACH, 1993 Cumulative Supplement, at 22.

72. In re Thompson Medical Co., Inc., 104 F.T.C. 648 (1984).

73. *Id*. at 844.
74. *Id*. at 723.
75. F.T.C. Guidelines §b at 96.
76. *Id*.
77. U-Haul International, Inc. v. Jartran, Inc., 522 F. Supp. 1238, 1245 (D. Ariz. 1981); *aff'd* p.127.
78. In re Dannon Milk Products, 61 F.T.C. 840 (1962).
79. In re Better Living, Inc., 54 F.T.C. 648 (1957); *aff'd* 259 F.2d 271 (1958).
80. *Id*. at 653.
81. Gillette Co. v. Wilkinson Sword, Inc., 1991 U.S. Dist. LEXIS 21006 (S.D.N.Y. 1991).
82. *Id*. at 54.
83. 16 C.F.R. §419 (1989).
84. *Id*. at §225 (a) (1987).
85. *Id*. at §255 (b).
86. Fed. Trade Comm'n, The FTC's Endorsement Guides: What People Are Asking, www.ftc.gov/tips-advice/business-center/guidance/ftcs-endorsement-guides
87. Fed. Trade Comm'n, Guides Concerning the Use of Endorsements and Testimonials in Advertising, 16 CFR Part 255.
88. In re Cliffdale Assoc., 103 F.T.C. 110, 174 (1984).
89. *Id*. at 136.
90. *Id*. at 169.
91. *Id*. at 171-172.
92. In re Cooga Mooga, 92 F.T.C. 310 (1978).
93. 16 C.F.R. §255.3 (b) (1987).
94. In re Leroy Gordon Cooper, 94 F.T.C. 674 (1979).
95. *Id*. at 680.
96. Niresk Industries, Inc. v. Federal Trade Com., 278 F.2d 337 (7th Cir. 1960).
97. 16 C.F.R. §233.1-5 (1990).
98. *Id*. at §238.
99. 80 CFR Part 221 (2015), www.ftc.gov/system/files/documents/federal_register_notices/2015/11/151117fplafrn.pdf.
100. 15 U.S.C. §§160-1614 and 1661-1665 (a) (1990).
101. Bruce E. H. Johnson & Kaustuv M. Das, *Recent Developments in Commercial Speech and Consumer Privacy Interests*, in 2 Communications Law, (Practising Law Institute, New York, 2006.
102. In Re Matter of BJ's Wholesale Club, F.T.C. Case No. 042 3160 (2005).
103. *Id*.
104. Fed. Trade Comm'n, Fighting Identity Theft With the Reg Flags Rule: A How-to-Guide for Business, www.ftc.gov/tips-advice/business-center/guidance/fighting-identity-theft-red-flags-rule-how-guide-business
105. *Id*.
106. *Id*.
107. Red Flag Program Clarification Act, 15 U.S.C. 1681m(e)(4).
108. 15 U.S.C. §45 (b) (1973).
109. F.T.C. v. Pharmtech Research, Inc., 576 F. Supp. 294 (D.D.C. 1983).
110. 15 U.S.C. §45 (m).
111. United States v. Reader's Digest Assoc., 464 F. Supp. 1037 (D. Del. 1978); *aff'd*, 662 F.2d 955 (3d Cir. 1981).
112. Sears, Roebuck & Co. v. F.T.C., 676 F.2d 385, 391 (9th Cir. 1982).
113. Codified in the Federal Cigarette Labeling and Advertising Act, 1965.
114. Warner-Lambert Co. v. F.T.C., 562 F.2d 749 (D.C. Cir. 1977); *cert. denied*, 435 U.S. 950 (1988).
115. *Id*. at 762.
116. Chrysler Corp. v. F.T.C., 561 F.2d 357 (D.C. Cir. 1977).

117. *Id.*

118. *Id.* at 364.

119. *Id.*

120. ITT Continental Baking Co. v. F.T.C., 532 F.2d 207 (2d Cir. 1976).

121. American Medical Association v. F.T.C., 638 F.2d 443 (2d Cir. 1980).

122. *Id.* at 452.

123. Standard Oil Co. v. F.T.C., 577 F.2d 653 (9th Cir. 1978).

124. *Id.* at 659.

125. What We Do, www.fcc.gov/about-fcc/what-we-do.

126. Red Lion Broadcasting Co., Inc. v. Federal Communication Commission, 395 U.S. 367 (1969).

127. Fed. Trade Comm'n, FAQs About Robocalls, www.fcc.gov/consumers/guides/stop-unwanted-robocalls-and-texts

128. Fed. Trade Comm'n, FCC Proposes $37.5 Million Fine for Spoofed Telemarketing Calls, www.fcc.gov/document/fcc-proposes-375-million-fine-spoofed-telemarketing-calls

129. Fed. Trade Comm'n, Consumer Guide, Broadcast Contests, Lotteries and Solicitation of Funds, http://transition.fcc.gov/cgb/consumerfacts/contests.pdf

130. 21 U.S.C. §352.

131. *Id.* at §353 (b)(1)(g).

132. *Id.* at §353 (b)(1)(c).

133. *Id.* at §321 (m).

134. Nature Food Centres, Inc. v. United States, 310 F.2d 67 (1st Cir. 1962).

135. United States v. Articles of Drug, etc., 263 F. Supp. 212 (D. Neb. 1967).

136. United States v. Guardian Chemical Corp., 410 F.2d 157 (2d Cir. 1969).

137. United States v. Diapulse Mfg. Corp., 269 F. Supp. 162 (D. Conn. 1967).

138. Va. St. Bd. of Pharmacy v. Va. Citizens Consumer Council, 425 U.S. 748 (1976).

139. Abbott Laboratories v. Celebrezze, 352 F.2d 286 (3d Cir. 1965)

140. 21 C.F.R. §202.1 (e).

141. *Id.* at §202.1 (e)(3)(iii).

142. *Id.* at §202.1 (3)(i).

143. *Id.*

144. *Id.* at §202.1 (3)(iii)(a).

145. *Id.* at §201.6 (i).

146. 21 C.F.R. §202.1 (6)(xiv).

147. *Id.* at Ch. 1 (4-1-94 Edition) §202.1 (6)(xv).

148. *Id.* at (7)(v).

149. *Id.* at (6)(xiii).

150. *Id.* at (6)(xvii).

151. *Id.* at (6)(xix).

152. 21 U.S.C. §352 (n).

153. *Id.* at (7)(viii).

154. 21 U.S.C. §352 (n).

155. *Id.*

156. 15 U.S.C. §77z.

157. *Id.* at §78gg.

158. *Id.* at §78c (a)(18).

159. Sarbanes-Oxley Act of 2002, Pub. L. No. 107-204, 116 Stat. 745, 758 (2002).

160. Securities and Exchange Comm'n, The Work of the Securities and Exchange Commission (1974) at 1.

161. Ernst and Ernst v. Hochfelder, 425 U.S. 185 (1976).

162. *Id.*

163. 15 U.S.C. §77 (a)(8), at §78 (c).

164. 17 C.F.R. §230.134.

165. S.E.C. v. Arvida Corporation, 169 F. Supp. 211 (S.D.N.Y. 1958).

166. In re Carl M. Loeb, Rhoades & Co., 38 S.E.C. 843 (1959).

167. *Id.* at 851.

168. *Id.* at 853.

169. Arvida, 169 F. Supp. at 215.

170. 17 C.F.R. Ch. 11 (4-1-94 Edition) §240.10b-1.

171. Complaint at 2, S.E.C. v. Elon Musk, (No. 1:18-cv-8865) (2018) www.sec.gov/litigation/complaints/2018/comp-pr2018-219.pdf

172. *Elon Musk Settles SEC Fraud Charges: Tesla Charged with and Resolves Securities Law Charge*, www.investor.gov/additional-resources/news-alerts/press-releases/elon-musk-settles-sec-fraud-charges-tesla-charged

173. 15 U.S.C. §§78 (m), 78 (n).

174. Gillette Co. v. RB Partners, 693 F. Supp. 1266 (D. Mass. 1988).

175. Long Island Lighting Co. v. Barbash, 779 F.2d 793 (2d Cir. 1985).

176. *Id.* at 794.

177. *Id.* at 797.

178. Long Island Lighting Co. v. Barbash, 625 F. Supp. 221 (E.D.N.Y. 1985).

179. *Id.* at 226.

180. Barbash, 779 F.2d 793.

181. *Id.* at 796.

182. *Id.*

183. *Id.* (citing Rule 14a-6 (g), 17 C.F.R. §240.14a-6 (g)).

184. *Id.* (citing Medical Comm. for Human Rights v. S.E.C., 432 F.2d 659 (D.C. Cir. 1970)).

185. S.E.C v. Texas Gulf Sulphur Co., 401 F.2d 833 (2d Cir. 1968).

186. *Id.* at 845.

187. 17 C.F.R. Ch. 11 (4-1-94 Edition) §240.10b-5.

188. Texas Gulf Sulphur, 401 F.2d at 856.

189. *Id.* at 852.

190. *Id.* at 848.

191. *Id.* (citing 17 C.F.R. Ch. 11 (4-1-94 Edition) §240.10b-5).

192. Carpenter v. United States, 484 U.S. 19 (1987).

193. For further discussion, *see* I. B. Bromberg, *Disclosure Programs for Publicly Held Companies—A Practical Guide*, 1970 Duke L.J. 1139-1179 (1970).

11 Other Federal and State Regulation of Commercial Speech

Corporate communicators who successfully wend their way through the tangled maze of federal regulations have avoided only a portion of the potential legal pitfalls of their profession. In addition to federal regulations and decades of common law pertaining to commercial speech (discussed in earlier chapters), corporate communicators must be equally aware of numerous obligations and responsibilities defined by federal and state statutory laws as well as industry-specific regulatory agencies. This chapter discusses the unfair competition provisions of the federal Lanham Act and other specific statutes and agencies concerned with commercial speech. Additionally, the chapter explores some common elements of state unfair competition and false advertising laws that should be of particular interest to corporate communicators.

The Lanham Act

In 1946, Congress passed the Lanham Act[1] (named after Representative Fritz C. Lanham) that substantially revised the Trademark Act of 1905.[2] The Lanham Act, also known as the Trademark Protection Act of 1946, provides a means for registration and protection of trademarks and remedies for the disparagement of products and services. Section 43(a) of the Act says that "any person who believes that he or she is or is likely to be damaged by such [a disparaging] act" can sue for damages.[3]

With the 1988 passage of the Trademark Law Revision Act and a subsequent revision in 1992,[4] the second purpose of the Act, *regulation of false and deceptive advertising*, became much more explicit. In part, the revised Act not only protects trademarks but also now includes causes of action for "any false designation of origin, false or misleading description of fact, or false or misleading representation of fact."[5] The phrasing, "any person who believes that he or she is or is likely to be damaged by such act," remains the same in the revised Act, but the statute defines *any person* as including "any State, instrumentality of a State or employee of a State or instrumentality of a State acting in his or her official capacity."[6]

In 1993, the Third Circuit U.S. Court of Appeals, in a case involving lawsuits brought by consumers for ads promoting premium gasoline and rust inhibitors for automobiles, said the intent of Congress in approving the revised Act was not to provide a remedy for consumers. The court noted that the wording including "a consumer" was originally proposed to be included in the Act but was dropped from the final draft.[7]

Exclusion of consumers from bringing suits under the Lanham Act underscores a substantial difference between the Act's provisions and more traditional remedies for false advertising. Although the Lanham Act's false advertising provisions do seek to protect consumers from the potential harms of marketplace confusion, the Act's core function is much more aligned with its intellectual property roots—preserving a fair market for those endeavoring to engage in commerce.

Remedies for a Lanham Act plaintiff (e.g., a business competitor) are generally divided into three categories: (a) injunctive relief; (b) market (actual) financial damages; and (c) court-ordered corrective advertising. The first, injunctive relief, only requires that a plaintiff show consumer confusion and "likelihood of damage" resulting from the defendant's deceptive advertising. No actual proof of harm, such as documentation of lost sales or consumer confusion, is necessary for injunctive relief.

When a Lanham Act plaintiff seeks financial damages or asks the court to order correc-tive advertising, however, the burden of proof generally increases to require a showing that the defendant's false or deceptive advertising materially affected the plaintiff's bottom line or customer base in a negative way. Courts have generally required plaintiffs to offer compelling expert testimony and independent consumer research that provide a causal link between the competitor's campaign and actual consumer confusion.

The Lanham Act's false advertising provisions are open to interpretation, however, as two federal appellate court decisions illustrate. The first, *Balance Dynamics Corp. v. Schmitt Indus-tries, Inc.,*[8] addressed the "likelihood [of harm] versus actuality" distinction. Balance Dynamics filed a lawsuit against the defendant Schmitt for implying in direct correspondence with corpo-rations in the machining industry that Balance Dynamics' industrial products would soon run afoul of the federal Environmental Protection Agency's ban on ozone-depleting substances. In its correspondence to corporations, Schmitt Industries suggested that, unlike its competitors, including Balance Dynamics, Schmitt Industries offered a line of quality, ozone-friendly replace-ments for that technology.

Balance Dynamics took exception to this communication and eventually filed suit in federal district court. The plaintiff claimed no actual damage as a result of Schmitt Industries' allegedly deceptive campaign but instead requested that it be compensated by the defendant for "dam-age control" efforts (i.e., funds to cover Balance Dynamics' own corrective measures). The dis-trict court, determining that the plaintiff had not provided evidence of a single consumer who was confused by Schmitt Industries' communications, ruled in favor of the defendant.[9]

The Sixth Circuit Court of Appeals vacated the decision and remanded to the district court for further proceedings. The appeals court noted that, based on its own analysis of Lanham Act false advertising claims, plaintiffs seeking "damage control" compensation do not need to show evidence of actual harm or consumer confusion. This relaxation of the proof burden for Lanham Act plaintiffs should serve as a warning for any corporation or agency engaging in comparative advertising. *Balance Dynamics* is also worthy of note because the "advertising" in question was not advertising at all; rather, it was direct correspondence with actual and potential consumers of the two corporations' products. Just as with the common law of commercial speech, courts seem to possess varying definitions of "advertising," creating additional uncertainty for corpo-rate communicators.

The uncertainty surrounding Lanham Act unfair competition litigation increased in subse-quent cases. In *Pizza Hut v. Papa John's International, Inc.,*[10] decided by the Fifth Circuit Court of Appeals, the pendulum seemingly swung back toward an approach that was more defendant-friendly. After Papa John's began to make a dent in Pizza Hut's market share with its "Bet-ter Ingredients. Better Pizza" slogan and a series of comparative advertisements touting the superiority and freshness of Papa John's dough and tomato sauce, Pizza Hut filed a Lanham

Act lawsuit in federal district court. Although offering no actual proof of the claim, Pizza Hut successfully argued that the combination of Papa John's new slogan and comparative advertising related to the production of the corporations' pizza crusts and sauce constituted false or deceptive statements of fact likely to confuse consumers. The court ordered Papa John's to immediately cease using its "Better Ingredients. Better Pizza," slogan which the corporation had spent millions of dollars printing on its boxes and other promotional materials, as well as awarding Pizza Hut a settlement of almost a half million dollars.[11]

The case was reversed on appeal in the Fifth Circuit. The court determined that the Papa John's slogan, taken by itself, was not a quantifiable material statement of fact (i.e., it was akin to puffery) and was therefore not actionable under Lanham Act provisions. In combination with the dough and sauce advertisements, however, the appeals court agreed with the lower court that "Better Ingredients. Better Pizza" acquired a new meaning that was indeed deceptive. The appeals court deviated from the lower court, however, in determining that Pizza Hut did need to present evidence that consumers' pizza-buying decisions had been and likely would continue to be affected by the deceptive campaign and slogan. On this ground, the court overturned the lower court's decision. This case left some legal observers scratching their heads because the court seemingly suggested that it cannot be assumed that consumers make their food-consumption decisions based on taste and quality.

The Lanham Act unfair competition jurisprudence remains somewhat difficult to predict. As *Pizza Hut* and *Balance Dynamics* illustrate, federal district and circuit courts have wrestled with fault standards for the various Lanham Act remedies, and, at a more elemental level, have not completely disposed of the question of what constitutes an "advertisement" under the Act's provisions. This latter uncertainty mirrors the California Supreme Court's determination in *Kasky v. Nike*[12] (discussed in Chapter 3) that Nike's non-advertising public relations efforts could be characterized as regulable commercial speech.

Regulation of Commercial Speech and the Federal Fair Housing Act

The Federal Fair Housing Act of 1968[13] makes it illegal to discriminate in the sale or rental of housing. Section 804(c) of the Act also "prohibits the making, printing, and publishing of advertisements [or other commercial speech] which state a preference, limitation or discrimination on the basis of race, color, religion, sex, handicap, familial status or national origin."[14] The prohibition applies to publishers, such as newspapers and directories, as well as to people and entities who place real estate advertisements.

Practices that have run afoul of provisions of this statute, or of the regulations promulgated by the Department of Housing and Urban Development (HUD), the federal agency charged with enforcing fair housing laws, include (a) exclusively employing white models in photographs or illustrations accompanying advertisements depicting potential clients in marketing campaigns for housing developments; (b) showing only adult couples in brochures describing rental property; or (c) specifying preferences for gender ("males preferred") or religion ("a Christian community") in advertising copy. Classified advertisements by individuals seeking roommates are exceptions.

Advertising and public relations professionals should be alert to possible trouble when using terms such as *exclusive* or *private, mature* or *adult, no children* or *couples preferred* (or *only*), and *only kosher meals served* or *close to (named denominational) church* in commercial speech related to the sale or rental of housing properties. Exceptions are recognized for commercial speech related to housing that is specifically designed for the elderly or the physically challenged or is restricted to members of a religious sect, although such speech cannot discriminate by race or other characteristics unrelated to the specific exemption.

HUD's expansive interpretation of the Federal Fair Housing Act's regulation of discriminatory commercial speech has been ratified by the courts. In *Ragin v. The New York Times*,[15] a Second Circuit federal Court of Appeals in New York disagreed with the trial court and upheld the viability of a discrimination claim based on the failure to use minorities as models in housing advertisements. The plaintiffs had claimed the ads indicated a preference for whites as purchasers or renters in certain neighborhoods and rental complexes. Finding that such evidence might cause a jury to conclude that *The New York Times* had violated the Fair Housing Act's provisions, the court remanded the case for further consideration. The Supreme Court of the United States elected not to hear the newspaper's appeal.

Regulation of Commercial Speech by Other Federal Laws and Agencies

Simply listing the federal statutes and regulations governing commercial speech, in addition to those involving the FTC, the FDA, the FCC and the SEC (discussed in the preceding chapter), could take up much of the rest of this book. For example, there are more than 800 federal statutes affecting commercial speech about everything from atomic energy to Woodsy Owl, including burial of veterans, currency usage in advertising, eavesdropping devices, foods from avocados to watermelons, use of insignias of the Girl Scouts and the Olympics, railroads, the Swiss Federation coat of arms and water hyacinths (transportation thereof). In addition, thousands of federal regulations cover these subjects in more detail, as well as specify procedural and technical requirements for satisfying these regulations. Prudent advertising and public relations professionals would be wise to review the list of these laws and regulations to determine which pertain to their commercial speech efforts.

Nonetheless, there are a number of subjects covered by federal statutes and regulations that deserve brief special mention because of the problems they might cause for significant numbers of those engaged in commercial speech. These include commercial speech about employment, banking, billboards and alcoholic beverages.

Employment Issues

Various civil rights statutes make discrimination by race, age and other characteristics illegal in employment practices. These same strictures often apply to commercial speech publicizing these subjects. The Civil Rights Act of 1964[16] forbids employment notices that appear to discriminate by race or sex and gives those harmed by such advertising the right to file civil suits seeking money damages both against those who place the notices and, in some cases, against those who publish them.

For example, in *Hailes v. United Air Lines*,[17] a federal appeals court upheld a claim that an employment notice seeking women for flight attendant positions had reasonably been interpreted by a man as discouraging his application for such a position. In *Pittsburgh Press v. Pittsburgh Commission on Human Relations*[18] (discussed in Chapter 2), the Supreme Court of the United States found that the newspaper's help-wanted advertisements, segregated by male and female headings, were not protected by the First Amendment. Congress enacted similar restrictions against discrimination by age in the Age Discrimination in Employment Act of 1967[19] and against physical and mental disabilities in the Americans with Disabilities Act of 1990.[20]

Complaints about discrimination involving these characteristics are often generated by use of such terms in commercial speech employment notices as *young, recent college graduate* or *able-bodied*. Advertising and public relations professionals should also be alert to terms like *junior assistant, first-time* or *beginner* in describing the position level that is the subject of the commercial speech.

Even potentially more dangerous for those engaged in commercial speech about employment opportunities are the sections of federal laws banning activities indicating "any preference ... based on race," including advertising and other publicity. Until *Ragin* (discussed earlier), most authorities had agreed with the logic of the court in *Housing Opportunities Made Equal v. Cincinnati Enquirer, Inc.*[21] that civil rights claims should be limited to statements constituting a "campaign of discrimination" or indicating a "preference, limitation, or discrimination based on race, color ... or national origin."[22] The expansive interpretation by the federal court in *Ragin*, holding that the use of models lacking racial diversity could constitute discrimination, should be a warning signal for advertising and public relations professionals to take a second look at common practices or thoughtless actions that could be considered discriminatory, particularly when viewed through the eyes of groups that historically have experienced the effects of discrimination.

Financial Issues

Advertising and public relations related to the banking industry are closely regulated by a variety of federal agencies. Both the Federal Reserve System and the Federal Deposit Insurance Corporation set policies for the operation of member banks and financial institutions, including regulations involving commercial speech. Similarly, the Federal Home Loan Bank Board regulates the commercial speech of federal thrift institutions, while the National Credit Union Administration oversees federal credit unions.

Each federal agency's concerns with commercial speech arise primarily with enforcement of various provisions of the federal "Truth in Lending Act,"[23] which regulates commercial speech involving offers of consumer credit. Both regulatory agencies and the courts have broadly defined commercial speech under the Act, including, for example, media advertising, direct mail solicitations and messages accompanying loan applications or checking account statements. The Act forbids commercial speech designed to encourage offers of credit that are not of a "usual and customary" nature, such as offers of low interest that actually are unavailable to the average consumer.[24]

The statute also requires commercial speakers to include "disclosures" in a "clear and conspicuous" manner about actual finance charges and other charges not specified in the finance program (e.g., membership fees and annual percentage rates) if the subject of the speech is the offer of a credit card or charge plan that entails continuing offers of credit at a specified interest rate. Terms that may "trigger" these disclosure requirements include promotional come-ons like *six months at no interest and then a small monthly charge* or *no money down* or *easy credit terms available*.[25]

Those engaged in commercial speech involving financial institutions also should be aware of the provisions of the Federal Consumer Leasing Act,[26] which regulates the offering of leases on personal property (e.g., automobiles); the antidiscrimination provisions of the Equal Credit Opportunity Act[27] and the Federal Deposit Insurance Corporation,[28] which make it illegal to deny credit or provide loans based on such characteristics as race, gender or age; and the Fair Credit Reporting Act[29] and related legislation (discussed in Chapter 13), which require certain creditors to dispatch privacy notices to their customers at regular intervals.

Outdoor Advertising Issues

Although most laws regulating outdoor advertising and signage are state laws, several federal statutes and regulations–notably the Federal Highway Act[30] and the Highway Beautification Act[31]–limit the location and size of billboards along federal highways. Because billboards and other signage often run afoul of community or environmental groups on aesthetic grounds, there have been frequent efforts to limit or ban such signs either by zoning regulations or laws forbidding all outdoor advertising. Objections to such laws and regulations based on a First Amendment rationale have met with mixed results.

In *Metromedia, Inc. v. City of San Diego*[32] (discussed in Chapter 2), the Supreme Court of the United States rendered a mixed opinion regarding the constitutionality of the city's efforts to limit billboards for safety and aesthetic reasons. The Court held that efforts to limit otherwise protected commercial speech must serve an important government purpose and be no more extensive than necessary to carry out the government's legitimate interests. As more outdoor advertising signs are erected, complete with eye-catching graphics and high definition, electronic displays that move and change, the question of whether purely aesthetic reasons will suffice for governments constitutionally to ban or limit billboards is yet to be determined.

Alcoholic Beverage Issues

Unlike billboard advertising, commercial speech involving alcoholic beverages has historically been the subject of extensive federal and state regulations. Because of the controversial nature of the effects of drinking alcoholic beverages, regulations involving its production, consumption and promotion date back two centuries. Although a complete discussion of the myriad laws and rules regulating commercial speech about alcohol is beyond the scope of this text, advertising and public relations professionals involved with these products should be aware of the more significant federal statutes and regulations that impact the promotion of alcoholic beverages.[33]

After the 1933 repeal of Prohibition with passage of the Twenty-First Amendment, Congress approved the Federal Alcohol Administration (FAA) Act,[34] which gave the United States Treasury Department the responsibility for regulating the alcohol industry. Since 1935, that responsibility has shifted among federal agencies and departments, with some focusing on the beverages themselves and others concerned with the marketing and promotions of alcohol. In 2003, significant aspects of the oversight of alcohol were transferred from the Bureau of Alcohol, Tobacco and Firearms[35] (ATF) to the newly formed Alcohol and Tobacco Tax and Trade Bureau (TTB). In addition to the collection of alcohol-related taxes, TTB's mission includes the prevention of misleading alcohol labeling and advertising, as authorized by the FAA Act. The Act itself allows the TTB to impose regulations on the advertising of distilled spirits, wine or malt beverages designed to "prevent deception of the consumer with respect to the products advertised."

Figure 11.1 Customers at a Philadelphia bar in 1933 celebrate the end of Prohibition. With passage of the Twenty-First Amendment, Congress gave the United States Treasury Department the responsibility for regulating the alcohol industry. Responsibility has shifted among federal agencies and departments, with some focusing on the beverages themselves and others concerned with the marketing and promotions of alcohol.

Credit line: Everett Historical/Shutterstock.com

The Bureau generally requires that all commercial speech about alcoholic beverages contain information that includes (a) required government warnings about the effects of consumption; (b) the company that has produced the product and paid for the speech; and (c) whether the beverage is considered to be a malt beverage, wine or distilled spirit. Prohibited statements include disparagement of a competitor's products, claims of a health or medicinal nature and messages considered false, misleading or indecent.

In addition, the TTB strictly regulates such marketing activities as cooperative advertising schemes and the purchase of advertising in publications produced by retailers. It also has interpreted an Internal Revenue Service ruling as prohibiting the use of athletes in distilled liquor commercial speech and limits their use in wine or beer promotions, and extended its advertising regulations to social media, the latter of which are outlined in Chapter 13.

Because the federal government acquired unique control over alcohol following the repeal of Prohibition,[36] the status of Constitutional protection for commercial speech involving intoxicating beverages is somewhat hazy. Although the *Central Hudson*[37] four-part test (discussed in Chapter 2) normally would be applicable to such commercial speech, those wishing to regulate speech promoting alcoholic beverages typically argue that, by definition, the government's interest in regulating such speech outweighs the First Amendment interests of the commercial speaker. For a time in the early to mid-1990s, these anti-alcohol speech arguments often were found persuasive by courts hearing such cases. However, since the Supreme Court's decisions in *Rubin v. Coors Brewing Co.*,[38] *44 Liquormart v. Rhode Island*[39] (see Chapter 2) and a number of "vice activity" cases subsequently decided by the Court, such arguments have largely fallen on deaf ears.

Overview of State Regulation of Commercial Speech

Because of the federal First Amendment issues inherent in government attempts to restrict commercial speech as well as the prominence of federal regulatory agencies like the FTC and SEC, many of those working in advertising or public relations lose sight of the role that state statutes and regulations play in the overall regulation of commercial speech. However, in the same way that much of the law that impacts our everyday existence is found at the state level, state regulation of commercial speech is both comprehensive and extensive.

With the California Supreme Court's 2002 decision in *Kasky* (discussed in Chapter 3), state efforts to regulate false and deceptive corporate messages took center stage. If nothing else, *Kasky* serves notice to all for-profit corporate communicators that they should be just as intimately acquainted with state statutes, court decisions and state regulatory agencies regarding their communication practices as they are with federal statutes and regulations.

Many of these laws and regulations are discussed in other parts of this text. However, a number of state statutes and administrative regulations deserve special mention here because of their impact on advertising and public relations professionals and because they parallel the federal regulations discussed in this and the preceding chapter.

False, Unfair or Deceptive Commercial Speech: The State Approach

Beginning in the early 1900s, states tried to regulate the negative effects of wildly extravagant advertising claims by passing "Printers' Ink" statutes. These efforts largely proved ineffective, however, because they neither allowed consumers or competitors to bring private causes of action nor established effective state agencies or commissions to oversee and enforce the law. Instead, most of these early state laws left to local prosecutors the option of instigating criminal proceedings against those accused of violating commercial speech statutes—a process that proved cumbersome because of the long and detailed procedures necessary to carry out criminal investigations and prosecutions.[40]

Therefore, it was not surprising that federal regulation, either by federal laws or federal agency rules, became the method of choice by those who wished to regulate commercial speech. The development of federal statutes and regulations, however, did not mean that states surrendered complete control of commercial speech to the federal government. Today, all 50 states have their versions of "mini" Federal Trade Commission/Lanham Acts that prohibit various deceptive commercial-speech practices, although generally without the provisions for separate regulatory commissions or agencies. In addition, numerous state statutes, common laws and administrative rules regulate many specific products, occupations and services, either co-extensively with federal law or in addition to federal regulation.

Sorting out exactly who has jurisdiction in a commercial speech case, or whether and in what circumstances both the federal and state legal systems can each have a hand in regulating a commercial speaker's efforts, creates the kinds of problems that form the bases of final exams in law schools. Generally, federal law prevails if Congress either has exclusive jurisdiction conferred on it by the Constitution (e.g., the power to determine the copyright status of an original creative work) or if a federal statute specifically or implicitly is meant to reserve regulation for the federal government, such as various federal statutes regulating over-the-air broadcasting.

In those areas in which both the federal government and a state may regulate commercial speech, the federal rules will exclusively apply if the state regulation conflicts with an express federal statutory provision. Although conflicts of a jurisdictional nature might help a defendant in the procedural development of a lawsuit claiming injury suffered because of false or deceptive commercial speech, perhaps the wisest course of action for advertising and public relations professionals is to be familiar with both state and federal regulations, assume that both apply and act accordingly.

Most state statutes mimicking the Federal Trade Commission/Lanham Acts' provisions regulating false, unfair or deceptive commercial speech allow competitors to pursue private lawsuits in state courts in addition to suits brought under the appropriate federal statutes. Some states have even gone a step beyond allowance of private causes of action. California's Business and Professions Codes,[41] for example, allow any Californian (like Marc Kasky) to file an unfair competition lawsuit on behalf of the state's citizens. Unlike other states, however, the creation in California of a "private attorney general" allows an unfair competition plaintiff to recover damages even though he or she was not personally damaged by the unfair practices.

The allowance of private actions reflects the historical antecedents of much of state regulation of commercial speech in English common law focusing on stopping one manufacturer from "passing off" his or her goods as the product of another. Often called "unfair competition" or "palming off," these statutes almost always come into play when speech negligently or intentionally misrepresents a product in ways that have a tendency to cause confusion on the part of a potential consumer.[42]

State statutes against "passing off" generally require a complainant to show that the defendant has actively and directly engaged in some action designed to mislead. Interestingly, although such efforts may run afoul of other state laws, using "trade dress" (distinctive design or packaging) that resembles another product is usually not considered "passing off." Similarly, removing a label from one's own product or simply failing to label a product generally does not invoke the provisions of state anti-"passing off" statutes.

In addition to laws and regulations prohibiting "passing off," a significant number of states today have either modified existing statutes or passed additional laws to permit private lawsuits by consumers and, in some instances, competitors. These statutes, often referred to as "consumer protection" or "consumer fraud prevention" acts, usually are based on claims of harm other than "passing off" that allegedly result from detrimental reliance on false, unfair or deceptive commercial speech. A number of states also permit the filing of class-action suits by consumers in such cases. In many states, these consumer-oriented statutes authorize the state's attorney general or other state officials to bring suits to prevent false or deceptive commercial speech practices as either representatives of consumers, competitors or on their own initiative.

Variations in these laws from state to state make it difficult to summarize them in any meaningful manner. For example, some states require that suits can only be brought by those somehow directly connected with defendants (sometimes referred to as "privity of contract"), either by being in actual competition with the defendants or by being a recipient of their false or deceptive commercial speech. Other states permit suits by those only indirectly related to, or affected by, the defendant's disputed commercial speech practices as well. Wise advertising and public relations professionals should both take note and seek interpretation of the applicable statutes in the states in which they practice to minimize unpleasant legal encounters with disgruntled state officials, consumers or competitors.

Perhaps not surprisingly, many state courts, faced with adjudicating cases under state laws prohibiting false, unfair or deceptive commercial speech, look to the interpretations of the FTC or the federal courts for guidance in defining these terms so as not to produce a jumble of confusing and possibly conflicting decisions. Similarly, state courts often take their cue for determination of "unfairness" from cases involving interpretation of FTC regulations. For example, numerous state courts follow the lead of the Supreme Court of the United States in *F.T.C. v. Sperry & Hutchinson*.[43] In this case, the Court approved a definition of *unfairness* that looked at the extent of harm to those relying on commercial speech claims that are either offensive to public policy or in violation of some legal definition of immoral activity.

Although federal regulatory agency and commission interpretations are influential when it comes to the definition of terms, state courts typically do not incorporate federal policy requirements (e.g., the FTC's prior substantiation doctrine) into the substantive language of state mini-FTC/Lanham Act statutes.

State Remedies for False, Deceptive or Unfair Commercial Speech: "Passing Off"

Remedies provided by state statutes for those harmed by false, deceptive or unfair commercial speech include the possibility of injunctive relief (a court order), money damages for actual or statutorily defined harm and/or court costs and attorney fees. (The possibility of remedies in state law for other kinds of injuries from false or deceptive commercial speech is discussed elsewhere in earlier chapters.)

Injunctions or court orders prohibiting or limiting commercial speech are inherently suspect because of First Amendment issues. However, these concerns may be overcome in situations in which states have approved statutes that make "passing off" goods a criminal offense. In such cases, the normal requirements for injunctive relief typically would apply (i.e., the threat of irreparable injury and the unavailability of other remedies that might prove effective to provide the relief sought by the plaintiff). Court orders in other circumstances may be available if directed at general business practices so as to prohibit a defendant from linking its product or service to those provided by the plaintiff.[44]

Although it is common to compensate any plaintiff who can demonstrate injury caused by the actions of the defendant with money damages, this remedy is frequently unavailable in cases in which plaintiffs are alleging harm amounting to "passing off" of products or services based on false or deceptive commercial speech. The problem lies in the difficulty of establishing the causal relationship between the defendant's actions and the plaintiff's claimed economic losses. Almost all states require evidence that either the economic loss by the plaintiff or the monetary gain by the defendant could not have been caused by anything other than the defendant's false or deceptive commercial speech. Short of providing testimony by individuals that they had been deceived into making their purchasing decisions solely by the defendant's bogus commercial claims, the burden of convincing a court to award damages in a "passing off" case often is too difficult for plaintiffs to meet.

Most state courts have the power to award plaintiffs' attorney fees and other financial costs associated with bringing a cause of action against the defendant. The possibility of such often substantial awards, coupled with the possibility of injunctive relief, frequently provide a strong deterrent for those guilty of using commercial speech to pass off a product or service as that of another. This should be sufficient to caution the prudent public relations or advertising professional to avoid the possibility of such practices.

Four Examples of State Regulation of Commercial Speech

To fully discuss the statutes, rules and regulations that control commercial speech in each state would require an additional chapter for each state. Although many of these state regulatory schemes look similar because they mirror their federal counterparts, almost every state statute or rule is worded slightly differently from those of its neighbors, creating nuances requiring state-by-state legal interpretations of how such laws apply.

Four examples of commercial speech regulation at the state level involving controversial, tightly controlled or currently socially relevant products or services that are also regulated by the federal government (and discussed in this and the preceding chapter) are discussed next to illustrate the breadth and complexity of such state regulatory efforts.

State Regulation of Environmental Advertising

During the past three decades, environmental issues, ranging from a diminishing ozone layer to reports of the accumulating garbage in dumps and landfills and the resulting problem of what to do with this increasing waste, have served as the basis for extensive public debate and discussion. Partially in response to these problems, environmental activists and others have pushed for the adoption of environmentally friendly policies by providers of products and services.

Many companies have found that significant numbers of consumers are more prone to purchase items if they are publicized as environmentally safe. Additionally, consumers can be persuaded to recycle containers (as long as doing so is not too expensive or inconvenient) and they will participate in programs to reuse or recycle packaging materials. These findings have led companies to provide environmentally friendly products and services and to make such efforts part of their advertising and public relations campaigns as well.

Using the environmental angle as a means to promote a product or service can create negative legal repercussions, however, if the dissemination of information about environmentally friendly practices does not comport with state statutes that spell out how and in what circumstances such claims may be made. Even neighboring states may differ considerably on how they regulate commercial speech regarding environmental issues including, for example, the legal definitions of such key terms used to describe a product as *environmentally friendly* or *recyclable*.

Compounding the issue is the inability of states to agree on a common set of standards or procedures for solving environmental problems. This has led to confusion in the enforcement of regulations regarding environmental issues and the packaging and advertising of a product. For example, the bottom of most plastic containers features a triangle of recycling arrows with a number in the middle. This number refers to the ingredients in that type of plastic and also provides a grouping number for workers sorting the containers so that they can ascertain which plastics can be melted together for recycling. However, not all states recycle all types of plastic.

The result is that in Oregon, for example, marketing a detergent as bottled in a recyclable container may be truthful and non-deceptive, whereas an identical advertisement in Tennessee for the same product in the same container with the same environmental claim might be judged as an example of deceptive commercial speech.

Concerns about such commercial speech-related environmental issues have inspired a number of states to prepare guidelines for companies that wish to tout the environmental benefits of their products or services. For example, Minnesota's guidelines state that:

- Marketers should be wary of tie-ins with environmental groups because their long-term aims may not be compatible.
- Marketers should distinguish between green claims for products and those for packaging.
- Marketers should not make an environmental claim unless the claim covers all their products.
- Marketers should avoid generalizations and half-truths in claims.[45]

Because such efforts are relatively new, state statutes and rules involving commercial speech and environmental issues are still awaiting final enactment or interpretation by the courts in many states adopting such regulations. Perhaps the safest policy for advertising and public relations professionals is to double-check the current status of environmental regulations in the states in which marketing or other communication campaigns are planned to confirm that contemplated commercial speech claims involving environmental issues do not run the risk of being judged as false or deceptive. Corporate communicators can rest assured that environmental activists will have already done their homework.

State Regulation of Securities Advertising

Mention was made in the preceding chapter that the origin of the SEC could be found in early attempts to regulate commercial speech at the state level under "Blue Sky" laws. The term *blue sky* came from the get-rich-quick schemes of fraudulent promoters whose "speculative schemes ... have no more basis than so many feet of blue sky."[46] Many times, the only information consumers received about securities came from a promoter's commercial speech. Because investments and securities are, for the most part, intangible products, promoters found it easy to twist information, omit some information or otherwise deceive gullible buyers all too ready to believe claims of easy money to be made through investments.

Eventually, state "Blue Sky" laws were enacted to provide at least some protection for consumers from the more outrageous examples of fraudulent or deceptive commercial speech practices involving securities. Today, although federal regulation of commercial speech about the offering or trading of securities overshadows efforts at the state level, "Blue Sky" laws still substantially impact the commercial speech practices of advertising and public relations professionals.

Although in the past, individual state "Blue Sky" laws varied considerably, most such regulatory schemes involved one or more of three methods for preventing false or deceptive commercial speech related to offering or trading securities. These were: (a) creating a regulatory scheme to regulate who can deal in securities; (b) requiring registration for those who sell or offer securities within a state; and (c) requiring that securities be registered before being offered to the public. As may be imagined, determining which state had adopted any of the three methods and exactly how each was interpreted by an individual state became extremely taxing for commercial speakers engaged in communicating on a regional or national level. Recognizing this difficulty, and to "avoid the complexities involved in satisfying the varying requirements of several states when offering securities for sale,"[47] the Uniform Law Commission in 1956 promulgated a Uniform Securities Act that 37 states adopted in whole or in part.[48] The Act, which provides for variations on all three methods mentioned above, gave states a pattern from which to mold and shape their individual approaches to securities regulation.

Advertising and public relations practitioners should note that although most states now base their statutes regulating securities-related commercial speech on the Uniform Securities Act, there still remain individual variations in state law that need to be understood before disseminating securities information in a particular state. For example, some states, including Alaska, Colorado, Montana, North Dakota and Washington, require a filed notification five days prior to the publication of any commercial speech regarding securities. Other states may also require prior notification, but the filing deadlines differ from state to state. In addition, the steps to be followed in each state during this filing period may vary considerably. In Alaska, for example, the law requires that a copy of the material to be distributed must be submitted for approval. In Montana, the five-day filing period is often waived. In Washington, the five-day filing period does not apply to all types of commercial speech, such as reports to shareholders, tombstone advertising without photographs or illustrations as well as some other kinds of sales literature.

In addition, 17 states have adopted or are considering adopting a newer version of the Uniform Securities Act presented in 2002. The new version features provisions designed to modernize state securities regulations and bring them more in line with newer federal provisions. Until widely adopted, however, the influence of several sets of uniform rules requires those doing business in multiple jurisdictions to pay attention to the controlling laws of each place.

Many states also address unfair practices in the insurance industry in much the same fashion. States that have articulated separate unfair competition laws for insurers operating within their borders generally cite as a rationale for these laws the high potential for confusion in insurance policy "fine print" (e.g., "term" versus "whole life" insurance, denial of coverage under certain conditions, deductible and premium structures, etc.). Additionally, because insurance companies also often provide consumers with avenues of investment (e.g., annuities), state unfair competition laws pertaining to insurance often bear remarkable similarity to legislation regulating their securities counterparts.

Advertising and public relations practitioners should be alert to these nuances in state law before engaging in securities or insurance-related commercial-speech practices, or risk unpleasant legal sanctions.

Lotteries, Sweepstakes and Games of Chance

A few states, including Nevada and New Jersey, have legalized casino-style gambling. Significantly more states allow supervised betting on sporting events. Some states have begun to get in on the action by creating state-run lotteries. In all cases, however, gambling is a highly controlled activity with detailed state laws specifying who can own or run lottery and/or gambling establishments, how wagers are placed or lottery tickets purchased and so forth.

It is common for providers of products and services to use contests such as sweepstakes or other games of chance as a marketing technique. For example, offering incentives in advertising

Figure 11.2 Even in states that have legalized casino-style gambling or state-run lotteries, such activities are highly controlled, with detailed laws specifying their ownership and operation.

Credit line: Gabriel Petrescu/Shutterstock.com

or as part of marketing special events attracts potential consumers by suggesting that the possibility of a prize may accompany a purchase. The focus of the commercial speech is not on a benefit of the product or service, but rather on the possible gain the purchaser might realize by winning a contest. Advertising and public relations professionals must be extremely careful about how such contests are presented, or legal action by state regulatory agencies could quickly put an end to the game.

All 50 states prohibit private lotteries. However, many types of contests, sweepstakes and other promotional devices may be legal if they follow the rules established by individual state legislatures. As discussed in the preceding chapter, three key elements help determine if a promotional device is a lottery: (a) if there is "consideration" or an effort made on the part of the consumer (e.g., buying a product or traveling to a destination to pick up a contest application); (b) if a prize is awarded; and (c) if winning is based on chance as opposed to a demonstration of at least some level of skill. If a proposed promotion or contest contains these elements, an advertising or public relations professional would be wise to seek advice from competent legal counsel before proceeding with the commercial campaign.

Like commercial speech about environmental issues and the offering or selling of securities, definitions of key terms in commercial speech about promotions vary from state to state and between the various states and the federal government. Some of these terms include *promotional device*, *chance*, *prize* and *consideration*. Additionally, most states have specific statutes or rules regulating games of chance. For example, Arkansas and Alabama allow promotional contests as long as the chances of winning or the prizes awarded do not depend on the payment of money or purchase of products by contest participants. Virginia has specific instructions about the information that must be disclosed to conduct a promotional contest, including the number of prizes to be awarded, odds of winning and the retail value of the prizes. Nevada prohibits gasoline and other motor-vehicle fuel dealers and sellers from sponsoring games of chance or contests as a means of promotion.

Although contests, sweepstakes and games of chance are popular promotional and advertising tools, advertising and public relations professionals should be familiar with the regulations imposed on such contests in each state where their commercial speech may be disseminated and should tailor their messages accordingly.

Commercial Speech About Alcoholic Beverages

As noted earlier, the manufacture and sale of alcoholic beverages historically have raised important social issues as illustrated by the enactment and ultimate failure of Prohibition in the 1920s. State laws regulating commercial speech about alcoholic beverages differ widely because of many factors, including the drinking age recognized by the state, rules about the sale of alcohol and statutes punishing drinking and driving.

Only a few states have no restrictions on commercial speech involving alcoholic beverages; most handle the sale and distribution of alcohol within their borders with the exception of bars and restaurants. The remaining states allow alcoholic beverages to be sold by private enterprises but under control by state commissions or agencies. Although for the most part state regulations parallel federal regulations, details of such regulatory schemes vary widely. Advertising and public relations professionals involved in disseminating commercial speech about alcoholic beverages might consider reviewing the *Code of Responsible Practices for Beverage Alcohol Advertising and Marketing* published by the Distilled Spirits Council of the United States.[49]

Conclusion

Add together federal and state regulations, rules and statutes that range from the national FTC Act to state laws regulating commercial speech about everything from automobiles to zoological parks and it is clear that even prudent advertising and public relations practitioners face formidable challenges in safely fulfilling their professional obligations in the decades ahead. Although the task may appear daunting, only the irresponsible practitioner would respond by claiming "it's all just too complicated" and trust only to luck to avoid legal entanglements. The appropriate way to meet these challenges is to check the applicable state and federal laws and regulations so practitioners can identify when it is necessary to seek the advice of legal counsel. This knowledge should sharply reduce the chances of accidentally running afoul of legal restrictions on commercial speech that could injure organizations, clients and professional careers.

Notes

1.   15 U.S.C. §1125 (1946) (also referred to as Lanham Act §43(a)).
2.   *Id.*
3.   *Id.*
4.   *Id.* §1125(1)(b) (1992).
5.   *Id.* §1125(1).
6.   *Id.* §1125(2).
7.   Serbin v. Ziebart Int'l Corp., 11 F.3d 1163 (3d Cir. 1993).
8.   Balance Dynamics Corp. v. Schmitt Indus., 204 F.3d 683 (6th Cir. 2000).
9.   Balance Dynamics Corp. v. Schmitt Indus., 1997 U.S. Dist. LEXIS 17253 (E.D. Mich. 1997).

10. Pizza Hut v. Papa John's Int'l, 227 F.3d 489 (5th Cir. 2000).

11. Pizza Hut, Inc. v. Papa John's Int'l, Inc., 80 F. Supp. 2d 600 (N.D. Tex. 2000).

12. Kasky v. Nike, Inc., 119 Cal. Rptr. 2d 296 (Cal. 2002).

13. 42 U.S.C. 3603(b).

14. *Id.*

15. Ragin v. New York Times Co., 923 F.2d 995 (2d Cir. 1991); *cert. denied*, 112 S. Ct. 81 (1991).

16. Pub. L. No. 88-352, §70 et seq., 78 Stat. 241, Title 42 U.S.C. §2000e et seq.

17. Hailes v. United Air Lines, 464 F. 2d 1006 (5th Cir. 1972).

18. Pittsburgh Press Co. v. Pittsburgh Comm'n. on Human Relations, 413 U.S. 376 (1973).

19. Pub. L. 90-202, 80 Stat. 602 (29 U.S.C. §621), as amended in Pub. L. 95-256 (A.D. in Employment Amendments of 1978), 92 Stat. 189.

20. 42 U.S.C. §12101 et seq.

21. Housing Opportunities Made Equal v. Cincinnati Enquirer, 943 F.2d 644 (6th Cir. 1991).

22. *Id.* at 646.

23. Pub. L. 96-240, 90 Stat. 257 (1976); codified at Table 15 U.S.C. §§1667-1667e (1982).

24. *Id.*

25. *Id.*

26. Pub. L. 93-495, Title V, 88 Stat. 1521 (1974); codified at 15 U.S.C. §§1691-1691f (1982).

27. 15 U.S.C. §1811 (1982).

28. See Housing Opportunities Made Equal v. Cincinnati Enquirer, 943 F.2d 644 (6th Cir. 1991).

29. 15 U.S.C. §§1681, et. seq.

30. 49 U.S.C. §303 (1956).

31. 23 U.S.C. §131 (1965).

32. Metromedia, Inc. v. City of San Diego, 453 U.S. 490 (1981).

33. 15 U.S.C. §§1601-1614 and 1661-1665a (April 1990).

34. 27 U.S.C. §§ 201-211.

35. In 2003, as part of the creation of the Department of Homeland Security, the ATF's focus was expanded to include explosives. Still known as ATF, the bureau's official name is the Bureau of Alcohol, Tobacco, Firearms and Explosives.

36. U.S. Const. amend. XXI.

37. Central Hudson Gas & Elec. Corp. v. Public Serv. Comm'n, 447 U.S. 557 (1980).

38. Rubin v. Coors Brewing Co., 514 U.S. 476 (1995).

39. 44 Liquormart v. Rhode Island, 517 U.S. 484 (1996).

40. *See* G. E. Rosden & P. E. Rosden, The Law of Advertising (Matthew Bender & Co. Inc., New York, 1991).

41. *See* Cal. Bus. & Prof. Code §17200 et seq.; Cal. Bus. & Prof. Code §17500 et seq.

42. Rosden at vol. 2, §13-14.

43. F.T.C. v. Sperry & Hutchinson Co., 405 U.S. 233 (1972).

44. Rosden at vol. 2, §13-29.

45. *Id.* at vol. 3, §26-47.

46. *Id.*

47. *Id.* at vol. 4, §57-29.

48. Unif. Sec. Act §§101-102 (1956) (amended 2003).

49. *Code of Responsible Practices*, The Distilled Spirits Council of the United States, www.distilledspirits.org/wp-content/uploads/2018/03/May_26_2011_DISCUS_Code_Word_Version1.pdf (last retrieved Nov. 20, 2018).

12 Access to Information, Free Press/Fair Trial, Journalist Privilege

Although the principal focus of this text is on the laws and regulations affecting commercial speech, advertising and public relations professionals should also be aware of a number of legal issues related to the news-gathering and disseminating processes. These issues include conducting public business "in the sunshine" by allowing public and press access to public records and meetings. They also include the inevitable tensions involved in protecting the freedom of journalists to fully and accurately report on the criminal and civil law processes while also ensuring that those parties actually involved in a case are afforded the right to the fair and unbiased judicial proceeding guaranteed by the Constitution. Finally, the chapter addresses the controversial issue of whether journalists have a constitutional or statutory "privilege" to withhold information sought by law enforcement, legislative or judicial authorities.

This chapter is purposely written from the perspective of the journalist because the issues discussed most directly impact the news-gathering process. However, these issues have implications for public relations practitioners and, to a lesser extent, advertising professionals as well.

Freedom of Information and Access to Places

Although the Supreme Court has expanded a right of public access to trials and other criminal proceedings (discussed later in this chapter), the First Amendment provides no general right of access. In *Pell v. Procunier*[1] and *Saxbe v. The Washington Post*,[2] for example, the Court specifically rejected claims that journalists have a special right to gain access to prisons and other government facilities, holding that the mass media have no greater right of access than the average citizen.

Lower federal and state courts have followed the Court's lead, ruling in almost every instance that journalists have no greater access rights to enter property, gain entrance to crime scenes or be admitted to meetings than those afforded the general public. The limited exception to this rule is for situations where public access—often represented by journalists—has been the rule historically and adds legitimacy to the situation.

What is true for access to physical places is also true for access to records (including digital files and data) and other information. With the exception of some categories of material related to criminal proceedings, particularly evidence or supporting matter introduced in open court, the courts consistently have held that the mass media have no greater right of access to records and documents than do members of the general public.

The Federal Freedom of Information Act (FOIA)

Although the First Amendment has not been interpreted as providing a special right of access for journalists and the public, this does not mean that the reasons for allowing access to records and places are without merit. To accomplish by statute what could not be achieved by constitutional interpretation, Congress passed the Freedom of Information Act (FOIA) in 1966,[3] supplemented by the 1974 Privacy Act[4] and the Electronic Freedom of Information Act Amendments adopted in 1996.[5] These laws provide a qualified right of access to information maintained in the files of federal agencies. All 50 states have now followed suit with their own freedom of information laws to provide a statutory right of access to state records.

The federal FOIA mandates that all federal executive departments and federal regulatory agencies disclose how and from whom their records may be obtained by the public for viewing and/or photocopying. According to the Act, the term "agency" includes "any executive department, military department, Government controlled corporation, or other establishment in the executive branch of the government (including the Executive Office of the President), or any independent regulatory agency."[6]

Government information covered by the Act is any agency record maintained by an agency in any format, including electronic format, and any information "maintained for an agency by an entity under Government contract, for the purposes of records management."[7] This includes, but is not limited to (a) printed records or printouts of computer files; (b) photographs, illustrations and graphs/charts; and (c) electronically recorded information including data stored in

Figure 12.1 Congress passed the Freedom of Information Act (FOIA) in 1966, supplemented by the 1974 Privacy Act and the Electronic Freedom of Information Act Amendments adopted in 1996. All 50 states have now followed suit with their own freedom of information laws to provide a statutory right of access to state records, as well as meetings of public governmental bodies. Shown here is a plaque at the City Hall and County Building in Chicago, Illinois.

Credit line: FeyginFoto/Shutterstock.com

electronic databases. Note that both federal and state freedom of information acts apply to existing records and documents. Even though bits of information may exist in a number of different government files, an agency is not required to create a new document that compiles this information in meeting FOIA requirements.

The federal FOIA covers documents and records in the possession of, and controlled by, a government agency. Disputes, sometimes leading to legal challenges, have arisen about the definitions of "possession" and "control." If the records sought were created by agency personnel and remain within the agency that created them, both requirements likely will be satisfied. Grayer areas involve records created by outside contractors or those technically no longer under the jurisdiction of the agency to which the FOI request is made.

The statute specifies that (a) all final court opinions and orders related to agency matters; (b) policy statements; and (c) interpretations of regulations, documents and records about agency actions or proposed actions that are not exempted from disclosure by the nine specific exceptions in the Act (discussed later in this chapter) must be made available for public inspection.[8] Even if some parts of a document might be exempted, the Act requires the government agency producing the document to make a reasonable effort to ensure that the non-exempted portions are provided to members of the public seeking the information.

Information Exempt From Disclosure

The federal FOIA contains a number of exceptions (or exemptions) from the general disclosure rule. The first exemption is material designated by an executive order to be kept secret in the interests of national defense or foreign policy and is "in fact properly classified pursuant to such Executive order."[9] This has proven in practice to be a rather large exception because Congress and the courts have given great deference to the executive branch in determining what is classified. The current test is simply whether disclosure could reasonably be expected to endanger national security. Not only can the government maintain a document as classified under the national security/foreign policy exemption, but it also can even reclassify a document formerly in the public domain as secret after an FOIA request has been made.

The second exemption is for information that is related solely to the internal personnel rules and practices of an agency. The third is for documents already exempted under other federal statutes.

The fourth exemption to the federal FOIA is for "trade secrets and commercial or financial information obtained from a person and privileged or confidential."[10] The degree of discretion given an agency in following this exemption gave rise to a decision by the Supreme Court in *Chrysler Corp. v. Brown* (1979)[11] that has proven significant to corporate public relations professionals. The case involved a request for information about Chrysler Corporation's affirmative action policies. This information had been provided to the U.S. Department of Labor by Chrysler under federal statutory provisions requiring such submissions from any company with multiple contracts with the federal government. Before the information could be made public, Chrysler sought an injunction in a federal district court in Delaware to block its release. The Court held that the federal FOIA permits, but does not require, an agency to withhold documents that arguably fall within one of the exemptions.

In 1986, President Ronald Reagan issued an executive order requiring federal agencies to routinely notify companies if information they have supplied is to be released to the public because a FOIA request has been filed. Organizations are permitted a 10-day period to protest

Figure 12.2 In 1986, President Ronald Reagan, shown here in the Oval Office, issued an executive order requiring federal agencies to routinely notify companies if information they have supplied is to be released to the public because a FOIA request has been filed. Organizations are permitted a 10-day period to protest such release and, if unsuccessful, to seek injunctive relief in federal district courts to stop the information from being divulged.

Credit line: Carol M. Highsmith, Library of Congress, Prints and Photographs Division, Washington, D.C.

such release and, if unsuccessful, to seek injunctive relief in federal district courts to stop the information from being divulged.

Exemption five to the federal FOIA protects

> inter-agency or intra-agency memorandums or letters that would not be available by law to a party other than an agency in litigation with the agency, provided that the deliberative process privilege shall not apply to records created 25 years or more before the date on which the records were requested.[12]

This exemption has been interpreted as protecting working papers and other documents produced as part of an agency's ongoing decision-making process, as well as the "work-product" of government attorneys normally protected as privileged communications under rules of legal civil procedure.

Exemption six protects personnel, medical and other similar government files, the disclosure of which would constitute a clearly unwarranted invasion of privacy. This includes information of a normally private nature about specific individuals. This exemption has produced considerable controversy and litigation. For example, a federal appellate court sided with a U.S. Department of State decision to deny FOIA disclosure to requests for information about the citizenship status of foreign nationals. The Supreme Court unanimously upheld the lower appellate court decision, ruling that information disclosure, which involved whether two Iranian nationals living in Iran had valid U.S. passports, could be an unwarranted invasion of personal privacy.[13] Another federal court, on the other hand, allowed *The New York Times* access to the last seconds of recorded conversations among the seven crew members of the space shuttle *Challenger* before the space craft crashed to earth, killing all aboard.[14]

Exemption seven has also seen its share of litigation and controversy. With the continuing focus on the reporting of crime and actions by law enforcement officials by American mass media, the exemption created by the federal FOIA for records or other documents compiled for law enforcement purposes frequently is challenged when agencies decline to provide journalists with information about criminals or criminal investigations. Government agencies wishing to classify information under this exemption must demonstrate either that disclosure could reasonably be expected to interfere with enforcement procedures or could deprive a person of a right to a fair trial. Also, exemption seven often affords protection for information constituting an unwarranted invasion of privacy, identifying a confidential source, revealing law enforcement techniques or endangering the life or physical safety of an individual.

The eighth exemption, permitting classification of information related to the examination, operation or condition of a financial institution, and exemption nine, concerning documentation of geological and geophysical investigations, have produced relatively little litigation.

Exemptions in state FOIA laws typically parallel their federal counterpart (e.g., law enforcement documents, confidential business data and individual privacy interests). Although a comprehensive discussion of these state statutes is beyond the scope of this text, those interested in learning more about a state's FOIA provisions are advised to access the website of the individual state's press association for advice about how to employ the act.

Requesting Information

Although procedures for requesting information vary, most FOIA laws, including the federal statute, require that (a) those requesting information submit a written or online request for specific records, although visiting the agency and asking the FOI officer politely to see a record sometimes works; (b) the government agency must provide the desired records within a specified time period or explain why the information is being withheld; and (c) the government normally be permitted to charge a reasonable fee for compiling and photocopying documents, although the fee may be waived upon request.

Among the frequently encountered problems in requesting government documents are delays, excessive redaction, requests ignored, excessive fees (including for search, redaction and copying), lack of enforcement, overuse of exemptions, and data and technology issues.[15] In the 2017 annual Freedom of Information issue of *Quill*, freelance data-journalism consultant Hilary Miles offered three major tips on how to overcome hurdles to FOI requests: (1) remember, public records are just that: public; (2) train your contacts to respond to you because you're you, not because you may be reporting for any particular organization; and (3) become your own best advocate.[16]

Among the tips Niles suggests for trimming costs of fees are (1) "Request fee waivers based on your credentials, not on your clients"; (2) "Call their bluff" when confronted with excessive cost estimates for producing documents; and (3) "get organizational buy-in," including making "the case for why these records are worth investigating."[17]

Open Meeting Laws

All states have passed statutes mandating open meetings of public bodies such as city commissions, state regulatory agencies, school boards, etc. Most of these "sunshine laws" also provide for closed door sessions when officials are discussing legal matters, property acquisitions, individual personnel matters and similar issues, although no official business may be finalized, nor may finalized votes be taken behind closed doors. Access to federal government agency meetings is provided by the "Government in the Sunshine Act" of 1977[18] that provides rights and exemptions, similar to state laws.

Notification of public meetings must be posted to give enough time for the public to attend. Although emergency meetings are allowed, the emergency must be genuine. "Informal" meetings, such as cocktail parties, backyard barbecues or early-morning breakfasts (where lawmakers "just happen" to get together), tend to be treated as public meetings by open meeting statutes and therefore subject to the same requirements as regular meetings.

Ad and Public Relations Professionals and FOIA Requests

FOIA and open meeting laws are not just for journalists. Knowledgeable advertising and public relations practitioners often can find valuable information (e.g., who has a government contract, business dealings by competitors or data about consumer behavior) from census and other government sources obtained through the strategic use of freedom of information requests.

Equally important, as the people to whom a freedom of information inquiry often is made or referred, public relations professionals in government organizations should make themselves intimately familiar with the requirements of both federal and applicable state FOIA statutes and counsel senior management and others in the organization about the rights and responsibilities of those to whom a FOIA or open meeting request is made.

Those responding to freedom of information requests should note that attempts to hide information created or maintained in websites, e-mails or other digital media technologies most likely will be futile. Whether in new media or old, court decisions to date tend to treat "documents" alike when it comes to FOIA inquiries. Also, prudent public relations staffs of most government agencies generally find it a wise policy to accommodate the requests of journalists and others making information requests if at all possible, even if technically not required to do so by FOIA provisions.

Free Press Versus Fair Trial Issues

At the heart of the free press/fair trial issue is the conflict between the courts' responsibility to ensure the criminally accused and, to a lesser degree, the people (represented by the prosecutor) the right to a fair and unbiased trial on the one hand, and the responsibility of the mass media to accurately and comprehensively report the news and to carry out this task free from unwarranted government interference, on the other. For much of the nation's history, this conflict was only theoretical. The media disseminated what they wanted and if the rights of the criminally accused were diminished, it was just too bad. But as concerns about protection of civil liberties increased during the 1950s, courts became more and more worried about the prejudicial publicity problem.

Things came to a head with the Supreme Court's decision in *Sheppard v. Maxwell*.[19] Dr. Sheppard, an osteopathic surgeon, was charged with murder in the slaying of his wife. Sheppard claimed an intruder had invaded their home, knocked him unconscious and killed Mrs. Sheppard, but police soon made Sheppard their number one suspect. In what today would likely be called a "media circus," the newspapers covering the case employed sensational headlines suggesting his guilt, officials made public statements of a similar nature prior to trial, and the news media were given almost free rein inside and outside the courtroom during the trial.

Found guilty and sent to prison, Sheppard pursued the appeal of his conviction all the way to the Supreme Court. In a landmark decision, the Court overturned Sheppard's conviction and ordered a new trial on the basis that the trial judge failed to "fulfill his duty to protect [Sheppard] from the inherently prejudicial publicity which saturated the community and to control disruptive influences in the courtroom."[20]

Many of the Court's suggestions for trial courts to use as remedies for alleviating potential bias are familiar to most readers today. These include (a) maintaining order inside the courtroom; (b) intensive screening of the jury pool to root out bias; (c) instructions to the jury to avoid reading or viewing the news media while the case proceeds; and, in more extreme cases, (d) sequestering the jury for the length of the trial. With these tools at a judge's disposal, once the jury pool is chosen, arguably there should be little reason to worry about prejudicial publicity reaching the jury unless the judge fails to do his or her duty. Unfortunately, the remedies that are most effective in minimizing bias require the judge to have control over the jury members. These measures are largely ineffective in preventing *pre*-trial prejudicial publicity from reaching *potential* jurors.

This conundrum—trial court judges charged by the Supreme Court with minimizing prejudicial publicity or risk having their cases overturned on appeal yet being unable to effectively use the remedies for prevention suggested by the Court—led to the first great confrontation between the legal system and the press over the issue of free press/fair trial: the use of prior restraints or "gag orders."

Use of Prior Restraint to Ensure Fair Trials

Charged by the Supreme Court with the responsibility for mitigating the effects of prejudicial pre-trial publicity, but lacking effective means to carry out this responsibility, beginning in the late 1960s, a few trial courts began to experiment with restraining orders directed at the press. These orders, placed on news media representatives in the early stages of a criminal case, usually allowed the press to be present at pre-trial hearings or other proceedings and to obtain information from law enforcement officials, but mandated that the press not publicize certain kinds of potentially prejudicial information. Journalists violating such orders ran the substantial risk of being found in contempt of court and made to pay fines and/or spend time in jail. Additionally, their media organizations could be fined as well.

The effectiveness of these court orders, quickly dubbed "gag rules" by the news media, made their use attractive to other judges and the number of courts across the country employing these court orders in some form quickly snowballed. Because these court orders also undeniably were examples of government agencies employing prior restraint (as discussed in Chapter 1, the most constitutionally suspect method of government abridgement of speech), it was only a matter of time before a challenge to their use arrived at the Court's door.

The case that presented the Court with the opportunity to speak about the legitimacy of the use of such restraints was *Nebraska Press Association v. Stuart*,[21] an appeal of a decision by the Nebraska Supreme Court. The sensational facts of the case included the murder of all six members of a family living in the small town of Sutherland, Nebraska (population 850). Police almost immediately suspected Erwin Simants, who turned himself in to authorities the next day. Because mass murder was not a common occurrence in Nebraska, the case garnered widespread attention from both regional and national print and broadcast media.

After three days of constant media attention, both Simants' attorney and the county prosecutor asked a county court judge to issue an order prohibiting the media from divulging "news which would make difficult, if not impossible, the impaneling of an impartial jury and tend to prevent a fair trial."[22] The judge granted the motion that "prohibited everyone in attendance from 'releasing or authorizing the release for public dissemination in any form or manner whatsoever any testimony given or evidence adduced.' "[23]

After a preliminary hearing, Simants was bound over for trial to the state district court presided over by Judge Hugh Stuart. Various journalist organizations, including the Nebraska Press Association representing the state's newspapers, asked Judge Stuart to lift the restraining order issued by the county court. Finding that there was "a clear and present danger that pre-trial publicity could impinge upon the defendant's right to a fair trial,"[24] the judge refused the request to lift the restraint on publication but modified the county court's original order to reflect the Nebraska Bar-Press Guidelines. These guidelines for disseminating information had been created earlier by print and broadcast media associations in cooperation with various law enforcement personnel and judicial officers.

The Nebraska Bar-Press Guidelines, like those that had been adopted by many other states, suggested that in criminal cases it would be inappropriate to report information about a suspect's confession or other admissions, the results of physical tests that might be inadmissible in court (e.g., a lie-detector test), opinions by officials about guilt or innocence and other statements that might inflame or influence potential jurors to which the actual jury members hearing the case might not be exposed because a court might exclude the evidence as being too prejudicial.

Although the Nebraska Press Association had participated in the drafting of these guidelines, it, along with other news media representatives, appealed to the Nebraska Supreme Court asking that the restraining order be overturned on the premise that making voluntary guidelines mandatory violated free speech/press rights. When the Nebraska high court refused, the press association took its appeal to the Supreme Court.

Characterizing the "problems presented by this case [as] almost as old as the Republic,"[25] Chief Justice Burger, writing for the majority (all nine justices agreed on the outcome), traced problems of prejudicial publicity surrounding criminal proceedings back to the trial of Aaron Burr for treason in 1807. The Chief Justice noted that even back then, Chief Justice Marshall had expressed concern about the problems in selecting an unbiased jury, and he observed that the "speed of communication and the pervasiveness of the modern news media have exacerbated these problems."[26] Nonetheless, the Court concluded that such sensational cases "are relatively rare, and we have held in other cases that trials have been fair in spite of widespread publicity."[27]

Observing the existence of a number of other measures to minimize the effects of prejudicial publicity, including changing the venue (location) of the trial, delaying the proceedings, interrogating potential jurors to determine bias, instructing jurors as to how they should view the evidence in a case and restraining other participants in the case (e.g., lawyers, defendants, witnesses) from discussing it with the news media, the Court overturned the ruling by the Nebraska Supreme Court and struck down the restraining order on First Amendment grounds.

In so holding, however, the Court did not rule out the limited use of judicial restraining orders in future cases. Instead, the Court created a three-part test for determining the constitutionality of such restraints of the media. First, said the Court, the judge issuing a restraining order directed against the press must be able to show a clear record of "intense and pervasive"[28] news coverage that demonstrates prejudicial pre-trial publicity has occurred, is likely to continue and that such "publicity might impair the defendant's right to a fair trial."[29] The second part of the test requires the judge to demonstrate on the record that he or she has investigated the feasibility of employing one or more of the alternatives to prior restraint noted above but has found that no other method or methods would be sufficient to protect the defendant's right to a fair trial.

Part three of the test relates to "the probable efficacy of prior restraint on publication as a workable method of protecting [the defendant's] right[s]."[30] Noting that, as a practical matter, a court must have jurisdiction over the parties involved in a case if its orders are not to be ignored, the Court pointed out that in a sensational case (e.g., the O.J. Simpson murder trial) it would be of little avail for a judge to issue a restraining order that could apply only to local or regional media but not control the coverage of the case by national media.

From the point of view of the news media, the results of the *Nebraska Press Association* case produced two important results, one good and one bad. The good news was that, although not prohibiting so-called gag rules completely, the Court's three-prong test signaled a clear message to lower courts seeking to enforce such rules that it was extremely unlikely the constitutionality of such prior-restraint orders directed against the news media would be sustained on appeal. This has proven to be the case.

Note, however, that the Court explicitly suggested that such restraints would be justifiable if imposed on other participants in the case, including public relations professionals representing clients involved in the litigation. The reader is cautioned not to trifle with or ignore a court order. The savvy public relations practitioner would be wise to follow such orders to the letter in releasing information to the public and, if in doubt, consult with the court before speaking and advise clients about their responsibilities to do likewise.

The bad news for the news media in *Nebraska Press Association* was contained in language in the Court's majority opinion that seemed to view with approval the Nebraska Supreme Court's suggestion that closing the proceedings to the public, including the news media, was an acceptable alternative to prior restraint.[31] Soon, trial courts, discouraged from using gag rules except in rare circumstances, began to deny the press and public access to pre-trial judicial hearings and other proceedings.

Closing the Courtroom to Ensure Fair Trials

It was only a matter of time before closing the courtroom doors (and thus denying to the public the ability to scrutinize the workings of the judicial process) also was challenged in the courts as a violation of the Constitution. The case presenting this opportunity was *Gannett Co. v. DePasquale*.[32] One day, Wayne Clapp and two of his buddies went fishing on Seneca Lake in upstate New York. Only his buddies returned. Police, alerted to Clapp's disappearance by his family, found his bullet-riddled boat and surmised that Clapp had met a violent end. Newspapers in the area, including one owned by Gannett Co., reported the story of Clapp's apparent death and the apprehension of the two suspects in Michigan several days later. The stories included details about the case against the suspects, including statements made by them to police.

As the case against them developed, both defendants moved to suppress various pieces of evidence, including much of the information they had given to police, on the grounds "that those statements had been given involuntarily. They also sought to suppress physical evidence seized as fruits of the allegedly involuntary confessions,"[33] specifically, a revolver said to have been involved in the alleged killing.

At a pre-trial suppression-of-evidence hearing before Judge Daniel A. DePasquale, defendants' attorneys asked that the press be barred from the proceedings, based on the already significant adverse publicity about the case and the possibility of a threat to the fair trial rights of the accused if the media were allowed to report on evidence that later might be excluded at trial. Neither the prosecution nor representatives of the press opposed the motion to close, although a reporter for the Gannett newspaper was present in the courtroom. Judge DePasquale granted the defendants' request and closed the hearing to the public.

When Gannett's attorneys later objected to the closure, Judge DePasquale, although noting that the press had a limited constitutional right of access, refused to lift the closure order on the basis that allowing the press to report on the outcome of a hearing to suppress evidence "would pose a 'reasonable probability of prejudice to these defendants'…[and] that the interest of the press and the public was outweighed in this case by the defendants' right to a fair trial."[34] When the New York Court of Appeals upheld Judge DePasquale's ruling, Gannett took its case to the Supreme Court.

The Court's majority opinion rejected First Amendment arguments in favor of overturning Judge DePasquale's closure order because media representatives had been present when the order was issued and had failed to object at that time, a subsequent hearing had been granted to the newspaper company in which to argue for openness, and the closure order was "only temporary. Once the danger of prejudice had dissipated, a transcript of the suppression hearing was made available."[35] Chief Justice Burger, in a concurring opinion, specifically noted that a First Amendment-based claim of access was inapplicable in this case because *Gannett* involved a pre-trial proceeding unknown at the time the First Amendment was adopted.

Based on *Gannett*, lower courts across the country increased their use of closure as a means of ensuring defendants a fair trial. This movement finally culminated in *Richmond Newspapers, Inc. v. Virginia*,[36] in which a judge closed an actual criminal trial. This set the stage for a second chance for First Amendment-based arguments in favor of public access to judicial proceedings.

The case involved the fourth trial of a defendant accused of murdering a hotel manager. His conviction in the first trial was reversed on appeal because a blood-stained shirt was improperly introduced as evidence. A second trial ended when a juror was forced to retire and no alternate was available. The third trial was aborted when it was discovered that a prospective juror had read about the earlier attempts to try the defendant, including the bloody-shirt evidence, and informed other jurors about these efforts.

At the beginning of trial four, defense counsel, citing the possibility of prejudicial publicity, asked the judge to close the proceedings to the press and public. When neither the prosecution nor the journalists present objected, the judge cleared the courtroom "of all parties except the witnesses when they testify."[37] At a subsequent hearing, requested by Richmond Newspapers, Inc. to protest closure, the trial judge refused to vacate his order, finding the criminal defendant's arguments about the number of trials to date and the smallness of the community persuasive, and the trial continued with the press and public barred. The defendant was eventually found not guilty of murder. The Virginia Supreme Court upheld the validity of the trial court's closure order and Richmond Newspapers, Inc. took its case to the Supreme Court.

Although the Court was fragmented in deciding on an overall rationale for its decision (Chief Justice Burger's opinion was joined by only two other justices and no other opinion represented the views of more than two justices), seven justices agreed that the lower court's order should be overturned on First Amendment grounds. The Chief Justice's opinion began by observing that

> this precise issue ... has not previously been before this Court. ... [H]ere for the first time the Court is asked to decide whether a criminal *trial* itself may be closed to the public upon the unopposed request of a defendant [absent] any demonstration that closure is required to protect the defendant's superior right to a fair trial. (emphasis added)[38]

Tracing the origins of a tradition of openness for such trials to before the Norman conquest of England in 1066, Chief Justice Burger noted that this tradition had been brought over to the English colonies in America and had become part of the American legal system. Based on this evidence, the Chief Justice concluded "[f]rom this unbroken, uncontradicted history, supported by reasons as valid today as in centuries past, ... a presumption of openness inheres in the very nature of a criminal trial under our system of justice."[39]

Despite this presumption, Virginia officials argued that no explicit provision of the Constitution guarantees that the press and public should be permitted access to all criminal trials. Although agreeing in principle, the Chief Justice found that

> [i]n guaranteeing freedoms such as those of speech and press, the First Amendment can be read as protecting the right of everyone to attend trials. ... "[T]he First Amendment goes beyond protection of the press and the self-expression of individuals to prohibit government from limiting the stock of information from which members of the public may draw."[40]

Although not providing a general right of access, Chief Justice Burger held that

> [t]he right of access to places traditionally open to the public, as criminal trials have long been, may be seen as assured by the amalgam of the First Amendment guarantees of speech and press; and their affinity to the right of assembly is not without relevance.[41]

The Chief Justice concluded that despite the failure of the Constitution to enumerate a guarantee of access,

> the right to attend criminal trials is implicit in the guarantees of the First Amendment; without the freedom to attend such trials, which people have exercised for centuries, important aspects of freedom of speech and "of the press could be eviscerated."[42]

Although the Chief Justice, in fashioning a limited First Amendment-based right of access, was careful to maintain the distinction between pre-trial proceedings and actual criminal trials, the limitation almost immediately began to suffer erosion. In *Globe Newspaper v. Norfolk County Superior Court*,[43] the Court struck down a state law mandating closing of trials involving victims of sexual offenses under the age of 18 on the basis that the law permitted no judicial discretion. Such a law, said the Court, could not be squared with the constitutional presumption of openness of criminal proceedings.

In *Press Enterprise Co. v. Riverside County Superior Court*,[44] the Court held that jury selection was so integral to the criminal trial process and was so intimately related to the actual trial that it too was presumptively open to the press and public, despite arguments that, in addition to prejudicial pre-trial publicity, potential jurors and witnesses might be intimidated or embarrassed by media reports.

In a later case with the same name, often referred to as *Press-Enterprise II*,[45] the Court was presented with the rather unusual situation of a pre-trial preliminary hearing that continued for 41 days in a case involving a nurse charged with multiple murders of patients under his care. Unlike a typical preliminary hearing, which generally lasts no more than a day or two, the proceedings in *Press-Enterprise II* involved presentation of extensive medical and scientific evidence, as well as testimonial evidence from the defendant's co-workers, which was then subjected to searching cross-examination by the defendant's legal counsel.

At the beginning of the proceedings, the defendant asked that the preliminary hearing be closed. The trial judge granted the motion—which was unopposed—on the basis that "closure was necessary because the case had attracted national publicity and 'only one side may get reported in the media.'"[46] At the end of the preliminary hearing, *Press-Enterprise* asked that the transcript of the proceedings be made public, but the judge denied the request. The appeal of the closure and sealing of the transcript was taken to the California Supreme Court, which upheld the lower court. The Supreme Court of the United States subsequently overturned the lower court's decisions on First Amendment grounds.

The Court recognized the lower courts' concerns about ensuring the defendant's rights to a fair trial and that its own rulings in earlier cases might be construed as to deny First Amendment claims of access to pre-trial proceedings. However, said the Court, despite the fact that the closure order involved a pre-trial proceeding, "the First Amendment question cannot be resolved solely on the label we give the event, i.e., 'trial' or otherwise, particularly where the preliminary hearing functions much like a full-scale trial."[47] Instead, said the Court, a possible constitutional right of access must be based on "two complementary considerations. First, ... we have considered whether the place and process have *historically* been open to the press and general public" (emphasis added).[48] The Court added, "[we have also] traditionally considered whether public access plays a significant *positive role* in the functioning of the particular process in question" (emphasis added).[49]

Finding that although in California proceedings like grand jury deliberations had not been open to public scrutiny, "there has been a tradition of accessibility to preliminary hearings of the type conducted in [this case]."[50] In fact, noted the Court, "[f]rom [the case of Aaron] Burr until the present day, the near uniform practice of state and federal courts has been to conduct preliminary hearings in open court."[51]

Although some states have allowed preliminary hearings to be closed on occasion, the Court observed that "even in these States, the proceedings are presumptively open to the public and are closed only for cause shown."[52] Based on its decisions in *Richmond Newspapers* and *Press-Enterprise I* that public access "is essential to the proper functioning of the criminal justice system,"[53] the Court held that, when conducted like those in California, "preliminary hearings are sufficiently like a trial to justify the same conclusion."[54]

After the series of cases ending in *Press-Enterprise II*, lower courts apparently got the message that closing criminal court proceedings to minimize prejudicial publicity should not be the method of choice, except in unusual situations. Lower courts, therefore, have increasingly turned to delay, change of venue and especially to the use of gag rules on police and trial participants to prevent them from talking to the press. Although there have been no significant recent cases for the Court to expand on its rulings in this area, it seems a safe bet that there is little enthusiasm on the part of the current members of the Court for narrowing the trend to openness recognized for criminal proceedings.

There remains the question, however, of whether this trend will be extended to provide a constitutional right of access to civil proceedings. Although most civil trials are routinely open to the public, lower courts, at least for the time being, still retain a greater ability to deny access if they so choose. Arguably, however, the benefits of public access to criminal proceedings articulated by the Court in cases ranging from *Richmond Newspapers* to *Press-Enterprise II* should apply to civil proceedings with equal validity.

Cameras in the Courtroom: A Special Access Problem

In 1927, Charles Lindbergh captured the imagination of the world when he flew his airplane, the *Spirit of St. Louis*, solo between New York and Paris. He returned to the United States a hero, and his fame increased as he toured the country and then foreign nations as well, with his bride, Anne Morrow Lindbergh. Tragically, their lives were shattered in 1934 when their infant son was kidnapped and later killed. The details of the kidnapping, the arrest of a suspect, Bruno Hauptmann, and his subsequent trial for murder created a news media frenzy, so much so that

Figure 12.3 The double-murder trial of former football star and actor O.J. Simpson in Los Angeles in 1995 attracted unprecedented media coverage. The Supreme Court of the United States has pointed out that in a sensational case such as the Simpson trial it would be of little avail for a judge to issue a restraining order that could apply only to local or regional media but not control the coverage of the case by national media.

Credit line: Joseph Sohm/Shutterstock.com

the American Bar Association was moved to adopt Canon 35 of its code of legal ethics, which banned broadcast coverage (as well as still photography) in courtrooms.

This prohibition of cameras and microphones in the courtroom continued to be enforced for more than four decades and continues in most federal courtrooms today. Beginning in the late 1970s, however, recognizing that modern technology had reduced the intrusiveness of broadcasting and photography, state courts began to experiment with allowing photographers and electronic journalists access to pre-trial and trial proceedings. In *Chandler v. Florida*[55] in 1981, the Supreme Court held it was not an inherent abridgement of a defendant's rights to a fair trial to allow cameras and microphones in the courtroom. However, the Court did not find a blanket right of access for such technology, leaving it to lower courts to establish rules and guidelines for allowing or prohibiting their presence.

Today, live coverage of trials on cable and satellite news channels has become routine and some channels are devoted primarily to court coverage. Among the trials broadcast live on network and cable television have been those of Casey Anthony (acquitted of killing her young daughter) and O.J. Simpson (found not guilty of killing his former wife and an acquaintance). In fact, the presence of cameras in the courtroom has become fairly common, especially in the more sensational trials.

Susan Smith: A Case Study

Perhaps nowhere are the ongoing tensions between the courts and the mass media demonstrated more dramatically than in the events surrounding Susan Smith, a 22-year-old South Carolina mother charged with the drowning deaths of her two young sons. Although the murder of children by a parent is not considered as newsworthy in America as it once was, the events surrounding the Smith case—including Smith's story that her children had been abducted by an African-American man, her tearful requests that her children be returned broadcast on network television, and then the startling revelation that all of this was a lie and that she herself had steered her automobile into a lake near her home with her two children strapped in their car seats—ensured that the subsequent proceedings to determine her fate (there was no doubt of her guilt) would be a major media event.

Recognizing the high probability of possible pre-trial publicity (although Smith's hometown, Union, S.C., has a population of about 10,000, a total of only 40,000 people live in all of Union County), police initially were extremely cautious about giving out information during their investigations but eventually did release the news that Smith had confessed to the crimes and permitted the news media to view the crime scene.

While all this was transpiring, the pre-trial proceedings, including evidence hearings and jury selection, were moving forward. And so were the preparations for covering the trial by the major television networks, syndicated tabloid news programs and local and regional television stations from Charlotte, N.C., to Atlanta. As the trial date neared, the broadcast media commandeered much of the rental property in the town to house its personnel, built a fortress-like system of makeshift broadcasting booths on risers stretching the length of one city block in front of the Union County courthouse, and incessantly interviewed Union residents brave enough to venture downtown about their opinions of the possible penalty Susan Smith should face.

Perhaps this build-up of media presence caused a last-minute decision by the trial judge to grant the Susan Smith defense team's request to ban all electronic and photographic equipment from the courtroom, despite the fact that extensive modifications of the courtroom requested by the judge to facilitate the electronic media had already been completed. The judge cited the possible reluctance of witnesses to testify truthfully if their testimony were shown on television as the principal reason for his decision. It is fair to speculate, however, given that everyone in the small town would almost immediately be aware of such testimony, that the judge was more concerned with losing control of the proceedings and risk becoming another Judge Lance Ito (the trial judge in the O.J. Simpson case, criticized for his performance and satirized on widely viewed late-night television shows).

Because in South Carolina, the admittance of electronic media and photographic cameras in the courtroom is left to the discretion of a trial judge, the judge's exclusion of electronic media in this case could not be appealed. As a result, the reporting of the trial was left entirely to print media and to the broadcasts of renderings by courtroom artists.

Although the memory of the O.J. Simpson murder trial has long faded (not to mention the subsequent cases involving Kobe Bryant, Michael Jackson and Martha Stewart), courts and legal commentators continue to regard requests to broadcast criminal proceedings and expansive interpretations of journalist privilege with suspicion. The negative media-related results of the Susan Smith trial should serve as a sobering reminder of the fragile nature of the free-speech protections for journalists when they seek access to courtrooms to report on the criminal or civil law processes.

Reporter's Privilege

Journalists, especially investigative reporters, routinely uncover or encounter information from tipsters and other sources about criminal activities or malfeasance in office by public officials. Often, these sources are willing to provide information to journalists on the condition that the reporters do not reveal their names or other identifying information because they fear retaliation in the workplace or physical harm to themselves or their families or, in some cases, concern that they may find themselves in trouble with the law.

Not surprisingly, members of law enforcement and the judiciary not infrequently express interest not only in this information but also in who supplied it to the journalists. This has led to numerous high-profile scenarios over the decades in which judges have attempted (often successfully) to force journalists to disclose the identities of their sources and other confidential information under threat of civil contempt punishable by fines or jail time. Such cases have created a demand by many journalists and their organizations for the creation of a "reporter's privilege" to withhold information demanded by a court, grand jury or government commission or committee. The recognition of such a privilege would permit a reporter to refuse to disclose information an average citizen normally would be obliged to surrender when called upon to do so by members of law enforcement and the judiciary.

Privilege and the Search for Truth

Being granted a privilege in the law usually means that the person accorded the privilege is permitted to engage in an activity or excused from following normal legal rules except under certain specific instances or, more rarely, excused from complying with such requirements in all circumstances. The granting of such a privilege when it comes to withholding information requested by a legally constituted authority is especially controversial because it flies in the face of the bedrock principle that in the American legal system, every person who possesses information that could assist in the administration of justice must come forward and provide that information if required by law. Courts, grand juries and other investigative government bodies could hardly function if people were free to flout this principle. Failure to provide such information, or to do so untruthfully, usually constitutes a serious criminal offense.

Because acquiring the most accurate and comprehensive information possible is so vital to the administration of justice, and because those who wish to exert a privilege not to provide testimonial evidence often possess information that would materially aid the search for truth, it is no surprise that the rule has developed that *"all privileges of exemption from this duty* [to testify] *are exceptional* and are therefore to be discountenanced."[56]

Yet some privileges do exist. The privilege to not provide information that could lead to self-incrimination is recognized as a fundamental liberty and enshrined in the provisions of the Fifth Amendment to the federal Constitution. Additionally, reaching far back into our antecedents in the English legal system, American common law today continues to recognize that privileged communications exist in the interactions between husband and wife; attorney and client; physician and patient; and priest (or other member of the clergy) and penitent.

Although the extent and nature of each of these privileged situations varies, if the relationships satisfy the definitions specified by law, the confidences shared in these relationships remain privileged and may not be subjected to judicial or investigative scrutiny. Each of these privileged relationships is based on a societal view that says we consider that other values (e.g., family harmony, the ablest legal representation or the health of the body and the soul) are of more importance than acquisition of the information that could be obtained by revealing the confidences shared in each of these relationships.

We should not lose sight, however, of the tremendous assistance obtaining such information would provide to those charged with ascertaining truth and administering justice. That's why many jurists and legislators resist creating any new privileges in the law to protect the confidences shared in other relationships. Journalists are by no means alone in requesting that privilege be extended to them. Spiritual advisers, school counselors, social workers and individuals in a wide variety of other occupations and professions advance similar arguments. Faced with these demands, it should come as little surprise that courts and legislatures show marked reluctance to opening the door even slightly to recognize additional privileges beyond those long recognized by the Constitution or the common law.

Journalists face other formidable obstacles in obtaining widespread acceptance of a privilege to protect their sources of information. Although credentialing or accrediting procedures often serve to officially designate those eligible to practice in specific professions or occupations, no such procedures exist to certify who is and who is not a journalist. In fact, most journalists actively resist the notion of any such licensing scheme, arguing that such a system would be a violation of the First Amendment. Extending privilege to journalists, therefore, presents difficult definitional problems. Such issues often arise when a journalist privilege is asserted by such individuals as a freelance writer, an academic preparing a scholarly manuscript, a documentary filmmaker or a blogger.

Another problem relates to the rationale usually advanced for protecting those relationships already recognized by the law. The extension of privilege in such situations generally protects the nonprofessional party in the relationship. For example, the confidentiality of the relationship between an attorney and client is meant to ensure that a client may speak openly and candidly to a legal representative without fear that the attorney subsequently will be forced to reveal these confidences. A privileged situation normally comes into existence the moment the professional nature of the relationship is established, as opposed, for example, to a casual conversation at a social gathering. If, however, clients do not object to revealing the contents of a privileged conversation, attorneys normally will not be exempted from providing information to a court or other legal body by claiming their own privilege.

Those in favor of recognition of a journalist privilege suggest that, unlike other relationships, the privilege should protect the journalist (e.g., the professional) and not the source. According to this argument, journalists should be able to make the decision as to whether a privileged situation exists, the nature and extent of the privilege and whether to withhold information or reveal it, at times irrespective of the wishes of the source.

Another problem with the recognition of a journalist privilege is the skepticism of many jurists and others in the legal community about the need for such a privilege. These critics argue that promises of confidentiality may be too easily given and there is little hard evidence that the flow of important information to the public would be seriously lessened if sources, instead of talking to journalists about wrongdoing, simply reported it to the proper authorities.

Additionally, because the shielding of sources often prevents law enforcement officials from identifying individuals who themselves have committed an illegal or unethical act, many in the legal community worry about a privilege that permits journalists to rise above the law by ignoring their civic responsibility to immediately report criminal activity or malfeasance in office. As Justice Byron White noted in the seminal Supreme Court decision in this area, "[W]e cannot seriously entertain the notion that [a privilege should exist] on the theory that it is better to write about crime than to do something about it,"[57] including providing timely information to investigators or courts.

Practical Reasons for Recognition of a Journalist Privilege

The arguments for granting a journalist the privilege to withhold information from government authorities are based both on the practical difficulties faced by a reporter in gathering information without such legal protection and the possibility that, in the absence of such a journalist's privilege, information with important implications for public policy might never reach the public.

In an era of serious eroding of public trust in government and business, it should come as no surprise that, for reasons ranging from the honorable to the most mean-spirited self-interest, many individuals with information about perceived wrongdoing or malfeasance in office are reluctant to reveal that information to government authorities. Whether they fear retaliation on the job, physical harm to themselves or their families, prosecution for criminal activity or just unwanted involvement in an uncomfortable situation, people "in the know" often will not complain or publicly blow the whistle. They may confide in a journalist, however, with the idea that the journalist, in making the information public, can set the wheels of reform in motion. Often the price of that information is a promise by the reporter never to reveal anything that could lead to the source of the information.

The ability and legal right of the reporter to make and keep such a pledge of confidentiality is an important weapon in the arsenal of journalists to ensure the news media effectively fulfill their function as a community watchdog. That important societal role would be made much more difficult if a journalist were forced to reveal the source of the information. Not only would the journalist lose an important and reliable informant in the current as well as in subsequent investigations (and bear the moral responsibility of possibly placing that source in jeopardy), but it is likely that other potential sources would be reluctant to divulge information to the news media if they believed their confidences also might be disclosed. Additionally, journalists argue, the watchdog role of the news media could be subverted by turning reporters into de facto agents of the government by routinely subpoenaing journalists to appear before legislative or judicial bodies and forcing them to reveal with whom they had spoken and the subject matter of such conversations.

An issue of even greater concern is the harm caused by the failure of the reporter to acquire the information, and thus never place it before the public, when confidences cannot be kept between reporter and source. Although it is true the reporter's job becomes more difficult if confidential sources are afraid or unwilling to provide information without a guarantee of confidentiality, the fact remains that journalists still will be able to produce a product at the end of the day, albeit perhaps an inferior one. For that reason, many supporters of a journalist privilege argue the public is the most important beneficiary of the recognition of such a privilege.

This argument is buttressed by the numerous instances of wrongdoing that have come to light only through the collaborative efforts between confidential sources and investigative reporters. Examples range from the Watergate investigations of the early 1970s that eventually resulted in the resignation of President Richard M. Nixon to frequent revelations of illegal or unethical behavior by state and federal legislators and other government officials throughout the country. Even college and professional sports are not immune from charges of fraud and corruption. For example, it was disclosures about the possible use of steroids by professional baseball players in 2005 that led to congressional hearings and a crackdown on performance-enhancing drug use by Major League Baseball.

Legal Arguments for Granting Journalist Privilege

Many supporters of a privilege for journalists not to testify in legal proceedings ground their advocacy in the language of the First Amendment. Although admitting that requiring journalists to provide information to legal authorities is not a direct, content-based "abridgment" of speech, these advocates argue that the inhibition of sources, the threat to journalist integrity and the resulting restriction on the free flow of information of importance to the public raise significant First Amendment issues.

The idea that journalists should be granted a legal privilege to withhold information gained popular support within the news media community by the late 1960s. Several states passed so-called shield laws recognizing a journalist privilege. Many of these laws then became the subject of court challenges when judges and grand juries, nonetheless, ordered reporters to reveal sources or face punishment for contempt. In many of these cases, as well as in cases in the federal courts, reporters argued that in addition to any statutory protection, the First Amendment should be construed as conferring constitutional protection. It was only a matter of time before the Supreme Court was asked to determine the extent, if any, of a First Amendment-based journalist privilege.

The opportunity presented itself in *Branzburg v. Hayes* (1972),[58] a consolidated appeal of three cases involving reporter privilege, two from state supreme courts and one from the federal Court of Appeals for the Ninth Circuit. In the lead case, the facts involved Branzburg, a reporter for the *Louisville (Ky.) Courier Journal*, who, while working on a story about local drug dealing, promised confidentiality to informants whom he had observed and photographed synthesizing hashish from marijuana. Subpoenaed by a county grand jury investigating illegal drug sales, Branzburg refused to reveal the names of the persons he had observed. A second story resulted in another subpoena, but this time the reporter refused to appear before the grand jury at all. In each instance, Branzburg's attorneys, in addition to the practical arguments in favor of recognizing a privilege for journalists, argued that there were three legal bases why the reporter should not be forced to testify: the federal First Amendment, Kentucky's state constitutional protections of speech and the state's shield law.

Ultimately, the Kentucky Supreme Court rejected all of these arguments, holding that the First Amendment did not provide a federal constitutional shield and that nothing in the state constitution could be construed as creating a privilege for journalists. The Kentucky court further held that Kentucky's shield law provided "a newsman the privilege of refusing to divulge the identity of an informant"[59] but added that "the statute did not permit a reporter to refuse to testify about events [the reporter] had observed personally."[60] Branzburg then took his appeal to the Supreme Court of the United States.

The second case in the *Branzburg* trilogy, *In re Pappas*, involved a reporter working for a New Bedford, Massachusetts, television station. Pappas was permitted to enter and report from inside the local headquarters of the radical Black Panthers group during a period of social unrest on the condition that he not "disclose anything he saw or heard inside ... except an anticipated police raid."[61] The raid never materialized, and Pappas never prepared a story. Nonetheless, a county grand jury summoned him to appear and to tell all he had learned by being inside the headquarters. Pappas refused, citing both the state and federal constitutional protections of speech. (Massachusetts had no shield law.)

On appeal, the Supreme Judicial Court of Massachusetts upheld a lower court's decision ordering the requested information be provided, noting that a privilege to avoid testifying in Massachusetts was "limited" and that "[t]he principle that the public 'has a right to every man's evidence'" was the general rule recognized by the state.[62] The state high court also concluded that the federal Constitution provided no privilege to avoid testifying in such circumstances. Like Branzburg, Pappas appealed this latter ruling to the Supreme Court.

U.S. v. Caldwell, the third of the three cases in the consolidated appeal, involved a reporter for *The New York Times* who also was covering the activities of radical groups, including the Black Panthers. A federal grand jury in California, investigating the causes of recent civil unrest in that state, subpoenaed Caldwell, ordering him to appear and bring with him "notes and tape recordings of interviews ... reflecting statements made for publication by officers and spokesmen for the Black Panther Party."[63] Caldwell refused, citing the First Amendment.

A federal district court then ordered the reporter to be jailed for contempt of court, but the Ninth Circuit reversed that decision, holding that the First Amendment did, in fact, provide at least a qualified constitutional privilege for news gathering. Faced with state court decisions denying the existence of a First Amendment-based journalist privilege in Kentucky and Massachusetts and a federal appeals court holding to the contrary in the states covered by the federal Ninth Circuit, the Supreme Court combined the three cases for consideration of the issue.

Those hoping that the Court's decision in *Branzburg* would provide a definitive answer as to whether the First Amendment provides a privilege for journalists were to be disappointed. In a divided opinion, the Court upheld the orders directed against the three journalists but, at the same time, appeared to hold that there was at least some First Amendment-based protection for reporters to protect their sources from forced disclosure.

Justice White, in an opinion joined by Chief Justice Burger and Justices Blackmun and Rehnquist, strongly rejected the notion of constitutional privilege. "[T]hese cases involve no intrusions upon speech ... no prior restraint or restriction on what the press may publish, and no express or implied command that the press publish what it prefers to withhold."[64] "The sole issue before us," said Justice White, "is the obligation of reporters to respond to grand jury subpoenas as other citizens do and to answer questions relevant to an investigation into the commission of crime."[65] Justice White added that

> [u]ntil now, the only testimonial privilege for unofficial witnesses ... in the Federal Constitution is the Fifth Amendment privilege against compelled self-incrimination. We are asked to create another by interpreting the First Amendment to grant newsmen a testimonial privilege that other citizens do not enjoy. This we decline to do.[66]

In contrast to the opinion authored by Justice White, Justice Stewart, writing for two other justices (Justice Douglas filed his own dissenting opinion), argued that the reasons for a constitutional privilege were compelling enough to warrant recognizing a privilege to protect journalists and their sources in most circumstances. Such a privilege was qualified, however, meaning that it could be overcome if (1) a court or other government agency seeking to compel the reporter's testimony could demonstrate the information sought was highly relevant, (2) the information could be obtained from no other source and (3) the information was essential to a substantial government interest (often referred to as the *Branzburg* three-part test). Unless the government can show such evidence, said Justice Stewart, a journalist has a First Amendment privilege to refuse to testify.

With four justices in *Branzburg* firmly committed to the position that the First Amendment does not provide a privilege for journalists and four others just as convinced that it does, all eyes turned to the swing vote of Justice Lewis F. Powell, Jr. Unfortunately for those seeking a decision that would settle this issue once and for all, Justice Powell contributed an opinion that seemed to come down squarely in the middle. He concurred with Justice White's opinion that a First Amendment-based privilege would be inapplicable in cases like those on appeal in which the journalists had actually witnessed criminal activity. On the other hand, Justice Powell seemed to find at least some constitutional basis for according journalists privilege in other (unspecified) situations, noting that "[t]his Court does not hold that newsmen ... are without constitutional rights with respect to the gathering of news or in safeguarding their sources."[67]

The upshot of Justice Powell's enigmatic opinion is that today those who argue the First Amendment provides no privilege for journalists cite *Branzburg* as authority for their position, and those who argue that indeed there is such constitutional protection also cite *Branzburg* as upholding their view. Lower federal and state courts have been confused when encountering such arguments and, predictably, some have recognized a First Amendment privilege, whereas others have not. The majority of courts that have recognized some form of journalist privilege usually have adopted the *Branzburg* minority's three-prong test, often applying it in a way that results in the journalist having to testify.

In a subsequent case with serious ramifications for journalists (and of interest to public relations practitioners as well), the Supreme Court upheld a breach of contract-like claim by a source against a Minnesota newspaper that revealed the man's identity after promising him it would not do so. That case, *Cohen v. Cowles Media Co.* (1991),[68] would appear to place journalists who promise confidentiality in the unfortunate position of facing contempt of court citations, involving possible jail terms and/or fines, if they do not reveal information when called to testify, and the possibility of payment of substantial money damages to the now-named aggrieved source if they do.

Even those who are strong supporters of the general concept of a reporter privilege by no means unanimously support a First Amendment rationale as the basis for a privilege. Those who object to a constitutionally based privilege argue such a position requires an interpretation of the First Amendment to provide one level of constitutional protection for "typical" individuals and a second, higher level for "journalists," a position these critics find untenable.

Those in favor of a journalist privilege, but who reject a First Amendment-based rationale, generally instead opt for achieving their objective by statutory means, urging legislatures to pass so-called shield laws. Some 40 states and the District of Columbia have already passed such laws, but their protection varies considerably. Most create a *Branzburg*-like, qualified privilege that provides protection for reporters under most circumstances, but can be overcome if a government body seeking information from the reporter can justify its request by meeting the requirements established in the statute.

Applying the Privilege

With so many news outlets soliciting and posting anonymous, often unedited reader opinions, serious issues can arise regarding the legal ability to protect the outlets from this anonymous commentary, especially from potential lawsuits by the targets of the commentaries who claim they have been libeled or suffered an invasion of their privacy or other similar grievance.

Because the Communications Decency Act (see Chapter 13) generally protects the sponsor of the website, the original poster of the message may be the only target available to outraged potential plaintiffs. One may imagine their increased anger upon finding that the website is attempting to exert a privilege to protect the anonymity of the sources of the comments, which, in effect, bars the potential plaintiffs from suing at all. Courts in different states have employed a range of different rationales in determining if potential plaintiffs will be able to discover the sources of anonymous comments. How other lower courts and, perhaps, ultimately the U.S. Supreme Court will deal with this issue will be interesting, particularly for public relations professionals looking to engage in reputation management for an organization damaged by such anonymous speakers.

A major emerging issue in journalist privilege is the potential passage of a federal shield law. Bills creating a reporter privilege at the federal level have been discussed over the years in both the U.S. House of Representatives and the Senate, and professional media organizations such as the Society of Professional Journalists and the Reporters Committee for Freedom of the Press have lobbied long and hard for such a statute. One of the more promising but, so far, unsuccessful efforts is the proposed Free Flow of Information Act of 2013, which has been introduced in both the House and the Senate with co-sponsors from both major political parties. Former President Barack Obama promised to sign such a bill into law should it make its way out of the Congress, but his term ended before any bill reached his desk.

Even with relatively strong bipartisan support in Congress for some form of a federal shield statute during President Donald J. Trump's administration, however, the prospects of passage have likely dimmed. As a President who frequently tangles with the press in highly contentious fashion, it appears highly unlikely he would sign such a bill if presented to him.

Other privilege issues that continue to pop up from time to time involve (a) subpoenas directed at broadcast "outtakes," (b) how thorough a court or other government entity must be in exhausting all other avenues to obtain information before establishing that the reporter is

Figure 12.4 Bills creating a reporter privilege at the federal level have been discussed over the years in both the U.S. House of Representatives and the Senate, with relatively strong bipartisan support for some form of a federal shield statute. The prospects of passage seem to come and go with each new administration, including that of President Donald J. Trump, shown here at a 2018 press conference.

Credit line: Nicole S. Glass/Shutterstock.com

the sole source, and (c) the remedies legally available to a court if privilege is asserted by the journalist in a libel trial to protect the source of the allegedly libelous statements.

Conclusion

Public relations professionals dealing with the news media in situations in which they request that the information provided is on a confidential basis should be aware that despite a pledge of secrecy, a journalist may be placed under tremendous pressure to reveal the source of the information. The prudent public relations professional, therefore, would be well advised not to provide confidential information to the news media if such provision is conditioned on a promise that the journalist will not reveal the source.

Notes

1. Pell v. Procunier, 417 U.S. 817 (1974).
2. Saxbe v. Wash. Post Co., 417 U.S. 843 (1974).
3. 5 U.S.C. §552 (2019).
4. *Id*. §552a (2019).
5. *Id*. §552a (1974).
6. *Id*. §552(f)(1) (2019).
7. *Id*. §552(f)(A)-(B) (2019).
8. *Id*. §552(a)(2)(A)-(E) (2019).

9.   *Id*. §552(a)(1)(B)(1) (2019).
10. U.S.C. §552(a)(1)(B)(4) (2019).
11. Chrysler Corp. v. Brown, 441 U.S. 281 (1979).
12. U.S.C. §552(a)(1)(B)(5) (2019).
13. United States Dep't of State v. Wash. Post Co., 456 U.S. 595 (1982).
14. New York Times Co. v. National Aeronautics & Space Admin., 287 U.S. App. D.C. 208 (D.C. Cir. 1990).
15. *Id*. at 25.
16. Hilary Niles, *Learn to Overcome Record Request Hurdles*, QUILL, Sept./Oct. 2017, at 29.
17. *Id*.
18. 5 U.S.C. §552b.
19. Sheppard v. Maxwell, 384 U.S. 333 (1966).
20. *Id*.
21. Nebraska Press Assn. v. Stuart, 427 U.S. 539, 553 (1976); quoting Sheppard v. Maxwell, 384 U.S. 333, 363 (1966).
22. *Id*. at 542.
23. *Id*.
24. *Id*. at 543.
25. *Id*. at 547.
26. *Id*. at 548.
27. *Id*. at 555.
28. *Id*. at 561.
29. *Id*.
30. *Id*. at 565.
31. *Id*. at 568.
32. Gannett Co. v. DePasquale, 443 U.S. 368 (1979).
33. *Id*. at 375.
34. *Id*. at 376.
35. *Id*. at 393.
36. Richmond Newspapers v. Va., 448 U.S. 555 (1980).
37. *Id*. at 560.
38. *Id*. at 564.
39. *Id*. at 573.
40. *Id*. at 576; quoting First Nat'l Bank of Boston v. Bellotti, 435 U.S. 765, 783 (1978).
41. *Id*. at 577.
42. *Id*. at 580; quoting Branzburg v. Hayes, 408 U.S. 664, 681 (1972).
43. Globe Newspaper Co. v. Superior Court, 457 U.S. 596 (1982).
44. Press-Enterprise Co. v. Superior Court of California, 464 U.S. 501 (1984).
45. Press-Enterprise Co. v. Superior Court, 478 U.S. 1 (1986).
46. *Id*. at 4.
47. *Id*. at 7.
48. *Id*. at 8.
49. *Id*.
50. *Id*. at 10.
51. *Id*.
52. *Id*. at 11.
53. *Id*. at 12.
54. *Id*.
55. Chandler v. Fla., 449 U.S. 560 (1981).
56. COMMUNICATIONS LAW (Vol. 3 1994) at 429.

57. Branzburg v. Hayes, 408 U.S. 664, 690 note 29 (1972) (quoting B. J. Wɪɢᴍᴏʀᴇ, Eᴠɪᴅᴇɴᴄᴇ (McNaughton rev. ed.), 1961, §2192, at 73).

58. Branzburg v. Hayes, at 692.

59. The case consolidated Branzburg with In re Pappas and U.S. v. Caldwell.

60. *Id.* at 669; quoting Branzburg v. Pound, 461 S.W.2d 345 (1970).

61. *Id.*

62. *Id.* at 672.

63. *Id.* at 674; quoting In re Pappas, 266 N.D.2d 297, 299, 358 Mass. 604, 607 (1971).

64. *Id.* at 681.

65. *Id.* at 682.

66. *Id.* at 689-690.

67. *Id.* at 709.

68. Cohen v. Cowles Media Co., 501 U.S. 663 (1991).

13 The Internet and Advertising and Public Relations Speech

This chapter provides an overview of Internet-related laws, some that have been mentioned briefly in previous chapters, that most directly impact the practice of advertising and public relations. It discusses how existing laws have been applied to accommodate technological innovation and summarizes new laws and regulatory schemes created to address issues presented by online communications.

The Internet has evolved into a global information infrastructure with far-reaching implications for business and commercial speech. Regulating the Internet and its use is difficult because it is a sprawling, decentralized mass of computers and networks. Further complicating matters, those computers and networks are originated and maintained by a variety of private and public entities and governmental institutions around the world. As one court has said,

> [N]o single entity—academic, corporate, governmental, or non-profit—administers the Internet. ... There is no centralized storage location, control point, or communications channel for the Internet, and it would not be technically feasible for a single entity to control all of the information conveyed on the Internet.[1]

The body of law that applies to the Internet and its larger environment (the World Wide Web) is sometimes called "cyberspace law," but cyberspace law does not operate in isolation; laws that apply to communications in other contexts generally apply to communications that rely on cyberspace. In some areas, however, the world of online communications has exerted pressure on established law, resulting in special rules for the Internet. For example, the tort of defamation (see Chapter 4) is defamation, whether it is published online or in a traditional print newspaper. But the realities of how people use the Internet prompted Congress to pass special laws that impact who may be successfully sued for defamation based on online postings.

The notion that the Internet may warrant special regulation has produced a special designation: "Internet exceptionalism." As Professor Eric Goldman notes, "Internet exceptionalism can cut both ways—we could give legal preferences to Internet actors ... or we could burden Internet actors more than other media actors." As this chapter illustrates, Internet-specific regulation does both, but for different reasons at different times.

The Internet and Jurisdiction

When online activity inspires some kind of legal action, a necessary first question is, Which court or enforcement authority has jurisdiction over the case? Professional communicators should be aware of the concept of jurisdiction because, in some cases, websites, e-commerce

Figure 13.1 The Internet has evolved into a global information infrastructure with far-reaching implications for business and commercial speech.

Credit line: James Teohart/Shutterstock.com

and other communications with customers or clients in other states can require an organization to defend itself in court in those other states.

For litigation purposes, jurisdiction over an individual or entity (such as an agency or corporation) may be established in one of several ways. The most common is through residency or domicile; for organizations, this is satisfied by having a place of business in a particular state. Another way is for an entity to agree to be subject to legal action in a particular state, perhaps upon the signing of a contract or other agreement. Jurisdiction over a defendant also may be established when the defendant has sufficient "minimum contacts" within the forum state where the litigation is being brought, and the legal action has something to do with those contacts. The "minimum contacts" requirement means that the defendant has "purposely availed" itself of the state's offerings by conducting activities there that "invoke[e] the benefits and protections of its laws."[2] An additional requirement is that the nature of the defendant's contacts be such that it would be reasonable to anticipate "being haled into court" there.[3]

Early in the development of the Internet as a place for businesses to interact with consumers, courts were asked to determine if the operation of a website equated to the kind of activity needed to produce the minimum contacts needed for jurisdiction. In *Zippo Manufacturing Co. v. Zippo Dot Com*,[4] a federal district court said the exercise of jurisdiction over a defendant should be evaluated in terms of a relative scale that measures commercial interactivity through the defendant's website. The *Zippo* court held that personal jurisdiction exists where a defendant is (1) clearly doing business through its website in the forum state (that is, the state where the lawsuit was filed) and (2) the legal claim is related or connected to the use of the website. Such commercial interactivity, according to the court, reflects the kind of specific, intended interaction with residents of the forum state to merit jurisdiction there.[5] It should be noted that simply operating a website that is visible to potential consumers in a particular geographic area is likely not enough; some kind of specific action establishing commercial interactivity must be present. This might include activity such as the processing of applications or the assignment of customer passwords. Other courts have described the necessary element for jurisdiction as the "manifested intent of engaging in business or other interactions within the State."[6]

Use of the Internet also may establish personal jurisdiction when the effects of the online communications produce harm of the type that might cause a plaintiff to sue for defamation or invasion of privacy or one of the other torts discussed earlier in this book. Courts considering this type of jurisdiction have used an "effects test" that gauges the harm caused to the plaintiff in the state where the lawsuit is brought, even if the defendant has not agreed to be sued there or engaged in sufficient minimum contacts. A prominent example of the "effects test" involved a lawsuit filed in California by Shirley Jones, a California-based actress and resident, against a Florida publication. The ruling was that intentional tortious actions (in this case allegedly defamatory statements that caused harm within California entertainment circles) that were aimed at the forum state (in this case California) gave rise to personal jurisdiction.[7] As with the minimum contacts requirement discussed above, simply posting defamatory content about someone on the Internet is likely not sufficient to establish personal jurisdiction in the state where the lawsuit is filed; it will need to be shown that the defendant was intentionally aiming the remarks at the forum state and not just the resident plaintiff.[8]

Defamation Online

The concepts of "publication" and "republication" in traditional defamation law (discussed in Chapter 4) are well established: one who originates a libel is responsible for any ensuing reputational harm, as is one who chooses to "republish" the defamatory content, even though it originated elsewhere. When the defamation is disseminated online, however, special republication rules apply, thanks to Section 230 of the Communications Decency Act[9] (CDA), which became law in 1996. In the traditional media context, the classic example of a defamatory "letter to the editor" published by a newspaper illustrates republication. In such a case, the letter writer is the originator of the libel and publishes it to the newspaper when it is submitted for potential inclusion in the printed edition. The newspaper, if it decides to print the letter, then republishes the defamation when the letter appears on its pages. In the print arena, both the author of the letter and the newspaper that made a decision to publish it are potentially liable for any reputational harm that may have inspired the letter's subject to file a lawsuit.

If, however, the defamatory statements about the plaintiff appear online, the potential liability shifts from the publisher and is focused only on the one who posted the commentary. Suppose an organization hosts a website in which it publishes a variety of content, including posts contributed by readers who are invited to comment upon certain subjects. Section 230 (c)(1) of the CDA says, "No *provider or user* of an interactive computer service shall be treated as the publisher or speaker of any information provided by another information content provider."[10] This language provides that the website's sponsor is not liable for any defamatory comments posted there by users of the site. The protection remains in place even if the sponsor undertakes some editorial control by attempting to screen user comments prior to their being posted. The impact of Section 230 (c)(1) is significant: it means that operators of websites and other *providers* of online services are generally not liable for content posted by third parties. It also protects *users* of interactive computer services, like YouTube or Facebook, from liability for sharing content posted by others. Posting a defamatory statement to Facebook, for example, may result in liability for the one who posted the harmful message, but typically not for Facebook or for its users who "like" or share the defamation with others. This statement about *user* immunity comes with a caveat, however: some courts may regard "retweets" to be legally actionable if the retweet contains added information provided by the retweeter and not simply the original post. This area of republication law is unsettled and should give likers, retweeters and sharers of defamatory social media posts some pause.

For organizations seeking to establish a dynamic online presence that invites customer interaction, Section 230's protections provide a welcome cloak of immunity from liability for user-provided content. On the other hand, if it is your organization's reputation—or perhaps a client's reputation—at issue, the other side of the Section 230 coin is that it limits the number of potential defendants who may be held responsible, even though multiple online voices may have been involved in amplifying the harm. And because many online comments are posted anonymously, the potential challenge of identifying the original poster enhances the degree of difficulty involved in bringing the litigation at all. Many interactive service providers have adopted policies against disclosing user-identifying information to third parties, particularly when that disclosure is likely to result in their users being named in a lawsuit or other legal proceeding.

Although libel plaintiffs may obtain court orders requiring service providers to provide user-identifying information, courts tend to require those plaintiffs to first demonstrate that their lawsuit has merit. As a practical matter, these limitations may make defamation plaintiffs reluctant to file lawsuits over online content. In particular, public relations professionals who work with interactive service providers should contribute to their organizations' policies regarding the unmasking of users. When the sullied reputation is that of your organization or client, it is advisable to consider whether the potential reward of a successful lawsuit outweighs the time, expense and hassle associated with unmasking and suing the poster for defamation.

An additional way that online publication has impacted defamation actions has to do with content that was originally offered in print form but later finds its way onto a website or online archive. The statutes of limitations for defamation lawsuits vary from state to state, but most, along with courts considering these cases, have adopted the position that the clock for filing a lawsuit begins to tick on the day of the original publication, even for content posted on the Internet that is accessible even many years later. These states recognize a "single publication" rule in which any later dissemination is tied to the original and considered a single publication for purposes of the statute of limitations. Liability for republication online is still a possibility, however. If the defamatory statements are repackaged or republished in a new form or new edition that substantially changes or modifies their presentation from its original state, the statute-of-limitations clock may begin to tick all over again.

Online Content and Copyright Law

Think about how online services like YouTube work. Can you imagine how cumbersome it would be, and how different YouTube would be, if YouTube were potentially liable for copyright infringement every time a user posted copyrighted video or other content without first obtaining permission from the copyright owner? Recognizing the unique nature of certain online services, Congress passed the Digital Millennium Copyright Act[11] (DMCA) in 1998. Just as the Communications Decency Act protects online service providers from liability for the defamatory postings of their users, the DMCA limits liability for copyright infringement by third parties if certain conditions are met. To qualify for this protection, an entity must meet the definition of "service provider" as defined in the statute: "A provider of online services or network access, or the operator of facilities therefor."[12] Under Section 512(c) of the DMCA, service providers are protected from liability for infringing material on their websites placed there at the direction of a user. To be eligible for this protection, the following is required:

- The provider must not have the requisite level of knowledge of the infringing activity. This means the service provider may not have actual knowledge of the infringement, or be aware of facts or circumstances from which infringing activity is apparent. Moreover, if the service provider becomes aware of apparent infringing activity, it must move quickly to take the material down or block access to it.
- If the provider has the right and ability to control the infringing activity, it must not receive a financial benefit directly attributable to the infringing activity.
- Upon receiving proper notification of claimed infringement, the provider must expeditiously take down or block access to the material.[13]

The law also requires a service provider to designate an agent, whose name is kept on file with the United States Copyright Office, to receive notification of claimed infringement on the service provider's site. A form for designating an agent and a list of registered agents is available through the Copyright Office via www.copyright.gov.

If properly followed, the "notice and takedown" procedure outlined in Section 512(c) prevents service providers from monetary liability for copyright infringement; it also prevents the poster from seeking to hold the service provider liable for having erroneously removed his or her posted content from the service. Additional rules apply as well. For example, it is a violation for a party to falsely claim that posted material is infringing. The upshot of the DMCA is that service providers who become aware, because of a good faith notification, of material posted to their sites that may violate copyright laws are protected as long as they follow the procedures set forth in the DMCA.

Trademarks and Cyberspace

Organizations that make use of cyberspace to communicate or do business with customers no doubt appreciate the value of Internet domain names that are readily associated with them. Like trademarks and service marks (discussed in Chapter 8), which enable consumers to identify the sources of goods and services in the marketplace, relatable domain names tend to make it easier for consumers to locate organizations online. Not surprisingly, entities (e.g., Pepsico, Inc.) with established trademarks (e.g., Pepsi) typically seek to register Internet domain names that feature those trademarks (e.g., www.pepsi.com) to identify websites where information about the trademarked goods may be found. Equally unsurprising is the tendency for entrepreneurial individuals to try and register popular, or even potentially popular, trademarks as domain names before the trademark owner may do so. As mentioned in Chapter 8, this practice of "cybersquatting" on domain names featuring trademarks in order to later sell them for a profit prompted Congress to enact legislation aimed at this practice. The Anticybersquatting Consumer Protection Act[14] (ACPA), passed in 1999, states that an owner of a distinctive trademark or service mark may seek to hold a person liable via civil action for the "bad faith intent to profit from that mark."[15] This Act may be implicated by "registering, trafficking in, or using a domain name" that is "identical or confusingly similar" to a mark that is distinctive at the time the domain name is registered.[16] The "bad faith" part of the law features nine factors for courts to possibly consider in determining the presence of bad faith in a domain name registration. Among these are an intent to divert consumers from the mark owner's online location; an offer to transfer, sell or otherwise assign an unused domain name to the mark owner for financial gain; and the providing of false contact information when applying for the registration of a domain name.[17]

Registering domain names featuring others' *famous* marks carries additional risk; owners of famous marks may use the ACPA to file civil lawsuits addressing domain names whose use might dilute the good will associated with the famous mark or that have the effect of diminishing a mark's distinctiveness. Dilution may occur even when the unauthorized use of the mark is not identical or confusingly similar to the famous mark. An example of trademark dilution involving a famous mark under the ACPA was the registration of the domain name www.fordrecalls.com by an individual selling pornographic material. According to the United States District Court for the Eastern District of Michigan, "There is not dispute that Ford is a famous name and a strong mark." It noted that courts have "uniformly held, and this court agrees, that the use of a famous trademark in a domain name used to purvey pornography constitutes dilution."[18] Such "tarnishes the goodwill developed by a trademark holder by causing it to become associated with pornographic material that is fundamentally inconsistent with the otherwise wholesome ... nature of the mark."[19] In this case, the court concluded Ford was likely to win its dilution claim, even though visitors to the naughty site were not likely to confuse it for something sponsored by the automobile manufacturer.

Not all unauthorized (and undesirable) domain name registrations are actionable under the ACPA. There are numerous examples of websites (sometimes called "gripe sites" or "suck sites") launched by disgruntled individuals or entities whose content is critical of certain trademark owners and whose domain names include identifiable marks. Courts have been reluctant to punish purveyors of these websites where it is clear that the website is unaffiliated with the trademark owner and the trademark-containing domain name is not used in association with goods or services in the commercial marketplace. Such critical expression aimed at a trademark owner may be protected as a fair use of a trademark or service mark and curtailing it likely creates undesirable First Amendment concerns. Also, websites that masquerade as "gripe sites" but in reality seek to take advantage of established trademarks for commercial or self-serving purposes are likely to find disfavor in the courts.

Trademark owners should note that settling disputes over domain names does not always require litigation. A public–private partnership, the Internet Corporation for Assigned Names and Numbers (ICANN), oversees the global registration of Internet domain names.[20] In 1999, ICANN adopted the Uniform Domain-Name Dispute Resolution Policy (UDRP) to help resolve domain name disputes that allege abusive, bad faith registration of a domain name. Disputes that do not include allegations of abuse or bad faith are not handled under the UDRP; these must be resolved through lawsuits or other negotiations.

Organizations seeking to manage their trademarks have options for taking control of domain names featuring marks that are similar or dilutive. Although the First Amendment requires that fair comment and criticism directed at trademark owners and associated domain names be tolerated, bad faith disregard for trademarks themselves may result in the forfeiture or cancellation of the registration, and even the transfer of the domain name to the trademark owner.

Meta Tags and Keywords

Owners of trademarks and service marks also may encounter the use of trademarked terms in meta tags, which are elements used in the coding of websites that describe the contents of web pages; the more specific the meta tags, the more highly a page will rank in the returned search results on a particular subject or topic. Meta tags are provided by website creators and used by search engines to identify and index pages. They may feature either keywords that describe the contents of the web page or descriptions consisting of a few sentences that describe a particular page.

Some courts have held that the use of trademarked terms in meta tags can constitute trademark infringement. The theory is that the use of specific keywords in meta tags, keywords that are trademarks that identify the goods or services of others, can cause confusion on the part of consumers. In one case, for example, an organization called Axiom Worldwide, Inc. used meta tags that apparently included the terms "Accu-Spina" and "IDD Therapy," which were trademarks for medical services provided by North American Medical Group, a competitor. When Internet users conducted web searches for those services using the Google search engine, the Axiom website ranked highly in the results. The moral of the story is that organizations should take care in selecting meta tag keywords and descriptions and avoid using trademarked terms.

A similar risk occurs with the use of trademarks in services such as Google's AdWords program and similar programs offered by other search engines, such as Bing. With AdWords, for example, Google allows advertisers to buy certain keywords likely to be used as search terms by those seeking information online. When a search-engine user enters one of these keywords, websites whose operators have purchased the keyword appear at the top of the search results. Sometimes, the purchased keywords consist of trademarked terms owned by someone other than the keyword purchaser. Trademark owners who have objected to this practice have filed infringement lawsuits against the advertisers, with mixed results. Courts finding trademark infringement related to keywords have focused on the likelihood of confusion caused by the information that appears *following* the search.[21] The purchase of keywords alone will likely not be considered trademark infringement.[22]

Organizations are advised to monitor the use of their trademarks online, even those uses that are behind the scenes in the form of meta tags and keywords. Purchasing keywords associated with your own trademarks is one practical strategy for dealing with this practice; lawsuits for trademark infringement may be another, especially if polite requests, usually delivered in a cease-and-desist letter from legal counsel, are unsuccessful.

Engaging With Consumers Online

Unsolicited E-mail: CAN-SPAM

Early in the Internet's development, consumers and Congress turned their attention to electronic mail (e-mail). Jurisdictional issues concerning the Internet make the regulation of e-mail and other world-wide-web-based communications challenging, to say the least. That, however, has not prevented Congress from trying to get a handle on annoying online marketing practices that have grown along with the Internet. In particular, "phishing" e-mails, which are messages sent to hook consumers into a scam, rather than a legitimate sale, have drawn regulatory attention.

Anyone who checks his or her e-mail for business-related or personal messages only to discover multiple unsolicited and unwanted marketing solicitations likely can relate to the frustration engendered by "spamming," defined as the practice of sending unwanted e-mail to unsuspecting e-mail users that is often misleading and obnoxious (and sometimes for illegal purposes or pornographic in nature as well). In 2003, President George W. Bush signed the

Figure 13.2 In 2003, President George W. Bush signed the Controlling the Assault of Non-Solicited Pornography and Marketing Act (CAN-SPAM Act) to address the problem of deceptive or fraudulent commercial e-mail. The CAN-SPAM Act became effective Jan. 1, 2004, and created a single set of rules designed to apply nationwide to commercial e-mails.

Credit line: Afanasev Ivan/Shutterstock.com

Controlling the Assault of Non-Solicited Pornography and Marketing Act (CAN-SPAM Act)[23] to address the problem of deceptive or fraudulent commercial e-mail. The CAN-SPAM Act became effective Jan. 1, 2004, and created a single set of rules designed to apply nationwide to commercial e-mails. The Act specifically preempts state laws regulating the use of electronic mail.

The CAN-SPAM Act is enforced by the Federal Trade Commission (FTC) and other federal and state agencies (see Chapters 10 and 11) that have jurisdiction over specific organizations. The Act provides for criminal sanctions enforceable by the United States Department of Justice (DOJ) and allows companies that provide Internet access to sue those who violate the Act. The DOJ has made several high-profile arrests of professional spammers who are alleged to have sent billions of spam messages in violation of CAN-SPAM.[24] It is important to note that the CAN-SPAM Act does not ban unsolicited commercial e-mail. Rather, it establishes requirements for those who send such e-mail, spells out potential penalties for violators and allows consumers to demand that e-mailers stop sending spam.[25]

Some observers suggest the CAN-SPAM Act may have had the unintended consequence of actually increasing the volume of spam e-mails by giving commercial e-mailers clear instructions for allowable e-mail behavior, thereby emboldening them to "spam away." Skeptics of the law's actual effectiveness also note that the FTC lacks the resources to aggressively enforce CAN-SPAM, a limitation that gives the law more bark than bite. Proponents of CAN-SPAM, nonetheless, applaud the effort and point to the availability of a private right of action the Act gives to Internet service providers and others seeking to hold violators accountable. Even with these challenges, the FTC takes spam e-mail seriously, particularly those that are sent by scammers and fraudsters, and is on the lookout for new varieties of e-mail that seek to deceive recipients.

For example, in 2016, the Commission highlighted the practice of using multiple online "masks" to deceive consumers about the source of emailed solicitations. This common masking tactic involves sending messages that "falsely convey they were sent by a friend of family member, including misleading FROM: addresses."[26] In some cases, the sender implies familiarity with the recipient by including the recipient's name in the subject line. Another type of masking is found after a recipient opens the e-mail and encounters a link to what looks like real news sites. According to an FTC complaint about one such spammer, the sites are "paid ads that mimic the look of media outlets and include links to drive consumers to the sites where defendants sell their diet products."[27]

The relative anonymity of the Internet makes it difficult to know who is sending, receiving and viewing what. This presents particular problems for those concerned about shielding children from inappropriate messages. The CAN-SPAM Act addresses some of these concerns, and several states (Michigan and Utah, among the most notable) have also passed laws designed to keep adult-oriented computer content away from children.[28] These laws have been drafted to avoid conflict or overlap with CAN-SPAM. Prudent marketing communications and public relations professionals who attempt to reach children by computer should understand both CAN-SPAM and any state laws that may apply.

Solicitation by Text Message

Recall the Telephone Consumer Protection Act[29] (TCPA) discussed in Chapter 10. When it comes to "robotexts," solicitations made via autodialed text messages, the position of the Federal Communications Commission (FCC) is that the law applies not only to voice calls but also to text messages sent to cell phones using any equipment that may be dialed "without human intervention."[30] The FCC has said it is "committed to protecting consumers from harassing, intrusive, illegal, and unwanted robotexts to cell phones and other mobile devices."[31]

As for robocalls, the TCPA prohibits:

> autodialed text messages unless made with the prior express consent of the called party, to any telephone number assigned to a cell phone or other mobile device (such as a pager), unless the calls or text messages are: 1) made for emergency purposes; 2) free to the end user and have been exempted by the Commission, subject to conditions prescribed to protect consumer privacy rights; or 3) made solely to collect debts "owed to or guaranteed by the United States."[32]

Organizations seeking to contact consumers via automated texts have the burden of proving they obtained express consent prior to sending the robotext. For robotexts that include or introduce an advertisement, the prior express consent must be in written form, unless an exemption applies. Two exceptions to the advertising requirement are for certain health-care calls and calls sponsored by a tax-exempt nonprofit organization. Also, express consent is not permanent consent: recipients may revoke their consent to be robotexted "at any time using any reasonable method."[33] When a text recipient asks to be removed from the text list, the regulations allow the sender of the text message to send a final autodialed text to confirm the opt-out request, but no other robotexts may be sent.

The FCC also addresses the procedure for handling reassigned numbers when consent was given by the number's prior owner. Its position has been that for robotexts to reassigned numbers for which consent had been previously obtained, the sender of the text is not liable for the first text to the new called party. Any continued text messages to a reassigned number, however, may result in forfeiture penalties approaching $20,000 per violation. Because of numerous court challenges in this area, users of robotexting should frequently consult FCC guidelines regarding the proper procedure for reassigned numbers. In addition to the FCC, robotexters also should check and follow state laws (discussed in Chapter 11) that may address robotext violations.

As with "phishing" e-mails, the FCC warns against deceptive text messages–called "smishing" (a combination of short message service, or SMS, and phishing) sent to smart devices. The FCC describes a typical smishing scam as one that "may seem like it's from a bank–maybe your bank–and include a link or phone number to bait you into clicking or calling. If you do, you stand a good chance of being hooked."[34] Once hooked, consumers' personal information and devices may be at risk. Smishing attempts are prohibited whether delivered by robotext or one at a time.

Influencers: Blogs and Social Media

As first noted in Chapter 10, FTC monitors the use of endorsements and testimonials by celebrities or other non-company spokespersons to promote products and services. The reach and potential impact of "influencers" on blogs and social media has heightened this focus. In 2009 and again in 2015, the Commission released information to aid marketers who seek to reach their online audiences by leveraging the popularity of influencers.

The use of paid influencers by Lord & Taylor, the fashion retailer, illustrates how the FTC regards influencer campaigns. After Lord & Taylor paid 50 online fashion commenters to post photos on Instagram or other social media sites of themselves wearing the same style of dress from the store's new collection, the FTC filed a complaint. According to the FTC, the influencers' failure to clearly disclose that they had been given the dresses and been paid (some of them handsomely) in exchange for their endorsements amounted to deceptive trade practices.

Figure 13.3 Photographing a movie star in public presents no invasion of privacy issues. Certain unconsented uses of the photograph, however, may invite a right of publicity/invasion of privacy lawsuit from the celebrity, and a copyright infringement lawsuit from the photographer.

Credit line: Yuganov Konstantin/Shutterstock.com

The updated *FTC Guides Concerning Use of Endorsements and Testimonials in Advertising*[35] primarily impacts the use of disclaimers to accompany true endorsement claims that do not reflect the average experience, and the types of endorsements companies can receive from new media sources like blogs and message boards. The Guides do not create law, but they do explain the way the FTC will interpret the law. The Guides state that an endorsement is "any advertising message (including verbal statements, demonstrations, or depictions of the name, signature, likeness, or other identifying personal characteristics of an individual or the name or seal of an organization) that consumers are likely to believe reflects the opinions, beliefs, findings or experience of a party other than the sponsoring advertiser."[36] Online reviews posted by influencers with some kind of material connection to the marketer clearly fall within the reach of the Guides. According to the FTC, the Guides "reflect the basic truth-in-advertising principle that endorsements must be honest and not misleading."[37] The FTC has emphasized the need for online endorsements to make clear when there is a connection between the endorser and marketer the consumers would not expect, especially when knowledge of the connection may affect how consumers evaluate the endorsement. Said the FTC's Director of the Bureau of Consumer Protection: "Consumers have the right to know when they're looking at paid advertising."[38] Social media influencers, for example, who tout the benefits of certain products must disclose to readers or viewers if they have been paid or given something of value in exchange for mentioning the product. FTC standards regard such endorsements as constituting misleading advertising unless the connection has been clearly disclosed. Both advertisers and their endorsers "may be subject to liability for false or unsubstantiated statements made through endorsements, or for failing to disclose material connections between themselves and their endorsers."[39] In short, statements of endorsement, whether offered on blogs or social media or via more traditional media vehicles must meet the same substantiation requirements as other material claims.

Hashtag Promotions, Online Contests and Sweepstakes

As with the paid-for endorsements of online influencers, the FTC also monitors hashtag promotions in which consumers are encouraged to use specific hashtags in exchange for some kind of incentive. According to the FTC, a failure to make clear that the use of the hashtag is because of an incentive and not an organic gesture by the consumer violates Section 5 of the FTC Act. An example of a problematic hashtag promotion that attracted the FTC's attention involved the shoe manufacturer Cole Haan, which sponsored a contest in which the means of entry involved the use of a hashtag. The contest itself required contestants to (1) create boards on the social media site Pinterest; (2) include five shoe images from the company's "Wandering Sole Pinterest Board"; (3) post five images of the contestants' "favorite places to wander"; and (4) use "#WanderingSole" in each pin description. In exchange for engaging in the hashtag promotion, the contestant was eligible to win a $1,000 shopping spree.

In a letter to Cole Haan, the FTC said it believed "that the participants' pins featuring Cole Haan products were endorsements of the Cole Haan products."[40] It also said it did not believe the hashtag "adequately communicated the financial incentive—a material connection between contestants" and the brand.[41] Because the FTC had not publicly addressed whether entry into a contest is a form of material connection or whether a pin on Pinterest could serve as an endorsement, it declined to take further action against Cole Haan, which changed its social media policy. The letter did, however, provide notice that promotions of this nature should satisfy both the FTC's *Guides Concerning Use of Endorsements and Testimonials in Advertising* (discussed above) and its *.Com Disclosure Guidelines* (discussed below).

For the most part, the rules for online contests and sweepstakes (see Chapter 10) mirror those of "old-fashioned" sweepstakes conducted offline. Contests, whether online or not, are games of skill. Asking participants to calculate the number of jelly beans in a jar, for example, would be a skills-based challenge. To avoid the risk of being regarded as an illegal lottery, rather than a legal contest, such games must not leave open the possibility that a participant may win purely as a result of chance.

Sponsors of online contests also should take care in determining how winners will be decided. State laws governing contests may require that qualified judges be tapped to evaluate the entries, which may preclude using public voting to choose the winner. Public voting is easy to solicit online and can be good for encouraging consumer engagement. If, however, public voting results in a winner being chosen because of popularity, rather than skill, it may corrupt the contest. Allowing the public to choose the winner also may encourage "vote farming," which both consumers and regulators disfavor. With vote farming, entrants solicit ("farm for") votes in what essentially becomes a popularity contest that can leave more legitimate entrants (and the consuming public) feeling resentful of the brand that sponsored the contest in the first place.

Sweepstakes, in contrast to contests, are based purely on chance: sweepstakes winners must be randomly selected. In addition, sweepstakes entries may not be conditioned upon the receipt of any kind of consideration, or something having economic value (see Chapter 9's overview of contracts). Some states require that consideration in the sweepstakes context be some kind of monetary payment; others regard consideration more broadly to include something offered to the detriment of the entrant and the benefit of the participant. In general, sweepstakes require sponsors to offer a method of entry that allows people to participate without making some kind of purchase.

Before computers were widely available in libraries, Internet cafes and other places of public access, lawyers debated about whether an online sweepstakes that requires people to possess or have access to a computer to participate equates to requiring some form of consideration. The answer to that question is likely "no," but sweepstakes that require smartphones and apps, and phone plans that charge for data access, present similar concerns. Observers who focus on this area of law suggest that a simple smartphone-and-app requirement is likely not consideration. A more complicated means of entry, however, could present enough hurdles to amount to consideration.[42] If the required app is not offered as a free download but must be purchased, for example, the sponsor is advised to create an alternate means of entry for those who wish to enter but do not wish to purchase the app.

Native Advertising

The concern that consumers be given information that signals when an endorsement has been paid for reflects a general concern about consumers' ability to distinguish between commercial content and editorial content. In the digital age, the FTC has devoted significant attention to native advertising, which imitates the form and style of the media in which it's featured. The Commission defines native advertising as "content that bears a similarity to the news, feature articles, product reviews, entertainment, and other material that surrounds it online."[43]

In the complaint against Lord & Taylor over its influencer campaign, discussed above, the FTC also charged that Lord & Taylor had "deceived consumers by paying for native advertisements" without disclosing that the posts actually were paid promotions for the company's new clothing collection. The native advertising included a seemingly objective article in an online publication and Instagram post. Ultimately, Lord & Taylor reached a settlement with the FTC over both the native advertising and the influencer campaign.

The FTC has noted that digital media presents advertisers with many ways to present brand information to consumers, some of which is advertising that "has moved past the banner ad into advertising that is more seamlessly and inconspicuously incorporated into digital content."[44] According to the FTC, approximately 75 percent of online publishers feature native advertising on their sites, and most of the remainder are or have considered using native advertising. Many brands and advertising agencies also use, or plan to use, native advertising, citing the ability to "provide more relevant messages, increase consumer engagement and generate awareness and buzz about products."[45]

Frequently, native advertising consists of advertisements whose style and presentation mimic editorial content of their host environments. In some cases, content is formatted to falsely suggest it was from news reports that had appeared in bona fide news programming. Other examples include websites featuring editorial content created solely for presentation by a sponsor; in addition to the Lord & Taylor complaint, the FTC also expressed consternation with American Express, which presented an online series featuring videos, articles and info-graphics created solely to appeal to the female small-business owners the company wanted to reach.

The FTC's concern about native advertising stems from the potential for it to exploit consumers' trust in a publisher or improperly influence purchasing decisions. From that perspective, the FTC has stated that native advertising, like other forms of advertising it regulates under the Federal Trade Commission Act, must not mislead consumers. It has created specific guidelines for native advertising in digital media that attempt to strike a balance between advertisers and publishers and the protection of consumers.[46] In particular, the FTC holds advertisers responsible for ensuring that native advertising is identifiable as such before consumers arrive at the main advertising page. Once consumers arrive at the advertising content, the commercial nature of the material must be clear and not misleading. The FTC considers factors such as

> an ad's overall appearance; the similarity of its written, spoken or visual style or subject matter to non-advertising content on the publisher site on which it appears; and the degree to which it is distinguishable from other content on the publisher site.[47]

The FTC's preferred mechanism for alerting consumers to native advertising is "clear and prominent disclosures." The Commission's business guidance document, *.comDisclosures: How to Make Effective Disclosures in Digital Advertising*,[48] explains what advertisers should do to comply. In general, disclosures should be:

- In a clear and unambiguous language.
- As close as possible to the native ads to which they relate.
- In a font and color that's easy to read.
- In a shade that stands out against the background.
- For video ads, on the screen long enough to be noticed, read and understood.
- For auto disclosures, read at a cadence that's easy for consumers to follow and in words consumers will understand.[49]

Advertisers should note that these are guidelines; advertisers have flexibility about how to identify native advertising as native advertising. The important consideration is whether a reasonable consumer will "notice and process the disclosures and comprehend what they mean."[50]

Dot.Com Disclosures and Small Screens

According to the FTC, "the same consumer protection laws that apply to commercial activities in other media apply online, including activities in the mobile marketplace."[51] As consumers have increasingly relied on their smartphones as conduits for information, however, the FTC's rules regarding online advertising have been tested by the physical limitations of small screens and "space-constrained" modes of communication, like Twitter. FTC advisory materials provide that when a space-constrained ad requires a disclosure, the disclosure should be incorporated into the ad whenever possible. In some cases, however, the use of a hyperlink to a separate page featuring the disclosure may be acceptable, provided the disclosure is clear and conspicuous. According to the FTC, when a hyperlink is used to lead to a disclosure, the following ground rules should be observed:

- Make the link obvious.
- Label the hyperlink appropriately to convey the importance, nature and relevance of the information it leads to.
- Use hyperlink styles consistently, so consumers know when a link is available.
- Place the hyperlink as close as possible to the relevant information it qualifies and make it noticeable.
- Take consumers directly to the disclosure on the click-through page.
- Assess the effectiveness of the hyperlink by monitoring click-through rates and other information about consumer use and make changes accordingly.[52]

Certain information, like the full cost of a product or service, should be offered in the initial ad. The FTC's position is that consumers should "not have to click on hyperlinks to understand the full amount they will pay."[53] Cost information, therefore, including any additional, applicable fees, "should be presented to [consumers] clearly and conspicuously prior to purchase."[54] Also, when the advertised product is offered for sale in a brick-and-mortar store or through a third-party online retailer, meaning one can purchase the product without clicking through to the hyperlinked disclosure, the FTC regards hyperlinked disclosures as inadequate.

The following hypothetical Tweet offered by the FTC satisfies its expectations regarding disclosures on platforms like Twitter: a celebrity whose Twitter handle is @JuliStarz tweets the following:

> Ad: Shooting movie beach scene. Had to lose 30lbs in 6 wks. Thanks Fat-away Pills for making it easy. Typical loss: 1lb/wk.

Because the space-constrained message signals that Juli is a paid endorser by beginning with "Ad:" and discloses "Typical loss: 1lb/wk," the disclosure requirements are satisfied.

Product Reviews and Other Online Feedback

In addition to the "gripe sites" described above, organizations concerned about protecting their reputations sometimes must contend with the posting of unflattering customer reviews on social media or websites like Yelp. As one means of combatting negative customer reviews online, some organizations have attempted to use contract language to prevent consumers from submitting negative remarks. To address this practice, Congress in 2016 enacted the Consumer Review Fairness Act[55] (CRFA), which prohibits sellers from using "form contracts" in this context. According to the Act, form contracts—that feature standardized provisions—between sellers and individual consumers are "void from the inception" if designed to restrict customer reviews. Specifically, the CRFA prohibits form contracts if the provisions: (1) prohibit or restrict individuals from reviewing sellers' goods, services or conduct; (2) impose penalties or fees on individuals for such reviews; or (3) require individuals to transfer intellectual property rights in such reviews.[56]

Not all contract language between seller and consumer is prohibited, however: the Act contains certain exceptions, "including for contract provisions that bar the submission of confidential, private, or unlawful information."[57] In other words, the CRFA does not grant a consumer a blanket license to reveal information protected by some other law or valid agreement. Also, the law protects the sharing of "honest opinions" related to the company's products or services; organizations are permitted to remove or seek removal of opinions that are "clearly false or misleading" or "libelous, harassing, abusive, obscene, vulgar, sexually explicit, or inappropriate with respect to race, gender, sexuality, ethnicity or other intrinsic characteristics."[58]

The Federal Trade Commission pursues violations of the CFRA, treating them as unfair or deceptive acts or practices (discussed in Chapter 10) that deprive consumers of honest information related to purchase decisions. Penalties may include fines, as well as a federal court order requiring different conduct. In its first action enforcing the CFPA, the Commission charged the marketers behind an online money-making promotion with using provisions in form contracts to restrict consumers' ability to post reviews of their products, services or conduct.[59] To assure compliance with the CRFA, organizations should review the terms and conditions of all form contracts and remove provisions that seek to limit or impose penalties on those who share their honest reviews.

Real-Time Advertising

This chapter would be incomplete without some mention of real-time advertising (RTA). The Real-time Advertising Academy defines RTA as "the practice of connecting with a consumer audience to sell products and services with messages that are reactive to the environment."[60] *Advertising Age* has described it as "creating special moments for the right audiences at the right time."[61] As one agency representative put it, such campaigns allow advertisers "to get really precise around media moments—big epic moments, but also really tactical real-time moments, like somebody sneezes and needs allergy meds."[62]

Real-time advertising campaigns range from the simple to the complex, with the latter often featuring a number of moving parts. For example, Johnson & Johnson, the maker of Neutrogena brand products, used RTA to drive sales to brand-loyal consumers while courting first-time buyers. Working with an agency that specializes in RTA, the company used shopper and buying data to display targeted content to individual shoppers. The resulting video and in-store-display content, which they called "Perfect Pairing," featured the products targeted consumers were already buying, along with complementary goods.

The type of RTA used by Johnson & Johnson for its Perfect Pairing campaign combines data analytics, media planning and media buying with original advertising messages delivered digitally. Those campaigns require significant planning to deal with the legal issues—copyrights, trademarks and publicity rights among them—that occur with the production of any communications campaign. In addition, they require attention to data privacy laws (discussed below) that impact how, for example, information about individual shoppers may be collected and used.

A type of RTA nicknamed "newsjacking" attempts to leverage current events (and popular culture) by pairing them with brand messages delivered via social media. Newsjacking has fewer components than the in-store content delivered to individual consumers, but it may be more fraught with potential legal liability if not handled thoughtfully. A successful example of newsjacking involved the use of Twitter to promote Oreo cookies, which consumers often dunk in milk prior to eating. When the lights in the football stadium went out during the 2013 Super Bowl, Oreo's digital brand agency jumped on the opportunity to remind consumers with a tweet that "You can still dunk in the dark."

Similarly, Arby's, the fast-food chain whose trademark features an image of a Western-style hat with a tall crown, received rave reviews for its use of Twitter during the live television broadcast of the 2014 Grammy Awards. In its Tweet, Arby's remarked on the hat singer Pharrell Williams wore, asking, "Hey @Pharrell, can we have our hat back? #GRAMMYs." Williams was amused and eventually posted his tall hat for sale on eBay, where Arby's bought it for $44,100. The proceeds went to a charity of Williams' choice.

At the other extreme, two social media posts by Duane Reade, the drugstore chain, invited a $6 million lawsuit from actress Katherine Heigl. The brand posted on Twitter and Facebook a paparazzi photo of Heigl leaving one of its stores with a shopping bag along with the message, "Love a quick #DuaneReade run? Even Katherine Heigl can't resist shopping #NYC's favorite drugstore . . ." Heigl eventually settled her right-of-publicity invasion-of-privacy lawsuit (see Chapter 6) with the company. Details were confidential, but Duane Reade ended up making a donation to benefit the Jason Debus Heigl Foundation.

In the Arby's example, the featured celebrity, it turned out, did not mind being tagged in the tweet and in fact leveraged it himself. But if the Twitter post had suggested that Pharrell's hat must mean "he loves Arby's" the implied endorsement may not have gone over as well. To successfully navigate this type of RTA, brand managers and their social media teams must have a clear sense of their own brand identity and should have some mechanism for evaluating RTA posts (albeit quickly) before they are dispatched. The Oreo "dunk in the dark" tweet was conceived of and approved by a team operating from a "social-media war room" staffed with people who had a strong sense of the brand's digital personality. According to the agency head who oversaw the war room, "Oreo didn't just wake up and join the conversation for the Super Bowl. Oreo has behaved like a digital brand for years, giving it the foundation to easily adapt."[63]

Advertisers seeking to use real-time advertising effectively without enhancing their legal jeopardy should devote adequate resources, e.g., experienced copywriters, brand experts and sometimes lawyers, to help ensure that their in-the-moment social media posts hit home instead of hitting a sour note.

Data Privacy

As noted above, real-time advertising's reliance on data analytics in the identification and targeting of individual consumers likely raises privacy concerns. Data privacy is one of the fastest-growing areas of communications law, and one likely to flourish as the interconnectivity of "smart devices" other than phones or computers (e.g., televisions, appliances, medical devices, etc.)—sometimes called the Internet of Things (IoT)—becomes more prevalent. Although advertising and public relations professionals are likely more focused on the messaging than on the collection and storage of the data that informs it, some knowledge of data privacy and its implications is advisable, if for no other reason than data breaches can quickly turn into public relations and brand-tarnishing nightmares.

The current slate of data privacy laws is best described as a patchwork of regulations and penalties for the collection, storage and use of consumer information. In some cases, Congress has taken direct action in response to activities in cyberspace. In others, the FTC or other regulatory agencies have used their existing authority to address questionable practices where the Internet is involved.

In the data collection sphere, the FTC has been active in urging businesses to fully inform consumers about their data collection practices. By the end of 2017, the FTC had brought more than 500 enforcement actions over the privacy of consumer information, many of which focused on online and mobile environments.[64] In late 2018, new FTC chairman Joseph Simons described data security as "a very serious issue" for the FTC, which will seek privacy enforcement that "strike[s] a proper balance for consumers and competition."[65] He said the Commission would "continue to closely follow privacy issues and act quickly in the case of any anticompetitive conduct"[66] and could seek clarification from Congress about its enforcement authority in this area, possibly to include authority to levy fines against offenders to "create a sufficient deterrence and … incentive for companies."[67]

Several cases from 2017 illustrate the types of practices the FTC aims to deter. In one, the FTC alleged that Lenovo, one of the world's largest computer manufacturers and one that recently had begun doing business in the United States, was selling laptops preinstalled with software that interfered with how a user's browser interacted with websites. In the process, the complaint alleged, consumers' personal information was accessible via the Internet. This included log-in credentials, Social Security numbers, medical information and financial and payment information.[68]

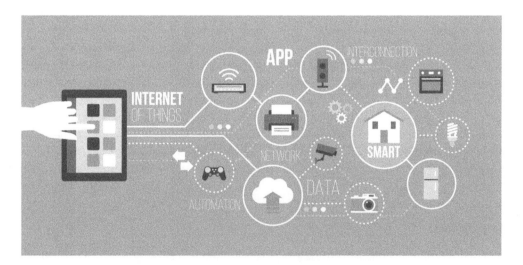

Figure 13.4 Data privacy is one of the fastest-growing areas of communications law, thanks to the growth of the Internet of Things ("smart devices" other than phones or computers, e.g., televisions, appliances, medical devices, etc.).

Credit line: Elen Absi/Shutterstock.com

Another case involved Uber, the ride-sharing company, which settled charges that "it deceived consumers by, among other things, failing to live up to its claims that it closely monitored employee access to consumer and driver data."[69] A third case involved a service designed to convince consumers to save for college. According to the FTC, Upromise encouraged consumers to download a toolbar that failed to "clearly and prominently disclose … the data collection and use," among other failures.[70]

The FTC has brought numerous cases against companies that have failed to properly safeguard consumers' personal data. The 2017 complaint against Uber, for example, included charges that it "deceived consumers by failing to reasonably secure sensitive consumer data stored in the cloud."[71] This was contrary to Uber's claims to customers that the data was secure within its databases. Another case focused on D-Link, a manufacturer of computer networking equipment. That complaint alleged the company had "failed to take steps to address well-known and easily preventable security flaws."[72]

A number of data-breach cases have been brought by the FTC enforcing the Fair Credit Reporting Act[73] (FCRA), which specifies the use of data in financial matters like creditworthiness, insurance eligibility and such. Financial institutions covered by the FCRA must, as part of corollary legislation known as the Gramm-Leach-Bliley (GLB) Act,[74] implement "reasonable security policies and procedures" and dispatch privacy notices to customers at regular intervals. Customers also must have an opportunity to "opt out of sharing their information with unaffiliated third parties."[75] An example of FTC action under the FCRA involved the online tax-preparation service TaxSlayer, which, according to the FTC, ran afoul of the legislation in several ways. Among them: failing to develop a comprehensive, written security program and failing to implement safeguards against potential cyberattack.

As noted in Chapter 11, FTC enforcement is sometimes accompanied by actions levied by state attorneys general. For example, lawsuits in Massachusetts and West Virginia claimed that Equifax, which also was under investigation by the FTC, had violated state-level consumer protection laws in those states. The Massachusetts complaint, for example, complained that Equifax turned a blind eye to its systems' potential vulnerability to hacking and neglected to deploy existing resources to prevent data breach.[76]

Companies that deal in data are advised to follow closely the schedule for disseminating privacy notices and take affirmative measures, such as requiring customers using online services to adopt strong passwords. When problems or breaches occur, consumers should be notified as quickly as possible.

The FTC and state attorneys general have focused on data privacy and security largely by using their existing authority to deal with unfair trade practices. In addition, some states have enacted specific legislation to address data security for their residents. California's legislation is among the most comprehensive and is likely to be a model for other states. The California Consumer Privacy Act[77] (COPPA) of 2018, effective Jan. 1, 2020, applies to businesses (1) whose annual gross revenues exceed $25 million; (2) that annually purchase, receive, transfer or sell personal information of more than 50,000 consumers; (3) who derive at least 50 percent of their annual revenues from selling personal information; and (4) that control or are controlled by a covered business if they share common branding. California residents engaged with these businesses can control how their personal information is used. Among other protections, the law "allows consumers to demand that certain businesses disclose any personal information they have collected, delete that information, and refrain from selling or transferring it to third parties."[78] It also provides for a "Do Not Sell My Personal Information" list (similar to the Do Not

Call list discussed in Chapter 10) to allow consumers to opt out of having their data sold. In addition, affected businesses must update their privacy policies annually and must include a link to the website featuring the opt-out page. Affected businesses may charge differing rates or prices and offer different tiers of services to customers who opt out but may not discriminate against them. Any additional fees or revenue collected must be "reasonably related to the value of the consumer's data."[79]

Several bills introduced in Congress in 2018 related to the Internet of Things indicate increased attention to consumer privacy concerns. For example, the State of Modern Application, Research, and Trends of IoT Act[80] (SMART IoT) required the Secretary of Commerce to commission a study of the IoT industry overall.[81] The National Institute of Standards and Technology Reauthorization Act of 2018[82] includes calls for expanded research into security and privacy concerns.

Abroad, the European Union has adopted a new General Data Protection Regulation (GDPR) that attempts to standardize privacy requirements across member states. The GDPR's idea of private information is "any kind of information that anyone could use to identify anyone," even if a name is not attached to the data.[83] The scope of the GDPR is broader than similar efforts in the United States, and its consent requirements are more stringent. The European law allows consumers to request any data about them and allows for the correction of errors or misrepresentations. Individuals also may control where their data reside and may request that their data be transferred from one platform to another. The GDPR also features the much-discussed "right to be forgotten" provisions that allow individuals to direct that their data be deleted if no valid reason exists for its being stored.

Observers have noted that international privacy laws often conflict with Americans' conception of the First Amendment (see Chapter 1). While California and other legislative bodies have no doubt been influenced by the more stringent approach to individual privacy adopted in Europe, full integration of more stringent approaches among governmental regulatory agencies is likely some distance away. Businesses with a global focus and customer base, however, will likely have to navigate the differences on their own if they wish to establish a degree of uniformity among their operating entities. Attorney Seth Blinder, who has advised on data privacy issues across several industries, suggests that any organization dealing with consumer information have a clear understanding of the data and the technology it possesses, especially as both are "getting more complicated."[84] He recommends those responsible for legal compliance and customer interactions know exactly what kind of data they are gathering and using, how the data are obtained, where the data are flowing and whether interactions with third-party vendors or customers in other forums (like California) present issues to be addressed.[85] Privacy policies and disclosures provided to individuals about the collection, storage, transfer and use of their data should be accurate and updated regularly to account for changes in technology and business relationships.

Interacting With Children Online

Compared to rules regarding data privacy and children, the privacy regulation described above is somewhat late to the party. Historically, lawmakers, judges and members of the general public have been more tolerant of laws that treat children differently from adults, even when those laws curtail otherwise constitutionally protected conduct or speech. As the Internet evolved into an integral part of daily American life, Congress took special action to govern the collection of data from and about children and their Internet usage.

The Children's Online Privacy Protection Act[86] (COPPA), enacted in 1998, gives parents tools to control what information is collected from their children online. In two decades of COPPA enforcement, the Federal Trade Commission has collected more than $10 million in civil penalties from misusers of such information. COPPA addresses all manner of online activity, including social networking, online access via smartphone and geolocation tracking of children. The data collection practices covered include text as well as information in the form of photos, video or audio files that contain a child's image or voice.

Website operators should note that COPPA applies to websites for children, but also may apply to other sites if "the operators have 'actual knowledge' they are collecting personal information from users of another site or online service directed to children under 13."[87] Actual knowledge of a user's age is presumed if "the site or service asks for–or receives–information from the user that allow it to determine the person's age."[88] According to the FTC, this provision could make COPPA applicable to "advertising networks, plug-ins and other third parties."[89]

The commission's COPPA regulations provide for some flexibility with input from affected companies, but the "centerpiece of COPPA" is the parental consent requirement.[90] The rules require operators of commercial websites and online services directed to children under 13 to:

* Notify parents of their information practices.
* Obtain verifiable parental consent for the collection, use or disclosure of children's personal information.
* Let parents prevent further maintenance of use or future collection of their child's personal information.
* Provide parents access to their child's personal information.
* Not require a child to provide more personal information than is reasonably necessary to participate in an activity.
* Maintain reasonable procedures to protect the confidentiality, security and integrity of the personal information.[91]

Parental consent must be "verifiable."[92] This means the method for obtaining consent must be "reasonably calculated, in light of available technology, to ensure the person providing consent is the child's parent."[93] Approved methods are included in the rules, but the list is not exhaustive; the Commission encourages companies to develop new, effective ways to obtain verifiable parental consent.

The FTC also encourages those interacting with children online to self-regulate in the spirit of the law; a "safe harbor" provision in the regulations allows industry groups and others to create their own guidelines for compliance and submit them to the FTC for approval. According to the FTC, providing an incentive for companies to self-regulate helps streamline compliance and keeps the focus on protecting children instead of the regulations themselves.[94]

Recent enforcement actions by the FTC have been directed at connected toys (part of the Internet of Things) and an online talent agency, for example. In the connected-toy case, the FTC alleged that Vtech, operator of an online learning platform for children, failed "to take reasonable steps to protect sensitive data collected from children."[95] The problem "came to light only after a hacker stole personal information about kids and parents who used the company's products."[96] In another action, the FTC sought a permanent injunction, civil penalties and "other relief" against the owner of Explore Talent, an online talent search network based in Nevada whose clientele includes children under 13. According to the complaint, the company "disclosed children's personal information without notifying or obtaining consent from the children's parents."[97] It also, said the complaint, "falsely has represented to consumers in its Privacy Policy that it does not knowingly collect personal information from children under the age of 13."[98]

Because of society's heavy emphasis on protecting children, organizations whose online presence depends on children, or whose content may be especially attractive to young consumers, are advised to know and understand COPPA compliance. An advisable first step would be to consult the FTC's online resources, including its *Six-Step Compliance Plan for Your Business*[99] and its list of answers to frequently asked questions.[100]

Conclusion

As the areas of law discussed here suggest, technological innovation frequently requires that "old" laws or regulations be applied in ways not necessarily intended when the regulation was born. In some situations, the unique characteristics of online communications have prompted regulation that affects the preparation and delivery of messages to online audiences and the outlook is for more of the same. Because of the fast pace of technological change in this area, it is foreseeable that data privacy concerns will continue to demand significant attention, both behind the scenes and in outwardly directed interactions with consumers and prospective clients.

Notes

1.   American Civil Liberties Union v. Reno, 929 F.Supp. 824 (E.D. Pa 1996).
2.   Eric Goldman, Internet Law: Cases & Materials loc. 1008 (2018) (ebook).
3.   *Id.*
4.   Zippo Mfg. Co. v. Zippo Dot Com, Inc., 952 F. Supp. 1119 (W.D. Pa. 1997).
5.   *Id.*
6.   ALS Scan v. Digital Service Consultants, Inc., 293 F.3d 707 (4th Cir. 2002).
7.   Calder v. Jones, 465 U.S. 783 (1984).
8.   Burdick v. Superior Court, 233 Cal. App. 4th 8 (Cal. App. Ct. 2015).
9.   47 U.S.C. §230.
10.   *Id.* (emphasis added).
11.   17 U.S.C. §512(a)-(d)).
12.   *Id.* §512(k)(1)(B)
13.   *Id.* §512(c).
14.   15 U.S.C. §1125(d)(1)(A).
15.   *Id.*
16.   *Id.* §1125(d)(1)(a)(ii)(I).
17.   *Id.* §1125(d)(B)(i).
18.   Ford Motor Co. v. Lapertosa, 126 F. Supp. 2d 463 (E.D. Mich. 2001).
19.   *Id.*
20.   *Internet Corporation for Assigned Names & Numbers*, ICANN Referrals Page, www.ICANN.com (last accessed Nov. 20, 2018).
21.   Hearts on Fire Co., LLC v. Blue Nile, Inc. 603 F. Supp. 2d 274 (D. Mass. 2009); Network Automation v. Advanced Systems Concepts, 638 F.3d 1137 (9th Cir. 2011) (emphasis added).
22.   Alzheimer's Disease and Related Disorders Assoc., Inc. v. Alzheimer's Foundation of Am., Inc., 307 F. Supp. 3d 260 (S.D.N.Y. 2018)]
23.   15 U.S.C. §7701 *et seq.*

24. *Id.*
25. Fed. Trade Comm'n, The CAN-SPAM Act: A Compliance Guide for Business, http://www.ftc.gov/bcp/edu/pubs/business/ecommerce/bus61.shtm
26. Fed. Trade Comm'n, CAN-SPAM: A Study in "Mask" Communication, www.ftc.gov/news-events/blogs/business-blog/2016/06/can-spam-study-mask-communication
27. *Id.*
28. MCL §752.1061 et seq. and Utah Ann. Code §13-39-101 *et seq.*
29. 102 P.L. 243
30. Fed. Communications Comm'n, Text Message Senders Must Comply with the Telephone Consumer Protection Act, FCC Enforcement Advisory, DA 16-1299 (Nov. 18, 2016), https://docs.fcc.gov/public/attachments/DA-16-1299A1.pdf
31. *Id.*
32. *Id.*
33. *Id.*
34. Fed. Communications Comm'n, Avoid the Temptation of Smishing Scams, www.fcc.gov/avoid-temptation-smishing-scams
35. Fed. Trade Comm'n, Guides Concerning the Use of Endorsements and Testimonials in Advertising, 16 C.F.R. §225 (a) (2009).
36. *Id.* at §255 (b).
37. Fed. Trade Comm'n The FTC's Endorsement Guides: What People Are Asking, www.ftc.gov/tips-advice/business-center/guidance/ftcs-endorsement-guides
38. Fed. Trade Comm'n, Lord and Taylor Settles FTC Charges It Deceived Consumers Through Paid Article in an Online Fashion Magazine and Paid Instagram Posts by 50 'Fashion Influencers,' www.ftc.gov/news-events/press-releases/2016/03/lord-taylor-settles-ftc-charges-it-deceived-consumers-through
39. Fed. Trade Comm'n, *supra* note 35.
40. Fed. Trade Comm'n, Closing Letter to Christie Grimes Thompson, Counsel for Cole Haan, Inc., www.ftc.gov/news-events/press-releases/2016/03/lord-taylor-settles-ftc-charges-it-deceived-consumers-through
41. *Id.*
42. Tsan Abrahamson, *Re-Gramming, Hashtagging, and Like-Gating: Sweepstakes in the New Digital Age, and How New Laws May Actually Improve Your Promotions*, reprinted from the Practising Law Institute (PLI) Course Handbook, TechLaw Institute 2016: The Digital Evolution (Item #149277).
43. Fed. Trade Comm'n, Native Advertising: A Guide for Business, www.ftc.gov/tips-advice/business-center/guidance/native-advertising-guide-businesses
44. Fed. Trade Comm'n, Blurred Lines: Advertising or Content?–An FTC Workshop on Native Advertising, Dec. 2012, remarks of Chairwoman Edith Ramirez, transcript, www.ftc.gov/system/files/documents/public_events/171321/final_transcript_1.pdf
45. *Id.*
46. Fed. Trade Comm'n, *supra* note 43.
47. *Id.*
48. Fed. Trade Comm'n,.com Disclosures: How to Make Effective Disclosures in Digital Advertising, www.ftc.gov/system/files/documents/plain-language/bus41-dot-com-disclosures-information-about-online-advertising.pdf
49. *Id.*
50. *Id.*
51. *Id.*
52. *Id.*
53. *Id.*
54. *Id.*
55. Pub. L. No: 114-258, Dec. 14, 2016.

56. *Id.*

57. Fed. Trade Comm'n, Consumer Review Fairness Act: What Businesses Need to Know, www.ftc.gov/tips-advice/business-center/guidance/consumer-review-fairness-act-what-businesses-need-know

58. *Id.*

59. Fed. Trade Comm'n, First Consumer Review Fairness case takes on promoter's 'big bucks on Amazon' claim, www.ftc.gov/news-events/blogs/business-blog/2018/08/first-consumer-review-fairness-case-takes-promoters-big

60. http://rtaacademy.com/about/

61. Alexandra Bruell, *Media Agency of the Year*, 87 Advertising Age, Jan. 25, 2016, 45.

62. *Id.*

63. E.J. Schultz, *Digital A-List 2013; OREO*, Advertising Age, Feb. 25, 2013, https://advance-lexis-com.pallas2.tcl.sc.edu/api/document?collection=news&id=urn:contentItem:57VN-7XR1-DYFH-V1XB-00000-00&context=1516831

64. Fed. Trade Comm'n, Privacy & Data Security Update: 2017, www.ftc.gov/system/files/documents/reports/privacy-data-security-update-2017-overview-commissions-enforcement-policy-initiatives-consumer/privacy_and_data_security_update_2017.pdf

65. Senate Committee on the Judiciary, *Oversight of the Enforcement of the Antitrust Laws*, Oct. 3, 2018, Questions for Joseph Simons, Chairman, Federal Trade Commission, www.judiciary.senate.gov/imo/media/doc/Simons%20Responses%20to%20QFRs1.pdf

66. *Id.*

67. *Id.*

68. Fed. Trade Comm'n, *supra* note 64.

69. *Id.*

70. *Id.*

71. *Id.*

72. *Id.*

73. 15 U.S.C. §§1681, et seq.

74. The Gramm-Leach-Bliley (GLB) Act, Pub. L. 106-102, 113 Stat. 1338, enacted Nov. 12, 1999.

75. Fed. Trade Comm'n, *supra* note 64.

76. Complaint, *Commonwealth of Mass. C. Equifax, Inc.*, No: 17-cv-3009N ¶ 7, Sept. 19, 2017, www.mass.gov/ago/dpcs/press/2017/equifax-complaint.pdf.

77. 2018 Cal. Legis. Serv. Ch. 55 (A.B. 375)(West).

78. Jane E. Kirtley, *Privacy and Data Protection–2018*, p.171 in Communications Law in the Digital Age 2018 Course Handbook, sponsored by Practising Law Institute (PLI).

79. *Id.* at 174.

80. SMART IoT Act, H.R. 6032, 115th Cong. (2018).

81. *Id.*

82. National Institute of Standards and Technology Reauthorization Act of 2018, H.R. 6229, 115th Cong.

83. Seth Blinder, Panel Presentation at Practising Law Institute on Hot Topics in Advertising Law: Key Issues in Privacy and Data Collection for Advertisers (June 2017).

84. *Id.*

85. *Id.*

86. 15 U.S.C. §§6501-6506.

87. Fed. Trade Comm'n, Children's Online Privacy Protection Rule: Not Just for Kids' Sites, www.ftc.gov/tips-advice/business-center/guidance/childrens-online-privacy-protection-rule-not-just-kids-sites

88. *Id.*

89. *Id.*

90. Peter Magee, *Happy 20th Birthday, COPPA* (Oct. 22, 2018, 10:30 am), www.ftc.gov/news-events/blogs/business-blog/2018/10/happy-20th-birthday-coppa

91. Fed. Trade Comm'n, Children's Online Privacy Protection Act, www.ftc.gov/enforcement/statutes/childrens-online-privacy-protection-act

92. *Id.*

93. *Id.*

94. Magee, *supra* note 9.

95. Fed. Trade Comm'n, VTech Settlement Cautions Companies to Keep COPPA-Covered Data Secure, www.ftc.gov/news-events/blogs/business-blog/2018/01/vtech-settlement-cautions-companies-keep-coppa-covered-data

96. *Id.*

97. United States v. Prime Sites, Inc., d/b/a/ Explore Talent, Complaint for Permanent Injunction, Civil Penalties and Other Relief, www.ftc.gov/system/files/documents/cases/1623218exploretalentcomplaint.pdf

98. *Id.*

99. Fed. Trade Comm'n, Children's Online Privacy Protection Rule: A Six-Step Compliance Plan for Your Business, www.ftc.gov/tips-advice/business-center/guidance/childrens-online-privacy-protection-rule-six-step-compliance.

100. Fed. Trade Comm'n, Complying with COPPA: Frequently Asked Questions, www.ftc.gov/tips-advice/business-center/guidance/complying-coppa-frequently-asked-questions

Appendices

Appendix A

The Constitution of the United States

September 17, 1787

We the People of the United States, in Order to form a more perfect Union, establish Justice, insure domestic Tranquility, provide for the common defense, promote the general Welfare, and secure the Blessings of Liberty to ourselves and our Posterity, do ordain and establish this Constitution for the United States of America.

Article I

Section 1. All legislative Powers herein granted shall be vested in a Congress of the United States, which shall consist of a Senate and House of Representatives.

Section 2. The House of Representatives shall be composed of Members chosen every second Year by the People of the several States, and the Electors in each State shall have the Qualifications requisite for Electors of the most numerous Branch of the State Legislature.

No Person shall be a Representative who shall not have attained to the Age of twenty five Years, and been seven Years a Citizen of the United States, and who shall not, when elected, be an Inhabitant of that State in which he shall be chosen.

Representatives and direct Taxes shall be apportioned among the several States which may be included within this Union, according to their respective Numbers, which shall be determined by adding to the whole Number of free Persons, including those bound to Service for a Term of Years, and excluding Indians not taxed, three fifths of all other Persons. The actual Enumeration shall be made within three Years after the first Meeting of the Congress of the United States, and within every subsequent Term of ten Years, in such Manner as they shall by Law direct. The Number of Representatives shall not exceed one for every thirty Thousand, but each State shall have at Least one Representative; and until such enumeration shall be made, the State of New Hampshire shall be entitled to choose three, Massachusetts eight, Rhode Island and Providence Plantations one, Connecticut five, New York six, New Jersey four, Pennsylvania eight, Delaware one, Maryland six, Virginia ten, North Carolina five, South Carolina five, and Georgia three.

When vacancies happen in the Representation from any State, the Executive Authority thereof shall issue Writs of Election to fill such Vacancies.

The House of Representatives shall choose their Speaker and other Officers; and shall have the sole Power of Impeachment.

Section 3. The Senate of the United States shall be composed of two Senators from each State, chosen by the Legislature thereof for six Years; and each Senator shall have one Vote.

Immediately after they shall be assembled in Consequence of the first Election, they shall be divided as equally as may be into three Classes. The Seats of the Senators of the first Class shall be vacated at the Expiration of the second Year, of the second Class at the Expiration of the fourth Year, and of the third Class at the Expiration of the sixth Year, so that one third may be chosen every second Year; and if Vacancies happen by Resignation, or otherwise, during the Recess of the Legislature of any State, the Executive thereof may make temporary Appointments until the next Meeting of the Legislature, which shall then fill such Vacancies.

No Person shall be a Senator who shall not have attained to the Age of thirty Years, and been nine Years a Citizen of the United States, and who shall not, when elected, be an Inhabitant of that State for which he shall be chosen.

The Vice President of the United States shall be President of the Senate, but shall have no Vote, unless they be equally divided.

The Senate shall choose their other Officers, and also a President pro tempore, in the Absence of the Vice President, or when he shall exercise the Office of President of the United States.

The Senate shall have the sole Power to try all Impeachments. When sitting for that Purpose, they shall be on Oath or Affirmation. When the President of the United States is tried, the Chief Justice shall preside: And no Person shall be convicted without the Concurrence of two thirds of the Members present.

Judgment in Cases of Impeachment shall not extend further than to removal from Office, and disqualification to hold and enjoy any Office of honor, Trust or Profit under the United States: but the Party convicted shall nevertheless be liable and subject to Indictment, Trial, Judgment and Punishment, according to Law.

Section 4. The Times, Places and Manner of holding Elections for Senators and Representatives, shall be prescribed in each State by the Legislature thereof; but the Congress may at any time by Law make or alter such Regulations, except as to the Places of choosing Senators.

The Congress shall assemble at least once in every Year, and such Meeting shall be on the first Monday in December, unless they shall by Law appoint a different Day.

Section 5. Each House shall be the Judge of the Elections, Returns and Qualifications of its own Members, and a Majority of each shall constitute a Quorum to do Business; but a smaller Number may adjourn from day to day, and may be authorized to compel the Attendance of absent Members, in such Manner, and under such Penalties as each House may provide.

Each House may determine the Rules of its Proceedings, punish its Members for disorderly Behavior, and, with the Concurrence of two thirds, expel a Member.

Each House shall keep a Journal of its Proceedings, and from time to time publish the same, excepting such Parts as may in their Judgment require Secrecy; and the Yeas and Nays of the Members of either House on any question shall, at the Desire of one fifth of those Present, be entered on the Journal.

Neither House, during the Session of Congress, shall, without the Consent of the other, adjourn for more than three days, nor to any other Place than that in which the two Houses shall be sitting.

Section 6. The Senators and Representatives shall receive a Compensation for their Services, to be ascertained by Law, and paid out of the Treasury of the United States. They shall in all Cases, except Treason, Felony and Breach of the Peace, be privileged from Arrest during their Attendance at the Session of their respective Houses, and in going to and returning from the same; and for any Speech or Debate in either House, they shall not be questioned in any other Place.

No Senator or Representative shall, during the Time for which he was elected, be appointed to any civil Office under the Authority of the United States, which shall have been created, or the Emoluments whereof shall have been increased during such time; and no Person holding any Office under the United States, shall be a Member of either House during his Continuance in Office.

Section 7. All Bills for raising Revenue shall originate in the House of Representatives; but the Senate may propose or concur with Amendments as on other Bills.

Every Bill which shall have passed the House of Representatives and the Senate, shall, before it become a Law, be presented to the President of the United States: If he approve he shall sign it, but if not he shall return it, with his Objections to that House in which it shall have originated, who shall enter the Objections at large on their Journal, and proceed to reconsider it. If after such Reconsideration two thirds of that House shall agree to pass the Bill, it shall be sent, together with the Objections, to the other House, by which it shall likewise be reconsidered, and if approved by two thirds of that House, it shall become a Law. But in all such Cases the Votes of both Houses shall be determined by yeas and Nays, and the Names of the Persons voting for and against the Bill shall be entered on the Journal of each House respectively. If any Bill shall not be returned by the President within ten Days (Sundays excepted) after it shall have been presented to him, the Same shall be a Law, in like Manner as if he had signed it, unless the Congress by their Adjournment prevent its Return, in which Case it shall not be a Law.

Every Order, Resolution, or Vote to which the Concurrence of the Senate and House of Representatives may be necessary (except on a question of Adjournment) shall be presented to the President of the United States; and before the Same shall take Effect, shall be approved by him, or being disapproved by him, shall be repassed by two thirds of the Senate and House of Representatives, according to the Rules and Limitations prescribed in the Case of a Bill.

Section 8. The Congress shall have Power To lay and collect Taxes, Duties, Imposts and Excises, to pay the Debts and provide for the common Defense and general Welfare of the United States; but all Duties, Imposts and Excises shall be uniform throughout the United States;

To borrow Money on the credit of the United States;

To regulate Commerce with foreign Nations, and among the several States, and with the Indian Tribes;

To establish an uniform Rule of Naturalization, and uniform Laws on the subject of Bankruptcies throughout the United States;

To coin Money, regulate the Value thereof, and of foreign Coin, and fix the Standard of Weights and Measures;

To provide for the Punishment of counterfeiting the Securities and current Coin of the United States;

To establish Post Offices and post Roads;

To promote the Progress of Science and useful Arts, by securing for limited Times to Authors and Inventors the exclusive Right to their respective Writings and Discoveries;

To constitute Tribunals inferior to the Supreme Court;

To define and punish Piracies and Felonies committed on the high Seas, and Offences against the Law of Nations;

To declare War, grant Letters of Marque and Reprisal, and make Rules concerning Captures on Land and Water;

To raise and support Armies, but no Appropriation of Money to that Use shall be for a longer Term than two Years;

To provide and maintain a Navy;

To make Rules for the Government and Regulation of the land and naval Forces;

To provide for calling forth the Militia to execute the Laws of the Union, suppress Insurrections and repel Invasions;

To provide for organizing, arming, and disciplining, the Militia, and for governing such Part of them as may be employed in the Service of the United States, reserving to the States respectively, the Appointment of the Officers, and the Authority of training the Militia according to the discipline prescribed by Congress;

To exercise exclusive Legislation in all Cases whatsoever, over such District (not exceeding ten Miles square) as may, by Cession of particular States, and the Acceptance of Congress, become the Seat of the Government of the United States, and to exercise like Authority over all Places purchased by the Consent of the Legislature of the State in which the Same shall be, for the Erection of Forts, Magazines, Arsenals, dock-Yards, and other needful Buildings; And

To make all Laws which shall be necessary and proper for carrying into Execution the foregoing Powers, and all other Powers vested by this Constitution in the Government of the United States, or in any Department or Officer thereof.

Section 9. The Migration or Importation of such Persons as any of the States now existing shall think proper to admit, shall not be prohibited by the Congress prior to the Year one thousand eight hundred and eight, but a Tax or duty may be imposed on such Importation, not exceeding ten dollars for each Person.

Privilege of the Writ of Habeas Corpus shall not be suspended, unless when in Cases of Rebellion or Invasion the public Safety may require it. No Bill of Attainder or ex post facto Law shall be passed.

No Capitation, or other direct, Tax shall be laid, unless in Proportion to the Census or enumeration herein before directed to be taken.

No Tax or Duty shall be laid on Articles exported from any State.

No Preference shall be given by any Regulation of Commerce or Revenue to the Ports of one State over those of another; nor shall Vessels bound to, or from, one State, be obliged to enter, clear, or pay Duties in another.

No Money shall be drawn from the Treasury, but in Consequence of Appropriations made by Law; and a regular Statement and Account of the Receipts and Expenditures of all public Money shall be published from time to time.

No Title of Nobility shall be granted by the United States: And no Person holding any Office of Profit or Trust under them, shall, without the Consent of the Congress, accept of any present, Emolument, Office, or Title, of any kind whatever, from any King, Prince, or foreign State.

Section 10. No State shall enter into any Treaty, Alliance, or Confederation; grant Letters of Marque and Reprisal; coin Money; emit Bills of Credit; make any Thing but gold and silver Coin a Tender in Payment of Debts; pass any Bill of Attainder, ex post facto Law, or Law impairing the Obligation of Contracts, or grant any Title of Nobility.

No State shall, without the Consent of the Congress, lay any Imposts or Duties on Imports or Exports, except what may be absolutely necessary for executing it's inspection Laws: and the net Produce of all Duties and Imposts, laid by any State on Imports or Exports, shall be for the Use of the Treasury of the United States; and all such Laws shall be subject to the Revision and Control of the Congress.

No State shall, without the Consent of Congress, lay any Duty of Tonnage, keep Troops, or Ships of War in time of Peace, enter into any Agreement or Compact with another State, or with a foreign Power, or engage in War, unless actually invaded, or in such imminent Danger as will not admit of delay.

Article II

Section 1. The executive Power shall be vested in a President of the United States of America. He shall hold his Office during the Term of four Years, and, together with the Vice President, chosen for the same Term, be elected, as follows:

> Each State shall appoint, in such Manner as the Legislature thereof may direct, a Number of Electors, equal to the whole Number of Senators and Representatives to which the State may be entitled in the Congress: but no Senator or Representative, or Person holding an Office of Trust or Profit under the United States, shall be appointed an Elector.

The Electors shall meet in their respective States, and vote by Ballot for two Persons, of whom one at least shall not be an Inhabitant of the same State with themselves. And they shall make a List of all the Persons voted for, and of the Number of Votes for each; which List they shall sign and certify, and transmit sealed to the Seat of the Government of the United States, directed to the President of the Senate. The President of the Senate shall, in the Presence of the Senate and House of Representatives, open all the Certificates, and the Votes shall then be counted. The Person having the greatest Number of Votes shall be the President, if such Number be a Majority of the whole Number of Electors appointed; and if there be more than one who have such Majority, and have an equal Number of Votes, then the House of Representatives shall immediately choose by Ballot one of them for President; and if no Person have a Majority, then from the five highest on the List the said House shall in like Manner choose the President. But in choosing the President, the Votes shall be taken by States, the Representation from each State having one Vote; A quorum for this purpose shall consist of a Member or Members from two thirds of the States, and a Majority of all the States shall be necessary to a Choice. In every Case, after the Choice of the President, the Person having the greatest Number of Votes of the Electors shall be the Vice President. But if there should remain two or more who have equal Votes, the Senate shall choose from them by Ballot the Vice President.

The Congress may determine the Time of choosing the Electors, and the Day on which they shall give their Votes; which Day shall be the same throughout the United States.

No Person except a natural born Citizen, or a Citizen of the United States, at the time of the Adoption of this Constitution, shall be eligible to the Office of President; neither shall any Person be eligible to that Office who shall not have attained to the Age of thirty five Years, and been fourteen Years a Resident within the United States.

In Case of the Removal of the President from Office, or of his Death, Resignation, or Inability to discharge the Powers and Duties of the said Office, the Same shall devolve on the Vice President, and the Congress may by Law provide for the Case of Removal, Death, Resignation or Inability, both of the President and Vice President, declaring what Officer shall then act as President, and such Officer shall act accordingly, until the Disability be removed, or a President shall be elected.

The President shall, at stated Times, receive for his Services, a Compensation, which shall neither be increased nor diminished during the Period for which he shall have been elected, and he shall not receive within that Period any other Emolument from the United States, or any of them.

Before he enter on the Execution of his Office, he shall take the following Oath or Affirmation: "I do solemnly swear (or affirm) that I will faithfully execute the Office of President of the United States, and will to the best of my Ability, preserve, protect and defend the Constitution of the United States."

Section 2. The President shall be Commander in Chief of the Army and Navy of the United States, and of the Militia of the several States, when called into the actual Service of the United States; he may require the Opinion, in writing, of the principal Officer in each of the executive Departments, upon any Subject relating to the Duties of their respective Offices, and he shall have Power to grant Reprieves and Pardons for Offences against the United States, except in Cases of Impeachment.

He shall have Power, by and with the Advice and Consent of the Senate, to make Treaties, provided two thirds of the Senators present concur; and he shall nominate, and by and with the Advice and Consent of the Senate, shall appoint Ambassadors, other public Ministers and Consuls, Judges of the supreme Court, and all other Officers of the United States, whose Appointments are not herein otherwise provided for, and which shall be established by Law: but the Congress may by Law vest the Appointment of such inferior Officers, as they think proper, in the President alone, in the Courts of Law, or in the Heads of Departments.

The President shall have Power to fill up all Vacancies that may happen during the Recess of the Senate, by granting Commissions which shall expire at the End of their next Session.

Section 3. He shall from time to time give to the Congress Information of the State of the Union, and recommend to their Consideration such Measures as he shall judge necessary and expedient; he may, on extraordinary Occasions, convene both Houses, or either of them, and in Case of Disagreement between them, with Respect to the Time of Adjournment, he may adjourn them to such Time as he shall think proper; he shall receive Ambassadors and other public Ministers; he shall take Care that the Laws be faithfully executed, and shall Commission all the Officers of the United States.

Section 4. The President, Vice President and all civil Officers of the United States, shall be removed from Office on Impeachment for, and Conviction of, Treason, Bribery, or other high Crimes and Misdemeanors.

Article III

Section 1. The judicial Power of the United States shall be vested in one Supreme Court, and in such inferior Courts as the Congress may from time to time ordain and establish. The Judges, both of the supreme and inferior Courts, shall hold their Offices during good Behavior, and shall, at stated Times, receive for their Services a Compensation, which shall not be diminished during their Continuance in Office.

Section 2. The judicial Power shall extend to all Cases, in Law and Equity, arising under this Constitution, the Laws of the United States, and Treaties made, or which shall be made, under their Authority; to all Cases affecting Ambassadors, other public Ministers and Consuls; to all Cases of admiralty and maritime Jurisdiction; to Controversies to which the United States shall be a Party; to Controversies between two or more States; between a State and Citizens of another State, between Citizens of different States, between Citizens of the same State claiming Lands under Grants of different States, and between a State, or the Citizens thereof, and foreign States, Citizens or Subjects.

In all Cases affecting Ambassadors, other public Ministers and Consuls, and those in which a State shall be Party, the Supreme Court shall have original Jurisdiction. In all the other Cases before mentioned, the Supreme Court shall have appellate Jurisdiction, both as to Law and Fact, with such Exceptions, and under such Regulations as the Congress shall make.

The Trial of all Crimes, except in Cases of Impeachment, shall be by Jury; and such Trial shall be held in the State where the said Crimes shall have been committed; but when not committed within any State, the Trial shall be at such Place or Places as the Congress may by Law have directed.

Section 3. Treason against the United States, shall consist only in levying War against them, or in adhering to their Enemies, giving them Aid and Comfort. No Person shall be convicted of Treason unless on the Testimony of two Witnesses to the same overt Act, or on Confession in open Court.

The Congress shall have Power to declare the Punishment of Treason, but no Attainder of Treason shall work Corruption of Blood, or Forfeiture except during the Life of the Person attainted.

Article IV

Section 1. Full Faith and Credit shall be given in each State to the public Acts, Records, and judicial Proceedings of every other State. And the Congress may by general Laws prescribe the Manner in which such Acts, Records and Proceedings shall be proved, and the Effect thereof.

Section 2. The Citizens of each State shall be entitled to all Privileges and Immunities of Citizens in the several States.

A Person charged in any State with Treason, Felony, or other Crime, who shall flee from Justice, and be found in another State, shall on Demand of the executive Authority of the State from which he fled, be delivered up, to be removed to the State having Jurisdiction of the Crime.

No Person held to Service or Labor in one State, under the Laws thereof, escaping into another, shall, in Consequence of any Law or Regulation therein, be discharged from such Service or Labor, but shall be delivered up on Claim of the Party to whom such Service or Labor may be due.

Section 3. New States may be admitted by the Congress into this Union; but no new State shall be formed or erected within the Jurisdiction of any other State; nor any State be formed by the Junction of two or more States, or Parts of States, without the Consent of the Legislatures of the States concerned as well as of the Congress.

The Congress shall have Power to dispose of and make all needful Rules and Regulations respecting the Territory or other Property belonging to the United States; and nothing in this Constitution shall be so construed as to Prejudice any Claims of the United States, or of any particular State.

Section 4. The United States shall guarantee to every State in this Union a Republican Form of Government, and shall protect each of them against

Invasion; and on Application of the Legislature, or of the Executive (when the Legislature cannot be convened), against domestic Violence.

Article V

The Congress, whenever two thirds of both Houses shall deem it necessary, shall propose Amendments to this Constitution, or, on the Application of the Legislatures of two thirds of the several States, shall call a Convention for proposing Amendments, which, in either Case, shall be valid to all Intents and Purposes, as Part of this Constitution, when ratified by the Legislatures of three fourths of the several States, or by Conventions in three fourths thereof, as the one or the other Mode of Ratification may be proposed by the Congress; Provided that no Amendment which may be made prior to the Year One thousand eight hundred and eight shall in any Manner affect the first and fourth Clauses in the Ninth Section of the first Article; and that no State, without its Consent, shall be deprived of its equal Suffrage in the Senate.

Article VI

All Debts contracted and Engagements entered into, before the Adoption of this Constitution, shall be as valid against the United States under this Constitution, as under the Confederation.

This Constitution, and the Laws of the United States which shall be made in Pursuance thereof; and all Treaties made, or which shall be made, under the Authority of the United States, shall be the supreme Law of the Land; and the Judges in every State shall be bound thereby, any Thing in the Constitution or Laws of any State to the Contrary notwithstanding.

The Senators and Representatives before mentioned, and the Members of the several State Legislatures, and all executive and judicial Officers, both of the United States and of the several States, shall be bound by Oath or Affirmation, to support this Constitution; but no religious Test shall ever be required as a Qualification to any Office or public Trust under the United States.

Article VII

The Ratification of the Conventions of nine States, shall be sufficient for the Establishment of this Constitution between the States so ratifying the same.

Done in Convention by the Unanimous Consent of the States present the Seventeenth Day of September in the Year of our Lord one thousand seven hundred and Eighty seven and of the Independence of the United States of America the Twelfth In witness whereof

We have hereunto subscribed our Names,

GEO. WASHINGTON–President and deputy from Virginia

New Hampshire

John Langdon
Nicholas Gilman

Massachusetts

Nathaniel Gorham
Rufus King

Connecticut

Wm Saml Johnson
Roger Sherman

New York

Alexander Hamilton

New Jersey

Wil. Livingston
David Brearley
Wm Patterson
Jona. Dayton

Pennsylvania

B Franklin
Thomas Mifflin
Robt Morris
Geo Clymer
Thos Fitzsimons
Jared Ingersoll
James Wilson
Gouv. Morris

Delaware

Geo Read
Gunning Bedford Jun.
John Dickinson
Richard Bassett
Jaco. Broom

Maryland

James McHenry
Dan of St Tho Jenifer
Danl Carroll

Virginia

John Blair
James Madison Jr.

North Carolina

Wm Blount
Richd Dobbs Spaight
Hu Williamson

South Carolina

J. Rutledge
Charles Cotesworth Pinckney
Charles Pinckney
Pierce Butler

Georgia

William Few
Abr Baldwin
Attest
William Jackson

Amendments to the Constitution of the United States

Note: The first ten amendments (the Bill of Rights) were ratified effective December 15, 1791.

Amendment One

Congress shall make no law respecting an establishment of religion, or prohibiting the free exercise thereof; or abridging the freedom of speech, or of the press, or the right of the people peaceably to assemble, and to petition the Government for a redress of grievances.

Amendment Two

A well regulated Militia, being necessary to the security of a free State, the right of the people to keep and bear Arms, shall not be infringed.

Amendment Three

No Soldier shall, in time of peace be quartered in any house, without the consent of the Owner, nor in time of war, but in a manner to be prescribed by law.

Amendment Four

The right of the people to be secure in their persons, houses, papers, and effects, against unreasonable searches and seizures, shall not be violated, and no Warrants shall issue, but upon probable cause, supported by Oath or affirmation, and particularly describing the place to be searched, and the persons or things to be seized.

Amendment Five

No person shall be held to answer for a capital, or otherwise infamous crime, unless on a present- ment or indictment of a Grand Jury, except in cases arising in the land or naval forces, or in the Militia, when in actual service in time of War or public danger; nor shall any person be subject for the same offence to be twice put in jeopardy of life or limb; nor shall be compelled in any criminal case to be a witness against himself, nor be deprived of life, liberty, or property, without due process of law; nor shall private property be taken for public use, without just compensation.

Amendment Six

In all criminal prosecutions, the accused shall enjoy the right to a speedy and public trial, by an impartial jury of the State and district wherein the crime shall have been committed, which dis- trict shall have been previously ascertained by law, and to be informed of the nature and cause of the accusation; to be confronted with the witnesses against him; to have compulsory process for obtaining witnesses in his favor, and to have the Assistance of Counsel for his defense.

Amendment Seven

In Suits at common law, where the value in controversy shall exceed twenty dollars, the right of trial by jury shall be preserved, and no fact tried by a jury, shall be otherwise re-examined in any Court of the United States, than according to the rules of the common law.

Amendment Eight

Excessive bail shall not be required, nor excessive fines imposed, nor cruel and unusual punish- ments inflicted.

Amendment Nine

The enumeration in the Constitution, of certain rights, shall not be construed to deny or dispar- age others retained by the people.

Amendment Ten

The powers not delegated to the United States by the Constitution, nor prohibited by it to the States, are reserved to the States respectively, or to the people.

Amendment Eleven

February 7, 1795

Note: Article III, Section 2, of the Constitution was modified by Amendment Eleven.

The Judicial power of the United States shall not be construed to extend to any suit in law or equity, commenced or prosecuted against one of the United States by Citizens of another State, or by Citizens or Subjects of any Foreign State.

Amendment Twelve

June 15, 1804

Note: A portion of Article II, Section 1 of the Constitution was superseded by Amendment Twelve.

The Electors shall meet in their respective states and vote by ballot for President and Vice-President, one of whom, at least, shall not be an inhabitant of the same state with themselves; they shall name in their ballots the person voted for as President, and in distinct ballots the person voted for as Vice-President, and they shall make distinct lists of all persons voted for as President, and of all persons voted for as Vice-President, and of the number of votes for each, which lists they shall sign and certify, and transmit sealed to the seat of the government of the United States, directed to the President of the Senate; the President of the Senate shall, in the presence of the Senate and House of Representatives, open all the certificates and the votes shall then be counted; The person having the greatest number of votes for President, shall be the President, if such number be a majority of the whole number of Electors appointed; and if no person have such majority, then from the persons having the highest numbers not exceeding three on the list of those voted for as President, the House of Representatives shall choose immediately, by ballot, the President. But in choosing the President, the votes shall be taken by states, the representation from each state having one vote; a quorum for this purpose shall consist of a member or members from two-thirds of the states, and a majority of all the states shall be necessary to a choice. [And if the House of Representatives shall not choose a President whenever the right of choice shall devolve upon them, before the fourth day of March next following, then the Vice-President shall act as President, as in case of the death or other constitutional disability of the President.]* The person having the greatest number of votes as Vice-President, shall be the Vice-President, if such number be a majority of the whole number of Electors appointed, and if no person have a majority, then from the two highest numbers on the list, the Senate shall choose the Vice-President; a quorum for the purpose shall consist of two-thirds of the whole number of Senators, and a majority of the whole number shall be necessary to a choice. But no person constitutionally ineligible to the office of President shall be eligible to that of Vice-President of the United States.

*Superseded by Section 3 of Amendment Twenty.

Amendment Thirteen

December 6, 1865

Note: A portion of Article IV, Section 2, of the Constitution was superseded by Amendment Thirteen.

Section 1. Neither slavery nor involuntary servitude, except as a punishment for crime whereof the party shall have been duly convicted, shall exist within the United States, or any place subject to their jurisdiction.

Section 2. Congress shall have power to enforce this article by appropriate legislation.

Amendment Fourteen

July 9, 1868

Note: Article I, Section 2, of the Constitution was modified by Section 2 of Amendment Fourteen.

Section 1. All persons born or naturalized in the United States, and subject to the jurisdiction thereof, are citizens of the United States and of the State wherein they reside. No State shall make or enforce any law which shall abridge the privileges or immunities of citizens of the United States; nor shall any State deprive any person of life, liberty, or property, without due process of law; nor deny to any person within its jurisdiction the equal protection of the laws.

Section 2. Representatives shall be apportioned among the several States according to their respective numbers, counting the whole number of persons in each State, excluding Indians not taxed. But when the right to vote at any election for the choice of electors for President and Vice-President of the United States, Representatives in Congress, the Executive and Judicial officers of a State, or the members of the Legislature thereof, is denied to any of the male inhabitants of such State, being twenty-one years of age,* and citizens of the United States, or in any way abridged, except for participation in rebellion, or other crime, the basis of representation therein shall be reduced in the proportion which the number of such male citizens shall bear to the whole number of male citizens twenty-one years of age in such State.

Section 3. No person shall be a Senator or Representative in Congress, or elector of President and Vice-President, or hold any office, civil or military, under the United States, or under any State, who, having previously taken an oath, as a member of Congress, or as an officer of the United States, or as a member of any State legislature, or as an executive or judicial officer of any State, to support the Constitution of the United States, shall have engaged in insurrection or rebellion against the same, or given aid or comfort to the enemies thereof. But Congress may by a vote of two-thirds of each House, remove such disability.

Section 4. The validity of the public debt of the United States, authorized by law, including debts incurred for payment of pensions and bounties for services in suppressing insurrection or rebellion, shall not be questioned. But neither the United States nor any State shall assume or pay any debt or obligation incurred in aid of insurrection or rebellion against the United States, or any claim for the loss or emancipation of any slave; but all such debts, obligations and claims shall be held illegal and void.

Section 5. The Congress shall have the power to enforce, by appropriate legislation, the provisions of this article.

*Changed by Section 1 of Amendment Twenty-Six.

Amendment Fifteen

February 3, 1870

Section 1. The right of citizens of the United States to vote shall not be denied or abridged by the United States or by any State on account of race, color, or previous condition of servitude.

Section 2. The Congress shall have the power to enforce this article by appropriate legislation.

Amendment Sixteen

February 3, 1913

Note: Article I, Section 9, of the Constitution was modified by Amendment Sixteen.

The Congress shall have power to lay and collect taxes on incomes, from whatever source derived, without apportionment among the several States, and without regard to any census or enumeration.

Amendment Seventeen

April 8, 1913
   Note: Article I, Section 3, of the Constitution was modified by Amendment Seventeen.
   The Senate of the United States shall be composed of two Senators from each State, elected by the people thereof, for six years; and each Senator shall have one vote. The electors in each State shall have the qualifications requisite for electors of the most numerous branch of the State legislatures.
   When vacancies happen in the representation of any State in the Senate, the executive authority of such State shall issue writs of election to fill such vacancies: Provided, That the legislature of any State may empower the executive thereof to make temporary appointments until the people fill the vacancies by election as the legislature may direct.
   This amendment shall not be so construed as to affect the election or term of any Senator chosen before it becomes valid as part of the Constitution.

Amendment Eighteen

January 16, 1919
   Note: Amendment Eighteen was repealed by Amendment Twenty-One.

   Section 1. After one year from the ratification of this article the manufacture, sale, or transportation of intoxicating liquors within, the importation thereof into, or the exportation thereof from the United States and all territory subject to the jurisdiction thereof for beverage purposes is hereby prohibited.

   Section 2. The Congress and the several States shall have concurrent power to enforce this article by appropriate legislation.

   Section 3. This article shall be inoperative unless it shall have been ratified as an amendment to the Constitution by the legislatures of the several States, as provided in the Constitution, within seven years from the date of the submission hereof to the States by the Congress.

Amendment Nineteen

August 18, 1920
   The right of citizens of the United States to vote shall not be denied or abridged by the United States or by any State on account of sex.
   Congress shall have power to enforce this article by appropriate legislation.

Amendment Twenty

January 23, 1933
   Note: Article I, Section 4, of the Constitution was modified by Section 2 of this amendment. In addition, a portion of Amendment Twelve was superseded by Section 3.

Section 1. The terms of the President and the Vice President shall end at noon on the 20th day of January, and the terms of Senators and Representatives at noon on the 3d day of January, of the years in which such terms would have ended if this article had not been ratified; and the terms of their successors shall then begin.

Section 2. The Congress shall assemble at least once in every year, and such meeting shall begin at noon on the 3d day of January, unless they shall by law appoint a different day.

Section 3. If, at the time fixed for the beginning of the term of the President, the President elect shall have died, the Vice President elect shall become President. If a President shall not have been chosen before the time fixed for the beginning of his term, or if the President elect shall have failed to qualify, then the Vice President elect shall act as President until a President shall have qualified; and the Congress may by law provide for the case wherein neither a President elect nor a Vice President shall have qualified, declaring who shall then act as President, or the manner in which one who is to act shall be selected, and such person shall act accordingly until a President or Vice President shall have qualified.

Section 4. The Congress may by law provide for the case of the death of any of the persons from whom the House of Representatives may choose a President whenever the right of choice shall have devolved upon them, and for the case of the death of any of the persons from whom the Senate may choose a Vice President whenever the right of choice shall have devolved upon them.

Section 5. Sections 1 and 2 shall take effect on the 15th day of October following the ratification of this article.

Section 6. This article shall be inoperative unless it shall have been ratified as an amendment to the Constitution by the legislatures of three-fourths of the several States within seven years from the date of its submission.

Amendment Twenty-One

December 5, 1933

Section 1. The eighteenth article of amendment to the Constitution of the United States is hereby repealed.

Section 2. The transportation or importation into any State, Territory, or Possession of the United States for delivery or use therein of intoxicating liquors, in violation of the laws thereof, is hereby prohibited.

Section 3. This article shall be inoperative unless it shall have been ratified as an amendment to the Constitution by conventions in the several States, as provided in the Constitution, within seven years from the date of the submission hereof to the States by the Congress.

Amendment Twenty-Two

February 27, 1951

Section 1. No person shall be elected to the office of the President more than twice, and no person who has held the office of President, or acted as President, for more than two years of a term to which some other person was elected President shall be elected to the office of President more than once. But this Article shall not apply to any person holding the office of President when this Article was proposed by Congress, and shall not prevent any person who may be holding the office of President, or acting as President, during the term within which this Article becomes operative from holding the office of President or acting as President during the remainder of such term.

Section 2. This article shall be inoperative unless it shall have been ratified as an amendment to the Constitution by the legislatures of three-fourths of the several States within seven years from the date of its submission to the States by the Congress.

Amendment Twenty-Three

March 29, 1961

Section 1. The District constituting the seat of Government of the United States shall appoint in such manner as Congress may direct:

> A number of electors of President and Vice President equal to the whole number of Senators and Representatives in Congress to which the District would be entitled if it were a State, but in no event more than the least populous State; they shall be in addition to those appointed by the States, but they shall be considered, for the purposes of the election of President and Vice President, to be electors appointed by a State; and they shall meet in the District and perform such duties as provided by the twelfth article of amendment.

Section 2. The Congress shall have power to enforce this article by appropriate legislation.

Amendment Twenty-Four

January 23, 1964

Section 1. The right of citizens of the United States to vote in any primary or other election for President or Vice President, for electors for President or Vice President, or for Senator or Representative in Congress, shall not be denied or abridged by the United States or any State by reason of failure to pay poll tax or other tax.

Section 2. The Congress shall have power to enforce this article by appropriate legislation.

Amendment Twenty-Five

February 10, 1967
Note: Article II, Section 1, of the Constitution was affected by the Twenty-Fifth Amendment.

Section 1. In case of the removal of the President from office or of his death or resignation, the Vice President shall become President.

Section 2. Whenever there is a vacancy in the office of the Vice President, the President shall nominate a Vice President who shall take office upon confirmation by a majority vote of both Houses of Congress.

Section 3. Whenever the President transmits to the President pro tempore of the Senate and the Speaker of the House of Representatives his written declaration that he is unable to discharge the powers and duties of his office, and until he transmits to them a written declaration to the contrary, such powers and duties shall be discharged by the Vice President as Acting President.

Section 4. Whenever the Vice President and a majority of either the principal officers of the executive departments or of such other body as Congress may by law provide, transmit to the President pro tempore of the Senate and the Speaker of the House of Representatives their written declaration that the President is unable to discharge the powers and duties of his office, the Vice President shall immediately assume the powers and duties of the office as Acting President.

Thereafter, when the President transmits to the President pro tempore of the Senate and the Speaker of the House of Representatives his written declaration that no inability exists, he shall resume the powers and duties of his office unless the Vice President and a majority of either the principal officers of the executive department or of such other body as Congress may by law provide, transmit within four days to the President pro tempore of the Senate and the Speaker of the House of Representatives their written declaration that the President is unable to discharge the powers and duties of his office. Thereupon Congress shall decide the issue, assembling within forty-eight hours for that purpose if not in session. If the Congress, within twenty-one days after receipt of the latter written declaration, or, if Congress is not in session, within twenty-one days after Congress is required to assemble, determines by two-thirds vote of both Houses that the President is unable to discharge the powers and duties of his office, the Vice President shall continue to discharge the same as Acting President; otherwise, the President shall resume the powers and duties of his office.

Amendment Twenty-Six

July 1, 1971

Note: Amendment Fourteen, Section 2, of the Constitution was modified by Section 1 of the Twenty-Sixth Amendment.

Section 1. The right of citizens of the United States, who are eighteen years of age or older, to vote shall not be denied or abridged by the United States or by any State on account of age.

Section 2. The Congress shall have power to enforce this article by appropriate legislation.

Amendment Twenty-Seven

May 7, 1992

No law, varying the compensation for the services of the Senators and Representatives, shall take effect, until an election of representatives shall have intervened.

Appendix B

The United States Court System

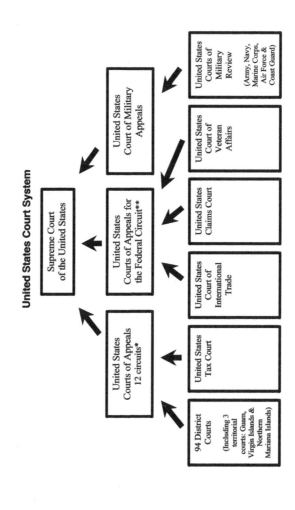

United States Court System

* The 12 original Courts of Appeals also review cases from a number of federal agencies.

** The Court of Appeals for the Federal Circuit also receives cases from the International Trade Commission, the Merit Systems Protection Board, the Patent and Trademark Office, and the Board of Contract Appeals.

Appendix C

Sample Model Release Forms

ADULT MODEL RELEASE

For valuable consideration received, I hereby grant to _____
("Photographer") the absolute and irrevocable right and unrestricted permission, in respect of photographic portraits or pictures that he/she has taken of me or in which I may be included with others, to copyright the same, in his/her own name or otherwise; to use, re-use, publish and republish the same in whole or in part, individually or in conjunction with other photographs, and in conjunction with any printed matter, in any and all media now or hereafter known, and for any purpose whatever, for illustration, promotion, art, editorial, advertising and trade, or any other purpose whatsoever without restriction as to alteration; and to use my name in connection therewith if he/she so chooses.

I hereby release and discharge Photographer from any and all claims and demands arising out of or in connection with the use of photographs, including without limitation any and all claims for libel or invasion of privacy.

This authorization and release shall also inure to the benefit of the heirs, legal representatives, licensees and assigns of the Photographer, as well as the person(s) for whom he/she took the photographs.

I am of full age and have the right to contract in my own name. I have read the foregoing and fully understand the contents thereof. This release shall be binding upon me and my heirs, legal representatives and assigns.

_____   _____

Date   Name

                                                                  _____

                                                                  _____

                                                                  Address

_____

Witness

MINOR MODEL RELEASE

In consideration of the engagement as a model of the minor named below, and for other good and valuable consideration herein acknowledged as received, upon the terms hereinafter stated, I hereby grant to _____ ("Photographer"), his/her legal representative and assigns, those for whom Photographer is acting, and those acting with his/her authority and permission, the absolute right and permission to copyright and use, re-use, publish and re-publish photographic portraits or pictures of the minor or in which the minor may be included, in whole or in part, or composite or distorted in character or form, without restriction as to changes or alterations from time to time, in conjunction with the minor's own or a fictitious name, or reproductions thereof in color or otherwise, made through any medium at his/her studios or elsewhere, and in any and all media now or hereafter known, for art, advertising, trade, or any other purpose whatsoever. I also consent to the use of any printed matter in conjunction therewith.

I hereby waive any right that I or the minor may have to inspect or approve the finished product or products or the advertising copy or printed matter that may be used in connection therewith or the use to which it may be applied.

I hereby release, discharge and agree to save harmless Photographer, his/her legal representatives or assigns, and all persons acting under his/her permission or authority or those for whom he/she is acting, from any liability by virtue of any blurring, distortion, alteration, optical illusion, or use in composite form, whether intentional or otherwise, that may occur or be produced in the taking of said picture or in any subsequent processing thereof, as well as any publication thereof, including without limitation any claims for libel or invasion of privacy.

I hereby warrant that I am of full age and have every right to contract for the minor in the above regard. I state further that I have read the above authorization, release and agreement, prior to its execution, and that I am fully familiar with the contents thereof. This release shall be binding upon me and my heirs, legal representatives and assigns.

_____
Date

_____   _____
Minor's Name   Father/Mother/Guardian

_____   _____
Minor's Address

                                                              _____
                                                              Address

_____
Witness

Appendix D

Sample Copyright Agreements

SAMPLE EXCLUSIVE COPYRIGHT AGREEMENT

_____ [John Doe] _____ (hereinafter "Licensor") is the author and owner of the rights of _____ [Photograph A] _____ (hereinafter the "Work"). ____ [Jane Roe] _____ (hereinafter "Licensee") intends to acquire the right to use the Work as specified in this agreement (hereinafter "the Agreement").

1. LICENSEE PUBLICATION. The Work will appear in _____ [Great Photos in Sports]._____

2. GRANT OF RIGHTS. Licensor grants to Licensee and Licensee's successors and assigns, the exclusive right to reproduce and distribute the Work, in all foreign-language versions of the Work, in all media now known or later devised, and in promotional materials published and distributed in conjunction with the Work.

3. FEES. Licensee shall pay Licensor a fee of _____ [$X,XXX.XX] _____ as full payment for all rights granted. Payment shall be made upon execution of this Agreement or in other manner agreed to by the Parties.

4. CREDIT AND SAMPLES. All versions of the Work shall attribute the Work to Licensor by including the following statement conspicuously displayed: By _____ [John Doe] _____. Licensee shall have discretion over any additional, accompanying attribution or credit to accompany the Work.

   Upon publication, Licensee shall furnish _____ X _____ copies of the Work to Licensor.

5. REPRESENTATIONS AND WARRANTIES. Licensor warrants that he/she has the right to grant permission for the uses of the Work and the Work does not infringe the rights of any third parties.

6. MISCELLANEOUS. This Agreement may not be amended except in a written document signed by both parties. The Parties agree that any court proceedings related to this Agreement shall be held in the exclusive jurisdiction of either the state or federal courts located in ____ [Your State, USA] _____.

This Agreement expresses the complete understanding of the parties with respect to the subject matter and supersedes all prior representations and understandings.

LICENSOR : _____

                         Name   Date

LICENSEE: _____

                         Name   Date

SAMPLE NON-EXCLUSIVE COPYRIGHT AGREEMENT

_____ [John Doe] _____ (hereinafter "Licensor") is the author and owner of the rights of ____ [Photograph A] _____ (hereinafter the "Work"). _____ [Jane Roe] _____ (hereinafter "Licensee") intends to acquire the right to use the Work as specified in this agreement (hereinafter "the Agreement").

1. LICENSEE PUBLICATION. The Work will appear in a book entitled _____ [Great Photos in Sports] _____.

2. GRANT OF RIGHTS. Licensor grants to Licensee, and Licensee's successors and assigns, the non-exclusive right to reproduce and distribute the Work in _____[Great Photos in Sports] _____ and in printed and online advertising materials that specifically promote the sale of _____ [Great Photos in Sports] _____. All other rights are reserved to the Licensor.

3. FEES. Licensee shall pay Licensor a fee of _____ [$X,XXX.XX] _____ as full payment for all rights granted. Payment shall be made upon execution of this Agreement or in other manner agreed to by the Parties.

4. CREDIT AND SAMPLES. All versions of the Work shall attribute the Work to Licensor by including the following statement conspicuously displayed: Photo by _____ [John Doe] _____. Licensee shall have discretion over any additional, accompanying attribution or credit to accompany the Work.

    Upon publication, Licensee shall furnish _____ X _____ copies of the Work to Licensor.

5. REPRESENTATIONS AND WARRANTIES. Licensor warrants that he/she has the right to grant permission for the uses of the Work and the Work does not infringe the rights of any third parties.

6. MISCELLANEOUS. This Agreement may not be amended except in a written document signed by both parties. The Parties agree that any court proceedings related to this Agreement shall be held in the exclusive jurisdiction of either the state or federal courts located in __[Your State, USA] _____.

This Agreement expresses the complete understanding of the parties with respect to the subject matter and supersedes all prior representations and understandings.

LICENSOR : _____

                Name   Date

LICENSEE: _____

                Name   Date

Glossary

Absolute Privilege – in the context of defamation, the freedom to discuss certain aspects of the public's business without fear of liability.

Affirmative Defense – a defense in which defendants admit to the truth of a plaintiff's complaint but claim they should not be liable for harm.

Appeal – the process of requesting that a higher court review a court judgment or outcome from a lower court.

Bait-and-Switch Advertising – advertising that features of a product for sale that the seller has no intention of selling but promotes for the purpose of selling an alternative item instead, often at a higher price.

Beyond All Reasonable Doubt – the burden or standard of proof in a criminal case. See also *Burden of Proof*.

Burden of Proof – in a legal dispute, the requirement that a party present evidence sufficient to meet the standard required by law to support a conviction or finding of liability. See *Beyond All Reasonable Doubt* (criminal) and *Preponderance of the Evidence* (civil).

CAN-SPAM Act – a federal law that sets rules for commercial e-mail, establishes requirements for commercial e-mail messages, gives recipients the right to have commercial senders stop emailing them and spells out penalties for violations.

Cause of Action – the existence of facts that may allow a plaintiff to file a particular kind of lawsuit such as one for defamation or invasion of privacy.

Censorship – the process of prohibiting or preventing the dissemination of certain messages or content. See also *Previous Restraint* and *Prior Restraint*.

Civil Lawsuit – a lawsuit filed by an individual or entity (e.g., company) against another in which the plaintiff seeks some kind of legal relief or compensation, typically money damages.

Collective Work – in the context of copyright law, a work, such as a newspaper, magazine or encyclopedia, in which a number of separate and independent works have been contributed for assembly into a new, collective whole.

Commerce Clause – language in Article I, Section 8 of the United States Constitution that states, "The Congress shall have Power To... regulate Commerce with Foreign Nations, and among the several States, and with the Indian Tribes."

Common Law – a body of "judge-made" law based on court decisions and opinions rather than legislative enactments.

Compelling Interest – the governmental rationale needed to withstand strict scrutiny; a rigorous type of judicial review of government actions. Ordinarily required when the government seeks to restrict the content of a communicator's expression.

Compensatory Damages – money awarded to a plaintiff in a legal action to compensate for injuries and/or losses caused by the defendant. See *Punitive Damages*.

Compilation – in the context of copyright law, a work formed by the collection and assembling of preexisting materials in such a way that the resulting work constitutes an original work of authorship. Includes *Collective Works*.

Complaint – the document filed by a plaintiff in a civil lawsuit that spells out the allegations against the defendant.

Concurring Opinion – an opinion filed by an appellate court judge or justice indicating agreement with another opinion filed in the same case, often stating his or her reasons for agreeing.

Conditional Privilege – in the context of defamation, the freedom to discuss certain aspects of the public's business without fear of liability, as long as certain conditions are met, such as not making a mistake in reporting the contents of public records. See also *Qualified Privilege*.

Confidentiality Agreement – a binding legal contract that requires a party or parties to maintain the confidentiality of information obtained from another party to the agreement. See also *Nondisclosure Agreement*.

Consideration – something of value given in exchange for something else in a contractual relationship.

Constructive Contract – see also *Quasi Contract*.

Content-neutral – a law or regulation that regulates conduct, but not any expression or viewpoint that accompanies the conduct.

Contract – a private agreement that is backed by consideration and defines the behaviors, risks and obligations of the parties who have entered into it.

Conviction – the result of a criminal trial in which the defendant is found to be guilty of the offenses charged.

Copyright – according to the Copyright Act of 1976, the exclusive right of authors to reproduce their works, prepare derivative works, distribute copies by sale, lease or other transfer and publicly perform or display their works of authorship.

Copyright Act of 1976 – the federal law that governs copyrights as authorized by Article I, Section 8 of the Constitution of the Unites States. See *Intellectual Property Clause*.

Copyright Infringement – the act of depriving copyright owners of one or more of their exclusive rights. See *Copyright*.

Court of Appeals – a higher (or superior) court that has the authority to review a court judgment or outcome from a lower court.

Crime – taking of action, or failing to take action, that is in violation of the obligations imposed by society upon the individuals within it.

Cybersquatting – the bad faith practice of claiming Internet domain names in order to deprive another Internet user of the name or require that the other user pay to have the name transferred to them.

Damages – money awarded to civil plaintiffs who successfully sue another for personal or property injury. See *Compensatory Damages* and *Punitive Damages*.

Declaratory Judgment – a judgment in which the presiding judge declares the rights of the parties regarding a particular question of law.

Defamation – published statements, usually false, about another person or organization that question their character and harm their reputation. Includes the torts of *libel* (for written or broadcast statements) and *slander* (for spoken statements). See also *Libel* and *Slander*.

Defendant – in a criminal or civil proceeding, the one who is in the position of defending against the charge(s) or complaint.

Disclaimer – a statement, usually written, in which parties state their lack of affiliation with other parties or deny responsibility for their actions or potential outcomes.

Dissenting Opinion – an opinion filed by an appellate court judge or justice indicating disagreement with another opinion filed in the same case, often stating reasons for dissenting.

Distortion – a variety of *False Light Invasion of Privacy* that creates an inaccurate portrayal of someone by distorting aspects of his or her life or accomplishments.

Embellishment – a variety of *False Light Invasion of Privacy* that creates an inaccurate portrayal of someone by adding details that are not necessarily true to make aspects of his or her life or accomplishments seem more interesting.

Emotional Distress – a type of civil lawsuit in which the defendant's outrageous, persistent conduct is alleged to have been intended to cause the plaintiff emotional distress.

Endorsement – in advertising, a message that consumers are likely to believe indicates the opinions or experiences of a person other than the sponsor of the message.

Equal Protection Clause – a portion of the Fourteenth Amendment to the United States Constitution that requires states to treat everyone within their jurisdictions equally with respect to the law.

Exacting Scrutiny – a rigorous type of judicial review of government action in which a court looks for the presence of a compelling governmental interest. Normally applied when the government seeks to restrict the content of a communicator's expression or interfere with some other fundamental liberty. Also known as *Strict Scrutiny*.

Express Contract – a legally binding agreement in which the parties have actually expressed the terms of their expected conduct in relation to each other.

False Light – a type of *Invasion of Privacy* that involves false, but not defamatory, portrayals of people, usually as a result of distortion, embellishment or fictionalization.

Federal Trade Commission (FTC) – the federal administrative agency empowered by Congress to regulate trade practices, including advertising and promotions.

Fictionalization – a variety of *False Light Invasion of Privacy* that creates an inaccurate portrayal of someone by fictionalizing aspects of his or her life or accomplishments.

Food and Drug Administration (FDA) – the federal administrative agency empowered by Congress to regulate certain foods, drugs, biologics, medical devices, radiation-emitting electronics, cosmetics, veterinary and tobacco products.

Freedom of Information Act (FOIA) – at the federal level, a law that provides the public with a right of access to records produced or kept by federal agencies. Similar state laws provide a right of access to records and meetings of public governing bodies. See also *Sunshine Act*.

Gag Rules – court-imposed orders that forbid certain actors, usually parties to a legal case, from disclosing information about the case or a matter related to it.

Implied-in-Fact Contract – an "after the fact" contract based on circumstantial evidence of the parties' actual intentions to enter into such an agreement.

Implied-in-Law Contract – a "fictitious" contract that imposes an obligation on one party to compensate another party, even when there is no express or implied contract in place and the parties did not necessarily intend for one to exist. Also known as a *Quasi Contract*.

Intellectual Property Clause – language contained in Article I, Section 8 of the United States Constitution that states, "The Congress shall have Power ... To promote the Progress of

Science and useful Arts, by securing for limited Times to Authors and Inventors the exclusive Right to their respective Writings and Discoveries."

Interlocutory Appeal – an appeal made regarding some aspect of a case during the process of a legal dispute that does not, by itself, determine the overall outcome of the dispute.

Intermediate Scrutiny – a type of judicial review of government action in which a court looks for the presence of a substantial or important governmental interest. In advertising or public relations, ordinarily applied when the government seeks to restrict commercial expression or impose regulations as to the time, place or manner of political expression.

Intrusion – a type of *Invasion of Privacy* that involves the highly offensive physical or electronic intrusion upon the solitude or seclusion of another in his or her private affairs or concerns.

Invasion of Privacy – an area of tort law that includes misappropriation, false light, public disclosure of private facts and intrusion.

Joint Work of Authorship – in copyright law, a work prepared by two or more authors with the intention that their contributions be merged into a unitary whole.

Jurisdiction – the authority of a court or governmental body to make and enforce laws and direct how legal matters are handled.

Lanham Act – the federal law that governs trademarks, service marks and claims of unfair competition. Also known as the *Trademark Act of 1946*.

Lawsuit – a cause of action initiated by one party against another in a court of law.

Liability Without Fault – the imposition of civil liability without a showing of negligence or some other breach of conduct. See also *Strict Liability*.

Libel – written, broadcast or other enduring statements (as opposed to transitory spoken words), usually false, about other persons that harm their reputations. See also *Defamation*.

Libel by Implication – defamation that results not from direct statements, but from the reader's or listener's logically inferred interpretation.

Libel *Per Quod* – a false, defamatory statement that is not on its face harmful to reputation but is made so by the addition of independent information known by the reader or listener.

Libel *Per Se* – a false, defamatory statement that is on its face harmful to reputation.

Litigation – deciding a dispute or conflict using the legal system.

Majority Opinion – an opinion filed by an appellate court and endorsed by more than half of the judges who have been asked to decide a particular legal matter.

Marketplace of Ideas – a view of free speech that suggests ideas, like goods and services in a free economic marketplace, should be made freely available and subjected only to the approval or disapproval of "consumers" of the ideas rather than governmental censors.

Minimum Scrutiny – a deferential type of judicial review of government action in which a court looks for the presence of a rational or reasonable governmental interest. Ordinarily applied when the government seeks to restrict everyday activities (or expression not protected by the First Amendment).

Minority Opinion – an opinion or opinions filed by an appellate court and endorsed by fewer than half of the judges who have been asked to decide a particular legal matter.

Misappropriation – a type of *Invasion of Privacy* in which the plaintiff alleges the defendant used, without consent, the plaintiff's image for commercial purposes or personal gain and caused the plaintiff emotional harm. See also *Right of Publicity*.

Motion – a request, often written, asking that a court take some kind of action or make some kind of ruling in a particular legal dispute.

Motion to Dismiss – a request, usually written, asking that a court dismiss the plaintiff's case because it is legally insufficient or violates some kind of procedural rule and cannot be successful.

Negligence – failure to act with the degree of care that a reasonable person would have used under similar circumstances.

Non-Compete Agreement – an agreement between two parties in which one agrees not to compete against the other in a similar business or market for a certain period of time.

Nondisclosure Agreement – a binding legal contract that requires a party or parties to maintain the confidentiality of information obtained from another party to the agreement. See also *Confidentiality Agreement*.

Open Meeting Laws – statutes requiring that the public be allowed a right of access to most meetings of public governing bodies.

Opinion – a judge's written explanation of a judgment in a particular case.

Oral Argument – in-court statements by attorneys in support of their client or made to rebut the statements of the opposing party.

Ordinance – the term used generally for a local law passed by a county, city or other municipality.

Parody – in copyright and trademark law, a secondary work that intentionally comments upon an original work while necessarily reproducing or parroting all or some of the original.

Patent – the exclusive right of control granted in Article I, Section 8 of the Constitution of the United States to an inventor of a unique device, process or system. See also *Intellectual Property Clause*.

Patent Infringement – the process of interfering with the exclusive right or control of a patent owner. See also *Patent*.

Plaintiff – in a civil lawsuit, the party who initiates the legal action by filing a complaint.

Precedent – a legal outcome that serves as a model for subsequent cases dealing with similar matters.

Preponderance of the Evidence – the burden, or standard, of proof typically employed in a civil case, often expressed as "more likely than not." See also *Burden of Proof*.

Previous Restraint – a law or regulation intended to prevent a speaker or publisher from disseminating content. See also *Prior Restraint* and *Censorship*.

Prior Restraint – a law or regulation intended to prevent a speaker or publisher from disseminating content. See also *Previous Restraint* and *Censorship*.

Prior Substantiation – a requirement of the Federal Trade Commission that advertisers be able to substantiate any material advertising claims prior to making them.

Private Plaintiff – in the context of defamation, a plaintiff who is neither a public official nor a public figure.

Product Disparagement – damaging statements about products or services that harm their position in the marketplace. See also *Trade Libel*.

Public Disclosure of Private Facts – a type of *Invasion of Privacy* in which truthful, private and usually embarrassing facts about an individual are disclosed at least negligently in a manner that offends ordinary decency and causes mental anguish to the plaintiff.

Public Plaintiff – in the context of defamation, a plaintiff who is a public official or a public figure.

Puffing – in advertising, exaggerated, opinion-based statements that reasonable consumers recognize as just "sales talk" or "puffery" and not material statements of fact.

Punitive Damages – money awarded to a plaintiff in a legal action that is designed not to compensate the plaintiff but to punish the defendant. See *Compensatory Damages*.

Qualified Privilege – in the context of defamation, the freedom to discuss certain aspects of the public's business without fear of liability, as long as certain conditions are met, such as correctly (and not erroneously) reporting the contents of public records. See also *Conditional Privilege*.

Quasi Contract – a "fictitious" contract that imposes an obligation on one party to compensate another party, even when there is no express or implied contract in place and the parties did not necessarily intend for one to exist. Also known as an *Implied-in-Law Contract*.

Rational Basis – the governmental rationale needed to withstand minimum scrutiny; a relaxed type of judicial review of government action. Ordinarily required when the government seeks to regulate everyday activities (or restrict types of speech that have no First Amendment protection).

Regulation – a rule having the force and effect of law, often imposed by regulatory agencies such as the Federal Trade Commission.

Remand – the action of a higher court to send a case back to a lower court so that additional action may be taken.

Restatement of Torts – a published treatise that summarizes various legal causes of action arising under tort law in the United States.

Retraction – in the context of defamation, to withdraw or "take back" the offending statements.

Right of Publicity – a type of *Invasion of Privacy* in which the plaintiff alleges the defendant used, without consent, the plaintiff's image for commercial purposes or personal gain and interfered with the plaintiff's own property rights in his or her image. See also *Misappropriation*.

Satire – a type of expression in which humor, exaggeration, irony or sarcasm are used to comment upon, ridicule or criticize aspects of culture.

Securities and Exchange Commission (SEC) – the federal administrative agency empowered by Congress to oversee investments, markets, securities and the formation of capital.

Service Mark – a name, symbol or color that identifies the source of services in the commercial marketplace. See also *Trademark*.

Sine Qua Non – in copyright law, the requirement that, to be protected, works of authorship must be original and not copied.

Slander – orally disseminated statements, usually false, about other persons or organizations that harm their reputation. See also *Defamation*.

Standing – the ability to file a particular lawsuit based upon a personal stake in the outcome.

Stare Decisis – in law, the principle that lower courts should follow decisions that have already been made by higher courts in previous cases.

Statute – the term generally used for a law passed by a legislative branch of government.

Strict Liability – the imposition of civil liability without a showing of negligence or some other breach of conduct. See also *Liability Without Fault*.

Strict Scrutiny – a rigorous type of judicial review of government action in which a court looks for the presence of a compelling governmental interest. Normally applied when the government seeks to restrict the content of a communicator's expression or interfere with some other fundamental liberty. Also known as *Exacting Scrutiny*.

Subpoena – an order backed by a court requiring a person to appear in a legal proceeding as a witness or provide materials relevant to the dispute.

Substantial Interest – the governmental rationale needed to withstand intermediate scrutiny, a type of judicial review of government action that is less rigorous than strict scrutiny. Ordinarily required when the government seeks to restrict commercial expression or impose regulations as to the time, place or manner of political expression.

Summary Judgment – an order entered by a court in early or intermediate stages of litigation that determines the outcome based on the judge's assessment of undisputed facts.

Sunshine Act – the Government in the Sunshine Act at the federal level gives the public a right of access to meetings of certain federal agencies. Also, a nickname for state-level Freedom of Information Acts (FOIAs), sometimes called "sunshine laws." See also *Freedom of Information Act*.

Supreme Court of the United States – the highest court in the United States, with jurisdiction over all federal and state courts as to matters concerning federal laws or issues and the United States Constitution.

Testimonial – in advertising, a message that consumers are likely to believe indicates the speaker's personal experience with a product or service.

Time, Place or Manner (TPM) Restrictions – rules or laws that may be imposed by governmental entities to dictate how and when expression occurs but not to regulate the content of the expression itself.

Tort – the term for legal harm that causes injury and may be addressed with the filing of a civil lawsuit.

Trade Libel – damaging statements about products or services that harm their position in the marketplace. See also *Product Disparagement*.

Trademark – a name, symbol or color that identifies the source of goods in the commercial marketplace. See also *Service Mark*.

Trademark Act of 1946 – the federal law that governs trademarks, service marks and claims of unfair competition. Also known as the *Lanham Act*.

Trademark Dilution – the act of diluting or weakening the value of a distinctive, famous trademark by using a similar mark in a way that blurs the original mark's distinctive characteristics or tarnishes the reputation of the famous mark.

Trademark Dilution Revision Act of 2006 – the federal law that allows owners of distinctive, famous trademarks to sue over the use of similar marks that blur or tarnish their trademarks. See also *Trademark Dilution*.

Trade Secret – information (e.g., formulae, plans, processes, devices, compounds) with commercial value derived from the fact that competitors do not have access to it.

Trade Secret Misappropriation – the process of making unauthorized use of a trade secret and thus depriving the owner of its value.

Trespass – to enter another's property without permission.

Trial – the process during which facts and law related to a legal dispute are presented in court and decided by a jury or a judge standing in the shoes of the jury.

Trial Court – the court in which trials related to a legal matter are conducted.

United States Court of Appeals – federal appellate courts that have authority to review court judgments from United States District Courts.

United States District Court – federal trial courts in which trials related to legal matters implicating federal law, or sometimes involving parties from different states, are conducted.

Vacate – in law, to set aside or void a decision by a lower court.

Witness – a person who provides evidence in a legal dispute or matter.

Work Made for Hire – in the context of copyright, an original work of authorship prepared by an employee within the scope of his or her employment.

Written Brief – a document summarizing legal arguments and presented for a court's consideration.

Table of Cases

Index